The Rule of Law in Japan

The Rule of Law in Japan

A Comparative Analysis

Third Revised Edition

Carl F. Goodman

Wolters Kluwer
Law & Business

Published by:
Kluwer Law International
PO Box 316
2400 AH Alphen aan den Rijn
The Netherlands
Website: www.kluwerlaw.com

Sold and distributed in North, Central and South America by:
Aspen Publishers, Inc.
7201 McKinney Circle
Frederick, MD 21704
United States of America
Email: customer.service@aspenpublishers.com

Sold and distributed in all other countries by:
Turpin Distribution Services Ltd
Stratton Business Park
Pegasus Drive, Biggleswade
Bedfordshire SG18 8TQ
United Kingdom
Email: kluwerlaw@turpin-distribution.com

Printed on acid-free paper.

ISBN 978-90-411-4125-5

To Beatrice Delphine Goodman who has followed me across the country and around the world and inspired my interest in Japanese law.

About the Author

Carl F. Goodman is Adjunct Professor of Japan/United States Comparative Law at Georgetown University Law Center and also at George Washington University School of Law, in Washington D.C. He has been a Visiting Professor at the University of Washington in Seattle Washington and Temple University Tokyo Faculty of Law and was a Fulbright Researcher at Tokyo University. He is the 2005 recipient of the Georgetown University Law Center Charles Fehy Distinguished Adjunct Professor Award. In private law practice he was a partner in the International firms of Surrey and Morse and Jones, Day. While in private practice Professor Goodman had an active international practice based in part on representation of Japanese clients. He is a retired partner of Jones Day and upon retirement became Professor of Anglo-American Law at Hiroshima University, Faculty of Law in Hiroshima Japan. He was on the Hirodai faculty from 1992–1995.

Professor Goodman started his legal career as an Honors Program hire in the United States Department of Justice. As a Foreign Service Reserve Officer he represented the United States as the United States Agent before the International Lake Ontario Claims Tribunal (United States and Canada)—a claims arbitration dealing with certain problems related to the St. Lawrence River and Lake Ontario. Professor Goodman's exposure to Japan began in the mid 1960's when, as a member of the Legal Advisor's Office he represented the State Department in negotiations with Japan concerning air routes to and from Japan and the United States. He ended his government career as General Counsel of the then United States Civil Service Commission.

Before teaching Japan/United States Comparative Law, Professor Goodman had been Adjunct Professor of Administrative Law at the Brooklyn Law School and was Adjunct Professor of Public Personnel Law at Georgetown University when he was General Counsel of the Civil Service Commission. He is the author of *Handbook on Public Personnel Law* Published in 1978, as well as *Justice And Civil Procedure in Japan* published in 2005.

Professor Goodman is a life member of the American Law Institute, a former Chairman of the Administrative Law Committee of the Association of the Bar of the City of New York and a former Member of the Council of the Administrative Law Section of the American Bar Association. He has participated in panels at the Woodrow Wilson International Center for Scholars and at various United States Law Faculties, he has lectured on Japanese law at the Sigur Center for Asian Studies of the Elliott School of International Affairs of the George Washington University as well as in Canada and Santiago, Chile. Since his return to the United States from Japan in 1995 he has visited Japan on several occasions and lectured at various Japanese Law Faculties. Professor Goodman lives in Bethesda Maryland and Becket Massachusetts with his wife Beatrice.

Table of Contents

Perface

Much has happened in Japan since the publication of the Second Revised Edition four years ago. The long ruling Liberal Democratic Party (LDP) was ousted from power in the Upper House of the Diet just prior to the publication of the Second Revised Edition creating political instability. The LDP lost control of the Lower House to the Democratic Party of Japan (DPJ) in 2009, only to regain control of the Upper House in the summer 2010 elections. The string of short serving Prime Ministers continued with DPJ Prime Ministers Hatoyama and Kan making way to PM Noda in a three year period. Nonetheless, the emergence of a political force strong enough to oust the long ruling LDP was a momentous event. The emergence of a local party in Osaka with national ambitions whose leadership, unlike the DPJ, is not composed of former LDP members and that threatens to take on both the LDP and DPJ in the forthcoming national election has excited the public and caused both the ruling and opposition parties to consider how to deal with this new threat from "outside." Meanwhile grid lock has settled over the Diet where the LDP's control of the Upper House has put it in a position to block Bills passed by the Lower House while the DPJ lacks a strong enough Lower House majority to override such rejection. The Supreme Court's ruling that the system for election of members of the Lower House was in a state of unconstitutionality and the failure of the special committee of the Diet created to rewrite the constituencies to bring the system back into constitutionality appears to mean that the next election will, like those before it, be held under an unconstitutional system. However, unlike previous elections held while the system was in a state of unconstitutionality, if the next election is held under the current unconstitutional system there will have been time for the Diet to correct the imbalance. Whether that would spur the Supreme Court to finally take some action other than coaxing the Diet to act remains to be seen.

The most significant event was, of course, the Great East Japan Earthquake and Tsunami and the Fukushima Nuclear Disaster that followed in its wake. The need to find funds for payment for reconstruction efforts and to compensate those left adrift by the events in Tohoku resulted in the establishment of claims processing procedures and both government and TEPCO programs designed to provide assistance and compensation. There was no rush to the courthouse as would be expected in the United States and no Representative Actions filed in the hope of creating a mass tort class to litigate the compensation question, although delay by the government in providing compensation has caused some to sue. Prefecture concern over the hosting of nuclear facilities has raised new issues regarding Prefecture / National Government issues and the use of mandamus when a Prefecture official refuses to carry out a national government directive. The continuing debate over the Futenma Airbase on Okinawa raises similar questions. More fundamentally the Fukushima Nuclear Tragedy has raised questions concerning the use of Administrative Guidance through which the Japanese Bureaucracy administers the law and has raised fundamental questions about the relationship between "descent from heaven" and the lifetime employment system with its corollary early mandatory retirement. As the same mandatory retirement system and lifetime employment system apply to private enterprise similar questions have been raised about those systems and their relationship to corporate governance. While more companies have adopted the new "company with committees" model of governance the pace of adoptions has slowed and the number of such companies remains small. Suggestions that "Outside Directors" be replaced by "Independent Directors" have been rejected by companies and by the task force set up by METI to review the issue.

The law itself changed in many other respects discussed in this Third Edition. The Supreme Court in holding Part of the Nationality Act unconstitutional continued its somewhat more accelerated recognition of its role in providing constitutional judicial review. Not only did the court deal with the question of unconstitutionality but it also dealt with the effect of such an unconstitutional finding, exposing a sharp difference in opinion between the Justices as to the role of the court vis-à-vis the Diet. After the court's determination the Diet amended the Nationality Law to conform to the Supreme Court's holding. The Nationality Act case also raises the question of whether the Supreme Court of Japan is moving away from a "reasonableness test" for constitutional determinations to a more nuanced "proportionality" approach, at least in certain areas as well as the question as the reach of the court's rationale in the Nationality Act case.

The Supreme Court dealt with how to determine the jurisdictional amount in a Representative Action brought in the District Court where each claim was less than the JPY 1.4 million limit of the Summary Court's jurisdiction but the total far exceeding this sum. The court considered the question of whether a Chief Justice who has publicly commented on the court's administration of a judicial reform law should recues himself when the constitutionality of that law is before the court. International jurisdiction provisions were added to the Civil Procedure Code to codify former rules and make them more understandable to both judges and foreign entities. These rules contain excessive jurisdiction provisions, especially in the consumer and labor area but also as regards quasi in rem jurisdiction. But the Code reserves the court's ability to reject cases where fairness would not be served by retaining jurisdiction.

The Supreme Court took aim at the disconnect between a lay juror function at the District Court trial level and a retrial of facts at the High Court level in cases handled by the new Saiban'in trial system and required that the High Court give deference to the findings of the mixed panels. The Supreme Court's language is broad enough to encompass cases heard by a single judge or panel of judges and may not be limited to Saiban'in cases. (Being a Petty Bench decision the decision may not reflect the views of the Grand Bench and it is to be expected that prosecutors will seek an opportunity to present the issue of deference to another Petty Bench and try to get the Grand Bench to lessen the burden on prosecutor appeals, at least in non-Saiban'in tried cases).The court set forth an exacting standard of burden of proof in circumstantial evidence cases, affirmed a lower court acquittal of a defendant finding that while he was probably guilty of the crime the finding of not guilty by the trial and High Court should be affirmed and reversed a criminal conviction on the basis that there was reasonable doubt as to guilt notwithstanding that prosecutors had presented a cigarette stub with the defendants DNA on it located in the stairwell of the house where the crime was committed—there were over 70 other butts in the stairwell without the defendant's DNA and since the defendant's child and grandchild lived in the building every reason for him to have at some time been present at the building for family rather than criminal purposes or for his child to have emptied an ash tray from her apartment containing his DNA. The Tokyo High Court allowed the retrial of a foreigner convicted of murder after it was learned that DNA of another person was found by prosecutors at the scene of the crime notwithstanding the prosecution's argument (previously accepted by the High Court and Supreme Court) that it was not believable that some other person was at the scene of the crime. A former Judge commented that Judges can only act on evidence that is presented to the court apparently suggesting that the court system should not be blamed for the prosecutor's failure to present the exculpatory evidence to the defendant and his counsel until 15 years after conviction. Perhaps this opens the door for a judiciary that feels free to be less deferential to the prosecution and more concerned with the rights of the accused.

The trial of DPJ kingpin Ichiro Ozawa and the trial of three of his Aides highlighted problems with the amended Prosecution Review Commission process and opened a window into the aggressive actions of the Special Investigation Units in the public prosecutor offices, especially in Tokyo and Osaka. The court appointed prosecutors' appeal of Ozawa's acquittal complicated the political scene and Ozawa's role in the DPJ. The secret taping of the prosecutor's interrogation by an Ozawa aide and the disclosure of the tactics used and an inaccurate report of the questioning session prepared by the Special Investigation Unit and submitted to the PRC coming on the heels of other well publicized cases involving false confessions and/or prosecutor misconduct has resulted in the full recording of interrogation of suspects by some Special Investigation Units, albeit on a limited "experimental" basis. Although the Constitutional right to counsel remains applicable only to those already indicted, a change in the Code of Criminal Procedure provides greater access to counsel by those suspected and remanded to questioning beyond the two days allocated to police and one day allocated to prosecutors before an extension may be requested.

The standing rules and rules for what constitutes a disposition subject to judicial review have been widened to provide greater review of administrative action in accord with the suggestions of the Judicial Reform Council, although the rules remain significantly less accommodating than standing in the United States. The concept of notice and opportunity to be heard as a part of "due process" or fairness in the Civil Procedure realm has been specifically utilized by the Supreme Court and the court continues to slowly but continuously open up the areas where production of documents may be obtained—while preserving the confidentiality of decision making documents of ongoing business entities.

Family Law has seen changes brought about in part by international pressure on Japan to accede to the Hague Convention on the Civil Aspects of Child Abduction. These changes not only affect transnational divorce but also domestic custody issues. The Diet enacted legislation that for the first time recognizes (but does not mandate) visitation by a divorced spouse without Parental Control and that recognizes rights of the child in visitation and custody. Nonetheless, visitation still is based on the consent of divorcing parties and remains, when granted, an infrequent and short time span event. Domestic legislation designed to carry out Japan's Hague Convention obligations will necessitate a rethinking of old ideas by the Family Court, highlight the question of "best interests of the child" and are likely to also affect domestic cases. Assisted Reproduction Technologies continue to raise and require the courts to deal with previously inconceivable legal issues that are tied to Japan's Family Register law. How to register the child of a couple where one of the parties has had a sex change operation because of Gender Identity Disorder; who is the father when a child is conceived via in vitro fertilization and this fact is known to the Family Registrar; who is the mother when a fertilized egg is transplanted into a woman who cannot produce eggs but can carry a child to term and wishes to do so? The effect of the Supreme Court's determination that part of the Nationality Act was unconstitutional on inheritance rights of children born out of wedlock was considered by the High Court in Osaka and by two Petty Benches of the Supreme Court with different results. As the case headed for the Grand Bench the issue was settled prior to Grand Bench decision and the matter was dismissed for failure to present a case or controversy.

Although the birth of a son to the younger brother of the Crown Prince postponed legislation dealing with the issue of a female ascension to the Chrysanthemum Throne, the dearth of male children in the Emperor's immediate family line has raised the question of amending the Imperial Household Law to permit female descendants to create branch families where male heirs can rise to the Throne. This in turn raises the more fundamental issue of the conflict between the Imperial Household Law's male only Imperial provisions and the Constitution's prohibition of discrimination based on sex.

With a changing political landscape and a Lower House election due to be held no later than 2013 the effect of Japan's restrictive election campaign laws on restricting freedom of speech by candidates under the rubric of a "level playing field" is more relevant than in the past. This is especially so as the laws forbid active use of the Internet and social media by candidates and their supporters during the all important campaign period between the closing of the Diet and the holding of a new election. So too, the Supreme Court's decisions in 2011 and 2012 concerning teachers' freedom of conscience and belief and what level of punishment is permitted for refusal to stand and sing the National Anthem and the Pledge to the Flag answer some questions but leave others unanswered. The thinking behind the court's decisions in this area tracks to some extent the thinking of Ito Hirabumi when writing about Freedom of Religion and raises fundamental freedom questions.

Actions by North Korea and the buildup of Chinese military forces, including a blue ocean naval capability and presence has brought about modifications in Japan's interpretation of Article 9 of the Constitution and for the first time Japan has established a base outside of Japan and entered into joint military production arrangements with a country other than the United States. While the issue of how to provide a truly mutual defense posture while Article 9 retains its solely self defense interpretation remains, Japan has taken steps to coordinate its military with that of neighboring countries including South Korea. While a Constitutional Amendment Referendum Law is now on the books, there have been no interparty discussions of Amendment since the DPJ took control of the government, although the LDP has been working on Amendments that can garner support of all factions of the Party. This may be part of a strategy to make Constitutional Amendment a political issue in the next Lower House election. Amongst other things the LDP draft would redefine the Emperor's Role to that of Head of State (immediately raising interpretation questions) and make singing of the National Anthem and the saying of the Pledge of Allegiance a Constitutional requirement for public employees (including teachers) and others. The Futenma Airbase issue claimed a Japanese Prime Minster and continues to be an issue between the national government and the prefecture government as well as the United States. Administrative changes in the status of forces agreement have been made to give Japanese authorities greater jurisdiction in criminal cases involving American military and non-military personnel while attempting to protect what the United States sees as "due process" rights of service personnel accused of crimes. These cases continue to raise an echo of the consular jurisdiction of the unequal treaty era. Okinawa was also the subject of suggested textbook modifications regarding the role of the military on Okinawa in the suicide deaths of Okinawans in the wake of the Battle of Okinawa. Public demonstrations not Freedom of Speech litigation forced the national Ministry of Education to back down.

The rise of one and perhaps two realistic contenders for political leadership brings Japan's election laws and restrictions on campaign activities into sharp focus and it is expected that political campaigns will be more meaningful in the post LDP domination era. These laws, passed in the early days of the Meiji era for the purpose of restricting the activities of the rising political parties seeking to challenge the Meiji Oligarchs' rule did not contemplate the communications channels and technology that exist in today's "e-world" just as Japan's Civil Code provisions dealing with parenthood could not contemplate the modern world of Assisted Reproduction Technology. Both place law at the cutting edge of understanding the common sense of the public as to these issues—indeed whether there is any common sense judgment of the society as to these issues.

The Supreme Court of Japan, as is the case with the Supreme Court of the United States, has found itself having to deal with the question of "separation of Church and State." This time the court has dealt with separation law outside the context of the Yasukuni Shrine or other shrines that have a relationship with the SDF. In cases arising in Hokkaido the court has had to deal with Church/State issues involving Shrines located on land owned by local governments. At the same time, the new political leadership has refrained from visits to Yasukuni out of deference to Japan's neighbors and trading partners in East Asia (although some Cabinet Ministers broke ranks with the Prime Minister and visited Yasukuni in October 2012).

The corporate governance model in Japan and the debate about whether and if so how has governance in Japan converged with governance in the United States has seen developments in the past several years. The scandal involving the camera maker Olympus that brought down the leadership of the company and heralded a mass change of its Board of Directors has rekindled the debate about whether Japanese companies need more "outside directors" or whether "independent directors" are required to protect the interest of shareholders—as well as other stakeholders.

The Supreme Court of Japan has rendered decisions allowing for Judicial Review of Administrative Actions that carry forward the reforms adopted at the suggestion of the Judicial Reform Council that have widened the area of those who have standing to sue, although not to the extent as in the United States; has more broadly defined what is a *shobun* (determination or order) that is ripe for review and has required that reasoning be given for a *shobun*. How these determinations will affect administrative law going forward remains to be seen but these steps are consistent with the Judicial Reform Council's proposals that judicial review of administrative action be more accessible.

So too, The Great East Japan Earthquake and Tsunami followed by the Fukushima nuclear disaster has had an effect on Japanese administrative law, including an effort to separate the advocacy and licensing function of METI with the safety and regulatory function of NISA (formerly a branch of METI). Failures of supervision and regulation by NISA have raised questions about administrative guidance and the close ties between regulators and the regulated and the effect of the lifetime employment system on regulation and "descent from heaven." The failure of the central government at several levels and the lack of credible and timely acknowledgment of the extent of the nuclear tragedy by the government has caused local authorities to demand greater say in future policy decisions concerning nuclear power throwing into question the issue of whether the mandamus authority of the national government extends beyond the military and security field to, for example, the restart of nuclear facilities closed for scheduled maintenance checks in the year after the Fukushima tragedy.

The above and other advances, changes and modifications in the law during the past four years are discussed in this Third Revised Edition. Legal discussion of numerous issues both in terms of United States and Japanese law has been brought up to date both in textual materials and in footnotes tracking recent developments. In addition, new Chapters have been added to deal with Freedom of Expression and Conflict of Laws rules. Family Law issues have been spun off into a separate chapter. Extensive new subchapter headings have been added to make the Table of Contents more "user friendly" and make it easier for the reader to find material and to navigate the text and a separate discussion of "communitarianism" as it relates to Japanese law has been added to the Chapter on Unifying Factors.

CHAPTER 1

Introduction

In the United States there are numerous "national law schools" notwithstanding the fact that like politics most law is local. It is of course, true that some law is federal in nature and thus uniform throughout the federalism system that is the U.S. political system. But once we are past administrative law, Constitutional law and some of the elective federal law subjects like anti-trust, bankruptcy, or SEC law, etc., we are left with a basically local legal terrain. Contracts, torts, substantive criminal law—the basic building blocks of U.S. law—are local in nature. American lawyers take national law schools for granted and rarely if ever think of how it is that a school such as Harvard can be the training grounds for lawyers in California, Georgia, New York, Texas, etc.

How is it that American lawyers can be adequately trained in national law schools? Why can lawyers in national law firms easily assist colleagues in "out of their state" offices when the need arises? The answer lies in the Rule of Law, grounded in notions of the English Common Law that bind our legal system together. This is true for the "original" 13 colonies and applies to those states that were colonies of civil law countries and thus had a civil law base. This is not to say that real estate notions in New York and Texas are uniformly the same or that there are not regional legal theories such as the difference in water rights law in the Northeast compared with Southwest. Such differences exist; and each state has its own state law concepts. Nonetheless, the Rule of Law fashioned on basic notions of the English Common Law system act as a kind of glue holding the divergent state systems together and making national schools and transferable legal talent possible. We are all subject to the Rule of Law and can base our decisions—both personal and business—on the existing Rule of Law.

In Japan federalism issues and conflicting state law issues do not arise because Japan has a unitary government system. Law is national in nature. Of course, there are local ordinances and even prefecture rules to be considered. But law is a matter of national authority and to the extent that local ordinances come into play it is because the national government has delegated power to the prefecture or the local authority. While national/state "law" issues tend not to arise in Japan (conflict can arise between national and prefecture authorities and courts may be called on to resolve such questions in limited cases), Japan does have its own conflicting ideas about law. When viewed by Americans the Japanese legal system seems a bouillabaisse of civil law rules and Codes, common law concepts and Constitution, a common law adversarial style prosecutorial system trying cases under a civil law style substantive criminal law and a common law style judiciary staffed with civil law selection process judges. Is there a similar "glue" that holds this mixture of legal concepts together? I suggest that there is—the "glue" is Japan's feudal past and the influence that that past and myths about that past have on Japanese life and law. That past is interpreted to stress relativity, harmony, group identity, substantive justice and a form of communitarianism wherein individual rights are subordinated to group or societal rights. Judges are ordinary men and women who are learned in the law and have as their business the application of legal principles to the dispute before them. But because they are persons in their own society they bring the ideas, notions, mores, cultural values and myths of their society to the problem at hand. This is the process of judging. Some call it judicial judgment, others common sense, others discretion, etc. But whatever label we place on it the fact remains that all judicial decisions are infected by the bias, education, training, experience, culture and background of the judicial officer. To American judges trained under a case law system that places primacy on the decisions of judges and stresses continuity and stability of legal principles, part of that "discretion" is logical application of prior decisions—and by extension logical applications of statutory language and legislative history—to the problem before them. But to Japanese judges, whose experience is fundamentally different the discretion to be exercised must be exercised in a way that is satisfactory to the Japanese public—in a manner consistent with cultural values, myths (if need be), and societal norms that may be different from norms that exist in the United States. To be consistent with these values, a decision may not reflect a syllogistic analysis of abstract logic. A decision must take account of the circumstances in which the parties presently find themselves and legal rules must be pliable to reflect the context in which the parties and the rule exist. Application of logical norms borrowed from Greek philosophers may have to be rejected in favor of application of notions that are part of the Japanese culture. The result of this process, to American eyes, may be that what you get in the application of a code, statute or Constitutional provision may not be what you see when you read (with Western eyes and Western notions of logic) the provision at issue.

American judges will sometimes rely on a "strained" reading of a statute to reach a result that is consistent with their philosophical view or with the court's perception of society's view. If abstract logic were the be all and end all of American law there would hardly be the numerous split decisions by appeals courts that characterize the American appellate system. Holmes is not the only one to appreciate the fact that the Common Law is based more on experience than on logic. But it is precisely that experience factor which forms the background for a syllogistic approach to law. One leg of the syllogism at work in most appellate cases is the experience that the legal system has had with similar issues. In other words, law has its own history and it is this history that plays a major role in deciding new cases.

Japan's legal history is fundamentally different from legal history in England, Europe and the United States. If indigenous legal experience is one leg of an American jurist's chair then in Japan that leg would simply be missing. The legal history of Japan is mostly a "borrowed" history with feudal Japan's notions of the function and purpose of law being fundamentally at odds with a "Rule of Law" society. It is simply asking too much to ask that such a society adopt as its own the cultural values that underlie the Codes that were borrowed from a fundamentally different society.

Moreover, the reasons for the borrowing of Codes may lead one to accept the Code in its entirety or to reject the notions in the Code that conflict with indigenous values—or at least with what are currently perceived as indigenous values. Some European countries willingly borrowed or adopted the notions of the Napoleonic Code and thus they wholeheartedly adopted the values underlying that Code. Japan's reasons for borrowing Western Codes is more complicated. A Western-style legal system was needed for Japanese society to leap forward from the feudal society imposed by the Tokugawa rulers and some saw the borrowing of Western Codes as a necessary step in Japan's economic and social development. But it is also true that Western Codes were borrowed for a less idealistic reason—namely as a means of getting the "barbarians" to relinquish the advantages they had forced Japan to give them under the unequal treaties extracted at the point of cannon on "black ships". If the Codes and concepts underlying the Codes are viewed as adopted out of necessity not because they were determined by the Japanese to be better than a home grown legal system then it is reasonable for judges to give the Codes an "imaginative" interpretation to make them consistent with Japanese values.

The Japanese Constitution is an example. The present Constitution was not written by and adopted by the Japanese political system because it was deemed as appropriate for the Japanese. Rather, the Constitution was written by Americans who were trying to change Japanese society through the Rule of Law represented by the Constitution. Prior to the adoption of the present Constitution the Japanese had prepared a post-World War II Constitution. The Occupation authorities rejected this document, which represented an amendment rather than a complete re-writing of the Meiji Constitution, and American talent was called upon to write a Constitution for Japan. The question is not whether the average Japanese is better off with the American drafted Constitution than she would be if the Occupation had approved the Japanese draft; nor whether the great mass of the Japanese population preferred the American draft to the Japanese draft. The answer to these questions while interesting does not change the fact that judges are being asked to interpret laws, Codes and Constitutions written by other societies with other values and, in a sense forced on Japanese society. When these Codes, Constitutions and laws are deemed to conflict with fundamental Japanese values or with Japanese historic norms or with myths accepted by the Japanese it is natural for judges to read these laws in a way which is consistent with these norms, values and myths. More is involved here than a strained interpretation of words. If need be a wholesale re-writing of the law by the judge may be called for and written provisions of the law will be sacrificed for the "greater Japanese good".

Japanese society has been struggling with the question of what it means to be Japanese since the Meiji Restoration and Japan's emergence as a global power. Japan having been subdued by the West's greater military might naturally turned to the creation of a strong military based on Western models. Once it had established itself it turned to the same imperialistic methods used by the Western powers. At the same time it was necessary for the Japanese Empire to define its borders—bringing what had been the Ryuku Kingdom into Japan and assuring that Hokkaido would be Japanese and not become Russian. This meant incorporating into greater Japan the Ryuku people and the Ainu of Hokkaido. After the conquest of Korea and Taiwan, the peoples of these territories also became part of the Empire. But the Empire consisted of a Nation State that had as one of its unifying principles the idea of the Emperor as the father figure in a Family-State and it thus became necessary to come up with a theory that would enable the family-state to incorporate the diverse peoples that now were part of the Empire. This was done through considering the Japanese people as a multicultural people that included traits of the various peoples in the Empire. These peoples were thus part of the Japanese family but differed because they did not follow the prevailing Japanese culture. To "remedy" the situation it was necessary for them to adopt Japanese culture—such as the Japanese language, names, diet, etc. In time they would then become full-fledged Japanese. After World War 2 the myth of the Japanese being a homogeneous ethic group replaced the prior myth. Homogeneousness thus put peoples who had previously been Japanese citizens (such as ethnic Koreans and Taiwanese) as well as those who were seen by the mainstream majority Japanese as "different" (such as the Ainu and Burakumin or *geikokumin* (people from a foreign land) "outside" the Japanese population, as they did not fit the alleged homogeneous mold. Post-World War 2 myths of homogeneousness result in a narrow view of discrimination when it affects those "outside" the mainstream Japanese model.[1] At the same time the myth of a homogeneous Japan supported and in turn was supported by the idea of a single national Japanese community with community values that are both uniquely important and ubiquitous to the Japanese, reflecting "Japanese values", including legal values. Since the community values in Japan may be different than the community values in the United States it should be expected that Japanese approaches to law and decisions of the Supreme Court of Japan will take into account factors different from an American court presented with the same problem and legal issue. It also will affect the Court's unwillingness to strike out on its own to create new law when the Diet as the representative of the people has not acted because there is as yet no known consensus among the community as to how to act.

Since the Western imports contained concepts for which there was no Japanese language equivalent it is impossible for a Westerner to get what the Westerner sees. The Japanese judge reads the words but must come up with an interpretation that is understandable in Japanese terms. Meiji-era judges were interpreting the borrowed Codes with an injunction from the Emperor to utilize custom and reason when necessary. Pre-war judges sought to do justice between the parties as Tokugawa magistrates had and sought to have parties reach a just resolution of their dispute. Post-war judges, many of whom were pre-war judges continuing in office under a

1. *See Transcultural Japan, At the borderlands of race, gender and identity* (Willis & Murphy-Shigematsu ed., Routledge 2008). *See also*, Chaihark Hahm & Sungn Ho Kim, *To Make "We the People": Constitutional Founding in Postwar Japan and South Korea*, 8 I•CON 800, 818,839–840 (2010).

newly formulated Judicial Bureaucracy, also sought a just result to the dispute before them, a practice followed by the judiciary today. Sometimes this means an interpretation that appears to be fundamentally different from the written word. With these thoughts in mind it should come as no surprise that "what you see may not be what you get" when an American reads a Japanese Code or law or Constitutional provision. While a disconnect between written law and law in practice may exist in any legal system, including the United States system, the fact is that this disconnect is much more marked in Japan than in the West.[2]

This text attempts to compare Japanese and American legal principles in selected areas with the above thoughts in mind. The format is designed to discuss the legal principles as applied in each society and provide material so that the reader can see how the Japanese interpretation may not reflect the conclusion of an American lawyer and vice versa. Examples are also given of situations in which "what you see may not be what you get" in United States law. However, the primary focus is on the Japanese law questions and the United States discussion is for perspective and comparative purposes. Thus, after a discussion of the legal principles in each society the text will discuss or raise questions as to whether "what you see is what you get" from the written Japanese law.

Like Japanese law this third edition must be viewed in context. The relevant context is the change that has been taking place in Japan over the past several years. Many of the recommendations of the Judicial Reform Council, which called upon the government to adopt the Rule of Law as the guiding principle for Japanese society and suggested the strengthening of the Rule of Law, have been enacted into statute law. Those suggestions dealt with the Judicial System and the participants in that system but also specifically dealt with the civil, administrative and criminal law systems and were designed to extend outward like the ripples caused by a stone thrown into a pond to affect the entire society. How fast change has been made is a subject of debate and how far these changes reach still remains to be seen. However, there are signs of change as the rules for opening the courts for judicial review of administrative action have actually opened the courts for review that would have been impossible in previous years and the Saiban'in criminal trial system has had spin off effects likely not anticipated but certainly welcome. Earlier disclosures to the defense of evidence to be used by the prosecution and calls for closer examination of confessions have been influenced by the new system. The current indigenous movement for judicial reform holds the possibility for revolutionary change. Some of that change can already be seen in specific areas of the law, but as the current failure of the reforms in matters affecting legal education disclose, whether what you see is actually what you get is another question.

2. Kenzo Takayanagi, *A Century of Innovation: The Development of Japanese Law, 1868–1961* in Arthur Taylor von Mehren, *Law in Japan* 5, 39 (Harvard University Press 1963).

CHAPTER 2
Foundations of the Legal System

§2.01 UNITED STATES

[A] Common Law System

The Declaration of Independence of the 13 colonies that later became the United States sets forth numerous matters relating to the nature of law as understood in the colonies and by the drafters. The Declaration recites, "all men [...] are endowed [...] with certain unalienable rights". This declaration is a continuation of prior Western theories of natural rights that can trace their roots to pre-Christian philosophies as well as the philosophy of early Christian writers.[1] The Declaration takes the position that these rights are not secondary to the notions of government or to the rules established by government but rather that it is the function of government "to secure these rights". In its catalogue of causes for the declared separation of the colonies from Great Britain, the Declaration refers numerous times to the legal requirements that Great Britain has failed to uphold. The king is accused of refusing to assent to laws necessary for the public good; of interfering with legislative bodies by calling them together in "unusual, uncomfortable and distant places"; of obstructing the Laws of Naturalization; of obstructing the Administration of Justice; of making judges "dependent on his will alone, for the tenure of their offices, and the amount and payment of their salaries"; of depriving those who lived in the colonies of the right to trial by jury in many cases and of "abolishing the free system of English Laws in a neighboring Province [...]" and threatening to do the same in the colonies.

Far from rejecting the notion of a Rule of Law the Declaration is founded on the assumption that the Rule of Law applies in the colonies (later to be the United States) and further that it is not just any law that applies but rather it is the "free system of English Laws" that applies. The colonies, while objecting to British rule were not

1. William Noel, *The Right to Life in Japan* 3 (Routledge 1997).

objecting to the English Common Law, they were basing their rebellion on the common law and their rights under law.

When the United States comes into being it does not come into existence in a legal vacuum. It comes into existence with an already established system of laws and a system for administering those laws; namely, the British system of Law and Equity. The newly established government could have rejected in its entirety the English system and written its own—perhaps it could have borrowed from the civil law systems of the continent of Europe—but it did not. This was a choice made by the United States, not a situation thrust upon the new government. It was a choice made based on the notion that the legal system was a good system and did not need to be fundamentally changed or rejected. After independence the pre-existing legal system continued in major part. Of course the substantive law was amended and changed to meet the new governing conditions and was further amended, as the various states deemed appropriate. This change continues to this day but no one would suggest that because substantive and procedural changes are taking place the basic legal system has changed.

At the heart of the United States system of government is the concept of law. Law is what binds the now 50 states together as one country. In essence the United States is created by a contract that we call a Constitution. Being the formative document of the government, this contract has attributes that make it a kind of "super contract" and thus there may be special rules applied to its interpretation, but in essence the document is a contractual undertaking by otherwise sovereign States to give up part of their sovereignty to a new entity called the United States. It contains all of the elements that the common law typically requires of a contract—it is an offer that only has binding effect when it is accepted ("the Ratification of the Conventions of nine States, shall be sufficient for the Establishment of this Constitution between the States so ratifying the Same") and we can impute "consideration" through the mutual promises of the accepting States to be bound by the terms of the Constitution. Like most contracts it is subject to amendment when the parties to the contract agree to its amendment, and the terms of agreement are set forth in the contract document. Most issues of interpretation are decided as would any contractual question by a court of law and to assure that parochial "State" concerns do not infect the judicial interpretation of the Constitution a Federal Court system is established with jurisdiction to decide cases arising under the Constitution, Treaties and laws made by the newly created government (Article III). Like most contracts this one did not foresee all future issues and did not provide for all contingencies. In most cases these blanks are determined by judicial decision but the most fundamental of legal questions—whether a consenting state could withdraw its consent and leave the federation—was ultimately decided by a civil war.

[B] History as Relevant to the American System of Law

To understand the system of laws that the colonies and thus the new United States government accepted, one must understand something of the history of English law;

that is the history of United States law and one must understand something of the nature of the society that was transplanted from England to the "New World". The conquest of England by the French Duke of Normandy in 1066 at the Battle of Hastings led to a fundamental difference between the rulers of France (to whom the Duke was supposed to owe fealty under the rules of the feudal legal system) and the new rulers of England who, while claiming their ancestral rights in France declared themselves rulers in their own right in England. This schism brought about a further schism when the rulers in England began the process of creating their own legal system for their newly acquired kingdom. Unable to rule through armed occupation in such a large territory the early English kings used the legal system to further the king's rule. To assure that the king's writ ran throughout the kingdom, the traveling judges of the king's court used local custom and communication between themselves to establish a common law throughout the kingdom. To know what this law was, decisions were written down and future judges referred back to these decisions in deciding cases later brought to the courts for decision. Few "statutes" were enacted in the early days—the Statute of Uses (the basis for the law of trusts) and the Statute of Frauds (designed to prevent fraud by requiring that certain contracts be in writing), etc. To determine what the law is that should be applied to the facts at hand, the judges were assisted by the parties to the case who marshaled the evidence and arguments (including prior precedents) and presented them to the judge. The adversarial common law system based on precedent that exists in the United States today is based on this model.

Because the king of England utilized the legal system and his Royal Court and traveling judges to extend his rule throughout England it was important that the populous view the Royal Court as fair and honest. Consistency of decision making was one method of demonstrating honesty. Rules applied in earlier cases were applied again in later cases demonstrating that the rules had not changed simply to aid a particular party to the litigation. The king welcomed the rise of professionals who created forms (writs) to be used by litigants and who provided advice on how to deal with litigation. These early professionals tended to come from the local inns that catered to litigants who had traveled to the site of the court in order to be heard (hence the English Bar's relationship to the Inns of Court). The resulting system came to be viewed with favor and litigants lined up to have disputes resolved by the king's judges who traveled on circuit throughout England (hence the rise of Circuit Court judges—American judges also traveled on circuit in the early days of the Federal Judiciary).[2]

2. The Judicial system was a moneymaker for the King: the fees for filing suit were a source of income as was the requirement that the losing party pay a penalty to the crown even in a civil case. "Free men" paid taxes to the king; Peasants to their local Lord to be paid to the King. Some of these monies inevitably found their way into the local Lord's coffers. As only "free men" could file suit it was in the crown's interest to have litigants declared free men subject to the King's tax. The Royal Judges complied benefiting the King's treasury while local Lords lost power that accumulated to the King as the peasantry became free men. Taken together with the statute quai emptores (1290) this hastened the decline of the land tied feudal system and sped up the process of movement to a land based capitalistic system.

This process of law making may be viewed as a "bottom-up" system where the law is created (or "found") as a consequence of lawsuits brought by individuals (later corporations and other juridical entities). Precedent is created from earlier cases and it is the bringing of these cases that result in the development of the law. Judges do not have the option of declining to decide a case because of uncertainty as to the law; new cases arising out of new circumstances have to be decided based on previous rules in analogous or at least somewhat relevant or similar cases. These new decisions in turn created new rules to be applied in future cases. In essence the development of the law was based on the types of cases brought to the court by the public.

One effect of this type of system is to remove from public officials and place in the hands of the litigating public the ability to determine the agenda for the development of law. Of course, the public officials have the power through the passage of legislation (adoption of statutes) to change or influence the law made by the judges. When a statute was adopted it was made in the setting of pre-existing rules "found" or adopted or created by the law courts. Statutes were not written "on a clean slate" nor were they viewed as the totality of the law. The pre-existing "common law" was the foundation on which the new statute was engrafted and the statute was not viewed as "occupying the entire field". In the common law model statutes were viewed as modifications of the existing body of law and were interpreted based on the existing body of law and the intention of the statute to modify that pre-existing law. The intent of the statute was not to completely obliterate the pre-existing law.[3] Only those parts of the existing law that were intended to be changed were affected and only to the extent of the intended change. To determine what part of and how the law was changed society looked to the judges who then applied the statutes to new fact patterns brought before them by litigants. In essence the same judiciary that had created the original common law was called upon to interpret just how far the new statute was intended to change the common law. It is not surprising that these judges were not always hospitable to an interpretation of the statutes that worked a substantial modification of the rules the judges had earlier created.

There are, of course, situations in which a federal law "occupies the entire field" and thus displaces the common law. Thus, where Congress delegates to a federal agency the authority to deal with a specific problem and specifically speaks to that problem in delegating authority the federal common law that may have existed prior to the delegation is displaced by the delegation.[4]

[C] Comparison to the Civil Law System

The civil law system that was developed on the continent of Europe was a system based on a different philosophy. Here was no "bottom-up" system but rather a "top-down" system of law making. The "top-down" model has a long and honorable tradition. The Code of laws found in the Bible's first five books of Moses represents a "top-down"

3. See, *Samantar v. Yousof*, 560 U.S. ___ (2010).
4. *American Electric Power Co. v. Connecticut*, 564 U.S. ___ (2011).

model of law making whether from a Godhead or from Moses that depends neither on public involvement nor judicial determinations for either its validity or its agenda. Numerous well-respected Codes given to the public by "law givers" are important in the history of Western culture. Roman law modeled on the Code of Justinian was a Code based system. Similarly the Canon Law was a Code-based system.

In the thirteenth Century Justinian's *Corpus Juris Civilius*, as preserved in Italian Universities—particularly the University of Bologna—was "rediscovered" as scholars from continental Europe came to Bologna and returned to their home countries bringing back the learning of the *Corpus Juris Civilius*. This became the foundation for the law systems of the various lands in Continental Europe. These lands had their own Germanic folk legal systems, which melded the old Roman law (or such parts of it as could be recalled after the fall of Rome) with local customs and decrees of local rulers. England, having been conquered by the Germanic Angles and Saxon tribes similarly had a Germanic folk law system that melded the old Roman law with Germanic customs, but unlike the Continent it did not accept the *Corpus Juris Civilis* to the same extent as Continental Europe did.

Two models of modern civil law systems developed in Europe. The system of the French Republic embodied the ideals of the French Revolution and the concept that the law should be contained in a Code that was easily understood by the people.[5] The Napoleonic Code and the Napoleonic Wars spread this civil law model to most of what is now modern Western Europe. In the nineteenth century, the German Principalities were being drawn together into a form of Federation and developed a more "scientific" approach to law as a means of harmonizing the Constitution that was bringing them into a unified country and the laws of the various principalities that were now brought under a single unified Code. This approach brought logical reasoning to the fore in giving a unified legal Code meaning and was considered more of a scientific discipline than the French approach.[6]

Under both the French and German top-down civil law model judges were neither as important nor as influential as judges in the common law system. This was especially so in the French model as pre-revolution judges were seen as supporters and upholders of the ancient regime whose powers were to be closely cabined. The Code, as adopted by the representatives of the people, was the law and the judges were simply to apply that law. The role of the judge was not to make the law—the law was contained in the Code—but rather to apply the law as found in the Code to the facts presented. Judges in this system were interpreters of the law made by others. The entire body of the law was to be found in the Code handed down to the judges for their use in deciding cases. When a change or modification or addition was made to the Code that new provision became the law and what had preceded it was of no further consequence. The statutes or Code changes were not viewed as "floating" on a body of

5. Arthur Taylor von Mehren & James Russel Gordley, *The Civil Law System* 48 (2d ed., Little Brown and Co. 1977).
6. Carl Steenstrup, *German Reception of Roman Law and Japanese Reception of German Law*, 1:1 Intercultural Communications Stud. (1991). For a recent article on the science of German Criminal Law see, Markus Dirk Dubber, *The Promise of German Criminal Law: A Science of Crime and Punishment*, 6 German L. J. No. 7, 1049 (2005).

pre-existing law but rather were viewed as completely replacing the pre-existing law.[7] Judges applying the Code to facts presented had no vested interest in preserving pre-existing rules, as the judges had not made those rules just as the judges also did not make the newer rules.

On the other hand, civil law judges were (and are) more important than common law judges when it comes to determining the facts and rendering a decision in a case. Civil law judges are not seen as lawmakers but rather as "law finders" or appliers. It is true that lower court judges will want to follow precedents made by appellate courts and thus precedent has significance. However, precedent is not considered as binding since the binding law is the Code. For the common law judge, the law is contained in the precedents and Codes are at best mere modifications of the precedent law. The judge is a lawmaker and the Code is simply one tool, albeit a very significant tool (since the judge has an obligation not to eviscerate the statute law) used in the making of the law. Civil law judges are also fundamentally different from common law judges because they have the responsibility of ultimately deciding the cases before them. Common law judges, however, may rely on the jury in a jury trial to decide the case. In a jury trial system, the judge is more an umpire between the adverse parties and their advocates (the lawyers)—who ultimately have the responsibility of presenting evidence to the jurors who will decide the facts in the case and will determine the winner and loser based on the rules of law that will be told to them by the judge umpiring the dispute. The common law trial judge's umpiring function makes him/her a less important player in the courtroom drama than is the civil law judge who decides questions of both law and fact and has the responsibility for gathering the relevant facts.

In another sense civil law and common law judges are quite similar—this is the sense of the ultimate purpose of their sitting on a case. Both have the obligation to see that the right and wrong of the case before them is resolved. Both have the obligation to apply the law (whether it be Code or statute on the one hand or judge made or common law on the other) to the facts presented so that the winner and loser of the case before the judge may be determined. Litigation in both the civil law and common law systems is not a "zero sum" game—rather it is a game with a winner and a loser. The determination of winner and loser is based on a professional application of a body of rules—namely the Rule of Law. But, the common law judge has no responsibility to see to it that the party who is right actually wins—that is a matter for the party's counsel and counsel's presentation of facts and witnesses to the jury. A civil law judge, however, may be seen as the representative of the state with responsibility to find the relevant facts and determine the case in such a way that the party who is in the right ultimately wins.

Because of its "bottom-up" nature, some view the common law system as a more democratic system than the civil law system. "Bottom-up" law tends to derive its rules from the actions of the general public and from judges who are a part of that general public. "Top-down" law is viewed by some as law imposed by a ruling hierarchy on the

7. *Hemi Group v. City of New York*, 559 U.S. ___ (2010).

public and thus hostile to democratic ideals. Such notions may have had validity in the days preceding the American Revolution and the rise of democratic government, and it may well be that this difference in legal system is one of the reasons why democratic ideals arose in England and the United States before they were adopted on the European Continent. In fact, this notion may be one of the reasons why the colonies accepted the common law system of England for the new nation they were creating. In modern times where legislative bodies are democratically elected and where judges are appointed not elected, it can be argued that the civil law system better represents the democratically assented to will of the people.[8]

The difference in the civil law and common law systems results in differing thought processes of legal professionals. The common law judge and lawyer is focused on the facts of the case as determining the law applicable to the case because if the facts are considered as distinguishable (substantively different) from the facts of the precedents that made the existing law then a new legal rule must be made and applied to those new facts. The common law judge not only can, but is required, to act more quickly than the civil law judge to changing circumstances such as new technologies. While the civil law judge looks back to statutes made during an outdated technology period as the guiding principle of law and must wait for the legislature to act to determine what law applies to a new technology era the common law judge must resolve the new facts (including the new technology facts) as calling for her to create the new law that applies because the precedents, while useful are no longer controlling and thus are not the applicable law. [This distinction may help to explain the reticence of the Japanese judiciary to claim new ground in the family law areas of posthumous in vitro fertilization and surrogate pregnancy and birth as discussed in Chapter 9.]

In pre-colonial England the common law system was viewed as a good system for resolving disputes and was supported by the general public as well as by public officials. When, in 1215, King John was forced by rebellious nobles to sign a peace treaty with them to resolve disputes that document contained provisions granting legal rights to the nobles that could be enforced against the king in the king's own courts. The Magna Carta thus became the first great "Constitutional" document of England and many of its concepts may be found in English and thus United States law today.

When the king's inquisition into matters in his kingdom through use of a jury of freemen whose obligation was to advise the king as to the goings on in his dominion was modified to determine who had and who had not committed crimes (through adoption of the Petite Jury system of English and United States criminal law), the

---

8. Federal Article 3 Judges are appointed by the president with the advice and consent of the Senate and serve during "good behavior", which has come to mean life tenure. In some states, judges are elected raising judicial independence questions when special interests pour money into contested Judicial campaigns. See e.g., Justice O'Connor in *Republican Party of Minnesota v. White*, 536 U.S. 765 (2002). In *Caperton v. A. T. Massey Coal*, 556 U.S. ___ (2009) the Supreme Court held that an elected judge was required to recuse himself from sitting on a case involving a major campaign contributor. In States where judges of the highest state court are subject to "retention elections" unpopular decisions may result in loss of such an election especially when a determined organized interest group opposes the decision. While democratic this can have negative effects on the Rule of Law if judges tailor their judicial opinions to remain on the bench rather than be faithful to the rule of law.

methodology of fact-finding through use of a jury of lay persons found its way into the common law. This jury system also applied to certain non-criminal cases. As compared to the religiously based trial by battle or trial by ordeal system that it replaced, trial by jury was seen as fairer and more rational.

When the king extended the right to trial by assize[9] a group of local freemen assumed to know the facts needed to resolve the dispute, because the facts were presumed to be known to the local community (and if they did not personally know the facts they could talk to other locals to discover the facts)- to persons in possession of land who were in danger of being dispossessed from that land (the function of the Great Assize)[10] he not only diminished the power of the nobles in relation to his own power (by subjecting their land decisions to the king's court and local people who might be expected to side with other locals in possession of the land) but also increased the rights of ordinary people against the wealthy landed aristocracy. The Assize morphed into the jury as locals comprising the assize sought the facts from knowledgeable people in the community when they did not personally know the facts. Trial by assize and later by jury thus became a weapon that could be used by ordinary people against their rulers, first the local nobles and later—especially when tied together with language in Magna Carta granting the nobles certain land rights and a judgment of their peers when those rights were threatened—against the king himself. At first the assize was assumed to know the facts in its own community or if not personally knowledgeable of the facts the assize was given authority to investigate into the facts itself.[11] Later it became the responsibility of the parties to litigation to ferret out the facts and present those facts to the jury.[12] The civil law system on the other hand did not develop a jury system for determining the facts. It became part of the judge's function to find and determine the facts. A more inquisitional system with the judge at the head having the responsibility of fact locator and fact finder as well as law finder arose in civil law societies. In the inquisitional type fact-finding system the role of the advocates for the parties was diminished as compared to the common law system.

---

9. The Great Assize likely preceded Magna Carta and likely was adopted by the King in Council in the 1170s. The date of the Great Assize, J.H. Round, 31 English History review 268 (1916), http://ehr.oxfordjournals.org/content/XXXI/CXXII/268.extract.
10. Archer M. White, *Outlines of Legal History* 69 (Swan, Sonnenshein and Co., Macmillan & Co. 1895) –White puts the date of the Grand (or Great) Assize as 1177.
11. The respect given to the fact finder at the trial level in ancient England carries forward to this day in the United States where facts found at the trial level by a judicial officer such as a magistrate cannot be overturned except in unusual situations. *Knowles v. Mirzayance*, 556 U.S. ___ (2009).
12. *Greenlaw v. United States*, 554 U.S. 237 (2008) ("In our adversary system, in both civil and criminal cases, in the first instance and on appeal, we follow the principle of party presentation.... But as a general rule, '[o]ur adversary system is designed around the premise that the parties know what is best for them, and are responsible for advancing the facts and arguments entitling them to relief.' *Id.*, at 386 (SCALIA, J., concurring in part and concurring in judgment)."); see also, *Wood v. Milyard*, 566 U.S. ___ (2012).

§2.02 JAPAN

[A] An Historical Analysis

[1] Pre-Meiji Japan

The history of law and the role of law in the history of Japan are fundamentally different from the United States. Modern Japan is generally considered to begin with the Meiji Restoration of 1868. Prior to the Meiji Restoration Japanese history can be categorized in any number of ways but for purposes of this text it is sufficient to consider pre-Meiji Japan in two large pieces: (a) the *Tokugawa Shogunate* and (b) pre-*Tokugawa* Japan. Pre-Tokugawa history may itself be divided into periods and for our purposes it is sufficient to note that Tokugawa was not the first shogun, rather a Shogunate existed in Kamakura (a small town outside of today's Tokyo) long before Tokugawa established his Shogunate government in Edo, today's Tokyo. The Kamakura government was a successful government that defeated Kublai Khan's attempts to conquer Japan in 1274 and 1281 (with the help of a propitious typhoon that became known as a divine wind or *Kamikaze*). The Kamakura government governed the entirety of the three main islands of Japan[13] under a military regime where loyalty was based on feudal notions. While the administrative government resided in Kamakura, the military leaders allowed the Imperial line to continue and the Emperor resided in Kyoto.

When the Kamakura government finally fell and the Emperor was unsuccessful in attempting to govern directly, Japan entered the warring states period during which, although there was a Shogun in name, there was almost continuous warfare between the various warlords in Japan. First Oda Nobunaga and later Toyotomi Hideoshi finally succeeded in bringing the entire country under one rule. After Hideoshi's death Tokugawa Ieyasu won the battle of Sekigahara in 1600 and became Shogun in 1603. Thus began a family rule of some 250 years. While in some ways modeled on the success of the Kamakura government, Tokugawa Japan represented a very high form of feudal society. At the top of this society was the warrior class, or samurai.[14] In addition Tokugawa closed Japan to most foreign influence. In such a setting, Japan was not exposed to the ideas that influenced Western law and both the civil and common law systems. The model for "law" in Tokugawa Japan came from Kamakura and the warring states period that preceded Tokugawa. These models were, in turn, influenced by China and modified to meet Japan's situation. China itself had a legal system that was fundamentally different from the West and where the Rule of Law as understood in the West was not significant. More important were ethical concepts. In addition,

---

13. Hokkaido became the fourth main island of Japan at a later date.
14. The origin of the samurai class was the decision of the Imperial Court in the late 8th Century to rely on privately trained and equipped mobile elite warriors to maintain order and track down both criminals and warring bands. These highly mobile warriors became known as Samurai and eventually they banded together in groups that overwhelmed the power of their prior employers so that they eventually became the samurai rulers of Japan. See, Karl Friday, *Once and Future Warriors: The Samurai in Japanese History*, 10 Educ. Asia 31 (2005).

Hideoshi had adopted rules that stratified Japanese society along class lines, dividing the classes into four broad categories. Tokugawa continued and froze the status differences between classes. Status differences also existed within the same class. One's class and one's status within one's class were important determinants of the rules one was subject to. Status rules, rather than legal rules, were at the heart of Tokugawa society.[15]

The Kamakura government was housed in Kamakura, a small village about an hour by train from today's capital, Tokyo. To successfully rule the entire country, the Kamakura government had local officials throughout Japan. Such "law" as there was in Kamakura Japan took the form of instruction from the Kamakura rulers to these subordinates.

During the warring states period the various warlords (Daimyo) adopted their own "household rules" of conduct that bound members of their household. Daimyo also adopted rules and edicts that bound people living in the territory controlled by the Daimyo. Such rules would not be recognized in the West as law since they did not control relations between people but rather were directions to officials and others as to how to act. Moreover, the local Daimyo retained the right to modify the edicts as they chose and the edicts had no binding force against the Daimyo himself. By taking the form of rules to be followed by subordinates these edicts did not set forth a set of norms that independent judges could apply based on principle and reason to fact patterns brought before them.

Moreover, Japanese feudalism both before and during the Tokugawa period was fundamentally different from Western feudalism—a difference that affects the notion of law in the West and the notion of law in the East. In Europe, feudalism was grounded in what modern Westerners would recognize as contract.[16] Lords owned the land (or held it under higher feudal Lords) and farmers lived on and produced from the land—in exchange they provided the Lord with services and other payments. If the Lord needed to raise an army to assist the king the tenants on the land were required to serve in the army, at other times they provided labor to construct projects for the Lord and they paid the Lord a percentage of their produce. In return the peasants were allowed to live on and work the land and the Lord provided them with protection from potential warring Lords and outlaws.

In the West, this notion of corresponding rights and obligations between Lord and peasant was replicated in rights and obligations flowing between the Lord and his higher Lord, ultimately to the king himself. When a peasant died, a question arose as to the rights and obligations of his inheriting child to the Lord. To bind this new relationship, Western feudalism adopted a formal process under which the new "tenant" paid a fee or tax to the Lord to bind the new arrangement. In time, peasants came to feel that that they had enforceable rights against the Lord—after all, they paid

15. See Herman Ooms, *Tokugawa Village Practice-Class, Status, Power, Law* (University of California Press 1996); John W. Hall, *Rule by Status in Tokugawa Japan*, 1 J. Japanese Stud. 39 (1974).

16. Toon Peters, *Law and Society*, in *Japan in Communitarianism in Law and Society* 49, 51 (Paul van Seters ed., Rowman and Littlefield 2006).

an inheritance fee to the Lord and as long as they met their part of the bargain—to work the land and pay the required crops and labor—the Lord was seen as required to meet his part of the bargain. In time, peasants saw themselves as having the right to sell the land they farmed as long as the new farmer paid the Lord what was due to him in exchange for the Lord's obligation of protection from outlaws, there was seen to be no complaint that the Lord could make. The Statute of Quai Emptores enacted in 1290 embodied this concept and specifically allowed holders of land under a superior Lord to sell the land without the consent of the superior Lord as long as the purchaser assumed the seller's obligations to the superior Lord. A contractual regime of land ownership and land use can be seen to arise from and to underlie Western feudalism—although the ability to freely sell land would eventually lead to the demise of the feudal system in the West.

In Japan on the other hand, contract played no role in the feudal system. (The prohibition on the sale of land was only abolished in 1873 and personal property (as distinguished from ownership of property by the Japanese Family Unit the *Ie*) came into being as a consequence of changes made after the Meiji Revolution.)[17] Here the "glue" that held the feudal system together was a kind of family or kinship relationship together with Japanese notions of neo-Confucianism. If necessary, myths about kinship had to be developed to allow the glue to serve its purpose. Such a myth conveniently existed in pre-Tokugawa Japan and had been utilized to legitimize the original Yamato rule of a unified Japan. This myth was based on the supposed relationship of the Yamato clan to Amaterasu, the Sun goddess, whose grandson Ninigi was sent to the islands of Japan. In turn, Ninigi's great-grandson, Jimmu, became the first ruler of a unified Japan and the progenitor of the Yamato clan. It is in this context that Tokugawa finally comes to power and the basic model of the Tokugawa regime, which lasted some 250 years, is developed.

When he first came to power, Tokugawa was confronted with a serious question of legitimacy. The Emperor system was still in existence and the Emperor resided in Kyoto. Tokugawa's legitimacy had to be based on something other than "kingship". Of course Tokugawa had some legitimacy through the fact that the Emperor had named him "shogun" but this in itself was insufficient. Some other means of legitimacy and a basis for exerting power needed to be found for Tokugawa's claim to rule all of Japan. Tokugawa relied on three basic pillars to support his rule:

(a) a philosophic base grounded on Chinese Confucianism but interpreted in such a way as to support Tokugawa rule—neo-Confucianism;
(b) power over local Lords through devices that made them subordinate to and "willing" partners in carrying out Tokugawa's instructions; and
(c) autonomy over day-to-day activities of rural districts as long as they followed, or at least appeared to follow, the rules made by the central authority.

17. *History of Law in Japan Since 1868* at 311 (Wilhelm Rohl ed., Brill 2005).

The interpretation of Confucianism used by the Tokugawa rulers included the notion that the peasant (or any subordinate Lord) owed obligations to his higher Lord. In such a philosophical setting, contract played little role. Rights were not important nor did they exist—rather the system was based on dividing society into five basic groupings—one of which was ruler and subject; another husband and wife; etc.—and emphasized the *obligations* within the groups. One such obligation was the obligation of the subject to the ruler, another of the wife to the husband. Rights as understood in Europe simply were not part of the system. Rulers, in turn, had an obligation to justly rule but this notion of obligation was not transformed into "rights" of the ruler's subjects.

Japan was too large for Tokugawa to rule on his own. To carry his authority throughout the "empire", Tokugawa appointed members of his family as Lords in various parts of Japan, gave lands to loyal Lords who had supported him at Sekigahara, and left in place some Lords who later swore allegiance to Tokugawa rule. The Tokugawa Shoguns used a "hostage" system (the alternative residence or *sankin-kotai* system) to assure that not only family members but also the other Lords would in fact be loyal. Local Daimyo were required to build homes in Edo (today's Tokyo) and to have their families reside in Edo while they were in the territory of their fiefdom. The Lord himself was required to spend every other year in Edo. This placed the Daimyo under the power of Tokugawa and also made the Daimyo dependent on Tokugawa largess, as it was expensive to maintain a residence in Edo. Here again the Daimyo had obligations to Tokugawa (and kinship played a role since many of the local Daimyo were now relatives of Tokugawa) but no corresponding rights. [In contrast, in England the Lords lived on the land and directly controlled the area under their control and authority. The local Lord was literally the "Lord of the Manor"]. Tokugawa Shoguns recognized that if the local Lords (Daimyo) banded together they could topple the Shogunate, and thus granted local Lords great autonomy (within the limits of Tokugawa authority) in their own domains.

The third pillar of Tokugawa rule is in many respects the most interesting from the perspective of modern Japanese law. While Tokugawa Japan was a highly centralized administrative state, the local villages and towns—and in some cases the cities that developed—were given a great deal of autonomy, as long as they paid their "rents" and taxes and did not appear outwardly to be violating any of the central government's edicts.[18] Rule in such communities was basically a local matter with local headmen and the "*gonin-gumi*" (Five-Man Group) responsible for maintaining order and seeing that Edo had no cause for complaint.[19] Such local autonomy resulted, in part, from the absence of the local Lord whose presence in Edo was required every other year. A crucial element of maintaining autonomy was to be seen as complying with the demands of the central authority. By appearing to comply there was no need for government officials to visit or maintain order in the community. The basic rule for these semi-autonomous entities was to keep the Tokugawa and even local officials

18. James L. McClain, *A Modern History of Japan* 100 (WW Norton & Company 2002).
19. George Sansom, *A History of Japan, 1615–1867*, 100–103 (Stanford University Press 1963).

away and to resolve disputes—that in feudal England would be settled by the king's circuit riding judges—without interference from the government.

Of course disputes could and did arise between members of the local village. Having no "charter" under which they could act to resolve such disputes (and thus no "courts" or "litigation") these semi-autonomous entities found other means for dispute resolution. Resolution was important as the village headman could be punished for the failures of the village.[20] Typical among the methods used to settle disputes were conciliation by respected members of the community, compromise between the parties—either voluntary or compelled[21] by such means as threats of ostracism or even banishment, and other "extra-judicial" mechanisms.[22] Ostracism was particularly powerful because the villages typically were involved in wet rice production—a communal affair involving communal water sources and communal assistance in planting, harvesting, etc. A farmer required the assistance of the entire community, and contributed to that assistance for other farmers. Ostracism could mean inability to farm, and thus inability to make a living. Similarly banishment was a severe penalty as there was no "right to travel" and peasants could not simply leave village A and set up shop in village B. A peasant banished from his village was in serious trouble.

Tokugawa Japan adopted its own set of edicts to control the conduct of subordinate officials. As a highly centralized governing force, Tokugawa adopted edicts to bind the conduct of the various classes in the feudal society. But unlike in England these edicts were not based on rights. The government set the rules and those governed by them were required to follow the rules. Of course, in Tokugawa Japan disputes arose that might require resolution by either Daimyo or Tokugawa officials. Typically such disputes might involve disputants who came from different villages. In such a situation, the first step was for the village leaders in the two villages to attempt to resolve the dispute through compromise and agreement. But if no resolution could be arrived at it was possible to seek relief from the local Daimyo's Magistrate. However, to do so the complaining party needed to get consent from his village. As villages sought to stay below the governing authorities' radar such consent was not easily obtained and infrequently given.

If the dispute could not be amicably resolved and was between villages in different Han [the territory controlled by each Daimyo] the dispute could be taken to the Tokugawa Magistrate. Here consent was required from the village and from the Daimyo's officials. Even if the needed consents could be obtained there was no assurance that the Magistrate would hear the matter as there was no "right" to a Magistrate's decision.

---

20. Sansom, *A History of Japan, 1615–1867*, 106 (Stanford University Press 1963). For a discussion of village life in Tokugawa Japan with references to apology, the need for cooperation and village autonomy, see Marius B. Jansen, *The Making of Modern Japan* 111-116 (The Belknap Press of Harvard University Press 2000).
21. Jeffrey E. Morrison, *Legal Foundations of the Tokugawa Bakufu and Post Colonial United States* 21–24, http://www.sewha.org/Paper%20SEWHA%202006%20Competion%20(Morrison).pdf.
22. John Owen Haley, *Authority without Power: Law and the Japanese Paradox* (Oxford University Press 1991).

Magistrates in Edo or in the local Han acted in such cases but action by the magistrate was not favored and numerous roadblocks were set up to try to get the parties to resolve the dispute amicably. The prevailing philosophy was that if parties could not resolve their dispute peaceably without interference from the governing authority both parties were at fault. It was the existence of the dispute itself—that is to say the dispute that could not be resolved—that was the fault for which the parties could and should be punished[23].

If the Magistrate heard the case the first impulse would be to get the parties to resolve the matter through agreement rather than through a resolution by the Magistrate. Disputes between town inhabitants were handled in a similar fashion with each town divided into blocks and districts that were similar to the villages in the previous discussion. Moreover, even this limited form of "litigation" did not apply between members of different social classes. This was particularly significant, as samurai were not merchants. Merchants were members of a lower social class and disputes between samurai and non-samurai could not be resolved through a "litigation" process. As for disputes between merchants, as was true for disputes between members of different villages, the parties and their local communities did not wish to involve either the Daimyo or the central government in such matters, but instead fell back on the methods utilized in the semi-autonomous villages and towns to resolve such disputes—mediation and compromise. In such a setting, a vibrant legal system could not and did not arise. Nonetheless, by late Tokugawa times a body of "case" authority was being developed by the Tokugawa Magistrates. This "precedent" was known to the Magistrates but not known to the public in general.

The Tokugawa period began in approximately the year 1600. While in the West the Renaissance had begun and Nation States were beginning to assert centralized control based on a legal system governing relationships based on rights and obligations, be it the common law system of England or the civil law model based on the *Corpus Juris Civilius*, Tokugawa Japan followed a very different path. By the eighteenth century we can see the foundations of Western legal systems as applied in England and the American colonies that were about to embark on revolution. Law is seen in the West as over arching—it limits the power of the government and allows individuals to set the rules that will govern their relationships through contract. The Rule of Law becomes firmly established. But in Tokugawa Japan no such similar path is taken. Instead of a system under which parties can establish their own "law" to govern their relationship (a contract), under which rights are the key ingredient of the system and under which rules exist that can be applied on a principled basis by independent judges, Tokugawa Japan still either follows the commands of a centralized government with no formal legal system that would apply principled rules and allow persons to form their own governing law for their relationships, or follows an informal system of

23. See, e.g., Tsuyohshi Kinoshita, *Legal System and Legal Culture in Japanese Law*, 44 Comp. L. Rev. 25, 87–93 (2011).

dispute resolution that relies on compromise to re-establish harmony between the disputing parties.[24]

[2] Meiji Japan's Adoption of Western Legal Models

In the nineteenth century the imperial West turned its eyes and its military might towards the East. China was divided into spheres of influence of the major Western powers and through the device of "consular jurisdiction" over Western citizens and businesses established in these Western enclaves, lost much of its sovereignty over its own territory. The United States was no idle witness to this phenomenon. It participated in the dismemberment of China and was a principle player in the attempt to do the same to Japan. Before the American Civil War, Commodore Perry arrived in Tokyo Bay with four ships (known to the Japanese as black ships because of the black smoke that belched from their smokestacks) and a demand for a commercial treaty that would "open" Japan to the West. Such opening was seen as required by American interests because of the importance of the whaling trade and the need to provision whaling ships far from the United States. The Tokugawa Shogunate had no desire to "open" Japan but also had no power to match Perry's warships. When Perry returned six months after his first visit with eight "black ships", Tokugawa officials negotiated a treaty opening Japan. Soon other Western powers (and Russia) signed "unequal" treaties with Japan. As all these competing treaties contained Most-Favored-Nation provisions, Japan was in a downward cycle insofar as loss of its authority over tariffs, loss of authority over trade, loss of authority over territory where Westerners could live and trade in Japan, loss of control over its monetary system, etc. A group of rebels (centered mostly in western Japan, an area that historically opposed the eastern Tokugawa regime) saw this as an opportunity to topple the Tokugawa government. These rebels took advantage of the unequal treaties and built on indigenous objections to Tokugawa rule to mount a revolution against the Tokugawa government.

Under the unequal treaties Westerners living in treaty zones were not subject to Japanese jurisdiction but rather to jurisdiction of Consular courts.[25] When the rebels succeeded in their revolution, one of their principle objectives was to undo these unequal treaties and regain sovereignty. Under the banner of throw the barbarians out and restore the Emperor, the rebels succeeded in toppling the Tokugawa government. Upon doing so they moved the Emperor (who had selected Meiji as the title for his era of rule) from Kyoto to Tokugawa's capital, the newly-named Tokyo (Eastern capital—to distinguish it from Kyoto which had been the Imperial capital).[26]

24. Toon Peters, *Law and Society in Japan in Communitarianism in Law and Society* 49 et seq. (Paul van Seters ed., Rowman and Littlefield 2006).
25. For a discussion of the history of consular jurisdiction in Japan and its impact on the policy of the Meiji Oligarchs see, Par Kristoffer Cassel, *Grounds of Judgment* (Oxford University Press 2012) Chapter 4 Exporting Extraterritoriality.
26. For a discussion of the joinder of anti-western views and indigenous concerns in the overthrow of the Tokugawa regime see George Sansom, *A History of Japan, 1615–1867*, 236–242(Stanford University Press 1963).

The rebels who engineered the Meiji Restoration took over control of the government in the Emperor's name and set about "Westernizing" Japan. They recognized that Japan required a Constitution and for this purpose they used a Prussian model. Moreover, the rebels, who now were the de facto government of Japan, recognized that Japan needed a legal system. This recognition stemmed from two notions. First, consular jurisdiction by the Western powers could only be abolished if the Japanese could show the Western powers that Japan had a sophisticated legal system and thus the argument for consular jurisdiction could be blunted. Second, without a legal system Japan could not advance economically, politically and socially to rival the Western powers. The new Japanese government briefly flirted with looking toward China (its historical cultural font) but determined that it should look further west. Two routes to creating a new "Westernized" legal system were followed: (a) Western scholars were invited to Japan as advisors to the new government and (b) Japanese scholars were sent to the West to study Western legal systems (law was simply one of many topics that were studied and numerous scholars were sent west to study other aspects of Western life).

One of the problems confronted by both the Japanese scholars and their Western advisors was language. It was not simply that there were some words in the Western codes that had no Japanese counterparts—although this was clearly one problem—but more significantly some words could not be translated into Japanese because the concept that the word intended to convey simply did not exist in the Japanese language.[27] For example, the French word "*droit*" and the German word "*recht*" may have a companion in the legal word "right" since both express a similar idea, but since the idea expressed by the terms was unknown in Japan a literal translation of the words "*droit*", "*recht*" or "right" would not carry the same meaning to a Japanese reading the translation.[28] Moreover, there existed a fundamental difference between the Japanese and Western scholars over the conceptual basis of "rights".[29] In the West, "rights" were viewed as protecting individual interests while in Japan "rights" were to be considered in a contextual setting so that as circumstances changed so too might the "right".[30] Although the concept of "natural rights" that underlies the American Declaration of Independence and the Constitution was introduced into Japan in the early Meiji period, the doctrine did not take root and it was rejected when the Constitution of 1889 was

27. Even when words existed to capture Western ideas, those words were used in a Chinese/ Confusion context giving them different meanings. See e.g., Takeshi Ishida, *Fundamental Human Rights and the Development of Legal Thought in Japan*, 8 L. Japan 39, 44–51 (Wagatsuma & Braverman translation 1975) [Understanding of Nature law].

28. For a discussion of the creation of Japanese words attempting to capture western legal concepts through the use of existing characters see Kenneth L. Port, *The Japanese International Law 'Revolution': International Human Rights Law and Its Impact in Japan*, 28 Stanford J. Intl. L. 139, 166 (1991).

29. Eric A. Feldman, *The Ritual of Rights in Japan* (Cambridge University Press 2000) argues that the Western notion of rights is not inconsistent with indigenous Japanese constructs (pages 16–19). Nonetheless Feldman concedes that *kenri*, the word typically used for legal right, is derived from the characters for *ken*-that has a connection to authority and power and *ri*, which can be associated with "profit, gain, benefit and advantage" (19).

30. Kenneth L. Port, *The Japanese International Law 'Revolution': International Human Rights Law and Its Impact in Japan*, 28 Stanford J. Intl. L. 139, 166 (1991).

adopted.[31] There existed between the Japanese scholars and their Western counterparts a fundamental gap related to the function of law in Western society and the function that the Japanese saw the law as performing in a "modern" Japan.

As a general matter Western law is "permissive" rather than compulsory. The law allows the parties to determine their own "law" to govern their relationship. Only when the parties have failed to select the governing principle (or when mandated by public policy or specific prescription) does the law enter the equation. Thus, while a civil law Code (or a United States statute or series of court decisions) may appear to completely dominate a field and prescribe conduct relating to that field, in most cases this is simply a "fall back" position that comes into play when the parties have failed to spell out the governing principle. Such a notion was fundamentally at odds with the interpretation of "household rules" and other prescripts handed down by Daimyo or Tokugawa officials directing their subordinate's actions. To Japanese scholars the Codes of Western Europe appeared as good vehicles to assert the authority of the new government, as they appeared to control almost all conduct. To the Japanese oligarchs of Meiji Japan, law was not seen as a means to resolve the issue of how to rationalize individual freedom on the one hand with the need for structure and discipline on the other. Rather, law was seen as a devise that could be used to enforce structure and discipline.[32] To the civil law lawyers who assisted the Japanese the Codes served a fundamentally different purpose.

Having decided that Western Codes should be utilized to form the basis of a new legal system, the Japanese turned to the French and German models. For purposes of this text it is not necessary to detail the debate between the French school and the English school and then the role of the German school, nor is it necessary to go into the debate over the adoption of the Civil Code, originally a French model but ultimately a German model built on a French base. What is significant is that the Meiji government borrowed in wholesale parts from Western civil codes[33] to create the basic Japanese legal system—both its substantive and procedural rules (although they were careful to leave the family law system of the *Ie* (the samurai family system) in place (and indeed to extend it to all classes of society). Those Codes were adopted by the new government and succeeded in their basic purpose of getting the Western powers to renegotiate the unequal treaties forced on the last Tokugawa Shogun and give up their consular jurisdiction. In 1890 the Civil Code was promulgated (effective 1893) and in 1894 the Anglo-Japanese Commercial Treaty provided for the abolition of extraterritoriality in five years. By 1897 the other Western powers had followed suit.[34] Through adoption of

31. William Noel, *The Right to Life in Japan* 3 (Routledge 1997).
32. Takeshi Ishida, *Fundamental Human Rights and the Development of Legal Thought in Japan*, 8 Law in Japan 39, 55 (Wagatsuma and Braverman translation 1975).
33. The late Tokugawa period Magistrates had begun a process that was not dissimilar from the process that created the British Common Law. There was an English Law faction urging adoption of a Western common law system. But a westernized common law takes time to produce while civil law Codes can be quickly adopted to form a new legal system. The civil law system was a natural solution for Japan's need to acquire a western legal system quickly.
34. James L. McClain, *A Modern History of Japan* 256, 299 (WW Norton & Company 2002). After WW2 the United States Occupied Japan and even after returning sovereignty to most of Japan it retained authority over Okinawa for another 20 years. The American military maintains

a Western form of legal system the Japanese had regained their sovereignty. In the process they had created a new Japanese legal system based on the civil law model. This system looked very much like the German legal system and many of its provisions were borrowed wholesale from the German (or French) system.

§2.03 WHAT YOU SEE MAY NOT BE WHAT YOU GET

[A] "Restoration"?

Modern Japan begins with the Meiji Restoration. But, was there in fact a restoration? This question involves two issues; first, was there any power to be restored to the Emperor in the sense that prior to Meiji did the Emperor have any power that could be restored to him? And, second, was power actually given to the Emperor Meiji and his successors or did the oligarchs who took control of the government and acted in the Emperor's name exercise power? If either of these scenarios accurately reflects either the role of the Emperor prior to or subsequent to the "restoration", then in fact there may have been a Meiji revolution but hardly a "restoration" of power to the Emperor.[35]

From an historical prospective one would have to look far back in history to find a time when the Emperor of Japan had any real power. Surely at least from the time of the Kamakura government the Emperor, while held in high esteem and deemed to have great authority, had no real power. The military (administrative) government in Kamakura held the real power in Japan and the Emperor in Kyoto was subordinate in real power terms to the Shogun and the Shogun's government. While there was a period when the Emperor sought to assert his authority—indeed when competing Emperors supported by competing military forces attempted to assert authority—the fact is that even during the warring states period the Emperor had no real power. Throughout the 250 years of Tokugawa rule the Emperors of Japan held no real power. Kyoto may have been the cultural capital of Japan but the real economic and political capital of Japan was Edo, the Shogun's city and the real power resided in the Tokugawa shogun. Indeed, it has been suggested that even the term "Emperor" fell into disuse after the thirteenth century and was not restored until the early nineteenth century.[36]

---

significant bases in Japan, mostly on Okinawa, and under the Status of Forces Agreement between Japan and the United States the United States maintains certain legal rights in connection with such matters as asserted criminal activity by American Service Personnel and accidents involving military equipment. Some in Japan view this retention of rights by the United States military under SOFA as a continuation of extraterritoriality and a denial of Japanese sovereignty. Ian Roberts McConnel, *A Re-examination of the United State-Japan Status of Forces Agreement*, 29 B.C. Intl. & Comp. L. Rev. 165 (2006). In 2011 the United States and Japan came to agreements under the SOFA that gave Japan significantly more authority over American personnel in Japan such as jurisdiction over traffic incidents involving military personnel under the influence of alcohol off base. Additionally administrative agreements now allow the Japanese government to interrogate American service personnel prior to indictment (as is the case with Japanese who are arrested) but permit an American legal advisor to be present during interrogation (a right not granted to Japanese nationals).

35. James L. McClain, *A Modern History of Japan* 154 (WW Norton & Company 2002).
36. Marius B. Jansen, *The Making of Modern Japan* 61 (The Belknap Press of Harvard University Press 2000).

Far from being a significant political player, Emperors during the Tokugawa period were rarely seen in public, never spoke in public and lived quietly in Kyodo under the Tokugawa Shogun's control. Not having had any real power prior to the revolution, the Meiji Emperor could hardly have had power restored to him.[37] Indeed, because of the relative obscurity of the Emperor during the preceding 250 years the Meiji oligarchs engaged in a process of having the Emperor, under whose authority they had claimed to rule, show himself to the public by traveling around the country so he could be seen by the public.

On its face, the Meiji Constitution appears to answer the second of the above questions by saying that power resides in the Emperor and not in the oligarchs. For starters, the Constitution is seen as a gift from the Emperor to the people. The Imperial Oath makes it clear that the Emperor is giving the Constitution as "an exposition of grand precepts for the conduct of the government". And, in Chapter I, "The Emperor", virtually the entirety of governmental power is placed in the hands of the Emperor. The Emperor is at one and the same time the head of the empire, sacred and inviolable. He exercises the legislative power (with the consent of the Imperial Diet), he orders laws to be promulgated and executed, he appoints and dismisses as well as sets the salaries of all civil and military officials, he is supreme military commander, he declares war, makes peace and concludes treaties, he convokes and has the power to dissolve the Diet and its House of Representatives and in their absence can rule by Imperial Ordinance in place of law. While the Constitution provides for Ministers of State, their responsibility is to "give their advice to the Emperor" although they are responsible for their advice.

In reality, the Meiji Emperor and his successors did not rule, although they did have somewhat more say in political consultation than their predecessors. Rather the oligarchs controlled the reins of government and as they died out it became difficult to find real leaders, as the political system was not particularly effective in providing a strong civilian government. Ultimately, the military government that brought Japan into conflict first with China and later with the West succeeded them. Thus the Emperor could neither be restored to a power the Imperial House never had, nor was the Emperor given any real power in the new "modern" Japanese government.

[1] The Emperor System, Sex Discrimination and the Supremacy Clause of the Constitution

The Imperial Household Law adopted in Meiji times (1889) and carried forward after the war limits the Imperial throne to male successors and restricts the Imperial family to the male line. Thus when a female descendant of the Emperor marries a commoner she automatically leaves the Imperial family (reminiscent of the pre-war *Ie* family law system under which the wife became a part of the husband's family). The Constitution on the other hand declares that sex discrimination is not permitted. This raises the

37. For the view that the Meiji Restoration did not conform to Japanese tradition by recognizing power in the Emperor but actually created a new authority for the Emperor see, Christian G. Winkler, The Quest for Japan's New Constitution 26–28 (Routledge 2011).

question whether the restriction against a female on the Imperial throne violates the Constitution. The issue is not merely theoretical. Until the birth of Prince Hisahito in 2006 to the Crown Prince's brother and sister-in-law there was real debate in Japan as to how to deal with the fact that there was no male heir to the crown after the current crown Prince's generation. Although the Crown Price was married and had a daughter his younger brother had two daughters but no son. The debate was in part historical—there had been Empresses in Japanese history but had they ruled in their own right or were they simply in office marking time until a male heir came along—and part traditional—was there really a tradition of only allowing a male to ascend to the throne as there had been no formal rules regarding succession until the Meiji Restoration and the oligarchs had created a male line as part of their need for legitimacy. But it also had "sexist" connotations as some argued that the male only accession provisions reflected the second-class citizenship of women in Japan and legitimatized sex discrimination against women.

The sex discrimination aspects of the succession debate do not appear to have implicated the supremacy clause of the Japanese Constitution. In the United States a Supremacy clause is needed as there needs to be some understanding of the relationship of federal law and the federal Constitution to state law and state Constitutions as the states are themselves bodies containing sovereignty within the federal system. Thus the Constitution, laws made in accordance with it and treaties agreed to by the Executive and consented to by the Senate (i.e., the states at the writing of the Constitution as the Senate was designed to be the representative of the state governments—a power lost when Senators were no longer appointed by states but rather were elected by the people on a state basis) are supreme law—supreme over state law and Constitutions. Japan is a unitary state and thus has no need to differentiate between national and local law—sovereignty resides in the people and is given by them to the national government. In such a situation what does a supremacy clause in the Constitution mean?

It would seem clear that the function of the supremacy clause at a minimum is to require that all other laws—the various Codes of a civil law system as well as special statutes—are subordinate to the Constitution. This then gives meaning to the power of judicial review given to the judicial system. Laws that are in conflict with the Constitution are unconstitutional and the court may set them aside. As the Imperial Household Law is not part of the Constitution a strong argument can be made (and in some circles in Japan is made) that the provisions of the Law that conflict with the Constitution (such as male succession) are unconstitutional. On the other hand the Emperor system is specifically continued by the Constitution (i.e., technically an amendment of the Meiji Constitution) and this leads to both interpretation and intent arguments. There are some who argue that the Japanese language version of the Constitution allows for a male only line of succession since the terms are similar to terms used in certain spheres of Japanese life that had traditionally been male only and remained so after the adoption of the Constitution (i.e., the succession of male kabuki actors). Others argue that the Constitution must be read in historic and cultural terms and that these relate back to the Meiji male only Imperial Line.

From an American legal perspective the stronger argument would appear to be that the male only provisions of the Imperial Household Law are on their face in conflict with the prohibition against discrimination based on sex contained in the Constitution and thus are unconstitutional. However, the debate about succession appears not to relate to sex discrimination in all its aspects—there does not appear to be serious challenge to the fact that Prince Hisahito will be first in line after the Crown Prince notwithstanding the Crown Prince has a daughter and is older than Prince Hisahito. This male preference would appear to be accepted—the only debate was what to do if there were no male successor. Thus sex discrimination in the Imperial line would appear to be an accepted idea although the Constitution would appear to prohibit all sex discrimination whether preferential or exclusive.

Under the Meiji regime, the Imperial Household Law was "Constitutional" in nature and on a level with the Constitution. If considered as "Constitutional" an argument could be made that the Imperial Household Law exists side by side with the Constitution and is not subject to the Constitution. Such an argument would need to confront the supremacy clause and would need to argue that the Constitution is supreme as a general matter but equal to the Imperial Household Law

Although the debate has been postponed, there is no assurance that it will not arise again. The Government has initiated discussion about whether a female member of the Imperial family may be considered as remaining a member of the Imperial line, at least for purposes of having her male children considered for Imperial status in the absence of a "direct" male heir, as well as discussion as to whether a commoner marrying a female member of the Imperial House should be considered as a member of the Imperial family.

The debate over Imperial succession also raises Family Law issues. As noted in Chapter 9 Japan has a Family Register law. When a couple marry they must advise the Registrar of their marriage—indeed marriage is not legal marriage until the Registrar is notified and the marriage entered in the newly married couples newly created Family Register. Generally either party may be the Head of the House of the Register or they may choose either party's family name as the House name. But, female members of the Imperial line cannot set up a branch family register of their father's family Register. In effect, on marriage the daughter is expelled from the Imperial Family Register and relegated to the husband's family register. As the vast majority of married couples choose the husband as Head of House and the husband's family name as their family name the practice of the Imperial family is similar to that of the vast majority of Japanese. And as the plight of the princess discloses the effect of the Family Register law is to perpetuate the feudal practice where the daughter was thrust out of her family register and placed into the husband's family register. Many have argued that the current Family Register system perpetuates and legitimizes sex discrimination in Japan. The debate about whether to allow female members of the Imperial Family to create Branch Imperial families thus not only affects the question of succession to the Throne but also raises fundamental issues of Japanese family law.

[B] A Western Legal System?

Second, was the new legal system really a Westernized civil law system, as it appeared to be on its face? It can be argued that it was not.

Fundamental to the idea of the civil law or common law systems is the notion of the binding nature not just of the agreements made between parties but also of the law that governs those agreements. The "Rule of Law" carries with it the idea that the law—as written or if unwritten as created by the Judicial Branch—has a life of its own and as such, when it comes into play, it must be obeyed. Both civil law and common law would recognize that we are a country of laws and not of men. The law may, in some cases, be inequitable and even may appear ridiculous when applied to the facts of a particular case, but the law must nonetheless be followed. Most legal systems have a safety valve to handle such inequitable or grossly unfair situations—that was a primary role played by equity and it is a role that equity plays in modern common law systems. But equity is not a "freewheeling" system that can simply "right wrongs", rather equity itself is bound by rules, by the maxims of equity, and can right wrongs within the scope of those rules.[38] Special legislation—private bills that become law when accepted by the political branches—also can fill the gap. Of course, not all decisions of a court are based solely on the "law" as it existed prior to the decision—common law courts while bound by stare decisis have the power to reverse themselves or, as is more commonly the case, to restrict an earlier decision to the facts of the earlier case.[39] It is well recognized that "bad facts create bad law". Civil law courts are not so bound and have both ability and some would argue a duty to reinterpret the Code when conscience demands that the judge interpret the Code differently from her predecessor. Nonetheless, the general rule and the guiding principle of the common law and civil law is to give way in the face of the law and to follow the law even if the result is other than what the judge or the society as understood by the judge would prefer.

---

38. The rules of equity were developed by the King's Chancery. Initially Chancery was responsible for issuing the various writs that enabled people to institute suit in the King's courts. As a consequence of the turmoil brought about by the Black Death in 1348 and its various recurrences, the Chancellor issued many new writs resulting in a great expansion of the jurisdiction of the King's courts because once the Black Death struck Parliament was out of session and the King devoted his time to holding together the society. As a consequence the King decreed that various issues be directed to the Chancellor. This marked, if not the beginning of the equity court system at least the start of the great expansion of equity. This same period saw the development of the "use" that later was transformed into the modern trust document and the enforcement of uses by the Chancellor's court. Robert C Palmer, *English Law in the Age of the Black Death, 1348–1381* (University of North Carolina Press 1993) (Chapter Nine, The Chancellor's Court).
39. In *Citizens United v. Federal Election Commission*, 558 U.S. 50 (2010) the Supreme Court reversed a prior decision. Speaking for the Five Justice Majority, Justice Kennedy stated: "Our precedent is to be respected unless the most convincing of reasons demonstrates that adherence to it puts us on a course that is sure error. 'Beyond workability, the relevant factors in deciding whether to adhere to the principle of stare decisis include the antiquity of the precedent, the reliance interests at stake, and of course whether the decision was well reasoned.'... We have also examined whether 'experience has pointed up the precedent's shortcomings.'"

The "Rule of Law" also has at its root a respect for the "professionalism" of the law. Only those trained in the law—whether through educational institutions or through practical experience—are viewed as permitted to appear before the courts, to give legal advice or to serve as judges. In the common law system, laypersons may play a significant role in deciding cases through their service on a jury (and the civil law also permits, in some cases, lay participation in decision making) but in such cases the lay person is limited to making factual determinations and swears an oath to follow the law as told to the jury by the professional judge. The law court may have been the King's Court but early in the development of the common law the king was prohibited from appearing before the court and arguing cases on his own because he lacked the necessary professionalism and qualifications. Similarly, while the King's Chancellor presided over the equity courts, these courts lost their religious backing as early as the fifteenth century when common law lawyers replaced the clerics. This requirement for professionalism separates the law from other aspects of government—legislators may come from all walks of life and need have no particular education or even any education at all. Indeed, there is an argument that can be made that legislators should, because they represent the general public, come from all aspects of the society. But no similar argument would be made for judges in a common law or civil law system. While bakers may have served as judges in the early "pie powder" courts at medieval English fairs, no one would seriously argue today that they should have been permitted to serve as judges in the House of Lords when that House constituted the highest court in England. Nor would it be argued that the Law Lords should not have been learned in the law.

This professionalism has led at least one scholar to reject the typical taxonomy under which law is categorized as common law, civil law, socialist law, etc. and substitute for it the categories of: Rule of Professional Law, Rule of Political Law and Rule of Traditional Law. Professor Mattei in his *Three Patterns of Law: Taxonomy and Change in the World's Legal Systems*[40] places the common law and civil law systems firmly in the Professional Law camp. He notes that both the common law and civil law distinguish between law on the one hand and politics, morality and religion on the other. Less firmly, but nonetheless with some conviction, Professor Mattei places Japanese law in the Traditional Law camp. Of course at the time of its adoption of Western Codes as the prevailing judicial system, Japan had no legal professionals who could serve as either judges or lawyers representing parties. But Mattei's reasoning goes further. He notes the comparatively small numbers of lawyers in Japan and notes that others such as mediators, conciliators, wise men, trusted seniors, etc. perform the same function that is performed by lawyers in the Western Professional Law systems. Mattei's list of common aspects of Traditional Law societies could have been hand tailored for the Japanese legal system.[41] Among the factors he cites are: greater authority by mediators than lawyers, adoption of Western Codes as a consequence of outside influence rather than indigenous change, significance of homogeneity; group

40. Ugo A. *Mattei, Three Patterns of Law: Taxonomy and Change in the World's Legal Systems*, 45 Am. J. Comp. L. 1 (1997).
41. *Ibid.*, 39.

identity rather than individualism as a norm of society, the predominance of duties over rights, etc.

This does not mean that Traditional Law societies in Mattei's taxonomy do not have law or legal institutions—far from it. But, the manner in which such institutions operate in such societies is fundamentally different from how they operate in Western/ Professional law societies. Moreover, it should be noted that in Japan context plays a more significant role in legal culture and the definition of legal "rights" than in a Western society such as the United States.[42]

The United States Constitution is a legal document and, as a general rule courts utilizing what Mattei would call the Rule of Professional Law apply the principles contained in that document. However, certain aspects of the Constitution do not easily lend themselves to a Rule of Law application and it can be argued that the United States has not always applied the Rule of Professional Law to dealing with Constitutional principles. For example, Article II section 4 provides that the president may be removed from office on "Impeachment for, and Conviction of, Treason, Bribery, or other high Crimes and Misdemeanors". On its face, this provision appears to call for application of the Rule of Law. Treason, bribery, crimes and misdemeanors are all words well known to the law and are words that judges apply in litigated situations. The Constitutional provision would appear to call for application of legal principles in a trial for Impeachment. Indeed, the procedural rules contained in the Constitution appear to support application of a Rule of Professional Law. The House of Representatives is given the sole power to actually impeach a president and the Senate "shall have the sole power to try all Impeachments". On its face it appears that a trial for the crimes and misdemeanors outlined in Article II section 4 is called for, a purely legal procedure. Indeed, the "legal" as distinguished from political nature of Impeachment is underscored by the requirement that the Chief Justice of the United States is to preside.

History has, in some ways, treated impeachment differently from what one would expect from the Rule of Professional Law. The impeachment of the first President Johnson concerned itself with Johnson's refusal to go along with what was clearly an unconstitutional Congressional grab for power. The law that Johnson refused to obey would have given the Senate the power to determine whether the Executive could discharge an Executive Branch official responsible for assisting the president in his duty to see that the law is faithfully executed. While Congress, through the Senate, is a player in the appointment process through its power of advice and consent, there is no provision in the Constitution giving the Legislative Branch any power in the removal process. Johnson's actions were clearly constitutional and indeed the actions of the Congress, not the Executive, crossed the line. Johnson was not accused of any crimes but rather was accused of the political act of failing to accede to congressional will. Fortunately for the United States, Johnson fought the impeachment and was found not guilty by one vote.

42. Joseph Sanders & Lee Hamilton, *Legal Cultures and Punishment Repertoires in Japan, Russia, and the United States*, 26 L. & Socy. Rev. 117 (1992).

The case of President Nixon was more closely tied to legal questions. The impeachment articles debated by the House did in fact accuse the president of crimes and misdemeanors. Rather than fight, Nixon resigned.

The case of President Clinton was more complicated. Clearly there was an argument that he had committed a crime—perjury—and thus his actions might technically fall under the crimes and misdemeanors section of the Constitution, but the issue debated was not so much a legal question as a political and philosophical question. Arguments were raised that if there had been a crime it did not matter since it related to a personal affair and not an affair of State; or in any event it was understandable because of the nature of the accusation, or that the accusers were themselves guilty of similar actions, or that......... An objective look at the Clinton matter discloses an excess of politics on both sides of the issue, split down both sides of the political aisle. The question of impeachment was basically a political issue. Each political party placed its own spin on events and on interpretations of the Constitution.

Perhaps the statement of former House leader and later Vice President and President Ford, when the Congress was considering the Nixon impeachment, comes closest to explaining the political aspects of impeachment. As Ford put it, what was an impeachable offense was what Congress said was an impeachable offense. If this is so, then impeachment becomes a political and not a Rule of Law issue and falls into Mattei's definition of the Rule of Political Law. But, impeachment is a very special case under United States law—the three presidential impeachments are illustrative of the unique position of impeachment in the political system. In the cases of Johnson and Clinton a Congressional block whose political agenda was substantially different from that of the Executive Branch utilized the impeachment process as part of a plan to carry out its political agenda. In both cases policy differences played a significant role in the impeachment process. Yet, in both cases the issues were framed as legal issues and in both cases the Senate found the President "not guilty" of committing an impeachable offense. In the Clinton case, both prosecutors and defenders appealed to the public in legal terms, phrasing their arguments in language readily understandable by courts—intention of the Framers, interpretation of "high crimes", the nature of perjury and whether it fit into the category of a high crime, whether "criminal intent" (*mens rea*) was required for the crime of perjury, etc. In other words, while the process may have had a political agenda behind it, the Rule of Professional Law was still given at least lip service in the way the matter was debated and the way its decisions were presented to the public.

Similarly the case of President Nixon ultimately was a vindication of the Rule of Professional Law. Impeachment by the House ultimately resolved itself based on the facts and a legal determination based on those facts. Politics did not save the Executive when his actions were viewed against the legal requirements. Indeed, it can be argued that the beginning of the end of President Nixon's presidency was the decision of the Supreme Court requiring him to deliver up the tape recordings of conversations undertaken in the White House. This was a quintessential Rule of Law decision and the President recognized that he could not both disobey the order of the Court and remain in office. It was the tapes that eventually resulted in the impeachment and resignation and it was the Rule of Law that required him to deliver up the tapes.

While Japanese law borrowed extensively from European Codes, the population was unconcerned with this new legal order and the new rulers of Japan appear to have been unconcerned about the popular view of the law. It can be argued that there existed a fundamental disconnect between the new legal regime created by the Meiji oligarchs and interpreted by the Meiji courts and the realities of Japanese life in the cities and villages of Japan.[43] For example, it was not until the American occupation-inspired Constitution that Japanese Codes and laws were written in a form that was understandable to the population in general. In 1996, the new Civil Procedure Code came into effect in Japan—one of the major changes brought about by the new Code was that it was written in more modern more understandable Japanese and the new Corporations Law adopted shortly after the turn of the twenty-first century brought under one statutory roof the corporation provisions of the Commercial Code and more recent amendments—and did so by use of Japanese writing familiar to the general reading public.

Finally, whereas Western societies had developed a Rule of Law system by utilization of their codes and Constitutions, in Japan a rule by use of law system seems to have developed.[44] It was the intent of the Justice System Reform Council to significantly modify the Japanese legal system and create a system imbued with the Rule of Law.[45] This new focus on law as a means of ordering affairs arose contemporaneously with Japan's utilization of law as a mechanism to protect its position as a world economic power—especially the legal procedures available under the World Trade Organization.[46] This recent focus has given greater impetus to the Rule of Law.

[C] A Civil Law System?

In the dichotomy of common law and civil law systems there is no question that Japan is closer to a civil law system than a common law system. Japan has all the hallmarks of a civil law system—a civil service career judicial system, Codes setting forth the civil law, the criminal law, the commercial law, and procedural codes. Yet in many ways the Japanese legal system operates like a common law system. Because the Americanized Constitution contains the *Marbury v. Madison* version of judicial review and the common law aversion to specialized courts, Japan's unitary legal system allows all courts to exercise the power of judicial review of the Constitutionality of laws. Modern civil law systems have, after the Second World War, adopted the idea of a modified role for a court in dealing with issues of Constitutionality. Thus many civil law systems

43. Yosiyuki Noda, *Introduction to Japanese Law* 59 (University of Tokyo Press 1976). There are differences in the values that different Western societies place on the Rule of Law and differences among "Western" legal cultures. See James L. Gibson & Gregory A. Caldeira, *The Legal Cultures of Europe*, 30 L. & Socy. Rev. 55 (1996).
44. Takeshi Ishida, *Fundamental Human Rights and the Development of Legal Thought in Japan*, 8 Law in Japan 39, 56 (Wagatsuma and Braverman translation 1975).
45. See, Recommendations of the Justice System Reform Council–For a Justice System to Support Japan in the Twenty-First Century, June 12, 2001.
46. For a general discussion of Japan's use of law as a part of its trade policy see, Pekkanen, *Japan's Aggressive Legalism* (Stanford University Press 2008).

today have a specialized Constitutional Court (consistent with civil law ideas separating the public law realm from the private law realm this public law Constitutional issue is placed in a special public law Constitutional Court) that performs functions along the whole range of Constitutionalism from outright declaration that a law passed by the legislature is unconstitutional to limited review of Constitutionality in cases brought by specified public parties prior to enactment of a law. But Japan has no specialized Constitutional Court and the Supreme Court of Japan's determinations of Constitutional issues must be granted a stare decisis affect if judicial review is to mean anything. But stare decisis is the defining characteristic of the common law system.

As is true in the United States, Japan's judicial system is limited to deciding cases and controversies—a hallmark of a common law adversary system. [Without a case or controversy there can be no guaranty that the adverse parties will present the issues that need to be presented for a proper judicial decision.] But civil law systems are characterized by an inquest or at least a modified inquest type procedure. And Japan's civil procedure code gives the judge most of the powers and responsibilities of the inquest judge—including varying the order of questioning so that the court may first question witnesses leaving the parties a subsidiary role in witness examination. Japanese judges while having most of the powers and responsibilities to properly decide cases of the classical inquest judge, lack the power to sua sponte call witnesses and are bound by the political question, case and controversy and standing rules familiar to the American common lawyer and necessary to make a common law adversary system work properly.

Nor is judicial law making foreign to the Japanese Judge[47]. As discussed in greater detail in Chapter 12 dealing with Contract Law, Japan's law governing certain continuing relationship contracts such as leaseholds, employment contracts and distributorship agreements is primarily judge made law. Indeed, the more recent amendment to the Labor Contract Law adopts the judge made law and leaves it to the courts to continue to develop the law appropriate to the employment relationship—a common law legislative approach. The growing and developing law governing what measures are acceptable to ward off a hostile takeover is being made by the courts (see Chapter 13) as there is no legislation defining what is and what is not acceptable. The METI guidelines may prove useful in the judicial analysis of poison pills, but they are not binding and unlike American rules and regulations made after notice and comment rule-making conforming to the Administrative Procedure Act, do not have the force and effect of law. On the other hand when it comes to such matters as how to deal with modern reproductive methodologies (in vitro fertilization and surrogate pregnancy) the courts have adopted a very civil law attitude, refusing to enter the field by placing a modern interpretation on a civil code written before such procedures could have been imagined, until the legislature has spoken.

47. An interesting development in characterization of legal systems is China's recent adoption of a "guiding cases" system under which the decisions in guiding cases are to be used as controlling authority in later cases involving similar issues or arguments. This will limit the discretion of judges in later cases, reduce uncertainty as to the law and will serve to unify the law and thus make the law "common". See, Stanford Law School, China's Guiding Cases Project, https://cgc.law.stanford.edu/why-guiding-cases-matter/.

Even in procedural law areas the Japanese judicial system has not been a passive interpreter of Codes. Unlike the United States that has semi-sovereign States and thus must have rules as to the territorial jurisdiction of State courts, Japan is a unitary country and need not have jurisdictional rules for domestic litigation. The Civil Procedure Code defines the proper venue for cases filed in Japan but had no provision for how to deal with jurisdiction over transnational cases until 2011. A strict reading of the Code would have allowed Japanese courts to handle cases where the defendant has an office in Japan even if the transaction had no contacts with Japan and the local Japan office had nothing to do with the transaction giving rise to the litigation. However, Japanese courts did not treat such venue provision as jurisdictional but rather engrafted on Japanese law a kind of "due process" requirement under which the courts could decline jurisdiction if they found that retaining jurisdiction was unfair to the defendant. And, as a corollary could uphold jurisdiction where the court found that it was not unfair to the defendant to litigate in a Japanese court even though the statutory basis for jurisdiction was absent.[48] Recent legislative changes in jurisdiction in Japan recognize this court made law by providing that even when the court has jurisdiction it may decline to handle the case where to continue would be unfair to a defendant.[49]

Japan's Administrative Law system requires a disposition before a party can seek judicial review of administrative action. But what constitutes a disposition and what procedures are required? As Justice Mutsuo Tahara has noted, Japanese courts have created a case law doctrine requiring fairness in the rendering of administrative dispositions. He tells us that this doctrine has developed over a long period of time through decisions of lower courts and precedents established by the Supreme Court.[50] That is how common law was and continues to be made.

Whether the Japanese legal system has developed its hybrid civil/common law characteristics as a consequence of the American Occupation or for more indigenous reasons (the abortive Tokugawa Magistrates' initial steps towards development of a legal system was similar to the common law development in England), the reality is that Japan's legal system may be characterized as a civil law system with common law characteristics. As such it provides much food for thought and potential lessons to both common law and civil law professionals.

---

48. *Jurisdiction Fairness case, Family KK v. Miyahara*, Case No. 1993 (O) No. 1660) 51 Minshu 4055 (Sup. Ct., Nov. 11, 1997) http://www.courts.go.jp/english/judgments/text/1997.11.11-1993-O-No.1660.html.); *Malaysian Airline System v. Michiko Goto*, 35 Minshu 1224 (Sup. Ct., Oct. 16, 1981), http://www.courts.go.jp/english/judgments/text/1981.10.16-1980-O-No.130.html; Tasuku Matsuo, Jurisdiction in Transnational Cases in Japan, 23 Intl. Lawyer 6 (1978); Akihiro Hironaka, Jurisdictional Theory "made in Japan": Convergence of U.S. and Continental European Approaches, 37 Vanderbilt J. Of Transnational L. (2004); The Draft Convention on Jurisdiction and Foreign Judgments in Civil and Commercial Matters, UIA Seminar, Edinburgh (2001), http://www.cptech.org/ecom/jurisdiction/Dogauchi.pdf.; see also, Goodman, *Justice and Civil Procedure in Japan* 246–247 (Oceana Publications 2004).
49. Article 3-9 Amended Code of Civil Procedure.
50. *Fairness in Rendering a Disposition Required by Court made Doctrine Case*, Case No. 2009 (Gyo-Hi) No. 91, Minshu Vol. 65, No. 4 (Sup. Ct. Petty Bench June 7, 2011) (Concurring Opinion of Justice Mutsuo Tahara), http://www.courts.go.jp/english/judgments/text/2011.06.07-2009.-Gyo-Hi-.No..91.html.

CHAPTER 3

Constitutional Ideology

§3.01 UNITED STATES

[A] Creation of the Constitution

The United States Constitution did not spring forth as full born after the Revolutionary War. The American Revolution was fought by a group of states united in a cause and with a unified army under the command of General Washington. But in no sense was the Constitutional Congress a governing body for the states that were fighting England. In truth there was no unity and there was no unified government nor were these separate states part of any single government. Vermont, for example, would not join the union of states till several years after the war was won and a new government installed.

The successful colonies determined that their new government should take the form of a confederation of separate and independent states. To carry out this goal, Articles of Confederation were drawn up and accepted. These Articles created the new government and gave that new central government precious little power. Power resided in each of the autonomous (for all practical purposes) sovereign states. It is only when this form of government proved itself to be unworkable that efforts were made to create a new central government with real powers. For this purpose a Constitutional Convention was organized and met to determine how to amend the Articles of Confederation. The representatives of this convention were sent by their states to represent the states in this new enterprise. A group of these representatives became convinced that amendment of the Articles could not resolve the issues that confronted the newly victorious colonies (now states) but rather an entirely new form of government, a Federation of states as distinguished from a Confederation of states, was called for. Throwing off the instructions to amend the Articles they set out to draft a new document that would create a new government. In doing so they attempted to deal with the practical problems that had arisen during the Articles of Confederation period and give the new central government those powers required to deal with real and perceived issues. But, there existed among the delegates a concern that the new government not exceed the powers to be given to it and further that its powers be limited by the document they were drafting. These were, after all, representatives of the states and they were representatives who had fought against rule by a central government that was far from the people it ruled. In seventeenth century terms, the scope of the new government's territory was great indeed and the delegates were concerned that this new government that would be far from the people it was to govern not replicate the problems that had existed with England. They knew that a central government with real power was required but they were fearful of making that government too powerful. This idea—fear of the central government and fear of government's power to oppress—resonated with the delegates and resonated with the public in general. It continues to resonate in the United States today.

[B] Limits on the Power of the National Government

To limit the powers of the new government they were creating, the Framers of the Constitution adopted several mechanisms: first, they made it clear that the government they were creating was a government of limited powers. The powers of the new central government were enumerated in Article 1 section 8 of the Constitution. In addition to the 17 specific powers enumerated in the section the new government was given the power to "make all Laws which shall be necessary and proper for carrying into Execution the foregoing Powers, and all other Powers vested by this Constitution in the Government of the United States, or in any Department or Officer thereof". It is important to note what was not given to the new government. The government was not given the power to make all laws necessary and proper as it saw fit. Rather the necessary and proper clause is limited to laws necessary and proper "for carrying into Execution the foregoing Powers" and all other powers vested in the new government by the Constitution.[1] Thus, even the necessary and proper clause was limited in its scope so as to limit the power of the new government. While they were about it, the Framers also wrote in some provisions to limit the powers of the various states that would make up the new union. Such limits included some limitations necessary to enable the new central government to carry out its functions, such as the prohibition of states from entering into agreements with foreign powers or making war themselves or enacting import duties or certain types of tax measures. Others limited the states from enacting laws that the Framers found particularly offensive to their notions of the

1. The Supreme Court (in a 5 to 4 decision) held that neither the Commerce Clause nor the Necessary and Proper clause was a constitutional basis for the Health Care Reform Legislation enacted in 2010. However, the Supreme Court upheld the law. The Chief Justice, while rejecting the Commerce Clause and Necessary and Proper Clause rationales joined the 4 Justices who would have found authority to legislate under the Commerce Clause concluded the challenged provision was authorized by the taxing power, thereby making a majority of 5 Justices finding the law Constitutional, although on differing grounds. *National Federation of Independent Business v. Sebelius*, 567 U.S. ___ (2012).

proper role of government. Principle among these limits was the prohibition against state laws "impairing the Obligation of Contracts".

Second, the Framers created a bicameral legislature and placed the states in control of the Senate. The original Constitution protected state power—and accordingly reduced federal power unless the majority of states agreed—by giving the states the power to appoint the members of the Senate. When this state power over one of the two branches of the legislature is added to the Great Compromise under which each state, regardless of size, is given two Senators and the power given to the Senate to "advise and consent" in regard to federal government senior appointments, it is clear that the states were to act as a "brake" on runaway "power grabs" by the newly created central government. To a great extent this limit on federal power has been undone by the Seventeenth Amendment (1913), under which senators are elected by popular vote in each state.

Third, the powers of the new federal government were limited by the doctrine of Separation of Powers. By diffusing the power of the new government, the Constitution serves to limit the power of any branch of that government and thus to limit the power of the new government itself. This was especially true when one branch (the Legislature) was partially appointed by the states, but still holds true today. The very structure of the newly created government was designed to slow down operations of the government and to create tensions that had the effect of limiting the ability of the new government to take away from the people their liberties. Thus, the Framers created a presidential governmental structure rather than the parliamentary structure they were used to under English rule. The president was to be popularly elected but his powers were severely limited in the Constitution. He lacks the power to make laws and indeed he cannot directly offer his own legislative proposals to the legislature in the form of a legislative Bill. All legislation must originate in the legislature itself and be offered by a member of the legislature. No official of the government (with the exception of the Vice President who is also the President of the Senate and may vote to break tie votes) may, at the same time, be an official of the Legislative Branch. The president's most impressive power on the domestic scene is his power to veto legislation coming to him from the Congress—but even this power is limited since it can be overridden by a supermajority vote of both houses of the Congress.

The Congress, in turn, is completely separated from the Executive function. Congress may pass laws but it cannot execute the laws that it has passed. This is left to the president. By giving the Executive Branch power to execute laws the Constitution places a limitation on the authority of Congress and prevents a "congressional dictatorship". While the Senate has the power to advise and consent over appointees, once appointed the official is no longer subject to Congressional power but typically is subject to the president's power of removal[2] (except in situations involving officials of certain "independent government agencies"—an entity that did not exist at the time of the Constitution's creation nor one that the Framers could have envisioned at the

2. *Myers v. United States*, 272 U.S. 52 (1926).

time[3]). While Congress can appoint its own officials to perform functions for the Congress itself, it cannot appoint officials to execute laws and cannot use congressional officials as supervisors of executive functions.[4] Nor can Congress retain to itself the interpretation of congressional enactments except through the vehicle of creating new laws to better carry out congressional intent or change an interpretation of the laws already passed.[5] Members of Congress cannot accept temporary appointments in the Executive Branch. If a member wishes to serve in the Executive, he or she must resign their seat in the Legislative Branch.

The Judicial function is also separated from the Legislative and Executive function. The judicial authority is given to a separate Judicial Branch consisting of the Justices of the Supreme Court and the various other courts created under Article 3 of the Constitution. To protect their independence, the judges of these courts are given life tenure (during good behavior) and salary protection. Judges are assigned to judicial districts or circuits (if appellate judges) and are not subject to geographic relocation by either the Executive or Legislative Branch. Once appointed to a district, the District Judge serves in that district and while he/she may consent to or ask to serve for a time in a different district, the judge may not be relocated without consent. While the Supreme Court has permitted the Legislature to grant the Judicial Branch power to select Special Prosecutors in certain limited situations involving alleged political corruption or malfeasance,[6] the Judicial Branch cannot itself prosecute cases nor can it enact laws (although it can make rules of procedure to govern cases brought before the federal courts).[7] The Judicial Branch early established itself as the final arbiter of the interpretation of the Constitution (such interpretation being deemed a legal question fit for judicial determination) and in *Marbury v. Madison*[8] concluded that it had the power of judicial review to determine whether a federal or state law was consistent with the Constitution.[9] While the court under this power may declare a law unconstitutional and therefore of no validity, the court lacks the power to create a new law to replace the

3. While Congress may create "Independent Commissions" by limiting the President's removal power (in some situations) to good cause removal, the Congress cannot insulate an Executive Officer from removal except for good cause when the removing official(s) are themselves only removable for good cause. This double layer of good cause tenure deprives the President of the Power given to him to see that the laws are faithfully executed. *Free Enterprise Fund v. Public Company Accounting Oversight Board*, 561 U.S. ___ (2010).
4. *Bowsher v. Synar*, 478 U.S. 714 (1986).
5. *I.N.S. v. Chadha*, 462 U.S. 919 (1983).
6. *Morrison v. Olsen*, 487 U.S. 654 (1988).
7. This rule making power extends beyond procedural rules and permits housing the United States Sentencing Commission in the judicial branch. *Mistretta v. United States*, 488 U.S. 361 (1989).
8. *Marbury v. Madison*, 5 U.S. 137 (1803).
9. Argument exists as to the proper role of the Executive when Congress enacts a law that the President deems unconstitutional either in whole or in part. Presidents have, when signing legislation, appended statements making clear their view that some portion of the law is unconstitutional and retaining the authority to refuse to obey or follow such portions of the law. Such statements have no legislative authority. But is it an impeachable offense for a President to refuse to execute or follow a law the President deems unconstitutional? It would seem clear that the President's action should not be deemed an impeachable act because otherwise there would be no way to challenge the assertion of authority by the Legislative Branch.

voided law or to modify the law to make it conform to the Constitution.[10] This legislative function is a prerogative of the Congress subject to the president's veto power.[11]

[C] Historic Texts to Aid in Interpretation of the Constitution

Although the Framers of the Constitution were drafting a document among and between the states, adoption of the Constitution required the ratification of the Constitution by "Conventions of nine states" before it could be placed into effect. This ratification process was done by popular votes in the various states. Debate about the Constitution was vigorous, and much of that debate dealt with legal points concerning the powers and the limitation on the powers of the new government. Supporters of the Constitution wrote articles and other tracts explaining the provisions of the Constitution these tracts were contained in a volume called the Federalist Papers and are used today in Constitutional litigation to help explain the meaning of the Constitution. Notes taken by James Madison during the drafting of the Constitution are also regularly used in litigation to help explain what the drafters meant by a provision. Eventually the Constitution was adopted but the Constitutional debates left us with two basic items of use today. One is the Federalist Papers discussed above. The other is the Bill of Rights—the first 10 Amendments to the Constitution. These Amendments were promised by the supporters of the Constitution to placate the concerns of people who worried that the new government would possess too much power. In effect, the Bill of Rights became another method by which the Constitution limited the power of the newly created government.

§3.02 JAPAN

[A] Constitution of the Empire of Japan

The Meiji Constitution was written by the new government of Japan and presented to the Japanese people as a gift of the Emperor. Under the Constitution power was supposed to reside in the Emperor and the institutions of civilian government were quite weak. One of the major short falls of the Meiji system was the requirement that the Cabinet contain representatives of the military branch. As the military viewed itself

---

10. Although the Framers were primarily concerned with cabining the power of the new federal government they recognized that that government needed officials who could undertake the duties properly given to them without fear of State retribution. Thus one of the powers of the federal courts is to handle litigation against federal officials for acts taken under color of their office. Similarly, those who assist the federal authorities in carrying out their duties and for this reason find themselves sued in State Courts may have the action removed to federal court. See *Watson v. Phillip Morris Cos.*, 551 U.S. 142 (2007);*Osborn v. Haley*, 549 U.S. 225 (2007).
11. Administrative Agencies are a new addition to government and are part of the Executive Branch although created by legislation. Their role in the tripartite government has been a subject of some dispute. See Justice Scalia's concurring opinion in *United States v. Home Concrete and Supply*, 566 U.S. ___ (2012).

responsible directly to the Emperor, it could simply resign from the Cabinet causing a government crisis. To resolve the crisis and form a new government the Cabinet would have to find a compliant military representative and this meant compromise (or capitulation) with the demands of the military. This severely limited civilian rule and may be one of the bases on which the military government of pre-Second World War Japan came into being.

Another major shortcoming of the Meiji system was the limitation on the rights of the Japanese public rather than a limitation on the rights of the government. Although Article II of the Meiji Constitution is entitled Rights and Duties of Subjects, it really is a litany of duties rather than rights. Every right supposedly granted by the Constitution is, in fact, limited so that the government may by legislative action or Imperial Order having the force of law, take away the supposed right. This cataloguing of rights and simultaneously limiting those rights to legislative action can be viewed as a reflection of the diametrically opposing views of Western law and the Japanese concept of law in Meiji Japan. The Meiji reformers viewed the Western legal system they were adopting as a means of ordering all forms of interaction and a means by which the government could control all activities rather than a means of setting the populous free to order their own relations with the law as a fall back to cover provisions the parties had failed to provide for—and utilizing the law as a means of regulating government power.

[B] The American Occupation and the Constitution

When the United States military authorities occupied Japan they determined to fundamentally change the Constitution. Before the U.S. military authorities became involved in the Constitution-writing business the Japanese themselves drafted several proposed Constitutions. An official draft was presented to the Americans and rejected by the occupation authority. Instructions were given to the legal staff at General Headquarters to prepare a Constitution for the Japanese. This Constitution was drafted by Americans in six days and given to the Japanese who commented on it and made some changes. Attempts to more significantly modify the American draft were countered by American threats about the status of the Emperor and threats to take the American draft directly to the Japanese people for a popular election. The Japanese government understood that its role was to accept the new Constitution. The government also understood that if the American draft were presented to the people alongside the official government draft the American draft would be overwhelmingly approved. The new Constitution (as drafted by the Americans with some modifications made by the Japanese committee to which it was referred by the prime minister—and which modifications were agreed to by the Americans—and some modifications made via translations that were slipped by the Occupation) was promulgated by the Showa Emperor on 3 November 1946, which happened to be the 94th anniversary of the birth of the Meiji Emperor.[12]

12. James L. McClain, *A Modern History of Japan* 539–542 (WW Norton & Company 2002).

The new Constitution thus had a very different history from that underlying the United States Constitution.[13] There were no serious debates reflected in documents such as the Federalist Papers. There were no drafting committee reports such as those reflected in Madison's notes on the debates at the Constitutional Convention. In short there was no Japanese "legislative history" that could be relied on by a court to interpret the intention of the Framers. More significantly, since the Framers were not Japanese the question arises: Is the intent of the Framers relevant to issues of Constitutional construction?

The American Framers of the Japanese Constitution sought to create a Rule of Law society paralleling that of the United States. It was an overriding belief of the Occupation that Japan should adopt a political system based on the democratic ideals of the victors. Such a political society, it was felt, would serve as a bulwark against future militarism. The American Framers were not unaware of Japan's history and while they sought to embody in the Constitution the ideals that they felt defined a democratic society, they did not try to completely dissociate Japan's new governing law from Japan's history. The rights set out in the Constitution differed substantially from the Meiji Constitution in that these rights were not nearly as limited as was true in Meiji.

It is of course true that the Constitution does provide that the Japanese people "shall refrain from any abuse of these freedoms and rights and shall always be responsible for utilizing them for the public welfare" (Article 12) and further that "Their right to life, liberty and the pursuit of happiness shall, to the extent that it does not interfere with the public welfare, be the supreme consideration in legislation and in other governmental affairs" (Article 14). Such provisions have the potential for abuse and could be read to be a limitation on all of the Constitutional rights granted to the people under the Constitution. However, the Supreme Court of Japan has for the most part[14] rejected such interpretation and it is to be hoped that such provisions will never be distorted to return to the Meiji Constitution's limitations on rights. In context it is clear that these limitations were designed to be narrow in scope and that it was surely not the intent of either the Americans who drafted the Constitution or of the post-war Japanese government that enacted the Constitution to return to Meiji doctrine.

Like the structure of the United States Constitution, the structure of the Japanese Constitution is instructive. The United States Constitution begins with the Article governing the Congress—the branch of government that the Framers felt would have the greatest power and then moves to the Executive and finally the Judicial—the least powerful branch. After defining the structure of the new government, the United States Constitution moves onto other issues such as, full faith and credit, amendment, supremacy etc. The Japanese Constitution begins with the institution of the Emperor and defines the Emperor's role as a symbol of the Japanese State, it then moves to Renunciation of War—considered a very important Article by the victorious American

13. For a brief statement of the American role in the drafting of Japan's Constitution, see Theodore McNelly, *The Japanese Constitution: Child of the Cold War*, 74 Pol. Sci. Q. 176–195 (1959).
14. See Chapter 7 for cases in which the Court used Article 12 to limit expression through mass demonstrations.

authorities who did not want to confront a future war in the Pacific and saw the demilitarization of Japan as a primary object of the war. Article III deals with the Rights and Duties of the People, followed by the Articles that define the structure of the government—the Diet, the Cabinet and finally the Judiciary. The Japanese Constitution retains the British parliamentary democracy model of government rather than changing the system to the American presidential model. Thus, the Diet is the repository of State power and has the exclusive power to make laws. (Article 41) The Diet is to consist of members elected by and to be representative of the people (Article 43). The Constitution retains the bicameral model that had existed prior to the war. (This represents a change from the original American proposal—the American drafters saw no need for a two-House legislature since Japan is a unitary State and thus did not have the same need for a second House as was the case for the United States Senate.) Consistent with the parliamentary democracy model, the prime minister is to be a member of the Diet (Article 67) and is to be elected by the Diet. The prime minister in turn selects the remainder of the Cabinet (a majority of whom but not all of whose members need to be members of the Diet and whose number is limited to 17 by legislation), all of whom must be civilians, thus eliminating military officer representation in the Cabinet and thus reversing one of the perceived shortcomings of the Meiji Constitution. (Articles 68, 66(2)) The primacy of the prime minister is reinforced by the Constitutional provision giving the prime minister the unfettered authority to discharge other Cabinet members at will.[15] (Article 68(2)) The Cabinet in turn is subject to removal by no-confidence vote by the Lower House. (Article 69)

Although the Diet is a bicameral legislative body the two bodies do not have equal power. The superior House is the Lower House or the House of Representatives, which can put a budget in place without the consent of the Upper House, can appoint the prime minister without approval by the Upper House and can by a two-thirds vote override a rejection of legislation by the Upper House. (Articles 59, 60, 67) This does not make the Upper House powerless—an amendment to the Constitution requires a two-thirds vote of each of the Upper and Lower House, certain appointments require approval by both Houses and overriding the "veto" of the Upper House implicates political questions, although in recent years the majority Party in the Lower House being different from the majority party in the Upper gridlock has become as common in Japan as in the United States. If the Lower House passes a Bill late in its session there may not be sufficient time for action in the Upper House and then override in the Lower House. In 2007 this was the situation the Fukuda government faced when control of the Upper House passed from the LDP to the opposition DPJ and the Lower House passed a Bill to permit Japan to continue to be a coalition partner in connection with refueling ships to aid the American effort in Iraq. Although the LDP had sufficient votes to

15. Although the Prime Minister may remove a Cabinet Minister if the Minister fails to follow the PM's direction, the Prime Minister may not directly manage the Minister's department. This is similar to the distinction invoked by then Attorney General Richardson and Deputy Attorney General Ruckelshaus when each refused to discharge Special Watergate Prosecutor Cox after being directed to do so by President Nixon. Each refused to obey the President out of moral conviction and each resigned believing that the President had a right to have a Cabinet Member who would follow his direction.

override a rejection by the Upper House, the 2007 year ended before the Upper House was required to act on the Bill and Japan's participation in the refueling operations ended. While the Lower House can on its own pass the budget, it cannot pass the many bills that are required to put the budget plan into effect. This is particularly important because of Japan's continuing budget deficits that require funding through the issuance of government bonds. The passage of bond legislation is considered an ordinary legislative matter and thus the Lower House does not have complete authority over such bills, unless it can muster the 2/3 vote needed to override Upper House rejection or inaction.

The Cabinet as a whole is invested with the Executive power (Article 65) and when a no-confidence motion is passed, the Cabinet as a whole must resign. (Article 69) The Constitution allows the cabinet to remain in office after a no-confidence motion if the government dissolves the House of Representatives and in such case a new election for the House must be held within 40 days (Article 54). There is no Constitutional requirement that the prime minister resign if his party loses an Upper House election (50% of the Upper House is elected every three years for six-year terms) but the prime minister as the leader of his party may feel compelled to "accept responsibility" for his party's loss by resigning. This does not signal a change in government, as the Lower House is not dissolved nor has the prime minister lost the confidence of the Lower House. In such a situation the Lower House will simply elect a new prime minister, who in turn will bring in his new Cabinet. This is what occurred when in 2007 the LDP lost the Upper House election to the DPJ and then Prime Minister Abe succumbed to party pressure and resigned. On the other hand, when the DPJ lost control of the Upper House in August 2010 Prime Minister Kan refused to step down and survived an internal party challenge to his leadership of the DPJ only to resign in the summer of 2011 (to be succeeded by Prime Minister Noda) as a consequence of the March 11, 2011 Great East Japan Earthquake and Tsunami and the Fukushima Nuclear Disaster.

The LDP had ruled Japan continuously from its formation as a coalition of conservative Parties (1955) until the revolt of Ichiro Ozawa and his faction in 1993.Their defection on a vote of confidence brought down the LDP government and in the ensuing general election the LDP remained the largest party but it did not command a majority in the Lower House. Ozawa cobbled together a coalition of eight Parties and Morihiro Hosokawa became the first non-LDP Prime Minister in almost 40 years. The coalition could not hold together and the LDP formed a coalition with their historic rivals the Japan Socialist Party (JSP) and retook control. The JSP faded away and it would not be until 2009 when the LDP lost a general election to a majority party—the DPJ formed via a merger of Ozawa's party with the party of Yukio Hatoyama (the Democratic Party of Japan or DPJ). The DPJ has had problems governing because of weak leadership in the Prime Minister position, financial scandal and divided government as a consequence of loss of the Upper House to the LDP in 2010.

Chapter VI of the Constitution creates the Judicial Branch and unlike the Meiji Constitution prohibits the creation of special courts. (Article 76(1)(2)) Judges are specifically granted independence (Article 76(3)) and judges of the Supreme Court are subject to popular referendum vote both at the first general election of members of the Lower House after their appointment and again 10 years later (Article 79). Judges do not serve life tenures. Judges of inferior courts are appointed by the Cabinet for terms of 10 years and may be reappointed (Article 80) and all judges are subject to mandatory retirement based on age as that age is determined by law. (Articles 79, 80) Judges may be removed if judicially declared to be mentally or physically incapacitated but otherwise removal is limited to public impeachment and the Executive Branch is specifically prohibited from administering disciplinary actions against judges. (Article 78) Instead, the Judicial Branch through the Supreme Court is empowered by rule to control the judicial system and the Bar. (Article 77)

The Japanese Constitution specifically gives the Supreme Court the power of judicial review (Article 81). As the drafters were representatives of the American New Deal, which had seen some of its most far-reaching reform legislation stricken down by the Supreme Court on Constitutional grounds, the original draft of the Japanese Constitution limited the power of judicial review to the Rights and Duties portion of the Constitution. The final version was not so limited.

The Constitution also contains provisions for local self-government pursuant to which provincial governors and councils and other legislatively determined local officials are to be elected by direct popular vote. (Article 93(2)) Such a provision may appear somewhat anomalous considering that Japan is a unitary state and that these locally elected officials lack the authority that similar local officials would have in the United States where the primary local authority—the state—is semi-sovereign. The United States drafters, in the belief that public election of local officials would serve as a bulwark for democratic rule, added this provision. Some in the Occupation wanted to strengthen the provisions to give local authorities both taxing and law making authority, but such a change from a unitary government system to a form of federation was considered too revolutionary and was rejected. Although for the first 50+ years after the adoption of the Constitution the ruling LDP structured grant programs in such a way that elected local officials became, in essence, campaigners for LDP candidates in national elections, electoral reform and mergers of municipalities in more recent years may have broken the hold that the LDP had on such local officials. It is likely that the defection of local officials from the LDP and the election of reform minded local officials had a significant effect on the DPJ's electoral victory in 2009 when, for the first time, the LDP was voted out of office by an opposition party.[16] In 2012 a local political party led by a charismatic governor and then mayor of Osaka transformed itself into a national party and is seen as a real challenge to the established LDP and DPJ in the forthcoming fall 2012 or 2013 Lower House election.

Article IX sets up a procedure for amendment of the Constitution that requires action by a supermajority of each House of the Diet (two-thirds vote) and popular acceptance by referendum or other vote. Chapter X makes the Constitution the

16. See, Sherry L. Martin, *The Influence of Voters* in *Routledge Handbook of Japanese Politics* (Routledge 2011) ch. 8; Jun Saito & Kyohei Yamada, *Local Government* in *Japan in Routledge Handbook of Japanese Politics* (Routledge 2011), ch. 10.

Supreme Law and laws, ordinances, imperial rescripts, or other act of government inconsistent with the Constitution are deprived of legal force and effect. (Article 98)

Notably lacking in the Constitution is any provision dealing with the effectiveness of pre-Constitution laws. This may be accounted for by the fact that the Constitution was not a "new" document in law but rather an amendment of the Meiji Constitution following the amendment provisions of the Meiji Constitution. Accordingly pre-Constitution laws were considered as remaining in effect but subject to the Supreme Law provision of the newly amended Constitution. This required some changes in basic laws such as the Family Law and subjected other laws to examination in court cases to determine whether the old laws were consistent with the new Constitution. As will be seen, the Supreme Court of Japan has been very restrained in holding laws unconstitutional, and this includes pre-war laws that were designed to stifle freedoms that the new Constitution was supposed to enshrine. Thus the election law passed as a counterweight to the 1920 laws opening up the franchise to almost universal male suffrage and restricting electioneering activities remains on the books and has been upheld in every challenge mounted against it in the post-war period.

A review of the Japanese Constitution shows that, like the United States Bill of Rights, it contains many provisions designed to protect the people from the potential oppressive power of the government. However, unlike the United States people in Japan do not appear to be overly concerned about the potential for government abuse of its powers. While Americans, whether liberal, conservative or unaligned and not capable of being categorized in such easy terms, are concerned that government not exceed its bounds and trample on individual liberties, the Japanese, on the whole, respect the government and do not fear it. In this respect the Constitution seems to protect against something for which protection is not sought. In a sense we are presented with a contradiction—Americans who have never seen military government or totalitarian regime revere the protections against such potential; Japanese whose history is filled with military government and whose World War II government may be categorized as authoritarian, do not appear concerned about such protections.

§3.03 WHAT YOU SEE MAY NOT BE WHAT YOU GET

[A] Executive and Legislative Power

The American Executive's Constitutional power in the domestic arena is quite limited. The President has no independent power to compel consideration of legislation. Nor can the president vote on legislative matters. His Constitutional role in the legislative process is a negative power—a veto authority—and a limited negative power since Congress retains the power to override a presidential veto. Notwithstanding, the president has emerged as a powerful legislative force and as a powerful domestic political figure whose power exceeds that which the Framers envisioned.

The president cannot on his own do what he may wish to do on the domestic scene. He is bound by the Constitution to follow the law and can only exercise such powers as may be given to him through legislation. Thus, even in the midst of the great depression President Roosevelt found himself at the mercy of Congress in getting legislation passed to aid his New Deal programs and this legislation in turn was captive to the Supreme Court's power of judicial review. In the midst of the Korean War, President Truman was found to be without power to seize the steel mills to prevent a shut down as a result of a threatened labor strike.[17] Congress, not the president, had the power to deal with such threats through legislation that the president could then administer and the president had no power on his own—not even during a time of fighting abroad and in the name of national security—to seize the mills to keep the steel rolling to make the munitions needed to prosecute the war.

In the final analysis the power of the president is severely limited by the Constitution and he is left with the all-important power of persuasion. While recent authority has permitted the Congress to delegate more and more power to the Executive Branch, the fundamental Rule of Law and separation of powers principle applies—the president cannot legislate, he can only execute.

Similarly, the Congress is limited in the power it can exercise. Congress has only the authority to pass laws; it cannot itself execute those laws. If the president or other Executive Branch officials interpret those laws differently from the initial congressional intent then the proper role of Congress is to pass new legislation making its intent clear. Third persons affected by the supposed improper interpretation may, of course, seek relief from the Judicial Branch if they have standing to sue and can present a justiciable question in the context of a case or controversy.[18] But Congress as an institution is limited to legislating. Nor can Congress retain any authority after it has legislated to determine whether the Executive is properly exercising the authority given to it. Thus, an attempt to write a legislative veto under which either one House or both Houses could reverse a rule or regulation proposed by the Executive Branch to carry out a legislative directive is unconstitutional.[19] Similarly an attempt to have a legislative officer such as the Comptroller General of the United States play a role in administering a statute is unlawful and will not be permitted.[20] The issue in each case is not whether Congressional or Executive activity is wise or useful or helpful in light of modern concerns or the facts of the day. The issue in each case is whether the law as set out in the Constitution permits the branch to exercise the power or authority it seeks to use. In short, the Rule of Law will determine the outcome.

As a practical matter the separation of power between the executive and legislative works, as a general rule, in a manner consistent with the intent of the

17. *Youngstown Sheet and Tube v. Sawyer*, 343 U.S. 579 (1952).
18. As a general rule the Supreme Court is agreed that taxpayer status is not sufficient to grant standing. *DaimlerChrysler Corp. v. Cuno*, 547 U.S. 332 (2006). Differences exist on how to apply the taxpayer rule when the government acts at issue in a Constitutional case involve Freedom of Religion and Separation of Church and State issues. See *Hein v. Freedom From Religion Foundation, Inc.*, 551 U.S. 587 (2007). and *Arizona Christian School Tuition Organization v. Winn*, 563 U.S. ___ (2011).
19. See *INS v. Chadha*, 462 U.S. 919 (1983).
20. *Bowsher v. Synar*, 478 U.S. 714 (1986).

Framers.[21] This may be, in substantial part, as a result of the United States voter's willingness to split her vote between the political parties. Thus, it is common—indeed it is the rule rather than the exception—for power to be divided between the political parties. Even where both houses may be in the same political hands, the president's veto acts as a check on legislative power and the ability of senators to "filibuster" a bill to death by endless debate serves to check legislative action.

The Japanese Constitution does not contain the same separation of powers provisions as the United States Constitution. In a parliamentary democracy the separation between Executive and Legislative power that exists in a presidential system is simply inapposite. It is expected that "political party discipline" at work in the election of a party leader as prime minister will, assuming that there is not a severely split coalition government, result in a strong Executive. The Japanese Constitution gives the prime minister far greater power than the American president. The prime minister can dissolve the House of Representatives and compel members to stand for election—an impressive power as politicians are not known for wanting to have to run any more often than is necessary for fear that they might be voted out of office. The prime minister appoints the Cabinet and may remove Cabinet ministers all without Diet input. He has the power to submit Bills to the Diet (of which he is a member) and he is in charge of the administrative organs of the State (Article 72).

While separation of powers would appear to be inapplicable to the Executive and Legislative Branches in a parliamentary democracy since there is no real separation between the two—indeed, members of the one are also members of the other and exercise their powers as members of each branch (thus members of the Cabinet who are also elected members of the Diet vote on legislation and then may be responsible for administering the law passed by the Diet)—Japanese scholars insist that the structure of the Japanese government is based on separation doctrine and principles. It is said:

> The national government of Japan is formed according to the doctrine of separation of powers, which is also found in other Constitutions including that of the United States.[22]

The Constitution of Japan divides power into three categories: legislative, executive and judicial power. Each power is vested in separate organs, namely the Diet, the Cabinet and the Supreme Court and other courts. Article 41 provides that the Diet shall be the exclusive law making body, while Article 65 simply states that the executive power is vested in the Cabinet. It is laid down in Article 76 that complete judicial power reposes in the Supreme Court and in inferior courts established by law.

Although it is recognized that a "pure" separation of powers cannot exist in a parliamentary democracy Japanese scholars maintain that a "'practical' doctrine of separation of powers" exists. In fact, however, most legislation passed by the Japanese Diet is legislation that has its genesis in a Cabinet Bill, i.e., a Bill introduced in the Diet

21. For a general discussion of Separation of Powers in the United States system, see Carl F. Goodman, *Separation of Powers: An Experiment in Pragmatic Constitutional Interpretation*, 17 Hiroshima L. J. No. 2, 512 and No. 3, 448 (1993).
22. Hiroyuki Hata & Go Nakagawa & Takehisa Nakagawa, *Japanese Constitutional Law* pt. 2, sec. 1 (Kluwer Law International 2001).

by the Executive Branch. Unlike the United States Legislative Branch, Diet members have relatively small staffs and must rely on the Executive to submit legislative proposals. The elected Executive in turn relies on the Departments and Agencies to come up with legislative language and proposals. The end result is Executive action but a type of Executive action not anticipated by the Constitution, which does not contemplate the extensive power of the Japanese bureaucracy.

Typically legislative action in Japan has its beginnings in study groups or consultative groups composed of competing interests whose views must be heard and reconciled in the ultimate legislation. These groups are organized by the Executive and invariably have on them representatives of the government agency with responsibility in the area. The agency representatives in turn mold the agenda, do the paper work, and while the individuals may change the agency policy objectives remain the constant in a process that may take several years. Any bill that emerges from the group process will be highly influenced by the bureaucracy and its views on the subject. Elected officials do not have legislative staffs of their own that can or do draft legislation for Diet action. Here again the bureaucracy is at work. The DPJ government elected in 2009 set as one of its principle goals the limitation of the power of the bureaucracy and a transfer of power from senior administrative officials to elected officials. This policy has not been carried out to date.[23]

Whereas in the United States most legislation that calls for administrative action sets out at least a general outline of policy directives that must be followed and provides for judicial review of Agency action to assure that at least the Judicial Branch has a chance to review whether agency action conforms to the policy directives of the elected Executive and Legislative Branches, Japanese legislation rarely has such safeguards. It is simply too much to expect that bureaucrats will write specific legislation that ties their own hands or provides for a judicial review of their actions. These essential elements of a Rule of Law society are not commonly found in Japanese legislation. Moreover, the long consultative process that looks for accommodation of competing interests tends to result in less "compulsory" legislation than would be expected under the Japanese Constitution. Rather, much legislation is couched in general policy terms or contains terms "requiring parties" to "endeavor" to take certain actions or fail to take such actions. If parties do not take the actions involved, their inaction is not subject to judicial enforcement, but rather the bureaucracy is given power to "push" the recalcitrant party towards cooperation in carrying out the legislative goal. Accordingly, while legislation may appear to embody a national consensus on a subject there is not an effective legal mechanism to compel a party to follow this consensus. The "law", in the form of legislative intent, may be clear but the legal remedy is less clear, thus making the "law" that must be applied less clear.

Further, it is generally believed that in a parliamentary system the Executive has much greater powers than in a presidential system controlled by checks and balances. This would appear to be especially true in a system where one party, the Liberal Democratic Party (LDP), had been in power for almost all of the post-war period until

23. Akira Minami, Noda makes key concession to bureaucrats, Asahi Shimbun Sept. 11, 2011, http://www.asahi.com/english/TKY201109100201.html.

2009. But that was not the case in Japan where ministerial posts under the LDP were distributed based on "factional" political realities and where ministers changed frequently.[24] In part the reasons for this anomaly may lie in the fact that what you see in the LDP is not what you get. Far from being a monolithic political party that held power for almost all of the post-war period, the LDP is really a group of political parties or factions who stuck together to exercise power. While it is probably true that there is a fundamental "conservative" bias that holds the various factions together, the fact is that the LDP represents within itself a "coalition" party and thus LDP governments represented coalition governments in fact, if not in name. In such a setting, the prime minister tended to be an acceptable "least common denominator" political figure. Someone whom all the coalition partners can deal with and whom none are fearful of. Even when a prime minister is popular, he may not be able to translate that popularity into policy. The coalition nature of the LDP and its various governments created a power vacuum that was quickly filled by Japan's bureaucracy.

The DPJ, formed primarily by disaffected LDP power brokers and members, similarly has within it factions, although Prime Minister Noda is attempting to establish party discipline under his leadership, going so far as to expel party powerbroker Ozawa and his followers from the party. In its short time in office the DPJ has had three Prime Ministers, demonstrating the weakness of the post.

Once the government resolves its internal factional disputes over legislation and policy, it must then negotiate with the minority parties. This "two-stage coalition consensus process" dilutes strong action by compromising away strong provisions in order to get consensus. So too, divided government wherein one party controls the Lower House and Government and the other the Upper House has led to compromise, weakening policy positions or deadlock resulting in weak or no legislation. Thus a "lowest common denominator" Executive (the Cabinet headed by the prime minister) has typically put forward a "low common denominator" legislative program. This "political weakness" tends to increase the power of the bureaucracy that must step in to fill the gaps on weak legislation and also to draft the legislative language that encompasses the various compromises made. The end result is a powerful bureaucracy, a weakened Executive and a weak Legislative Branch. Not what one would expect from the language of the Constitution that gives the prime minister substantial powers including the power to appoint the Cabinet and discharge Ministers at his sole discretion.

For most of the post-war era the LDP had been the ruling party in Japan and the Social Democratic Party (SDP) had been the formal opposition party. Many Japanese voters withheld support from the left leaning SDP out of concern that the SDP could not affectively govern or could not be trusted to govern. When the SDP joined a coalition with the LDP under which the leader of the SDP became prime minister it was forced to abandon some of its cherished positions, such as the asserted illegality of the Self-Defense Force. After the coalition collapsed the SDP became a splinter party with virtually no membership in the Diet. A new opposition emerged (the DPJ) Although the

24. See Lawrence W. Beer, *Japan's Constitutional System and its Judicial Interpretation*, 17 L. Japan 7, 18 (1984).

DPJ unseated the LDP in the Lower House election of 2009 its margin of victory in the Lower House did not permit it to override a rejection of legislation by the Upper House. The LDP regained control of the Upper House in 2010 and deadlock on most issues has been the result. Some have suggested that the reform of Japan's election system brought about in part by the Supreme Court's apportionment decisions and in major part by the efforts of Ichiro Ozawa may lead to a stronger Prime Minister. The Hosokawa government interlude of nine months when the LDP was out of power before reemerging as a coalition with the SDP, created election reform with a single-seat electoral district system complimented with a proportional representation system, the current system. This has made Japanese politics somewhat more like American or British politics in the sense that the proportional representation portion of the election system relies on a strong Party leader who is seen as the face of the Party while the single-seat districts allows for direct competition between candidates and parties. Candidates who lack Party support are at a disadvantage in campaigning as Japan's campaign laws are very restrictive but grant Parties more flexibility then single seat candidates in campaign practices (see Chapter 7). This in turn is seen as elevating the role and power of the Party leader, especially as the political parties have greater electioneering speech rights than do individual candidates in Japan.[25]

[B] Limits on National Government Powers: Local Government Powers

The Bill of Rights in the United States Constitution constitutes a clear and unambiguous attempt to limit the powers of the new federal government. Thus Amendment 1 can hardly be clearer in its attempt to limit the new government's authority—" Congress shall make no law ... "As interpreted by the courts, the Bill of Rights granted citizens direct rights against the excessive use of power by the new federal government. Thus, if Congress makes a law abridging the freedom of speech granted by the First Amendment a newspaper or a news reporter party in interest who has standing to challenge the law may do so in a case or controversy to be heard by the federal courts. It is governmental action that the Bill of Rights was intended to protect against as distinguished from personal or private action. Thus a news reporter who objects to her paper's editorial policy has no First Amendment right to sue her paper claiming that the paper has denied her freedom of speech.

The Bill of Rights was enacted in 1791. It soon became clear that excessive federal powers could be exercised by way of the newly formed judiciary. Thus, the states became concerned that judicial action against a state by citizens of a different state or a foreign State (thus creating a diversity of citizenship that gave federal courts the authority to act) could give the new Federal government power over state actions. The Eleventh Amendment was designed to deal with this issue by limiting the judicial powers of the new federal government and prohibiting the new judiciary from handling such suits.

25. See Roy Christiansen, *Election Systems and Campaign Rules* in *The Routledge Handbook of Japanese Politics* 63 ch. 6 and ch. 7 herein, Freedom of Expression.

The Bill of Rights limits on the federal power taken together with the fact that the new government was a government of enumerated powers, i.e., only those powers given to it by the Constitution, were designed to limit federal authority. Yet today it is clear that more and more issues that at one time might have been considered state issues have been subsumed by the federal government. Health care and the Supreme Court's sharply divided ruling in 2012 upholding the federal health care reform law is but the latest example. Is this a case of "what you see may not be what you get?"

This process has been, in part, a function of changing Constitutional law through amendment of the Constitution itself and changing judicial interpretation of the Constitution. However, at all times the process has been one dominated by legal considerations and the legal battle over the proper power of the states vis-à-vis the Federal government continues.

The most substantial weakening of the state power and a resulting expansion of the Federal Power is to be found in the Civil War Amendments (Thirteen, Fourteen and Fifteen) that both prohibited the states from engaging in certain activities and also expanded the Federal Power to deal with issues dealt with in the Amendments (e.g., "Congress shall have power to enforce this article by appropriate legislation").

The inevitable result of the victory of the Union forces in the American Civil Law was that the rebellious states were once again states in the federalism system and thus retained the rights that all states previously possessed. As a consequence, after the war the Constitution was amended to limit the power of the states in certain regards and to extend the powers of the Federal Government in connection with those matters. The next major diminution of state power was the Amendment calling for direct election of Senators. Under the original Great Compromise scheme of the Constitution all states were granted two Senators to permit equality among the large and small States. But, in addition, the States themselves were to appoint the Senators who serve six-year terms. When direct appointment by state legislatures was abolished and Senators were elected by statewide ballot, the views of the state government in the state where the Senator was elected no longer became a primary consideration for Senators who now became a part of the central government mechanism with no responsibilities or ties to the state government—although they retained ties to voters in the state from which they were elected. This difference between perceived obligations to the voters as distinguished from the state as an institution works in favor of expanding the federal government role and if necessary doing so at the expense of state governmental interests.

The greatest increase in central government power probably started in the period of the Great Depression of the 1930s when the New Deal administration of President Roosevelt began a series of economic measures at the federal level to try to deal with the economic crisis. At first these efforts were met with Supreme Court decisions limiting the role of the central government. However, whether as a consequence of the threat to increase the size of the court to get more "friendly to the president's plan" Justices or simply because of changes on the court, the court changed its philosophical approach and new federal agencies and new federal powers were approved, typically using commerce clause language. By this time the direct election of Senators was in place and it cannot be said that this expansion was to be unexpected.

The next great increase occurred as a consequence of the "Civil Rights Revolution" of the 1960s. The federal government took a direct role in the effort to fight race discrimination in the United States, especially in the southern states. Many times these efforts were in direct contradiction to state laws that either permitted or required the discrimination at issue. This clash of *federal v. state authority* uniformly resulted in victory for the federal government. Once again there was a federal Constitutional basis for this victory, namely the Civil War Amendments. What did not change in the 1960s was the argument that these amendments did not give individuals direct rights against personal conduct undertaken in the states. Consistent with the original Constitutional view that the restrictions of the Constitution applied to "government power" not individual action, civil rights cases found themselves dealing with the "state action" doctrine.[26] Individual discriminatory actions were not prohibited by the Constitution but if that action could be tied to the state so as to make the action involved state action then the Constitution was applicable and such state action would be held unconstitutional and unlawful. Only when a federal statute prohibiting discrimination by private parties was enacted was such private discrimination unlawful as a matter of federal law. Once again, such victory of federal law over state law was a matter of victory for the Rule of Law. At first the central government's authority to pass such laws was squarely based on the Constitution's interstate commerce clause and thus the first cases in this arena involved interstate transportation. Later cases applied the authorization of federal law contained in the Civil Rights Amendments themselves.

The federal government has also intruded into traditional state authority through use of the federal government's taxing and spending powers. Thus the federal government may provide funds to the states and attach conditions to the funding—thus asserting federal standards on the state use of the monies. In essence the rules of contract apply in that the agreement between the state and Federal authorities determines whether the state can get the money and the conditions that attach to the receipt and use of the money. Because the conditioning of the funds is contractual and voluntary in nature: 'Congress has broad power to set the terms on which it disburses federal money to the States...but when Congress attaches conditions to a State's acceptance of federal funds, the conditions must be set out "unambiguously"'.[27] The 2012 Health Care Law decision prohibits the federal government from requiring the States to pay a penalty if they refuse the federal monetary grant.

Today there is a debate in the Supreme Court both as to how far the federal government's power to give individuals rights to sue the states can reach and how broad the Commerce Clause authority of the federal government reaches.[28] While the federal government itself may sue states to carry out federal legislative mandates, Constitutional issues are raised under the Eleventh Amendment as to private monetary claims against the states. These issues are raised whether the state action sought to be

26. *Brentwood Academy v. Tennessee Secondary School Athletic Assn.*, 531 U. S. 288 (2001).
27. *Arlington Central School District v. Murphy*, 548 U.S.291(2006).
28. In *National Federation of Independent Business v. Sebelius*, 567 U.S. ___ (2012) a 5 Justice Majority held that the Health Care law could was not authorized by the Commerce Clause, a different 5 Justice majority upheld the law on differing grounds.

set aside by private parties is in the civil rights field (broadly defined) or in other fields. By a bare majority the Supreme Court supported the rights of states to be free of some such lawsuits because of the wording of the Eleventh Amendment. The court has recognized that when Congress, acting under authority given to it by the Fourteenth Amendment specifically has abrogated Eleventh Amendment immunity and authorized suit against a state by a private party there is no Eleventh Amendment immunity from such suit.[29] Thus, the court has held that when a State Courthouse design is such that paraplegics cannot gain access to a courtroom on the second floor without the indignity of being carried, there is a violation of the Americans With Disabilities Act, a statute wherein Congress specifically abrogated state Eleventh Amendment immunity, and that Congress had authority to abrogate the immunity as it was acting under its Fourteenth Amendment power to protect a disadvantaged minority in a situation where there was a history of discrimination and a Congressional effort to remedy that discrimination.[30] In *Lane* the court specifically mentioned and distinguished other recent cases where a closely divided court had found that the Congressional abrogation involved went beyond Congresses remedial powers under the Fourteenth Amendment.

Finally, there remains an area where the separation of federal and state authority remains inviolate. Namely, while the federal government may pass legislation in areas under its Constitutional authority, the federal government cannot make the state government its instrumentality or agency to carry out the legislation. Thus, in *New York v. United States*[31] the Supreme Court found the effort of the federal government to, in essence, make the state an agency of the federal government for the purpose of carrying out a federal program unconstitutional—even in the face of state acceptance of that role in the negotiations leading up to the federal legislation. The state could not waive its sovereignty and the federal government was required to recognize that the state government was a sovereign and not merely an agency of the federal government. Several Justices view federalism as a significant protection of liberty in the American system.[32]

In Japan there are no sovereign states. The various local government entities, beginning with the highest form of entity, the prefecture (typically the "ken" although there are different names for the Tokyo government and certain other large bodies), may be provided for in the Constitution but the Constitution neither gives these entities any powers nor are there any powers to be reserved for these entities. Japan is, in the truest sense, a "unitary state" with government power in the hands of the central or national government. What then is to be made of the Constitutional provisions requiring that governors of prefectures and certain other local officials must be popularly elected? Popular election would seem to imply a political power base and moreover would seem to imply that the elected official has some policy role to play in governmental affairs. Moreover this direct election requirement was placed in the

29. *Board of Trustees of Univ. of Ala. v. Garrett*, 531 U. S. 356, 363–364 (2001); *United States v. Georgia*, 546 U.S. 151 (2006).
30. *Tennessee v. Lane*, 541 U.S.509 (2004).
31. 505 U.S. 144 (1992); see also *Printz v. US*, 521 U.S. 898 (1997).
32. See, e.g., *Bond. United States*, 564 U.S. ___ (2011).

Constitution by the Occupation to further expand the new democracy that the Constitution was to give the Japanese people. By diffusing power through having local officials popularly elected there would, the Occupation believed, be a check on runaway central power in the event of a movement away from democratic ideals. It was the intent of the Occupation and the Constitution drafters to give significant power to local governments and the popular election of local officials was designed with this end in mind.

That has not been the case.[33] The Japan government negotiators took steps during the negotiations and later to stifle local autonomy, including steps that made the prefectures and other local governments dependent on the national government for financing.[34] Local authority in Tokyo and Osaka are challenging the current system and the government has joined opposition parties in endorsing a Bill that gives large municipalities greater self-governing authority.[35]

The prefecture governments and the governments of cities and other municipalities have only such powers as are delegated to them by the central government. Delegations that might be viewed as treating a local government unfairly in comparison with other local authorities must have such government's approval. Even if a popularly elected provincial governor wanted to act vigorously in an area where the local government is given authority, the central government has a second chance to limit local autonomy through the central government's power over local finances. Local governments do not have their own taxing powers and must get needed funding from the central authority. While Prefectures and other local governments have authority to challenge national government directives by suing the national government there is no corresponding grant of authority to the national government to sue the local entity—although mandamus suit may be brought against the head of the entity to require him (her) to carry out the national government mandate.

Unlike the United States where the semi-sovereign States cannot be made administrative arms of the central government, in Japan the local authorities can be made such administrative arms and in fact are utilized as central government agencies for purposes of enforcing or carrying out central government policy. Thus, such clearly central government responsibilities as immigration and visa matters are routinely delegated to the local government to carry out.[36] Once given the responsibility to carry out the function the local government becomes, in essence, an agency of the central government but unlike most agencies there may not necessarily be additional funds allocated to pay the local government for carrying out this policy function.

33. Shigenori Matsui, *The Constitution of Japan* 32–33 (Hart Publishing 2011).
34. See, Takemae Eiji, *The Allied Occupation of Japan* 301–304 (Robert Ricketts & Sebastian Swann trans., Continuum International 2002).
35. Kyodo, Japan Times, July 31, 2012, Bill to transform Osaka government jointly submitted to Diet, http://www.japantimes.co.jp/text/nn20120731a2.html.
36. In 2012 an amendment to the immigration law went into effect that required that alien registration cards be issued by the national government rather than by the Prefectures and/or local authorities. This caused many persons in Japan past their visa status to object because of concern that the government would not issue special resident permits. See, Ayako Mie, *Visa Overstayers Rally to Maintain Privileges after Immigration Revision*, Japan Times, Mar. 27, 2012, http://www.japantimes.co.jp/text/nn20120327a8.html.

What you see when you look at the Constitution are local popularly elected officials—whom one would presume have some real authority and power because otherwise why have them elected in the first place. What you get are local governors and other officials who have in the past had little or no power to affect policy decisions and local governments that in many respects are administrative arms of the central government. The *Okinawa Mandamus* case of 1966, *Prime Minister v. Governor of Okinawa*,[37] illustrates the limits on local authority and the requirement that local authority comply with national government orders to execute national government policy. The recent actions of the Governor of Osaka and his local political party in readying themselves for an active role in the next Lower House election as well as the actions of Prefecture governors and mayors of towns since the Great East Japan Earthquake and Tsunami of March 11, 2011 may herald a change as local authorities are attempting to influence Japan's national elections and evolving nuclear power debate. Enhancing local officials' authority may be one of the changes brought about by the Fukushima nuclear disaster.

[1] Okinawa Mandamus Case

Okinawa is the largest island in the Ryukyu chain of islands. These islands were a separate sovereignty unified in the fifteenth century under their own kingdom. They were eventually defeated in a battle by Daimyo from Kyushu in 1609 and fell under Kyushu domination and thus under Japanese rule. After the Meiji Restoration, as part of Japan's policy to establish itself as a self-ruling nation state, the Ryukyu's were annexed (1879) and given the prefectural name of Okinawa. Ryukians became Japanese citizens. Many residents of the Ryukyu's feel "left out" of matters decided by the national government in Tokyo and in many ways residents feel themselves to be "second-class citizens". This situation was exasperated during the Second World War because the battle of Okinawa was one of the bloodiest of the War and many noncombatants on Okinawa lost their lives.[38] After the war the United States occupied Okinawa and built air and naval bases as part of its global defense strategy. Even after the signing of the peace treaty with Japan, Okinawa remained an occupied area,[39] and the 1951 security treaty permitted the United States to govern Okinawa directly while recognizing Japan's "residual sovereignty" to the island. When Okinawa was finally returned to Japan and the occupation ended in 1972, the United States insisted on

37. Case No. 90 of 1996 (GB Aug. 28, 1996), http://www.courts.go.jp/english/judgments/text/1996.08.28-1996-Gyo-Tsu-No.90.html.
38. There is evidence that Japanese military commanders on Okinawa were involved in the mass suicide of Okinawa civilians in the final days of the Battle of Okinawa. The extent of the military's involvement and responsibility for such suicides has been a subject of fierce debate in Japan as well as a subject implicated in textbook censoring in Japan. The Supreme Court on procedural grounds dismissed an appeal from a High Court ruling that had found an author not responsible for libel when writing of such commander's responsibility. See, "Okinawa Notes" suit Favors Oe, Japan Times, Apr. 23, 2011, Kyodo News, http://search.japantimes.co.jp/cgi-bin/nn20110423b1.html.
39. Hugh Cortazzi, *The Japanese Achievement: A Short History of Japan & its Culture* 262 (Sidgwick & Jackson Great Civilization Series, St. Martin's Press 1990).

retaining bases on Okinawa. The United States remains in bases on Okinawa to this day under mutual defense treaty arrangements with the government of Japan. These bases are the largest in all of Japan and take up a significant area on Okinawa.[40] They are a source of mixed feelings among Okinawa residents who, on the one hand enjoy the economic benefits that come from the bases but on the other object to being a garrison for the United States and would prefer to see some of the bases relocated to other areas of Japan.[41] The military bases are a major political issue in Okinawa. It is in this political context that *Prime Minister v. Governor of Okinawa* must be considered.

The American bases are located on leased land on Okinawa. These leases were due to expire in 1996 and 1997. The owners of the land refused to extend the leases so the Government of Japan determined that it would expropriate the land pursuant to statutory and Constitutional provisions. As part of the process it was necessary to obtain some documentation from local officials who refused to sign the documents. To bypass these officials, the national government directed the Governor of Okinawa to sign the documents and take certain other necessary steps. He in turn refused. The government, in the name of the prime minister then sued in mandamus to compel the governor to act.[42]

The Supreme Court recognized that governors are elected officials. But, their elected status does not mean they have complete autonomy. Rather they can, consistent with legislative enactment, be made organs of the national government subject to the control of the national government.

The court recognized that this role, as a subordinate organ of the national government subject to the power of the responsible national ministerial officials was not consistent with the independence typically thought to apply to a popularly elected official. To "harmonize" these conflicting roles, a system of judicially ordered mandamus was established under which the court could compel the governor to act as ordered. In exercising its power, the role of the court is limited. The court determines whether the national minister has met his statutory obligations and whether the act ordered is Constitutional. Since both these conditions were met in this case the governor was ordered to follow the instructions given to him by the national government. Moreover, the governor could not continue to refuse on the ground that carrying out the instructions given to him was inconsistent with local autonomy. Local autonomy goes only so far and if the order of the national government minister to the governor is lawful, the governor must comply regardless of local sentiment. In effect, the governor becomes a subordinate national official.

---

40. James L. McClain, *A Modern History of Japan* 611 (WW Norton & Company 2002).
41. For an interesting discussion of the unique position of Okinawa in the Japanese society, see Glenn D. Hook & Gavan McCormack, *Japan's Contested Constitution: Documents and Analysis* 23–24 (Routledge 2001).
42. Two issues were presented in the case. The first dealt with the authority of the national government to order the governor to act–*a question of national v. prefecture power and relations*. That question is discussed above. The second dealt with the validity of the expropriation proceeding. The Court rejected this argument–it is not discussed in this section but is discussed in Chapter 10.

With Okinawa residents and local government officials opposed to the move of the Futenma Airbase to some other place in the Prefecture (wanting to see the base located in some other part of Japan) the prospect of another Okinawa Mandamus Case is presented unless a resolution is found. So too, with some prefecture and other local officials opposed to restart of nuclear plants after the Fukushima nuclear disaster, the potential for an Okinawa Prefecture type case dealing with nuclear startups is possible. Such case would be the first time the Okinawa Prefecture decision might be applied in a non-military base setting.

The Local Autonomy Law was initially designed to carry out the objectives of the American Occupation of giving local elected officials greater power and thus reducing the power of the central government. One mechanism for increasing the authority of local officials was the reduction of local governmental units. Thus today there are 47 prefectures in Japan while in the pre-war period there were as many as over 300 prefectures. Similarly the number of municipalities was dramatically reduced. The reality is that local governments are dependent on the national government for their finances and this financial dependency has been translated into a loss of power in favor of the national government. Reform efforts have been mounted to decentralize governmental operations by giving greater independence to the prefectures and other local governments. Because of the use that the ruling LDP could make of local government candidates in support of Diet candidates supported by the LDP, the LDP was not supportive of such reform efforts but the short interregnum during the early 1990s when a coalition government not dominated by the LDP was in power resulted in significant reform that was in turn adopted by the LDP when it returned to power as part of a coalition government. Thus in 1995 a Decentralization Promotion Act was adopted. The policies of the Koizumi Administration in the early 2000 period reduced the reliance of local governments on national government grants and subsidies and caused many local government entities to merge in order to reduce expenses. Merger was supported by national government policies that allowed merged municipalities to issue bonds for public projects and when repaid the national government would repay 70% of the principal of the bonds. Moreover merged entities would not suffer a loss of funds because of the merger (such loss might otherwise have occurred because of the nature of the formula under which certain grants were given to municipalities based on population ranges). Merger was also supported by a squeeze on municipal finances through a reduction in the amount of funds available to municipalities in general. In the first decade of the twenty-first century there were more than 600 municipal mergers affecting more than 2000 municipalities. Because local politicians were the ground troops for the LDP in national elections, the merger of municipalities and its consequent reduction in the number of local elected officials has adversely affected the LDP from a political standpoint and may have contributed to both the need for the LDP to find coalition partners when in power as well as the successful election campaign by the DPJ in 2009.

[2] *Fukushima Disaster and Prefecture Governor Influence on Nuclear Power Debate*

Although nuclear policy in Japan is set at the national level, it is the Prefectures that act as "host" to the various nuclear power facilities in Japan. This "host" arrangement is in the form of a contract between the Prefecture and the nuclear power company operating the facility. Under the terms of such contracts, when a nuclear facility is placed off line, the operator is to obtain the consent of the Prefecture Governor before placing the facility back on line. Such contracts had little effect on nuclear policy prior to Fukushima—plants go off line on a revolving basis every 13 months for technical review of operations and safety checks and typically after such review simply come back on line with no prefecture interference. But since the Fukushima disaster, and especially after the national government put in place a new series of "stress tests" Prefecture officials have become more involved in determining whether to grant permission for facilities to come back on line. Some Governors have been resisting. Whether the Okinawa Governor case would be applicable should a Minister order a Governor or a local mayor to allow a nuclear generator back on line is uncertain. On the one hand, the issue is one of national significance as the loss of power as a consequence of Fukushima on Japan's exports and economy has shown; on the other the issue could be argued to be a private law contract matter between the Governor and the Power Company and thus not subject to the public law rationale of the Okinawa case. Such litigation is unlikely and a compromise under which at least some of the plants come back on line is likely to be reached. Exactly how the process will work remains to be seen but clearly the Governors and mayors as well as local assemblies are having an effect on the nuclear power debate through their "authority" under the "host" contracts between their prefecture and the power company.[43]

[C] Limitations on Private Actions Deemed in Violation of the Constitution

Unlike the United States government the Japanese government is not a government of "enumerated powers". Rather it has the complete government power because there are no semi-autonomous States. Moreover, the rights of the people set out in the Constitution are not drafted as limitations on the powers of the government as is the case in the United States system. Rights are simply drafted as rights that the people have. This raises the question as to whether the "state action" doctrine has any relevance to the Japanese situation. For example, the Japanese Constitution contains several references to the equality of the sexes and it is undeniable that one of the things that the American occupying authorities wished to do was to dramatically change the role of women in Japan. Pre-war and Second World War Japan treated women in a mostly feudal way and the feudal institution of the *Ie* remained the basic family law institution. In such

43. See, e.g., Eric Johnston, *Debate Growing Over "Local" Reactor Consent*, Japan Times (Apr. 6, 2012), http://www.japantimes.co.jp/text/nn20120406x1.html.

circumstances women were hardly more than possessions of their husband's family. To change this, the Constitution prohibited discrimination based on sex and provided that marriage was to be based on mutual equality of the partners to the marriage. The language appears to have universal applicability and not to be limited to state action. Does this mean that the Japanese Constitution prohibits sexual discrimination by private parties? The short answer would appear to be—no; sort of; and in certain situations, all at the same time.

Although there is no state action doctrine under Japanese law that does not mean that constitutionally protected rights are "self-executing" rights nor does it mean that the rights are applicable as between private parties. Direct applicability is viewed as inconsistent with the nature of Constitutions in that Constitutional language is considered as setting the framework for government and its direct application between private parties can lead to unintended results.[44] As a consequence "direct application" doctrine is not the prevailing view.[45] Does this mean that the Constitutional protection against sexual discrimination is not applicable as between private parties? Not necessarily.

While most Japanese law scholars and judicial decisions may reject direct applicability theory, an "indirect theory" may lead to a similar result. Under the indirect theory, Constitutional provisions can be used to interpret and define legislative enactments. The basic building blocks of the Japanese legislative system are the "six Codes" meaning the Constitution and the Civil Code, the Criminal Code, the Code of Civil Procedure, the Code of Criminal Procedure and the Commercial Code.[46] These Codes form a hierarchy under which the provisions of the more specific Code take precedence over the more general Code.[47] Thus, for example, if both the Civil Code and the Commercial Code have provisions dealing with the same subject, the Commercial Code would govern in a commercial situation since it is considered more specific than the Civil Code. The placement of the Constitution in this hierarchy is more complicated because Constitutions by their nature are more general than the Codes but the Constitution is specifically stated to be the Supreme Law. In any event, the Civil Code contains general "contra bones mores" and prohibition against abuse of rights

44. While Constitutions do set the framework for the government and the relations between the government and the citizenry, modern (post WW2) Constitutions also have as their function the statement of "universal" rights enjoyed by the populace-even in their relations among each other. See, e.g., South Africa-http://www.Constitutionalcourt.org.za/text/rights/bill.html. Modern application of Constitutions or Constitutional type documents such as human rights treaties raise the question of both horizontal (among the people) and vertical application. See, e.g., Jonathan Cooper, *Human Rights are for People*, 20 Stat. L. Rev. 238 (1999).
45. This view fails to take into account that many more Constitution provisions were drafted but were rejected by the Steering Committee in the belief that they were too specific and thus better suited for statutes. Takemae Eiji, *The Allied Occupation of Japan* 278 (Continuum International 2002) (translation by Robert Ricketts and Sebastian Swann).
46. It is possible that the future will recognize a seventh code-namely, the new Companies Law which was spun out of the old Commercial Code and designed to house all the laws dealing with corporate functions such as corporate democracy, governance, shareholders' suits, etc.
47. Legal research in Japan is based on navigation through the various Codes and specific statutes to find the applicable law.

provisions under which actions against good morals are not permitted. Admittedly these are general provisions and require interpretation.

In the *Nissan Motor* case[48] the Japanese Supreme Court held that in interpreting the contra bones mores provision of the Civil Code in a lawsuit brought by employees of a motor company against their employer objecting to the company's the retirement policy that required women to retire at an earlier age than men it was proper to look at the Constitutional grant of sexual equality rights. Since company policies were inconsistent with the Constitutional norm of equal treatment, the unequal treatment of employees by the company was inconsistent with the Civil Code and thus the employees were successful. Note that the court did not hold that the company had violated the Constitution nor did the court hold that the Constitutional right to equal treatment of women and men was binding against the private company involved. The court "indirectly" applied the Constitutional norm by interpreting the Civil Code's provision against activity inconsistent with good morals to include a prohibition against the sex discrimination involved in the case. The conclusion of the court was that the sex discrimination practiced against the company employees was in violation of the Civil Code, Article 90. [Similarly, in 2006 the Supreme Court of Japan found that a private Commons Association requirement limiting payment of funds received for use of common land to male Heads of Houses in certain situations violated Article 90 because it was male gender based discrimination that, because of the Constitution, is unreasonable and inconsistent with public policy.[49]]

This holding, while it is to be applauded by all who believe in equal treatment for women may be inconsistent with specific statutory enactments that appear to permit certain sex based discrimination.[50] Note that the court's decision *was not Constitutionally based but was based on the Civil Code.* Under the Japanese rules for applying law, the Civil Code as a general law is subordinate to specific statutes. Accordingly, if a specific statute allows discrimination, the Civil Code should not be used to find that discrimination unlawful. This may thus be a case of "what you see is not what you get".

Does this mean that a private company cannot discriminate, as a matter of Constitutional law, against women because of their sex? Not necessarily—the answer is "it depends". In the motor company case the Civil Code was applicable because of the contractual relationship that existed between the motor company as employer and the workers who were its employees. But what if an employer/employee relationship did not exist? In the *Mitsubishi Jushi (Resin)* case[51] an applicant for employment had hidden from the company his student activities as a political activist. During the probationary employment period the company discovered the true facts and

48. *Nissan Motors Inc. v. Nakamoto*, 35 Minshu 300 (Sup. Ct. PB Mar. 24, 1981). An English language translation of this decision may be found at Lawrence W. Beer & Hiroshi Itoh, *The Constitutional Case Law of Japan, 1970–1990* at 179 (University of Washington Press 1996).
49. *Common Funds Distribution case*, Case No. 2004 (Ju) No. 1968, 60 Minshu No. 3, Mar. 17, 2006, http://www.courts.go.jp/english/judgments/text/2006.03.17-2004.-Ju-.No..1968.html.
50. Frank K. Upham, *Visions of Justice in Postwar Japan: A Preliminary Inquiry*, L. E. & W. 145, 157 (Waseda University 1988).
51. *Mitsubishi Jushi K.K. v. Takano*, 27 Minshu 1536 Case No. 1968 (O) No.932 (G.B., Dec. 12, 1973). http://www.courts.go.jp/english/judgments/text/1973.12.12-1968-O-No.932.html.

discharged the probationary employee. The court refused to apply the Constitutional provision in Article 14 making all people equal as a matter of law and prohibiting discrimination in economic and social relationships. The court found that Article 14—and indeed all provisions of Chapter 3 of the Constitution—was intended to guaranty rights against the state and did not apply directly to private conduct and relationships. To apply Constitutional provisions as between private parties in this context would violate the employer's right to contract, i.e., the right of the employer to decide not to enter into an employment relationship based on the application or the true facts sought in the employment application. The employer's freedom of contract was thus given precedence over the indirect application of Article 14.

No contractual relationship between the parties existed, as the employment was provisional during this probationary period. Thus, *Mitsubishi Jushi* and *Nissan Motors* are consistent to this extent: both refuse to directly apply the Constitutional provision as between private parties, in *Nissan* the provision is indirectly applied through application of the Civil Code because of the existence of an employer/employee relationship to which the Civil Code's public policy provisions could apply, in *Mitsubishi* there was no such contract and thus the Civil Code did not apply.[52] Thus, it would appear that discrimination in making the initial hiring decision would be permissible, absent some special statutory provision to the contrary. Indeed, when Japan enacted its first Equal Employment Opportunity Law that statute distinguished between existing contractual relationships—where discrimination based on sex was prohibited—and pre-hiring discrimination—where equal treatment was encouraged but not required. Amendments to the law now prohibit sex discrimination in hiring decisions.

Similarly, in the *Gokoku Shrine Enshrinement* case[53] (see Chapter 11) involving an allegation of violation of Article 20's freedom of religion guaranty when a Shinto Shrine enshrined the complainant's deceased husband over her objections, the court utilized Article 20 to determine whether the public order and good morals provision of Article 90 of the Civil Code had been violated by the shrine. Again the court utilized an "indirect" application of Constitutional principles analysis in a case involving what the court found to be purely private activity.

There are some Constitutional provisions that appear to be directly applicable and would not appear to require statutory language to bring them into effect. Thus, one would hope that Article 15(4) requiring ballot secrecy in elections and protecting voters from punishment of any type for the manner in which the voter voted is self-executing. However, it is not certain that this provision would apply as between private parties. What if a voter publicly acknowledges that he (or she) voted for a particular candidate

52. See also, Yuji Iwasawa, *International Law, Human Rights and Japanese Law* 200–201 (Oxford University Press 1998) discussing the Yokohama District Court decision in 1974 holding a company had violated Article 90 of the civil code when it fired an employee when it learned he was Korean. The court distinguished this case from a situation where an employer refuses employment to an applicant because of his nationality. In this case the firing took place after the probationary period and at a time when there was a contractual relationship.

53. Case No. (0) 902 of 1982 (G.B. June 1, 1988). http://www.courts.go.jp/english/judgments/text/1988.06.01-1982-O-No.902.html.

and then applies for employment with company X? If company X, which has good reason to believe that the candidate of the voter's choice is antagonistic to company X's industry and would support legislation and other programs that could dramatically adversely affect the profits of company X, refuses to hire the voter because of his support of the candidate is that actionable under the Constitution? Could a court apply the reasoning of *Mitsubishi Jushi* and *Nissan Motor* and uphold the right of the company to contract finding the Constitutional provision not self-executing between the voter and a private employer? Might a court hold that if self-executing at all, the provision only prohibits an employment decision by a public employer? Might a court hold that where a "patronage" political position is involved the provision is not self-executing even where public employment is involved?

The Japanese Constitution protects the secrecy of all forms of communications.[54]

Although the Article would appear on its face to be an absolute protection for the privacy of all forms of communication, there is no doubt but that under appropriate conditions the police may obtain wiretaps and warrants for the purpose of searching computer email communications. Even without a warrant the police were allowed to electronically listen in on the deliberations of the Japan Communist party, because such listening was considered to be for a legitimate investigative purpose.[55] In mid-2011 the Diet enacted legislation that makes creation or distribution of a computer virus criminal activity. The law also makes it a crime to send certain email messages with pornographic images attached. Although the law was passed to enable Japan to meet commitments to be undertaken under the Convention against Cybercrime, there is debate in legal circles in Japan as to whether the law violates the Constitutional protection of all forms of communication[56]. Another significant question is whether the Constitutional provision applies as between private parties? On its face the provision would appear to prohibit a company from adopting a policy under which it can review emails sent by employees on the company's computers. But such an interpretation could lead to complications for employers whose property is being inappropriately used. In the United States (where no similar Constitutional right is contained in the language of the Constitution and the extent of the right to privacy is a subject of debate) there may be good legal reasons for employers to monitor their employees' email sent on company computer terminals—for example, failure to stop sexually harassing email communications on company computers could subject the employer to sexual harassment liability. In such cases United States law appears to be headed in the direction of permitting such "violation" of privacy concerns provided there is a clearly announced privacy policy disclosing that the company may look at employee email communications (based on the general nature of United States law as permitting the parties to set their own "law" on a matter but requiring that employees not be "blindsided" by having their communications read when they had reason to believe such

54. Constitution Article 21.
55. *Japan Communist Party Electronic Eavesdropping case*, 9 Hanji 3, Tokyo High Court 77/53.
56. Kyoto News, *Domestic Cybercrime Bill Passed*, Japan Times (June 18, 2011), http://search.japantimes.co.jp/cgi-bin/nn20110618a3.html.

communications were privileged or private).[57] So too in Japan there can be good reason for employers to monitor the use of their own property even if that means violating the secrecy of an employee's communication. This is especially so now that the EOL prohibits sexual harassment by either conduct or speech.[58] Regardless of the Constitutional language, what you see may not be what you get and this prohibition probably will not be applied in full force in either a private sector or public sector employee/employer relationship. Whether Japan will adopt a right of privacy for communications using company equipment similar to that of the United States and base its legal prohibition on notice remains to be seen. The Supreme Court of Japan held that the secret recording of a conversation by one party thereto was not unlawful in circumstances where the party recording the conversation suspected that he was a victim of fraud.[59]

Article 19 of the Constitution provides that neither freedom of thought nor of conscience may be violated by act of the government. This provision would seem to be self-executing. But the thrust and meaning of the Article is open to debate. The public school teachers union in Japan has typically been a liberal organization well to the left of the government in its ideology. Ever since the war the issue of teaching various subjects directly or indirectly has been a source of conflict between the union and the government. Central to this dispute has been the Japanese national anthem (*Kimigayo*) and the flag. Teachers have objected to the requirement that they sing or play the anthem or salute the flag viewing the anthem and flag as remnants of the Second World War era and the emphasis on patriotism prior to and during the war.[60] When a public school music teacher refused to play *Kimigayo* on the piano at a school enrolment ceremony arguing that her freedom of thought and conscience was violated by the school's order that she play the anthem, she was subjected to discipline. She brought suit. The Supreme Court, in 2007, denied relief noting that playing the anthem did not in and of itself deny the teacher her right to hold any view of history that she wanted; it is a typical part of a music teacher's function to play the national anthem at school functions and thus the playing of the anthem does not convey any message regarding

57. Government employer/employee relations and communications are covered by the Fourth Amendment to the Constitution of the United States. The Supreme Court has so far refused to broadly comment on the right of a government employer to read communications of its employees when they use employer-supplied equipment. But the Court has held that when the government employer acts reasonably and for a governmental purpose its action is not in violation of the fourth Amendment. *City of Ontario v. Quon*, 560 U.S. ___ (2010).
58. 2006 Amendment of the EOL Article 11 makes it compulsory that employers act to prevent sexual harassment–whether that harassment be in the form of speech or conduct.
59. *Recording of Conversation Case*, Case No. 1999 (A) No. 96 (P.B. July 12, 2000) http://www.courts.go.jp/english/judgments/text/2000.07.12-1999-A-No.96.html. The recording was not illegal and was allowable in evidence in a later criminal proceeding. In 2012 the District Court in the trial of Ichiro Ozawa accepted in evidence the surreptitious recording of a police interrogation by the subject of the interrogation to show that a prosecutor's report of events was inaccurate.
60. In the United States there have been cases arguing that separation of Church and State is violated by the language "under God" placed in the pledge of allegiance during the cold war. In *Elk Grove Unified School District v. Newdow*, 542 U.S. 1 (2004) the non-custodial parent of a school child sued to prohibit the saying of the pledge. The Court avoided the issue by finding that the non-custodial parent lacked standing.

the teacher's thoughts concerning the anthem; and teachers are public servants and as such are obligated to perform functions for the entire community and that a public servant's personal views does not excuse the servant from performing duties for the community as a whole. In such role the teacher has the obligation to carry out lawful orders of the school and the playing of the anthem was not a violation of her Constitutional rights.[61] A concurring Justice was greatly concerned about the obligation of a public servant to perform a service for the entire community and the conflict with that duty that would be caused if the public servant could avoid that duty because of an inner conflict of conscience. One Justice dissented.[62]

Although limited to public servants, the *National Anthem Playing* case has overtones of earlier, pre-war thinking. The Meiji Constitution contained several Articles giving citizens certain rights under legislation (meaning that these rights could be provided for by legislation and thus also limited by legislation). One of these rights was freedom of religion. It was the view of leading scholars of the Meiji era that such freedom was limited to one's personal thoughts and that one could still be compelled to engage in public Shinto rituals without violating the freedom of religion. People were free to believe what they wanted but the "external effects" of their beliefs were not covered by the Constitutional grant.[63] In the 2007 case the teacher was allowed to have whatever internal belief she wished while at the same time required to perform the external effect of playing the anthem. The Court's conclusion that a public servant is required to carry out lawful orders begs the question—namely whether an order to perform an act that is inconsistent with the public servant's beliefs is a lawful order.

In May and June 2011 all three Petty Benches of the Supreme Court upheld Orders by school principals that required teachers to stand before the Japanese flag and sing the national anthem. The Court recognized that singing the anthem was somewhat different from playing the anthem on the piano and that singing is a form of expression including a statement by the singer. As such this case was distinguishable from the piano case and was recognized by the Court as involving an indirect restraint on freedom of thought and conscience. The Court nonetheless upheld the requirement to show respect to the flag and sing the words of the anthem. The Court balanced the indirect constraint on teachers against the requirement that public servants (teachers) observe the requirements of their job, including showing respect for the flag and singing the anthem, and found the requirement of singing and showing respect as public servants participating in a school ceremony to outweigh the teachers' rights and

61. *National Anthem Playing Case*, Case No. 328 (Gyo-Tsu) 2004, 61 Minshu No. 1, http://www.courts.go.jp/english/judgments/text/2007.02.27-2004.-Gyo-Tsu-.No..328.html, (P.B. Feb. 27, 2007).

62. Teachers continue to protest. *Kyodo News, Rebuked ex-teachers lose "Kimigayo" suit*, Japan Times (Jan. 29, 2010), http://search.japantimes.co.jp/cgi-bin/nn20100129a3.html Japan Times, Jan. 29, 2011, http://search.japantimes.co.jp/cgi-bin/nn20110129a2.html. In January 2012 the Supreme Court upheld a school principal's decision to discipline teachers who refused to stand and sing but also held that suspension or reduction of pay was too severe, although a reprimand was acceptable. The *Kimigayo Punishment Case* is discussed in Chapter 7.

63. See Hirobumi Ito, *Commentaries on the Constitution of the Empire of Japan* 60 (2d ed., Chuo-o University 1906); Shinichi Fujii, *The Essentials of Japanese Constitutional Law* 165 (University Publications of America Reprint ed., 1979) 165.

the harm to teachers as a result of this infringement[64]. These cases did not decide what level of punishment was appropriate when teachers refuse to follow an Order to stand before the flag and sing the anthem. The level of discipline is not within the sole discretion of the public[65] or private employer[66] but like the lifetime employment system discussed in Chapter 12, has roots in and is limited by the abuse of rights good faith doctrines of the Civil Code. A Petty Bench in the June 2011 *National Anthem Singing Case* upheld the City's decision to refuse to rehire teachers who had refused to sing the anthem. Although recognizing that the discipline involved adversely affected the teachers' right to thought and conscience, the court found the order Constitutional and necessary and rational[67]. In 2012 however a different Panel while recognizing that a principal acting in accord with a school district rule could reprimand teachers who refused to stand and sing also held that punishment of loss of pay or suspension as too severe—reprimand was acceptable.[68] Whether and if so what more severe punishment may be exacted for multiple violations is uncertain.

refuse to rehire

but ↓ pay is too severe.

[The issue of teaching "patriotism" in Japanese schools arises in part from the history of the Meiji Emperor's Prescript on Education and its effect pre-Second World War. This subject is discussed in Chapter 7.]

Although it is generally recognized that there is no state action doctrine in Japanese Constitutional theory, the fact is that there may in fact be a state action doctrine in reality. By this is meant that certain Constitutional provisions may be self-executing when applied against the Japanese government. Thus, for example, the provision of Article 15(4) protecting the sanctity of secret voting probably applies directly to prohibit public officials from violating a person's right to a secret ballot.

64. *National Anthem (Kimigayo) and Flag (Hinomaru) case, May 2011)(* 2010 (Gyo-Tsu) No. 54, Minshu Vol. 65, No. 4, May 30, 2011), http://www.courts.go.jp/english/judgments/text/2011.05.30-2010.-Gyo-Tsu-.No..54.html (P.B. June 6, 2011); *National Anthem (Kimigayo) and Flag (Hinomaru) case, June 6, 2011,* (2010) (O) No. 951, Minshu Vol. 65, No. 4, http://www.courts.go.jp/english/judgments/text/2011.06.06-2010.-O-.No..951.html (P.B. June 6, 2011); *National Anthem (Kimigayo) and Flag (Hinomaru) case, June 14, 2011,* (2010) 2010 (Gyo-Tsu) No. 314, Minshu Vol. 65, No. 4 (June 14, 2011), http://www.courts.go.jp/english/judgments/text/2011.06.14-2010.-Gyo-Tsu-.No..314.html (P.B. June 14, 2011). Makoto Inagaki, Long-fought battle over "Kimigayo" at an end / Top court calls order "indirect constraint of rights, but recognizes importance of school ceremonies, Daily Yomiuri, June 1, 2011, http://www.yomiuri.co.jp/dy/national/T110531004880.htm. Where a person who had previously been a teacher at a school attended a graduation ceremony and handed out pamphlets and caused a commotion and refused to leave the hall so that ceremonies could proceed, the Supreme Court affirmed the former teacher's conviction for disrupting the ceremony. *National Anthem Disruption of Graduation Ceremony Criminal Case,* Case No. 2008 (A) No. 1132, Keishu Vol. 65, No. 5, http://www.courts.go.jp/english/judgments/text/2011.07.07-2008.-A-.No..1132.html (P.B. July 7, 2011).
65. See, *Penalties require careful approach,* The Yomiuri Shimbun, June 1, 2011, http://www.yomiuri.co.jp/dy/national/T110531004199.htm, noting that the Tokyo High Court had held that discipline including a loss of pay was unreasonable when teachers refused to stand before the flag and sing the anthem.
66. *Reporter who Overslept* case, *Shioda v. Kochi Broadcasting* 268 Rodo Hanrei (Sup. Ct. Jan. 31, 1977) discussed in Frank K. Upham, *Visions of Justice in Postwar Japan: A Preliminary Inquiry* 145, L. E. & W. (Waseda University Press 1988).
67. *Top Court Again Backs "Kimigayo" Orders,* Japan Times (June 8, 2011), http://search.japantimes.co.jp/cgi-bin/nn20110608b1.html.
68. The *Kimigayo Punishment Case* is discussed in Chapter 7.

Likewise Article 18's prohibition against involuntary servitude (except as punishment for a crime) probably applies directly against public bodies but may or may not apply directly to private parties.

[D] Hortatory Rights: Public Welfare Restraints

It is generally understood that United States Constitutional prohibitions are not hortatory in terms but are meant to have discreet and legally binding effect on state action. Thus the courts may enjoin government action in violation of the language of the Constitution when a case is brought by a party having standing to sue (generally an injured party whose injury is separate from that of the public in general) and such case presents a justiciable issue. The same may not be said for all of the rights and Constitutional prohibitions contained in the Japanese Constitution.

Article 25(1) grants all people a minimum standard of living. If government policies fail to provide all citizens of Japan with sufficient funds to maintain such minimum standards, may a citizen sue to require that the law be changed to meet these minimum levels? On its face it would appear to represent a right of the Japanese people and thus to give rise to a remedy if that right is violated. Is this provision, in fact, binding on the government or is it simply hortatory and an expression of national policy without legal "bite?"

It appears that the answer is somewhere between hortatory and a rule that has some bite. The obligation to provide minimum standards is a legislative and not a judicial function—and this is especially true in a "civil law" country where courts typically exercise less power than in a common law jurisdiction. In fact, all attempts to require the legislature to provide additional benefits through litigation have proven unsuccessful.[69] Nonetheless, the courts have indicated that the provision is not meaningless. Rather the provision, as is true of other provisions in the Constitution while not "binding" on the Legislative and Executive Branches is "directive" and points the legislature in the direction in which it should be moving. The court has indicated that *when it is enacting a law in the social policy area* the legislature must consider Constitutional provisions. In fact, in dictum the court holds out the possibility (although today that possibility is remote at best) that the court might intervene if the legislature strays too far from the Constitutional direction.[70]

First, the court reaffirmed its prior decision in the *Staple Food Control Act* case and held that Article 25, while stating the responsibility of the state to carry out national policy in such a way that all people can enjoy at least a minimal standard of cultured and healthy living, does not create any legally enforceable rights. In other words, the state has an obligation to society in general but this obligation does not translate into a grant of individual rights. Next, the court considered how this generalized "right"

69. See e.g., *Staple Food Control Act Case*, 2 Keishu 1235 (Sup. Ct. 929/48) for an English language translation see John M. Maki, *Court and Constitution in Japan* 253 (University of Washington Press 1964).
70. *Asahi* case, Case No. 14 of 1964, 21 Minshu 1043, http://www.courts.go.jp/english/judgments/text/1967.05.24-1964-Gyo-Tsu-No.14.html (G.B. May 24, 1967).

was affected by the passage of the Livelihood Protection Law, which gives eligible persons a right to receive payments based on a schedule of payments to be established by the Minister of Health and Welfare. The court found that amounts set out in such schedule of payments are, in the first instance, a matter of discretion for the minister in charge and a political rather than a legal question—notwithstanding Article 25. However, the court holds out the possibility of judicial review of the amounts set out in the schedule in the event of egregious action by the minister that could rise to the level of judicially reviewable abuse of power.

The Supreme Court revisited the issue of welfare rights in a somewhat different Constitutional setting in the *Horiki* case.[71] Here a handicapped mother who received handicap benefits and also sought juvenile allowance benefits confronted the court with an equal protection argument when the Juvenile Allowance Law prohibited "double dipping" of welfare benefits. After the district court found such provision was in violation of equal protection—a mother in a childless home received handicapped benefits but a mother in a home with a child only received juvenile benefits—the Diet amended the law to permit double dipping. On appeal the character of the challenge resembled more of an Article 25 challenge since the equal protection issue had been resolved by legislation.[72] The Supreme Court affirmed the High Court's rejection of the district court determination finding that the legislature had broad discretion in the social welfare arena and that discretion had not been abused. Once again the Court kept a "string" on legislative action by holding out the possibility that an egregious case of abuse of discretion could be reversed. The *Horiki* case reasoning was reaffirmed in 2007.[73]

Even this limited "right" to have legislation that is enacted reviewed for abuse based on the Constitutional grant may be illusory because the Court has been quite deferential to the Government in the welfare arena. Indeed in 2012 the Court reversed a Fukuoka High Court ruling that had favored elderly residents on welfare who complaining that a cut in benefits to the elderly by local government brought about because of national government policy was unconstitutional. The Supreme Court held that the national government had the power to decide to cut benefits to seniors on welfare and to determine the means by which such cuts should be put into effect.[74]

Another illustration of a hortatory Constitutional "right" is Article 27, paragraph 1, which grants all people both the right and obligation to work. Such a provision could be interpreted to require that the government be an employer of last resort. Under such a rule, persons who could not obtain employment in the private sector could exercise their "right" to work by insisting on a government job. However, no such obligation to

71. 36 Minshu 1235, Case No. 1976 (Gyo-Tsu) No. 30. (G.B. July 7, 1982), http://www.courts.go.jp/english/judgments/text/1982.07.07-1976.-Gyo-Tsu-.No..30.html.
72. That the Court treated the matter as an Article 25 issue is clear from its opinion and its reliance on its previous decision in the *Staple Food Control Act case* that had been the basis for the Asahi decision.
73. *Benefits case*, Case No. 246 Gyo-Tsu of 2005, 61 Minshu No. 6, http://www.courts.go.jp/english/judgments/text/2007.09.28-2005.-Gyo-Tsu-.No..246.html (P.B., Sept. 28, 2007).
74. Kyodo, *Welfare cuts ruling reversed*, Japan Times (Apr. 3, 2012), http://www.japantimes.co.jp/text/nn20120403a5.html.

provide employment exists and thus this right is similarly a programmatic directive rather than a right, as that term is understood in United States law. [The Constitutional *obligation* to work creates additional problems. Surely the Constitution does not permit involuntary servitude—so what remains of the obligation to work as a legal matter?]

The fundamental idea of "rights" of individuals as being protected by the Constitution may not mean the same thing to Americans and Japanese. American notions of "rights" have their basis in natural law concepts that did not take root in Japan after the Meiji Restoration. This "natural law" concept is predicated on the idea that each person—each individual—has naturally given rights that adhere to the individual. In Japanese law the "rights" of individuals may have to give way to the rights of the "group", i.e., the Japanese society. A "public welfare" philosophy surrounds the Japanese Constitution both because of the appeal of such doctrine at the end of the Second World War and also the group identification philosophy of Japan. It is also consistent with Confucian philosophy and can be traced back as far as the Seventeen Article Constitution of Prince Shotoku, written in 604.[75]

Public welfare was a rallying call for the New Deal, which had sought to bring the United States out of a great depression and in attempting to do so was imbued with a public welfare mandate and philosophy. A similar philosophy was specifically written into Article 13 of the Japanese Constitution where the rights to life, liberty and the pursuit of happiness are specifically limited by public welfare considerations. More overarching in its reach is Article 12, which places a responsibility on the Japanese people to use the rights granted by the Constitution for the benefit of the public welfare and which calls on the people of Japan not to abuse their constitutionally granted freedoms and rights so as to damage the public welfare.[76] In considering the concept of public welfare, it has been suggested that the role of each individual as it relates to the larger group of which that individual is a part must be considered.[77] Even outside the "welfare" area there is confusion as to whether the government has an obligation to legislate in areas that appear on their face to be constitutionally mandated. Thus, the right to vote is a Constitutional right. Nonetheless, the Supreme Court has upheld the action of the Diet in abolishing certain procedures that had enabled handicapped persons to vote and then failed to create new procedures to enable such voting. Not only could plaintiffs not compel government action to provide them with special procedures so that they could exercise the franchise but so too a suit for damages was unavailable.[78]

75. See, http://www.sarudama.com/japanese_history/jushichijokenpo.shtml.
76. See Christopher A. Ford, *The Indigenization of Constitutionalism in the Japanese Experience*, 28 Case W. Res. J. Intl. L. 3, 28 (1996).
77. William Noel, *The Right to Life in Japan* 92–93 (Routledge 1997).
78. *At Home Voting case*, Case No. 1978 (O) No. 1240, 39 Minshu No.7, http://www.courts.go.jp/english/judgments/text/1985.11.21-1978.-O-.No..1240.html (P.B. Nov. 21, 1985). The Court found that Diet members were exempt from liability for their legislative acts or failure to act and thus concluded that with the rare and not likely exception of acting in a manner that is clearly contrary to the Constitution the State cannot be held responsible for failures to enact legislation. In *Overseas Voting Case*, Case No. 82 and 83 (Gyo-Tsu) and 76 and 77 (Gyo-Hi) of 2001, http://www.courts.go.jp/english/judgments/text/2005.09.14-2001.-Gyo-Tsu-.No..82%2C.2001.-Gyo-Hi-.No..76%2C.2001.-Gyo-Tsu-.No..83%2C.2001.-Gyo-Hi-.No..77.html (G.B.,

Thus, while the Japanese Constitution contains a number of provisions that appear mandatory on their face, what you see is not what you get. Social policy provisions are viewed as directional rather than as legally binding imperatives and are subjected to a "greater societal good" analysis that makes them subject to legislative rather than judicial enforcement. No such directional provisions are to be found in the United States Constitution and the idea of hortatory Constitutional "rights" is foreign to American lawyers. Rather than making most Constitutional rights subject to legislative enforcement the United States Constitution subjects legislative action dealing with such rights to a searching judicial analysis that places primacy not on societal rights but rather on the rights of the individual.

Sept. 14, 2005) plaintiffs were awarded damages finding this was the unusual and unlikely case that it had posited in the earlier decision.

CHAPTER 4
The Legal Profession

§4.01 UNITED STATES

The principal author of the Declaration of Independence, Thomas Jefferson, was a lawyer. The principal force behind a unified colonial response to British occupation of Boston, and hence the Revolutionary War, John Adams, was a lawyer. Both received their legal education in the Colonies, although they were trained in English common law. One went to Harvard, in Massachusetts and the other to William & Mary in Virginia. The Constitutional Convention was filled with lawyers, as was the Continental Congress. The footprints of the legal profession are evident in the basic documents of the Revolution and the basic documents establishing the United States. Lawyers have been a "power" in state legislatures, the Federal Congress and State and Federal Executive Departments from the start of the Republic.

The history of American lawyers is, of course, the history of English lawyers. The legal profession in England goes back hundreds of years. Starting as Innkeepers who assisted parties in litigation and progressing to Writ writers who needed knowledge of what Writs the courts would and would not accept, the profession divided into two parts in England—Barristers who actually appeared in courts and represented clients in front of the courts and solicitors who provided advice to clients but did not actually appear in front of the judges. (In modern England the distinction between Barristers and Solicitors is being blurred as Solicitors are allowed to appear in court in connection with certain matters. This blurring is likely to accelerate in light of the European Union and its affect on legal professions throughout the Union.) In the United States such distinctions have never existed.

The legal profession has always been subject to state as distinguished from federal law and the various states set the terms and conditions for allowing persons to practice law before their courts. In most states applicants for the Bar are graduates of accredited law schools[1] and upon passage of a bar examination and approval by a character committee are allowed to enter the profession. A lawyer admitted to practice in one state is not permitted to practice in another state unless she is admitted to the bar of that state or has been granted special approval to appear in the court either for the specific case being handled or more generally.[2] Federal courts typically allow a lawyer licensed in the state where the court sits to "waive" in and thus to be admitted to the bar of the federal court. Federal courts, including the Supreme Court of the United States, do not have their own bar examination system.

Law schools in the United States, like most universities and colleges, are of two types—private and public. There are no predetermined limits on the number of students these schools may admit to their law school. Law schools are a graduate faculty and entering students typically have an undergraduate Bachelors degree—although some schools will accept a student who has had three years at an undergraduate faculty of the same school.[3] Typically law school is a three-year program[4] at the end of which the student graduates with a JD degree. Generally speaking the teaching method in United States Law Schools is the confrontational, Socratic question and answer method. While most law schools have a required first year curriculum, students are granted great latitude in choosing the courses they wish to take. The use of clinics, where students get "hands on" experience representing real clients with real problems as part of their legal education, has accelerated as more and more schools utilize more clinics and students are allowed (compelled in some cases) to take more clinical courses in their final year of school. The Judicial Branch is supportive of clinical education and third year students in a clinic are typically allowed to appear in court (under supervision of an admitted lawyer/professor) to argue various matters.

While law schools tend to be national in character, teaching general principles of law and the legal method of thinking and researching, bar examinations are local in character, focusing on the applicant's knowledge of the state's law. After law school the typical student will attend a short, intensive bar review program to prepare the student to take the bar examination in the state where the student seeks to be admitted. These review courses focus their attention on the law of the state involved and seek to prepare the student to pass the State Bar Examination.[5]

1. In some places an applicant need not be a graduate of a law school but may, through experience and apprenticeship apply for the exam.
2. Many states have reciprocity agreements under which lawyers of one state may be admitted to the Bar of the other state without having to take the entire bar examination. Typically in such situations lawyers must take an examination in procedural law to demonstrate ability to handle the procedural requirements on the state in which they seek to practice.
3. A new trend is to offer a joint graduate degree program so that the graduate will graduate with an MBA and a JD at the same time.
4. Four years if the student attends classes at night.
5. In some few states, graduates of the state university's law faculty do not need to take the bar examination to be admitted to practice. Such procedure is considered non-discriminatory to out of state students on the theory that the State Supreme Court is the governing body of the university's law faculty and by graduation has certified that the student is competent in the state's law.

While a large part of the Bar in the United States is composed of lawyers in private practice, many of whom work for themselves in one-person law firms, licensed lawyers also staff the in-house law departments of many companies. All judges are licensed lawyers and the vast majority (if not all) law professors are admitted to the bar. Many lawyers practice law as part of a law partnership (law firm.) Taking note of the recent wave of lawsuits against law firms, many states have provided for a new type of law partnership, the Limited Liability Partnership, under which partners are each responsible in damages for their own malpractice but not for the malpractice of other partners in the firm. A recent trend in the American practice has been the creation of "national law firms" and more recently of "international law firms" consisting of several hundreds of lawyers in offices located throughout the United States and in many cases in offices abroad. Most law partnerships operate as true partnerships in the sense that all fee income is pooled and, after deducting expenses, the profits are distributed to the partners under a formula agreed to in accordance with the applicable partnership agreement. In addition to partners, associate lawyers who, it is hoped will one day become partners in the firm staff law firms. Many firms operate on an "up or out" philosophy under which an associate who is not elected to partnership after a certain number of years is asked to leave the firm. Partnership decisions involve numerous factors, some having nothing to do with the applicant (such as the finances of the firm or its need for additional partnership staff, etc.), and failure to be elected a partner is not a reflection on the lawyer's ability.

Many lawyers in the United States have had a multi-organizational career. Thus it is not uncommon for a young lawyer to spend several years working for the government before going into private practice. Similarly, later in life it is not uncommon for such a lawyer to return to government service for a few years in a senior position either as a lawyer or administrator in a government agency. Lawyers in private practice may move into corporate law departments and vice versa. Senior criminal law prosecutors similarly have typically had both private practice and government prosecution practice in their careers and most criminal defense lawyers were at one time government prosecutors.

Most judges in the United States were, earlier in their careers, practicing trial lawyers. In recent years the salary gap between judges and lawyers in private practice (especially with major litigation or national firms) has created a certain tension between the litigating Bar and the judges, although lawyers have been great supporters of the need to better compensate American judges.

§4.02 JAPAN

One will not find the name of Japanese lawyers among the leaders of the Meiji Restoration for the simple reason that at the time of the Restoration there was no legal profession in Japan. There were no law schools, no *bengoshi* (licensed lawyers) and there was no legal system similar to the Western model. Accordingly, lawyers were not leaders of the revolution, were not the drafters of the original Constitution or the various Codes placed into effect following the Western model. The oligarchs who ruled in the name of the Meiji Emperor were not lawyers. Until well into the second half of the nineteenth century there were no Japanese law faculties and no Japanese lawyers, as we understand lawyers to be a learned profession.

The embryonic roots of the legal profession in Japan were similar to those in England, namely innkeepers who advised customers who were engaged in a dispute (typically with a government tax office). While such persons were unable to actually represent their customers before the tax office they could and did help in the drafting of documents and in provided advice as to arguments to be made. Because the longer a matter was pending at the tax office the longer the customer needed to stay at the inn, questions arose as to the objectivity of the innkeepers who performed this role.[6] In 1872 "*daigennin*" were permitted to represent clients. But there were still no law schools and no professional licensing methods. In 1876 *daigennin* received professional qualification through passage of an examination. Those who failed the examination were still permitted to provide advice and assistance but they could not take the title *daigennin*. In 1880 a further effort was made to regulate lawyers and a kind of bar association to regulate lawyers was created. The Lawyers Law of 1893 created the modern lawyer or *bengoshi*.

The first law faculty in Japan was established in the 1870s at the Imperial Tokyo University. Tokyo University's Faculty of Law remains the dominant force in the legal community and is the most prestigious law faculty in Japan today. Most *bengoshi* and most judges are graduates of Tokyo University—as are a significant number of the senior executives in the Japanese bureaucracy.

Although the legal profession in Japan is only about 100 years old, the fact is that it attracts only the best of the best. Those who have passed the Japanese bar examination have passed one of the most exacting and difficult tests. (This remains the case after the reforms to legal education and the new bar exam and the increase in numbers of applicants admitted to the Bar). *Bengoshi* have one of the highest social statuses in Japan and are entitled to be called by the honorific "sensei".

The training and experience of a Japanese *bengoshi* differed dramatically from that of an American lawyer. Japanese universities contain law faculties and until 2004 all aspiring lawyers attended those undergraduate faculties. The system changed in 2004 so that while there are still undergraduate law faculties (*hogakubu)* there are also new graduate law schools loosely based on the United States model. Nonetheless, most professors, whether of the undergraduate or graduate law faculties are graduates of *hogakubu* law faculties who have pursued masters and other advanced degrees but they are not practicing lawyers and they are not *bengoshi* who have been licensed to practice as lawyers. Many of the new graduate law schools have hired a limited number of practicing *bengoshi* to try to get some practical experience into the classroom. Teaching methods however continue to follow the typical Japanese pedagogy, namely lecture, although some clinical studies are permitted and embraced by some schools. Unfortunately the Judiciary does not permit third year students to actually argue matters before the court, as does the American judiciary. The teacher expounds and the

6. Richard Rabinowitz, *The Historical Development of the Japanese Bar*, 70 Harvard L. Rev. 61 (1956).

student is expected to absorb. It was anticipated that a more Americanized methodology based on the Socratic Method and clinics would be emphasized in the new schools.

The curriculum of new law schools is, for the most part, a national curriculum in which the government, through the Ministry of Education, has a great say. Most students in a *hogakubu* law faculty have no intention of ever competing for the *bengoshi* exam. Most wish to pursue a career in business and a background in a law faculty is considered as good training for the business world. Members of an in-house law department in Japan are typically not *bengoshi* but rather are graduates of the law faculty who have either decided not to compete for *bengoshi* licensing or have not passed the *bengoshi* exam and have given up trying. Indeed, the *Bengoshi-ho* (the lawyers' law) frowns upon full time employment of *bengoshi* in corporate departments and requires Bar Association permission for such a position.[7] As a condition of such approval the Bar requires that the lawyer devote a certain percentage of time to pro bono activities.[8] This requirement is consistent with the ethical rules for lawyers that recognize that part of a *bengoshi's* function is the realization of social justice and the protection of fundamental human rights.[9] Although not licensed lawyers, these *hogakubu* graduates are learned in the law and perform many of the same functions as in-house lawyers in the United States such as document preparation, advice to operating departments in the company, negotiation, etc.

Just as *bengoshi* are generally not permitted to work full time as a company employee so too *bengoshi* may not, as a general rule,[10] work full time as a government employee (with limited exceptions). Accordingly Japanese prosecutors and judges are not *bengoshi*—although they have passed the necessary qualifying exams and have attended the Legal Training Institute. Those who leave the prosecutor or judicial service may apply to the Bar Association for admission as *bengoshi* and will typically be granted such permission. But, Japanese government agencies have no equivalent of the in-house general counsel's office staffed by lawyers that are ubiquitous in American government agencies. To make up for this unavailability the ministries and agencies may "borrow" on temporary assignment members of the Judicial Branch, i.e., judges, who have the necessary qualifications. This leads to separation of powers questions, even if the judges temporarily "resign" from the Bench, as they know they will return at the end of the assignment and are still considered by colleagues as judges. Indeed, the Judicial Secretariat has designated these assigned judges for assignment.

7. Lawyers Law Article 30.
8. Toshiro Nishimura, *Speech at Temple University (Tokyo) Professional Ethics in International Business*, http://www.tuj.ac.jp/newsite/main/law/lawresources/TUJonline/Japan'sLegalProfession/benethics.html, last accessed Sept. 14, 2012.
9. Japan Federation of Bar Associations, Basic Rules on the Duties of Practicing Lawyers, Article 1. (Awareness of Mission). (Adopted at an Extraordinary General Meeting on Nov. 10, 2004).
10. Bengoshi may perform legal services for the government as a client. Even when a *bengoshi* is permitted to be a full time government employee (such as when she is a Diet member or has been retained for a limited number of years for a special assignment) the *bengoshi* must refrain from practicing law while in such government position. Article 30, Practicing Attorney Law (Bengoshi-ho). In 2011 the Ministry of Health retained a lawyer to advise the Ministry on how to avoid litigation. The lawyer will work for the Ministry for two-years. It is apparently the first time the Ministry retained a lawyer to advise it. Kyodo, *Besieged Health Ministry Lawyers Up*, Japan Times (Oct. 1, 2011), http://search.japantimes.co.jp/cgi-bin/nn20111001b2.html.

Unlike the situation in the pre-war period when *bengoshi* were under the control of the Ministry of Justice, the post-war lawyer system makes Bar Associations (*bengoshi-kai*) independent of the Executive Branch of government. The Supreme Court is given authority to regulate the practice and, as a practical matter Bar Associations are independent. All *bengoshi* must belong to the Bar Association and the Japan Federation Bar Associations (JFBA) is the national body of all Bar Associations.[11] The JFBA has jurisdiction to handle disciplinary cases against lawyers and its determinations will not be overturned by the courts unless based on illegality, lacking in a factual basis or such an unreasonable exercise of discretionary authority so as to constitute an abuse of discretion.[12] While members of the public as well as other *bengoshi* can file disciplinary charges against a lawyer,[13] if a *bengoshi* makes a charge in bad faith or without investigation that an ordinary person exercising ordinary care would make before filing, the filing constitutes a tort and the charged *bengoshi* has a right to sue for damages.[14]

The Bar Association is more "liberal" than is the Secretariat and typically will engage in certain activities in opposition to the government to assure that a more liberal Japanese view is heard. Thus it is common for the Bar Association to file its own "report" to various United Nations bodies taking a different approach and setting out a different view from the official government of Japan report.

---

11. If a local Bar Association refuses to register an applicant who has passed the Bar exam and Training institute Course the applicant can appeal to the Japan Federation of Bar Associations which may reverse the local Association's determination. If the JFBA does not reverse the applicant can appeal to the Tokyo High Court. Grounds for refusal are limited–reason to believe that admission can hurt the reputation of the Bar and/or Bar Association, mental incompetence or previous discipline by a Bar Association or certain other professional organizations.
12. Teruki Tsunemoto, *Commentary on Important Legal Precedents for 2006–Trends in Constitutional Law Cases*, 9 Asian-P. L. & Policy J. 213, 216 (2008).
13. The ability of ordinary citizens to file charges can result in charges being brought that have no basis–for example, in 2007 over 7,500 charges were filed against attorneys who represented a defendant in a heinous criminal case in Hiroshima. Total charges in that year exceeded 9,500. Almost all were dismissed by the end of 2008. In 2007, 2008 and 2009 only 1 attorney in each of these years was disbarred and a total of 8 attorneys were ordered to withdraw from the association in total for the three-year period, although a total of over 13,000 charges were made in the same time frame. In 2009 there were a total of 76 disciplinary actions of which the great majority were admonishments (40) and suspension from practice of one year or less (27). JFBA, While Paper on Attorneys 2010, page 62, http://www.nichibenren.or.jp/library/en/about/data/WhitePaper2010.pdf. The request for charges in the Hiroshima case brought forth a suit by the attorney's involved against a bengoshi who was on a TV program and recommended that viewers write in and request an investigation of the attorneys. The Supreme Court held that the attorney making the suggestion was not subject to a tort action. One Justice specifically referred to the *Unwarranted Disciplinary Charge Against Bengoshi May Constitute a Tort Case,* Case No. 2126 (Ju) of 2005, 61 Minshu No. 3 (Sup. Ct. 24 April 2007), http://www.courts.go.jp/english/judgments/text/2007.04.24-2005.-Ju-.No..2126.html discussed in the text. *Suggestion that Public Ask Bar Association to Discipline Attorneys case,* Case No. 2009 (Ju) No. 1905 and 1906, Minshu Vol. 65, No. 5, http://www.courts.go.jp/english/judgments/text/2011.07.15-2009.-Ju-.No..1905.and.1906.html (P.B., July 15, 2011).
14. *Unwarranted Disciplinary Charge Against Bengoshi May Constitute a Tort Case,* Case No. 2126 (Ju) of 2005, 61 Minshu No. 3 (P.B., Apr. 24, 2007), http://www.courts.go.jp/english/judgments/text/2007.04.24-2005.-Ju-.No..2126.html.

In addition to licensed lawyers and in-house legal departments Japan has professionals known as judicial scriveners who prepare documents much as an American lawyer. In addition there are patent and tax professionals who perform many functions that in the United States are handled by lawyers and who as a consequence of recent reforms are now allowed to appear in court in some specialized litigations under the supervision of a *bengoshi*. As a consequence it is inappropriate to compare the number of licensed lawyers in each country to draw a comparison about the size of the legal professions therein. However, even when taking account of these other professionals in Japan the fact remains that there are many more lawyers in the United States than in Japan. This may be accounted for by the fact that until the 1990s Japan only licensed 500 new lawyers every year.[15] In the 1990s the number began to climb to a total of about 1,000 new admissions by 2000; and in 2007 a total of 2,099 people passed the Bar Examination of who 1851 had gone to the new graduate level law schools. It was the objective of the Reform Council that the number of persons passing the bar would continue to rise to 3,000 by the year 2010. However, that objective requires both an objective passing grade that can be achieved by 3,000 test takers and an Education Ministry that, together with the Bar, wishes to have the law school system experiment succeed. Only 2043 graduates passed the Bar Examination given in 2009—a decline from 2007 figures—and the passing percentage in 2009 was a low 27.6%.[16] In 2010 only 2074 graduates passed and the passing rate had fallen to 25.4%.[17] This marked the fourth year in a row in which the passing rate had declined—an indication that the Ministry is not anxious to see 3,000 new lawyers licensed each year. Moreover, the percentage of students passing the exam who had taken their undergraduate degree in the *hogakubu* (undergraduate law) faculty was more than double that of students coming from other faculties—also undermining the intent of the Law Reform Council that new lawyers have a broader educational experience than had *bengoshi* of the past.[18] The low passing rate taken together with the adoption of a "three strikes and you're out" policy under which graduates have only three opportunities to pass the bar within a five year period after graduation, means that the odds are seriously against graduates passing the exam and becoming lawyers. Such policies are likely to lead to the same type of self elimination that characterized the former exam system as well as to reduce the likelihood that

15. The number is actually less than 500 as in this number are included judges and prosecutors. This would bring the number of new practicing lawyers down to approximately 425 each year.
16. Jonathan David Marshall, *Democratizing the Law in Japan*, in *Routledge Handbook of Japanese Politics* 92, 97 (Alisa Gaunder ed., 2011).
17. Kyodo News, *Bar exam success rate at record low*, Japan Times (Sept. 10, 2010), http://search.japantimes.co.jp/cgi-bin/nn20100910b2.html; Bar exam pass rate falls for 4th year, The Yomiuri Shimbun, Sept. 11, 2010, http://www.yomiuri.co.jp/dy/national/T100910002851.htm. In 2012 the passing rate was only 25.06%. Yomiuri Shimbun, Sept. 13, 2012, 70% of preliminary exam passers successful in bar exam, http://www.yomiuri.co.jp/dy/national/T120912004614.htm.
18. Of the five schools that had more than 100 graduates pass the 2010 exam, four were located in Tokyo (Tokyo University, Chuo University, Keio University and Waseda University) and one in Kyoto (Kyoto University). (See, http://www.yomiuri.co.jp/adv/chuo/dy/news/20100909.htm) This too was inconsistent with the reforms' intent to more widely disburse legal professionals.

non-*hogakubu* undergraduates will opt to go to law school (while increasing the likelihood that Law Schools will gear their entrance exams to eliminate non-*hogakubu* entrants in order to increase their overall pass rate) thereby limiting the experience and exposure of lawyers, judges and prosecutors leading to the same type of tunnel vision that the Law Reform Council had sought to change.

After passing the bar examination a *bengoshi* candidate is required to attend the Legal Training and Research Institute, which is operated by the Japanese Supreme Court. Students receive a government grant while at the Institute. All judges, lawyers and prosecutors pass through the Institute. Upon graduation a second test is given but virtually all who take it pass the examination. Upon graduation new lawyers choose to be either *bengoshi* in private practice, judges or prosecutors. The government makes the decision as to who will be accepted as judges and prosecutors. The Institute thus gives the Judicial Secretariat the opportunity to determine at the outset whether a judicial candidate is likely to conform to Secretariat views.

Most Japanese lawyers are individual practitioners. Even where there are law firms they have tended to operate more as individual practices with shared expenses than as true partnerships. Branch offices were forbidden. There are some large firms (and some now contain over 100 lawyers) but there are certainly no national firms to rival those of the United States. With changes in the *Bengoshi-ho* to allow for lawyer's companies and changes permitting mergers between Japanese firms and foreign firms, a number of international firms have merged with Japanese firms and become a presence in the Tokyo legal scene. Although the requirement that lawyers be Japanese citizens has been lifted because the *bengoshi* exam is given in Japanese (and for other reasons) it is almost impossible for an American to become a member of the Japanese bar.[19] On the other hand, it is not uncommon for a Japanese *hogakubu* graduate working in the American office of a Japanese company to take a state Bar Review course and then pass the State Bar Examination and become a lawyer in the United States.

As Japan is a unitary state there is only a national licensing requirement and a lawyer once licensed can practice anywhere in the country. Most Japanese lawyers practice in Tokyo or Osaka (and surrounding cities) and there is a dramatic shortage of lawyers in small communities in Japan.[20] Unlike American lawyers who tend to specialize in specific areas of the law, Japanese lawyers tend to be generalists (except for tax and Intellectual Property practices) who handle litigation as well as other general corporate work.

---

19. There are reports of a single individual who was able to bridge the gap and become a Japanese lawyer. Lifting the citizenship requirement has made it easier (but by no means easy) for Korean permanent residents of Japan to become bengoshi.
20. Recognizing this problem, especially as it affects those accused of committing crimes, the JFBA has attempted to staff outlying offices to bring at least some professional legal services to small communities in Japan.

§4.03 WHAT YOU SEE MAY NOT BE WHAT YOU GET

In the United States law schools have become "profit centers" for universities. As law firm entry level salaries have escalated into the over USD 100,000 mark, top law schools found it relatively easy to increase tuition and this trend has been followed by other schools. As the rate per student that can be exacted increases, so too does the school's desire to expand its programs and size of student body to a manageable but still large size. The result has been an explosion in the number of graduating law students. To make it worthwhile for students to attend law school there must be a reasonable probability of success on the bar exam—why go to law school and pay high tuition fees if the chances of becoming a lawyer are small? In the United States there is no absolute score required to pass a State Bar Examination and it is typical for about 60% of applicants to be successful. Such a large number of law graduates and lawyers raise issues of quality and competence.

In Japan, on the other hand, the public is well aware of the historic difficulty in passing the bar examination. With only some 1,000 successful lawyer candidates each year until recently, the number of students competing to be *bengoshi* self excluded those who are not the cream of the crop.[21] With so few lawyers being admitted and with the system designed to accommodate only the best of the best one would expect to find that Japanese lawyers are considered to be highly qualified to practice their profession. And, it is the author's experience that they are.

But the reputation of lawyers in Japan is mixed. On the one hand they are respected as highly intelligent and the brightest of the brightest. On the other, they have acted, at times, in ways that makes the public wonder about them. In representing clients in the various criminal cases that arose out of the riots protesting the Japan/ United States Mutual Defense Treaty, the lawyers concluded that the courts were biased against their clients. They engaged in delaying tactics, they were unruly and they were insulting towards the courts. The reputation of the bar suffered and, in 1979, the JFBA apologized to the public. The bar began an internal self-analysis and rewrote its rules of ethics in 1990.[22]

The Law Reform Council's initial 2001 Report "Points at Issue" identified more and better training of lawyers as a necessary component of legal reform.[23] The Final Report of the Council recommends a complete overhaul of the methods of training the legal profession and suggests—and Japan has adopted these suggestions—a graduate law school program for *bengoshi* candidates. These schools should have a standardized three-year course of study (this was reduced to two years for students who enter after

21. The difficulty in passing the exam also serves to self-exclude many who are the "cream of the crop". Moreover, by having an absolute and small number of passes each year, the majority of those taking the exam will be forced to fail and as a result it may be many years before these highly qualified candidates achieve success on the exam. Many candidates may simply give up rather than wait until they finally succeed.
22. For a discussion see Sherill A. Leonard, *Attorney Ethics and the Size of the Japanese Bar*, Japan Q. (January-March 1992) reprinted in Koichiro Fujikura, Japanese L. & Leg. Theory 501(New York University Press 1996).
23. Carl F. Goodman, *The Somewhat Less Reluctant Litigant: Japan's Changing View towards Civil Litigation*, 32 L. & Pol. Intl. Bus. 769, 804-805 (2001).

completing undergraduate work in a law faculty), and most significantly should provide a practical education. Theory should be combined with the actual practical requirements of law practice. Moreover, the lecture method should be replaced with interaction between students and professors as well as interaction between the students themselves.

In other words, Japan appeared to be on the brink of introducing the Socratic Method to its law school system and appeared to have adopted the basic graduate law faculty approach of the United States. In addition suggestions have been made to try to bring more practicing lawyers onto law faculties so that students can get a better understanding of the actual practical aspects of the law. Moreover, it appeared that an effort would be made to bring into the profession students whose undergraduate work was in other than law faculties and there will be an emphasis on expanding the geographic base of new lawyers by establishing law schools in various parts of the country and by accepting candidates from various parts of the country. The goal was to have 70% to 80% of law school students pass the bar examination and enter the profession as *bengoshi*. The reality has not lived up to expectations. The 2012 passing rate of only 25.06% is a function of both too many law schools and an unrealistically high (and one might note arbitrary) passing grade. This low passage rate places pressure on Law Schools to compete with each other on the basis of how many of their graduates pass the Bar—this in turn has led to more students entering law schools from undergraduate law faculties (as statistically these students do better in passing the Bar) thus the number of lawyers with non-law undergraduate degrees remains minimal and it is likely that the reform objective of having lawyers with a broader base of education will not be achieved. So too this process results in most law students attending law school for only two and not three years as undergraduate law students who pass a knowledge exam need only attend two years. Law Schools in great measure have taken to "educating to the test" rather than in trying to educate "to the practice" and by some accounts have become the formalized *juku* (cram course) schools for *hogakubu* graduates who wish to become lawyers. It is too early to pronounce the law education reform as a failure because it is possible that economics will force sufficient numbers of Law Schools to fail so that the reform might eventually have hope of succeeding. By mid-2012 three law schools had announced that they would close.[24] Nonetheless it is not too early to note that they are not achieving the reform ends sought by the Council.

Considering that Japanese *bengoshi* are so highly talented and considering that their reputation among the public is so much better than United States lawyers,[25] why is Japan fundamentally restructuring its legal training system? The reasons are varied. There is recognition that *hogakubu* law faculties are neither designed to nor do they do a good job of training professional lawyers. Existing *hogakubu* faculties have as their major objective educating students who wish to go into the business world and see the

24. Meiji Gakuin planning to close law school in 5 years, The Yomiuri Shimbun (May 31, 2012), http://www.yomiuri.co.jp/dy/national/T120530004820.htm.

25. For a general discussion of the difference in reputation of Japanese and United States lawyers see Dal Pont, *The Social Status of the Legal Profession in Japan and the United States: A Structural and Cultural Analysis*, 72 U. Detroit Mercy L. Rev. 291 (1995).

law faculty as a good background for business. In the United States many of such students might take a BBA degree, wherein they are introduced to basic notions of contract and business law. In Japan the law faculty is the choice. As the faculty must support the needs of its students, teaching techniques as well as curriculum is geared to these students not the handful who may wish to make the practice of law their profession.[26] The general view of *hogakubu* law faculties is that their purpose is to provide a generalized legal education that is sufficient for business executives but while such a program may produce educated legal generalists is not sufficient for production of legal professionals.[27] Even the minority view on the Council stressed the "basic" nature of the legal education provided by *hogakubu* faculties. As law has become more specialized the providing of a basic general legal education is not sufficient for the practitioner.

If the *hogakubu* faculty was not providing a "vocational" education for lawyers, who was doing this job? This function appears to have been performed by two diametrically different types of organizations. First were the private tutoring schools (*juku*) that educated graduates of the *hogakubu* so that they can pass the bar examination. Second, the Legal Training and Research Institute operated by the Supreme Court. The function of this school is strictly "vocational" in the sense that it is designed to teach law and to teach the practical aspects of law. However, whereas this school used to provide a two-year education it changed to only one year and it cannot keep up with the demands that will be placed on it if the legal profession moves towards 3,000 successful bar exam passing mark. In addition, it is the assumption of the Institute that since their students have all passed the new bar examination they are prepared for the tasks of lawyering. Thus the Institute, while it has some classroom work, is more in the nature of an apprenticeship program and less in the nature of a true educational program. Japanese lawyers while highly educated have not been educated in what American lawyers—and now to a great extent Japanese businesses—view as the "legal method". The give and take of the Socratic method is more than simply a learning tool, it sharpens certain skills that clients expect their lawyers to possess, such as a certain aggressiveness in supporting a position taken even when it has been vigorously challenged, the ability to vigorously challenge a position; quick thinking on one's feet, etc.[28] As Japanese business has expanded to become a major player in world markets it can no longer rely on in-house legal generalists to do some of the work that is done by lawyers in most Western countries. This need for more lawyers finds reflection in the need to better educate students to perform these functions. Law firms in Japan can no longer be expected to be the training institutes for their new members. In addition, if law schools are to educate a new generation of lawyers on practical aspects of the law, then law schools must look to practitioners to assist them in this

---

26. Yukio Yanagida, *A New Paradigm for Japanese Legal Education–in Light of the Legal Education at Harvard Law School*, 1 Asian-P. L& Policy J. 1, 5 (2000).
27. Kaoru Matsuura, *Gakubu ni okeru hougaku kyoiku no mokuteki ni tsuite*, 1062 Hanrei Jiho 3, 5 (1983) quoted in Yukio Yanagida, *A New Paradigm for Japanese Legal Education—In Light of the Legal Education at Harvard Law School*, 1 Asian-Pacific Law & Policy Journal note 8 (2000).
28. Yukio Yanagida, *A New Paradigm for Japanese Legal Education—In Light of the Legal Education at Harvard Law School*, 1 Asian-Pacific Law & Policy Journal 1, 18 (2000).

function. The new Japanese graduate law faculties have sought practitioners as adjuncts and have introduced practical courses such as clinics to the law program. However, clinic programs have been hindered by an unwillingness of Bench and Bar to permit third year students to appear in court under the supervision of a *bengoshi* as well as an ingrained prejudice against allowing students to actually interact with clients rather than simply watch as licensed professionals interact in their presence. Moreover the new law schools while seeking to obtain more rounded professors who can teach several different courses and thereby bring together seemingly diverse subjects that may meld together at the client's or the courthouse's door were hindered by the necessity to find positions for *hogakubu* faculty members who were leaving to staff the new schools.

The vast majority of Japanese *bengoshi* (and judges) are graduates of a few law faculties located in the Tokyo or Kyoto regions. Greater geographic distribution of lawyers was one of the goals of legal reform. Recent results show that the vast majority of new lawyers continue to come from Tokyo and Osaka/Kyoto area law schools. While greater geographic distribution of *bengoshi* has not been achieved, there are significantly more female lawyers in Japan today than there were a decade ago.[29] The reality is that the Law School Reform has faltered and is on the brink of failure.[30]

There are still over 70 graduate law schools in Japan (an *increase* from the original number approved by the Ministry of Education in 2004). The average number of students in each yearly class totals approximately 5,700-5,800 students. The goal of 3,000 new lawyers a year beginning in 2010 was not achieved.

Although the low passing rate is not viable to achieve the ends sought by the Reform Council (and lower than the 70%–80% passing rate suggested by the Council) it is higher than the 20% passing rate originally suggested by the Ministry of Justice but lower than the compromise 30% rate proposed by the ministry after the storm of protest that greeted its 20% proposal. The government is unlikely to announce a new higher projected passing rate for the future, thereby further clouding the prospects for both new law schools and their prospective students.[31] It is likely that rather than lowering the passing grade to increase the number of lawyers the government will simply reduce its goal for new lawyers below the 3,000 agreed to when the Reform Council work was done.[32] This would be consistent with the views of the JFBA, which is concerned about the inability of the current system to find positions for newly

29. Eric Feldman, *Law, Society and Medical Malpractice Litigation in Japan*, 8 Wash. U. Global Stud. L. Rev. 257, 268 (2009).
30. For a critique of the Japanese bureaucracy's conservative approach to the new law schools and a discussion of the potential effect of costs on students and their families see Luke Nottage, *Reformist Conservatism and Failures of Imagination in Japanese Legal Education*, 2 Asian-P. L.& J. 28, 48–51 (2001).
31. See Peter A. Joy, Shigeo Miyagawa, Takao Suami & Charles D. Weisselberg, *Building Clinical Legal Education Programs in a Country without a Tradition of Graduate Professional Legal Education: Japan Educational Reform As a Case Study*, 13 Clinical L. Rev. 417 (2006) for a discussion of the debilitating effect of low passage rates on the Japanese Bar to law school reform and problems in clinical education.
32. See, Govt. may lower bar exam goal / Target of 3,000 passing law exam deemed risk to quality of lawyers, Yomiuri Shimbun, Jan. 6, 2010; http://www.yomiuri.co.jp/dy/national/20100106TDY02305.htm.

licensed lawyers. The actual number of lawyers in Japan has increased since the Reform Council's Report and while there were only 20,700 lawyers in Japan in 2000 by 2009 there were almost 31,500, putting a strain on established law firms that cannot absorb the new lawyers and placing a strain on the new lawyers who cannot find positions.[33] If the Bar Association's new goal of lowering the number of new lawyers to only 1,500 a year is achieved this will put even greater pressure on the fledgling new Law Schools.

In fact, no school achieved the 70%–80% passing rate suggested by the Council. The passing rate of the top 10 Law Schools in the country was only 57% and of the top 10 Law Schools in Japan only Tokyo, Kyoto and Hitobashi achieved a passing rate in excess of 50%. Nor did the Council's objective of having graduates from across the entire nation pass in sufficient numbers that lawyers could then return to their home communities thereby remedying the situation where most lawyers are in the main centers surrounding or close to Tokyo and Osaka. In 2009, 216 Tokyo University Graduates passed the Bar Exam followed by another Tokyo based school (Chuo University) which had 162 passing graduates. Of those passing the exam, 75% came from the top 16 laws schools in Japan.[34]

The granting of a special status to *hogakubu* students, so that those who pass an exam need only take two years at the new graduate faculty is subject to question. If the idea of reform was that a three-year graduate program was required so that new lawyers would be more properly educated for the Bar, then the implicit suggestion is that *hogakubu* faculties did not properly train students to be lawyers. Why then give graduates of the *hogakubu* a pass on the first year (probably a formative year and fully one-third of the time other students devote to law school) in the new law schools? The answer would appear to be totally unrelated to the question of educating the next generation of lawyers—rather, it appears to be related to preserving the viability of *hogakubu* schools and their faculties and staff. The symbiotic relationship between the undergraduate *hogakubu* faculty and the new graduate law school is demonstrated in many ways: (a) by giving students a one year credit in the new law schools, *hogakubu* faculties remain relevant for students who wish to become *bengoshi* and can serve as a "farm system" for the University's new law school; (b) the professors in the new law schools are graduates of and most were (and still are) professors at the *hogakubu* faculties; (c) the new graduate faculties are seen as a means of preserving the viability of *hogakubu* faculties since a school with a *hogakubu* faculty but no law school may be seen as less desirable or may have a lower reputation than a school with a new law school. Finally, *hogakubu* graduates who take the two-year law school program are more likely to pass the Bar Exam than graduates of other undergraduate faculties causing schools to increase the percentage of *hogakubu* graduates admitted to their law

---

33. Setsuko Kamiya, *Reformist bar head works to raise way lawyers serve*, Japan Times (July 24, 2010), http://search.japantimes.co.jp/cgi-bin/nn20100724f2.html. See, Yomiuri Shimbun, Aug. 14, 2010, 40% of trainee lawyers can't secure work / Crowded field leads to intense competition, http://www.yomiuri.co.jp/dy/national/T100813004341.htm.
34. Tomoya Ishikawa, Mitsusada Enyo & Daisuke Nakai, *Law Schools Troubled by Bar Exam Failure Rate*, the Asahi Shimbun (Oct. 27, 2009), http://www.asahi.com/english/Herald-asahi/TKY200910270110.htm.

school program.[35] If the *hogakubu* failed in its mission to properly educate lawyers the higher passing rate for *hogakubu* graduates would appear to be unrelated to their ability to perform legal tasks and more related to the nature of the Bar Exam.

Thus, what you see—a vibrant new three-year graduate law school system modeled after the American law school with clinics and Socratic teaching methods employing licensed lawyers as professors—is not what you get. Rather, the new schools are only two-year schools for an increasing number of their students, some are focusing on teaching to the test rather than providing a rounded law school education, clinics are a shadow of what they are in the United States (and what they could be in Japan) and most of the professors are the same professors who taught at and still teach at what were and are considered inadequate training grounds for lawyers. Practicing lawyers teaching in law schools have to a certain extent been marginalized, teaching courses like legal ethics (which are of course important) rather than the nuts and bolts courses required of a practicing lawyer. Nor have they been welcomed by the classic teaching profession with offers of tenure and other benefits. The schools and established faculties do not carry all the blame for the failure to utilize *bengoshi* resources to teach practical subjects. The schools initially intended to hire large numbers of *bengoshi* but the Ministry of Justice required that practical teachers (*bengoshi*) submit as part of their required qualifications research works so as to demonstrate their qualifications to teach.[36] It has been suggested that the experience to date raises serious questions as to whether the new law schools can survive.[37]

Associated with the notion of a more professionally educated class of lawyers was the idea of a better-informed public. Thus the concept of a "judicial support network" that would provide information to ordinary citizens was seen as an essential step in judicial reform. In 2004 a new Legal Support Law was enacted to carry out this goal. In April of 2006 a Legal Support Center was created within the Ministry of Justice and began operations in October of 2006. The Center provides information to the public on such subjects as how to get in touch with Bar Associations, or other professional associations as well as how to contact legal professionals. As part of Japan's emphasis on settlement of disputes through alternative dispute resolution the Center also provides information that it is hoped will enable disputing parties to reach an amicable resolution of their problem.

As early as 1952 the JFBA had established the Legal Aid Corporation to provide legal assistance to parties without financial means. The activities of this Corporation have been bundled into the operations of the new Center, which has authority *to make loans to litigants* to support the cost of civil litigation and also to provide free legal assistance to needy persons with non-criminal legal problems. It is anticipated that the

35. Tomoya Ishikawa, Mitsusada Enyo & Daisuke Nakai, *Law Schools Troubled by Bar Exam Failure Rate*, The Asahi Shimbun (Oct. 27, 2009), http://www.asahi.com/english/Herald-asahi/TKY200910270110.htm.

36. Masahiro Tanaka, *Ideals and Realities in Japanese Law Schools: Artificial Obstacles to the Development of Legal Education*, Higher Education Policy 195–206 (Palgrave Macmillan 2007).

37. Peter A. Joy, Shigeo Miyagawa, Takao Suami & Charles D. Weisselberg, *Building Clinical Legal Education Programs in a Country without a Tradition of Graduate Professional Legal Education: Japan Educational Reform As a Case Study*, 13 Clinical L. Rev. 417, 452 (2006).

Center will open offices in close proximity to each District Court as well as in outlying areas of Japan that have no or very few lawyers. These offices are to be staffed with at least one lawyer so that legal service will be immediately available. The structure is still a work in process. How much free legal advice and how large a staff these offices will have will be determined to a great extent by budget and professional talent availability considerations. In a limited number of situations the Center will also be able to provide assistance to indigent parties accused of crimes and in a smaller number of cases to indigent suspects. What is clear is that the Japanese system does not in fact provide free legal service to the poor—rather the poor can get loans to support litigation but are expected to pay back those loans. The JFBA recognizes its obligation to provide legal service to the poor but it also recognizes its need to be an advocate for lawyers and to see that lawyers are paid for the legal work they provide. One solution being urged by the JFBA is for the government to pay for legal services for the poor.

In 2001 the Lawyers Law was amended to allow for the incorporation of law firms in Japan and to allow such incorporated bodies to maintain branch offices.[38] The Judicial Reform Council recommended expansion of the incorporation of firms and their opening additional offices and further, suggested, that consideration should be given to permitting legal forms that would allow for the provision of both legal advice and business advice and would permit lawyers to share in fees generated from such non-legal advice.[39]

Japan presently allows foreign lawyers, under conditions, to practice as foreign law specialists in Japan, provided reciprocity is given to Japanese lawyers in the foreign lawyer's licensing jurisdiction.[40] Such foreign law experts may not provide advice as to Japanese law or law of jurisdictions other than their home country. Initially such lawyers were not permitted to hire Japanese lawyers in order to get Japanese law expertise in-house but this practice has changed. More recent changes have permitted the merger of Japanese and foreign law firms so as to allow for "one-stop" shopping by international clients. In addition, Japanese law firms have begun to grow in size as they provide a wide range of services and have lawyers who specialize in specific areas. Although not reaching the mega size of some United States firms, these local firms can have several hundred lawyers. Mega American firms have merged with Japanese firms creating Tokyo offices that dwarf the size of Japanese firms just a few years ago. As of April 2011 359 foreign lawyers were registered with the JFBA (JFBA). Foreign lawyers

---

38. Act No. 41 of 2001. Under the law lawyers will not only be permitted to have branch offices but for the first time will be able to hire lawyers to work for the firm. Previously lawyers worked as independent practioners even when working under a single firm name. It is hoped that "staff lawyers" will take temporary positions in government and the new emerging law schools and then be able to return to work for the firm. The *Japan Times*, Mar. 7, 2001 Changes to Attorney Law Allows Lawyers to Establish Legal Firms.
39. Recommendations of the Justice System Reform Council—For a Justice System to Support Japan in the twenty-first century, June 12, 2001, www.kantei.go.jp/foreign/judiciary/2001/0612report.html—see 66.
40. In the United States licensing jurisdictions are the states and some states may not provide such reciprocity. Moreover the conditions attached may be difficult to meet. For example, new lawyers cannot practice as foreign law experts as to be qualified the lawyer must meet certain minimum experience requirements.

have not been able to incorporate and operate as a law corporations but in 2012 the DPJ submitted a Cabinet Bill (supported by Japanese business interests) to allow such incorporation subject to supervision by the JFBA. Such corporations would be permitted to employ Japanese *Bengoshi* and could establish branch offices.[41] Although the Bill promises equality by allowing foreign law corporations to open branch offices in Japan just as local Japanese law corporations can, what you see may not be what you get. Only law corporations can have branch offices and most foreign firms in Japan are not organized on a corporate model nor can they effectively incorporate in Japan because doing so would have worldwide implications, including tax implications, for partners outside of Japan. As a consequence major foreign firms are unlikely to incorporate and thus unlikely to be able to open branch offices.[42]

The large number of lawyers in the United States has led to ethical problems. Each year numerous lawyers have either been suspended from practice or disbarred for a number of years or permanently for misconduct. In post-war Japan ethical issues involving lawyers have not been as great a problem, although there have been a few widely publicized scandals.[43] In the year 2000 only 44 lawyers were punished or reprimanded in Japan. This was a decline from 52 cases in 1999. Of the 44 punished, only eight were disbarred, 20 were reprimanded and 16 suspended for up to two years.[44] In 2009 76 lawyers were disciplined—40 received reprimands, 27 were suspended for 1 year or less, 3 suspended for 1–2 years, 5 ordered to withdraw from the Bar Association, and 1 formally disbarred[45]. As the size of the lawyer population grows in Japan methods for dealing with ethical lapses will have to be found, which both protect clients and the judicial process and assure that public perceptions of Japanese lawyers remains at the high level it is today.

In the United States there are extensive ethical codes to govern the conduct of lawyers and active bar counsel operating under the auspices of integrated bars with judicial supervision handle cases against lawyers charged with unethical conduct. Yet there are high rates of lawyer misconduct and discipline. The situation in Japan is different. There are few ethical rules and what rules there are, are widely considered irrelevant to the issue of lawyer ethics because ethics is considered a cultural imperative not a rule driven imperative. Yet with the increase in new lawyers it was anticipated that ethical problems would arise with more frequency than today. The Ministry of Justice as well as the JFBA considered how to deal with this potential

41. Jun Hongo, *Calls Mount for Restrictions on Foreign Lawyers to be Eased*, Japan Times (Mar. 7, 2012), http://www.japantimes.co.jp/text/nn20120307x3.html.
42. See, e.g., Minoru Matsutani, *Foreign Law Firms aim for Equal Treatment*, Japan Times (Apr. 5, 2012), http://www.japantimes.co.jp/text/nn20120405f1.html.
43. See Sherill A. Leonard, *Attorney Ethics and the Size of the Japanese Bar*, Japan Q. (January--March 1992) reprinted in Koichiro Fujikura, *Japanese Law and Legal Theory* 501(New York University Press 1996) for a discussion of the small number of lawyer discipline cases in Japan.
44. *Changes to Attorney Law Allow Lawyers to Establish Legal Firms*, Japan Times Mar. 7, 2001, http://www.japantimes.co.jp/text/nn20010307b8.html. Although only one lawyer was "dismissed", the seven lawyers who were ordered to leave the Bar Association were effectively dismissed.
45. Kyoko Ishida, *Ethics and Regulations of Legal Service Providers in Japan* 58–59, 132 (vdm Verlag, Dr. Muller 2011).

problem without overly defining ethical duties in a written code or overly regulating what has been a self-regulating (for the most part) profession. In 2004 the JFBA adopted its first ever "binding" as distinguished from hortatory ethics code. Although considered binding the Code makes it clear that disciplinary actions must be based on the *Bengoshi-ho* (Attorney's Law) rather than the Code.

CHAPTER 5
The Judiciary

§5.01 UNITED STATES

The American Colonies and then the States and the United States accepted the British common law model. However, the governmental structure of Parliamentary government with an all-powerful Parliament was not accepted. Instead, adopting the philosophy of separation of powers the United States Constitution creates a separate and co-equal federal Judicial Branch of government. The independence of this branch is protected by life tenure.[1] To assure that judges are not influenced by the Congressional power over the budget, salaries of judges are protected from diminution.[2] All District Court judges receive the same salary, just as all Circuit Court Judges receive the same salary and as all Associate Justices of the Supreme Court receive the same salary. Although the general jurisdiction of the courts of the new government of the United States is set out in the Constitution, the Constitution makes no mention of the court's ability to declare actions of the other branches of government unconstitutional. In short, the power of judicial review is not mentioned.

The federal Judicial Power is distributed over three levels of courts. The District Courts are the basic trial level courts. Their function is to determine the facts of a matter and make an initial decision in the case. Under the doctrine of stare decisis these courts are "required" to follow the law as established by the Circuit Court of Appeals for the Circuit in which they are located. Following the British distinction between "law" and "equity" the original judiciary had both law and equity courts but these courts were merged into one federal court system and today Federal Judges are both law and equity

1. "The Judges, both of the supreme and inferior Courts, shall hold their offices during good Behavior [...]" Article III section 1.
2. Article III section 1. Several federal judges sued arguing that refusal to take account of inflation in judges' salaries constituted an unconstitutional diminution of judges' compensation. The Court of Appeals rejected this argument and the Supreme Court, probably well aware of the political ramifications of ruling on its own as well as other federal judges' salaries, declined to hear the matter.

judges. Similarly, judges are both criminal and civil judges and handle both criminal and civil cases.

Depending on the nature of the case the role of the Federal District Judge will differ. Thus, in criminal and common law cases tried to a jury, the District Judge is not the determiner of the facts of the matter. The fact-finding function is the exclusive function of the jury with the judge retaining a limited right to overturn a determination that is clearly contrary to the evidence presented. Parties entitled to a jury trial may waive their right to a jury and in such case, as well as in equity cases; the District Judge becomes both a fact finder and law decider. In a jury case the role of the judge is essentially that of a neutral "umpire" who maintains order in the court, rules on evidentiary questions and, when the parties have finished presenting their respective cases, tells the jury the law that they must apply to the facts that they find.

The significance of the jury to the American judicial system cannot be underestimated. American courtrooms are built to accommodate the jury by providing a jury box that enables the jurors to see and hear the witnesses, the judge and the lawyers for the parties. American trials are typically day after day events at which witnesses testify by answering questions put to them by the lawyers. This is done to enable jurors to better understand what is happening than by having to stop and let each juror read a relevant document before the case can proceed. The emphasis on speed is related to the fact that jurors are laypersons who have been called away from their normal life activities such as work or family matters to become part of the judicial process. To the extent possible it is necessary to get them back to their normal life as quickly as possible. Trials must be continuous affairs or jurors will forget what has happened at an earlier session and in addition it is difficult, if not impossible, to have jurors take a day off from work this week and another next week and another next month. Once a jury is selected the idea is to get the trial over with as quickly as possible—consistent with the interests of a fair trial.

Moreover, since jurors are lay people who may be swayed by emotion and cannot be relied on to separate relevant evidence from that which is not relevant, the United States system has developed a complicated series of evidentiary rules, which are applied by the judge to decide if a witness should be allowed to answer a question or if a document, photograph, or other thing may be shown to the jury. While the judge makes evidentiary decisions the function of raising questions about the "admissibility" of evidence is a function for the lawyers. Thus a trial is characterized by a question and answer format wherein lawyers raise evidentiary objections to questions asked of a witness and the judge decides whether the witness should be permitted to answer. This adversarial system depends for its validity on the quality and diligence of the lawyers for the parties since the presentation of evidence, the order of witness presentation and the marshalling of evidence are all a part of the lawyer's function. The judge is a somewhat passive player—making rulings when called upon but not actively participating in the process of question and answer or objection. Once the parties have rested their case [they have no further evidence to present] the judge assumes a more active role since it is the judge's function to educate the jury as to the law that is relevant to its decision. This is done through a "charge" to the jury as to the law. The jury is then sequestered and left to decide the matter. The judge remains available to answer specific questions the jury may have as to the law or to provide them with pieces of evidence they may wish to review in the jury room.

The basic function of the District Court is to make a "record" of all the proceedings held in the court [a transcript of all testimony is prepared and copies of all documents introduced into evidence are made] and to have an initial decision entered in favor of one of the parties. The District Court is the trial court in the American system.

There is at least one Federal District Court in each of the 50 states and the District of Columbia (the national capital city). In one situation, where a Federal Park's borders include parts of three states, a District Court includes parts of each of these States. Some states are so large or have so much litigation that the state itself is divided into parts, each of which has its own District Court. In the case of New York, for example, there is a Southern District, a Northern District, an Eastern District and a Western District Court. Judges appointed to a District Court reside in their District and may not be moved to another District—although the judge may volunteer, on a temporary basis, to assist another District that may have an overload of cases. When there is a need, District Judges may be allowed to participate on a case-by-case basis at the Court of Appeals level.

The next highest level is the Circuit Court of Appeals. It is the function of the Courts of Appeal to hear appeals from decisions made at the District Court level and to review decisions of certain administrative agencies. The Court of Appeals is exclusively an appellate court and it decides cases on the basis of the record made in the District Court (or administrative agency) and does not receive new or additional evidence. Its function is basically a law making function as distinguished from the function of the District Court whose role is to try cases and make the record of the evidence.[3] Determinations of a jury are entitled to great weight at the appeals court level especially since the Constitution provides:

> and no fact tried by a jury, shall be otherwise re-examined in any court of the United States, than according to the rules of the common law[4]

The Court of Appeals is basically a "law court" in the sense that it determines the law (or rule of equity) that should be applied to a set of facts already determined in the case and decides cases on the basis of the record made in the trial court. Legal determinations of the Court of Appeals for a circuit are binding on all the District Courts located in that circuit and while not binding may be considered by District Courts and Courts of Appeals in other circuits.

The United States is divided into 12 geographic areas known as circuits. One circuit is in the national capital, Washington DC and hears appeals from the District Court for the District of Columbia. In addition, this court and other circuit courts (but

3. As an historic matter, appeals in England were also on a record basis. The job of the appeals court was to determine the correct rules of law and not to re-try a case.
4. Amendment VII. The rules of the common law gave great deference to jury determinations and such findings could only be set aside for clear error or because of an error of law resulting in the determination.

because of its location primarily this court) hears challenges to decisions of federal government agencies. Because government agencies have their own fact-finding mechanisms and create the factual record needed for a judicial challenge to the agency action, there is no need for a trial of such cases and thus no need to first proceed in the District Court. Review of most agency determinations is in the Court of Appeals either for the Circuit where a party challenging the government action resides or in the Court of Appeals for the District of Columbia since that is where the agency resides. Eleven other judicial circuits exist and they encompass all of the 50 states (and U.S. territories). Like the DC Circuit they hear appeals, on the record, from District Court decisions in their geographic area.

There is one special jurisdiction federal appeals court—the Federal Circuit. This is a relatively new court at the appellate level created to handle appeals involving federal government employee matters and most importantly patent law matters. The creation of this special court demonstrates the importance that intellectual property, especially patents matters, has assumed in today's technological world.

Courts of Appeals typically hear cases in three-judge panels. To avoid disputes within a circuit there are rules requiring that later panels adhere to rulings made by earlier panels of the circuit.[5] A dissenting judge may request that the entire court review a matter and if the judges of the court agree, the matter is heard en banc by all of the active judges on the Circuit Court of Appeals. A party who is unsuccessful in its appeal may also ask for an en banc hearing, but such relief is unusual. In unusual circumstances, such as the appeal in the *Microsoft antitrust* case, where the government sought to have the Supreme Court hear the case before an appeal to the Circuit Court was completed—an unusual procedure permitted by a special jurisdictional grant in the anti-trust laws—the Circuit Court of Appeals may hear a case en banc without any panel decision.

The Supreme Court of the United States is fundamentally an appeals court.[6] It hears appeals from decisions of the various Courts of Appeal. Appeal to the Supreme Court is by way of a writ of certiorari—which is a request from a party that the court exercise its discretion to hear the case on appeal. A Petition for Cert. (as it is commonly

5. The Supreme Court of Japan mostly sits in panels. En banc (called Grand Bench) decisions are rendered in a limited number of situations. There are no rules requiring Panels to follow the logic or reasoning applied by other Panels or of the Grand Bench. Thus, dissenting Justices in a Grand Bench determination when they make up a majority of a Panel may refuse to either acknowledge or follow the logic of the Grand Bench majority when presented with a case presenting the same logical arguments in a slightly different context. *"illegitimate" child Inheritance case 3*,Case No. 2009 (Ku) No. 1027, Minshu Vol. 65, No. 2 (Sup. Ct. P.B. Mar. 9, 2011), http://www.courts.go.jp/english/judgments/text/2011.03.09-2009.-Ku-.No..1027.html) dismissing a suit (settled while on appeal). Likewise panels of the same High Court are not required to follow the determinations of prior High Court panels dealing with the same legal issue. See, e.g., Kyodo News, Fine upheld for civil servant's political act, Japan Times, May 14, 2010. Following the earlier ruling would have resulted in a reversal of a guilty verdict. In the apportionment context dealing with the 2010 election, two Tokyo High court decisions were rendered by different panels on the same day-each with different results.

6. *Zivotofsky v. Clinton*, 566 U.S. ___ (2012) ("Ours is 'a court of final review and not first view.'... Ordinarily, 'we do not decide in the first instance issues not decided below.'") The Supreme Court has a very limited original jurisdiction and typically only hears original jurisdiction cases where one state sues another. See Article III section 2[2].

called) is granted when four Justices decide that the entire court should hear the case. Because Certiorari is discretionary the Supreme Court is in control of its own calendar and can decide what and how many cases it will hear each term. The court's term begins on the first Monday in October and continues through the month of June.

The function of the Supreme Court is not to act as a court of errors correcting mistakes of lower courts (i.e., the function of the Courts of Appeal); rather the function is to "settle the law of the United States". Because there are so many Circuit Courts of Appeal it is possible that different circuits will decide the same legal question in different ways. When this happens the law in the United States is not "common". It is the basic function of the Supreme Court to make the federal law throughout the country consistent. Most cases heard by the Court involve a conflict between different circuits on a principal of law. The Court may take a case even if there is no conflict if four Justices feel that the issue is of such importance that it should be decided by the Court immediately. Moreover, cases involving the Federal Circuit appear to be taken more frequently—perhaps because this court deals with a substantive issue (patent law) and there are not going to be disagreements between the Circuits. It may also be that in today's technology economy the Supreme Court feels intellectual property cases are sufficiently significant that it should deal with them quickly. The court meets en banc (all nine Justices) and never decides cases in panels.

Appeals are heard on the basis of the record made in the lower courts and the Supreme Court does not take evidence but simply receives written arguments and hears oral argument. Typically oral argument on a case is limited to one hour, divided equally between the two sides in the case, although the court may grant additional time to either or both or all parties as it did in the 2012 Health Care Reform case. Interested persons who are not party to the litigation may request permission to file "friend of the court" briefs and the Court may ask the United States government to comment on a matter when the Court wants to obtain the views of the government. The Solicitor General, an official of the Department of Justice, represents the United States government before the Court. It is the practice of the Court to decide all cases argued before it by the end of the argument term—June 30. However, the court may, and sometimes does, request additional argument on the matter the next term and thus can put off decision until the next year. Decisions on cases are reported as they are written and decisions are thus forthcoming during the term. Members of the Court can communicate with each other during the summer recess and if an important matter requiring immediate attention comes up during the summer the Court can deal with it on an emergency basis.

Exercising its control over its own docket, the Court has reduced the number of cases it agrees to hear. As a consequence, today's Court, while it receives thousands of Petitions for Certiorari hears less than 100 cases a year. The effect of this limited case review is to leave most "law making" or judicial interpretation of statutes to the Circuit Courts of Appeal.

The three tier system may be defined as one where the Courts of Appeals, under the supervision of the Supreme Court, are responsible for interpreting the law so that the District Courts can know what law should be followed when handling trials.

The president, with the advice and consent of the Senate appoints judges in the federal court system.[7] If the Senate is not in session, the president can make a "recess" appointment on his own but then the judge must be considered for confirmation when the Senate reconvenes. Judges are typically appointed after a successful legal career in the private practice and sometimes in academia. Many federal judges have previously served the government as United States Attorneys [the senior federal government lawyers located in the various Judicial Districts in the United States and part of the Department of Justice] or other high-ranking government legal officials. Appointees to the Circuit Courts of Appeals and the Supreme Court need not have had any prior judicial experience.[8] Because judicial salaries have failed to keep pace with the salaries of lawyers in private practice, many federal judges view their service as public service to be undertaken after a successful private practice. There is no federal judicial "civil or career service" and judges do not view appointment to a lower court as a stepping-stone to appointment to a higher court.[9]

§5.02 JAPAN

The Japanese Constitution is specific in granting judges independence. By Constitutional provision judges are bound only by their conscience, the Constitution and laws.[10]

To guaranty their independence, the salary of judges is protected.[11] Moreover, the Executive Branch is prohibited from dismissing judges who may only be removed by impeachment or a judicial finding of mental or physical inability to perform their duties. The Executive Branch can take no disciplinary action against judges.[12] In cases of impeachment, the Diet must establish a special impeachment court consisting of members of both Houses and whose proceedings must be public.[13] The details for dealing with judicial impeachment are set out in the Impeachment of Judges Act.[14]

7. Constitution Article 2, section 2. By giving the Senate the right to "advice and consent" for federal judges, the original Constitution retained the power of the states (who at the time appointed Senators) in selecting the federal judiciary.
8. Judges at the State Court level are selected depending on state law. In some cases judges are appointed and in others judges are elected. Judges at the state level typically do not have life tenure but rather are appointed for a period of years—typically sufficiently long to guaranty independence.
9. Recently there has been a tendency to appoint Justices of the Supreme Court from among those who have served in other Appellate Courts—Federal or State. This is not consistent with the historical pattern. Presidents may wish to appoint persons with a known judicial "track record" to keep surprise to a minimum. Justice Kagen had not previously served as a judge.
10. Article 76 (3).
11. Article 80 (2); Article 79 (6). None the less, in 2012 the salaries of judges as well as all civil servants were reduced so that funds could be applied to reconstruction efforts in Tohoku.
12. Article 78.
13. Article 64.
14. "The Act specifies impeachable offenses as follows: i) conduct in grave contravention of official duties or grave neglect of official duties; and ii) other misconduct seriously affecting the integrity of a judge. The Impeachment Committee consists of 10 members (plus 5 reserve members) from each House, while the Court of Impeachment consists of 7 members (plus 4 reserve members) from each House. Both the members of the Impeachment Committee and the

Judges are not appointed for life and have limited appointment tenure. In the case of Supreme Court Justices, who are appointed by the Cabinet,[15] the Constitution provides for voter approval of Supreme Court Justices both at the first general election for the Lower House after appointment and every 10 years thereafter.[16] Lower court judges are appointed by the Cabinet but from a list of nominees compiled by the Supreme Court.[17] Since this list contains only a few names more than the total number of judges to be appointed and since the list is presented to the Cabinet with only a very short time frame for consideration before appointment must be finalized, the selection is effectively in the Judicial Secretariat itself.[18] Lower court judges are appointed for 10-year terms and may be reappointed for additional 10-year terms.[19] Mandatory retirement is required of all judges at ages determined by law.[20] The retirement age for most judges is 65 (for Summary Court judges the retirement age is 70, thus permitting retired District and High Court judges to become Summary Court judges and serve an additional five years on the bench) but for Supreme Court Justices the retirement age is 70. The average appointment age for Supreme Court Justices has been rising and is presently about 64[21] meaning that time spent on the highest Court has been shrinking (the opposite of the trend in the U.S. where Justices have lifetime appointment so Presidents tend to want to appoint younger Justices who may reflect the President's philosophy further into the future). In the year 2006 there were a total of 2,535 judges (not counting summary court judges of whom there were 806) in Japan—Supreme Court = 15; "full" judges = 1,605; assistant judges (judges in their first 10-year training period) = 915.

The judiciary in Japan is a "career or civil service" and most judges are appointed immediately after admission to the Bar[22] and serve a term as assistant judges before

---

judges of the Impeachment Court are guaranteed that they can exercise their official power independently. A resolution of the Impeachment Committee and a judgment of the Court of Impeachment are determined by a majority of members or judges present, but to pass a resolution to proceed with an impeachment and to render a judgment of removal, a two-thirds majority is needed." Hiroyuki Hata & Go Nakagawa & Takehisa Nakagawa, *Japanese Constitutional Law* sec. 99 (Kluwer Law International 2001). The procedure of the Impeachment Court is special-it follows the classical inquest system rather than the modified system followed in civil and criminal cases in Japan.

15. Article 79 (1). The Chief Justice is appointed by the Emperor, but in reality the Chief is appointed by the Cabinet as the Emperor is required to appoint the person selected by the Cabinet. Article 6(2).
16. Article 79 (2).
17. Article 80 (1).
18. Takayuki Ii, *Japanese Way of Judicial Appointment and Its Impact on Judicial Review*, 5 Natl. Taiwan U. L. Rev. 73, 86–87 (2010), http://www.law.ntu.edu.tw/ntulawreview/articles/5-2/03-Article-Takayuki%20Ii.pdf.
19. Article 80 (1).
20. Article 79 (5); Article 80 (1).
21. Hiroshi Ito, *The Supreme Court and Benign Elite Democracy in Japan* 229 (Ashgate Publishing Ltd. 2010).
22. In the discussion herein reference is made to the District Court, Family Court and High Court judges. Judges of the Summary Court, a kind of "small claims court", are not included in this discussion.

being appointed as full judges.[23] As a consequence, judges typically have no experience in the trial of cases or the actual practice of the law. Efforts by the Bar Association to change the system to require judges to have at least five years experience as practicing lawyers or prosecutors have been rejected. Instead a new system that permits the Judicial Secretariat to assign assistant judges (i.e., judges in their first 10-year training term) to work for two years in the office of a *Bengoshi* was adopted in 2004. Judges of the High Court are typically appointed from among the judges of District and Family Courts but High Court judges may be reassigned to such courts after service on a High Court. This ability to move judges up and down the judicial system has the advantage of allowing judges at all levels to receive training and wisdom from senior members of the judicial corps. Because it is a career service, judges on the same court who have served more than 20 years in the Judiciary may and do receive different salaries

The Supreme Court is given extensive authority to administer the judicial system. Not only does the Court nominate lower court judges, and determine whether judges whose 10-year term has expired should be re-nominated, but it is vested with rule-making power, which extends beyond procedural rules for the courts to include rules concerning the legal profession and the administration of the Judicial Branch.[24] To assist it in handling its administrative function the Supreme Court appoints judges to a Secretariat, which is under the direct supervision of the Supreme Court.

It has been suggested that the Japanese system is designed to create and successfully creates a homogenous, uniform and conforming judiciary.[25] The point is debatable—especially as more women join the ranks of Japan's judges—up from 346 judges (11%) in 2001 to 499 (15%) in 2007. What is not debatable is the uniformly high character, integrity and intelligence of Japan's judges. It seems clear that the Judicial Secretariat uses the system to perpetuate its approach to the law.[26] The Judiciary's objection to the appointment of practicing lawyers as judges also serves to assure that the Secretariat can mold young neophyte judicial candidates to its way of thinking and then promote them through the system until some who conform to the Secretariat's view reach appointment to one of the six seats on the Supreme Court that are set aside for career judges.[27] The appointment of practicing *bengoshi* could affect the conservative tilt of the court because the Bar has a much more liberal tilt than the Judicial Secretariat. The short terms that Justices serve on the court gives a new ruling party

23. Because of the press of litigation in recent years, some judges act as full judges after only five years (rather than 10 as in the past). An assistant judge is usually the youngest member of a three-judge panel of judges that hears a case. In this way the young assistant judge gets "on the job training" from seniors.
24. Article 77 (1).
25. Catherine Burns, *Sexual Violence and the Law In Japan* at 61–66 (Routledge Curzon 2005); As of 1991 there were few women on the bench in Japan. There has been an increase in the number (and percentage) of female judges. It is to be expected that more women will continue to join Japan's career judiciary. This is turn is bound to change the judiciary and the law. See *Women In The World's Legal Professions* tbl. 3, xxxviii (Ulrike Schultz & Gisela Shaw eds. Hart Publications 2003).
26. See, Setsuo Miyazawa, *The Politics of Judicial Reform in Japan: The Role of Law at Last?*, Asian-Pac. L. & Policy J. 89 (Special Issue) (Spring 2001).
27. See, David S. Law, *The Anatomy of a Conservative Court: Judicial Review in Japan*, 87 Texas L. Rev. 1545 (part II The Screening of Japanese Supreme Court Justices) (2009).

ample opportunity to appoint Justices, ample opportunity to change the balance on the court and the leadership of the Secretariat and thus reorient the philosophy of the Secretariat, but that has not happened to date. The system by which the judiciary commands the process for selection of Justices makes change difficult.

The court system is a three tier system with the Supreme Court at the top, the High Court as an intermediate court and the District Court and Family Court as courts of first instance. (There is also a Summary Court[28] that handles small claim type matters as a court of first instance. Appeals can be had from the Summary Court to the District Court.) There are 50 District Courts (with 203 branch offices) as well as 50 Family Courts. These courts are geographically located in each prefecture of Japan. Unlike the United States where judges are assigned to cases through a lottery type system, District Courts in Japan can be organized with specialized panels to hear specialized cases. Thus there are special panels to hear intellectual property cases (in both Tokyo and Osaka), administrative law cases and more recently to hear medical malpractice cases.[29]

There are eight High Courts, organized on a regional basis, and one Supreme Court. The District and Family Courts are the first level trial courts in the system with the High Court serving as an intermediate Court of Appeals, although the High Court has original jurisdiction of cases involving treason and certain Election Law cases. Appeals to the High Court are not "on the record" and parties may raise new issues and introduce new evidence at the High Court level.[30] The High Court also hears cases coming directly from certain government agencies such as the Fair Trade Commission, Patent Office, etc. The High Court typically sits in panels of three to hear cases, although in reviewing determinations of the agencies mentioned above and in treason cases it sits in panels of five.

As part of the reform of the judicial system and recognizing the growing importance of patents and other intellectual property, a new High Court within the Tokyo High Court has been created to handle such cases. The new High Court is based on the Federal Circuit Court in Washington DC.

Although there is one Supreme Court, the Court consists of 15 judges and either sits as a Grand Bench (all 15 judges) or in panels of five (Petit Bench) (although one panel typically has only four Justices as the Chief has other, chiefly administrative, duties to perform).[31] The Supreme Court is a court of errors (although recent changes in the Civil Procedure Code have attempted to make it a more certiorari court) and the panels are designed to have expertise in specific areas of the law so that cases involving those areas are sent to the appropriate panel. Petit Benches handle most cases and the

28. The summary court is a first instance small claims court below the District Court. Appeals from the Summary Court may be taken to the District Court.
29. For a discussion of the introduction of specialized medical malpractice panels in District Court and their utility in speeding the resolution of medical malpractice cases see, Eric Feldman, *Law, Society and Medical Malpractice Litigation in Japan*, 8 Wash. U. Global Stud. L. Rev. 257, 273–275 (2009).
30. Yosiyuki Noda, *Introduction to Japanese Law* 125 (University of Tokyo Press 1976).
31. *Ibid.*, 126–127. David S. Law, *The Anatomy of a Conservative Court: Judicial Review in Japan*, 87 Texas L. Rev. 1545, 1569–1570 (2009).

Grand Bench handles very few cases each year.[32] A Grand Bench is required for cases wherein the court declares a law, regulation, executive order or administrative decision unconstitutional and when the court reverses a previous decision.[33] Decisions of the Supreme Court are by majority vote and unlike other courts, dissenting Justices may write dissenting opinions. The Supreme Court exercises "judicial power" and accordingly it can only handle cases or controversies[34] brought by parties with standing and which do not present a "political question".[35] Notwithstanding, it is not unusual for the Court to determine that it has no jurisdiction for reasons such as political question and then discuss the substance of the issues in extensive dicta.

Parties have a right to appeal a matter from a District or Family Court to a High Court.[36] However, recent changes to the Civil Code limit the right to appeal to the Supreme Court giving the Court more control over its docket.[37] The 1998 Code retains the right to appeal to the Supreme Court in certain Constitutional cases and in cases involving certain alleged procedural errors. Other appeals to the Supreme Court are discretionary with the Supreme Court.[38] However, the court is not in complete control of its docket since the High Courts may certify some classes of cases to be heard on appeal by the Supreme Court.[39] The Supreme Court is still besieged by cases and, the procedure under which "certiorari" and asserted appeal by right claims can be filed with one filing fee covering both has not significantly reduced the workload of the court[40] although the Justices now devote more time to fewer important cases.[41]

There is no jury trial in Japan. Trial by jury, of sorts, was attempted for some criminal cases after the First World War. However, the jury system was by request only and the judge was not bound by a jury decision and if the court disagreed the matter was re-tried. The system was not widely used and during the war the right was

32. Hiroshi Oda, *Japanese Law* 66–67 (Oxford University Press 1999).
33. *Ibid.*
34. *National Police Reserve Case*, Case No. 1952 (Ma) No. 23 (G.B. Aug. 10, 1952) 6 Minshu 783, http://www.courts.go.jp/english/judgments/text/1952.10.8-1952.-Ma-.No..23.html.
35. *Dissolution of House of Representatives case*, Case No. 1955 (O) No. 96 (G.B. June 8, 1955), http://www.courts.go.jp/english/judgments/text/1955.6.8-1955.-O-No.96.html.
36. Because new evidence and new arguments can be raised at this level some have considered this a continuation of the trial rather than an appeal. Carl F. Goodman, *The Somewhat Less Reluctant Litigant*, 32 L. & Policy Intl. Bus. 769, 795 N. 115 (2001).
37. Yasuhei Taniguchi, The 1996 Code of Civil Procedure of Japan—A Procedure for the Coming Century? 45 Am. J. Comp. L. 767, 779 (1997).
38. Civil Procedure Code, Article 318; see Yasuhei Taniguchi, *The 1996 Code of Civil Procedure of Japan—A Procedure for the Coming Century?*, 45 Am. J. Comp. L. 767, 779 (1997).
39. Civil Code Article 337. See Takeshi Kojima, *Japanese Civil Procedure in Comparative Law Perspective*, 46 Kansas L. Rev. 687, 717 (1998).
40. Carl F. Goodman, *Japan's New Civil Procedure Code: Has it Fostered a Rule of Law Dispute Resolution Mechanism*, 29 Brooklyn J. Intl. L. 511 (2004) (See chart re: appeal and certiorari cases filed in the Supreme Court 1997–2001).
41. It is estimated that individual Justices review over 1000 cases a year. Jonathan David Marshall, Democratizing *the Law in Japan*, in *Routledge Handbook of Japanese Politics* 92 at 93 (Alisa Gaunder ed. 2011). In the United States review of certiorari petitions is undertaken by Law Clerks retained by individual Justices with the Justices themselves being involved in few such reviews.

"suspended".[42] Although there is no jury trial there was general agreement that there should be some form of citizen participation in judicial proceedings in Japan. The form chosen was a mixed layperson/professional panel to decide certain categories of criminal cases. This *Saiban'in* system went into effect in 2009. It is discussed, along with whether what you see from looking at the system is likely to be what you get, in greater detail in Chapter 16. The Judicial Branch objected to the suggestion for a lay jury system. Preparation for lay panel cases has resulted in some positive changes in evidence production by Japanese prosecutors in both lay panel and other criminal cases and review of saiban'in decisions has resulted in new rules making it more difficult for prosecutors to rely on circumstantial evidence that is not compelling.

§5.03 WHAT YOU SEE MAY NOT BE WHAT YOU GET

[A] United States

The Framers of the United States Constitution saw the Judicial Branch as the least "dangerous" of the three branches of the new government they were creating. Unlike the Legislative or the Executive Branches, the Judicial Branch could not self-start a matter but was a responsive organ that responded to complaints brought to it. Thus it was seen as not having an agenda that it could press upon the government or the people. Its function was limited to "cases or controversies" brought to it and raising a justiciable question. Only matters of law brought to the court by parties with adverse interest could be considered[43]. On paper the powers of the court appear confined and its authority limited. The reality is, however, substantially different. Moreover, the court would be insulated from "politics" because of the life tenure of its judges, whose appointment was not subject to approval by a popularly elected political branch of government[44] and whose retention was not subject to popular vote or referendum.

When the Supreme Court asserted in *Marbury v. Madison* that the question of whether a law passed by Congress and signed by the president was consistent with or inconsistent with the terms of the Constitution was a legal question to be decided by the court, it was carving out for itself an expansive role in government. It is not self-evident that the Judicial Branch is the final repository of Constitutional authority to determine whether a law is or is not in conformity with the Constitution. There is room for

---

42. For a discussion of the prior "jury type" procedure see Yosiyuki Noda, *Introduction to Japanese Law* 137–138 (University of Tokyo Press 1976) and Hiroshi Oda, *Japanese Law* (Oxford University Press 1999) Chapter 4 the Administration of Justice, part 3 Lay Participation in Justice (1999).
43. Typically the case or controversy rule requires that only a losing party in the court below can file an appeal. However, that rule is modified, at least for Supreme Court certiorari review, where a defendant public official's action is held by the Court of Appeals to be unlawful but relief is denied and where the holding of illegality affects the official's future conduct creating a sufficient personal stake and adverse interest to meet the case or controversy requirement. *Camreta v. Greene*, 563 U.S. ___ (2011).
44. The Senate was initially an appointed body whose members were appointed by the State Legislatures.

argument that this is a basic political question and should be decided by the elected branches of government rather than an unelected lifetime appointed branch.

Moreover, the mere assertion of authority does not mean that the court has the power to carry out that authority. The Judicial Branch has no "power" mechanism of its own to carry out its orders but must rely on the Executive to carry out the determinations of the court on the theory that the Executive is to "take care that the laws be faithfully executed".[45] Failure of the president to carry out a court order may be the basis for an impeachment by the House and Impeachment trial by the Senate but again, the court must rely on a political branch to carry out its mandate. It has been suggested that President Jackson, the first western state president of the United States failed to carry out a court order in favor of the Indian tribes of the west because he disagreed with the court and suffered no consequences as a result. Not only has the court taken to itself the power of judicial review of legislative acts but it has also assumed the authority to determine whether action of the Executive Branch conforms to the Constitution.

Modern presidents have been constrained to follow the court's orders and do so. President Truman's attempt to seize the steel mills was found unconstitutional by the Court[46] and notwithstanding the existence of a war between the United States and North Korea at the time and the need for steel to prosecute that war Truman obeyed. President Eisenhower was confronted with a refusal by state government to obey a Supreme Court ruling ordering the racial integration of a public school in Arkansas. The president sent the military to Arkansas to insure that the order of the Court would be followed.[47] President Nixon was ordered by the Court to turn over tape recordings of White House conversations concerning the break in at the Watergate complex. Nixon could not refuse to obey because failure to obey would undoubtedly have led to his impeachment. More recently the Court has ruled that prisoners held as enemy combatants in the War against Terrorism at Guantanamo have a right to a forum for determining whether their detention is lawful and also have some rights granted to prisoners under the Hague Conventions. Although the Executive argued against these holdings it has complied.[48]

Not only the Supreme Court, but also all federal courts have the power of judicial review.[49] And, federal courts are not hesitant about using that power. Today it is common place for the Supreme Court to hear several cases each term that attack the

45. Article II, section 3.
46. *Youngstown Sheet and Tube v. Sawyer*, 343 U.S. 579 (1952).
47. In a speech to the American public the president explained his actions in terms of the requirement that he faithfully execute the laws whether or not he personally happened to approve or disapprove of the court's decision and called upon Americans to do the same.
48. *Hamdi v. Rumsfeld*, 542 U.S. 507 (2004); *Hamdan v. Rumsfeld*, 548 U.S.557 (2006).
49. All courts created by Article III of the Constitution have the power. Moreover, as the power is just a manifestation of what judges do—interpret laws of which the Constitution is one—State courts have the power to declare state laws and acts unconstitutional because inconsistent with either the State or Federal Constitution.

Constitutionality of federal and state laws and it is common place for the Court to strike down those laws that it feels are unconstitutional.[50]

When the power of judicial review is combined with the equity power of the court to order federal or state officials to do an act, it is readily seen that the Judicial Branch is quite powerful. This power has been demonstrated by the court's insertion of itself (of course at the instigation of parties who have initiated litigation) in some of the most vexing problems of American society. It was the Court that gave the "green light" to the civil rights revolution in its *Brown v. Board of Education*[51] decision, that changed the political equation between city and rural in its apportionment decisions,[52] that granted women the right to an abortion,[53] took religion out of the public school classroom,[54] and decided who had won the Presidency in the 2000 election[55] and in 2012 upheld the Health Care Reform legislation and part of Arizona's immigration law—both highly contentious political issues. Moreover, the Court has asserted the authority through its equity power to take over, if necessary, the functions of state officials to carry out the court orders. Federal courts have seen it as their responsibility to resolve political issues between the Congress and the president when there is a "justiciable" question that they can use to resolve the matter.[56]

In addition, the courts through an expansive reading of their jurisdiction have been significant players in setting the national agenda. Obviously the areas of abortion, same-sex relationships, apportionment, and civil rights fit into this category but so too are more "mundane" areas such as public health (through acceptance of tobacco litigation suits), public safety (through expansion of rules dealing with strict liability in product liability cases), etc. In Japan judges tend to defer to the legislature. Thus litigation in Japan tends to be used as an agenda mechanism through its public character highlighting issues for public debate and resolution.[57] Rather than litigants looking to judges to be the instrument for change (the American model), Japanese litigants use publicity as the instrument for agenda modification. Federal judges particularly are not afraid to use the broad powers asserted by the judiciary. These judges have life tenure as well as salary protection[58] and the power to punish those who

50. In its 2001–2002 term the Supreme Court held more than half as many federal statutes unconstitutional as the Supreme Court of Japan has held in its almost sixty-year history.
51. 347 U.S. 483 (1954).
52. See *Baker v. Carr*, 369 U.S. 186 (1962); *Reynolds v. Sims*, 377 U.S. 533 (1964). Although it has to date refused to enter the political gerrymandering arena, the Court has refused to determine that all political gerrymandering cases are outside its jurisdiction. *Vieth v. Jubelirer*, 541 U.S. 267 (2004); *League of United Latin American Citizens v. Perry*, 548 U.S. 399 (2006).
53. *Roe v. Wade*, 410 U.S. 113 (1973).
54. *Engel v. Vitale*, 370 U.S. 421 (1962).
55. *Bush v. Gore*, 531 U.S. 98 (2001).
56. See the one-house veto case, *INS v. Chadha*, 462 U.S. 919 (1983); the Budget power case, *Bowsher v. Synar*, 478 U.S. 714 (1986); the Special Prosecutor case, *Morrison v. Olsen*, 487 U.S. 654 (1988); the "line item veto" case, *Clinton v. City of New York*, 524 U.S. 417 (1998).
57. Compare the American judiciary's approach to the tobacco litigation with the Japanese judicial approach and the adoption of anti-smoking policies in both nations. See Eric A. Feldman, *The Culture of Legal Change: A Case Study of Tobacco Control in Twenty-First Century Japan*, 27 Michigan J. Intl. L. 1 (2006) and John O. Haley, *Comment, Law and Culture in China and Japan: A Framework for Analysis*, 27 Michigan J. Intl. L. 895, 913–914 (2006).
58. *Stern v. Marshall*, 564 U.S. ___ (2011).

disobey their orders through the contempt sanction.[59] As a consequence what you see may not be what you get since what you get is a much more assertive and powerful judiciary than anticipated by the Framers of the Constitution or than would appear from the language of the Constitution.

This "expanded" power of the court system is related to a second phenomenon, namely the "politicizing" of judicial appointments. United States judges serve on their courts for very long tenure because there is no mandatory retirement policy and further because they may be appointed at a relatively young age. This long tenure gives judges the opportunity to "mature" both personally and jurisprudentially. This is particularly important at the Supreme Court level where decisions have binding effect on the entire judiciary. It is quite common to see Supreme Court Justice moderate opinions over time. No doubt politics has always played a role in the selection of federal judges but as presidents have become "surprised" by the decisions of their appointees they have sought greater assurance of what to expect. This has led to appointments of Justices (and subsequently to lower appellate court judges) with a judicial record that provides some guidance to judicial philosophy. But such a record while reassuring to a president may be anathema to an elected Senate in the hands of the opposition party. As a consequence the judicial selection process has become very politicized. The result is a more politically oriented judiciary at all levels—but once appointed the life tenure judge has independence.

The concept that judicial appointments would be scrutinized via the advice and consent process by an unelected body and thus politics would not play as significant a role in appointment and confirmations of judges has also been undermined. The fact is that with the popular election of Senators the Senate's function in advice and consent—to express the will of the States—has been undone. Today there is no more reason to give the Senate advice and consent power than to give such power to the House of Representatives. Politicizing also exists at the state court level as in many states judges are elected or are subject to reappointment votes (similar to the vote required in Japan for a Justice who has served 10 years on the Supreme Court). Serious questions have been raised in the United States, especially by retired Supreme Court Justice O'Connor, concerning the effect of election of judges on judicial independence.[60] In 2009 the Supreme Court of the United States reversed the decision of the highest court of West Virginia finding that a Judge of the State court committed error when he refused to disqualify himself from sitting on a case where one of the parties (the eventual winner in State court) had made extremely high campaign contributions

59. Even if it ultimately determined that a court lacked jurisdiction to enter a temporary restraining order, a failure to follow that order while it is being judicially appealed can be punished as contempt. *United States v. United Mine Workers*, 330 U.S. 258 (1947).

60. See e.g., Sandra Day O'Connor, *Justice for Sale: How Special-Interest Money Threatens the Integrity of our Courts*, WSJ.Com, Opinion Journal, Nov. 15, 2007, http://opinionjournal.com/editorial/feature.html? id=110010864. See *NY State Bd. of Elections v. Torres*, No. 06-766 (Sup. Ct. 16 January 2008). See also, Justice Bee Ann Smith, *Third District Court of Appeals of Texas, International Association of Women Judge's Conference Appointment and Removal of Judges: Elective Systems*, http://iawj.org/what/Session3BSmith.doc.

to the judge's campaign during the time the case was pending on appeal.[61] Also in 2009 the O'Connor Judicial Selection Initiative was formed to attempt to abolish the election of judges.[62] Judges' reappointment elections have become a source of partisan campaigns by special-interest groups raising questions about the effect of such elections on judicial independence.[63] In the 2010 election voters in Iowa, which has a retention election system rejected three Judges who had voted to hold that a law limiting marriage to one man and one woman violated Iowa's Constitution. Some have raised concerns about the chilling effect the election results may have on judicial independence.[64] While conservatives politicized the Iowa election of Judges in 2010, liberals politicized the judicial election in Wisconsin in 2011.[65] Campaign contributions were also an issue in 2012 judicial elections.[66]

[B] Japan

[1] Judicial "Independence"[67]

[a] Institutional versus Individual Independence

In Japan, what you see is a constitutionally declared independent court with the power of judicial review and with authority to maintain its own bureaucracy to run the court system. But, it is submitted that what you get may not be what you see.[68]

61. *Caperton v. A.T. Massey Coal Co.*, 556 U.S. 868 (2009). A year after its Caperton decision a different 5 Justice majority explained the *Caperton* holding as follows: "*Caperton* held that a judge was required to recuse himself 'when a person with a personal stake in a particular case had a significant and disproportionate influence in placing the judge on the case by raising funds or directing the judge's election campaign when the case was pending or imminent.'. The remedy of recusal was based on a litigant's due process right to a fair trial before an unbiased judge. See *Withrow v. Larkin*, 421 U. S. 35, 46 (1975)." *Citizens United v. Federal Election Commission*, 558 U.S. 50 (2010).
62. Schwartz, *Effort Begun to End Voting for Judges*, New York Times (Dec. 23, 2009).
63. See, A.G. Sulzberger, *Voters Moving to Oust Judges Over Decisions*, New York Times (Sept. 24, 2010), http://www.nytimes.com/2010/09/25/us/politics/25judges.html.
64. See, A.G. Sulzberger, *Ouster of Iowa Judges Sends Signal to Bench*, New York Times (Nov. 3, 2010); Judges' Battles Signal a New Era for Retention Elections, Washington Post A8, Dec. 5, 2010.
65. Monica Davey, *Fueled by Protests Angry Wisconsin Voter show Up to Fight*, New York Times (Apr. 6, 2011), http://www.nytimes.com/2011/04/07/us/politics/07wisconsin.html?src=recg;Nicholas Riccardi, *Wisconsin Supreme court election: Republican, Democrat Neck and Neck*, Los Angeles Times (Apr. 6, 2011), http://www.latimes.com/news/nationworld/nation/la-na-wisconsin-election-20110407,0,5568333.story.
66. Brady Dennis, *Pac's, donors shaping judicial elections* 1, Washington Post (Mar. 30, 2012).
67. A distinction must be drawn between independence of the Judicial Branch and independence of individual judges. The Branch has asserted its independence in the past. Thus, when Diet hearings were held in connection with a judicial sentence and the Diet Committee adopted a resolution criticizing the sentence the Supreme Court objected claiming Judicial Independence was being challenged. Yet, the Judicial Branch permits judges to be "lent" to the Executive to serve in such important roles as membership on the Cabinet Legislation Bureau using the transparent ruse that the Judges appointed had "resigned" from the Judicial Branch during their tenure in the Executive Branch.
68. In the pre-war period the Judiciary had established its independence in ruling against the government in the *Otsu Incident case* (1891)—finding no crime by analogy when an attack was

The "problem" starts at the top—the Supreme Court.[69] While the Constitution contemplates that Justices of the Court will serve for an extended period[70] the fact is that Justices of the Supreme Court serve very few years on the Court. They are appointed late in life, which when combined with mandatory retirement at age 70 results in little time to develop a judicial philosophy in the highest court. By rotating Justices of the Supreme Court over a short time frame the LDP could effectively control the Court, the Secretariat and hence the judicial machinery, process and assure the career development and promotion of like thinking judges and Justices. While in the United States political parties attempt to perpetuate their philosophy to a time when they may lose an election by appointing young life tenured judges who will carry the party's views into the future, the LDP did not need to be concerned because of its belief (accurate for almost all of the post-war period) that it would remain in power.[71] The election of an opposition party in 2009 could change the dynamics,[72] although the role of the Justices and judges in the Secretariat in selecting their successors may inhibit change.[73]

Since the Supreme Court controls the judicial Secretariat, LDP control of the Supreme Court meant control of the Secretariat. The DPJ government elected in 2009 appears not to have sought to gain control over the Secretariat. The Judicial Branch is separate from the Legislative and Executive and thus appoints its own Secretariat. Of

---

made on a foreign Prince. While much heralded in the literature, the independence of the judicial system was found to be a thin shield in the later *Morito Incident Trial* of the 1920s in which a University of Tokyo Professor was convicted of violating the pre-war Newspaper Law's ban on acting in opposition to the Constitution through a scholarly writing dealing with communist ideology because the thought set forward was found to be dangerous—even though the means of achieving the objective was entirely Constitutional. It is suggested that this decision was the beginning of the end of judicial independence in the pre-war period. See, Richard H. Mitchell, *Japan's Peace Preservation Law of 1925: Its Origins and Significance*, 28 Monumenta Nipponica 317–345 at 327–328 (Autumn, 1973). The *Otsu Incident Case* did however apparently influence Western Powers to give up consular jurisdiction because of the perceived independence of the Japanese courts. Par Kristoffer Cassel, *Grounds of Judgment* 159 (Oxford University Press 2012).

69. It has been alleged that public statements by the Chief Justice concerning administration of the Saiban'in system had prejudged his position in the case. The Grand Bench rejected the challenge noting that the carrying out of the Chief Justice's administrative duties did not implicate his views regarding legal issues. *Chief Justice not Disqualified in Saiban'in case*, Case No. 2011 (Su) No. 220, Keishu Vol. 65, No. 4 (Sup. Ct. May 31, 2011), http://www.courts.go.jp/english/judgments/text/2011.05.31-2011.-Su-.No..220.html. Compare Justice Scalia's Memorandum rejected arguments that he should recuse himself in a suit where the Vice President was sued in his official capacity. *Cheney v. United States District Court, http://fl1.findlaw.com/news.findlaw.com/wp/docs/scotus/chny31804jsmem.pdf.*

70. This is seen in the requirement that Judges of the Supreme Court must be approved at a public referendum after ten years. Article 79.

71. For a discussion of the relationship between judicial independence and "one-party" rule, with a comparison of the United States and Japan see J. Mark Ramseyer, *The Puzzling (In)Dependence of Courts: A Comparative Approach*, 23 J. Leg. Stud. 721, 746–747 (1994).

72. For a discussion of the role of the Judicial Secretariat and the Supreme Court in reigning in the independence of judges in Japan, concluding that the recent election of the DPJ will likely have no effect on the Judiciary See, Hiroshi Itoh, *The Supreme Court and Benign Elite Democracy in Japan* 28–34 (Ashgate Publishing Ltd. 2010).

73. Shigonori Matsue, *Why is the Japanese Supreme Court so Conservative*, 88 Wash. U. L. Rev. 1375, 1406 (2011).

course, the ruling party gets to appoint the Chief Justice (once there is a vacancy) and the Chief holds great power over appointments to the Secretariat, including the important post of Secretary General of the Secretariat. This is significant as the Secretariat administers a civil service, career service judiciary whose members have not already enjoyed successful careers in private practice. The Secretariat not only controls promotions and thus salary levels of judges but, under Japan's rotation policy—under which judges are transferred to different localities every three or four years—it controls the place where the judge will work. This is significant—there are some locations that are more desirable to live in than others and some courts (e.g., District or High Court in Tokyo) that are more professionally rewarding than others, and some courts that are simply dead ends for judicial careers. Judges who head the Secretariat almost inevitably wind up as appointees to the Supreme Court.

Of course, the greatest power that the Secretariat and the Supreme Court wield over lower court judges is the power to reappoint or not reappoint after the 10-year term. Failure to suggest reappointment marks the end of a judicial career. It is true that there are few cases in which judicial careers have been sidetracked for political reasons. But, there are some cases and all that is needed are some so that all judges get the message to decide cases "properly"—although interviews with some young judges indicate that they are not aware of the previous cases and thus are not influenced by them. In 2003 the Supreme Court started to utilize a review board to examine whether judges should be appointed or reappointed. The Board consists of 11 members appointed by the Judicial Branch of whom 6 are to be academics and the balance judges and prosecutors. The Court is not required to but has stated that it will follow the advice of the board. The Board has acted to discipline judges by refusing reappointment. Perhaps the most significant step it took was to support the rejection of the reappointment application of a judge who had publicly criticized the Judicial Branch.[74] The Constitution by placing judicial administration and career advancement in the hands of the Judicial Branch, which exercises that power through its Secretariat, in a perverse way may lead to the subordination of the judicial independence decreed by that document.

This is not to say that parties in commercial litigation face a corrupt or non-independent court. Far from it. Rather, the problem appears to be at the "government" level, i.e., when challenge is made to government policy. In fact, when litigating against the government parties may face a further hurdle in that many times their adversary counsel is in fact a member of the judiciary assigned to the Ministry of Justice or even a Public Prosecutor's Office "to gain experience". However, once in the

74. See, Shigenori Matsui, *The Constitution of Japan* 125–129 (Hart Publishing 2011). See also, J. Mark Ramseyer, The Puzzling (In)Dependence of Courts: A Comparative Approach, 23 J Legal Studies 721, 727 (1994) discussing the sidetracked career of two judges who sided with leftists in certain cases. See also, J. Mark Ramseyer & Frances McCall Rosenbluth, *Japan's Political Marketplace, Chapter 9 Judicial Manipulation*, (Harvard University Press 1993); see Takuya Asakura, *A Judiciary Ruled by Conscience or Politics*, Japan Times (June 22, 2002) for the position that one of the biggest challenges to Judicial Reform in Japan is to take steps to improve the judicial personnel system so as to ensure independence and details independence problems.

ministry for a term of years—in some cases the term may extend for many years—the assigned judge may defend the government in litigation. This merging of the Judicial Branch with the Executive appears to be both inconsistent with the argument that there is a separation of powers and the argument that there is a judiciary independent of the executive.[75] In any event, it raises ethical and fairness questions. Nonetheless the policy was followed until 2011 when it was modified by the Justice Minister who stopped the swapping of jobs between prosecutors and judges out of concerns for fairness.[76]

In addition, judges are seconded to the Ministry of Justice and from there to other Ministries and even to the Cabinet Legislation Bureau ("CLB") where they perform various functions including legal drafting and other legal work. It has been estimated that at any one time as many as 140 Judges are working in the Executive Branch. Such judges are not simply "students" learning how agencies work but include judges holding such important executive positions as Director of the Civil Affairs Bureau and the Civil Liberties Bureau of the Ministry of Justice. In their work for the CLB they provide legal advice to other Executive Branch officials. This comingling of Executive and Judicial Branches is rationalized in either of two ways—first, the judges are not really working for the executive they are simply getting training in how the executive works (hardly a viable explanation of the heads of Bureaus in the Justice Ministry) or second, that the judge seconded to the executive is for the period of seconding not a judge. This too is form over substance as they have been seconded to the executive by the Judicial Secretariat and the assumption is that they will return to the Judicial Branch to take up their judicial future.[77]

In an effort to blunt the continuous demand of the Bar Association for a unified Judiciary/*Bengoshi* system under which *bengoshi* would eventually become judges and all judges would have *bengoshi* experience, the Supreme Court supported legislation that would permit young judges (while still in their training period, i.e., the first 10 years of service) to work for two years in a *bengoshi* office to garner *bengoshi* real life experience. Such a Bill passed in 2004 and the system has been placed in effect. Again, what you see may not be what you get. *Bengoshi* retaining such judges in their office cannot take advantage of having a judge on staff—raising questions as to whether the young judge is permitted to represent clients in litigation before the courts. A young judge in training is unlikely to be given direct contact with a firm's clients or allowed to handle significant matters. Training is likely to follow the training methods used in

75. In the United States, judges cannot serve in an Executive agency while remaining a judge. The closest the United States has come to breaching this separation wall was when Justice Jackson, a former Attorney General of the United States was selected to be the Nuremberg War Crimes Prosecutor. However, his appearance before an international court could not affect inter-United States government branch separation.

76. Tsuyoshi Tamura, Job swaps between prosecutors and judges abolished, Asahi Shimbun (Apr. 27, 2012), http://ajw.asahi.com/article/behind_news/social_affairs/AJ201204270070.

77. For a discussion of the seconding practice see, Kazuko Tanaka Country Paper for Japan, Organization and Management of Government Legal Services of Japan, (International Cooperation Department, Research and Training Institute, Ministry of Justice, Japan), http://www.adb.org/Documents/Reports/Consultant/33069-REG/33069-01-REG-TACR.pdf, last accessed Sept. 15, 2012.

the intern stage of the Legal Training Institutes program, namely watching others perform and learning through watching rather than doing. This is hardly likely to provide judges with the real life lawyer experience that the JFBA has been claiming is required for judges to properly understand cases and do justice. It may be that this law was designed as "cover" to allow the argument that there is no difference between sending judges to work in the Executive Branch and sending them to work in private practice—of course, there is no separation of powers issue when judges intern in private firms.

For the ordinary day-to-day civil litigation that makes up the vast majority of the court's docket, the parties can be confident that they are before honest, non-corrupt and in all likelihood incorruptible, intelligent, hardworking and dedicated judges. Moreover, in even "politically" charged cases the lower courts have shown a remarkable willingness to understand the "temper of the times" and adopt rules that result in a just decision.[78]

While there are substantial differences in how one gets to be a judge and how one is treated once one is a judge, it is interesting to note that both in the United States and Japan the Judicial Branch is the most respected branch of government. With all the criticism and potential for politicizing the judiciary, there is much to be said for Professor Haley's conclusion that the judiciary in Japan has maintained both cohesion and autonomy notwithstanding the potential of political control.[79] Yet cohesion and autonomy do not necessarily lead to independence any more than life tenure shields American judges from their own politics. The Judicial Reform Council suggested and the Supreme Court has agreed that an advisory panel should assist the Supreme Court in the process of appointing District Court and High Court Judges.[80] The panel makes recommendations and its decisions are not binding. The panel was previously discussed and it is questionable whether the panel has had any substantive effect on the appointment or selection process.[81] The key to change in the Japanese judicial system

78. For example, in the Big Four pollution cases, the lower courts, in the face of indications that the political establishment was supporting the companies, recognized that the plaintiffs were in the right and accordingly modified the pre-existing rules on burden of proof so as to make it possible for the plaintiffs to succeed. In criminal prosecutions brought against the leaders of demonstrations held in support of the Minamata disease plaintiffs, the courts found a way to dismiss the criminal cases even though the likelihood is that the defendants were technically guilty. See Frank K. Upham, *Law and Social Chance In Postwar Japan* (1987). For another illustration see the court's blistering criticism of the government's actions both past and in the circumstances of the case in the *Nibutani Dam* case, *Kayano* et al. *v. Hokkaido Expropriation Committee* (The Nibutani Dam Decision) [English translation can be found at 38 *International Legal Materials* 394 (1999)] See also Lawrence W. Beer, *Japan's Constitutional System and its Judicial Interpretation*, 17 L. Japan 7, 20 (1984 and Lawrence W. Beer & Hiroshi Itoh, *The Constitutional Case Law Of Japan, 1970–1990* at 25 (University of Washington Press 1996).

79. John O. Haley, *Judicial Independence in Japan Revisited*, 25 L. Japan 1, 18 (1995) arguing that those who maintain that the judiciary in Japan lacks autonomy and that politicians direct the actions of the courts mislead and distort the facts.

80. *Supreme Court accepts Advisory Panel on Judges*, Japan Times (Feb. 20, 2001).

81. For a view that the advisory panel has had no meaningful effect on judicial selections see, David S. Law, *The Anatomy of a Conservative Court: Judicial Review in Japan*, 87 Texas L. Rev. 1545 (2009).

is the appointment of *bengoshi* as judges and on that score little has been changed as few *bengoshi* apply and of those who apply even fewer are appointed.[82]

[b] A Democratized Court

Whether for good or for bad, the Japanese Constitution calls for a more "democratized" court than in the United States. Recognizing that Justices of the Supreme Court have a longer tenure and a more significant role than other Judges, the Occupation introduced the idea of retention elections to Japan's Supreme Court. Thus justices of the court must be presented to the public for referendum vote in the first general election after appointment and at the election every 10 years thereafter. Several factors combine to make this provision of the Constitution more apparent than real.[83] First, as Justices are appointed after reaching age 60 virtually no Justice need stand for referendum approval after 10 years of service. Most Justices are career judges or career bureaucrats unknown to the general public prior to their appointment and likely to remain unknown right up to the referendum election. The Court has held that a Justice retains the position to which appointed unless more voters vote against the Justice than vote in general. In other words abstentions are considered as votes in favor of retention. Since most voters lack interest in retention elections of Justices most abstain.

The role of mid-level judicial assistants to Supreme Court Justices also negatively affects the democratization sought by the Occupation. Unlike Supreme Court Justices in the United States, Japanese Justices do not have their own law clerks but share a pool of judicial assistants (all judges) assigned to Panels and matters by the Secretariat. Because of the large workload of the court, individual Justices must rely on the assistant assigned on a particular case and while the Justice can mold the view to be taken, unless the Justice is prepared to spend the time and energy required to do the work of opinion writing and research needed—thus taking time and energy from other cases equally or potentially more deserving—the ideas of the Justice may not be accurately reflected in the opinion.[84] It is not a question of neglect; it is a question of judicial resources and workload. Retention elections do not affect the core of assistants assigned to the Court (like other judges these assistants are regularly rotated to other judicial positions). Nonetheless, a retired Supreme Court Justice recently mounted a campaign to unseat at recall election two Justices for failure to take decisive action in the area of apportionment where (as discussed *infra*) the Court appears to have given up on providing any relief for unconstitutional elections. Even with such a campaign,

82. For a discussion of the workings of the panel process see, Takayuki Ii, *Japanese Way of Judicial Appointment and Its Impact on Judicial Review*, 5 Natl. Taiwan U. L. Rev. 73 (2010), http://www.law.ntu.edu.tw/ntulawreview/articles/5-2/03-Article-Takayuki%20Ii.pdf. The article notes that in 2003 of 11 Bengoshi who sought appointment as Judges only 4 were found by the panel to be qualified.

83. For the view that the recall provisions are "meaningless" see, Hiroshi Itoh, *The Supreme Court and Benign Elite Democracy in Japan* 23 (Ashgate Publishing Ltd. 2010).

84. See, *Judicial Allergy to Appeals, Sentaku Magazine*, Japan Times (Feb. 28, 2011), http://search.japantimes.co.jp/cgi-bin/eo20110228a1.html.

the Justice up for election received only a 7% negative vote thereby decisively defeating recall.[85]

[2] *Judicial Review*

[a] *United States*

The American concept and application of Constitutional judicial review has both common law and civil law attributes. The creation of the doctrine is pure common law. The court has the power of judicial review because it is a court. Courts apply the law and the Constitution is simply another law. It is true that the Constitution is special—but that is because it is the "supreme law" to which all other laws must comply but not because it is "public law" as distinguished from "private law"—the distinction that civil law would draw between the Constitution and other laws. And, as a necessary corollary the power of judicial review is not limited to some special public law court system but applies to all courts both federal and state. It is simply just another aspect of being a court.

While the doctrine is common law in character and thus was rejected by civil law systems until the end of the Second World War when a combination of American ascendency and the lessons of the fascist period that preceded and led up to the war convinced civil law societies that some form of judicial "brake" on executive and legislative power was necessary, the application of the doctrine has both civil and common law attributes[86] in that it relies both on the text of the Constitution and a common law reading of the applicability of the text.

This kind of approach has led the Supreme Court to use a textual approach to rights that are clearly delineated—thus the Court tries to read the right to free speech or the right to equal protection so as to emphasize the free speech and equality aspects of the rights. At the same time the Court attempts to categorize matters so that the text can be more readily carried out. Equal protection claims are typically viewed categorically—if the inequality is based on a suspect classification then a very stringent "compelling government interest" standard of review is utilized, if the inequality is economic in nature a more relaxed "reasonableness" standard is involved and in the middle a standard more demanding than reasonableness but not as demanding as compelling government interest. So too in the free speech area the Court attempts to categorize the standard of review—content neutral restrictions are treated less stringently than are content based restrictions; prior restraints are treated more stringently

85. David Law, Comparative Constitutions Blog, *The Japanese election: Much Ado About Very Little,* http://www.comparativeConstitutions.org/2009/09/japanese-election-much-ado-about-very.html (Sept. 8, 2009).

86. Civil law countries that have adopted a form of judicial review have done so in a civil law context. Thus special public law Constitutional courts have been established and in many cases limits have been placed on who can appear before such courts, when a case can be brought to the court (e.g., exhaustion of the ordinary court system), and the extent of the remedy that can be granted by the court.

than are after the event remedial actions (a libel action for damages may well lie in a situation where publication would not be prohibited).

The United States categorical approach differs from the approach of most other countries which tend to use a balancing and proportionality test. This is true in domestic law and is the approach favored by the European Court of Human Rights. Thus, for example, hate speech has to be balanced against the feelings of those affected and whether the restriction is proportional to the harm and governmental policy being furthered. In the United States hate speech restrictions are a form of content based restriction and cannot be prohibited. The content of the speech may be despised but as long as there is no clear and present danger generated by the speech the speech is to be countered by other more rational speech and is to be dealt with in the market place of ideas.

The Supreme Court of the United States has been an "activist" court in judicial review in the sense that it has not hesitated to strike down laws at both the federal and state level when it considers such laws to contravene the Constitution. Deference is to be paid to the Legislative and/or Executive Branch in Constitutional litigation only when there is a special basis for such deference such as greater knowledge available to the Congress and/or President that is not available to the court.[87]

[b] Japan

Unlike the United States Constitution the Constitution of Japan clearly and specifically grants the judiciary the power of judicial review. This would appear to contemplate an activist court sitting in judgment of legislative enactments that appear to conflict with the Constitution. In fact, that is not the case. Indeed, the Japanese Supreme Court is very solicitous of the government's authority.[88] This may arise out of a civil law notion that elected representatives are more properly entrusted to determine the will of the people and to carry out that will in a way that conforms to the Constitution, i.e., to interpret the Constitution through legislation, than is an appointed court.[89] Or, perhaps it is a combination of this civil law notion and a history in which the pre-war court gave great deference to the government.[90] It may be that the Supreme Court does not see the Constitution, the Supreme Law, as rising to the level of statutory law.[91] It may also be

87. See, e.g., *Holder v. Humanitarian Law Project*, 561 U.S. ___ (2010).
88. See, Ichiro Kitamura, *The Judiciary in Contemporary Society: Japan*, 25 Case W. Res. J. Intl. L. 263, 276 (1993) for a statistical analysis showing that the Supreme Court rarely deals with Constitutional issues (although such issues are frequently raised by litigants).
89. Professor Hata writes: "It might be safe to generalize that the Supreme Court of Japan has continued its judicial self-restraint in fear of judicial usurpation of the power of the political branches to establish and control public policy." Hiroyuki Hata & Go Nakagawa & Takehisa Nakagawa, *Japanese Constitutional Law* sec. 54(Kluwer Law International 2001).
90. See Hiroshi Itoh, *The Japanese Supreme Court Constitutional Policies* 212 (M. Wiener 1989).
91. See, Shigonori Matsue, *Why is the Japanese Supreme Court so Conservative*, 88 Wash. U. L. Rev. 1375, 1376, 1413–1416 (2011) suggesting that Judges in Japan do not view the Constitution as containing rules of positive law.

a reflection of the debate within the American drafting committee as to the proper scope of judicial review to be permitted in Japan.[92]

The reasons why the Supreme Court has failed to carry out its judicial review responsibilities are many and varied[93] and likely several of the reasons suggested by commentators are responsible, rather than a single reason.

There seems to be little doubt but that the Constitution contemplates a judicial review similar to that exercised by the Supreme Court of the United States under *Marbury v. Madison*. On the other hand, this reticence to find legislation inconsistent with the Constitution (the Supreme Law of the land under Article 98) may reflect deference to political parties. Such deference may explain why the Court appears to give greater weight to international treaties adopted by Japan than to the Constitution.[94] Professor Hata suggests that the:

> idea of judicial review is a bit too radical for the Japanese version of democracy, and because it cannot be traced to the traditional political values of the Japanese, the Supreme Court has almost never nullified or reversed governmental actions as unconstitutional.[95]

It has even been suggested that the failure to extensively use judicial review is part of a Supreme Court strategy to consolidate judicial power in the face of strong Executive and Legislative Branches.[96] It has been suggested that the real reason the Supreme Court does not become more engaged in Constitutional issues is the power of the Cabinet Legislation Bureau whose bureaucrat's rule on the Constitutionality of laws before they are passed by the Diet.[97] It is even suggested that the Supreme Court has acquiesced in the CLB's assumption of the Judicial Review function that the Constitution grants to the Court.[98] Although the role of the CLB would appear to be similar to the role of the Office of Legal Counsel ("OLC") in the United States Department of Justice[99], its decisions are given more respect outside the Executive Branch than are OLC's. At an early stage the DPJ government sought to change this and likely its determination to prohibit the head of the Bureau from appearing before the Diet to

Cabinet Legislation Bureau

92. Norikazu Kawagishi, *The birth of judicial review in Japan*, 5 ICON No. 2, 308–331 (Oxford University Press and New York University School of Law 2007).
93. See, David S. Law, *Why has Judicial Review Failed in Japan?*, 88 Wash. U. L. Rev. 1425 (2011).
94. See Kenneth L. Port, *The Japanese International Law "Revolution": International Human Rights Law and its Impact on Japan*, 28 Stanford J. Intl. L. 103, 139 (1991). See also discussion of women's rights and Ainu rights in Chapter 8 herein.
95. Hiroyuki Hata & Go Nakagawa & Takehisa Nakagawa, *Japanese Constitutional Law* sec. 54(Kluwer Law International 2001).
96. Hiroshi Itoh, *Judicial Review and Judicial Activism in Japan*, 55 L. & Contemp. Probs. 169 (1990). See also, David S. Law, *A Theory of Judicial Power and Judicial Review*, 97 Geo. L. J. 723, 778–785 (2009).
97. Jun-ichi Satoh, *Judicial Review in Japan: An Overview of the Case Law and an Examination of Trends in the Japanese Supreme Court's Constitutional Oversight*, 41 Loyola Los Angeles L. Rev. 603, 605, 624–625 (2008).
98. See, Jonathan David Marshall, *Democratizing the Law in Japan*, in *Routledge Handbook of Japanese Politics* 92, 94 (Alisa Gaunder ed., 2011); Jun-ichi Satoh, *Judicial Review in Japan: An Overview of the Case Law and an Examination of Trends in the Japan Supreme Court's Constitutional Oversight*, 41 Loyola of Los Angeles Law Review 603 (2008).
99. See the official website of the Cabinet Legislation Bureau for a statement of its functions at http://www.clb.go.jp/english/about.html.

answer questions and participate in debate[100] and the DPJ government's determination to have Constitutionality judgments by the Executive Branch made by the Cabinet itself[101] was part of that effort. The DPJ appears not to have been successful in this regard. It is argued that the Bureau is one of the most powerful organizations in the bureaucracy and that even Prime Ministers and Justices of the Supreme Court have in the past felt compelled to follow its Constitutional rulings.[102] The LDP opposed efforts to downplay the role of the Bureau, especially the Bureau's ability to answer questions in the Diet.[103] Prime Minister Noda sought to make peace of sorts with the LDP so that legislation could be passed and consequently stopped the process of downgrading the bureaucracy, including the CLB.

Undoubtedly the process for selecting Justices has contributed to a conservative Supreme Court that is not likely to trample on legislation passed by a conservative government and approved as Constitutional by a prestigious administrative organ of the Cabinet (the CLB)—as has been the situation for virtually all of the post-war period. The Conservative nature of the court is perpetuated by the Secretariat's selection of six career judges to serve as Justices,[104] and the Secretariat's hand in selecting the one academic typically appointed to the Court, the Prosecutor General's selection of two or three prosecutor's to serve on the court (prosecutors can be expected to be conservative and indeed are likely to be even more conservative than the career judiciary), the selection of two or three career bureaucrats (who may or may not have legal training and who likely neither took nor passed the Bar Examination) who are likely (but not inevitably) supportive of the Secretariat's conservative approach, and even the nominees of the JFBA for the positions on the Court generally reserved for *bengoshi* are first vetted with the Secretariat to assure that they are not "unacceptable"[105] and the Association's suggestions need not and have not always been followed.[106] This structure inhibits change from the established philosophy and practice of the court, including the Court's reticence to overturn legislation or previous decisions.

The Court's reticence may also be rooted in too close a relationship between the judiciary and the Executive Branch created by the assignment of judges to the Justice

100. Cabinet Legislation Bureau chief to be Excluded from Diet Debates, Kyodo News, Jan. 14, 2010, http://home.kyodo.co.jp/modules/fstStory/index.php?storyid=480437.
101. Cabinet Legislation Bureau chief to be Excluded from Diet Debates, http://www.breitbart.com/article.php?id=D9D7G4800&show_article=1.
102. JPRI Working Paper No. 99 (March 2004) Politics, Security Policy, and Japan's Cabinet Legislation Bureau: Who Elected These Guys, Anyway?* by Richard J. Samuels, http://74.125.93.132/search?q=cache:sUQmQziADgkJ:www.jpri.org/publications/workingpapers/wp99.html+japan+%22cabinet+legislation+bureau%22&cd=2&hl=en&ct=clnk&gl=us.
103. See, Kyodo News, *Bill Revision Would Boost Power of Politicians*, Japan Times (Oct. 19, 2010), http://search.japantimes.co.jp/cgi-bin/nn20101018a4.html.
104. See, Lawrence Repeta, *Reserved Seats on Japan's Supreme Court*, 88 Wash. U. L. Rev. 1713 (2011). (Repeta traces the change in composition of the Court from a relative balance between lawyers and bureaucratic judges to the present system that weighs heavily in favor of judges, prosecutors and bureaucrats and the political reasons for such changes and how such changes resulted in a change from a liberal leaning to a conservative court.)
105. David S. Law, *The Anatomy of a Conservative Court: Judicial Review in Japan*, 87 Texas L. Rev. 1545 (2009).
106. Shigonori Matsue, *Why is the Japanese Supreme Court so Conservative*, 88 Wash. U. L. Rev. 1375, 1407–1408 (2011).

Ministry[107] that likely instills a pro-government bias. So too, insecurity as to ability to carry out its decisions may limit the Court's judicial review powers. As discussed *infra* the Court appears to have "given up" in its attempt to make the Diet more representative of the people by providing a loose equality of vote between rural and metropolitan areas. Having thrown the issue of reapportionment back to the Diet the Diet has made changes on the edges of proportionality but not a single election since the court's decision has been held under a system that is Constitutional as the Diet has refused to carry out the Court's mandate.

Whatever may be the basis of the Court's restraint, the fact remains that the Court has infrequently struck down legislative enactments as being in violation of the Constitution even in cases that touch the basic civil liberties of the public when in conflict with government actions. It is of interest that the *Post Office Liability* case, the *Overseas Election case* and the *Portion of Nationality Law Unconstitutional* case (all finding laws unconstitutional) were decided during a period when the CLB's power was under attack. And, in both the election and Nationality Act case the Court goes to great length to recognize that at the time the laws involved were passed the rationale for the laws may have been justified, but that times had changed. On the other hand, it has been suggested that the *Portion of Nationality Law Unconstitutional* case eschews the prior jurisprudential approach of the Supreme Court that measured whether a law was Constitutional by the "reasonable relationship" or "rationality" test and replaced it with a modified version of the more dominant (in European and Canadian jurisprudence) "proportionality" test.[108] It is suggested that this change in approach may hold the seeds for a more robust analysis of Constitutionality where issues of human of rights are concerned. It has also been suggested that in the *Overseas Election* case the Court applied a compelling government interest test before the government could take away the right to vote of overseas Japanese[109]. It remains to be seen whether a new test is emerging, although it does appear that a new generation of Justices is more willing to strike down laws than their predecessors.[110] An analysis of the few judicial review cases in which laws were held unconstitutional follows.[111] However, these are the rare

107. See Yuji Iwasawa, *International Law, Human Rights, and Japanese Law* 157, 305–306 (Oxford University Press 1998).
108. The United States does not use a "proportionality" test. *United States v. Stevens*, 559 U.S. ___ (2010).
109. Shigenori Matsui, The Constitution of Japan 43–44 (Hart Publishing 2011).
110. Craig Martin, Glim*mers of Hope: The Evolution of Equality Rights Doctrine in Japanese Courts from a Comparative Perspective*, 20 Duke J. Comp. & Intl. L. 167 (2010) http://works.bepress.com/cgi/viewcontent.cgi?article=1002&context=craig_martin.
111. It is generally considered that the Supreme Court has had seven cases in which it struck down five laws. Two cases involved the same issue–electoral apportionment. These seven cases are discussed below. However, sometimes the Customs case of 1955 is considered as a judicial review case. Case Number (A) 2961 of 1955, *Nakamura v. Japan*, http://www.courts.go.jp/english/judgments/text/1962.11.28-1955-A-No.2961.html (G.B. Nov. 28, 1962). The customs statute failed to give third parties who claimed an ownership interest in forfeited property a right to be heard. After forfeiture a person sued to recover back his property. The court found that this third person was the actual owner and thus found the forfeiture unconstitutional. While the decision is an important recognition of "due process" type rights, it did not declare the Customs Law unconstitutional and hence is not herein considered as a judicial review case.

exceptions and in most cases the Court applies a "reasonableness" standard that is almost invariably met by the government[112].

[i] Pharmacy Location Case from Hiroshima[113]

A pharmacy company applied to the Governor of Hiroshima for permission to open a pharmacy near to a pre-existing pharmacy. The Pharmaceutical Affairs Law provided for the licensing of pharmacies and specifically allowed the licensing Prefecture Authority to consider location and closeness to other pharmacies in making the licensing decision.

Hiroshima Prefecture acted under the law to enact an ordinance requiring a 100 meter distance between pharmacies. The applicant was denied a license because his store would not be more than 100 meters from existing pharmacies. The Supreme Court held the law unconstitutional. The court reasoned that Article 22 of the Constitution granting people the right to choose their own occupation (provided that the choice is not contrary to the public welfare) was implicated in the licensing decision. As the denial of a license was contrary to the applicant's choice of occupation, the issue was whether the grounds for denial were consistent with the public welfare proviso of the Article. Hiroshima argued that it was, as the distance requirement was needed to assure quality of pharmaceutical products dispensed by a pharmacy. The court found that the real reason for the location requirement was anticompetitive and that it was designed to protect pre-existing pharmacies from new competitors.

Questions exist as to the scope of the decision. The geographic limitation had been challenged by a small storeowner, who wished to compete with other small stores. Article 22 was implicated because such a storeowner typically lived where the store was located so that a geographic limitation could be said to affect his ability to follow his chosen occupation. But what if the challenge had been made by a chain store operation? Would a geographic limitation that restricted a "Wal-Mart type" store from being located within a certain distance of another major store be unlawful? The *Pharmacy* case would not appear to answer this question, as Article 22 would not seem to be implicated. Would the case apply to other types of business establishments? It appears from a reading of the opinion that the Court was concerned that the geographic limitation was not based on a real concern that substandard pharmaceutical products would be sold absent the restriction. Rather the law, which had been lobbied for by other pharmacy owners out of economic concerns not public safety concerns,[114] was really designed to cut off competition and create monopolies in geographic areas, not to protect the public welfare. In the face of this purpose the government simply could

---

112. E.g., *Tokyo Supervisory exam limited to Japanese Citizens Case*, Case No. 1998 (Gyo-Tsu) No. 93, Minshu Vol. 59, No. 1 (G.B. Jan. 26, 2005), http://www.courts.go.jp/english/judgments/text/2005.01.26-1998.-Gyo-Tsu-.No..93.html.

113. *Sumiyoshi v. Governor of Hiroshima*, 29 Minshu 572 Case No. 1968 (Gyo-Tsu) No. 120 (G.B. Apr. 30, 1975). http://www.courts.go.jp/english/judgments/text/1975.04.30-1968-Gyo-Tsu-No.120.html.

114. See Hiroshi Itoh, *Judicial Review and Judicial Activism in Japan*, 53 L. & Contemp. Probs. 169, 175 (1990).

not marshal evidence to support a public welfare exception. But what of geographic limitations where a more reasonable public welfare argument could be made? Where the government can make a convincing case for a geographic limitation such a limit appears permissible. Thus, it may be lawful to have a geographic restriction on the location of public bathhouses since public health issues related to hygiene may be more directly implicated where bath houses are concerned. The Supreme Court had previously upheld geographic limitations on new bathhouses[115] and while there are indications that the *Pharmacy* case overruled a prior decision—which would be the *bathhouse* case—the decision itself does not specifically overturn the 1955 *bathhouse* case[116] and, since the decision is fact based, there exists good reason to believe that the *bathhouse* case remains good law for the facts involved with bathhouses.

[ii] Patricide Case[117]

In the *Patricide* case, the Supreme Court confronted a particularly bad fact situation. The defendant was charged with murdering her father who had abused her for many years even raping her when she was in primary school and forcing her to have children through incest. One night when he attacked her, she strangled him to death.

Under the criminal code, the crime of murder is punishable by not less than three years in prison but the crime of killing a lineal ascendant was subject to a much more harsh punishment. While the Court may modify this punishment, as it can modify the punishment for murder, even after modification the punishment remains quite severe and much harsher than for ordinary murder.[118] In an earlier case, the Supreme Court had upheld this unequal application of the laws.[119] However, in the *Patricide* case the Supreme Court reconsidered its previous ruling and found the provision unconstitutional.

The provision under review pre-dated the Constitution. It was based on Confucian ideas underlying the Tokugawa system. The provision was related to the family system in effect in Tokugawa times (the *Ie*[120]) which system had been abolished by the Constitution. As a result, the Criminal Law provision at issue had no "mooring" in the modern family system.

115. *Sakamoto v. Japan*, 16 Minshu 57 (Sup. Ct. Jan. 19, 1962) reported in *Hideo Tanaka* (assisted by Malcolm D.H. Smith), *The Japanese Legal System* 690 (University of Tokyo Press 1976); see also earlier *Bathhouse* case decided Sup. Ct. G.B. Jan. 26, 1955 for an English language translation see John M. Maki, *Court and Constitution in Japan* (University of Washington Press 1964).
116. See John O. Haley, *The Freedom to Choose an Occupation and the Constitutional Limits of Legislative Discretion*—K.K. Sumiyoshi v. Governor of Hiroshima, 8 L. Japan 188, 194 (1975).
117. *Patricide case, Aizawa v. Japan*, Case Number (A) No. 1310 of 1970, 27 Keishu 265, http://www.courts.go.jp/english/judgments/text/1973.04.04-1970-A-No.1310.html (G.B., Apr. 4, 1973) overturning an earlier Patricide decision, http://www.courts.go.jp/english/judgments/text/1950.10.11-1950-A-No.292.html (G.B. Oct. 11, 1950).
118. The ability of a court to modify a statutory penalty is discussed in Chapter 16.
119. Although in that case the Court had suggested the law be changed because the punishment provided was too harsh.
120. The *Ie* is discussed in Chapters 8 and 9.

Although the Court recognized that there is an especially pernicious nature to killing a lineal ascendant that may justify a stronger penalty then ordinary murder, the Court found that the difference in penalties for ascendant murder and ordinary murder was simply too great to survive a challenge under Article 14 of the Constitution. Article 14 will be searched for any provision that, on its face, appears to deal with the problem. However, Article 14 provides that all of the people are equal under the law and that people cannot be discriminated against because of race, creed, sex, social status or family origin. The Supreme Court found in this provision a general authority to strike down legislation that treats citizens differently and does not have a reasonable basis for such different treatment.

The decision in the *Patricide* case would appear to have broad application and would appear to pave the way for an activist court. However, the Court has not followed the *Patricide* case with other cases building on it to create an active judicial review precedent. And, the *Patricide* case may be limited to the special circumstances of a Code provision based on feudal concepts that was intended to be changed by the Constitution but was not.[121]

[iii] The Forest Division Case[122]

This case involved the conjunction of two laws. The Civil Code, which provides in Article 256 that each co-owner of joint property has the right to demand partition of the jointly owned property and the Forestry law, which prohibits partition of a jointly owned forest unless the holders of at least 50% of the forest request partition. In this case an owner of less than 50% sought partition and challenged the Constitutionality of the Forest Law claiming that it violated the terms of Article 29 of the Constitution which guarantees ownership rights in property and contains a just compensation clause similar to the United States Constitution. The Supreme Court noted that as a general matter Article 29 not only protects an individual's right in private property but also makes the guarantee of the property rights a fundamental human right. This fundamental right, in turn, is subjected to the limitation that the government through legislative action can regulate private property in the interests of the public welfare. With this as the general legal background the Court considered the challenge to the Forest Law.

The Forest Law, like the patricide provision of the Criminal Code discussed above, was virtually identical to the Forestry Law in force prior to the Second World War.[123] The purpose of the Law was found to be to stabilize forest management, preserve and nurture a forest and maximize the productivity of the forest. The court

121. In addition, the Supreme Court may, in part, have been reacting to the government's failure to follow an earlier suggestion by the Court that the statutory provision at issue should be modified.

122. *Forest Division case, Hiraguchi v. Hiraguchi*, 41 Minshu 408 (G.B., Apr. 22, 1987). For an English language translation see Lawrence W. Beer & Hiroshi Itoh, *The Constitutional Case Law of Japan, 1970–1990* at 327 (University of Washington Press 1996).

123. Article 186 was actually based on Article 6 of the old Forestry Law enacted in 1907 and only slightly modified when it was reenacted in 1951.

noted that where joint owners agreed to partition or where an owner of more than 50% demanded partition, the Law did not prevent partition. Partition was only prevented when joint owners, neither of whom owned a 50% interest, differed as to matters pertaining to management of the forest. In such case, the effect of the law did not resolve the difference between the joint owners in a manner consistent with the law's intent to maximize productivity of forests. Accordingly there was no "rational relationship" between carrying out the intent of the Law and the more than 50% requirement for forced partition. While the Court had respect for the legislature's judgment, it found that that judgment went beyond reasonable limits and therefore found the Forestry Law's limitation on the Civil Code to be in violation of Article 29 of the Constitution.

[iv] The Voting Rights Apportionment Cases

Japan's Supreme Court has been faced with several Constitutional challenges to the apportionment of seats in the Diet. The allocation of seats is a matter for the Diet under Article 47 of the Constitution, which gives the Diet authority to establish electoral districts by legislation and also to legislatively deal with other matters concerning elections for the Diet. The original voting districts were established at a time when Japan was mostly an agricultural country. But, as Japan became an industrial power a larger percentage of its population moved off the farms and into cities. Electoral districts, for the most part, remained the same. The movement to the cities created a great disparity in the value of the votes of rural dwellers and city residents. Litigation, similar to the United States' one-person, one-vote rationale, followed. Japanese litigants placed reliance on Article 14(1), which, in the *Patricide* case the Court had held was not limited in scope to the categories of group identification listed in the statute but rather generally provided for equal treatment. In its basic outline, plaintiff's argument was that failure to give each person's vote the same (or at least nearly the same) value in an election denied equality to those persons whose vote carried less weight.

In *Koshiyama v. Tokyo Metropolitan Election Commission*[124] the Supreme Court rejected a challenge to the districting law finding that a voter disparity of 1–4.09 did not violate the Constitution's equality clause. However, the Court held that it had jurisdiction over the case and that the issue presented was legal in character and not a political question. In 1976 the Court in *Kurokawa v. Chiba Election Commission*[125] found a Constitutional violation in the holding of the 1972 election for the Lower House because the value of a vote in the least populous district was entitled to 4.99 times the value of a vote in the most populous. This large disparity was found to exceed the discretion given to the Diet to establish electoral districts. Nonetheless, the Court, finding that to overturn the election would cause great harm to the general population refused to overturn the election results. The matter was placed back in the hands of the Diet to reapportion.

124. 18 Minshu 270 (Feb. 5, 1964).
125. 30 Minshu 223, Case No. 1974 (Gyo-Tsu) No. 75, http://www.courts.go.jp/english/judgments/text/1976.04.14-1974-Gyo-Tsu-No.75.html (G.B., Apr. 30, 1976).

While the *Kurokawa* case was pending, the Diet passed a reapportionment law that would have cut down the disparity to 1–2.92 if the election had been held when the law was passed. As it was, by the time of the election the disparity between the most and least populous districts was 1–3.94. In 1980 an election was held under this law—followed by another challenge based on Article 14. Again the Court found the disparity to conflict with the Constitution, although the Court indicated that it would have found a disparity of 1–2.92 valid.[126] Again it refused to overturn the election. This time the Court found that as the *Kurokawa* decision had been rendered in 1976 and the election held in 1980, the Diet had not been given sufficient time to change the procedure to one that conformed to the Constitution.[127] This decision was based on a reasonable period doctrine, under which, since demographic changes are always occurring, the legislature is given a reasonable time to fix an unconstitutional disparity. It is only when the Diet fails to act during the reasonable time frame that an issue of unconstitutionality can arise.[128]

Since then each election held in Japan has resulted in litigation challenging the voting disparity. In many of the cases the Supreme Court has found the system in a state of unconstitutionality but in no case has the Court upended an election. Rather the matter has always been sent back to the Diet for resolution.[129] As a consequence the current apportionment system is in a state of unconstitutionality but the Diet, which appointed a special committee to deal with the issue, has been unsuccessful in

126. In the United States a 1 to 2.92 disparity would be unconstitutional. See e.g., *Reynolds v. Sims*, 377 U.S. 533 (1964).

127. *Kanao v. Hiroshima Prefecture Election Commission*, 39 Minshu 1100, Case No.1984 (Gyo-Tsu) No.339, http://www.courts.go.jp/english/judgments/text/1985.07.17-1984-Gyo-Tsu-No.339.html (G.B. July 17, 1985).

128. See Toshihiko Nonaka, *The Significance of the Grand Bench Decision Concerning Proportional Representation in the House of Representatives and Related Issues*, 18 L. Japan 134, 139 (David Nelson trans., 1986) for a discussion of the "reasonable period" doctrine.

129. See, e.g., *Kawahara v. Tokyo Prefecture Election Administration Commission*, Case Number 111 of 1991,47 Minshu 67, http://www.courts.go.jp/english/judgments/text/1993.01.20-1991-Gyo-Tsu-No.111.html (G.B., Jan. 20, 1993); *Single Electoral and Prefecture Representation case*, Case No. 1998 (Gyo-Tsu) No. 7, http://www.courts.go.jp/english/judgments/text/1999.11.10-1999-Gyo-Tsu-No.7.html (G.B. Nov. 10, 1999); *Proportional Representation and Dual Candidacy case*, Case No. 1998 (Gyo-Tsu) No. 8, http://www.courts.go.jp/english/judgments/text/1999.11.10-1999-Gyo-Tsu-No.8.html (G.B. Nov. 10, 1999); 2001 Upper House Election Case, Case No 24 (Gyo-Tsu) of 2003, 58 Minshu No. 1, http://www.courts.go.jp/english/judgments/text/2004.01.14-2003-Gyo-Tsu-No..24.html (G.B. Jan. 14, 2004); *2005 Upper House election case*, Case No. 247 (Gyo-Tsu) of 2005, 60 Minshu No. 8, http://www.courts.go.jp/english/judgments/text/2006.10.04-2005.-Gyo-Tsu-.No..247.html (G.B., Oct. 4, 2006); *2007 Upper House Election Case*, Case No. 2008 (Gyo-Tsu) No. 209, Minshu Vol. 63, No. 7, http://www.courts.go.jp/english/judgments/text/2009.09.30-2008.-Gyo-Tsu-.No..209.html (G.B., Sept. 30, 2009); *2009 Lower House Election Case*, Case No. 2010 (Gyo-Tsu) No. 207, Minshu Vol. 65, No. 2, http://www.courts.go.jp/english/judgments/text/2011.03.23-2010.-Gyo-Tsu-.No..207.html (G.B., Mar. 23, 2011); Kyodo News, *Court Contradictory on Vote Disparity, July poll legit in morning ruling, Unconstitutional in the afternoon*, Japan Times (Nov. 17, 2010), http://search.japantimes.co.jp/cgi-bin/nn20101117x1.html; Kyodo News, *Courts Question 2010 Vote Validity*, Japan Times (Jan. 29, 2011), http://search.japantimes.co.jp/cgi-bin/nn20110129a7.html; *High Court Hits August 30 Vote Disparity*, Japan Times (Dec. 29, 2009); *Court Rules August Poll Not Constitutional*, Daily Yomiuri (Dec. 29, 2009); Kyodo News, *Vote Gaps illegal but poll isn't void: court*, Japan Times (Feb. 25, 2010), http://search.japantimes.co.jp/cgi-bin/nn20100225a1.html.

resolving the disparity. As the 2013 Lower House election approaches it appears that it will be held under an unconstitutional system. The unconstitutionality has even been used by the opposing ruling and opposition parties in their efforts to either delay an election until required by the Constitution or to demand an earlier snap election.

While not correcting the disparity the decisions of the Supreme Court have had an effect and influenced the changes in Japan's election system from a multi-seat election district system to single-seat districts with proportional representation.[130]The Court may be backing away from its previous stance, which gave precedence to a numerical calculation of voting strength rather than a consideration of other factors. The Court has noted that numbers alone were not controlling and the Diet could, in designing a "harmonious" election system, properly consider other factors beyond equality of a vote in designating electoral districts. The weight to be given to these "other factors" is uncertain as the Court failed to set any objective criteria to be used in evaluating other factors. The apportionment issue is difficult to solve and courts have refused to place blame on the Diet for failure to apportion the districts in accordance with the Constitution.[131]

[v] The Post Office Liability Case[132]

Under Japan's Constitution the government is responsible in damages for illegal actions taken by government officials in their official capacity.[133] The Constitutional right is carried out through a statute that more fully defines the cause of action. In the *Post Office liability* case the Supreme Court was confronted with a provision of the Post Office law that limited and in some cases absolved the Post Office from liability in connection with the failure to deliver registered mail. The limitation on Post Office liability was enacted as part of a broader plan to assure that mail service would be available to the general public at as low a cost as was possible. By reducing the liability of the Post Office, costs would be reduced and this reduction could be passed on to postal users.

Registered mail utilizes a system under which postal employees record the receipt of the mail and in some cases also record the delivery of the mail. In either event the customer using registered mail pays a higher fee than for ordinary mail. The limitation of liability provision applies to failure to properly deliver registered mail as well as other mail. The Supreme Court was presented with the question of whether the

130. The Diet under the first non-LDP government in almost 50 years (a coalition with Prime Minister Hosokawa at the head but Ichiro Ozawa a former leader of the LDP as the "shadow shogun") made major changes to the method of voting, creating a single-seat election system with a proportional representation component.
131. Kyodo News, *Vote Gaps illegal but poll isn't void: court*, Japan Times (Feb. 25, 2010), http://search.japantimes.co.jp/cgi-bin/nn20100225a1.html.
132. *Post Office Liability* case, Case No.1999 (O) No.1767, 56 Minshu No. 7 at 1439, http://www.courts.go.jp/english/judgments/text/2002.09.11-1999.-O-.No.1767.html (G.B., Sept. 11, 2002).
133. Constitution Article 17.

limitation (and in some cases immunity) of liability provisions applicable to registered mail were consistent with Article 17 of the Constitution.

The Supreme Court recognized that it was inevitable that in a system as large as the Post Office handling as much registered mail as the Post Office handles there would be mistakes and errors and that some mail would not be delivered. Moreover, the Court was of the view that mistakes in delivering registered mail could occur frequently as a consequence of negligence and thus limiting liability served the purpose of the legislation, namely keeping rates for registered mail lower than would be the case without the limitation provision. Accordingly for ordinary negligence the Court found that the limitations of liability provisions were reasonable and hence constitutional.

The Court took a different view of improper handling of registered mail that occurred as a consequence of either intentional or grossly negligent conduct on the part of postal employees. The Court asserted that failure of the system to deliver registered mail as a consequence of such intentional or grossly negligent conduct was rare. Consequently the limitation of liability provision was not necessary to protect lower postal rates and did not conform to the purpose the government had in mind when it adopted the postal law. Accordingly the provision limiting liability in cases of gross negligence or intentional conduct was unreasonable and thus inconsistent with Article 17. In reaching its determination the court pointed out that in the transportation business there were several laws that limited the liability of transportation companies but that in each case the law was limited to negligent conduct and did not limit liability in the event of grossly negligent or intentional conduct. The statute also limited Post Office liability for ordinary negligence involving "special delivery" mail. Because special delivery is an unusual and infrequent process the Court concluded that immunity for ordinary negligence was inconsistent with the Constitution since instances of ordinary negligence were so infrequent the goal of maintaining postal rates at a reasonable level would not be adversely affected by permitting suit for ordinary negligence.

In 2008 the Court decided the *Mapplethorpe Photographs Case*[134] holding that a book of photographs (some showing male genitalia) was not obscene. It required the Customs Authority to return the book to the publisher whose copy had been seized at Narita Airport. Five of the photographs in the book had previously been in a catalogue that the Supreme Court had held was obscene. Because of the context of the entire work the Court found no conflict between its 2008 decision and the earlier case. Nonetheless it refused to order the Customs Authority to pay damages to the publisher holding that the decision in the earlier case justified the Customs seizure and thus there was no illegality within the meaning of Article 17 and the statute designed to carry out the Constitutional mandate of Article 17.

Mapplethorpe did not cite the *Post Office* case but the two cases are consistent in that in both cases the court looked for some intent or gross negligence (as a surrogate

134. *Robert Mapplethorpe Photographs Case, Asai v. Japan,* Case No, 2003 (Gyo-Tsu) No. 157, 2003 (Gyo-Hi) No. 164, 62 Minshu No. 2 at 69, http://www.courts.go.jp/english/judgments/text/2008.02.19-2003.-Gyo-Tsu-.No..157%2C.2003.-Gyo-Hi-.No..164-103831.html (P.B., Feb. 19, 2008).

for intent) to assess liability and bring the Constitutional grant of redress against the government into play. In the *Post Office* case there was no intent for ordinary negligence and a limitation of liability was permitted—but for intentional wrongdoing or gross negligence (as a surrogate for intent) a remedy under Article 17 was required. No such intent was present in the *Mapplethorpe* case and damages were not permitted.

[vi] The Overseas Voting Case[135]

Under Article 15 of the Constitution the people "have the inalienable right to choose their public officials" and "Universal adult suffrage is guaranteed with regard to the election of public officials". As a consequence, the right to vote in national elections extends to all of "the people". The Constitution was originally drafted in the English language by MacArthur's forces. But as it is the Constitution of Japan the official version of the Constitution must be written in Japanese. To achieve this result the Occupation and the Japanese government held an extensive translation session during which disputes arose between the parties as to the proper translation of words used in the Constitution. Ultimately the word used to describe "people" who had Constitutional rights was "*kokumin*", a term, which while it means people also has the connotation of Japanese people.[136] The result of this translation is that unlike the American Constitution's Fourteenth Amendment that applies to all people affected by the action of the State, the Japanese Constitution does not apply to all people living in Japan. But, the provision clearly applies to all Japanese nationals and the provision has no temporal bounds. Still certain limits on the right to vote are potentially constitutional. Thus there is a relationship between Japan's criminal laws and its voting laws. Unlike the United States where many states prohibit persons who have been convicted of a felony from voting, in Japan the prohibition is much more narrowly confined to persons whose crime related to the voting process. The Supreme Court of Japan has nonetheless upheld voting legislation under which homeless Japanese citizens who have no residence address cannot register to vote and thus cannot vote.[137]

As noted earlier, the Hosokawa government interlude and Ichiro Ozawa's influence on that government ushered in a process of election law reform that resulted in a system where certain members of the Upper and Lower Houses were elected on a proportional representation basis and others on a single-seat constituency basis. In view of Japan's emergence as a major exporting country many Japanese executives are required by their companies to take up residence abroad to carry out the policy and business of the company. To deal with these overseas executives (and their families)

---

135. *Overseas Voting Case*, Case No. 82 and 83 (Gyo-Tsu) and 76 and 77 (Gyo-Hi) of 2001, http://www.courts.go.jp/english/judgments/text/2005.09.14-2001.-Gyo-Tsu-.No..82%2C.2001.-Gyo-Hi-.No..76%2C.2001.-Gyo-Tsu-.No..83%2C.2001.-Gyo-Hi-.No..77.html (G.B., Sept. 14, 2005).
136. Mark A. Levin, *Essential Commodities and Racial Justice: Using Constitutional Protection of Japan's Indigenous Ainu People to Inform Understanding of the United States and Japan*, 33 N.Y.U. J. Intl. L. & Pol. 420, 481–483 (2001).
137. *Homeless Persons no Right to Vote Case*, see, Setsuko Kamiya, *Park dweller loses address case*, Japan Times (Oct. 4, 2008), http://search.japantimes.co.jp/cgi-bin/nn20081004a2.html.

the Japanese election laws were amended to provide for the creation of an overseas voting register. This register was to be used in the proportional representation portion of the election process but was not to be used for the election of single-seat district elections. Overseas Japanese sued.

The Supreme Court utilized an "unavoidability" test to determine whether the system was unconstitutional. If the denial of the right to vote was "unavoidable", meaning that if the circumstances made it virtually impossible to overcome difficulties to the grant of the franchise, then denial could be upheld. The government attempted to justify the restriction on voting by noting that it was very difficult for Japanese residing abroad to receive information concerning the election of local officials running in single-seat election contests. As a result the government argued that it was impossible to provide overseas Japanese with the right to vote in single-seat elections. The Supreme Court noted that such a justification might have been valid when the single-seat system was first established and when the overseas voter register was first created. But it noted that two elections had been held in which it had proven practical to use the register for proportional representation elections. Moreover, advances in technology including communications technology made the government's argument, while perhaps valid when the system was originally designed, no longer valid. Accordingly the court found the restriction on voting contained in the election law unconstitutional.

In an earlier decision (that the Supreme Court found was not inconsistent with its latest ruling) the Court had found that handicapped people who could not vote because they could not get to polling places on Election Day were not entitled to relief. However, in a suit brought by Lou Gehrig's disease victims challenging the government's rejection of their write in votes (rejected because the sufferers could not personally write in the name of the candidate they choose but instead used proxies to write in the candidate's name) the District Court held that the rejection was unconstitutional. Although it rejected the plaintiffs' request for damages, the District Court suggested the law be changed. Thereafter the Diet amended the law to allow proxy write-ins by handicapped voters who cannot write.[138]

Even after the Supreme Court held that it was unconstitutional to deny overseas Japanese the right to vote in Diet elections, the Bureaucracy failed to take steps to allow overseas Japanese to vote in the Judicial Referendum that accompanied the Diet elections. The government used the same arguments that it had used to justify its failure to allow voting by overseas Japanese in single-seat district elections. The District Court rejected the argument using language similar to the Supreme Court language in the *Overseas Election* case. Nonetheless, it ordered no remedy leaving it to the Diet to remedy its own failure.[139]

138. See, *Disabled people get right to cast votes via proxy*, Japan Times (July 16, 2003), http://search.japantimes.co.jp/cgi-bin/nn20030716a3.html.

139. *Court Questions Exclusion of Overseas Japanese From Vote*, Japan Times (Apr. 28, 2011), http://search.japantimes.co.jp/cgi-bin/nn20110428a8.html.

[vii] The Nationality Act Case

Japan's Nationality law differs from American law. While under U.S. law a child may become a citizen either because its parent is American or because it is born in the United States, in Japan citizenship is based solely on the parent's nationality. Of course Japanese law permits the government, in its discretion, to grant nationality to "deserving" persons who apply for Japanese nationality (such persons are naturalized citizens—the United States law also contains naturalization provisions. These provisions are much more accommodating to acquiring United States citizenship than are the Japanese naturalization provisions.). Also, under United States law an "illegitimate" child of an American father whose father recognizes the child as his own may obtain citizenship as of right anytime before the child's 21st birthday. In Japan the Nationality Act provided that to gain citizenship the "'illegitimate' child" of a Japanese father and a non-Japanese mother[140] had to be recognized by the father prior to birth or the parents had to wed after the child's birth. In 2008 the Supreme Court of Japan held that this provision of the law was unconstitutional because it treated children born to unwed parents who did not later marry differently than children whose parents later married. The Court's decision was based on Article 14 of the Constitution, which requires equal treatment. The Court found that the unequal treatment between children whose parents marry after birth and those whose parents do not marry after the child's birth was unreasonable and therefore in violation of Article 14. The Court noted that the distinction drawn by the Nationality Act between children whose parents marry after birth and those who do not may have had reasonableness when the Act was first enacted because it tended to establish that the child had a strong relationship to Japan and significantly to the Japanese father. However, noting the change in social attitudes towards marriage as well as changes in family life and internationalization of Japanese travel and relationships since enactment of the Nationality Act, the Court found such rationale to be unreasonable in modern life. Finding that marriage did not establish any stronger bonds between the Japanese father and the child than a father (who acknowledged paternity) and mother who remained unmarried, the Court found the Act unconstitutional.

The Court's reasoning on this point appears strained. As an initial matter, it remains the fact that Japan has one of the lowest rates of "illegitimacy", one of the lowest rates of cohabitation without marriage and very few children born into a de facto as distinguished from de jure family.[141] It may well be that the real reason for the Court's decision is the Court's recognition of the changing international attitude towards treating legitimate and "illegitimate" children equally.[142] Thus the Court notes

---

140. The child of a Japanese mother, whether born in or out of wedlock, gets Japanese citizenship on birth.
141. Richard Ronald & Allison Alexy, *Continuity and Change in Japanese Homes and Families*, in *Home and Family in Japan* 1, 14 (Richard Ronald & Allison Alexy eds., Routledge 2011); Tadaki Matsukawa, *The Japanese Family between Tradition and Modernity*, in *The European Family* 139, 147 (Jacques Commaille & Francois de Singly ed., Kluwer Academic Publishers 1997).
142. See, 28 Waseda Bull. Comp. L. 134–141 (developments in 2008) http://www.waseda.jp/hiken/jp/public/bulletin/pdf/28/134-144.pdf at 140–141 noting that the Court applied the

that both the International Covenant on Civil and Political Rights as well as the Convention on the Rights of the Child (both of which have been ratified by Japan) contain provisions prohibiting discrimination against children because of their having been born out of wedlock[143]. Finally, the Court noted that by holding unconstitutional the portion of the Nationality Act at issue in the case it would be putting Japan into the same position of many other countries that had previously required both acknowledgment and parental marriage as conditions of citizenship but had changed their law to require only acknowledgment.[144]

The Court's reasoning may also be strained because of an unwillingness to directly address and change the Court's prior approach to discrimination jurisprudence. Prior to the Nationality Act case, in cases involving the claim of unconstitutionality based on an asserted violation of the equality provision of the Constitution the Supreme Court looked to see if the law challenged was "reasonable". Typically it found such reasonableness. In the Nationality Act claim the Court uses the language of reasonableness and finds the law unreasonable because of changed attitudes both domestic and international. At the same time it uses language that indicates that it finds that the means are not proportional to the ends in part because the victims of the discrimination (children) neither caused their situation nor could they cure the situation or achieve the goal that the Diet sought—and in part because the ends are to establish a nexus to Japan and the marriage of the parents simply was not relevant to nexus in the case of a "de facto mixed nationality marriage". It also looks to whether the purpose of the law itself is reasonable or whether a more nuanced approach is required to achieve the end. This *may be* the start of a new disproportionate analysis. If this is the springboard for a new approach to discrimination law (and perhaps Constitutionality determinations in general) then the Nationality Act case may have huge consequences for the future. This may herald a new judicial approach to Constitutional and discrimination challenges to legislation.[145] On the other hand, it may simply be the Court's application of the tried and true Japanese jurisprudence of applying the common sense of the society—in this case the common sense is demonstrated by the public's increased recognition and apparent acceptance of "de

principle of jus sanguine in a formalistic manner rather than looking for a link to the State for which nationality was claimed and that this accords with current international practice.

143. When a Japanese husband who could not produce sperm (because he had been born a woman and through treatment and operation became and was legally recognized as a man) sought to have his wife's child (conceived via in vitro fertilization) registered as the lawful child of his wife and himself the Registrar refused and the Justice Minister stated the child should be registered as born out of wedlock.

144. *Portion of Nationality Law Unconstitutional Case*, Case No. 2006 (Gyo-Tsu) No. 135, 62 Minshu No. 6, http://www.courts.go.jp/english/judgments/text/2008.06.04-2006.-Gyo-Tsu-.No..135-111255.html (G.B., June 4, 2008).

145. Craig Martin, Gli*mmers of Hope: The Evolution of Equality Rights Doctrine in Japanese Courts from a Comparative Perspective*, 20 Duke J. Comp. & Intl. L. 167 (2010) http://works.bepress.com/cgi/viewcontent.cgi?article=1002&context=craig_martin; for perhaps a less expansive but nonetheless positive view of the decision based on the remedy portion of the ruling see, Hitoshi Nasu, Constitutionality of the Japanese Nationality Act: A Commentary on the Supreme Court's Decision on 4 June 2008, ANU College of Law, Social Science Research Network, Legal Scholarship Network, http://papers.ssrn.com/sol3/papers.cfm?abstract_id=1402407.

facto marriage" including "de facto mixed nationality marriage" and modern family relations in order to reach a conclusion that puts Japan closer to international norms such as those recognized in International Covenants Japan has signed.[146] On its face it would appear that the American approach in dealing with such issues as discrimination based on illegitimacy may have influenced the Court—the child cannot be punished for the acts of its parents —although that would not explain the decision rendered several months later by a Petty Bench to again uphold discrimination against "illegitimate" children where inheritance is involved[147] although it may explain a later panel's determination to transfer another case involving the inheritance issue to the en banc Supreme Court for consideration. That later case was set for Grand Bench determination but the parties settled and the case was sent back to the Petty Bench which then dismissed it because of the settlement.[148] Since the Nationality Act case the Court has not held another law unconstitutional.

[c] The Effect of a Finding of Unconstitutionality

It has generally been viewed that even when the Court acts to find a law unconstitutional, the law does not "go away" nor is it null and void. This is because under the Civil Law philosophy followed in Japan, only the legislature can make or unmake a law.[149] However this view is not universal.[150] Article 200 of the Civil Code, which was struck down in the *Patricide* case remained on the books and no action was taken by the government to have it removed from the books until the amendment of the

146. Where there is no need seen to moderate law to meet international standards it may well be that the old rules rejecting the idea of having "illegitimate" children prevails allowing differently and unfavorably treatment notwithstanding the logic of the Nationality Act case.
147. The decision of the court in the Nationality Act case allowed acknowledged children of Japanese fathers and non-Japanese mothers who resided outside of Japan to be granted citizenship. Such children, it could be argued, may have little link to Japanese society since they reside abroad and may have little or no contact with their Japanese father. A Japanese father who acknowledged the child is sufficient link, perhaps supporting the notion that it is not reasonable for a law to punish the child for acts it cannot control and that society no longer considers relevant because of changing views both domestically and internationally. The amendment to the Nationality Act enacted after the Supreme Court's decision provides that *any* child born out of wedlock acknowledged before the child achieves age 20, by either a mother or father holding Japanese nationality at the time of the child's birth, acquires Japanese citizenship by notification to the Minister of Justice as long as the Japanese parent remains a Japanese citizen at the time of notification or if no longer alive was a Japanese citizen at the time of death. Nationality Act Article 3. http://www.japaneselawtranslation.go.jp/law/detail/?printID=&id=1857&re=02&vm=02.
148. *"illegitimate" child Inheritance case 3*, Case No. 2009 (Ku) No. 1027, Minshu Vol. 65, No. 2 (P.B. Mar. 9, 2011), http://www.courts.go.jp/english/judgments/text/2011.03.09-2009.-Ku-.No..1027.html.
149. Hiroshi Oda, *Japanese Law* 42 (Oxford University Press 1999).
150. Professor Itoh has identified four theories: 1) null and void with retroactive effect, 2) unconstitutional applied in the case at hand but only applicable to other cases based on their facts and on a case-by-case basis; 3) effect on other cases only after legislative action to conform to the decision and 4) some precedential value but not determinative of future cases. See, Hiroshi Itoh, *The Supreme Court and Benign Elite Democracy in Japan* 82 (Ashgate Publishing Ltd. 2010).

Criminal Code in 1995, although the Prosecutor General announced that he would not proceed under the law.[151]

The issue of the effect of a declaration that a law is unconstitutional presented itself in the Nationality Act case. Two Justices dissented. To these Justices the question of granting nationality was a matter left by the Constitution to the Diet and hence it was a violation of the judicial function for the Court to enter a decision that granted these children Japanese nationality. These Justices were of the view that the Court simply had a negating authority and lacked authority to "rewrite" the Nationality Act so as to make it Constitutional.

A concurring Justice specifically rejected this argument noting that acceptance would allow the unconstitutional condition to remain unless and until the Diet acted. To this Justice the Diet had acted and all judicial review did was to excise the unconstitutional condition and thereby allow the law to work in a Constitutional manner by granting citizenship to the children whose parents had not married. Another concurring Justice was of the view that the dissenters made a valid point but not one that could be accepted in this case because the Court was simply giving a broad interpretation to language that had already been adopted by the Diet.

These various opinions arose in the context of a finding that a portion of a law was unconstitutional. The remedy was thus to excise that portion of the law and leave the remainder of the law intact. The effect of the Nationality Act decision on the "effect" of unconstitutional laws remains to be seen. In any event, shortly after the Court's decision in the Nationality Act case the Diet enacted a new law removing the condition of marriage and allowing citizenship based solely on acknowledgment prior to the child's 20th birthday.[152]

In sum, while the Constitution gives the Supreme Court (and all courts in Japan) the power of judicial review that power is very sparingly used, although recently the court has been more willing to find a law unconstitutional—whether this represents a new approach remains to be seen. Even when it is used, the court is solicitous of the democratic institutions of government—the political branches (Cabinet and Diet)[153]and will defer to those institutions whenever possible and leave fundamental changes to those institutions. This solicitous attitude goes so far as to exercise judicial restraint so as to avoid ordering the government to make changes to conform to the Constitution.[154]

When one looks at the language of the Constitution, one sees an activist court exercising equal powers with other branches of government and holding the ultimate power of judicial review. This is a far different view than the one that arises from

151. Ichiro Kitamura, *The Judiciary in Contemporary Society: Japan*, 25 Case W. Res. J. Intl. L. 263, 277 (1993); See also Hiroshi Oda, *Japanese Law* 42 (Oxford University Press 1999).
152. To deal with acknowledged children who were older than 20 on the effective date the Law granted such children the right to acquire Japanese Nationality through notification to the Japanese Government before December 31, 2011.
153. See Christopher A. Ford, *The Indigenization of Constitutionalism in the Japanese Experience*, 28 Case W. Res. J. Int'l L. 3, 42 (1996).
154. The United States approach is fundamentally different. *United States v. Morrison*, 528 U.S. 598 (2000) and *Dickerson v. United States*, 530 U.S. 428 (2000).

looking at the Meiji Constitution. Yet, what you see is not what you get. Rather than an activist court wielding judicial review to keep the Legislative Branch in line, the Japanese Supreme Court is solicitous of the views of the legislature to a point where little of consequence has been set aside for Constitutional reasons.[155]

[d] A Constitutional Court?

Because of the passivity of the Supreme Court in Constitutional cases some have suggested that Japan should adopt a Constitutional Court modeled after the much more active German Constitutional Court. It is questionable whether such a change would achieve its stated objective—the problem is not that a court with judicial review authority does not exist, the problem relates to the Justices themselves who refuse to utilize their judicial review authority. These problems would need to be solved whether a Constitutional Court were created or not—although it is possible that a structural change could help usher in a change in appointment practice.

[e] Judicial Review: Restrictions

The Japanese Constitution confers all of the judicial power on the Judicial Branch and prohibits the establishment of extraordinary tribunals such as a Constitutional Court or Courts Marshall.[156] But what you see may not be what you get as the "circumstance decision", the deference given to the opinions of the CLB[157] and the prime minister's authority to set aside provisional remedies in some situations appear to impinge on the power of the Judicial Branch.

One reason for conferring all of the judicial power on the Supreme Court was to avoid the re-creation of the Administrative Court that had existed under the Meiji Constitution. The Constitution does not prohibit the exercise of "quasi-judicial" powers by an administrative agency[158] since such exercise is not final judicial action and may be appealed to the ordinary judicial courts.[159] Another was to provide the ordinary court system with the power of judicial review and thus avoid the civil law practice of creating a separate "Constitutional Court". The great discretion given to the CLB's

155. See Hideo Tanaka (assisted by Malcolm D.H. Smith), *The Japanese Legal System* 692 (University of Tokyo Press 1976) for the view that the Supreme Court may be following practices and philosophy used by the Great Court of Judicature notwithstanding the intended change in system sought to be brought about by the Constitution.
156. Article 76.
157. It has been suggested that the question is not a matter of deference given to the CLB but rather that the CLB's views serve to weed out unconstitutional statutes leaving the court with few if any laws to overturn. See, Jun-Ichi Satoh, *Judicial Review in Japan: An Overview of the Case Law and an Examination of Trends in the Japanese Supreme Court's Constitutional Oversight*, 41 Loyola of L.A. L. Rev. 602–623–625.
158. See Akira Mikazuki, Saibansho Seido (Judicial System) 5 Nihon-koku Kempo Taikei 73 quoted in Hideo Tanaka (assisted by Malcolm D.H. Smith), *The Japanese Legal System* 454 (University of Tokyo Press 1976).
159. Hiroyuki Hata & Go Nakagawa & Takehisa Nakagawa, *Japanese Constitutional Law* sec. 125 (Kluwer Law International 2001).

opinions as to the Constitutionality of laws given before enactment seems similar to the authority given to certain Constitutional Courts, while the circumstance decision and prime minister's power to temporarily suspend "provisional remedies" raise constitutional questions.

Technically the circumstance decision does not involve an exercise of power by the Executive Branch. It is an authority given to the Judicial Branch and thus may be said to be consistent with the notion of complete judicial power in the Judicial Branch. On the other hand, the legislative authorization of such a power (which would likely adhere to the judiciary as a matter of discretion with no need for legislation) can be seen as a message to the judiciary to utilize such power.

A circumstance decision (discussed in Chapter 17) is a decision that is limited to a finding of illegality on the part of the Executive and/or Legislative Branches, which the court then refuses to extend to give the supposedly prevailing party the relief requested. In such case, the circumstances are deemed such that the public interest is best served by allowing the unlawful action to continue in effect[160] In the United States courts of equity may, and indeed should, refrain from ordering the relief requested by a particular party when a "balancing of the equities" or a "balancing of the harms" leads the court to such restraint.[161] The circumstance decision is more than a balancing discretionary act by the judiciary. Rather, it reflect a "bias" in favor of permitting illegal administrative action to go forward, even when steps can be taken to remedy the situation, such as in the voter apportionment decisions discussed *supra*..

The Constitutionality of the Administrative Case Litigation Law (ACLL) provision dealing with the circumstance decision may itself be drawn into question by Article 98 of the Constitution, which provides that no law or other governmental act that is contrary to the Constitution shall have legal force or effect. Once the Supreme Court holds that an administrative act (or the election apportionment system and thus the election) is unconstitutional Article 98 appears to say that act shall have no legal force or effect, but the circumstance decision allows that unconstitutional act to have continuing force and effect. What you see is not what you get. The prime minister's power to suspend a provisional remedy ordered by a court appears unique and raises fundamental questions as to the exclusive nature of the judicial power and the Judicial Branch. Although Japanese courts lack the equity power of a common law court, they can issue provisional remedy orders that stop certain types of administrative action while the court is considering the case. The prime minister in turn may object to such a provisional remedy, giving his reasons why such a remedy is against the public interest. The court may not look behind or question the prime minister's objection and must decline to grant the provisional relief or if already granted must set aside its previous order.[162] In effect, the prime minister, not the court, has decided the provisional remedy request. This would appear to raise serious Constitutional questions as the Executive Branch rather than the Judicial Branch appears to be exercising

160. ACLL section 31.
161. See, e.g., *Monsanto Co. v. Geerseon Seed Farms*, 561 U.S. ___ (2010).
162. Hiroyuki Hata & Go Nakagawa & Takehisa Nakagawa, *Japanese Constitutional Law* sec. 374 (Kluwer Law International 2001).

judicial power. Further, the Constitution places judicial decisions in the hands of judges who are to be bound by their conscience and the Constitution. In the case of the prime minister's suspension power, the judge is not permitted to exercise judgment based on conscience.[163]

The Diet amended the ACLL to grant courts greater authority to grant provisional remedies in administrative cases but took no action in connection with the prime minister's power to suspend a provisional remedy.

163. The prime minister used his power to stay an order of the Tokyo District Court that would have permitted a demonstration in the streets surrounding the Diet building. The filing by the prime minister of a "motion of objection" had the effect of setting aside the restraining order issued by the District Court. Hideo Tanaka (assisted by Malcolm D.H. Smith), *The Japanese Legal System* 773–774 (University of Tokyo Press 1976).

CHAPTER 6

Treaties

§6.01 UNITED STATES

There is no question that the United States as a sovereign power has the right to enter into treaties. The Supreme Court has said that the power of the federal government to make treaties is inherent in national sovereignty and does not require a specific Constitutional grant.[1] Bearing in mind that the United States is a federal republic with semi-sovereign States and recognizing that at the creation of the federal union the States sought to protect their authority, it is not surprising that the States retained a power to reject treaties that they objected to. The mechanism selected was the limit placed on the Executive's power to make binding treaties. The president was given power to make treaties, but was required to seek the advice and consent of the Senate for treaties and further was required to get the consent of two-thirds of all senators present to a treaty before it could go into effect.[2] The States' need for protection was highlighted by the Supremacy Clause under which "all Treaties made, or which shall be made, under the Authority of the United States, shall be the Supreme Law of the Land; and the Judges in every State shall be bound thereby". This places treaties on parity with other federal law making (the Constitution itself and laws made pursuant to the Constitution). Since treaties could make law supreme to conflicting state law, the States required protection and a significant say in the matter. It is important to recall that at the time the Constitution was written the Senate was an appointed body that represented the interests of the various states and senators were appointed by state governments.

1. *United States v. Curtiss-Wright Export Corp.*, 299 U.S. 304 (1936).
2. The president may make various appointments for which he must get advice and consent but that consent is by a simple majority. The treaty power however requires agreement of two-thirds of the representatives of the states.

§6.02 JAPAN

Under Article 73 of the Constitution the Cabinet concludes treaties on behalf of the State.[3] However, the Cabinet must obtain approval of the Diet. That approval may precede or come after Cabinet action. Under Article 98(2) Japan is committed to faithfully observing its treaty obligations. Article 98, which is in "Chapter X. Supreme Law" makes no mention of treaties as Supreme Law and indeed makes no mention of the effect of treaties as domestic law in Japan.

§6.03 WHAT YOU SEE MAY NOT BE WHAT YOU GET

The Constitution of the United States appears, on its face, to call for a consultative role for the Senate prior to the president's acceptance of a treaty. As a practical matter the president does not seek formal advice from the Senate. The first real chance the Senate has to be deeply involved in a treaty matter occurs when the treaty, already negotiated by the Executive is presented for "consent".

The placement of treaties in the Supremacy Clause was an outgrowth of problems experienced in the Articles of Confederation period when Congress entered into treaties but some States simply failed to abide by the treaty terms. To avoid such embarrassment, treaties became part of the Supreme Law of the Land and there is evidence that the intent was to assure that treaty commitments were binding on the States and would be applied as domestic law by the judicial system.[4]

While treaties may be the Supreme Law of the Land in the United States, such a rule only applies when the treaty is deemed to be part of the law of the land and only when a later adopted law is not inconsistent with the treaty. In a real sense what you see in the Constitution is not what you get in many treaty situations. How does this come about? The United States only recognizes treaties as establishing a rule of domestic law when the treaty is self-executing. Most treaties to which the United States is a party are not considered as self-executing.[5]

While there is a certain amount of confusion in United States' law in determining when a treaty is and when it is not self-executing it is clear that if the United States government declares its view that the treaty is non-self-executing the courts will follow that view.[6] Such declarations have been attached to treaties submitted to the Senate to assure the non-self-executing nature of the treaty. Examples would be Covenant on Civil and Political Rights, International Convention on the Elimination of All Forms of

---

3. See, *American Society of International Law, National Treaty Law and Practice* 20 (Hollis, Blakeslee & Ederington eds., Martinus Nijhoff 2005).
4. 3 Story, Commentaries on the Constitution of the United States 696 (1833).
5. See, *Foster v. Nelson*, 27 U.S. (Peters) 243 (1829) and *United States v. Percheman*, 32 U.S. (Peters) 51 (1833).
6. Restatement (Third) of the Foreign Relations Law of the United States section 111, comment h; For a general discussion of the treaty making power and the effect of treaties and reservations on domestic law and the foreign relations obligations of the United States, see John Norton Moore, *Treaty Interpretation, the Constitution and the Rule of Law*, 42 Virginia J. Intl. L. 164 (2001).

Racial Discrimination, International Covenant on Economic, Social and Cultural Rights, and American Convention on Human Rights.[7]

Furthermore, while self-executing treaties may override federal or state statutory law existing at the time of the treaty's effectiveness, if federal legislation is later enacted that is inconsistent with the previously agreed to treaty the later adopted legislation controls and the treaty is simply not the Supreme Law.[8] Of course, to avoid international complications a later enacted law should, if possible, be construed to be consistent with a treaty obligation.[9]

Even where there is a treaty right, the method of enforcement of that right may be a question of domestic law. Thus, the state courts need not suppress a confession made by an arrested Mexican national who was not informed of his right to confer with the Mexican Consul prior to questioning—a right granted by the Vienna Consular Convention of which both the United States and Mexico are signatories. The Court concluded that as the Convention had no specific provision regarding how the right to confer was to be enforced, the Supreme Court would not establish a rule that state courts were required to follow in order to carry out the treaty provision. To do so would infringe the president's power to conclude treaties as it would grant a treaty right that had not been negotiated and agreed to. Accordingly suppression was not mandated, especially as the defendant had been given his *Miranda* warnings (in both English and Spanish) and advised of his right to counsel prior to his questioning and confession. The Court noted that if a self-executing treaty contains an enforcement mechanism then the state is required to comply with the enforcement mechanism under the Supremacy Clause and the Court would require the state to so comply.[10]

Nonetheless, there are situations in which treaties establish a rule that must be followed by the government and must be applied by the courts. In *Hamdan v. Rumsfeld*[11] the Supreme Court held that the structure and rules of procedure of the Military Commission established to try the defendant were inconsistent with both the Uniform Code of Military Justice and Common Article 3 of the Geneva Conventions and hence the Commission was not proper. Although the case does not deal with classical war situations of opposing armies representing sovereign States, the court found that Common Article 3 applied even though there was no conflict between signatories. Accordingly the government was required to follow the portions of the Conventions

---

7. See Carlos Manuel Vazques, *The Four Doctrines of Self-Executing Treaties*, 89 Am. J. Intl. L. 695, 706 note 54 (1995); Yuji Iwasawa, *The Doctrine of Self-Executing Treaties in the United States: A Critical Analysis*, 26 Virginia J. Intl. L. 627, 669 (1986).
8. *Whitney v. Robertson*, 124 U.S. 190 (1888); *Chinese Exclusion* case, 130 U.S. 581 (1899). Of course State legislatures could not pass superceding legislation, as the Federal Treaty is supreme over all state law whenever passed. Executive Agreements such as claims agreements *may* supersede State and Federal law, as the Congress has indicated that it approves of such settlement by Executive Agreement. See *Dames & Moore v. Reagan*, 453 U.S. 654 (1981) (The Court said it was "not prepared to say the President lacks the power to settle such claims."); see also, *U.S. v. Pink*, 315 U.S. 203 (1942); *U.S. v. Belmont*, 301 U.S. 324 (1937).
9. *Murray v. Schooner Charming Betsy*, 6 U.S. (2 Cranch) 64 (1804); *Weinberger v. Rossi*, 456 U.S. 25, 32 (1982).
10. *Sanchez-Llamas v. Oregon*, 548 U.S. 331 (2006).
11. *Hamdan v. Rumsfeld*, 548 U.S. 557 (2006).

that applied and the Commissions as constituted were invalid for failure to conform to the Convention.

As a general rule treaties in Japan that require approval by the Diet are subject to the promulgation requirement.[12] Treaties that are promulgated are considered as self-executing and have the force and effect of domestic law.[13] As such, they may give rise to rights in Japanese courts without any further action by the Legislature.[14]

Of course not all treaties are self-executing—regardless of the general rule. Thus treaties that require implementing legislation are said to be non-self-executing and the Japanese government has taken the view that non-self executing treaties require legislative or administrative action before such treaties become domestic law.[15] Yet the distinction between treaties that require implementing legislative action and those that do not appears strained, as all treaties in Japan that implicate legislative action (either to carry out the treaty or that require amendment of laws to conform to the treaty) require approval by the Diet—and the general rule is that such approval is given prior to the treaty being signed or ratified.[16] Accordingly, treaties that require domestic legislation would appear to have met that requirement when the Diet approves the agreement.[17] Japan is a parliamentary democracy so that "party discipline" at work in the approval of a treaty would appear to be the same discipline that would approve legislation required by a treaty. Why then demand two steps of some treaties but one step of others? The answer may lie in the role of the domestic law adopted prior to accession in defining the terms of the treaty—or at least Japan's understanding of what it is agreeing to. Thus, the Hague Convention on the Civil Aspects of International Child Abduction has not yet been acceded to (although the government several times committed to accession) because the domestic law needed to "carry out" duties under the treaty has not been agreed to by the LDP and DPJ. More relevant may be the fact that some treaties deal with societal rights and, similar to the hortatory interpretation given to provisions of the Japanese Constitution dealing with similar rights, such treaties require more specific Diet consideration. The typical procedure for treaty approval in Japan involves an examination of domestic laws that might be affected by

12. *American Society of International Law* (National Treaty Law and Practice, Martinus Nijhoff 2005) Hollis, Blakeslee & Ederington Ed., 424.
13. Yuji Iwasawa, *International Law, Human Rights And Japanese Law*, 28 (Oxford University Press 1998).
14. Sayoko Kodera, *Implementation of the Convention on the Elimination of All Forms of Discrimination against Women within Japan*, 39 Japanese Annual Intl. L. 149 (1996); see also, Japanese Report on International Law in Municipal Courts, *Reports of National Committees*, 36 Japanese Annual Intl. L. 103. There is some scholarly opinion that treaties lawfully entered into take precedence over the Constitution, although this is a minority view and would seem to lack rationality. In the United States the Constitution is always superior to a treaty. *Reid v. Covert*, 354 U.S. 1, 16–17 (1957).
15. Sayoko Kodera, *Implementation of the Convention on the Elimination of All Forms of Discrimination against Women within Japan*, 39 Japanese Annual of International Law 149, 150 (1996).
16. Yuji Iwasawa, *International Law, Human Rights and Japanese Law*, 13–14 (Oxford University Press 1998).
17. Most domestic law requires approval of both houses of the Diet. A treaty on the other hand may be approved by the Diet even if the Upper House disapproves. However, this same approval by the Lower House alone applies to the budget process and the selection of a prime minister so that this difference by itself should not account for different treatment of treaties.

the treaty to determine whether amendments or adoption of new laws are called for. If required, such new or amendatory legislation is prepared by the government and submitted to the Diet.[18] While most treaties receive Diet approval prior to their being signed or ratified, some treaties are signed and subsequently Diet approval is sought. When the Diet turns down such a treaty it cannot be considered as domestic law since it has failed to receive Diet approval. Moreover, it is probably the better rule that under such circumstances the treaty also lacks international effect since it has failed to be concluded as the law of the Japanese signatory requires.[19] The Diet has never turned down a treaty concluded by the Cabinet.[20]

The "black letter" law in Japan is to the effect that treaties are superior to inconsistent domestic law, whether such domestic law precedes or comes after the treaty is promulgated although there is a contrary school of thought.[21] The argument in favor of this view is premised on "internationalism" (specifically in connection with Japan's reliance on international norms of peace as it is "bound" by Article 9), the requirement in the Constitution that treaties be "faithfully observed" and government comments to the effect that treaties are superior to domestic law. However, none of these reasons appear compelling. Japan can support internationalism and still insist that for domestic matters domestic law controls if that law comes after the treaty is ratified; the Constitution also gives precedence to Diet passed laws; and the government comments could be applied to pre-existing law only. While the Tokyo District Court found a 1949 ILO Convention superior to a provision in the Public Corporation and National Enterprise Labor Relations Law in a 1966 case, by the time the Convention was ratified the statutory provision in question had been deleted from the law.[22]

As an initial matter before a treaty provision can be said to be part of domestic law and thus have the effect of overruling either a prior or later enacted domestic law, it must be determined that the treaty provision is self-executing. Again, it appears that scholarly opinion is to the effect that treaties in Japan are self-executing.[23] But, even if a treaty is considered as self-executing that does not necessarily mean that it has direct

18. Japanese Report on International Law in Municipal Courts, *Reports of National Committees*, 36 Japanese Annual Intl. L. 103, 103–104.
19. For a contrary view see Yuji Iwasawa, *International Law, Human Rights and Japanese Law*, 14–16 (Oxford University Press 1998).
20. See Hiroyuki Hata & Go Nakagawa & Takehisa Nakagawa, *Japanese Constitutional Law* sec. 412 (Kluwer Law International 2001) for a discussion of differing views as to whether a signed treaty rejected by the Diet has international effect and concluding that the majority view is to the effect that it does not.
21. Yuji Iwasawa, *International Law, Human Rights and Japanese Law*, 95 (Oxford University Press 1998); Hideo Tanaka (assisted by Malcolm D.H. Smith), *The Japanese Legal System* 57 (University of Tokyo Press 1976); Shigenori Matsui, *The Constitution of Japan*, 28–29 (Hart Publishing 2011).
22. See discussion in Yuji Iwasawa, *International Law, Human Rights and Japanese Law*, 95 (Oxford University Press 1998); Hideo Tanaka (assisted by Malcolm D.H. Smith), *The Japanese Legal System* 95, 110, 111 (University of Tokyo Press 1976). See also discussion of the *Kobe Jewelry* case at pages 95 n. 306 and 67, of Iwasawa, where it appears that the treaty was ultimately found to be inapplicable.
23. Yuji Iwasawa, *International Law, Human Rights and Japanese Law*, 95 (Oxford University Press 1998); Hideo Tanaka (assisted by Malcolm D.H. Smith), *The Japanese Legal System* 25, 27 (University of Tokyo Press 1976).

applicability and thus overrides domestic law. To determine if a treaty has direct applicability Japanese law recognizes two different types of treaties—those that are specific in requiring that the terms of the treaty take effect immediately and those where the terms of the treaty are directional and are to take effect over time. This latter category of treaty does not have immediate effect as domestic law.[24] This "escape valve" from domestic effect can be used by courts which can give lip service to the rule that treaties establish domestic law obligations and then find the treaty is merely directional or is characterized as having progressive character or setting a guiding principle, which would not override domestic statutes. Even if a treaty is considered as applicable to the Japanese Government it may be interpreted as not requiring action by local authorities. This is not quite the same as the argument that absent a supremacy clause a treaty may not affect sovereign states in a federation—Japan is a unitary government and local authorities have no sovereign or semi-sovereign status. When the government asserts that a treaty is merely of a progressive character the courts ultimately conclude that the treaty does not have immediate or direct effect. Thus the issue of whether the treaty takes precedent over domestic law simply never arises. And, this appears to be the situation even when scholarly opinion differs from that of the government and takes the view that the treaty is not progressive but has immediate effect.

If a treaty is imprecise in its terms it will not be found to override domestic law.[25] And, if the matter is considered one that properly belongs in the realm of the Legislative Branch the treaty will not be found to override domestic law. Finally, if the court is of the view that the domestic law rule is "reasonable" it appears that the treaty will not be found applicable—even if the court must simply disregard the treaty argument in its opinion.

Although Article 9 of the International Covenant on Economic, Social and Cultural Rights provides that everyone should have a right to social security, the Tokyo District Court in 1994 struck down a claim for social security by Korean permanent residents who had been injured when serving in Japan's armed forces during World War Two. In response to the treaty claim the court held it was "reasonable" for the legislature when restricting social security relief to injured Japanese soldiers to believe that Korean nationals would be taken care of in later agreements between Japan and Korea. In a 1995 case involving the same issue the court held that the question of relief was a matter of legislative discretion. Yet, these cases were decided some 30 years after an agreement between Japan and South Korea, which had not provided for such benefits.[26]

Similarly, the courts had upheld the Constitutionality of Pension Law provisions that granted pension benefits to Japanese nationals but denied similar benefits to permanent residents of Japan who were not citizens. Such laws were legislatively

24. This distinction is similar to the distinction drawn by Japanese courts between self-executing or immediately applicable Constitutional provisions and directional provisions that require legislation to bring them to fruition.
25. Yuji Iwasawa, *International Law, Human Rights and Japanese Law*, 47–48 (Oxford University Press 1998).
26. *Ibid.*, 182–183.

amended in 1982 to bring Japan into compliance with the International Covenant Related to the Status of Refugees [ICRSR] to provide pension benefits to permanent residents.[27] A court has found that the failure to make such change retroactive was not unconstitutional.[28] The Supreme Court affirmed that decision in late 2007. Similarly the Supreme Court on the same day held that the failure to make the 1982 legislative change that permitted permanent Korean residents of Japan over the age of 20 to receive disability benefits retroactive so as to cover such permanent residents who had already reached their 20th birthday was not unconstitutional.[29] In the *Courtroom Note Taking* case[30] an American lawyer doing research in Japan was prohibited from taking notes while watching a Japanese trial. He challenged the ruling based on the Constitution and Article 19 of the Human Rights Agreement. The Supreme Court found the limitation on note taking in court to be in accord with the Constitution and dealt with Article 19 summarily by simply recognizing the provision and stating that the judge's prohibition on note taking did not violate the treaty. The Court failed to consider the argument (urged by the plaintiff) that the treaty contained a requirement that restrictions on the right provided must be necessary to protect the rights of third parties or to protect national security, public health or good morals.[31]

Complications regarding application of international norms may arise when there is a treaty "right" that can be carried out by either of two or more countries but each relies on the other to perform. The consequences for the "right holder" may be that the right is not carried out. For example, Japan follows the *jus sanguines* rule under which a child's nationality is dependent on the parents' nationality. Many other countries follow the *jus soli* rule (place of birth). The different approaches to nationality by countries can create complications for children born abroad to non-national parents. If the parents' country of nationality follows *jus soli* and the country of birth location follows *jus sanguines* the child may fall in the gap between the two and be stateless. The treaty complication arises because the UN Convention of the Right of the Child provides that steps should be taken by signatories to prevent a child from being stateless.[32] The Convention does not place the burden of avoiding statelessness on either the *jus sanguines* or *jus soli* nation and has no enforcement mechanism. Nonetheless signatories have an obligation to mold domestic law to achieve the ends of the convention. Since it is obviously not the fault of the child that such a circumstance is presented the situation should be remedied by legislation in both countries giving the

27. See Kenneth L. Port, *Impact of Human Rights Law in Japan*, 28 Stanford J. Intl. L. 139, 159 (1991) for a discussion of the relationship between the treaty and judicial opinion as it affected the liberalizing legislation.
28. See *Naturalized Japanese Denied Disability Pension*, Japan Times (Mar. 14, 2001), http://www.japantimes.co.jp/text/nn20010314a6.html. When the pension law was amended in 1982 to permit benefits to non-Japanese the provision was not made retroactive.
29. Kyodo News, *Court rejects Koreans' appeal seeking disability benefits*, Japan Times (Dec. 27, 2007), http://search.japantimes.co.jp/cgi-bin/nn20071227a9.html.
30. *Repeta v. Japan*, 43 Minshu 89 (1989), Case No. 1988 (O) No. 436, http://www.courts.go.jp/english/judgments/text/1989.03.08-1988-O-No.436.html (G.B. Mar. 8, 1989).
31. Similarly, concurring Justice Yotsuya failed to discuss this point although he recognized the treaty argument made by plaintiff.
32. Article 7.

child the right to opt for citizenship at a specified age. However, such opt in legal provisions are not present in many countries, including Japan. Nor does Japan have bilateral treaties to deal with the issue with *jus soli* nations such as Brazil, which has a large ethnic Japanese population and has many nationals living, working and undoubtedly some are raising children in Japan.[33] Nationality may be a problem when a surrogate carries and gives birth to a child and the law of the place of birth does not grant citizenship to the child and the law of the "parents" providing the genetic material does not recognize them as the parents (see Chapter 9).

The Supreme Court appears never to have stricken a domestic statute because of a conflict between the statute and a treaty. The Court either finds that the treaty is consistent with domestic law, or the treaty is not specific enough to be considered as domestic law but rather is merely "progressive", or finds that the domestic law is "reasonable" and hence is acceptable. To reach its conclusion that the treaty does not displace the domestic law, the court will even simply disregard the treaty argument or fail to consider provisions of the treaty that might be applicable even when such arguments have been raised in the court below and presented to the Supreme Court on appeal. What you see (the rule of treaty supremacy) is not what you get (rule of domestic law supremacy).

The fact that Japanese appellate courts do not find treaties inconsistent with domestic law and thus do not strike down domestic statutes that conflict with treaties does not mean that international agreements have no effect on Japanese law. As in the case with hortatory Constitutional provisions, and with judicial suggestions for legislative changes based on the Judicial Branch's understanding of changing social attitudes, treaties have had a great influence on domestic law in Japan. In some cases the government of Japan has postponed ratification of a treaty in order to have time to change its domestic law to conform to the obligations to be undertaken in the treaty.[34] Many of the changes in domestic law bettering the condition of women in Japan can be traced to the UN Decade of the Woman and the ratification by Japan of the Women's Convention. Similarly many of the legislative changes bettering the condition of Korean permanent residents in Japan can be traced to agreements entered into between Japan and South Korea. The 1984 amendments to the Nationality Act, under which children of Japanese mothers automatically acquired Japanese citizenship when formerly only children of Japanese fathers acquired Japanese citizenship, were specifically designed to bring Japanese domestic law into conformity with the Convention on the Elimination of All Forms of Discrimination Against Women.[35] In its 2008 decision *Portion of*

33. Yasuhiro Okuda, *The United Nations Convention on the Rights of the Child and Japan's International Family Law including Nationality Law*, 18 Journal of Japanese Law (Feb., 2005), last accessed Sept. 15, 2012, www.law.usyd.edu.au/anjel/documents/ZJapanR/ZJapanR_15_08_Okuda.pdf.
34. Convention on the Elimination of All Forms of Discrimination against Women. It took Japan five years to get ready to ratify the Convention on the Elimination of All Forms of Discrimination against Women so that it could first amend its domestic law to conform to the Convention.
35. See Kiyoshi Hosokawa, *Amendment of the Nationality Law*, 28 Japanese Annual Intl. L. 11, 12 (1985). This Convention also worked to the advantage of Korean permanent residents in Japan by providing that the legitimate children of Korean/Japanese marriages were automatically citizens of Japan.

Nationality Law Unconstitutional Case the Court specifically referred to the International Covenant on Civil and Political Rights and the Convention on the Rights of the Child—both of which prohibit all forms of discrimination against a child as a consequence of birth.[36] Japan is a party to numerous multilateral treaties and to treaties, such as the WTO, that establish judicial machinery to interpret the treaty and determine whether there have been treaty violations. It is likely that determinations of such treaty judicial bodies are considered binding on Japan. Where less "definitive" enforcement bodies are established, such as is the case with the International Covenant on Economic, Social and Cultural Rights, then the determinations of such bodies are considered as advisory and are not considered as binding.

In 1987 Japan amended its Penal Law to provide for extraterritoriality in some situations in order to comply with various international conventions that Japan had entered into. These included, the Convention on the Prevention and Punishment of Crimes against Internationally Protected Persons, Including Diplomatic Agents, International Convention Against the Taking of Hostages, United Nations Diplomats Convention and United Nations Hostages Convention.[37]

The Human Rights Conventions to which Japan is party have exerted pressure to improve the living conditions of Japan's minority *Burakumin* community. And, the International Covenant on Civil and Political Rights had a great effect on the Act for the Promotion of Ainu Culture and Dissemination of Knowledge Regarding Ainu Traditions.

In 2004, in preparation for Japan's acceptance of the Protocol against the Trafficking of Persons Japan established a task force and action plan. Since then changes have been made in several domestic laws, including the Criminal Code, the Immigration Law, the Passport Law, the Law governing entertainment establishments, etc. to bring them into conformity with the Protocol and to criminalize the trafficking in persons.[38] But Japan's Diet was unable to pass a general conspiracy law, notwithstanding treaty commitments to do so to fight terrorism.

In 2007 the Supreme Court had to deal with claims made against the Government of Japan and companies in Japan arising out of Japan's prosecution of the Second World War. The Supreme Court referred to treaties as the basis for rejecting the suit.[39] The Court utilized the San Francisco Peace Treaty between Japan and numerous other parties as the template for resolution of reparations claims and noted that such treaty waived the claims of governments and citizens of the governments. While holding that there was no legal obligation to pay compensation the Court expressed the view that

36. *Portion of Nationality Law Unconstitutional Case*, Case No. 2006 (Gyo-Tsu) 135, 62 Minshu No. 6, http://www.courts.go.jp/english/judgments/text/2008.06.04-2006.-Gyo-Tsu-.No..135-111255.html (G.B.June 4, 2008.
37. Shigamitsu Dando, *The Criminal Law Of Japan: The General Part* 52–55 (B. J. George trans. Rothman & Co. 1997); see also, Kensuke Itoh, *The 1987 Penal Code and Other Special Criminal Laws Amendments Law: A Response to the Two U.N. Conventions Against International Terrorism*, 32 Japan Annual Intl. L. 18 (1989).
38. Ministry of Foreign Affairs, *The Recent Actions Japan has taken to combat TIP* (Trafficking in Persons) (October 2007), www.mofa.go.jp/policy/i_crime/people/action0508.html.
39. *Chinese Citizens Reparations* case, Case No. 1658 (Ju) of 2004, Minshu 61 No. 3, (Sup. Ct. Second Petty Bench, 27 April 2007).

compensation could be paid on a humanitarian basis and was justified on that basis and suggested that a payment should be made. It is likely that similar arguments would apply to claims of so-called comfort women.

In July 2007, Japan signed the Rome Statute establishing the International Criminal Court (ICC).[40] The Rome statute contains provisions relating to confessions. The Japanese Constitution prohibits the use of coerced confessions and gives suspects the right to counsel. The reality of criminal investigation is that suspects may be held in custody in substitute prisons for extensive periods of time during which time they are subjected to interrogation without counsel being present. (See Chapter 16) Japanese police and prosecutors may use aggressive questioning techniques. While it is unlikely that in any domestic criminal case there would be an issue that could be brought to the ICC, it is likely that the ICC will have to more clearly define the meaning of the Rules and will have to deal with admissions and the rights of the accused under the Rome treaty.[41] International bodies have objected to Japan's substitute prison system and the Japanese interrogation process.[42] It is possible that exposure to such issues through the ICC (especially as Japan now has a Judge on the ICC) could induce changes in the domestic system for interrogation and admission of confessions. Although that has not yet occurred, as Chapter 16 discusses, Japan is moving in the direction of recording the entirety of suspect interrogations.

Japan's determination to accede to the Hague Convention on the Civil Aspects of Child Abduction creates new ground for conflict between domestic law and international commitments. It is the purpose of the treaty to recognize the determination of the domestic court that makes the custody determination in Family Law adjudication rather than leave such matters open for debate in the court of the country to which the child has been abducted. There is, of course, an escape valve that allows the abducting country court to refuse to order return of the child when there is a "grave risk" to the child's physical or psychological well being from return. However, domestic legislation under consideration in Japan leaves flexibility in determining grave risk and specifies certain risks that would not appear to meet the Conventions understanding of grave risk.[43] Moreover, Japanese Family Court judges will need to dramatically change their attitude, especially the generally accepted attitude in Japan that a child of a divorced

40. See Ministry of Foreign Affairs, Election of Ms. Fumiko Saiga, Ambassador in Charge of Human Rights and Member of the Committee on the Elimination of All Forms of Discrimination against Women (CEDAW), as Judge of the International Criminal Court (ICC), www.mofa.go.jp/announce/announce/2007/12/1176491_840.html.
41. The United States is not a party to the Rome Treaty and hence interrogation of prisoners at Guantanamo is not subject to review by the ICC.
42. Concluding Observations of the Human Rights Committee (Nov. 19, 1998); www.mofa.go.jp/policy/human/civil_ccpr.html.
43. In *Neulinger and Shruk v. Switzerland* (No. 41615/07) Grand Chamber of the European Court of Human Rights, http://www.caselaw.ch/d/div/egmr%206-7-10.pdf held that under the unusual facts of that case the phrase grave risk had to be viewed with reference to best interests of the child. However, the Grand Chamber did not rule that in all cases grave risk and best interests were the same.

couple is better off with only one of the parents in his or her life, if the Convention is to be meaningful in Japan.[44] This subject is discussed in greater detail in Chapter 9.

While the "black letter" law in Japan would seem to suggest a different rule than in the United States as to the rank of treaties as domestic law, the two systems are closer than academics would choose to believe. For example, while Japan's courts have found ways to hold that various civil rights treaties are not binding as domestic law the United States has made the same determinations in connection with the same treaties through use of the non-self-executing doctrine and presidential or Senatorial declarations. Both countries find that treaties are not domestic law when they find that the treaties are merely directional or progressive. Courts in both countries appear to follow the lead of the government in determining whether a treaty is to be applied as domestic law. Finally, it is to be expected that in democratic government by elected leaders in the Legislative and Executive Branches, an unelected Judiciary, whether appointed for life as in the United States or selected as part of a bureaucracy as in Japan, is generally going to find mechanisms that permit the duly elected representatives of the people determine which international undertakings apply domestically and which have application solely in the international arena.

44. See, Tanase, *Hague Convention Ratification and Post-Divorce Parent-Child Law*, http://www.yomiuri.co.jp/adv/chuo/dy/opinion/20120611.htm.

CHAPTER 7

Freedom of Expression

§7.01 UNITED STATES

First Amendment law dealing with freedom of expression in the United States remains a work in progress, although the basic outlines of First Amendment jurisprudence appear secure. The original Constitution contained no provision regarding the fundamental questions of free speech and censorship. To those who argued that such omission was dangerous the supporters of the Constitution responded that as Congress was given no power to regulate speech or to censor materials there was no need for a Free Speech provision. Nonetheless the objections to this and other omissions dealing with fundamental rights led to the commitment to adopt a Bill of Rights and the eventual adoption of the first 10 Amendments to the Constitution.

Until after the Civil War the United States had virtually no Freedom of Expression jurisprudence. The First Amendment applied solely to Congress and there was no 14th Amendment Due Process clause that could be used to apply the freedom of expression provisions to actions by State governments. It was not until adoption of the 14th Amendment that a vehicle for applying the First Amendment to State legislation was available. The Amendment is directed solely to the Congress and Congressional action. Yet it is clear that it reaches all governmental action. The Supreme Court has applied First Amendment free speech concepts to private causes of action such as libel against a news reporter or news organization or public figures or involving issues of public debate. All forms of expression, including the arts such as painting, music, theater, movies, even video games are included in the term speech. While the Supreme Court is united on the general framework of its First Amendment jurisprudence issues arise on the fringes such as when action is speech and whether organizations are entitled to free speech rights and whether certain conduct is so reprehensible that it is not entitled to protection of the Amendment, etc.[1]

[A] Advocacy versus Material Support

The First World War demonstrated that the supporters of a Bill of Rights were correct in their demand to a guaranty of free speech rights.[2] The case of *Adams v. U.S.*[3] in 1919 upholding a conviction under the Espionage Act for urging workers to strike during the War brought forth a dissent by Justice Holmes which later became the "clear and present" danger doctrine in Holmes' opinion in *Schenck v. United States*[4].

In *Brandenburg v. Ohio*[5] the Court required not simply advocacy but also imminent unlawful action before restriction could be applied to speech bringing the law close to Justice Holmes' original idea of a clear and present danger. It reaffirmed its rejection of the idea that mere advocacy of the use of force could be prohibited in *NAACP v. Claiborne Hardware Company.*[6]

More recently in *Holder v. Humanitarian Law Project*[7] the defendants challenged a criminal statute that prohibited giving material support to terrorist organizations. That support was in the nature of speech that imparted information to and thus assisted terrorist groups—albeit information that was neither intelligence information nor otherwise unlawful information. The issue before the Court was whether that support via speech could be criminalized. The Court held it could, utilizing an imminent danger rationale.[8] The majority was influenced by the fact that Congress had expressly narrowed the speech that could be reached under the statute:

> Finally, and most importantly, Congress has avoided any restriction on independent advocacy, or indeed any activities not directed to, coordinated with, or controlled by foreign terrorist groups.

The Court concerned about the reach of its decision sought to cabin the decision to the specific advocacy and speech before the Court and to further limit the decision to aid to foreign terrorist groups.

---

1. The Supreme Court has even held that some false statements have constitutional protections and that it is unconstitutional to criminalize the false statement that the speaker has received a military honor or award. See, *United States v. Alvarez*, 567 U.S. ___ (2012).
2. The Alien and Sedition Laws of 1798 are properly seen as an attack on First Amendment rights. Although no court overturned the laws, the public performed a similar service by supporting Jefferson's election and throwing out the Federalist regime that had enacted the laws. See, Jeffrey E. Morrison, *Legal Foundations of the Tokugawa Bakufu and Post Colonial United States* 17, http://www.sewha.org/Paper%20SEWHA%202006%20Competion%20(Morrison).pdf.
3. 250 U.S. 616 (1919).
4. 249 U.S. 47 (1919). ("The question in every case is whether the words used are used in such circumstances and are of such a nature as to create a clear and present danger that they will bring about the substantive evils that Congress has a right to prevent.")
5. *Brandenburg v. Ohio*, 395 U.S. 444 (1969) See also, *Virginia v. Black*, 538 U.S. at 359.
6. 458 U.S. 886 (1982).
7. 561 U.S. ___ (2010).
8. The minority specifically utilizes *Brandenburg* and the imminent requirement in rejecting the majority's reasoning.

Thus the majority made clear (as Congress had done in the statute) that independent advocacy was not criminalized by the statute and that freedom of association was not criminalized:

> The statute does not prohibit being a member of one of the designated groups or vigorously promoting and supporting the political goals of the group... . What [§2339B] prohibits is the act of giving material support.... 205 F. 3d, at 1133.

[B] Activity or Conduct that Communicates

In the *Holder* case the Court was careful to distinguish the "speech" involved from statutes that criminalize activity.[9] Where activity is forbidden the issue becomes one of whether the prohibition is one of activity that can itself be prohibited or one of the communication of ideas, which then implicates First Amendment concepts. Thus in *Cohen v. California*[10] the Court reversed the conviction of a defendant who was convicted of disorderly conduct for wearing a shirt in public that used an obscenity to express his objection to the draft. The only conduct Cohen was charged with was his communication of an idea—his objection to the draft. And as this was speech pure and simple he could not be convicted for exercising his right of free expression. It was of course true that Cohen engaged in conduct, he did wear a shirt—but there was no prohibition against shirt wearing and he was not prosecuted for shirt wearing he was prosecuted because of what his shirt said.

Cohen's conduct/message is to be distinguished from the ability of the government to criminalize or prohibit conduct in a situation where the conduct—without reference to its communicative value—would otherwise be prohibited. Thus in *United States v. O'Brien*[11] the conduct involved—burning a draft card—was a crime because of the need to protect the draft and the necessity of persons with draft cards to carry them on their persons at all times. The fact that O'Brien burned his card to express his disagreement with the draft did not turn his criminal act of burning the card into a free speech activity. To put it in *Cohen* terms, it was the act of wearing a shirt that was criminalized not the communication of the message written on the shirt. Similarly burning of the American flag can be criminalized under a statute that prevents all burning of materials when there are high winds that make such conduct dangerous, but the burning of the flag cannot be prohibited because the message delivered by that burning is dislike of government policies.[12]

9. Both the majority and minority agreed that speech rather than activity was implicated in *Holder*.
10. 403 U.S. 15 (1971).
11. 391 U.S. 367 (1968).
12. *Texas v. Johnson*, 491 U.S. 397 (1989). *R.A.V. v. City of St. Paul*, 505 U.S. 377 (1992).

[C] Content Restrictions

As a general rule the content of a message cannot be regulated by the government unless the content falls into very narrowly defined fields that are held to be outside the protection of the First Amendment:

> These "historic and traditional categories longfamiliar to the bar," *Simon & Schuster, Inc. v. Members of N. Y. State Crime Victims Bd.*, 502 U. S. 105, 127 (1991) (KENNEDY, J., concurring in judgment)—including obscenity, *Roth v. United States*, 354 U. S. 476, 483 (1957), defamation, *Beauharnais v. Illinois*, 343 U. S. 250, 254–255 (1952), fraud, Virginia Bd. of *Pharmacy v. Virginia Citizens Consumer Council*, Inc., 425 U. S. 748, 771 (1976), incitement, *Brandenburg v. Ohio*, 395 U. S. 444, 447–449 (1969) (per curiam), and speech integral to criminal conduct, *Giboney v. Empire Storage & Ice Co.*, 336 U. S. 490, 498 (1949)—are "well-defined and narrowly limited classes of speech, the prevention and punishment of which have never been thought to raise any Constitutional problem." *Chaplinsky v. New Hampshire*, 315 U.S. 568, 571–572 (1942).[13]

In the *Stevens* case quoted above the government proposed that the categories listed could be enlarged and that a balancing test be used for this purpose The Supreme Court found such a proposed rule "startling and dangerous." A balancing test was rejected. The Court reaffirmed its ruling when it applied a "compelling government interest" and narrow tailoring while refusing to extend the categories outside First Amendment protection to the sale of violent video games to minors.[14]

The Supreme Court's virtually complete ban on restrictions on political speech has been generally accepted because political speech is an essential element of American views of democracy and the electoral process.[15]

[D] Commercial Speech

The rare exceptions where speech may be regulated deal more with the nature of the speech rather than its content. Thus, speech that incites immediate lawless action can be restricted as can the speech that presents a clear and present danger, speech that constitutes a true threat to a person can be punished as a means of protecting the person threatened (especially if the person is the President), and commercial speech does not have the same high level of protection as does political speech. Thus, the Court has said:

> In commercial speech cases, then, a four-part analysis has developed. At the outset, we must determine whether the expression is protected by the First Amendment. For commercial speech to come within that provision, it at least must concern lawful activity and not be misleading. Next, we ask whether the asserted governmental interest is substantial. If both inquiries yield positive answers, we

---

13. *United States v. Stevens*, 559 U.S. ___ (2010).
14. *Brown v. Entertainment Merchants Association*, 564 U.S. ___ (2011).
15. *Monitor Patriot Co. v. Roy*, 401 U.S. 265 (1971); *Buckley v. Valeo*, 424 U.S. 1 (1976).

> must determine whether the regulation directly advances the governmental interest asserted, and whether it is not more extensive than is necessary to serve that interest.[16]

The "not more extensive than is necessary" language requires narrow tailoring to carry out the government's objective so that there is a reasonable fit between the means chosen by the government and the lawful objective sought. The language does not require that the means used be the least restrictive means available.[17]

False and misleading advertising can be forbidden because as *Central Hudson* notes, "there can be no Constitutional objection to the suppression of commercial messages that do not accurately inform the public about lawful activity."

[E] Fighting Words

Similarly "fighting words" have been held to be outside the protection of the amendment. The fighting words exemption has been subject to severe narrowing in recent years. It is likely that there is little left of the fighting words exception in modern Constitutional law, except where the words are directed at a specific person and are likely to (and perhaps it is required that they in fact do) incite immediate reaction.

[F] Content Neutrality

So too the government can enact content neutral regulations that carry out a legitimate government objective unrelated to speech such as noise regulations designed to protect the hearing of citizens. Such regulations may have the effect of prohibiting loud sound trucks from blaring out a political message and thus may affect speech. It is not the speech but the level of noise that is regulated.[18] But, the regulation may not burden speech more than necessary to carry out the lawful purpose[19]. It is not permissible for the government to permit loud noise but prohibit loud noise that has a political message. In content neutral regulation situations an intermediate judicial review test is applied, requiring that the regulation be narrowly structured so as to carry out the important government interest it is supposed to further and also that the regulation allow for other means of communicating the message. Thus giving a police official complete discretion as to what level of noise is permissible is not constitutional.[20]

---

16. *Central Hudson Gas & Electric Corp. V. PSC,* 447 U.S. 557, 566 (1980).
17. *Board of Trustees of State University of New York v. Fox,* 492 U.S. 469 (1989).
18. *Grayned v. City of Rockford,* 408 U.S. 104, 116 (1972); *Kovacks v. Cooper,* 336 U.S. 77 (1949).
19. *Madsen v. Women's Health Center Inc.*, 512 U.S. 753, 773 (1994).
20. *Saia v. New York,* 334 U.S. 558 (1948).

[G] Overreaching Even where Obscenity Is Concerned

There are of course certain situations in which the pure expression may be regulated or prohibited. Obscenity[21] is one situation and child pornography another where the court has held the pure expression may be prohibited and thus is outside the protection of the First Amendment—although the Amendment is broad enough to reach attempts to restrict obscenity and child pornography that are not narrowly tailored to carry out their intended goal. Thus where a statute attempting to restrict child pornography is worded so broadly as to encompass protected speech it will be found unconstitutional.[22]

[H] Hate Speech

Other areas of United States freedom of expression law deserve special attention. The area of hateful speech or actions that deliver a hateful message is an area where the American rule is different from that of other liberal democracies and an area where although the speech is abhorred by the general populous it is protected.[23] When the content of the speech is regulated the Supreme Court does not balance the effect of the disagreeable content on the hearings or seeing of the content message against the free speech rights of the speaker/actor.[24] "Regulations which permit the Government to discriminate on the basis of the content of the message cannot be tolerated under the First Amendment."[25]

More recently the Court upheld the right of a group to demonstrate near a military funeral to protest against government policies that had nothing to do with the family of the dead soldier. The demonstrators did not violate any content neutral reasonable time, place or manner regulation but their means of relaying their message was objectionable to many, including the father of the deceased.

[I] Corporate Speech

What has been contested is whether corporations have a categorical right to free speech in the political arena—an issue decided in favor of speech and corporations in the

21. *Roth v. United States*, 354 U.S. 476 (1957).
22. *Ashcroft v. Free Speech Coalition*, 535 U.S. 234 (2002) holding that depictions of virtual child pornography can have literary, artistic, political or scientific value and thus criminalizing all such depictions violates the First amendment. Actual child pornography on the other hand involves child abuse and thus is not protected. *New York v. Ferber*, 458 U.S. 747 (1982); *Reno v. American Civil Liberties Union*, 521 U.S. at 875; *Sable Communications v. FCC, supra* at 130–131.
23. *R.A.V. v. City of St. Paul*, 505 U.S. 377 (1992).
24. Even such hateful and disturbing action as a march by neo-Nazi's in a neighborhood where many Holocaust survivors live cannot be enjoined although the march would cause suffering to the residents. *Collins v. Smith*, 578 F.2d 1197 (7th Cir. 1978). See also, *Snyder v. Phelps*, 562 U.S. ___ (2010).
25. *Simon and Schuster Inc. v. Members of New York State Crime Victims Board*, 502 U.S. 105,116 quoting *Regan v. Time Inc.*, 468 U.S. 641, 648–649 (1984).

Citizens United case.[26] So too, States that have election contests for judges cannot, on the claim that impartiality of the judicial system might otherwise be compromised, limit candidates from expressing their view on the law and on politics.[27] The answer is not to abandon Free Speech principles the answer may well be to abandon judicial elections.

[J] Door-to-Door Canvassing and Electoral Speech

Door-to-door canvassing in order to spread the canvasser's ideas has also been a subject of Supreme Court decision and, in the face of local attempts to license door-to-door canvassers has been given First Amendment protections.[28] The Court held that canvassing regulations or licensing requirements that are dependent on the content of the message being delivered are prohibited.[29] Localities cannot require that persons seeking to do door-to-door canvassing apply for a permit before canvassing and identify themselves in advance. Door-to-door canvassing has religious, political or other communication aspects. To pass Constitutional muster, the ordinance limiting or regulating door-to-door canvassing must be narrowly drawn to meet the legitimate concerns of localities. Most such ordinances fail to be so narrowly tailored.[30]

Door-to-door canvassing is just one aspect of electoral speech protected by the First Amendment. Because the electoral process is at the heart of democratic institutions electoral speech is highly protected.[31] This is particularly relevant when compared to the limits on electoral speech and the electoral process that exist in Japan and are discussed *infra*. Indeed, in the United States electoral speech is of such high value that anonymous speech urging a vote for a candidate or a referendum or other ballot matter is protected.[32] In addition to actual speech or communication of ideas, the First Amendment prohibits restrictions on how much money a party can spend to communicate its political ideas.[33]

[K] Chilling Effect

Government action that has a chilling effect on speech is prohibited.

26. *Citizens United v. Federal Election Commission*, 558 U.S. 50 (2010); reaffirmed in *American Tradition Partnership Inc. v. Bullock*, 567 U.S. ___ (2012).
27. *Republican Party of Minnesota v. White*, 536 U.S. 765 (2002).
28. *Martin v. City of Struthers*, 319 U.S. 141 (1943).
29. *Lovell v. Griffin*, 303 U.S. 444 (1938).
30. *Watchtower Bible & Tract v. Village of Stratton*, 536 U.S. 150 (2002). Requiring a permit would not prevent criminals from going door to door without a permit such as under the guise of being a census taker and a permit would not restore the privacy of the person visited whether the door-to-door canvasser had a permit or not.
31. *McIntyre v. Ohio Election Commission*, 514 U.S. 334 (1995) quoting *Buckley v. Valleo*.
32. *Abrams v. United States*, 250 U.S. 616, 630–631 (1919).
33. *Buckley v. Valeo*, 424 U.S. 1 (1976).

[L] Prior Restraint

Prior restraint is the essence of censorship and is not permitted except in the most unusual of circumstances.[34] Prior restraint is looked on with extreme caution and the general rule is that such restraints are prohibited.

Free speech is considered such an important principle of United States law that even though person's whose character is defamed may sue for damages to reputation they cannot prevent the publication.[35] Group libel is especially pernicious and yet is especially protected because prohibition would have the effect of stifling free expression.

Even when dealing with speech outside the protection of the First Amendment, a prior restraint is unlikely to be sustained except in the rarest of cases involving some clear and present danger or similar consequence. Obscenity is the rare situation where prior restraint is sometimes permitted. But even here there must be procedural safeguards to assure that the material is in fact obscene and these safeguards require a timely due process procedure and judicial proceedings to protect the interests of the defendant and the speech involved.[36]

Where an injunction against conduct that has an effect on communication (a demonstration outside an abortion clinic) rather than pure speech is involved, the Supreme Court applies a heightened scrutiny test to assure that "the challenged provisions of the injunction burden no more speech than necessary to serve a significant government interest."[37]

Even claims by the Executive that national security is at stake may not be sufficient to sustain a prior restraint on speech. The government bears a heavy burden of proving that such a restraint is necessary and the Court is not hesitant to deny that the government has made such a showing.[38] Thus New York Times could publish the classified report on the history of decision making concerning the Viet Nam War notwithstanding an Executive claim of harm.[39]

[M] Free Speech's Effect on Private Action: Public Concern versus Private Concern

Although the First Amendment forbids State action and does not prohibit personal action—so that an editor of a newspaper may properly drop a paragraph from a

---

34. *Near v. Minnesota*, 283 U.S. 697 (1931).
35. *Beauharnais v. Illinois*, 343 U.S. 250 (1952). Although libel is subject to suit for damages, this does not mean that censorship of statements that are libelous is permitted. The dissenting opinions of Justice Douglas and Black more accurately represent the rule in injunction cases. *Tory v. Cochran*, 544 U.S. 734 (2005).
36. *Freedman v. Maryland*, 380 U.S. 51 (1965).
37. *Madsen v. Women's Health Center, Inc.*, 512 U.S. 753 (1994).
38. Where a government employee in a position of trust has access to classified material and signs an agreement that any publication he makes concerning his employment will first be shown to his agency, the Court will enforce such an agreement. *Snepp v. United States*, 444 U.S. 507 (2000).
39. 403 U.S. 713 (1971).

reporters story without fear of First Amendment issues or an editor can refuse to publish letters to the editor or replies to editorials[40] and a public utility can refuse to place inserts in envelopes with bills to its customers because it disagrees with the views expressed in the insert[41] the idea of freedom of expression combined with the chilling effect that litigation may have on free speech has allowed the idea of free speech to intrude on an area of personal litigation particularly relevant to free speech ideas, namely libel and other torts involving speech.[42] To a great extent the scope of protection given to speech in these areas depends on whether the speech involved deals with matters of public or private concern.

New York Times v. Sullivan[43] set the standard that should be used in all state courts when libel action is brought claiming that a public official has been libeled by comment on the official's public duties. To be responsible for such a claimed libel the defendant must have acted with actual malice, meaning knowledge of the falsity of the material published or with reckless disregard of whether the material published was false. The *New York Times* standard of actual malice or reckless disregard applies to candidates for office and comments concerning their qualification for office.[44] "Public figures" but not private parties are covered by the *New York Times* standard.[45]

Not only libel but also the tort of intentional infliction of emotional harm when relied on by a public figure seeking damages because of speech directed at the individual is subject to the *New York Times* standard.[46]

Parody is another area of personal claim that is affected by free speech rights. Thus while material may be protected by copyright, the use of such material in parody is protected speech and a copyright action will not be sustained for parody.[47]

[N] Reporter's Privilege

Many States have provided for an evidentiary privilege that would allow a reporter to refuse to identify a source to which the reporter has given a pledge of confidentiality. Federal law does not compel such "shield law" protection in federal cases and the Supreme Court has held that there is no Constitutional right to such a reporter's privilege[48] although a privilege may be found on a case-by-case basis.[49] Producers of films have no Constitutional right to refuse to turn over to a party in civil litigation (and

40. *Miami Herald v. Tornillo*, 418 U.S. 241 (1976).
41. *Pacific Gas & Electric v. Public Utilities Commission*, 475 U.S. 1 (1986).
42. *Rosenblatt v. Baer*, 383 U.S. 75, 84 (1966).
43. 376 U.S. 254 (1964); *Rosenblatt v. Baer*, 383 U.S. 75, 85 (1966) (defining public official).
44. *Monitor Patriot Co. v. Roy*, 401 U.S. 265, (1972).
45. *Curtis Publishing Co. v. Butts and Associated Press v. Walker*, 388 U.S. 130, 164 (1967); *Gertz v. Robert Welch, Inc.*, 418 U.S. 323, 345 (1974); *Dun & Bradstreet, Inc. v. Greenmoss Builders, Inc.*, 472 U. S. 749 (1985).
46. *Hustler Magazine v. Falwell*, 485 U.S. 46, 56 (1988).
47. *Campbell v. Acuff-Rose Music Inc*, 510 U.S. 569 (1994); *Golan v. Holder*, 565 U.S. ____ (2012).
48. *Branzburg v. Hayes* 408 U.S. 665, 690 (1972).
49. 408 U.S. at 710. For an analysis of the state of the law as of 2005 and the suggestion that the time has come for the Supreme Court to recognize a reporter's privilege see, Jeffrey S. Nestler, *The Underprivileged Profession: The Case for Supreme Court Recognition of the Journalist's Privilege*, 154 U. PA. L. Rev. 201 (2005), http://www.acslaw.org/files/awardwinner.pdf; see also, Eric B.

also to prosecutors through use of a Grand Jury subpoena) outtakes from a documentary film.[50]

The Court of Appeals for the District of Columbia Circuit has held that there is no reporter's privilege in the District of Columbia relying on the Supreme Court's *Branzburg* decision.[51] The DC Circuit specifically rejected the argument that the concurring opinion of Justice Powel indicated that a privilege existed and that the lower courts should analyze a case to determine whether to allow the privilege based on the facts of the case. The Circuit found that as Justice Powell had joined the majority he concluded that there was no First Amendment privilege.[52] Other Circuits have come to a different conclusion, some even suggesting that the Court actually created such a privilege in *Branzburg*.[53] Newsrooms must comply with search warrants issued after a showing of probable cause.[54]

At all events the federal law as to a reporter's privilege is uncertain both as the existence of privilege and in the Circuits that have recognized a qualified privilege the extent of that privilege.

§7.02 JAPAN

[A] Pre-war Japan

The "right" to freedom of speech or press or to assemble was unknown in Tokugawa Japan. Even the Daimyo and other upper level samurai had no right to freedom of expression when it came to the regime. The Shogun could call a council of Daimyo Lords to assist in decision making but this system had dried up and it was not until Admiral Perry arrived in Japan that such a council was again called.

With the overthrow of the Shogunate, the ruling oligarchs took over control and rule of the country—in the Emperor's name. Within the ranks of the oligarchs there was disagreement as to how to rule and how much freedom to give to others in the society. The last battle of the Restoration was a naval engagement in 1869 but no Constitution was put in place until 1890. During this interregnum the oligarchs ruled and debated amongst themselves. Some leaders were expelled from the ruling counsel for expressing views found undesirable, and some of them formed political parties.[55] While these political parties engaged in debate and writings that opposed government

Easton, *A House Divided: Earl Caldwell, The New York Times and the Quest for a Testimonial Privilege*, 4 Utah L. Rev. 1293 (2009).

50. *Chevron v. Berlinger* 629 F.3d 297(2nd Cir, 2011).
51. *In Re Grand Jury Subpoena Judith Miller*, No. 04- 3138 (Feb. 15, 2005), http://www.jprof.com/law/inregjmiller21505opn.pdf. *cert. denied*, 125 S. Ct. 2977 (2005).
52. The Circuit Court found that there was no common law privilege.
53. For a discussion of some of the disagreement in the Circuits prior to the *Miller* case, see, Judge Posner's opinion for the Seventh Circuit in *McKevitt v. Pallasch*, 339 F.3d 530 (7th Cir., 2003).
54. *Zurcher v. The Stanford Daily*, 436 U.S. 547, (1978).
55. See, George Akita, *Foundations of Constitutional Government in Modern Japan* 31–57 (Harvard University Press 1967); See, G. B. Sansom, *The Western World and Japan* 333–353 (Vintage Books 1949); George M. Beckman, The Making of the Meiji 61–62 (University of Kansas Press 1957).

policy, others—notably Takamori Saigo, the leader of the Satsuma Rebellion, openly declared war against the new regime only to be decisively beaten by a non-samurai conscript army. Ito Hirabumi, who came to dominate such important subject matter as the nature and text of the Constitution and who became prime minister and leader of his own political party once party governments began to dominate the Diet became the most powerful of the Oligarchs until his assassination in 1909. Ito while a "reformer" was neither a liberal nor a believer in democratic government or in a rights based political system that favored open and free speech and press.

Political parties and elections for members of the Diet (but not of the government—the Cabinet was to be appointed by the Emperor and unlike a Westminster model Parliament was not subject to the confidence of the Lower House of the Diet) created a climate for views different from those of the Oligarchs in power. Even before the adoption of the Constitution the government took steps to, if not silence at least significantly weaken the potential opposition, through restrictions on the right to assemble and meet as well as to express views. As early as 1868 manuscripts had to be submitted to the governmental authority and permission granted for publication.[56] Almost immediately after deciding that a representative assembly would meet in 1890 the pre-Constitutional government passed laws that restricted the right of the people to assemble and hold public meetings[57] and before the holding of the assembly and adoption of the Constitution a Peace Preservation Law limiting freedom of speech and assembly was enacted.[58] To weaken the power of the press, the Newspaper Law was amended in 1883 giving the authorities the power to seize printing plants and in 1888 press regulations as well as publishing house regulations were put into force. The police were given authority to break up meetings in their discretion. Certain government officials were forbidden to be politically active, although they could join conservative political groups.[59]

The Imperial Constitution treated speech as it had other civil rights—it allowed such freedom as long as the freedom comported to law. Not only could the legislative arm (the Diet) restrict speech rights but so too under the Meiji Constitution the Emperor had a residual power to act through Ordinances in certain situations and such Ordinances could restrict free speech rights. Under the Constitutional regime, the government continued its policy of restricting the rights of the press, political parties and the right of association.

Prior to the War, the most sweeping legislation restricting communication rights was the Peace Preservation Law of 1925 that was intimately tied to the concept and debate over the status of the Emperor and the *kokutai*, the essence of being Japanese under the Emperor system. The law made it a crime to attempt to change any part of the

56. For a synopsis of the legal basis for censorship during the Meiji era see, Jay Rubin, *Injurious to Public Morals, Writers and the Meiji State* 15–31 (University of Washington Press 1984).
57. Whether the first such law was passed in 1882 or 1880 is disputed. Fairbank, Reischauer & Craig, *East Asia Tradition and Transformation* 539 (Houghton Mifflin Company 1973); George M. Beckman, *The Making of the Meiji Constitution* 45 (University of Kansas Press 1957).
58. W.W. Mclaren, *A Political History of Japan* 168–169 (1916, reissued 1965, Russell & Russell).
59. See generally, Goodman, *Justice and Civil Procedure in Japan* 25–30, 44–47 (Oxford University press 2004).

kokutai system.[60] Thus the status quo or the nature of the status quo as interpreted by the government could not be challenged. Equally significant is the distinction drawn by both Japanese Constitutional and legal scholars to the difference between freedoms of the mind and freedoms of action. Thus thought is free—it is when thought is put into action through such things as creating an organization to advocate for the thought or going to meetings dealing with debate over such thoughts or publishing such thoughts that a crime against the State was committed. Ito draws a similar distinction when dealing with Freedom of Religion in the Constitution—in conscience everyone can believe what they want about religion but all must attend to certain prayer services and events.[61] The Peace Preservation Law marked the end of what had been a period of "Taisho Democracy" in the early part of the 1920s and ushered in the more draconian restrictions on freedom of expression that would accompany the War.[62] During the War there was precious little free speech in Japan.[63] Indeed, even after the Occupation had issued its Press Code the Japanese authorities attempted to use the Peace Preservation Law to suppress the famous photograph of General MacArthur and the Emperor because it showed the Emperor in a subservient position to the General. The Occupation responded by ending all efforts by the Japanese government to censor the media and within a week of the photo incident issued a directive dealing with civil liberties that, among things rescinded the Peace Preservation Law. The Occupation engaged in censorship of its own.[64] Like pre-war censorship Occupation censorship relied to a great extent on self-censorship by Japanese media.[65]

Consistent with the Potsdam Declaration the Occupation set about dismantling the censorship and other free speech inhibiting systems established pre-war. In the fall of 1945 the Occupation voided all pre-war restrictions on freedom of speech.

[B] Post-war Japan

The Constitution of Japan provides for Freedom of speech, freedom of assembly and specifically prohibits censorship. Going beyond the text of the Constitution of the United States it provides for the confidentiality of communications and for freedom of conscience, assembly and academic freedom. But, as is the case with all the rights

60. For a discussion of the events leading up to the Peace Preservation Law of 1925 see, Richard H. Mitchell, *Japan's Peace Preservation Law of 1925: Its Origins and Significance*, 28 Monumenta Nipponica 317 (Sophia University 1973).
61. Ito Hirabumi, *Commentaries on the Constitution of the Empire of Japan* 60 (2d ed., Chuo University 1906).
62. See, Dolan, *Cultural Noise: Amplified Sound, Freedom of Expression and Privacy Rights in Japan*, 2 Intl. J. Commun. 662, 664 (2008).
63. Robert Trager & Yuri Obata, *Obscenity Decisions in the Japanese and United States Supreme Courts: Cultural Values in Interpreting Free Speech*, 10 U. C. Davis J. Intl. L. & Pol'y 247, 264 (2004).
64. See, Jay Rubin, *From Wholesomeness to Decadence: The Censorship of Literature Under the Allied Occupation*, 11 J. Japanese Studies 71 (1985).
65. Takemae Eiji, *The Allied Occupation of Japan*, 236–238, 384–396 (translated by Robert Ricketts and Sebastian Swann, Continuum International Publishing 2002).

granted by the Constitution this seemingly broad right is conditioned by the public welfare clause (Article 12) of the Constitution.

The Supreme Court of Japan has used the existence of Article 12 to formulate its "balancing test" in Constitutional rights litigation as well as its general Constitutional test, namely is the restriction complained of reasonable (Constitutional) or unreasonable (unconstitutional).[66]

§7.03 WHAT YOU SEE MAY NOT BE WHAT YOU GET

In the United States the law concerning freedom of expression hews quite closely to the Constitutional mandate. If anything it goes beyond what the language of the 1st Amendment requires. The Amendment's most recent application to hate speech at the funeral of a service member by an almost unanimous Court demonstrates the respect given to different views—even abhorrent views or views expressed in abhorrent ways. This interpretation was not pre-ordained. Other liberal democracies have approached the issue of freedom of expression with more understanding of the feelings of those personally affected by the speech and by the experience of the nation that is doing the interpreting.

Although it is clear that the American framers of Japan's Constitution sought to transplant the American view of Free Speech and Assembly on Japanese soil things have not turned out as anticipated. Although earlier decisions of the Supreme Court of Japan supported a strict scrutiny standard for laws that abridged speech rights, a dramatic change in court composition and court philosophy in the early 1970s replaced the strict scrutiny approach with the far more deferential reasonableness standard that has seen the Court become a virtual rubber stamp for government restrictions on free speech in the areas where speech is most important—political and election campaigning.[67] Unlike the United States that utilizes a categorical approach to free speech and assembly under which such stringent tests as compelling government interest and least intrusive alternative are utilized, Japan uses "reasonableness". If the objective sought by the Diet is reasonable and the law is rationally related to carrying out that objective, then it is Constitutional. Narrow tailoring is not required. From an American point of view this puts matters upside down—the statute passes Constitutional muster because

---

66. This general rule is under attack in certain areas. Thus the *Overseas Voting Case*, http://www.courts.go.jp/english/judgments/text/2005.09.14-2001.-Gyo-Tsu-.No..82%2C.2001.-Gyo-Hi-.No..76%2C.2001.-Gyo-Tsu-.No..83%2C.2001.-Gyo-Hi-.No..77.html (G.B., Sept. 14, 2005), utilized a more stringent test requiring a governmental showing that it was impossible or extremely difficult to hold a fair election without the restriction when a restriction on the right to vote was challenged and the *Portion of Nationality Law Unconstitutional Case*, Case No. 135 (Gyo-Tsu) of 2006, 62 Minshu No. 6, http://www.courts.go.jp/english/judgments/text/2008.06.04-2006.-Gyo-Tsu-.No..135-111255.html (G.B., June 4, 2008, used "reasonableness" language but appeared to apply a more nuanced balancing and proportionality test. To date this approach has not been used in the Free Speech Freedom of Association area where the reasonableness test holds sway.
67. For a discussion of the court's movement to the "right" in the early 1970s and the political reasoning behind such movement see, Lawrence Repeta, *Reserved Seats on Japan's Supreme Court*, 88 Wash. U. L. Rev. 1713 (2011).

it is reasonable not because it conforms to the Constitution.[68] In a sense the law defines the Constitution and is its own test of Constitutionality.

Even using the suggested Constitutional standard of balancing and means-end analysis[69] the decisions of the Japanese Supreme Court in the Free Speech area are suspect. The balancing called for is to balance the importance of the various governmental and private interests implicated by the law challenged. It is here submitted that in such balance the court should but does not consider the importance of the Constitutional grant under which the challenge arises. The Supreme Court of Japan appears to place equal weight on the Constitutional grant of a right and the Constitutional grant of authority of the Diet to legislate. The balance then becomes a balance between the asserted "public interest" as represented by the enactment of a law by the representatives of the public (even if those representatives were pre-war representatives elected in less than democratic circumstances) and the interest of the party suing to have the law set aside. In such a mismatch it is little wonder that Article 21 is yet to be meaningfully used by the Supreme Court of Japan to set aside a law or ordinance that restricts free speech rights. So too the means-end analysis by failing to take into account alternatives that are less intrusive on the free speech right handicaps the challenge to the means utilized by the government.

The Supreme Court's excessive deference to the Diet in the Free Speech and Assembly area leaves little room for the Constitutional mandate of free expression. Even speech of the most public nature—speech by or about political candidates—is severely restricted during the most relevant time period—the time of political campaigning just before an election.

Japan has numerous private newspapers and TV stations that carry the news and make their own editorial decisions. The media is not reticent about revealing corruption, objecting to government policy or expressing its views freely. Japan's libel laws are much more protective of personal reputation, even reputation of public figures and politicians, than is United States law and such figures can and do obtain libel judgments against the press from time to time.

Libel protects reputation but celebrities not only have a reputation to protect but a personal right to use their name, image and/or voice to publicize products. Those who use the publicity rights of a celebrity without first obtaining permission are free riding on the personality of the celebrity. In early 2012 the Supreme Court of Japan recognized a "right of publicity" for commercial uses belonging to the celebrity that required consent before it could be used by third parties —newsworthy events may be reported on by the press outside the right of publicity and the right of publicity does not prohibit a magazine from publishing photos of celebrities when the photos are not used for the commercial purposes set out by the court.[70] This right is similar to the "right of

68. For a discussion of how this circular reasoning affected the free speech and assembly as well as the due process arguments raised in the *Narita Airport Case* discussed *infra* see, P.A. Jones, *Narita Airport and the Japanese Constitution: A Case Study*, 24 L. Japan 39, 54–56 (1991).
69. David S. Law, *Generic Constitutional Law*, 89 Minnesota L. Rev. 652, 697–698 (2005).
70. *Right of Publicity not Violated by Magazine article that Explains a Weight Loss Program and includes Photos of Celebrities (Pink Lady Case)*, Case No. 2009 (Ju) No.2056, Minshu Vol.66, No.2, http://www.courts.go.jp/english/judgments/text/2012.02.02-2009.-Ju-.No.2056.html

privacy" that some State courts and legislatures have used in the United States to protect the right of famous people to the commercial use of their likeness.

Japan's inability or unwillingness to face directly the actions of its military during the Second World War has led to disputes about censorship in Japan—especially censorship of history textbooks and at least one case concerning whether the government owned TV station (NHK) bowed to political pressure and used its editorial rights to edit out parts of a documentary that were uncomplimentary of the prior Emperor and Japan's military during the war. And, government unwillingness to directly confront policies that may be required but are likely not pleasant to the general population has sometimes led the government to hide events from the public—even to the point of punishing reporters who obtain access to secret agreements and report about them in the press.[71]

[A] Political Speech

While its judicial decisions give lip service to the necessity to protect freedom of expression as a basic right to citizens in a Constitutional democracy, some critics have complained that the test used by the court is so obliging to government that in reality freedom of expression has not been protected.[72] Moreover, the full right to free speech is not given to non-citizens resident in Japan, including ethnic Koreans and Formosans who lost their Japanese citizenship at the end of the Pacific War. [In the United States resident aliens are also denied the full expanse of free speech rights allowed a citizen in the election context. Thus, the First Amendment rights that permit unlimited corporate or labor union spending in support of candidates upheld in the *Citizens United* case are not applicable to non-citizens, presumably including non-citizen corporations.[73]] For example, the Referendum Law that provides the framework for a potential vote on changes in the Japanese Constitution not only limits voting on such amendments to Japanese citizens but it also prohibits special permanent resident aliens (i.e., such ethnic Koreans and Formosans) from speaking freely about their opposition or support of the Referendum. While resident aliens may not have a right to vote on changes in the Constitution, they may well be affected by changes in the Basic Law and

---

(P.B., Feb. 2, 2012). *Decision seen curbing use of celebrities' images without OK*, Daily Yomiuri on Line (Feb. 11, 2012), http://www.yomiuri.co.jp/dy/national/T120210005845.htm.

71. For a general discussion of Freedom of Expression in Japan see, A. Mark Weisburd, *Comparative Human Rights Law (Vol. 1)* 25–27(Carolina Academic Press 2008); Krotoszynski, *The First Amendment in Cross-Cultural Prospective* 139–182 (New York University Press 2006); Beer, *Freedom of Expression in Japan* (Kodansha International Ltd. 1984); Beer, *Constitutional Revolution in Japanese Law, Society and Politics*, 16 Modern Asian Stud. 33 (1982); Beer, *Freedom of Expression: The Continuing Revolution*, 53 L. & Contemp. Probs. 39 (1990); Shigenori Matsui, *Freedom of Expression in Japan*, 38 Osaka U. L. Rev. 13 (1990).
72. Akiko Ejima, *Enigmatic Attitude of the Supreme court of Japan Towards Foreign Precedents–Refusal at the Front Door Admission at the Back Door* 15, http://www.juridicas.unam.mx/wccl/ponencias/12/200.pdf (2010) (workshop paper, World Congress of the International Association of International Law) updating article in 16 Meiji Law Journal (2009)), last accessed Sept. 15, 2012; David Beatty, *Protecting Constitutional Rights in Japan and Canada*, 41 Am. J. Comp. L. 535, 546 (1993).
73. See, *Bluman v. Federal Election Commission* (No. 11-275, Jan. 9, 2012, Summary Disposition).

should have the right to make their concerns known both to politicians considering a change in the Constitution and Japanese citizen voters who are voting in a referendum about whether to change the Constitution. So too Japanese citizens who are civil servants and school teachers are not permitted a full free speech right in connection with the Referendum, should one be held. Finally, although the Supreme Court has indicated that foreign nationals lawfully in Japan have a right to freely express their views, the Court has also held that as foreign nationals have no "right" to enter Japan the government can deny such residents a re-entry visa or an extension of their visa based on their exercise of their free speech rights.[74]

[1] Demonstrations, Assembly and Communications by Citizens

In the *Tokyo Metropolitan Public Safety Ordinance* case of 1960[75] the Supreme Court upheld the Constitutionality of an ordinance that required government (Police) approval of the holding of a political rally.

Unlike an earlier ordinance upheld by the Court[76] the Tokyo Ordinance did not require that the municipality make a decision as to whether to permit the mass demonstration prior to the date of the demonstration or failing to so act the demonstration would be deemed acceptable. The Supreme Court had no difficulty with the provisions of the ordinance that granted wide discretion to the police authorities in determining whether or not to grant permission although it found that permission should not unreasonably be withheld. The Supreme Court reaffirmed its decision in the *Kyoto City Ordinance* case[77]. Neither the Tokyo Ordinance nor the Kyoto Ordinance provided for judicial review of a negative determination by the government authority prohibiting the demonstration/march.

Unlike the Supreme Court of the United States there was no searching inquiry as to whether such a demonstration created a clear and present danger of rioting or whether what was involved was solely advocacy. And unlike the Supreme Court of the United States there was no consideration of whether the Ordinances were directed at content restrictions on speech. Notification is not unreasonable when the public way is involved—after all the public does have the right to reasonably use the public way and should at a minimum be notified that traffic will be halted for a period of time—but the Court's easy assumption that public safety was imperiled because marches *could*

74. *McLean Visa Case, McLean v. Minister of Justice*, Case No. 1975 (Gyo-Tsu) No. 120 http://www.courts.go.jp/english/judgments/text/1978.10.04-1975-Gyo-Tsu-No.120.html (G.B. Oct. 4, 1978).
75. *Tokyo Metropolitan Public Safety Ordinance case*, Case No. 1960 (A) 112, http://www.courts.go.jp/english/judgments/text/1960.07.20-1960-A-No.112.html (G.B., July 20, 1960).
76. *Niigata Public Safety Ordinance case*, 8 Keishu 1866 (G.B., Nov. 24, 1954).
77. *Kyoto City Ordinance case*, Case No. 1965 (A) No. 1187, 23 Keishu No. 12, at 1625 http://www.courts.go.jp/english/judgments/text/1969.12.24-1965.-A-.No..1187.html (G.B., Dec. 24, 1969).

degenerate into riot is questionable at best. Neither the Tokyo nor Kyoto Ordinance was a notification scheme. Both clearly call for a permit before assembly can be had.[78]

In 1953 the Supreme Court dismissed on mootness grounds a lower court decision upholding the government's decision to forbid a labor union May Day gathering outside the Emperor's palace on the grounds that it might disturb the garden outside the palace. The matter was considered moot since the date for the meeting had passed. Nonetheless in dicta the Court indicated that the refusal was Constitutional as the normal use of a garden was not for political gatherings.[79]

It is reported that the Supreme Court of Japan has never found a statute, ordinance or local law unconstitutional because it violates free speech principles.[80] Notwithstanding the permit requirement laws and the various cases upholding such laws the reality on the ground is that in recent times permits are hardly ever denied and that in fact Japanese demonstrate quite freely and frequently.[81] The Fukushima Nuclear Disaster and the government's plans to allow nuclear reactors back on line brought forth huge rallies on a regular basis in Tokyo.[82] Still, the permissive attitude toward permit regulations and the wide authority they give public officials to make freedom of speech and assembly determinations sets the framework for other restrictions on communication rights (such as political campaigning rights) as well as the right to assemble for purposes of expression. And, the assembly permit requirement has been used to stifle freedom of expression as recently as in the twenty-first Century. The Supreme Court upheld a criminal conviction for violation of an assembly permit when members of a motorcycle gang, without a permit, congregated in a public square wearing their motorcycle regalia and refused to disburse when requested by the authorities. The vague nature of the ordinance they were in conflict with was waived aside by the Court because they had been warned to disburse and thus there was no confusion as to the Ordinance's inclusion of them. (The idea that the administrative officials might have misread the Ordinance was not entertained by the Court). And the asserted violation of Article 21 of the Constitution was set aside because of the fear that motorcycle gangs raised among the general public. Balancing this fear against the Constitutional challenge the Court found the regulation to be reasonable.[83]

78. For a critical discussion of the Niigata and Tokyo Ordinance cases concluding that the determination would be different in the United States see, Ronald J. Krotoszynski, Jr., *The First Amendment in Cross-Cultural Perspective* 148–151 (New York University Press 2006).
79. Shigenori Matsui, *Freedom of Expression in Japan*, 38 Osaka University Law Review 13, 36 (1991).
80. Shigenori Matsui, *The Constitution of Japan* 210 (Hart Publishing 2011); Matthew J. Wilson, *E-Elections: Time for Japan to Embrace on line Campaigning*, Stan. Tech. L. Rev. 4, 22–23 (2011), http://stlr.stanford.edu/pdf/wilson-e-elections.pdf, last accessed Sept. 15, 2012.
81. E.g., Beer, *Freedom of Expression: The Continuing Revolution*, 53 L. & Contemp. Probs. 39, 48 (1990).
82. Setsuko Kamiya & Mizuho Aoki, Antinuke *demonstrators form human chain around Diet building, Ordinary citizens by the thousands join activists in protest rally*, Japan Times (July 30, 2012), http://www.japantimes.co.jp/text/nn20120730a1.html.
83. *Hiroshima Motorcycle Ordinance Case*, Case No. 1819(A) of 2005, 61 Keishu No. 6 http://www.courts.go.jp/english/judgments/text/2007.09.18-2005.-A-.No..1819.html (P.B., Sept. 18, 2007).

Although not a permit case as such, the Supreme Court's decision (*Narita Airport Case*) upholding a law designed to protect Narita Airport by preventing meetings at property close to the airport, bears similarities to the Permit cases.[84] As in the *Tokyo Ordinance case* the Court started its opinion with great respect for freedom of assembly and speech but quickly qualified that respect by noting that these freedoms can be subjected to restrictions in the interest of public welfare. In the case of the airport the welfare appeared to be the need to enlarge the airport so that greater use of the facility could be made by international air carriers.[85] The Court asserted that it balanced the right of freedom of assembly against the need and extent of the restriction. However a close reading shows that what was really being balanced was the restriction on assembly versus the desire of potentially violent and destructive activists to meet near the airport. In such a contest the interests of the presumably violent had to succumb. The Court did not take into account the fact that the so-called violent activists had been neither charged nor convicted of a crime nor that the police could assure that the assembly did not degenerate into violence.

Apparently concerned that its activity could on close analysis be seen to be a disregard for Freedom of Assembly the court rewrote the statute limiting assembly near the airport. It modified the definition of a violent activist by changing it from one who is "suspected" of engaging in violent activity to one who is highly likely to engage in such activity; redefined the meeting place from a structure suspected of being used for a meeting of such activists to a structure where it is highly likely that it will be used by such activists. But it provided no means for measuring whether such determinations by the government authorities were accurate and it found that due process could also be limited in administrative determinations such as this and accordingly no due process need be given.

In the *Narita Airport* case, as in the *Tokyo and Kyoto Ordinance* cases the Court allowed freedom of speech and assembly to be restricted based on an administrative determination made without transparency and neither subjected to prior or post hoc due process challenge.[86]

Japan has an excellent postal service that delivers mail on a regular basis to mail boxes all over the country. These mail boxes also receive various forms of advertisements, particularly advertisements from eating and other entertainment establishments. In litigation challenging the applicability of criminal trespass laws to placing antiwar pamphlets in mail boxes in buildings that were not in a separate compound and were not protected from "intruders" by gates or other obstructions but were owned

84. *Narita Airport* case, *Sanrizuka-Shibayama Anti-airport League*, Case No. 1986 (Gyo-Tsu) No. 11, http://www.courts.go.jp/english/judgments/text/1992.07.01-1986-Gyo-Tsu-No.11-163553.html (G.B. July 1, 1992).

85. The court attempts to make a public welfare case beyond economics by referring to the safety of passengers–although from the text of the decision it appears that what was really at stake was the continued operation of the airport.

86. *Narita Airport* case, *Sanrizuka-Shibayama Anti-airport League*, Case No. 1986 (Gyo-Tsu) No. 11 (G.B. July 1, 1992) The parties did eventually get a hearing on their challenge to the law (but not the determination of the Minister of Transportation) but that hearing was concluded some six years after the meetings were to be held. For a discussion of the *Narita Airport case* see, P.A. Jones, *Narita Airport and the Japanese Constitution: A Case Study*, 24 L. Japan 39 (1991).

by the Self Defense Forces and housed SDF members, no permits to deliver such materials were requested or required by law. The Tokyo District Court refused to find the defendants guilty but the High Court overturned the decision. On appeal the Supreme Court upheld the High Court finding that the mailboxes were in private property and that the tenants objected to such literature.[87] Although recognizing the free speech aspects of the delivery of such pamphlets the Court found that the right to free speech could be restricted when it violated the rights of others.[88]

[2] Electioneering in General

Japan's election law[89] is one of the most restrictive among democratic countries.[90] It dates back to pre-war times and has its roots firmly planted in the universal franchise (for men) adopted in 1925 (the same year as the Peace Preservation Law that contained provisions severely limiting freedom of speech and assembly).[91] The Occupation made few changes in the law, mostly to open up the ranks of the electorate to include women and to lower the voting age. Post-war changes to the law retained restrictions placed on campaign speech that individual candidates are subject to but which the parties are not subject to. The most far-reaching amendment was the introduction of single-seat election districts alongside proportional representation election seats in 1994.[92]

The law contains regulations as to what type of campaigning is permitted by candidates and political parties and restricts campaigning by ordinary citizen voters including regulations on the time allowed for an election campaign, delivery of campaign literature, posting of election materials, prohibition of door-to-door canvassing, restrictions on individual candidate's purchase of on-air and print advertising, delivery of campaign materials to eligible voters, prohibition against grass roots campaigning on behalf of a candidate, etc.[93] Besides leading to rather sterile election

87. *Mail Delivery Free Speech Case,* Case No. 2008 (A) No. 13, 63 Keishu, No. 9, http://www.courts.go.jp/english/judgments/text/2009.11.30-2008.-A-.No..13.html (P.B. Nov. 30, 2009).
88. David McNeill, Tachikawa, *Three Claim ruling marks crisis for Japan and its democracy*, Japan Times (May 20, 2008), http://search.japantimes.co.jp/cgi-bin/fl20080520zg.html; discussed in Daniel Dolan, *Cultural Noise: Amplified Sound, Freedom of Expression and Privacy Rights in Japan*, 2 Intl. J. Commun. 662, 665 (2008). See also David McNeill, *Chipping Away at Constitutional Freedoms*, Japan Times (Jan. 24, 2010), http://search.japantimes.co.jp/cgi-bin/fl20100124x5.html.
89. Public Officials Election Act, Law No. 100 (1950) as amended.
90. For a discussion of the limitations in the election law see, Shigenori Matsui, *The Constitution of Japan* 51, 53–54 (Hart Publishing 2011); Shigenori Matsui, *The Political Participation and the Election Process in Japan*, http://www.juridicas.unam.mx/wccl/ponencias/1/27.pdf;. See also, Zenichiro Kono, *Essay and Opinion: Citizens Have Right to Freely Campaign in Elections, Japan Institute of Constitutional Law*, (2008), http://www.jicl.jp/english/related/backnumber/20080512.html, last accessed Sept. 15, 12.
91. See, E.g., Kazuhiro Hayashida, *Development of Election Law in Japan* 38–39, Kyushu University Journal of Law and Politics (1967), https://qir.kyushu-u.ac.jp/dspace/bitstream/2324/1546/4/KJ00000742797-00001.pdf, last accessed Sept. 15, 2012.
92. This change was made by the Hosokawa Administration during the short interregnum when the LDP was out of power.
93. Masahiro Usaki, *Restrictions on Political Campaigns in Japan*, 53 L. & Contemp. Probs. 133 (1990).

campaigns in Japan[94] the law's effect is to limit the content of and nature of communications that both politicians and voters may make concerning elections.[95] Moreover, the effect of the restrictive provisions of the law are to enhance the power of political parties as organizations, to limit the rights of members of the Diet (those elected under the proportional representation portion of the election process cannot leave the party under whose wing they were elected to join an existing party, but may leave to form their own party[96]) and to foster a system of handing political power from one generation to another since the family name is well known and the restrictions on electoral speech make it difficult for a new candidate to become well known.[97] Particularly striking is the fact that in the technologically sophisticated world Japanese citizens live in and the high degree of technological sophistication in Japan, the law does not allow for use of modern mediums of communications for politicians to reach voters during the election campaign period.[98]

The Supreme Court of Japan has consistently found that as the purpose of the law is to run clean and equally fair elections the law is Constitutional. More recently when it has been clear that recent changes have substantially benefited party candidates for single-seat districts in competition with independent candidates, the Court has adopted a rationale that permits such advantage through finding that such unequal treatment makes for more policy oriented and party centered politics—a matter that is within the discretion of the Diet and while this results in different treatment for independents that difference is based on "reasonable" grounds, i.e., policy orientation and party centered politics[99] and has upheld the disadvantage meted out to independent candidates.[100]

This asserted purpose (asserted because an historic view of the election law will disclose that the pre-war government adopted the law for the purpose of restricting speech by politicians and parties opposed to the government rather than to have clean

94. See, Alex Klein, *The Puzzle of Ineffective Election Campaigning in Japan*, 12 Japanese J. Pol. Sci. 57, 59 (2011).
95. For a discussion of the provisions of Japan's election laws and the effect of restrictions on public participation in the electoral process see, Takaaki Ohta, *Fairness versus Freedom: Constitutional Implications of Internet Electioneering for Japan*, 11 Soc. Sci. Japan J. 99 (2008).
96. Some have questioned the Constitutionality of this provision (Shigenori Matsui, *The Constitution of Japan*, 55 (Hart Publishing 2011) but considering the deference shown to the Diet when the election law is concerned it is highly unlikely that a challenge would be sustained.
97. The passing of political seats from one generation to the next is reminiscent of feudal systems where children followed their parents in line of work. One of the 3 basic principles of the Occupation was to do away with all vestiges of Japanese feudalism.
98. See, Matthew J. Wilson, E-*Elections: Time for Japan to Embrace on line Campaigning*, Stan. Tech. L. Rev. 4 (2011) http://stlr.stanford.edu/pdf/wilson-e-elections.pdf.; see also, Wilson, Essay, *e-elections: Law in Asia & Online Political Activities*, 12 Wyoming L. Rev. 237 (2012).
99. *Lower House Election Case*, Case No. 2010 (Gyo-Tsu) No. 207, Minshu Vol. 65, No. 2, http://www.courts.go.jp/english/judgments/text/2011.03.23-2010.-Gyo-Tsu-.No..207.html (G.B., Feb. 23, 2011).
100. *Small Constituency Case*, Case, Case No. 1999 (Gyo-Tsu) No.35, Minshu Vol.53, No.8, at 1704, http://www.courts.go.jp/english/judgments/text/1999.11.10-1999.-Gyo-Tsu-.No.35.html, Nov. 10, 1999, affirmed, *Small Constituency Case*, Case No. 2006 (Gyo-Tsu) No.176, Minshu Vol.61, No.4, http://www.courts.go.jp/english/judgments/text/2007.06.13-2006.-Gyo-Tsu-.No.176.html, June 13, 2007. (Dissenting Justices Kawai, Endo, Fukuda, Motohara and Kajitanii noted several ways in which non-party candidates were disadvantaged in elections.)

or fair elections[101]) is diametrically opposed to the United States doctrine under which laws granting financial support to candidates to "equal the playing the field" have been struck down as restrictions on the free speech rights of the candidate with more money as well as the free speech rights of those who wish to contribute to a candidate.[102]

The Supreme Court of Japan has held that the hiring of personnel by a labor union to man phone banks seeking support for a candidate for election to the Diet during the election period constitutes a violation of the Public Officers Election Law.[103] So too, when a small newspaper put out a special election edition with comments that were critical of a candidate and was charged with a violation of the Public Office Election Law, the Court upheld its conviction finding that the legislation that prohibited "information or comment" on a candidate during the election period that might reasonably affect who the public voted for and thus might aid or hurt candidates[104] was Constitutional. On the other hand, it has long been recognized that corporations in Japan may make political contributions as such contributions are socially acceptable and are consistent with the corporation being a good corporate citizen.[105]

Similarly, in dismissing an appeal by a company executive who had invited a candidate to a meeting with company employees the Court made no searching inquiry as to whether the provision of the law impeded free speech or assembly. Instead it noted that the purpose of the law was reasonable, ergo the law was Constitutional.[106] The Court has even gone so far as to permit the government owned national television station to delete portions of a political broadcast made for influencing voters because of the station's conclusion that the words deleted while not obscene were offensive to some voters.[107] Of course, a television station has a right to refuse to broadcast a political advertisement because it disagrees with the position of the candidate or the

101. See, e.g., Louis D. Hayes, *Introduction to Japanese Politics* 124 (5th ed., M.E. Sharpe 2009).
102. See, *Davis v. Federal Election Comm'n*, 554 U. S. 724 (2008) striking down the so-called "Millionaires Amendment" to the Bipartisan Campaign Reform Act of 2002; *Arizona Free Enterprise Club's Freedom Club PAC v. Bennett*, 564 U.S. ___ (2011) (striking down Arizona's matching fund election legislation which was designed in part to level the playing field between candidates. ("Leveling the playing field" can sound like a good thing. But in a democracy, campaigning for office is not a game. It is a critically important form of speech.")
103. *Labor Union Campaign Activity During Campaign Period Violates Public Election Law Case*, Case No. 2004(A)No. 2031, 58 Keishu Vol. 9, http://www.courts.go.jp/english/judgments/text/2004.12.21-2004-A-No..2031.html (P.B., Dec. 21, 2004).
104. *Nonaka v. Japan*, 33 Keishu 7 (Sup. Ct. Petty Bench, Dec. 20, 1979). Japan's restrictions on independent campaign expenditures is directly the opposite of United States doctrine. *Arizona Free Enterprise Club's Freedom Club PAC v. Bennett*, 564 U.S. ___ (2011).
105. *Arita v. Kojima, The Yawata Steel Political Contribution Case*, Case No. 444 (O) of 1966, Supreme Court of Japan June 24, 1970. An English language translation may be found in Lawrence Beer & Hiroshi Itoh, *The Constitutioonal Case Law of Japan, 1970 through 1990* at 406 (University of Washington Press 1996). It is *ultra vires* for an association of licensed tax accountants to make political contributions, *Political Contributions by Accountants Ultra Vires Case*, Case No. 1992 (O) No.1796, http://www.courts.go.jp/english/judgments/text/1996.3.19-1992.-O-.No.1796.html (P.B., Mar. 19, 1996).
106. *Company Cannot Invite Political Figure to Speak During Campaign Period Case*, Case No. 1996(Gyo-Tsu) No.193, 51 Minshu No. 3 at 1453, http://www.courts.go.jp/english/judgments/text/1997.3.13-1996-Gyo-Tsu-.No.193-195652.html (P.B., Mar. 13, 1997).
107. *NHK Censorship* case, Case No. 1986 (0) No. 800, http://www.courts.go.jp/english/judgments/text/1990.4.17-1986.-0-.No..800.html (P.B. Apr. 17, 1990).

language used and indeed derogatory language can be prohibited by the station but in Japan political advertising is forbidden during the campaign period so the only way to reach the television audience is through the few short expositions permitted on the government owned national television station. Considering that candidates have such limited opportunity to reach their audience during the relevant time frame the action of the station (owned by the government) had a prior restraint effect and surely was not the least restrictive means for protecting a reasonable restriction on speech. Finally, the Court's conclusion that no censorship was implicated as the opinion of the government (to delete the language) was not "binding" on the government owned station is subject to question. Concurring Justice Sonobe noted the importance of the NHK broadcast as this was the sole opportunity the candidate had to directly communicate with voters via television. He noted that the deletion constituted a prior restraint on speech. In Justice Sonobe's opinion neither the government nor NHK had editorial right to engage in a prior restraint on the candidate's speech. NHK's role should, in his view, be limited to simply carrying the speech without any editorial control.

As recognition of the value of the Internet to voters, the Japanese government has determined that in elections held from 2012 forward The Internal Affairs and Communications Ministry will post on the internet candidate profiles that will include the picture of the candidate, some biographical information and campaign promises.[108] It is not yet clear as to what input candidates will have in the compilation of the profile.

Japan's restrictions on Free Speech during election campaigns have drawn international criticism.[109]

[3] Door-to-Door Canvassing

Closely aligned to the permit cases are the cases that prohibit free speech in political campaigns by such means as door-to-door solicitation and the posting of political signs and delivery of political literature during an election campaign.

The Supreme Court of Japan has uniformly upheld the prohibition of such direct campaign practices by finding that it was rational or reasonable to prohibit them. In the *Takatsu Canvassing Ban* case,[110] the Court acknowledged that such restriction could work a limit on free speech. Apparently the restriction on free speech brought about by the canvassing ban does not make the ban unreasonable.[111]

108. Online Profiles to be Allowed from Next election, The Yomiuri Shimbun (Apr. 6, 2012), http://www.yomiuri.co.jp/dy/national/T120405005577.htm. It is not yet clear as to what input candidates will have in the compilation of the profile.
109. See, Report of the Human Rights Committee, Volume I Ninety-fourth session (October 13–31, 2008) Ninety-fifth session (March 16 –April 3, 2009)Ninety-sixth session (July 13–31, 2009), http://www.ccprcentre.org/doc/ICCPR/AR/A_64_40(Vol%20I)_Eng.pdf, last accessed Sept. 15, 2012.
110. *Takatsu Canvassing Ban case*, 35 Keishu 5 at 568 (1981). An English language translation of Justice Ito's concurring opinion may be found in Beer & Itoh, *The Constitutional Case Law of Japan, 1970 through 1990*, 598 (University of Washington Press 1996).
111. For a critical analysis of the canvassing ban cases see, Masahiro Usaki, *Restrictions on Political Campaigns in Japan*, 53 L. & Contemp. Probs. 133, 139–143 (1990); Takaaki Ohta, *Fairness versus Freedom: Constitutional Implications of Internet Electioneering for Japan*, 11 Soc. Sci. Japan J. 99 (2008).

[B] Other Speech

[1] Mass Media

Japan has a large and active mass media distribution system. Daily newspapers run the political gamut from liberal to conservative and farther at each end. Japan has both national and local, public and private, TV and Radio outlets that provide news to the public. Satellite TV allows those who wish access to foreign broadcasts such as CNN, BBC and other outlets (French, German, etc.) both in Japanese and the native language of the original broadcast. There is no shortage of news. That does not mean that there is no constraint on news gathering and the presentation of views.

Japan's system of reporters press clubs allows members of the club to obtain news first hand from various government and political party sources. The system provides a free flow of information that the government wishes to get out to the public to club members—but membership is not "wide open" to foreign or domestic media such as alternative or Internet media. The system raises significant question as to whether the Japanese press club system has the effect of tilting the playing field with the press in favor of the government's position on issues.[112] The DPJ loosened to some extent access to briefings so that non-press club members could attend but membership in the clubs remains an indispensable element for a main line press organization.

Press club members share certain "ethical" standards and understandings regarding proper protocol for reporting events.[113] These standards are "enforced" by the need of press club reporters to curry favor with officials so that they are included in press announcements.[114] A system of "voluntary censorship" surrounds the clubs[115] and has the effect of limiting news coverage by the major media players in Japan.[116] Revelations concerning the Tokyo Electric Power Company's handling and reporting of information concerning the nuclear catastrophe that followed the March 11, 2011 Great East Japan Earthquake and Tsunami disclosed the "self-censoring" nature of Press Club press conferences attended almost exclusively by press club members who are beholden to the subjects of the news conferences.[117] NHK is the government owned broadcasting

112. *Judicial Allergy to Appeals, Sentaku Magazine*, Japan Times (Feb. 28, 2011), http://search.japantimes.co.jp/cgi-bin/eo20110228a1.html suggesting that reporting about court decisions may be affected by the press club system and its potential for co-opting reporters.
113. Declan Hayes, *The Japanese Disease: Sex and Slease in Modern Japan* 295–297 (2005).
114. For a discussion of the limiting nature of news reporting and the role of press clubs in such limitations see, Louis D. Hayes, *Introduction to Japanese Politics* 125–127 (5th ed., M.E. Sharpe 2009).
115. See, Beer & Maki, *From Imperial Myth to Democracy* 136 (University Press of Colorado 2002).
116. See, Laurie Freeman, *Japan's Press Clubs as Information Cartels*, Japan Policy Research Institute Working paper 18 (1996), http://www.jpri.org/publications/workingpapers/wp18.html;*Restrictive Self-censorship in Japan's Press Club System*, Center for International Media Ethics (Mar. 10, 2010), http://www.ammado.com/nonprofit/111249/articles/14027; *Let the Rising Sunshine In*, The Economist (Sept. 24, 2009), http://www.economist.com/node/14505541?story_id=14505541; Kanako Takahara, *Press Clubs, Exclusive Access to, Pipelines for info*, Japan Times (Jan. 30, 2007), http://search.japantimes.co.jp/cgi-bin/nn20070130i1.html.
117. See, Kanako Takahara, *Tight-Lipped TEPCO Lays Bare Exclusivity of Press clubs*, Japan Times (May 3, 2011), http://search.japantimes.co.jp/cgi-bin/nn20110503f1.html.

system and while its management is supposed to be separated from government and not be influenced by government policies and views there are times when the separation has broken down. NHK broadcast a documentary program concerning certain matters relating to the Second World War. The original documentary cast the former Emperor and certain aspects of the Military during the war in a less than favorable light. After meeting with Cabinet officials from the more conservative wing of the then ruling LDP the company determined to edit out the most objected to material. The Supreme Court held that the station had editorial right to modify what it would show. But the issue of whether there had been political pressure or influence on the government owned station remained unresolved.[118]

NHK has at times sought and acted in conformity with administrative guidance. The Supreme Court found that as NHK was free to either follow or decline to follow such guidance there was no "administrative action" that was subject to judicial review. Since there was no administrative action that compelled the deletion of the terms as to which guidance was sought (and apparently followed) there was no censorship.[119] (See Chapter 17 for a discussion of Guidance).

The Supreme Court of Japan has recognized a qualified news reporter's privilege to hold the identity of a source confidential in civil cases. The privilege is subject to a balancing test involving whether the news report concerns matters of public interest and concern; whether a fair trial could be had without disclosure of the source; whether the source refused to consent to disclosure and whether the means of information gathering were in conformity with the criminal laws and standards of good conduct recognized in Japan. In the case before the Court the reporter was allowed to refuse to identify the source.[120] Of particular significance was the Court's finding that the Constitutional right of free speech as set out in Article 21 of the Constitution extended beyond simply reporting the news and included means of gathering the news.

This case was followed in early 2011 by a High Court ruling that a reporter need not produce the audio tape of his interview with a government source in a libel case (*News Reporter's Privilege Case, High Court Osaka, 2011*). The reporter refused to produce the entire interview, arguing that disclosure of the entire interview would result in disclosure of the source that had been promised confidentiality, but did submit portions of the interview. The High Court in Osaka reversed the Kobe District Court

118. NHK Censorship ruling reversed, Japanese Law Blog, http://japaneselaw.blogspot.com/2008/06/nhk-censorship-ruling-reversed.html (June 14, 2008) (NHK Self-Censorship Case); Eric Johnston, *NHK A Font of Info, a Lot of It From the Government*, Japan Times (July 7, 2009).

119. *NHK Censorship case,* Case No. 1986 (0) No. 800, http://www.courts.go.jp/english/judgments/text/1990.4.17-1986.-0-.No..800.html (P.B. Apr. 17, 1990).

120. *News Reporter's Privilege* case, Case No. 19 (Kyo) 2006, 60 Minshu No. 8, http://www.courts.go.jp/english/judgments/text/2006.10.03-2006.-Kyo-.No..19.html (P.B., Oct. 3, 2006). Previously the Supreme Court had upheld a decision of the Sapporo High Court that had allowed a reporter to refuse to identify sources in a civil case on the basis of an evidentiary privilege relating to trade or business (occupation) secrets. *Hokkaido Newsman's Privilege case, Sasaki v. The Hokkaido News, Inc.*, 956 Hanrei Jiho 32 (P.B., Mar. 6, 1980). An English Translation may be found in Beer & Itoh, *The Constitutional Case Law of Japan, 1970 Through 1990*, 567 (University of Washington Press 1996).

noting that a reporter's pledge of confidentiality was similar to a trade secret in so far as the source was concerned.[121]

Whether the privilege itself applies in criminal cases is unclear and if applicable the extent of the privilege may be different as the court would undoubtedly take into consideration the right of the public to have the guilty convicted and potentially the right of the accused to a fair trial and thus access to evidence that might acquit. In the *Hakata Railway Station* case[122] the Court did not explicitly say that newsgathering was protected by Article 21 of the Constitution but it did say that the freedom to gather news must be respected in light of Article 21. This respect, like freedoms directly covered by the Constitution is not absolute and in the specific case had to be balanced against the right to a fair trial. In making the relevant balancing the Court should also consider the nature and seriousness of the crime alleged, the need for the evidence and the effect that requiring production by a news outlet may have on future news gathering operations. In the end the Court ordered the films were available for evidence.[123]

[2] Defamation

Japan has both criminal and civil libel prohibitions. The same tests are used for civil libel as are used for criminal libel. Libel is made a crime when a person's reputation is damaged even if the statement made is true.[124] Although Japan's Penal Code does not provide that truth is a defense the courts have established a rule qualifying Article 230 when the press is the defendant and the party asserting libel is a public official or a candidate for public office or otherwise the matter is a matter dealing with the public interest. Comments about public officials and public figures are matters of public interest covered by the rule.[125] In such cases truth, taken together with lack of malice and publication for public interest purposes, provides a defense. The press need not establish truth, it is sufficient if the press establishes a reasonable belief that the matter

121. High Court Upholds Protecting Sources, Japan Times, Jan. 23, 2011, http://search.japantimes.co.jp/cgi-bin/nn20110123a5.html.
122. *Hakata Railway Station case, Kaneko v. Japan,* Case No. 1969(Shi)No.68, 23 Keishu 1490 (G.B., http://www.courts.go.jp/english/judgments/text/1969.11.26-1969-Shi-No.68.html (G.B., Nov. 26, 1969).
123. The films were not sought by the prosecutor but by students who had been involved with the events at the Railway station who wanted prosecution against the police to be pursued and wanted the films so that the events as well as the identity of the police involved could be determined.
124. Penal Code Article 230.
125. In *Gekkan Pen v. Japan,* 35 Keishu 34 (Sup. Ct. Petty Bench, Apr. 16, 1981) (an English language translation may be found in Itoh & Beer, *The Constituional Case Law Of Japan, 1970 Through 1990* (University of Washington Press 1996)) The Supreme Court applied the rule to a magazine article accusing the leader of a Buddhist group affiliated with one of Japan's political parties (Soka Gakkai) of a sexual affair. Although there was witness testimony to support the news article, the court below discounted the testimony on the basis of lack of reliability. On remand the trial court found that the magazine had committed libel because it could not establish that the accusations were true and there was no showing of reasonable grounds to believe them true.

reported was true.[126] What constitutes reasonable belief is a subjective judgment based on facts and the lack of stare decisis makes reliance on earlier court authorities dangerous.[127] The burden of proof on truth or reasonable belief as well as showing that the matter was of public concern is on the media defendant.[128]

Thus, when an author relied on a District Court conviction of the plaintiff in a libel suit in setting forth the facts of the case and after publication the High Court reversed the guilty verdict, the Court held that the author had not libeled the plaintiff. Even though the book containing the subsequently reversed facts was written while the case was on appeal, the Court found that the author had substantial reason to believe the facts set out in his book were true since he relied on the judgment of the District Court.[129] But when a small media company that was not a member of the press club at the Police Department relied on a national news service that had a good reputation and had been in business for almost 50 years the defendant was held liable when the information turned out to be false. The only issue before the Supreme Court was whether reliance by the media outlet was sufficient to establish reasonable belief in truth. The court held that it did not.[130] The Supreme Court appears not to have made any analysis of whether their decision would have the effect of chilling speech that is in the public interest. In the *Gekkan Pen* case, the Supreme Court had indicated that unless the publisher believes that the matter reported is true with certainty, reasonable belief in the truth of the material published does not exist. This raised the question of whether there exists a rule requiring the publisher to do its own research even if it receives information from a reliable source such as a main stream press club member reporting service. If so, the ruling would make it extremely difficult for non-press club publishers to compete with press club members and increases the power of press clubs to self-censor news.[131]

---

126. *Kochi v. Japan*, Case No. 1962 (O) No. 815, 20 Minshu No. 5 at 1118, http://www.courts.go.jp/english/judgments/text/1966.06.23-1962.-O-.No.815.htmlP.B., June 23, 1966).
127. When dealing with personal matters that are not matter of public interest truth is not a defense. Private matters that damage a person's reputation are subject to damage awards for defamation. Japan's defamation law draws no distinction between libel and slander.
128. *Gekkan Pen v. Japan*, 35 Keishu 34 (Sup. Ct. Petty Bench, Apr. 16, 1981) An English language translation may be found in Itoh & Beer, *The Constitutional Case Law of Japan, 1970 through 1990*, 637 (University of Washington Press 1996); Jeffrey A. Ourvan, *Damage Control: Why Japanese Courts Should Adopt a Regime of Larger Libel Awards*, 21 N.Y.L.Sch. J. Intl. & Comp. L. 307, 313(2002).
129. *Author Reliance on Lower Court Fact Finding not Libel*, Case No. 1997 (O) No.411, 53 Minshu No. 7, at 1313, http://www.courts.go.jp/english/judgments/text/1999.10.26-1997.-O-.No.411.html (P.B., Oct. 26, 1999).
130. *Reliance on News Service not Defense to Libel Case*, Case No. 1995(O)No.1421, 56 Minshu No.1, at 185, http://www.courts.go.jp/english/judgments/text/2002.1.29-1995-O-No.1421.html (P.B., Jan. 29, 2002). It may well be that the decision was influenced by the practice of some news outlets of manufacturing news and then feeding it to a press club which then disseminates it to other outlets. See, Jeffrey A. Ourvan, *Damage Control: Why Japanese Courts Should Adopt a Regime of Larger Libel Awards*, 21 N.Y.L.Sch. J. Int'l & Comp. L. 307, 320 (2002).
131. The issue of self-censorship was raised in the wake of Japan's nuclear tragedy at Fukushima following the 2011 earthquake and tsunami in the Tohoku region. Hiroko Nakata, *Freedom of Press Hurt by Nuclear Crisis: Group*, Japan Times (Jan 26, 2012), http://www.japantimes.co.jp/text/nn20120126x3.html. See also, Mari Yamaguchi, *Govt failed to keep records of key nuke*

The Supreme Court of Japan threw additional light on the question of reasonable reliance on news agency reports in its April 2011 decision involving an inaccurate newspaper report of a purported botched medical procedure. The report clearly damaged the reputation of the innocent doctor who sued several newspapers, all of whom had based their reporting on a report from a news gathering organization of which they were all members. The Court rejected the argument that while the news reporting agency might be able to show reasonable belief in truth the same did not apply to the newspapers that reported the story from the news service as the papers had done no research of their own. The papers could in fact rely on the news gathering service because the papers were themselves members of the service and were actively involved in the management of the service. In essence the Court found the news service to be the equivalent of a department of the paper designed to gather facts about stories and hence there was a continuous line from gathering facts to reporting that involved the papers themselves and thus the papers were entitled to the rely on the reasonableness of the reporting service. The Court appears to have validated the major papers' reliance on news services such as Kyodo news. This is clearly a victory for free press as it applies to major papers but leaves lesser papers, who are mere subscribers but not involved in management decisions or otherwise have the close relationship with the news service that major publications have, at risk.[132]

Japanese publishers may be subject to prior restraint injunctions issued by the judicial system to protect a person's privacy, reputation and/or honor—even when the subject of the article is a prominent politician and even when the article can be viewed as parody designed to highlight the publisher's objections to the former Mayor's running for election as Governor. In the *Hoppo Journal* case the Court was presented with a newspaper article concerning a politician running for election. The article attacked him brutally and clearly was designed to convey the paper's view that he should not be re-elected. Acting on an ex parte application for a "provisional disposition" (the Japanese equivalent of a preliminary injunction) the District Court had considered only the application and statements in support by the plaintiff and his representatives. There is no indication that any effort was made to notify the news organization of the injunction request or to seek the views of the paper. Reading the article literally (rather than as parody) the courts involved in the matter concluded that the harsh statements were false and were not made for the sole reason of promoting the public interest. It concluded that the statements were defamatory and outside of protection and since there was imminent threat to the plaintiff's reputation an injunction should issue.[133]

---

meetings, Associated Press (2012), http://www.google.com/hostednews/ap/article/ALeqM5jVUDDVhQ-gjvgjpBFvnN89OUehwQ?docId=bf58ca73a73d4cd990738d8f6e883532.

132. *Reliance on News Service is Defense to Libel Case*, Case No. 2009 (Ju) No. 2057, Minshu Vol. 65, No. 3 (P.B., Apr. 28, 2011), http://www.courts.go.jp/english/judgments/text/2011.04.28-2009.-Ju-.No..2057.html.

133. See also, *Shirakawa v. Amano*, Supreme Court 3/ 28/80, discussed in Sugiyama, Japanese Copyright Law Development at http://www.softic.or.jp/en/articles/fordham_sugiyama.html and by Roderick Seeman at http://www.japanlaw.info/lawletter/april83/bcn.htm as well as Teruo Doi, *Parody, Fair Use, and Moral Rights from the Japanese Perspective*, AIPPI Journal at 16 (Jan. 1999) etc. in which the author's *moral right* trumped parody use of a photograph and

While the Supreme Court recognized that prior restraint involved freedom of expression issues that were qualitatively different from damage awards granted after publication, its decision opened the door to prior restraints even when matters of public debate are implicated. To get a prior restraint the court established criteria that on analysis are no more stringent than for a post publication damage award.[134]

It would appear that the real reason for the injunction in the *Hoppo Journal* case was the lack of civility in the attack on the candidate for Governor, including an attack on personal as well as public matters. The harshness of the language went beyond Japanese norms of politeness.[135] In short the language was inconsistent with community standards as to proper means of debate and disagreement, although the Court does not say this in its opinion.[136] Perhaps this also explains why no effort appears to have been made to give the media an opportunity to contest the granting of the prior restraint injunction.[137]

Prior restraint is the essence of censorship and the Japanese Constitution specifically provides "No censorship shall be maintained". The Court has narrowed the definition of censorship to permit the Judiciary to grant prior restraints and to find administrative guidance not censorship.[138] The Court has concluded that since a book had been published abroad there was no "censorship" when Japanese customs officials

---

thus the photographer was entitled to damages for violation of the moral right. Professor Doi notes that this moral right is separate from the question of whether fair use trumped the original photographer's copyright claim. Indeed, Professor Doi notes that under the Old Copyright act there were separate claims and separate damages for violation of moral right and copyright. In either event the Freedom of Speech argument was not accepted by the Court either for moral right nor apparently as part of the quotation defense to copyright claim allowed by the Act.

134. *Hoppo Journal Case*, Case No. 1981 (O) No. 609, http://www.courts.go.jp/english/judgments/text/1986.06.11-1981-O-No.609.html (G.B. June 11, 1986).

135. There can be no explanation for exceeding norms of politeness and language and hence no hearing was required. For a discussion of speech norms in the context of on-line speech and criminal libel in Japan see, Salil Mehra, *Post a Message and go to Jail: Criminalizing Internet Libel in Japan and the United States*, 78 U. of Colorado L. Rev. 767 (2007).

136. In the field of defamation Japan has favored politeness and reputation over vigorous public debate. See, e.g., Krotoszynski, *Defamation in the Digital Age: Some Comparative Law Observations on the Difficulty of Reconciling Free Speech and Reputation in the Global Village*, 62 Wash. & Lee L. Rev. 339, 349 (2005).

137. Post publication restraint is also a remedy that can be sought in a libel suit. Thus the descendents of former Pacific War military commanders sought a libel judgment that would also have forbidden future publication and sale of a book of essays that quoted other works that asserted these commanders were at best implicated in ordering civilians on Okinawa to commit suicide during the Battle of Okinawa. The High Court denied the requested relief finding that the assertions were true. The Supreme Court in 2011 refused to reverse the High Court on procedural grounds. See, Kyodo News, "*Okinawa Notes" suit Favors Oe*, Japan Times (Apr. 23, 2011), http://search.japantimes.co.jp/cgi-bin/nn20110423b1.html.

138. Pre-War Japan had an extensive administrative machinery to censor written materials and censorship relied on publishers to determine, in the first instance, whether material was fit for publication. If it was later determined published material should have been prohibited, it was collected, further publication prohibited and the publisher punished. The system while providing for prior restraint actually allowed much banned material to be published. Jay Rubin, *Injurious to Public Morals: Writers and the Meiji State* (University of Washington Press 1984).

refused to allow it into Japan[139] and that the government had not engaged in censorship when it refused to approve a textbook unless certain deletions were made—the book could be published and hence was not censored (although why one would publish a textbook that could not be used in schools was not explained).[140] Similarly censorship is not involved when a private party such as an Internet Service Provider blocks the transmission of messages when it has received knowledge of a communication that is defamatory or otherwise barred (such as obscene).[141]

Prior restraint may also be judicially obtained when a publication concerns the personal life of an individual who is not a public figure and has not consented to the publication. In such a case, the court simply weighs the damage to the author versus the damage to the person whose story is being told. If the damage to the privacy interest of the subject is deemed weightier a prior restraint injunction can be obtained.[142] In a 2002 decision affirming an injunction prohibiting publication of a book that contained personal information about a character in the book the Court utilized a more lenient standard balancing the individual's right of privacy against the publisher's right to free expression.[143]

While a prior restraint order may be obtained to protect a person's privacy, privacy in the sense of the right to be left alone appears to have little weight when speech is forced upon the public, especially by ultra conservative groups. Such groups drive in caravan around major cities blaring out their message through loud speakers placed on vehicles prominently displaying their name and loyalty. Ordinary citizens in the streets cannot escape the loud noise and message.[144] Yet no effort is made to protect the "privacy" of such residents and other people.[145]

---

139. *Customs Office Censorship Case, Matsu v. Hakodate Customs Director*, 38 Minshu 12 at 1308), http://www.courts.go.jp/english/judgments/text/1984.12.12-1982-Gyo-Tsu-No.156-163203.html (G.B., Dec. 12, 84).
140. *Textbook Screening Case*, Case No. 1986 (O) No.1428, Minshu Vol.47, No.5, at 3483, http://www.courts.go.jp/english/judgments/text/1993.03.16-1986-O.-No.1428.html (P.B. Mar. 16, 1993).
141. Article 3, Law No. 137 of November 30, 2001, http://www.soumu.go.jp/main_sosiki/joho_tsusin/eng/Resources/laws/Compensation-Law.pdf. Article 4 gives the alleged damaged party a right to obtain identification of the sender from the ISP notwithstanding Article 21 of the Constitution provides that the secrecy of any means of communications shall not be violated.
142. Minoru Nakamura, *Privacy: Current Status and Pending Issues in Japan*, NRI Papers No. 131 (2008) at 7, http://www.nri.co.jp/english/opinion/papers/2008/pdf/np2008131.pdf.
143. *Supreme Court upholds ban on book*, Japan Times (Sept. 25, 2002), http://search.japantimes.co.jp/cgi-bin/nn20020925a1.html.
144. In the 2010 local election a British subject grabbed a microphone at a political rally and complained about the noise level. He was arrested for violation of the Public Officials Election Act, Law No. 100 (1950) as amended. Minoru Matsutani, *Brit Held in Campaign Noise Protest*, Japan Times (Apr. 26, 2011), http://search.japantimes.co.jp/cgi-bin/nn20110426a8.html.
145. For a discussion of this phenomenon see, Daniel Dolan, *Cultural Noise: Amplified Sound, Freedom of Expression and Privacy Rights in Japan*, 2 Intl. J. Commun. 662 (2008). The privacy of employees is protected so that employers cannot force them to attend meetings and listen to political speeches and messages. See, Hisashi Okuno, *Captive Audience Speeches in Japan: Freedom of Speech of* Employers v. Workers' Rights and Freedoms, 29 Comp. Lab. L. & Policy J. 129, 144–145 (2008). The United States is not free of similar problems. See, Masako Iwamoto Washington, *What do we Want? For you to Turn it Down a Little*, Washington Post C6 (Mar. 27, 2011) (complaining about the continuous noisy labor picketing of a hotel in his neighborhood and the effect of the noise on his way of life).

Lack of a clear definition of "privacy" and a clear understanding of who is a private as distinguished from public figure and therefore entitled to greater protection in a defamation or privacy dispute has resulted in numerous injunction and damage actions against newspapers.[146] While damages in such cases remain low by United States standards, they are much higher than just a few years ago.[147]

[3] Obscenity

Obscenity is not covered by the free speech provisions of the Constitution. The rejection of obscene materials at the border is not an act of censorship. The common sense of the society as interpreted through the norms of people of "good" sense and morals defines obscenity. In early decisions the Court found that even works that in their entirety have redeeming value and are recognized as works of art may be rejected and banned if there are obscene portions.[148] The redeeming nature or artistic character of the work may minimize the obscenity to a point where the work is acceptable.[149] The Court utilizes a balancing test that balances the value of the work against public morals and the welfare of society. Thus purely scientific works that contain photographs that might be deemed obscene in artistic works are not obscene. This leads to some unusual late night "medical" programs on television in modern Japan.

In 1980 the Court returned to obscenity and attempted to moderate its earlier opinions in the *Chatterley* and *de Sade* cases. The Court recognized that it was important to look at the work as a whole in deciding whether it was obscene. Factors such as the writing style of the allegedly obscene portions of the work as well as the proportion of the work devoted to such portions and intellectual and artistic aspects of the work plus the connection of the alleged obscene portions to the story being relayed should be considered. This has the effect of significantly moderating the earlier attempts at defining obscenity and the failure to recognize the artistic qualities of the work as a whole as bearing on the obscenity issue.[150]

It may be that the Court has recognized that the norms of society have evolved from the very modest standard it set in the late part of the twentieth Century.[151] The

146. In addition to monetary damages Japan, consistent with some European countries, may require an apology in some cases of defamation. Such rule was unsuccessfully challenged as a violation of the freedom of conscience clause of the Constitution. Perhaps because of the low damages awards available in defamation cases and the ubiquitous nature of the Internet and the potential for "private" defamation over the Internet Japan has seen a rise in criminal defamation cases in recent years. Salil Mehra, *Post a Message and go to Jail: Criminalizing Internet Libel in Japan and the United States*, 78 U. of Colorado L. Rev. 767 (2007).

147. Declan Hayes, *The Japanese Disease: Sex and Slease in Modern Japan* 291–295 (2005).

148. *Lady Chatterley's Lover Case, Koyama v. Japan*, No.1953 (A) 1713, 11 Keishu (No. 3) 997, http://www.courts.go.jp/english/judgments/text/1957.03.13-1953-A-No.1713-112004.html (G.B. Mar. 13, 1957).

149. *Marquis de Sade Case, Ishii v. Japan*, 23 Keishu (No. 10) 1239 (Sup. Ct. G.B. Oct. 15, 1969).

150. *Sato* et al. *v. Japan*, 34 Keishu 433 (Sup. Ct., 2d P. B., Nov. 28, 1980), an English language translation may be found in Lawrence Beer & Hiroshi Itoh, *The Constitutional Case Law of Japan, 1970 through 1990*, 637 (University of Washington Press 1996).

151. For a comparative discussion of U.S. and Japanese obscenity approaches prior to the Supreme Court of Japan's recent *Mapplethorpe* decision discussed *infra*, see, Robert Trager & Yuri Obata,

Supreme Court's most recent foray into the obscenity area resulted in its finding that photographs of nude males, even photographs that contained close ups of male genitalia, were not obscene. The *Mapplethorpe Photographs Case*[152] involved the bringing into Japan a book of Mapplethorpe photographs. The issue before the Supreme Court was whether the book was obscene and thus subject to seizure and denial of entry. The Supreme Court: (a) reaffirmed its position that no censorship was involved as the book had been previously been sold (and distributed) in Japan; (b) although the book showed and indeed emphasized male genitalia, (i) the book was put together in an artistic fashion by a photographer of renowned reputation (ii) the objected to photographs appeared in only 19 of 384 pages of photographs (many being of flowers and other innocuous subjects and some being of female nudes) (iii) the photos were in black and white and did not show sexual intercourse. The Court concluded the photos did not appeal primarily to sexual interest of the viewer and the book was not against good morals—the definition for seizure under the Customs Law. The Court had previously found a catalogue of photographs containing five of the photos in the book against good morals but it concluded that the instant decision was not inconsistent with that earlier ruling. Because the decision explicitly confirmed the *Lady Chatterley decision* the extent to which the decision opens other materials to the Japanese market remains unclear[153] although the possibility exists for a more relaxed view by courts on the subject of obscenity. It is likely that younger lower court judges will see the decision as giving them room to exercise greater discretion in finding materials not obscene because of the artistic nature of the presentation.

Japan also has laws that prohibit distribution, sale or public display of child pornography.[154] Nonetheless there is a very large market for child pornography in Japan as possession of child pornography is legal; it is difficult to determine whether a publication is classified as child pornography as adults playing the role of children are not covered by the law and the government is not active in policing the sale of such pornography. Recently Japan's police have taken a more active role in trying to deal with child pornography and local governments have taken steps to attempt to stem the tide of such pornography through the use of local ordinances to prevent sale of such materials. On the national level child pornography has not been criminalized.[155]

Obscenity Decisions in the Japanese and United States Supreme Courts: Cultural Values in Interpreting Free Speech, 10 U. C. Davis J. Int'l L. & Pol'y 247 (2004).

152. *Mapplethorpe Photographs Case, Asai v. Japan*, Case No, 2003 (Gyo-Tsu) No. 157, 2003 (Gyo-Hi) No. 164, 62 Minshu No. 2 at 69, http://www.courts.go.jp/english/judgments/text/2008.02.19-2003.-Gyo-Tsu-.No..157%2C.2003.-Gyo-Hi-.No..164-103831.html (P.B., Feb. 19, 2008).

153. Yuri Obata, Public Welfare, Artistic Values and the State Ideology: The Analysis of the 2008 Japanese Supreme Court Obscenity on Robert Mappelthorpe, 19 Pacific Rim Law and Policy Journal 519 (2010).

154. *Law for Punishing Acts Related to Child Prostitution and Child Pornography, and for Protecting Children* at http://www.interpol.int/Public/Children/SexualAbuse/NationalLaws/csa Japan.asp.

155. In 2008 it was thought that Japan would bow to international pressure and ban possession of child pornography, exempting manga comics and animated films. However that did not materialize. Justin McCurry, *Japan to Outlaw Possession of Child Porn, Christian Science*

Manga are Japanese "comic" books or anime type books typically soft covered with mostly cartoon type (anime) pictures and little text. Some contain quite explicit pictures of amorous adventures. A Manga work was found obscene by the Tokyo District Court in 2002 and its decision was upheld by the Tokyo High Court that relied on the *Lady Chatterley's Lover* and *de Sade* decisions. The case started a public debate over Manga and especially Manga directed at children. The result was a classification of adult only Manga books.[156] The conflict continues as Manga can be quite explicit and quite disrespectful of women and children.[157] In December 2010 the Tokyo City Government passed a Youth Ordinance Bill that directly confronts Manga that may be considered dangerous or injurious to the moral of Japanese youth.[158] The Ordinance prohibits the sale to minors of manga comics and videos that show sexual acts by young girls in cartoon or manga depictions. The Ordinance relies on self-regulation by the Manga industry —the mechanism used for censorship by the pre-war government. As of July 2012 no Manga had been banned under the Ordinance.[159] An American collector of Manga that contained cartoon depictions of sexual abuse of children was arrested for possession of Manga showing sexual abuse of children and pleaded guilty. He received a prison sentence.[160]

[4] Textbooks and Teachers

The issue of teaching "patriotism" in Japanese schools arises in part from the history of the Meiji Emperor's Prescript on Education. The Occupation's objective of taking education out of the domain of the national government was not realized. The Ministry of Education exercises authority over what can and cannot be said in textbooks and has responsibilities for curriculum. Prime Minister Abe was successful in getting the Diet to pass a new education law that requires the teaching of patriotism in the public schools.[161] It is likely that this new legislation will lead to further litigation regarding Article 19.[162] It is also likely that the Supreme Court will reject such suits on a basis

Monitor, (Mar. 10, 2008), http://www.guardian.co.uk/world/2008/mar/10/japan; Justin McCurry, *Moves to Rein In child Pornography Meet Resistance in Japan*, Christian Science Monitor (Mar. 31, 2011), http://www.csmonitor.com/World/Asia-Pacific/2011/0303/Moves-to-rein-in-child-pornography-meet-resistance-in-Japan.

156. Frederik L. Schodt, *Dreamland Japan: Writings on Modern Manga* 51–59 (Stone Bridge Press 2002).
157. Takahiro Fukada, *Child Sex in Manga–Art or Obscenity? Graphic but Healthy Free Speech*, Japan Times (June 12, 2010), http://search.japantimes.co.jp/mail/nn20100612f1.html.
158. Tokyo enacts ordinance to regulate sexual comics, Mainichi Daily News, Dec. 15, 2010, http://mdn.mainichi.jp/arts/news/20101215p2g00m0et085000c.html.
159. See *No manga banned by Tokyo as too racy*, Ymiuri Shimbun (July 3, 2012), http://www.yomiuri.co.jp/dy/national/T120702004395.htm.
160. Anime news network, http://www.animenewsnetwork.com/news/2010-02-11/christopher-handley-sentenced-to-6-months-for-obscene-manga, last accessed Sept. 15, 2012. See *No manga banned by Tokyo as too racy*, Yomiuri Shimbun (July 3, 2012), http://www.yomiuri.co.jp/dy/national/T120702004395.htm.
161. Norimitsu Onishi, *Japanese Lawmakers Pass Two Laws That Shift the Nation Away From Its Postwar Pacifism*, New York Times (Dec. 16, 2006).
162. Article 19 "Freedom of thought and conscience shall not be violated."

similar to the *National Anthem Playing* case and its progeny[163] discussed in Chapter 3 §3.03 herein. The latest development in the National Anthem series of cases is a 2012 Supreme Court Panel holding that a rule that mandated a graduated schedule of penalties based on number of refusals by teachers to stand and sing the anthem with a second "offense" resulting in a reduced salary and a third in dismissal was too harsh and arbitrary a penalty although the requirement to stand a sing was not unconstitutional. It has been suggested that in light of this latest decision the strongest penalty that can be imposed for refusal to stand and sing the anthem is a reprimand.[164]

T he issue of textbook screening emerges periodically in Japan.[165] The roots of textbook "certification" by the government go back to the Meiji period but the American Occupation also established a textbook censorship program that relied on certification of approved texts.[166] That program continued after the Occupation. A Council appointed by the Ministry of Education reviews texts and "suggests" changes and rejects passages it finds objectionable. Professor Ienaga led the charge to challenge the textbook certification program on the grounds that passages deemed unacceptable stated the truth and thus unobjectionable.[167] Although he had some partial success he was unable to break the hold of the Ministry on the certification process. Diplomatic efforts by China and South Korea resulted in loosening of censorship to allow some greater objectivity in history textbooks. This created a conservative backlash and the recent certification of a nationalistic and revisionist history text adopted in 2009[168] and later adopted by the entire Yokohama school district causing angry protests from countries that had been occupied by Japan during the War[169] and sparked an interest in joint textbook writing that has had modest success.[170]

---

163. *National Anthem Playing Case*, Case No. 328 (Gyo-Tsu) 2004, 61 Minshu No. 1, http://www.courts.go.jp/english/judgments/text/2007.02.27-2004.-Gyo-Tsu-.No..328.html (P.B., /22/07) See, Takashi Kanazawa, Supreme Court Judgment in the *Kimigayo* Case, Waseda University Institute of Comparative Law, http://www.waseda.jp/hiken/en/jalaw_inf/topics2011/004kanazawa.html;, See, The Yomiuri Shimbun, *Board fears more "national anthem resisters" / Supreme Court rules salary cuts, suspensions "too harsh" for teachers who refuse to sing "Kimigayo"*, Daily Yomiuri (Jan. 18, 2012), http://www.yomiuri.co.jp/dy/national/T120117005934.htm; *Editorial: Supreme Court's national anthem decision a call for restraint*, The Mainichi Daily News (Jan. 17, 2012), http://mdn.mainichi.jp/perspectives/news/20120117p2a00m0na004000c.html;; *Board of Education Circular to Principals not a Disposition*, 2011 (Gyo-Tsu) No. 177 and No. 178, and 2011 (Gyo-Hi) No. 182, Minshu Vol. 66, No. 2 http://www.courts.go.jp/english/judgments/text/2012.02.09-2011.-Gyo-Tsu-.No..177.and.No..178%2C.and.2011.-Gyo-Hi-.No..182.html (P.B., Feb. 9, 2012).
164. Kotaro Kodama, *Ruling puts brake on severe punishments*, Daily Yomiuri (Jan. 18, 2012), http://www.yomiuri.co.jp/dy/national/T120117005932.htm.
165. For a general discussion see, Claudia Schneider, *The Japanese History Textbook Controversy in East Asian Perspective*, Annals Am. Academy Pol. & Soc. Sci. 107–122 (2008).
166. Kathleen Woods Masalski, *Examining the Japanese History Textbook Controversies, Stanford Program on International and Cross Cultural Education*, Freeman Spogli Ins. Intl. Stud., http://spice.stanford.edu/docs/134.
167. See Masakski for a discussion of Professor Ienaga's decades running dispute with the Ministry.
168. Kyodo News, Yokohama *Adopts Nationalistic Junior High History Textbook*, Japan Times Aug. 5, 2012, http://www.japantimes.co.jp/text/nn20090805a2.html, last accessed Sept. 15, 2012.
169. See, e.g., Kyodo, *Textbook row fires up China's media*, Japan Times (Aug. 8, 2011), http://search.japantimes.co.jp/cgi-bin/nn20110808a4.html.
170. Zheng Wang, *Old Wounds, New Narratives, Joint History Textbook Writing and Peacebuilding in East Asia*, 21 History & Memory 101 (Spring/Summer, 2009); Korea Times, Aug. 29, 2010,

The Supreme Court has held that the system of textbook screening is Constitutional[171] and has held that *suggestions* for changes by the ministry are permissible while mandatory change orders that are inconsistent with the weight of academic thinking are not.[172] While it was an abuse of discretion to *compel deletion* of material that was historical fact, the ministry has questioned statements in textbooks arguing that they are not proven and hence not historical fact and has objected to opinions in textbooks that conflict with the ministry's view.[173]

The ministry ordered references to the Japanese military's role in the mass suicides of Okinawa civilians during the Second World War deleted from textbooks.[174] As a consequence of public protests in Okinawa, the ministry reconsidered its order.[175] The libel laws have also been used by those who object to publications placing blame on the Japanese military for the deaths of Okinawa civilians through mass suicide in the final days of the Battle for Okinawa. In 2011 the Supreme Court turned down an appeal from the High Court which had found that the author of a book of essays had not libeled former military officers when he claimed in his book that they had issued orders for mass suicides on Okinawa. The Supreme Court did not render a judgment about the truth of the allegations but found that there was no Constitutional issue presented by the appealing parties and, thus no right to appeal. Discretionary review was denied.[176]

Bae Ji-Sook, *Korea, China Japan to Publish Joint History Book*, http://www.koreatimes.co.kr/www/news/nation/2010/10/117_72193.html, last accessed Sept. 15, 2012; Toru Higashioka & Yoshihiro Makino, *Panel Still Bickers Over History Issues*, Asahi Shimbun (Mar. 25, 2010), http://www.asahi.com/english/TKY201003240433.html.

171. *Textbook Screening Case*, Case No. 1428 (O) of 1986, 47 Minshu No. 5 at 3483, http://www.courts.go.jp/english/judgments/text/1993.03.16-1986-O.-No.1428.html (P.B., Mar. 12, 1993).

172. *Textbook Suggestions are Guidance but Mandatory Order Reversed*, Case No 1119 (O) of 1994, 51 Minshu No. 7, http://www.courts.go.jp/english/judgments/text/1997.8.29-1994-O-No.1119-170618.html (P.B., Aug. 29, 1997). At issue in the case was a reference in the textbook to Japan's Military Unit 731 and its activities during the Second World War. Nicholas D. Kristof, *Japan Bars Censorship of Atrocities in Texts*, New York Times (Aug. 30, 1997). See also, Hiroshi Fukurai, The Rebirth of Japan's Petit Quasi-Jury and Grand Jury Systems: A Cross-National Analysis of *Legal Consciousness and the Lay Participatory Experience in Japan and the U.S.*, 40 Cornell Intl. L.J. 315, 350 (2007), http://query.nytimes.com/gst/fullpage.html?res=9E06E6D71031F933A0575BC0A961958260&sec= &spon=&pagewanted=print.

173. See Alan Brender, *Japan's High Court Upholds Censorship, The Chronicle of Higher Education*, (Dec. 16, 2005), http://chronicle.com/weekly/v52/il7/17a04102.htm.

174. Norimitsu Onishi, *Japan's Textbooks Reflect Revised History*, New York Times (Apr. 1, 2007). www.nytimes.com/2007/04/01/world/asia/01japan.html.

175. Kyodo News, *Texts to restore army Okinawa mass suicide role*, Japan Times (Oct. 19, 2007), http://search.japantimes.co.jp/cgi-bin/nn20071019a3.html; Kyodo News, Texts reinstate army's role in mass suicides, Okinawa prevails in history row, Japan Times (Dec. 27, 2007), http://search.japantimes.co.jp/cgi-bin/nn20071227a1.html.

176. See, Kyodo News, *"Okinawa Notes" suit Favors Oe*, Japan Times (Apr. 23, 2011), http://search.japantimes.co.jp/cgi-bin/nn20110423b1.html.

The issue of what is a proven historic fact is also potentially confusing[177] especially when the fact relates to Japanese actions during the Second World War[178] or relates to the three non-nuclear principles.[179] In the Okinawa matter there is little questioning but that the military was if not responsible at least implicated in the mass suicide of citizens on Okinawa.[180] But the ministry refused to recognize this as a "fact" resulting in the objections by Okinawa's residents.[181] Japanese textbooks have denied the historic facts of the military's role in providing "comfort women" for Japan's fighting men[182] as well as the role of Japan's Unit 731.[183] The textbook controversies in Japan have both a domestic (*conservative v. liberal*) and an international (Japan vis. China, South and North Korea, Taiwan) aspect[184] similar to the domestic and international aspects of visits to the Yasukuni Shrine (See Chapter 11).[185] After the Fukushima nuclear disaster the ministry quickly approved changes in textbooks that downplayed the safety of nuclear power.[186]

Similarly the government had for years denied the existence of agreements regarding the Okinawa reversion, even after the agreements were declassified and

177. The United States is not immune from the attempt to recast history in its history text books to suit a particular view. See, Jamess C. McKinley Jr., *Texas Conservatives Win Curriculum Change*, New York Times (Mar. 12, 2010); *Associated Press, Texas Approves Textbook Changes*, New York Times (May 22, 2010), http://www.nytimes.com/2010/05/22/education/22texas.html.
178. Sven Saaler, *Politics, Memory and Public Opinion*, in *The Textbook Controversy and Japanese Society* (Deutschen Institut fur Japanstudeien 2005) discussing "historical revisionism" in Japan, including particularly revisionism regarding the Second World War.
179. For a firsthand discussion of the textbook controversy see, Saburo Ienaga, *The Glorification of War in Japanese Education*, 18 Intl. Sec. No. 3, 113–133 (Winter, 1993–1994).
180. Kim Hyun-chul, *Progress in Authorization of Japanese History Textbooks Related to Mass Suicide During the Battle of Okinawa*, http://english.historyfoundation.or.kr/main.asp?sub_num=93&pageNo=3&state=view&idx=254.
181. *Okinawa's war time wounds reopened*, BBC News (Nov. 17, 2007), http://news.bbc.co.uk/2/hi/7098876.stm.
182. See, Yoshiko Nozaki & Mark Selden, *Japanese Textbook Controversies, Nationalism, and Historical Memory: Intra- and Inter-national Conflicts*, 24-5-09 Asia-P. J., http://organizations.lawschool.cornell.edu/ilj/issues/40.2/CIN202.pdf (June 15, 2009). In the run up to the Lower House election that must be held by 2013 at the latest both former Prime Minister Abe and Osaka Mayor Hashimoto have again claimed that there is no evidence of Japanese military involvement in the provision of "comfort women" during WW2. See, Eric Johnston, *On sex slaves, Hashimoto on same page as Abe*, Japan Times, Aug. 25, 2012, http://www.japantimes.co.jp/text/nn20120825a4.html.
183. For a discussion of the activity of Unit 731 and the textbook review case See, Lawrence W. Beer & John Maki, *From Imperial Myth to Democracy* 170–174 (University s of Colorado 2002). For a discussion of the Occupation's use of personnel from Unit 731 to help with health conditions during the Occupation see Takemae Eiji, *The Allied Occupation of Japan*, 426–428 (translated by Robert Ricketts and Sebastian Swann, Continuum International Publishing 2002).
184. See, Claudia Schneider, *The Japanese History Textbook Controversy in East Asian Perspective*, 617 The Annals Am. Academy Pol. & Soc. Sci. No. 1, 107–122 (2008); Daiki Shibuichi, *Japan's History Textbook Controversy Social Movements and Governments in East Asia*, 1982–2006, http://www.japanesestudies.org.uk/discussionpapers/2008/Shibuichi.html.
185. See, Zheng Wang, Old *Wounds, New Narratives, Joint History Textbook Writing and Peacebuilding in East Asia*, 21 History & Memory 101 (Spring/Summer, 2009).
186. Yuta Hanano, *The Asahi Shimbun, Publishers Revise Textbook entries About Nuclear Energy*, http://article.wn.com/view/2011/12/17/Publishers_revise_textbook_entries_about_nuclear_energy/.

published by the United States and were revealed in a book by the Japanese negotiator. The DPJ government created a committee of experts to review the files of the ministry to determine whether there were such agreements.[187] Only after the family of the prime minister who had signed the agreements disclosed that they had the agreements in the private papers of their ancestor did the committee conclude that such agreements existed and that the historic fact of the agreements had been proven. The failure of the committee to locate the official documents in the files of the ministry was believed by some to be the result of destruction of such files in the lead up to Japan's adoption of a Freedom of Information Act.[188] In late 2010 the Ministry of Foreign Affairs declassified documents disclosing the secret agreements. Why these documents were not submitted to the Committee was not explained.[189] Why existence of the agreements was not established by the U.S. declassification and publication of the agreements is confusing—can it be that only Japanese files can be relied on to prove historic facts?

[C] Conclusion

There is no doubt but that Japan has a free society and that as a general rule freedom of expression is guaranteed. National newspapers representing "liberal", "conservative", and "independent" viewpoints are readily available; independent and NHK TV and radio news are available, foreign news in the form of papers and over satellite TV can be seen and read in both the Japanese and native language. Japanese are well educated and follow the news from these various sources. Academic debate is open and continuous—national, prefectural, local and private universities send their professors abroad to study and be exposed to other views and cultures. In short, Japan is a liberal democracy with mass media that is free and a population that can get its news from home and abroad.

Nonetheless the juridical basis for that freedom is less secure than in the United States and less broad than the Occupation intended. The prohibition of censorship contained in the Constitution is a case of what you see not being what you get. The standard for prior restraint is weak and injunctions against publication available.

Although there is no reason for Japan to have adopted the categorical approach to expressive freedom that the United States has adopted the present standard that gives at least as much weight to the public welfare clause as it does to the free speech clause is an unreliable reed on which to base a Constitutional right. The deference

187. See, Matsumoto Tsuyoshi, *Revealing "Secret U.S.-Japan Nuclear Understandings": A Solemn Obligation of Japan's New Government*, 51-3-09 Asia-P. J., http://www.japanfocus.org/-Matsumoto-Tsuyoshi/3273 (Dec. 21, 2009).

188. *Documents Concerning Secret Pacts Missing*, Daily Yomiuri (Jan. 13, 2010), http://www.yomiuri.co.jp/dy/national/20100113TDY02308.htm; Masami Ito, *Nuke Pact Fuiles May Have Been Chucked*, Japan Times (Mar. 20, 2010), http://search.japantimes.co.jp/cgi-bin/nn20100320a1.html; *Secret Pact Files Probably Shredded*, Asahi Shimbun (Mar. 20, 2010), http://www.asahi.com/english/TKY201003180400.html.

189. The Mainichi Daily News, *More than meets the eye in declassified Diplomatic documents* (Dec. 23, 2010), http://mdn.mainichi.jp/perspectives/news/20101223p2a00m0na001000c.html. The declassified documents also make it clear that some documents were destroyed but do not shed light on when or why.

given to the Diet in the conflict between freedom of expression and the public interest and the use of a loose "reasonableness" test could readily lead to the conclusion that the Constitutional grant is not significant. This is not to say that the Constitutional grant of free speech is meaningless—far from it. Undoubtedly the law has dramatically advanced from what it was prior to the Occupation and the decision as to "reasonableness" by the Court, Diet and Bureaucracy is made with one eye on the Constitutional grant. Still, jurisprudence more accommodating to free speech would advance the law as would a greater delving into reasonableness by the Supreme Court. The *Mapplethorpe Photographs Case* surely advances free speech and gives greater effect to literary or artistic worth. But the opinion is careful to preserve the test that was used in the *Lady Chatterley's* case. This may be a reflection of the Petty Bench's concern that elevating the case to the Grand Bench, a necessary step to set aside the earlier precedent would have led to a decision contra to the Panel's.

The greatest threat to free speech is in the areas where free speech is most needed, namely the election process and the recognition of and coming to terms with history. In the world of the Internet and mobile electronic communication devices, a law created in the Meiji era for the purpose of stifling political speech is inconsistent with a modern democracy.

CHAPTER 8

Equality and Issues of Discrimination

§8.01 RACIAL AND ETHNIC DISCRIMINATION

[A] United States

[1] Historic Background

The history of the United States and the legal concept of equal justice for all are stained by the American experience with slavery and the American treatment of African-Americans both before and after the Civil War. Although the founders of the United States righteously declared their acceptance of the ideal that "all men are created equal" neither the Colonies nor the newly declared independent States treated all men as equals. Slavery existed in the Southern Colonies long before the Declaration of Independence and while some in the North decried the practice others made their livelihood from it.

The blight of racial discrimination stained the Constitution, which permitted continuation of slavery as well as the continued importation of slaves in the southern states; stained the Presidency of the United States because George Washington, the first president, owned slaves while he was president (although his Will freed his slaves on the death of his wife) and Thomas Jefferson, the third president, was also a slave owner (who did not similarly free his slaves on his death); stained the Congress, which enacted numerous compromises designed to maintain the peace between the slave owning and free states of the Union; stained the Supreme Court whose decisions upholding the rights of southern slave owners to retrieve runaway slaves mark a low point for the Rule of Law in American history; stained American expansion to the west because the Northwest Ordinance allowed the expansion of slavery westward and maintenance of a balance of power between slave and free states.

Similarly, the Europeans who immigrated to the United States treated the indigenous peoples badly—invading their land and violating treaties that had been entered into.

[2] The Civil War Amendments

The Civil War worked a fundamental change in the legal status of the slaves. The Civil War Amendments and statutory provisions prohibiting discrimination in certain circumstances were a direct outgrowth of the war. The Fourteenth Amendment decreed that all persons born in the United States were United States citizens and citizens of the state in which they resided. States were prohibited from depriving any citizen of the privileges and immunities of citizens. Nor could States "deprive any person of life, liberty, or property, without due process of law; nor deny to any person within its jurisdiction the equal protection of the laws". The Thirteenth Amendment prohibited slavery and the Fifteenth Amendment prohibited the federal and state governments from denying a person a right to vote because of their "race, color or previous condition of servitude".

Nonetheless, following the death of President Lincoln and the withdrawal of federal troops from the South many former Confederate States enacted laws that had as their effect and purpose to treat African Americans differently (and worse) than other American citizens. Segregation of the races became the norm in the South and as African American citizens migrated to the North discrimination followed them. The segregation of the races received a legal stamp of approval when the Supreme Court decided *Plessey v. Furgeson.*[1] The doctrine of separate but equal opened the floodgates for laws that certainly treated the races separately, but those laws hardly treated African Americans equally.

Segregation infected many of the national institutions in American life, not the least of which was the American Army and Washington DC, the nation's Capital. During the Second World War, American authorities acting out of irrational fear that the Japanese American population on America's West Coast could form the basis for a Fifth Column or spy network segregated, imposed curfews on and later imprisoned American citizens solely on the basis of their Japanese ethnic origins. The courts turned their backs on the "equal protection" mandate of the Constitution and in a series of cases upheld the discriminatory imprisonment orders.[2]

[3] Post World War 2 Reforms and the Civil Rights Revolution

After the war some in America began a process of self-examination concerning racial policies. To many it appeared hypocritical to have fought against racial theories and policies of an "Aryan superman" only to find that segregationist policies based on the

1. 163 U.S. 537 (1896).
2. See *Kiyoshi Hirabayashi v. United States*, 320 U.S. 81 (1943); *Korematsu v. United States*, 323 U.S. 214 (1944).

same warped racial philosophy existed in the United States. President Truman by Executive Order ended discrimination in the military forces. Others turned to the judicial system to end discrimination.

In 1954, the Supreme Court gave the civil rights movement a boost when in *Brown v. Board of Education*[3] it rejected the reasoning of *Plessey v. Ferguson* and ruled that racial discrimination in education was inherently unequal. A series of cases followed in which the Court required schools systems to take aggressive steps, including bussing of children from one school to another, to integrate their schools. *Brown v. Board of Education* was a watershed decision and opened the way for the Civil Rights movement of the 1960s, which moved into high gear under the leadership of such people as the Reverend Martin Luther King Jr.

After the death of President Kennedy, President Johnson, himself a Southerner from Texas, used his enormous power to get Congress to pass the Civil Rights Act of 1964, which contained provisions prohibiting racial, religious, sex and national origin discrimination on the part of private parties in certain spheres. Although challenged by the supporters of segregation the courts uniformly upheld the Act and the segregated nature of American society took its first steps towards integration.

The basic philosophy of the Civil Rights Act and the various programs instituted since *Brown* is the same philosophy that underlies that decision. Namely, segregation is wrong and the goal of the legislation and programs is an integrated society. Persons are to be given equal opportunity in all walks of life without discrimination on the basis of race, color, religion, sex or national origin. Persons are to be judged on their individual merit and not on racial or sexual or religious or ethnic stereotypes. While this philosophy is yet to produce a society in which racism is wiped out, at least the juridical basis for an integrated society has been laid and the basis for a segregated society has been disowned. In more recent years the philosophy of the civil rights legislation and the court decisions has been extended to other areas including age discrimination and discrimination against the disabled and most recently discrimination based on sexual preferences. And while the Supreme Court may be divided on how far states may go in taking race into account in programs designed to integrate schools, the members of the Court appear in agreement with the ultimate aim of such programs, namely integration.[4] The Equal Employment Opportunity Act not only prohibits intentional discrimination but it seeks to prevent subtle or hidden discrimination through prohibiting roadblocks to hiring or advancement that may appear racially neutral on their face but that are discriminatory in practice. Thus, in *Griggs v. Duke Power Company*[5] the Supreme Court held that the use of a general IQ test for the hiring of workers violated the Act. The result of the test was to exclude from the work pool members of a racial minority when there was no showing that the result of the test had any relevance to the issue of how well the applicant would perform on the job. Even though the statute on its face permits the use of generalized professionally developed employment tests, the court held that only such tests as were valid for testing "job

3. 349 U.S. 294.
4. See *Parents Involved in Community Schools v. Seattle School District No. 1*, 551 U.S. 701(2007).
5. *Griggs v. Duke Power Company*, 401 U.S. 424 (1971).

related" qualifications were permitted by the Act. To hold otherwise would be to permit discrimination to exist under the cloak of a testing program.

While the thrust of the EEO Act is prohibitory the relief obtainable under the Act may be affirmative in nature. Thus, a discriminating employer may be required to take affirmative steps to end discrimination and increase the minority work pool or work force. President Nixon adopted a program of "Affirmative Action" requiring federal contractors on federal work projects to take affirmative steps to increase the size of their minority work force. While some actions, such as advertising in minority neighborhoods or abolishment of programs that hired only friends and family of existing workers, were seen by virtually all as progressive affirmative steps to integrate the work force, other steps such as the establishment of goals and timetables and the methods used to achieve such goals (including in some cases preferences based on race) were considered by some to be forms of discrimination prohibited by the law. Similar debate affects affirmative action programs in education.[6]

The Equal Employment Opportunity Act and similar laws in other fields (such as equal housing opportunity) have done much to limit discrimination in American society. These laws primarily operate on a private party basis to prevent private parties from engaging in certain types of discrimination—with integration as the ultimate goal. However, it is clear that much discrimination based on race continues to exist and that additional efforts are required, especially at the private and social level to wipe out racial discrimination. Still, since the 1960s there has been a concerted effort to wipe out the de jure basis for discrimination based on race and to integrate American society.

[a] Discrimination Based on Handicap: U.S. and Japan Different Approaches

The United States equal employment opportunity laws cover a broader spectrum of conduct than do the Japanese laws. In the United States there are laws prohibiting discrimination on the basis of age and disability[7] as well as the traditional classifications of race, color, religion, sex or national origin. The American with Disabilities Act ("ADA") was amended in 2008 to reverse several decisions of the Supreme Court and make relief under the Act more available to persons claiming discrimination based on disability[8] and the Genetic Information Nondiscrimination Act of 2008 prohibits discrimination in employment (including fringe benefits such as health insurance) based on genetic markers.[9]

6. *Regents of the University of California v. Bakke*, 438 U.S. 265 (1978); *Parents Involved in Community Schools v. Seattle School District No. 1*, 551 U.S. 701 (2007); *Grutter v. Bollinger*, 539 U.S. 306 (2003);see also, *Ricci v. DeStefano*, 557 U.S. ___ (2009).
7. For a comparison of the American equal opportunity approach and the Japanese "quota based" approach see, Tamako Hasegawa, *Equality of Opportunity or Employment Quotas?—A Comparison of Japanese and American Employment Policies for the Disabled*, 10 Soc. Sci. Japan 41–57 (2007).
8. Among the cases reversed was *Toyota Motor Manufacturing, Kentucky, Inc. v. Williams, 534 U.S. 184 (2002).*
9. See EEOC paper on GINA, http://www.eeoc.gov/laws/types/genetic.cfm.

Japanese law requires that business entities hire disabled people as a percentage of total hires. This "quota system" approach is fundamentally different from the approach of the U.S. ADA. The Japanese system uses a carrot and stick approach. Firms with over 200 employees are to hire the disabled at a rate of 1.8% of their workforces. If this percentage is not met default payments must be made. Firms that exceed the percentage are paid a bonus.[10] A 2010 study made by Japanese authors concluded that the Japanese quota approach resulted in more opportunity for the disabled than did the U.S. anti-discrimination approach.[11] Nonetheless, Japanese companies fail to meet their "quota" in 50% of cases, although the trend of failure has been declining since 2003. Larger companies have a better record of meeting the quota (required minimum employment) than do companies with less than 1,000 employees.

Japan permits citizen suits against the government challenging employment practices while in the United States because of the effect of the Eleventh Amendment suits by individuals alleging discrimination against the various States are limited, making relief unavailable under some federal anti-discrimination laws.[12] Although this trend has been moderated in more recent years[13] it has not been abandoned.[14]

[B] Japan

The establishment of a Japanese Empire during the Post-Meiji Restoration period brought many non-mainstream Japanese into the Japanese population. Included among these were Koreans, Formosans, the Ainu, Ryukians (Okinawans) etc. This influx required a rationalization myth to justify their recognition as Japanese citizens under the then prevalent Family-State system with the Emperor as the Head of such Family-State. This Pre-War myth was based on the concept of multiculturalism in which all of such peoples shared affinity with "main stream" Japanese and only needed assimilation through adopting main stream Japanese cultural values such as Shinto, Japanese diet, Japanese language, etc. to bring them within the main stream. This resulted in "integration" policies under which non-main stream Japanese were compelled to give up their indigenous culture and adopt Japanese culture, religion, dress, diet, etc. Integration did not go so far as to permit non-Japanese to be listed in the "Japanese" Family Register system. Separate Family Registers existed for Koreans and

10. Notwithstanding, failure to reach the quota percentage is in the neighborhood of 50%. See also, Naoko Moriya, *More firms opening doors to HIV positive / Infected people able to work until retirement age, help companies looking to fill disability quotas*, Yomiuri Shimbun (Aug. 19, 2010), http://www.yomiuri.co.jp/dy/national/T100818004459.htm.
11. Tadashi Kudo, *Japan's Employment Rate of Persons with Disabilities and Outcome of Employment Quota System*, 7 Japan Lab. Rev. 5 (2010). This higher percentage may be accounted for in part by differences in how "disability" is defined in Japan (narrowly) and the U.S. (broadly).
12. See e.g., *Board of Trustees of the University of Alabama v. Garrett*, 531 U.S. 356 (2001) [Americans with Disabilities Act not a waiver of Eleventh Amendment immunity]; *Kimel v. Florida Board of Regents*, 528 U.S. 62 (2000) [No waiver of Eleventh Amendment immunity in Age Discrimination in Employment Act].
13. *U.S. v. Georgia*, 546 U.S. 151 (2006); *Tennessee v. Lane*, 541 U.S. 509 (2004); *Nevada v. Hibbs*, 538 U.S. 721 (2003).
14. *Coleman v. Court of Appeals of Maryland*, 566 U.S. ___ (2012).

Formosans in Japan. The existence of these separate registers made it easy for Japan to deny these former citizens citizenship after the war.

With the collapse of the Empire Japan adopted a new myth of cultural homogeneity that excluded many of these non-mainstream peoples from the Japanese body politic. Thus, formerly Japanese citizens of Korean ancestry had their Japanese citizenship taken from them and now constitute a large group known in Japan as Special Permanent Residents. Similarly the large Japanese emigration to Brazil combined with the "economic miracle" in Post-War Japan resulted in many second and third generation Japanese-Brazilians returning to Japan to find work. While part of the mythical homogeneous society many of these returnees could not speak Japanese, had a Brazilian not a Japanese diet, lived in a Brazilian manner, dressed differently and generally were outside the cultural main stream. In short, Japan is presently made up of several different cultural communities besides the main stream Japanese community.[15] Many of these communities are seen both by government and many main stream Japanese as outside the communitarianism of the modern Japanese State.[16] In the twenty-first Century the homogeneous myth is both accepted by portions of Japanese society and is under attack by other parts of the society.[17]

Unlike the United States Constitution, the Constitution of Japan has no provision under which those born in Japan acquire Japanese citizenship. The citizenship of a child's parents determines its citizenship—if either the father or mother is a Japanese citizen then, in theory, the child acquires Japanese nationality.

Citizenship may also be acquired through nationalization provided the applicant has met certain conditions such as continuous residence in Japan for five years,[18] is able to support himself or herself, is a person of good behavior, is willing to give up non-Japanese nationality in exchange and is not and never has been a member of a political group that advocates or advocated overthrowing the Constitution of Japan. Various aliens with connections to Japanese nationals can become naturalized citizens, such as the spouse of a Japanese citizen who has resided in Japan for three years and is presently a Japanese resident, or adopted children of Japanese citizens, etc. Naturalization is a discretionary function of the Minister of Justice. The minister may, with Diet approval, grant Japanese citizenship to aliens who have made a special contribution to Japan —e.g., foreign Sumo wrestlers who have achieved special status

---

15. For a modern and nuanced discussion of the myth of homogeneousness both in the pre-war and post-war period see, Harumi Befu, *Concepts of Japan, Japanese Culture and the Japanese* in *The Cambridge Companion to Modern Japanese Culture* 21 et seq.(Yoshio Sugimoto ed., Cambridge University Press 2009).
16. For the view that the myth of homogeneousness is at least partly responsible for the discrimination against minorities in Japan today see, Mark Levin, Continuities of Legal Consciousness: Professor John Haley's Writings on Twelve Hundred Years of Japanese Legal History, 8 Wash. U. Global Studies L. Rev. 317, 327 (2009).
17. Yoshio Sugimoto, *Japanese /Culture, an Overview* in *The Cambridge Companion to Modern Japanese Culture* 1 et seq. (Yoshio Sugimoto ed., Cambridge University Press 2009). arguing that in the 21st Century the view of Japan as a homogeneous and unique culture has lost its monopoly position and that domestic diversity is a reality that cannot be denied.
18. The five-year provision may be waived in a limited number of cases. So too may some of the other requirements and all may be waived for an alien who has provided Japan with particularly meritorious service. See, Nationality Act Articles 5–9.

in the Sumo world. The post-war myth of "homogeneous" Japan negatively influences government officials (at all stages of the process and at all levels of the bureaucracy) making naturalization very difficult to achieve for the average applicant. Even after achieving naturalization, many are still considered as "outsiders" by the majority Japanese population. Large segments of the Japanese non-citizen population do not seek naturalization because of the loss of indigenous or ethnic cultural values that accompany it and the relatively few advantages it is seen as bringing because of their continuing "outsider" status even when naturalized.[19]

The indigenous peoples of Japan include the Ainu (some have written that the Ainu are the indigenous people of Hokkaido, others have suggested that the Ainu occupied Honshu at one time and were forced north to Hokkaido as the invaders occupied more Ainu land[20]) and Okinawans (Okinawa was originally the Ryuku Kingdom and most residents of Okinawa are ethnically Ryuku. Okinawans have been subjected to discrimination by the majority Japanese.[21]

The homogeneity myth does not mean that all Japanese have equal status in Japanese society. During the Tokugawa era, Japanese society was rigidly stratified. Buddhism was a principle religion. Under strict Buddhist philosophy the taking of life creates great ethical complications. This, in turn, created difficulty since the slaughtering of animals was required for both food and for leather and other products. Some persons were needed to perform these functions, which were indispensable for the public good. Unfortunately, Tokugawa society treated these persons as a lower class in Japanese society and this official discriminatory treatment continued into the Meiji era. Such discrimination continues in modern Japan. Members of this discriminated group are sometimes referred to as *Burakumin* because during the Tokugawa era they were forced to live in isolated villages known as *Burakus*.[22]

The Occupation sought to deal with the problem of "class" and ethnic discrimination by providing in Article 14 for equality and prohibiting discrimination on such familiar American basis as sex and race and including in the prohibited classifications discrimination based on family background and social status. The various rights and obligations set out in the Constitution were rights granted to the inclusive term "persons" in the American language version of the Constitution. However, the Occupation permitted changes in its draft that had the effect of watering down the extent of the Constitutional grant and limiting its effectiveness as a bar against

19. *Transcultural Japan, At The Borderline of Race, Gender, and Identity* xxiv, 12, 298–300 (David Blake Willis & Stephen Murphy-Shigematsu eds., Routledge 2008).

20. See, e.g., *Japan's Ainu fight for their cultural survival*, Taipei Times (Nov. 16, 2009) http://www.taipeitimes.com/News/world/archives/2009/11/16/2003458609.

21. For a discussion of the Okinawan experience see, Koji Taira, *Troubled National Identity, The Ryuku/Okinawans*, in *Japan's Minorities, the Illusion of Homogeneity* (Michael Weiner ed., Routledge, 1997) and *Transcultural Japan, At The Borderline of Race, Gender, and Identity* (David Blake Willis & Stephen Murphy-Shigematsu eds., Routledge 2008), Wesley Ueunten, *Okinawan Diaspora identities* 159 et seq. For the Empire period multicultural and latter post war homogeneous myth see, in addition to pages cited above, 9–10, 284–286.

22. James L. McClain, *A Modern History of Japan*, 101 (WW Norton & Company 2002); for a discussion of the classless people in the tightly class structured Tokugawa society see Marius B. Jansen, *The Making of Modern Japan*, 121–123 (The Belknap Press of Harvard University Press 2000).

discrimination. Most notably by removing its original draft language that would have prohibited discrimination on the basis of both caste and national origin and by changing the translation of the scope of the article to protections of *kokumin*—Japanese people—the Constitution left former colonial subjects such as Koreans and Formosans[23] as well as those who had previously been discriminated against such as Okinawan's, Ainu and so-called Burakumin outside Constitutional protection.[24]

[C] What You See May Not Be What You Get

The discussion below deals with various classes of discrimination in Japan including "outsiders" who suffer discrimination in Japanese society such as Japanese war orphans who were left in China after the Second World War and raised families in China (because they could not return to Japan until recently when relations between China and Japan became more normalized) and are now returning to Japan or their children are returning. This group has adopted characteristics from their stay in China that set them apart from the mainstream Japanese.[25]

[1] The Test for Unlawful Discrimination

As is true in the United States, so too in Japan not all discrimination is unlawful. While the United States has a complex multi-part test for determining when discrimination is in violation of the Constitution (e.g., economic discrimination typically involves a reasonableness standard, suspect classifications such as race or color is subject to a stringent test requiring a compelling government interest to permit discrimination, sex discrimination is somewhere between the two previously mentioned standards) in Japan only one standard—a reasonableness standard—has typically been applied. Further, in Japan the Court has not engaged in a probing in depth analysis of the rationale for the discrimination but simply has looked to see if there was a reasonable explanation for the discrimination being challenged. Almost always the Court has found that the discrimination was reasonable, even though on a deeper analysis reasonableness would not be found or other, non-discriminatory or less discriminatory means could be found to achieve the objective that theoretically supports the discriminatory classification.

Japan has no overarching general anti-discrimination laws. Thus the Japanese Equal Opportunity Law ("EOL") deals solely with employment discrimination based on

23. See, Chaihark Hahm & Sungn Ho Kim, *To Make "We the People": Constitutional Founding in Postwar Japan and South Korea*, 8 I•CON 800, 835–840 (2010).
24. For a discussion of the Occupation's approach to discrimination against Japan's minorities see, Takemae Eiji, *the Allied Occupation of Japan* 435–454 (Translated by Robert Ricketts and Sebastian Swann, Continuum International Publishing 2002).
25. Sara Oikawa & Tomoko Yoshida, *An identity based on being different: A focus on Bioethic Individuals in Japan*, 31 Intl.l J. Cultural Rel. 633 (2007). For a general discussion of discrimination in Japan see Canon Pence, *Japanese Only: Xenophobic Exclusion in Japan's Private Space*, 20 N.Y. Intl. L. Rev. 101 (2007).

sex. Nor is there any law that generally prohibits discrimination in rental or purchase and sale of residential housing[26] or discrimination against non-Japanese citizens, Special Permanent Residents, Burakumin, Ainu, Okinawans or those not seen as main stream Japanese. At best, these groups are left to seek judicial relief based on general tort (*delict*) theory or the amorphous "good faith" "good morals" clause of Article 90 of the Civil Code or in limited cases Japan's treaty obligations. But Article 90 requires a juridical relationship between parties for its application and good morals is determined based on the common sense of the Japanese public as understood by the judiciary. And, since virtually all of Japan's treaty obligations are deemed to be non-self-executing as domestic law, this too is a slender reed to rely on. Japan's failure to enact general anti-discrimination legislation has been a source of international criticism.

[2] Ethnicity and Citizenship

[a] Non-Japanese Citizens

[The discussion that follows deals with permanent resident aliens in Japan. For aliens who seek to visit Japan for a limited period, different rules apply. In *McLean v. Justice Minister*,[27] the plaintiff was an American citizen who went to Japan as a teacher. He sought to renew his one year visa when it expired but was turned down on the grounds that while in Japan he had engaged in activities, which while within the scope of freedom of expression granted by the Constitution to aliens, was not helpful to Japan. During his stay in Japan the plaintiff had engaged in anti-Vietnam War activities. He had also changed his place of work without advising the authorities as required. The plaintiff sought a revocation of the minister's denial of the renewal application on the basis of Article 22 of the Constitution, which grants persons the freedom to change residence and to make his/her own choice as to occupation provided the choice does not violate the interests of public welfare. The Supreme Court, Grand Bench upheld the minister's order. The Court found that Article 22 makes no provision for entry of aliens into Japan but simply deals with freedom of residence and movement once in Japan. As for entry, this is a matter committed solely to the discretion of Japan as the nation to which entry is sought[28] (the existence of a treaty might change this rule). As a matter of Constitutional law, aliens have no right to enter the country or a right once admitted of staying in Japan. In deciding whether to grant an extension the minister is given broad discretion. In addition to domestic considerations the minister may take into

26. The recent downturn in Japan's rental housing market, caused in part by the decline in population, has fueled an effort to make rental housing more available to non-Japanese residents in Japan. See, Mizuho Aoki, *Housing glut Opens Door to Foreign Tenants*, Japan Times (May 15, 2010), http://search.japantimes.co.jp/cgi-bin/nn20100515f2.html.
27. (The *McLean* case), *McLean v. Minister of Justice*, Case No. 1975 (Gyo-Tsu) No. 120, 32 Minshu 7 http://www.courts.go.jp/english/judgments/text/1978.10.04-1975-Gyo-Tsu-No.120.html (G.B. Oct. 4, 1978).
28. This is consistent with statements in Supreme Court of the United States decisions to the effect that entry of aliens into the United States is an inherent aspect of sovereignty. See e.g., *Nishimura Ekiu v. United States*, 142 U.S. 651, 659 (1892); *Kleindienst v. Mandel*, 408 U.S. 753, 762, 765 (1972).

account international concerns. The Court went on to generally agree that the fundamental human rights set out in Chapter 3 of the Constitution apply, as a general rule, to both aliens in Japan and Japanese nationals. But the Court recognized that some rights are inherently applicable only to citizens—such as the right to vote in national elections. Although aliens in Japan are free to engage in political activities,[29] such as those engaged in by McLean, aliens like McLean did not have a Constitutional right to stay in Japan and certainly had no right to get a continuation of their visa status to remain. The minister had discretion to determine whether McLean's residence in Japan was desirable or undesirable and if the minister concluded that it was undesirable, as he did in *McLean's* case, there was no Constitutional issue involved. The *McLean* decision *appears* to grant alien visitors in Japan even greater Constitutional rights than such visitors (or even long time alien residents) are permitted under the United States Constitution when the Federal Government acts to deport them pursuant to Federal legislation.[30]

The United States has a different alien experience than Japan and thus different legal problems are presented for aliens in the United States than is the case in Japan. But that should not disguise the facts that alien discrimination problems exist in the United States as well as in Japan. The form and reasons therefore may be different but aliens in the United States are not the same as citizens.

The United States also has a group of permanent resident aliens—principally those who have visas that allow them to remain in the U.S. for extended periods. Requirements to become a naturalized citizen are much easier to meet in the United States than in Japan. On the other hand, the United States has a much larger class of "illegal" or "undocumented" aliens who live in an underground society where they are denied many of the fundamental rights that United States citizens take for granted. As for "legal aliens" many of them enjoy Constitutional and statutory protections. However, many laws that prohibit discrimination do not prohibit discrimination against aliens.[31]

Many aliens in the United States are fearful of deportation. The Supreme Court has long held that deportation is a civil not a criminal process[32] and thus the Constitutional freedoms that adhere to United States criminal proceedings do not apply to deportation proceedings. Deportation of aliens who are already inside the United

29. As discussed in Chapter 10 Special Permanent Residents are denied the right of free speech in the Constitution Referendum Law-but then so too are citizens who are public employees.
30. *Galvin v. Press*, 347 U.S. 522 (1954). Cf. *Zadvydas v. Davis*, 533 U.S. 678 (2001).
31. See *Espinoza v. Farah*, 414 U.S. 86 (1973). For an interesting reversal of roles in discrimination based on being an American citizen working for an American subsidiary of a Japanese Company see *Sumitomo Shoji America Inc. v. Avagliano*, 457 U.S. 176 (1982) where the Court held that the provisions of the U.S./Japan FCN Treaty did not immunize an American corporation subsidiary of a Japanese parent company from claims that the company favored Japanese nationals over American citizens. The Treaty may protect branch offices of Japanese companies but as the defendant was a United States corporation it was not entitled to invoke the treaty. Compare, *Fortino v. Quasar Co.*, 950 F.2d 389 (7th Cir. 1991) for a practical distinction of Sumitomo Shoji.
32. *Bugajewitz v. Adams*, 228 U.S. 585 (1913).

States is subject to the less stringent due process requirements of civil cases.[33] The Supreme Court has held that Congress may deny aliens Medicare benefits[34] and held that the NLRB lacks authority to give an illegal alien an award for back pay in a situation where a citizen would be entitled to such an award. The Court's rationale was that allowing such awards would be inconsistent with immigration policy.[35] Under the "plenary power doctrine" the Court gives almost absolute discretion to the act of Congress and the Executive when dealing with aliens.[36] States however are limited in their authority to deal with aliens and the Supreme Court has struck down numerous state limitations on the rights of resident aliens.[37] What is clear is that the children of such aliens who are born in the United States are United States citizens.[38]

Citizenship under Japanese law is based on the principle of *jus sanguinis* and accordingly passes to a next generation based on citizenship of the parent. In form Japan does not permit dual nationality so that a Japanese citizen who voluntarily takes nationality of another state must give up Japanese nationality.[39] While there are many ways that a person can acquire Japanese citizenship, none give a *right* for the children of Koreans, a large number of whom were brought to Japan during Japan's annexation of Korea in the early twentieth century and during the Second World War, to become Japanese citizens. There are hundreds of thousands of persons of Korean ancestry, some of whose family has lived in Japan for generations, who are permanent residents of Japan but are not Japanese citizens. Some of these people, or at least their "Korean" parents became Japanese citizens because after the annexation of Korea in 1910. Japan has interpreted the 1951 Peace Treaty as resulting in such persons losing their Japanese nationality. The consequence of this loss of nationality is that their children and grandchildren, etc. are not Japanese nationals.[40] Taken together with the division of

33. See *Yamataya v. Fisher*, 189 U.S. 86 (1903); *Wong Yang Sung v. McGrath*, 339 U.S. 33 (1950). Moreover there are restrictions on the right of the federal government to indefinitely hold aliens subject to deportation in criminal type confinement. *Zadvydas v. Davis*, 533 U.S. 678, 150 L. Ed.2d 653 (2001)–although indefinite detention may be permissible for "suspected terrorists".
34. *Mathews v. Diaz*, 426 U.S. 88 (1976).
35. *Hoffman Plastic Compounds v. NLRB*, 70 USLW 4209 (27 March 2002).
36. See e.g., *Shaughnessy v. United States*, 345 U.S. 206 (1953).
37. See *Graham v. Richardson*, 403 U.S. 365 (1971) (but See *Mathews v. Diaz*, 426 U.S. 67 (1976) refusing to apply the heightened scrutiny test of *Graham* to aliens discriminated against by federal law); *Takahashi v. Fish and Game Commission*, 334 U.S. 410 (1948).
38. The question of how far States can go in taking action against aliens who are not properly documented to be in the United States was before the Supreme Court in *Arizona v. United States, Arizona v. United States*, 567 U.S. ___ (2012). where the Court found certain provisions of a State law dealing with illegal immigration inconsistent with the federal scheme and preempted by the federal law while other provisions were, on their face, constitutional.
39. See, Mie Murazumi, *Japan's Laws on Dual Nationality in the Context of a Globalized World*, 9 Pacific Rim L. & Policy J. 415 (2000).
40. This interpretation of the Peace Treaty has had discriminatory affect on Japanese women who married Korean men at a time when Korea was considered a part of Japan and hence the husband was considered a Japanese national. This comes about because such women would no longer be registered in their (Japanese) parent's Family Register but would be registered in the husband's Registry. When the husband lost citizenship the wife would ipso facto lose citizenship and could no longer claim nationality under the parent's Registry. See *Kanda decision*, Case No. 1955 (O) No.890, 15 Minshu No. 4 at 657, http://www.courts.go.jp/english/judgments/text/1961.04.05-1955.-O-.No.890.html (G.B., Apr. 5, 1961). Since Japanese

Korea into North and South, it has also resulted in "Koreans" living in Japan choosing between affiliating with North Korea or South Korea thereby dividing the Korean community and complicating Japan's relations with and about both Koreas.

As permanent residents but not citizens these persons are not entitled to all of the rights and benefits of citizens. This differing status has resulted in litigation testing whether Japan's Constitutional requirement that all persons be respected as individuals (Article 13) and the grant of equality in Article 14(1) applies to permanent residents whose families have resided in Japan for generations. The Supreme Court of Japan has found the foreign resident registration system is Constitutional as there is a rational basis for distinguishing between citizens and permanent residents. The rational basis of the difference was that foreign residents were not entered in the Japanese Family Register and thus a different system for such residents was permitted.[41]

Similarly, the Supreme Court has upheld the City of Tokyo's citizens only restriction of supervisory positions.[42] The plaintiff in the case was a nurse and had worked for the city in that capacity but was denied permission to take the test for advancement to a management position. The Supreme Court reversed the part of the High Court's decision[43] that allowed the nurse to take the exam reasoning that it was up to the Tokyo Government to determine whether it wished to have a unified employment system under which all supervisors were theoretically able to perform supervisory positions even in areas where they had neither specialty, knowledge nor experience. Since *some* supervisory positions in this unified system were positions that could properly be reserved for Japanese nationals, it was acceptable for the Tokyo government to prevent any non-Japanese national from competing for a supervisory position.[44] In using this generalized reasonableness formula the Court failed to consider the motives of the Tokyo city government that adopted the system only after 1972 when public service jobs in Japan were opened up to non-Japanese such as ethnic Koreans in Japan.[45]

---

husbands married to Korean women invariably set up their own Family Register the *Kanda decision*, while sex neutral on its face, has a discriminatory impact.

41. *Foreign Resident Registration System Constitutional Case*, Case No. 1994(A)No.687, http://www.courts.go.jp/english/judgments/text/1997.11.17-1994-A-No.687-172901.html (P.B., Nov. 17, 1997) The requirement for fingerprinting was dropped in 1993.
42. *Government Employment discrimination case*, Case No. 93 (Gyo-Tsu) 1998, 59 Minshu (No. 1) http://www.courts.go.jp/english/judgments/text/2005.01.26-1998.-Gyo-Tsu-.No..93.html (G.B., Jan. 26, 2005).
43. 960 Hanta 79 (26 November 1997 Tokyo High Court). For an English language discussion of the case on the Internet see Jody Chafee, www.Senrei.com. The Supreme Court of the United States has held that the U.S. Civil Service may disqualify aliens from civil service positions that have a policy making function–but merely being a management position is insufficient for such an equal protection violation. See *Mow Sun Wong v. Hampton*, 426 U.S. 88 (1976) discussed in Carl F. Goodman, *Handbook on Public Personnel Law* 180 (Law Journal Seminars Press 1978).
44. In the United States it is recognized that certain positions, e.g., policy making positions, may be limited to citizens. The Japanese approach is generalized and does not require that reasonableness be shown for each position restricted to citizens. See, *Mow Sun Wong v. Hampton*, 426 U.S. 88 (1976); *Sugarman v. Dougel*, 413 U.S. 634 (1973).
45. See, John Lie, *Zainichi (Koreans in Japan): Diasporic Nationalism and Post Coplonial Identity* 72–74 (University of California Press 2008), http://escholarship.org/uc/item/7qr1c5x7;jsessionid=A2036D57C28619D859892B711150D810#page-1.

Non-Japanese wives of Japanese nationals have also been subject to discrimination when they have had marital problems. Thus, when a Japanese national left his non-Japanese wife to live with his girl friend, the wife was denied a visa to remain in Japan on the grounds that since she and her husband were not living together she could not perform the functions of a Japanese spouse and thus did not fall within the category of a spouse for purposes of the immigration laws.[46] The Revised Immigration Control and Refugee Recognition Act of 2009 ameliorates this rule by granting visa status to foreign wives who live separate from their husbands for just cause. Just cause would include such matters as spousal abuse.

The Supreme Court, although it has approved the national prohibition against aliens voting in national elections, has also said that localities may permit aliens with ties to the community—such as permanent residents—to vote in local elections.[47]

Similarly, the courts had upheld the Constitutionality of Pension Law provisions that granted pension benefits to Japanese nationals but denied similar benefits to permanent residents of Japan who were not citizens. Such laws were narrowly amended in 1982 to bring Japan into compliance with the International Covenant Related to the Status of Refugees [ICRSR]. The Osaka High Court held in 2005 that the nationality requirements in the National Pension Law were not subject to any mandatory provisions of the international Covenants because the treaties were not self-executing and did not have effect as Japanese law.[48] The Supreme Court affirmed that decision in late 2007. On the same day the Court held that the failure to make the 1982 legislative change retroactive was not unconstitutional.[49] It has also been held that the rules prohibiting Permanent Resident Aliens from certain government pension systems is permissible because it is reasonable for a government to favor its own citizens to whom it has an overriding obligation. However, in 2010 the High Court in Fukuoka held that an elderly Chinese woman born and raised in Japan was entitled to welfare benefits.[50]

The problems faced by the non-Japanese population in Japan are rooted in history and the efforts of conservative elements in Japanese society (and government) to create a negative image of foreigners. The problem is reflected in Japanese attitudes towards the rising crime rate in Japan and the attempt by government to place the

46. *Non-Japanese Spouse Change in Status Determination*, Case No. 46 (Gyo-Hi) of 1999, 56 Minshu (No. 8) at 1823, http://www.courts.go.jp/english/judgments/text/2002.10.17-1999.-Gyo-Hi-.No.46.html (P.B., Oct. 17, 2002).
47. *Aliens Not Permitted Vote in National Elections Case*, Case No. 1993 (Gyo-Tsu) No. 163, http://www.courts.go.jp/english/judgments/text/1995.02.28-1993-Gyo-Tsu-No.163.html (P.B. Feb. 28, 1995).
48. *X et al. v. Japan*, Osaka High Court Judgment of Oct. 27, 2005. See also, Report of the Special Rapporteur on contemporary forms of racism racial discrimination, xenophobia and related intolerance, Jan. 24, 2006 COMMISSION ON HUMAN RIGHTS, UN Economic and Social Council, http://www.hrcompilation.org/documents/832/774/document/en/doc/text.doc.
49. Kyodo News, *Court rejects Koreans' appeal seeking disability benefits*, Japan Times (Dec. 27, 2007), http://search.japantimes.co.jp/cgi-bin/nn20071227a9.html.
50. (*Naturalized Japanese granted Pension case*) See, Kyodo, *High court rules foreigners are eligible for welfare benefits*, Japan Times (Nov. 17, 2011), http://www.japantimes.co.jp/text/nn20111116x1.html.

blame for the loss of security Japanese feel on the presence of "foreigners".[51] Thus bail is typically denied to non-Japanese criminal defendants who have been exonerated at the District Court level but whose case the prosecutor has appealed to the High Court.[52] Crime statistics are kept concerning crimes committed by non-citizens in Japan and crimes by foreigners are habitually referred to by politicians and the press. Yet, the rate of homicides committed by foreigners remained the same during the decade from the early 1990s through the early 2000s although the number of "foreigners" in Japan increased during this period.[53] And, statistical analysis shows that the crime rate for foreigners is not high, has remained relatively stable despite a rise in the number of non-citizens resident in Japan[54] that violent crimes are more likely to be committed by Japanese nationals than by non-Japanese and that much of the crime committed by foreigners are immigration violations. Crimes committed by foreigners has actually declined steadily for the last several years[55] falling 12.7% in 2011 with violations of the penal laws (as distinguished from the immigration laws) declining 10.2%.[56] Japanese crime statistics fail to take account of the facts that many foreigners in Japan are there to work, thus placing them in the very demographic age group for which crime in general is higher and that it is more likely for a crime committed by a foreigner to be reported than a crime committed by a Japanese—thus skewing any comparative analysis. [Under legislation adopted in 2007, employers are required to report to the government their activities concerning foreign workers such as hiring, firings, etc. As a consequence employers have an obligation to check the status of foreign workers in their employ. While there is no anti-discrimination law to protect the rights of foreign workers, the 2007 legislation mandates that employers of foreign workers endeavor to improve their management of foreign workers in such a way as to permit such workers to reach their potential within the employment context and when foreign workers are discharged to try to assist them in finding new employment (such as by introducing them to sister or related companies). The Labor Standards Act contains a prohibition against the discriminatory treatment of workers based on nationality when terms and conditions of employment are involved.]

In November 2007 Japan instituted a policy of both fingerprinting and photographing all foreign visitors to Japan. Special Permanent Resident Aliens are exempt

---

51. Apichai W. Shipper, *Criminals or Victims? The Politics of Illegal Foreigners in Japan*, 31 J. Japanese Stud. 299 (2005).
52. Hiroshi Matsubara, *Detention of Acquitted Prompts Legal Cross Fire*, Japan Times (Sept. 10, 2003).
53. Dag Leonardsen, *Crime in Japan: Paradise Lost?* 7 J. Scandinavian Stud. Criminology & Crime Prevention 185, 191 (2006).
54. Hussain Khan, *Japan's Foreignor Crime Fears*, Asia Times on line (2003), www.atimes.com/atimes/Japan/EK14Dh03.html.
55. Kyodo News, *Foreigners' crimes down again in '08*, Japan Times (Feb. 27, 2009); Kyodo News, *Sham Marriages with Foreigners Surged 14% in 2101 NPA Says*, Japan Times (Feb. 25, 2011), http://search.japantimes.co.jp/cgi-bin/nn20110225a3.html reporting that in 2010 cases involving criminal law and other penal law provisions were down 28% from a year earlier.
56. *No. of crimes by foreigners in Japan drops 12.7% in 2011*, The Maininchi Daily news (Feb. 23/2012), http://mdn.mainichi.jp/mdnnews/news/20120223p2g00m0dm011000c.html.

from this provision.[57] While Special Permanent Resident Aliens may have a right to travel outside the country that does not, ipso facto, give them a constitutionally guaranteed right to re-enter Japan. Needless to say, a refusal to permit re-entry results in a prohibition against resident aliens' ability to travel abroad.[58] Under the current re-entry system Special Permanent Resident Aliens can travel abroad and stay abroad for as long as five continuous years for work or educational purposes. A multiple re-entry permit can be obtained for this period.[59] Nonetheless there are restrictions on the right of Special Resident Aliens to travel. When North Korean leader Kim Jong Il died the leader of the pro-North Korean group in Japan sought permission to attend his funeral and was advised by the Japanese government that if he went he would be denied re-entry into Japan.[60] Some Japanese municipalities are experimenting with mechanism to provide permanent residents with voting rights for municipal elections. Some changes have been made such as the ending of the requirement that Special Permanent Residents be fingerprinted.[61] In addition, some courts have found that some forms of private discrimination against permanent residents are a violation of the good morals clause of the Civil Code.[62] Thus, a golf course could not limit memberships to persons of Japanese nationality. In reaching this decision the court utilized the indirect application of Article 14 finding that such a requirement violated the Civil Code.[63] And, an employer could not discharge an employee after learning that the employee was not a Japanese citizen but rather was a Korean permanent resident.[64] It has been found to be a violation of the Civil Code's "good faith" provision to refuse to rent property to a person because of his Korean nationality.[65]

But, Japanese courts are reluctant to recognize "discrimination" even when deciding that a discriminated against plaintiff has in fact been the victim of a *delict* and entitled to damages. Thus, when a shop keeper ordered an African-American looking in his shop window to leave because he hated "blacks" the High Court in Osaka held that the African-American was entitled to damages for the illegal act but refused to

57. Hussain Khan, *Japan's Foreigner Crime Fears*, Asia Times on line (2003), www.atimes.com/atimes/Japan/EK14Dh03.html.
58. See, *Vartelus v. Holder*, 566 U.S. ___ (2012) slip opinion page 9.
59. See Yuji Iwasawa, *International Law, Human Rights and Japanese Law*, 149, 157 (Oxford University Press 1998).
60. Kyodo, *Top Official of Pro-North Group Denied Re-Entry if he Attends Kim's Funeral*, Japan Times (Dec. 24, 2011), http://www.japantimes.co.jp/text/nn20111224a5.html.
61. Glenn D. Hook & Gavan McCormack, *Japan's Contested Constitution: Documents and Analysis* 22 (Routledge 2001).
62. Article 90 of the Civil Code.
63. 1531 Hanji 53, 874 Hanta 298 (23 March 1995 Tokyo District Court).
64. In 1974 the Yokohama District Court held that it was a violation of Article 90 of the Civil Code to fire an employee upon learning that he was of Korean nationality rather than Japanese. The Court however distinguished such a case from an employer's refusal to hire a person because of his Korean nationality. Yuji Iwasawa, *International Law, Human Rights and Japanese Law*, 157, 200–201 (Oxford University Press 1998). For a discussion of the *Pak Chong-Sok v. Hitachi Co.* case see Taimie Bryant, *For the Sake of the Country, For the Sake of the Family: The Oppressive Impact of Family Registration on Women and Minorities in Japan*, 39 UCLA L. Rev. 109, 127 (1991).
65. Teruki Tsunemoto, *Commentary on Important Legal Precedents for 2006: Trends in Constitutional Law*, 9 Asian-P. L. & Pol'y J. 213, 223 (2008)Yuji Iwasawa, *International Law, Human Rights, and Japanese Law* 157, 201 (Oxford University Press 1998).

characterize the act as racial discrimination.[66] And, when a naturalized Japanese citizen was denied access to a bathhouse on the grounds that he did not look Japanese, the Supreme Court refused to hear his appeal from a High Court decision holding that the city where the bathhouse operated had no obligation to adopt rules prohibiting such discrimination (notwithstanding an earlier ruling that the bathhouse itself had committed a tort by refusing entry.)[67]

While rights of aliens resident in Japan have improved in recent years[68] there are still numerous restrictions that apply to aliens that do not apply to citizens.[69] For example, while Japanese national children are compelled to get an education, such compulsion is not required of non-Japanese children living in Japan.[70] "Korean" students who are educated at Korean schools in Japan affiliated with a group that supports North Korea and is financially supported by North Korea, had not been considered as attending "accredited schools" and thus were subject to numerous disadvantages. However, this does not appear to be a discrimination based on ethnic origin because "Korean" students attending schools affiliated with the group associated with South Korea have been considered as attending "accredited schools".[71]

While steps are being taken in some municipalities to grant additional rights to Koreans resident in Japan and while some courts may be entertaining suits challenging Korean exclusionary policies,[72] the fact remains that unlike the thrust of United States law and policy, Japan's policy is not one of integration nor is it a policy based on "rights" of minorities. Indeed, discrimination may exist against Naturalized Japanese citizens as compared to citizens by birth—even when the Naturalized citizen is the daughter of a Japanese mother and non-Japanese father who first took the citizenship

66. Eric Johnston, *Plaintiff Gets Redress But Not For Racial Bias*, Japan Times (Oct. 19, 2006).
67. *High court rejects compensation claim over racial discrimination at bathhouse,* Japan Times, Sept. 17, 2004, http://www.japantimes.co.jp/text/nn20040917a3.html.
68. Yuji Iwasawa, *International Law, Human Rights, and Japanese Law* 157, 203–204 (Oxford University Press 1998).
69. See Yuji Iwasawa, *International Law, Human Rights, and Japanese Law,* 157, 166 (Oxford University Press 1998). A recent incident involving a South Korean's purchase of land near a Ministry of Defense installation has revived calls in some quarters to reconsider new limits on foreign land purchases that could implicate national security. See, The Yomiuri Shimbun, *Kan weighs limiting foreign land ownership* Oct. 17, 2010, http://www.yomiuri.co.jp/dy/national/T101016001545.htm.
70. The UN's committee under the International Convention on the Elimination of all Forms of Racial Discrimination has recommended that such non-Japanese children be included in compulsory education laws. Japan has resisted on the theory that it is not appropriate for it to force non nationals to receive an education. http://www.unhcr.org/refworld/type,CONCOBSERVATIONS,,JPN,3df9b15d4,0.html.
71. *Ibid.*, 196–197. In 2010 the new DPJ government began to provide free high school education in public high schools and to pay a stipend to parents of students who attend private schools that are accredited. This created a firestorm as to how to treat schools associated with the North Korean regime. See, Kyodo News, *Pro-North schools look to get fee waiver,* Japan Times (Apr. 4, 2010), http://search.japantimes.co.jp/cgi-bin/nn20100804x3.html.
72. The Nationality Law was amended in 1984 to provide for equal treatment of spouses of Japanese nationals who wish to acquire Japanese citizenship. Previously the female spouse of a Japanese citizen could acquire Japanese citizenship under relaxed conditions while the male spouse of such a citizen was treated the same as any foreigner. Kiyoshi Hosokawa, *Amendment of the Nationality Law,* 28 Japanese Annual Intl. L. 11, 17 (1985).

of her father and later took Japanese citizenship.[73] Japan appears to have adopted a legal/social policy that permits separate treatment as long as steps are taken to better the conditions of the minority group as a whole.[74] The situation involving so-called *Burakumin* is a good illustration.

[b] Burakumin

The history of *Burakumin* discrimination has been discussed previously. In summary, this discrimination began in Tokugawa Japan, which was a rigidly structured class society. Certain persons were placed outside the established class structure because of their occupations and were forced to live separated from the general population. These people, living in *Burakus* were discriminated against as a matter of official policy.[75] As a consequence of this history there has been and continues to be great social as well as economic discrimination against so-called *Burakumin*.[76] Because *Burakumin* are ethnically and racially identical with other Japanese a question may arise as to how a person can be identified as *Burakumin* and then subjected to discrimination. The answer lies in the Family Register system in use in Japan. All family events are required to be entered in the register—births, legitimacy, marriages, adoptions, etc. Newly married couples are required to establish their own Family Register. This Registry, in turn, is linked to the parent's Family Register making it possible to trace family history. Moreover, it is possible to trace the original location of the family through entries made in the Registry. Since *Burakumin* in Tokugawa Japan lived in separate communities it is possible to determine who is and who is not "Burakumin".[77] This tracing of *Burakumin* origins might be eliminated (if not immediately than within two or three

73. See, *Gaffe-prone Hiranuma Refers to Renho as "Not Originally Japanese"*, Japan Times (Jan. 19, 2010), http://www.japantimes.co.jp/text/nn20100119a7.html. After a former LDP policy maker referred to a DPJ Upper House member Renho as not originally Japanese and someone who later became naturalized, he stated that he did not mean to say something discriminatory.
74. Japan has seen an influx of foreign workers in recent years, some of whom overstay their visa requirements in order to work in Japan where wages are higher than in their home country. In *The Foreign Worker Disability Compensation Case*, 1993 (O) Case No.2132, 1996 (O) Case No.2382, http://www.courts.go.jp/english/judgments/text/1997.1.28-1993.-O-.No.2132%2C. 1996.-O-.No..2383-093444.html (P.B. Jan. 28, 1997) the Supreme Court held that citizens and foreign workers should be treated equally in making the calculation of lost future wages. Japanese wages should be calculated for the period when it is reasonably anticipated that the worker would have worked in Japan (even if that period exceeds the permitted visa given to the foreign worker) and that for the period thereafter lost wages should be calculated based on what the foreigner could expect to earn in his home country.
75. See *'Burakumin' Relief Funds to Be Halved from April*, Japan Times Mar. 6, 2002, http://www.japantimes.co.jp/text/nn20020306c1.html for a summary description of the background of Buraku discrimination and the occupations involved.
76. For a discussion of discrimination against Burakumin as well as a discussion of Buraku culture see, Hideo Aoki, *The Cambridge Companion to Modern Japanese Culture* 182 (Yoshio Sugimoto ed., Cambridge University Press 2009).
77. Theoretically it is possible to change the location of the Registry and this may cut the link to prior Registries and the link to location. However, if a change of location is undertaken this fact is noted on the Family Register and this in itself is sufficient to give rise to suspicion that the family involved is Burakumin. As a consequence non-Burakumin do not change the location and for Burakumin there is thus no point in changing the location.

generations) if the Family Register system were simply to require all new registrants to register in their present location with no links to previous family location or Registry. Rather than adopt such a policy the government changed the Family Register system in 1976 to limit access to the Registry. Nonetheless applicants for jobs, potential spouses and others may be asked to produce copies of the Family Register and while limited, access is not sufficiently prohibited so as to make it unavailable to those who are determined to find out whether a person is *Burakumin*.[78] (In 2009 Google Earth made available old maps that unwittingly made it possible to locate the present location of ancient *Burakumin* neighborhoods creating a firestorm because of the ability to use such maps to identify suspected "*Burakumin*".)[79] It is probably no coincidence that the Family Register system was adopted in 1872 while *Burakumin* were "liberated" in 1871. The Emancipation Edict left *Burakumin* with no formal status and the government required them to list themselves as "Former Eta" or "New Commoners" in the new Family Register system.[80]

Discrimination against *Burakumin* has taken many forms and continues to be a problem in Japan to this day.[81]*Burakumin* organizations have fought back against this discrimination using a variety of devices, including mass demonstrations in the 1960s and "denunciation" sessions wherein *non-Burakumin* have been subjected to "education" sessions to make them renounce their discriminatory actions and to better understand the *Burakumin* approach to an issue.[82] Such sessions may be extremely harsh for those who are subjected to it and in some cases may involve what in the United States would be considered the torts of false imprisonment and even assault and perhaps battery.[83] While such actions have been used by individuals in place of litigation as a means of dealing with individualized instances of discrimination, the governmental approach to such discrimination has not been to deal with individual rights of members of the discriminated against group.[84]

Beginning in 1969 the Japanese government enacted a series of Special Measures Laws that had as their objective the raising of living standards of *Burakumin* in Japanese society.[85] Legislative measures were adopted in 1969, 1982, and again in

78. Ian Neary, *The Buraku Issue And Modern Japan* 237–238 (Routledge 2010).
79. See, e.g., *Google Earth maps out discrimination against Burakumin Caste in Japan*, Times on Line (May 22, 2009), www.timesonline.co.uk/tol/news/world/asia/article6337499.ece.
80. For a discussion of the affect of the Family Register system on discrimination in Japan *see* Taimie Bryant, *For the Sake of the Country, For the Sake of the Family: The Oppressive Impact of Family Registration on Women and Minorities in Japan*, 39 UCLA Law Review 109 (1991).
81. See, e.g., Daniel A. Bell, *Beyond Liberal Democracy* 188 (Princeton University Press 2006).
82. James L. McClain, *A Modern History of Japan*, 385 (WW Norton & Company 2002). [Denunciation as a tactic to fight discrimination was first adopted in 1922].
83. See Frank K. Upham, *Law and Social Change in Postwar Japan* (Harvard University Press 1987) Chapter 3—Instructional Violence and the Struggles for Buraku Liberation, See also, James L. McClain, *A Modern History of Japan*, 624(WW Norton & Company 2002).
84. Discrimination against Burakumin would seem to be prohibited by Article 14, which specifically provides that all people are equal and prohibits discrimination based on "family origin".
85. Ian Neary, *The Buraku Issue And Modern Japan, The Dowa Policy Process* 226–230, The *Buraku liberation movement and Dowa Policy*, 237 et seq. (Routledge 2010); James L. Mcclain, *A Modern History of Japan*, 624 (WW Norton & Company 2002).

1987.[86] Under these measures, infrastructure projects were undertaken in areas where *Burakumin* lived and individual relief was provided to Buraku families through scholarship aid and other social welfare programs. These programs served to better the overall living standards of the subjects of Buraku discrimination[87] but did little to end separate treatment of Buraku community members and the social discrimination against *Burakumin*.[88] Some programs remain in effect at the local level, although Japan's economic troubles have caused the government to significantly scale back on the size of the programs.[89]

There is no effective legislation at the national level in Japan to deal with individualized discrimination against *Burakumin*.[90] No laws have been enacted to make it easier for *Burakumin* to sue to enjoin discriminatory acts or to recover substantial damages for such discrimination. In fact, there is no general legislation declaring such discrimination by private parties illegal.[91] Some steps making discrimination harder to practice have been undertaken (especially as affects "Burakumin lists") but discrimination against this group of ethnic Japanese continues.[92] Acting under the International Convention on the Elimination of all Forms of Racial Discrimination, the UN has raised questions concerning Japan's domestic treatment of people classified as *Burakumin*.[93]

[c] Ainu

In the case of the *Ainu*, the government adopted a program for "assimilation" whose effect was disastrous for the *Ainu* people. [In the United States a similar Native

86. Hiroyuki Hata & Go Nakagawa & Takehisa Nakagawa, *Japanese Constitutional Law* sec. 238 (Kluwer Law International,2001).
87. Frank K. Upham, *Law and Social change In Postwar Japan* 92–93 (Harvard University Press 1987).
88. Hiroyuki Hata & Go Nakagawa & Takehisa Nakagawa, *Japanese Constitutional Law* 238 (Kluwer Law International 2001); See also, Kenneth L. Port, *Impact of Human Rights Law in Japan*, 28 Stanford J. Intl. L. 139, 159 n.123 (1991).
89. *Japan Times* for March 6, 2002 reported that the fiscal 2002 budget for such programs had been cut by more than 50% to JPY 49 billion. The *Japan Times* also noted that thirty-nine prefectures and ten cities had such special programs.
90. For a discussion of the need for comprehensive civil rights legislation that would protect Burakumin rights, see Japan Federation of Bar Associations, Alternative Report to the Third, Fourth, Fifth and Sixth Combined Periodic Report of Japan on the International Convention on the Elimination of All Forms of Racial Discrimination Chapter 5 Burakumin Issues (July 2009), last accessed Sept. 15, 2012, http://www.nichibenren.or.jp/ja/kokusai/humanrights_library/treaty/data/Racial_discrimination_en.pdf.
91. Neary, *In Search of Human Rights in Japan*, in Roger Goodman & Ian Neary, *Case Studies on Human Rights in Japan* 13 (Japan Library, 1996).
92. For a highly critical analysis of Burakumin discrimination and government inaction see Kathianne Hingwan, *Identity, Otherness and Migrant Labour in Japan*, in *Case Studies in Human Rights in Japan* (Roger Goodman & Ian Neary Ed., Curzon Press 2003; Japan Library 1996).
93. *United Nations Committee on the Elimination of Racial Discrimination*, Questions by the Rapporteur (Nov. 17, 2009), http://74.125.93.132/search?q=cache:ZCVdkm4vg2sJ:www2.ohchr.org/english/bodies/cerd/docs/AdvanceVersions/CERD-C-JPN-6-Add1.doc+japan+ainu+discrimination+2010+buraku&cd=3&hl=en&ct=clnk&gl=us.

American assimilation program similarly had the disastrous effect of reducing Indian land holdings by approximately two-thirds,[94] while "integration" programs focused on children of Native Americans almost destroyed Native American communities and destroyed many Native American families[95].] The program was adopted in order to protect Japan's Northern flank from Russian encroachment by making the indigenous population "Japanese".[96] The government took from the Ainu their ancestral lands in Hokkaido; Ainu were required to give up their ancestral names as recorded in the Family Register; Ainu rituals were forbidden; worship of Japanese Gods required; Japanese diet, which eschewed meat, the prime ingredient in the Ainu diet, was instituted as was Japanese dress. The Ainu were settled on small farms that were insufficient to provide a reasonable living standard. All done under the rubric of assimilation[97] pursued to prove the residents of Hokkaido were "Japanese" and thus Hokkaido was an essential part of a greater Japan[98] and consistent with the then prevailing theory that the majority Japanese were multiethnic and thus all peoples within the Japanese Empire, including the Ainu were related. This theory held that through assimilation of diet, intermarriage, agricultural work, etc. eventually the distinctive nature of the Ainu would disappear and their descendants would be part of the Japanese Family whose Head of House was the Emperor. To achieve this end, all those things that distinguished the Ainu from the majority Japanese had to be changed. It was not until the Post-War period that the current prevailing myth of Japanese homogeneity was born.[99]

The few remaining Ainu in Japan have sought government recognition of their status as the aboriginal people of Japan and have sought protection of their heritage and culture. International treaties recognizing the status of aboriginal peoples has proven to be a source of legal protection for Ainu culture and the Japanese courts and legislature reacted to the international pressure to preserve the culture of aboriginal peoples in a manner that recognizes the Ainu claim.[100] In 2008 the Diet finally recognized the Ainu as an indigenous people of Japan.

94. Suzanne Garner, *"The Indian Child Welfare Act": A Review*, 9 Wicazo Sa Rev. 47 (1993).
95. For a discussion see, P. Kunesh, *Transcending Frontiers: Indian Child Welfare in the United States*, in *Families across Frontiers*, 347–355 (Nigel Lowe & Gillian Douglas eds., Martinus Nijhoff Publishers 1996).
96. See James L. Mcclain, *A Modern History of Japan*, 133 (WW Norton & Company 2002); see also, Marius B. Jansen, *The Making of Modern Japan*, 258–261(The Belknap Press of Harvard University Press, 2000).
97. Hiroyuki Hata & Go Nakagawa & Takehisa Nakagawa, *Japanese Constitutional Law* sec. 239 (Kluwer Law International 2001) "Years of government assimilation policy has not only deprived the Ainu of their native language (Ainu language) as a mother tongue for daily use, but also has made it difficult for the Ainu to leave their traditional culture to posterity".
98. Kathianne Hingwan, *Identity, Otherness and Migrant Labour in Japan*, in Roger Goodman & Ian Neary, *Case Studies on Human Rights in Japan* 60 (1996).
99. David L. Howell, *Making "Useful Citizens" of Ainu Subjects in Early Twentieth-Century Japan*, 63 J. Asian Studies 5, 6, 18, 24 (2004); *Transcultural Japan, At The Borderline of Race, Gender, and Identity* 10 (David Blake Willis & Stephen Murphy-Shigematsu eds., Routledge 2008).
100. See Kenneth L. Port, *The Japanese International Law 'Revolution': International Human Rights Law and Its Impact in Japan*, 28 Stanford J. Intl. L. 139 (1991) for an interesting discussion of the relationship of International agreements to progress in the civil rights area in Japanese law.

The *Nibutani Dam* case[101] (involving land expropriation to build a dam) was a major event in the recognition drive. The District Court concluded it was necessary to determine the nature of the legal rights that were claimed by the Ainu. The basis of the Ainu's claimed rights was contained in a multilateral treaty adopted by the UN and ratified by Japan—the International Covenant on Civil and Political Rights. Under that treaty, members of a minority ethnic group in a contracting State are entitled to enjoy their minority culture, religion, and language.[102] The court concluded that these treaty rights applied to the Ainu as the indigenous people of Hokkaido and that Japan had a duty to follow the treaty rights granted to the Ainu.[103] While rights granted by ICCPR Article 27 were found not to be absolute but rather subject to the general public welfare, the court found that limits on Article 27 rights must be kept to the minimum necessary for the public welfare. The court concluded that the Ainu were entitled to be treated as indigenous people of Hokkaido and that the Ainu had been the subject of discrimination by the majority population and by policies that failed to take into account the Ainu culture, language, customs and way of life. The court held that the expropriation of Ainu land for the Dam unlawful because the Hokkaido Expropriation Committee failed in its obligation to take into account numerous matters relating to the Ainu culture and the significance of the expropriated property to that culture. However, by the time the court decided the case the Dam had been constructed at a cost of tens of billions of yen and any effort to prevent its use could cause great damage from flooding because the construction obstructed the flow of the river. The court entered a "circumstance decision" in which it declared the expropriation action illegal but nonetheless permitted the dam to remain in place and be operated. Neither side appealed.[104]

The *Nibutani Dam* case was decided in March of 1997. In May the Diet enacted an Act for the Promotion of Ainu Culture & Dissemination of Knowledge Regarding Ainu Traditions.[105] The Act is significant both for what it does and what it does not do. It does not provide any new legal rights to the Ainu people and does not outlaw discrimination against the Ainu. It repeals the "Act for the Protection of the Previous Indigenous People of Hokkaido".[106] By repealing the old law there is an implication that the Ainu are in fact the indigenous people of Hokkaido. It confirms the status of the Ainu as indigenous people of Hokkaido by referring to communal Ainu property as

101. *Kayano* et al. *v. Hokkaido Expropriation Committee* 1598 Hanrei Jiho 33, 938 Hanrei Taimuzu 75, Sapporo District Court Mar. 27, 1997. For an English language translation see 38 *Int'l Legal Materials* 394.
102. Article 27. Article 26 of the Covenant also purports to guarantee equal treatment under law and requires legal enactments to prohibit discrimination on ground such as race, language, religion, and social origin, all of which would appear to be applicable to the Ainu situation.
103. Article 98(2) of the Constitution requires that Japan faithfully perform its international obligations.
104. For an in depth discussion of the Nibutani Dam case in the context of the Ainu experience in Japan see Mark A. Levin, *Essential Commodities and Racial Justice: Using Constitutional Protection of Japan's Indigenous Ainu People to Inform Understanding of the United States and Japan*, 33 N.Y.U. J. Intl. L. & Pol. 420 (2001).
105. Professors Ohata and Nagata suggest that the Act may have been passed in response to the decision of the Sapporo District Court. 18 Waseda Bull. Comp. L. 103 (1997).
106. Supplementary Provisions Article 2.

belonging to the indigenous people of Hokkaido.[107] The Act requires the government of Japan to take steps to promote the continuation of Ainu culture and to make the public aware of Ainu traditions.[108] Finally, the Act contains provisions calling for a program to return to the Ainu certain communal property that had been taken from them under the prior law. If the property is not returned under the law then it shall be used to promote Ainu culture.[109]

The provisions for return of communal property failed to contain procedural guarantees to assure an accounting for properties taken and placed under the trusteeship of the Hokkaido government. The Hokkaido governor's office adopted a procedure for returning cash assets in its possession but did not account for assets (primarily land) seized but not in its possession currently. Nor did it explain how it had arrived at the cash values to be returned. Ainu claiming communal property were required to file a claim seeking return within a one year period. Several Ainu filed claims, most of which were granted in full by the governor's office. Nonetheless these claimants filed suit under the ACLL seeking reversal of the decision to return arguing that the process was inherently unfair and that the governor's office had an obligation to account and explain. The Sapporo District Court rejected the suit on the narrow ground that all that was at issue in a case brought under the ACLL was whether the decision to return the assets was proper and since the determination granted the plaintiffs the total assets they sought there was no aggrieved party and hence plaintiffs lacked standing. The plaintiffs were in a classic Catch-22 situation. To recover the assets improperly held by the governor they had to file claims (failure to do so waived their claims) and once those claims were granted they lacked standing to challenge the basis on which the governor proceeded. What the plaintiffs wanted was not the small sums of cash that the governor listed in the claim procedure—what they wanted was an accounting and review of the methodology by which the yen value had been calculated.[110] What you see, a law requiring that Ainu assets be returned to the Ainu, is not what you get.[111]

In 2008 the government established a panel on Ainu policy composed mostly of non-Ainu,[112] that presented a final report in 2009 containing numerous recommendations most of which related to cultural matters. Missing from the report was any recommendation that legislation be enacted that would prohibit discrimination against Ainu or any recognition that as indigenous peoples the Ainu have certain rights under international agreements.[113] The DPJ government disbanded the panel and a new Ainu

---

107. *Ibid.*, Article 3(1).
108. Article 3 (Duties of the National Government and Regional Governmental Bodies).
109. Supplementary Provisions Article 3(1).
110. The property had been taken and placed in trust in the early 1900s and Japanese currency had undergone several changes in the intervening period. Clearly the conversion rates, interest calculations, etc. were relevant factors in determining what the proper yen values involved should be.
111. *Ogawa* et al. *v. Governor of Hokkaido*, an English translation may be found at Appendix B to Saeko Kawashima, *The Right to Effective Participation and the Ainu People*, 11 Intl. J. Minority & Group Rights 21 (2004).
112. Of the 8 panel members only one was Ainu.
113. See, *United Nations Committee On the Elimination of Racial Discrimination*, Questions by the Rapporteur (Npv. 17, 2009); See also, *Key Points of the Report of the "Panel of Experts on Ainu*

policy panel was established. This panel which has significant Ainu representation[114] submitted two reports: one dealing with discrimination against Ainu in Hokkaido and a report on discrimination against Ainu outside of Hokkaido. The report shows discrimination against Ainu remains widespread. Not only are Ainu outside of Hokkaido poorer than other Japanese but they have less education than other Japanese and are the subject of both employment and social discrimination.[115]

[d] Indigenous People of Okinawa

Like the Ainu the indigenous people of Okinawa were brought into Japanese society as a means of Japan defining its national boundaries. This necessitated that Ryukians become "assimilated" Japanese, following Japanese customs, diet, religion, etc. Residents of Okinawa claim that they are a discriminated against minority and that they have a right to be recognized as a distinct ethnic group.[116]

To close the economic gap between the residents of Okinawa and the main islands of Japan a Law on Special Measures for the Promotion and Development of Okinawa was enacted in 2002. However, no general law prohibiting discrimination against Okinawans has been enacted.

Part of the difficulties suffered by Okinawan's is caused by the large American military bases on the Island. (See Chapter 10)

[e] General Observations

While an individual subject to certain forms of discrimination may obtain judicial relief available under general tort principles, Japan does not aim for economic and social integration of discriminated groups into the general Japanese population. Japan attempts to raise living standards and the conditions of such groups through education and seeks to enhance respect for cultural differences (as in the case of the Ainu). In the United States integration is viewed both as an end in and of itself and also as a means to uplift the economic and social status of discriminated against group members.[117]

Policy Countermeasures", http://www.win-Ainu.com/Ainu%20Panel%20Experts%20Special%20Report%20Points.pdf, last accessed Sept. 15, 2012.

114. See, New Japanese Governmental Ainu Policy Promotion Panel to include 5 Ainu members, http://liralen42.xanga.com/718879137/new-japanese-governmental-ainu-policy-promotion-panel-to-include-5-ainu-members/.
115. Masami Ito, *Ainu outside Hokkaido also marginalized: poll*, Japan Times (June 25, 2011), http://search.japantimes.co.jp/cgi-bin/nn20110625a9.html.
116. Committee on the Elimination of Racial Discrimination, UN, 58th Session Mar. 6–23, 2001, http://www.unhcr.org/refworld/type,CONCOBSERVATIONS,,JPN,3df9b15d4,0.html, last accessed Sept. 15, 2012. *United Nations Committee on the Elimination of Racial Discrimination*, Questions by the Rapporteur (Nov. 17, 2009), http://74.125.93.132/search?q=cache:ZCVdkm4vg2sJ:www2.ohchr.org/english/bodies/cerd/docs/AdvanceVersions/CERD-C-JPN-6-Add1.doc+japan+ainu+discrimination+2010+buraku&cd=3&hl=en&ct=clnk&gl=us last accessed Sept. 15, 2012.
117. Roger Goodman & Ian Neary, *Case Studies On Human Rights In Japan* at 15 (Japan Library, 1996).

Integration in the American context does not require an assimilation of culture or diet to satisfy some perceived American norm while integration in Japan has been interpreted to mean the throwing off of culture, language, diet, heritage and adoption of the government recognized "Japanese way."

One of the greatest difficulties encountered by persons from abroad in Japan is language. Japanese has both a kanji character written language as well as two syllabic written languages (*hiragana* for indigenous Japanese words and *katakana* for foreign borrowed words). Foreigners invited to Japan to perform needed labor have been required to take examinations in written Japanese making passage impossible for most. Some exams while still being given in Japanese had many of the technical terms translated into English but this change did not increase the pass rate and consideration to giving the entire nursing examination in English or Indonesian[118] was stymied by the a Ministry of Health panel that recommended against such step.[119] Japan has decided to give foreign test takers more time to complete their exam papers, use *hiragana* and *katakana* replacements for kanji characters used in the test, but still give the test in the Japanese language.[120] Driver's license tests are offered in English throughout most of Japan and some locations allow tests using Chinese. Shizuoka Prefecture gives drivers license tests in Portuguese to make it possible for Brazilians in Japan to pass the exam.[121]

While the Japanese Constitution may grant rights to equality, because there is no effective generalized anti-discrimination legislation that grants a cause of action to those discriminated against the juridical reality is far different.[122] What you see when you look at the Japanese Constitutional prohibitions against discrimination and requiring equality is different from what you get in real life. The recent *Portion of Nationality Law Unconstitutional* Case (discussed in Chapter 5), may indicate that the test of unlawful discrimination in certain areas of equality may be changing.[123] Japan has still not enacted a national law prohibiting racial and other forms of discrimination (with the exception of the EEO Act that is limited to sex discrimination and discussed *infra*) notwithstanding international pressure to do so.[124] The failure to adopt such a law has seriously handicapped efforts to bar discrimination through legal avenues.

---

118. Jun Hongo, *Foreigner's Poor Test Grades Force Rethink of Nurse Tests*, Japan Times (Jan. 31, 2012), http://www.japantimes.co.jp/text/nn20120131a3.html.
119. Kyodo, *Panel advises keeping nursing test in Japanese*, Japan Times (Mar. 13, 2012), http://www.japantimes.co.jp/text/nn20120313f3.html.
120. Kyodo, *Foreigners to get extra time for caregivers' exam*, Japan Times (June 7, 2012), http://www.japantimes.co.jp/text/nn20120607b4.html; Kyodo, *Foreign Pass Rate for National Nurse Exam Triples*, Japan Times (Mar. 27, 2012), http://www.japantimes.co.jp/text/nn20120327b3.html. Although the rate tripled it only reached a passing rate of 11.3%.
121. *Driver's License Test in Portuguese*, Japan Times (Jan. 18, 2011), http://search.japantimes.co.jp/cgi-bin/nn20110118x3.html.
122. See James L. McClain, *A Modern History of Japan*, 627–628(WW Norton & Company 2002).
123. Craig Martin, *Glimmers of Hope: The Evolution of Equality Rights Doctrine in Japanese Courts from a Comparative Perspective*, 20 Duke J. Comp. & Intl. L. 167 (2010) http://works.bepress.com/cgi/viewcontent.cgi?article=1002&context=craig_martin.
124. See, e.g., *Recommendation 76 of the Report of the Special Rapporteur on contemporary forms of racism racial discrimination, xenophobia and related intolerance*, Commission on Human Rights (Jan. 24, 2006) UN Economic and Social Council, http://www.hrcompilation.org/documents/832/774/document/en/doc/text.doc.

And yet, by focusing its attention on the economic plight of *Burakumin* and Okinawans and the cultural heritage needs of the Ainu, the Japanese government has managed to provide programs that have uplifted both the economic and social status of these groups. This group oriented approach is not surprising in a group oriented society and, while much remains to be done, the same may be said for the United States where an individual oriented approach has bettered the lot of some but still left a large percentage of America's minority population with social stigma and economic deprivation. In the final analysis, in neither country do you get what the Constitution promises although it is fair to say that each society is slowly improving the status and condition of its minority population.

[3] Sex Discrimination

[a] The Equal Opportunity Law

Even before adoption of the new Constitution, the Occupation had started a program to grant equality to women. Women were permitted to vote in the 1946 election and 67% of them did[125] although the election law had not been amended and even though the new Constitution had not yet been promulgated.[126] After the adoption of the Constitution the Criminal Code was amended to eliminate the discriminatory provisions under which women but not men could be charged with adultery in certain situations and in 1947 the Labor Standards Law provided for equal pay for equal work but did not otherwise prohibit discrimination based on sex.[127] A second wave of legislative enactments designed to carry out equality of the sexes began in the mid 1980s when Japan acted to conform its domestic law to its obligations undertaken by ratification of the Convention on the Elimination of All Forms of Discrimination against Women. One major legislative change was the passage of an Equal Opportunity Law ("EOL"). This law, consistent with the Supreme Court's decision in the *Nissan Motor* case prohibited discrimination in the training, pension and welfare benefits of employees. However, in areas not covered by the *Nissan Motor* case the legislation simply required that employers (or prospective employers) endeavor to abolish discriminatory practices.[128]

The EOL of 1985 was a milestone in women's rights in Japan. Although it did not provide many new "rights" it did set out a program for gradual change in the treatment of women in the workplace. Complaints were to be resolved "in-house" and if that failed, a mediation procedure was adopted but both the employer and employee

125. Sarah Kovner, *Occupying Power Sex Workers and Servicemen in Postwar Japan* (Stanford University Press 2012).
126. Sayoko Kodera, *Implementation of the Convention on the Elimination of All Forms of Discrimination against Women within Japan*, 39 Japanese Annual Intl. L. 149, 155 (1996).
127. *Ibid.*
128. For a discussion of the EOL and the background to the Law See Loraine Parkinson, *Note, "Japan's Equal Employment Opportunity Law: An Alternative Approach to Social Change"*, 89 Columbia L. Rev. 604 (1989); Masako Kamiya, *A Decade of the Equal Employment Opportunity Act in Japan: Has it Changed Society?*, 25 L. Japan 40, 55 (1995); Jan M. Bergeson & Kaoru Yamamoto Oba, *Japan's New Equal Employment Opportunity Law* Brigham Young U. L. Rev. 865 (1986).

needed to agree placing the choice of mediation in the discretion of the employer. The EOL does not contemplate litigation as an enforcement device and it provides no mechanisms to assist an employee who might sue.[129] The Law served to better women's conditions but it still did not result in significant advancement for women. On the other hand the Law did have an effect on how women were thought about in terms of employment and the Law did have positive effects on the public perception of female employees.

In 1997 the EOL was amended to prohibit discrimination against women in recruitment, hiring, assignments and promotion. The amendment enlarged the bureaucracy's power to enforce the law by giving it authority to publish the names of companies that failed to comply with agency advice to cease discrimination.[130] The amended law called on employers to take into consideration prevention of sexual harassment.[131] Japanese courts had already recognized that women in a workplace had a tort (*delict*) cause of action for a human dignity violation when co-workers engaged in hostile workplace activities that constituted sexual harassment.[132]

The Amended EOL's anti-discrimination provisions did not have retroactive effect.[133] Continuation of overtly discriminatory hiring systems after the effective date of the EOL's 1997 Amendment was made unlawful but did not necessarily provide women who suffered damage after the effective date because of the effects of pre-amendment discrimination with monetary relief. The Tokyo District Court held that the overtly discriminatory recruitment and dual-track employment system in operation at a securities company in the 1950s and 1960s was consistent with public morals of the time. The court found that the difference in wages and promotions were caused by the fact that the company's system trained men, but not women, to be future managers. Nonetheless, the court dismissed the plaintiffs' claim for compensation for monetary damages resulting from the wage differences.[134]

The courts approach is significant. It did not analyze the employer's policy to see if it conformed to the Constitutional mandate of equal treatment but found that the employer's policy was consistent with the social order and good morals of the time —*even though such social order and good morals appears to contradict the Constitutional mandate of equality of the sexes.* Only when societal values—as determined by the judiciary—had matched those of the Constitution did the Constitutional norm take on legal significance.

129. See Masako Kamiya, *A Decade of the Equal Employment Opportunity Act in Japan: Has it Changed Society?*, 25 *Law in Japan* 40, 55, 56 (1995).
130. Carl F. Goodman, *The Somewhat Less Reluctant Litigant: Japan's Changing View towards Civil Litigation*, 32 L. & Policy Intl. Bus. 769, 774–775 (n. 21) (2001).
131. Shimada Yoichi & Naito Shino, *Labor Law—Major Developments*, 18 Waseda Bull. Comp. L. 59–61 (1997).
132. Christopher Uggen & Chika Shinohara, *Sexual Harassment Comes of Age: A Comparative Analysis of the United States and Japan*, 50 Sociological Q. 201, 203–204 (2009).
133. See *Sumitomo Women Lose Wage Bias Case*, Japan Times (Mar. 30, 2001) (*Sumitomo Dual Track Employment* case, Osaka District Ct.).
134. See *Nomura Securities Wage case*, Tokyo District Court February 2002 *Japan Times*, Nomura Securities Loses Discrimination Lawsuit (Feb. 21, 2002).

The 1997 EOL Amendments prohibit discrimination on the basis of sex in hiring. Such change has the perverse effect of employers creating or strengthening pre-existing two-track employment systems—a non-management track and a management track. Although both tracks are theoretically equally available to men and women, the reality is that such system institutionalizes sexual discrimination.[135] Women in the management track were required to meet the same overtime and transfer requirements as their male counterparts. This shortcoming in the Law was exasperated by the government's policy of supporting two-track systems and the Ministry of Labor even endorsed the "ability and willingness" concept as a part of such systems.[136] Since, as a societal matter, women are expected to and are pressured to be responsible for family matters (including children and parents) it was difficult for them to meet the requirements of the management track. As a consequence very few women opted for the management track leaving them to the non-management track. This placed them in "non-core" or "temporary" or "indefinite" work positions—all of which have fewer benefits than permanent employment, no "lifetime employment guarantees" and subjects them to "first out" layoff in times of economic downturn.[137] Some of these issues were addressed in the "third-wave" amendment to the EOL discussed in part §8.01[C][3][c] *infra*.

[b] The Family Register's Effect on Sex Discrimination

Only one spouse can be officially listed as the "Head of Household" in the Family Register. This registry is important in that it not only records all family events in order to give them legal validity, but it is also used by employers and officials when making decisions that may be dependent on family status or events that are required to be recorded. Since the husband is typically the main breadwinner and thus the Head of Household recorded in the registry, employment benefits that are based on Head of Household status typically accrue to the husband and not to the wife. This results in a subtle but real discrimination where married couples are living together—where the parties are separated it can result in severe hardship and discrimination.[138] No weight

135. For a discussion of two-track hiring See Leo Kanowitz, *Two-Track Hiring and the Japanese Equal Employment Opportunity Act: An American Perspective*, L. E. & W. 389, 392 (Waseda University 1988); for a similar Japanese perspective See Kazue Suzuki, *Equal Job Opportunity for Whom?*, Japan Q. 54 (July-September, 1996).
136. See Masako Kamiya, *A Decade of the Equal Employment Opportunity Act in Japan: Has it Changed Society?*, 25 Law in Japan 40, 65 (1995).
137. Helen A. Goff, *Glass Ceiling in the Land of the Rising Sun*, 26 L. & Policy in Intl. Bus. 1147, 1153 (1995).
138. *Suzuki v. Nissan Motor Co.*, 1301 Hanji 71, 694 Hanta 114 (Tokyo District Court, Jan. 26, 1989) holding benefits to the husband were not discrimination since wives could be registered as the Head of House. The case was settled on appeal and the company agreed to pay the women the benefits they sought. For a discussion of the *Suzuki* case, See Taimie Bryant, *For the Sake of the Country, For the Sake of the Family: The Oppressive Impact of Family Registration on Women and Minorities in Japan*, 39 UCLA Law Review 109, 115-116 (1991).

is given to the actual affect of the system on women.[139] Similarly, the government's use of the Family Register to make economic stimulus payments to the Head of House discriminates against women as a matter of fact, if not law.

[c] The 2006 Amendment to the EOL and Limited Recognition of "Indirect Discrimination"

In 2006 the EOL underwent another overhaul. This Amendment made clear that the discrimination prohibited was not simply discrimination against women but more fundamentally was discrimination based on sex.[140] Men were included within the equality provisions of the law. The Amendment restated permission for affirmative action in favor of women. Affirmative steps are permitted (under guidelines issued by the Ministry of Health, Labor and Welfare) when the percentage of women in the workplace is less than 40%. The 2006 Amendment permits the government to publish the names of companies that are deemed to have voluntarily adopted positive affirmative action programs.

The Amendment has several substantive and potentially far-reaching effects. For the first time the Act recognizes "indirect discrimination" or what would be referred to in United States law as discrimination that flows from the effect of actions that may appear neutral on their face.[141] Although the 2006 Amendment does not prohibit all discrimination against women based on the effects test it is a first (albeit limited) attempt to adopt an effects analysis. The Minister of Health, Labor and Welfare may set out policies or practices that have an adverse effect on women and thus result in discrimination against women.[142] When an employer nonetheless utilizes such practices the employer has the burden of showing that the practice is required for the performance of the job. The ministry has been modest in setting out practices that come within the reach of the law. This was to be expected as the provision limiting the effects doctrine to certified practices was designed to limit the reach of the law and was a compromise based on the commitment by the ministry to limit its initial reach to only three categories of practices. Nonetheless, now that the camel's nose is under the tent it may be possible for future governments to expand the reach of the law through administrative rather than legislative action. In reporting on its 6th periodic report to the UN Committee on the Elimination of Discrimination against Women in 2009, the

139. In the case of a marriage between a Japanese national and an alien only a Japanese national spouse can be the Head of Household, a program such as the motor company's program has a discriminatory affect on non-Japanese national employees in such a marriage.

140. For a discussion of the 2006 Amendment see Hiroya Nakakubo, *"Phase III" Of the Japanese Equal Employment Opportunity Act*, 4 Japan Lab. Rev. No. 3, 9 (Summer 2007).

141. The Committee on the Elimination of All Forms of Racial Discrimination established under the International Convention on the elimination of All Forms of Racial Discrimination (1966) views discrimination "in effect" as discrimination even if not intentionally discriminatory. While discrimination as a consequence of effect may sometimes be difficult to discern, in other cases it is easily recognized. See, Patrick Thornberry, *Confronting Racial Discrimination: A CERD Perspective*, 5 Human Rights L. Rev. 239, 256 (2005).

142. Article 7.

Japanese delegation noted that it was anticipated that new areas of indirect discrimination would be added to those already adopted.[143]

Under the ministry's regulation the three practices to which the "effects test" apply are: (a) height, weight and strength restrictions applied in the hiring process; (b) conditioning promotion on a workers experience in several different locations maintained by the employer; (c) conditioning acceptance of new hires in a career management track (when there exists a dual-track employment system) on willingness of the employee to accept transfers involving a change in location. The first of the above categories should assist women who are applying for jobs that involve manual labor or heavy lifting. The second and third categories both involve the issue of transfer of location. In each case there appears to be an implicit recognition that in Japanese society women have the primary responsibility for the family and thus transfer from one location to another is likely to have an adverse effect on women compared to men. These provisions, though limited in scope, appear to be consistent with recent attempts in Japan to create a more family friendly workplace. This, in turn, is likely related to concerns about the declining Japanese birth rate.

The 2006 Amendment compliments the Child and Family Care Leave Law by prohibiting either (a) demotion or other adverse treatment of women or (b) dismissal—based on pregnancy, birth of a child, leave taken prior to or subsequent to childbirth and taken as a consequence of maternity, or for any other reason that is listed by the Ministry of Health, Labor and Welfare as relating to pregnancy or childbirth and places the burden of proof on the employer to show that a dismissal during this period was not based on such prohibited reason. Employers are prohibited from causing a female employee to retire as a consequence of marriage, pregnancy or childbirth or from dismissing a female employee because she has married. As to these matters the law does not shift of the burden of proof. The Amendment expanded the reach of the previous law in the arena of sexual harassment[144] making harassment a sex discrimination issue rather than a woman's issue and thus men can now be the subjects of sexual harassment. The 2006 Amendment makes it compulsory that employers act to prevent sexual harassment—whether speech or conduct.

The 2006 Amendments to the EOL fail to provide effective administrative remedies to employees complaining of sex discrimination or harassment. The failure to adopt an effects test ("indirect discrimination") for all forms of sexual discrimination is another major shortcoming of the Law. Nonetheless, the Amended EOL creates a basis for future improvements As Japan's female labor force continues to expand and Japan's birth rate continues to decline greater understanding of the need to outlaw all forms of sex discrimination in the workplace, whether direct or indirect, may compel further amendments to the Equal Opportunity Law.

---

143. Committee on Elimination of Discrimination against Women Chamber B, 890th & 891st Meetings (AM & PM), http://www.un.org/News/Press/docs/2009/wom1742.doc.htm, last accessed Sept. 15, 2012.

144. For a comparative analysis of sexual harassment in Japan and the United States see, Christopher Uggen & Chika Shinohara, *Sexual Harassment Comes of Age: A Comparative Analysis of the United States and Japan*, 50 Sociological Q. 201 (2009).

In an effort to entice women workers to have children, the Japanese government has made several moves designed to make the workplace more compatible to the family responsibilities of women workers.[145] In 1991 a Child Care Leave Law[146] (now titled to reflect its coverage of family care as the Child and Family Care Leave Law) was enacted.[147] This law has been amended several times. Under the law a worker (male or female[148]) may take leave to care for a child during its first year (sometimes 18 months). During this period the employer has no obligation to pay the employee but the government is obligated to assure that the employee receives (from government funds) 30% of the pay received prior to taking leave, with an additional 10% allowed after the employee returns to work. The law applies to temporary or contract workers who were employed continuously for at least one year and are expected to return to work after the leave period, but it does not apply to workers who are part timers who were employed only two days a week (or less). The law allows parents of children who are not yet in elementary school (and who meet the requirements set out above) unpaid leave of five days a year to care for illness and a limitation on overtime and/or night work—although the limitation on overtime and night work is not applicable if the employer can show that to do so would adversely affect the operation of the business. In addition there has been a push by government to increase the availability of day-care to families where both spouses work. An employer is not permitted to either discharge or otherwise adversely affect the employment of a worker because the employee has taken child care leave. Significantly, however, there are long waiting lists for day-care facilities.[149] As a consequence, although more woman are taking child care leave (especially in large companies) the rate of retention of female workers after giving birth has not changed significantly and indeed has declined, especially for professional and technically trained female workers. It is likely that the failure to increase retention of professional and technical female workers is related to unavailability of child care

145. For a discussion of the demographic changes in Japan (both a falling birth rate and a rising elderly population) see Patricia Boling, Family Policy in Japan, 27 J. *Social Policy* 173–190 (Cambridge University Press 1998). See *Demographic Crisis, Robotic Cure? Rejecting Immigration, Japan Turns to Technology as Workforce Shrinks*, Washington Post (Jan. 7, 2008) A12.
146. Law No. 76 of 1991 (May 8, 1991).
147. For a discussion of the Child Care Leave Law and related statutes see Toshiko Kanno, *Act on the Welfare of Workers Who Take Care of Children or Other Family Members Including Child Care and Family Leave Care*, 4 Japan Lab. Rev. No. 3, 29 (Summer 2007).
148. The law assumes that non-working mothers will care for a child and thus if the mother is unemployed the father's leave under the law is limited to eight weeks after the child' is born. This period is considered the period during which a mother is not physically capable of taking care of a child. While the law allows fathers to take this leave father's rarely use any or all of the leave they are permitted.
149. See, *More than 25,000 children on waiting lists for day-care centers*, Japan Today (Oct. 5, 2011), http://www.japantoday.com/category/national/view/more-than-25000-children-on-waiting-lists-for-day-care-centers. For a discussion of efforts to make Japanese employment more woman friendly, see Michiyo Morozumi, *Special Protection, Equality, and Beyond: Working Life and Parenthood Under Japanese Labor Law*, 27 Comp. Lab. L. & Policy J. 513 (2006). See Suzannah Tartan, *Making Day Care Fit Real Needs*, Japan Times (Jan. 22, 2008).

centers.[150] Women who can take advantage of both child care leave and child care facilities have a significantly higher retention rate.[151]

The ministry's categorization fails to reach other aspects of dual-track employment systems that disadvantage women and fails to reach another real problem facing women, which is discrimination based on fringe benefits such as health insurance. Here employers may continue to favor the Head of House by limiting fringe benefits to the house head emphasizing the dependent position of married women.[152]

[d] *Conclusion*

Although Japan's Labor Law provides significant protections to Japanese full time workers such benefits are not present for part timers who are generally paid significantly less and have less security than full time workers. Approximately 33% of the entire Japanese workforce is composed of non-regular workers and only some 18% of male workers in Japan are non-regular while over 53% of female workers are non-regular,[153] disclosing that much more needs to be done in the area of providing women in Japan equal employment status.

Although Japanese law has been slow to meet the Constitutional demand for equality of the sexes, and what you see in the Constitution may not be what you get in practice, the fact is that Japanese society has undergone a sea change in sexual relations since adoption of the Constitution. It is to be expected that improvements will continue, especially as women are now better mobilized to make demands for change.

While women still are the mainstay of the home and support of ageing parents, there has been a societal change in which more women refuse to marry young, opting instead for years of freedom outside of marriage and even after marriage many refuse to have children or if they raise a family have smaller families than in the past.[154]

With the juridical recognition of the concept of sexual harassment in the 1997 amendments to the EOL, judicial recognition of sexual harassment increased. As the 2006 Amendment now prohibits some forms of sexual harassment it may be expected

---

150. See, *Child Care Leave System and Women's Job Continuity–JILPT Research report Number 109*, http://www.jil.go.jp/english/reports/documents/jilpt-research/no.109.pdf (Jan. 6, 2010 updated).
151. Shingou Ikeda, *Company Size and Childcare Leave: The Problems of Support for Women's Job Continuity*, 7 Japan Lab. Rev. 119, 127–131 (2010).
152. Because the Act fails to address significant issues that prevent women from attaining their true potential it is unlikely to significantly affect either the birth rate or employment advancement of women. See, *For Japan's Young Families, A Little Good News*, Washington Post A8 (Apr. 18, 2009). For a discussion of the connection between employment discrimination and the declining birth rate see Robbi Louise Miller, *The Quiet Revolution: Japanese Women Working Around the Law*, 26 Harvard Women's L. J. 163 (2003).
153. See Ministry of Internal Affairs and Communications, Annual Report for the Labour Force Survey (2006) Summary of Results, www.stat.go.jp/english/data/roudou/report/2006/dt/pdf/summary.pdf; see International Labor Organization statistics concerning the Japanese workforce for slightly different statistics for an earlier period but showing similar characteristics. See also Osawa Mari, *Comparative Social Policy Systems from a Gender Perspective*, Soc. Sci. Japan (Mar. 31, 2005) on the Web at http://newslet.iss.u-tokyo.ac.jp/ssj31/ssj31.pdf for slightly different statistics for an earlier period but showing similar characteristics.
154. James L. McClain, *A Modern History of Japan*, 616 (WW Norton & Company 2002).

that greater judicial recognition of the concept will follow. The courts have recognized that sexual harassment is against the law and have rendered significant judgments against men who have been found to harass women.[155] The 1997 law marked another turning point in the equality of the sexes recognized by the Constitution and the 2006 Amendment should have significant social implications in bettering the status of women.

While many changes in substantive law have brought women close to de jure parity with men, as a matter of fact women are still subject to discrimination in Japan. There is a severe under-representation of women in the Diet and those women who serve in the Diet tend not to have significant leadership positions on committees.[156] Even at the elected prefecture level there is inadequate female representation. Few women hold senior bureaucracy portfolios although the number of female ministers has been growing. As of 2011 when it was reported that only slightly less that 9% of the House of Representatives and only less than 18% of the Upper House are women while only 2 of the country's 48 Governors are women.[157] The number of women assigned to management positions in local government is similarly low.

Japan scores near the bottom of the list of countries where woman hold management and Board positions.[158] The wage gap between men and women remains quite high.[159] Since most women are classified as indefinite employees, even those who have long tenure in their positions and have less rights and protections than most men in the workplace. Two-track employment systems persist and disadvantage women. The modest attempt of the law and regulations to recognize "indirect" or "effects" discrimination still leaves most forms of indirect discrimination outside the reach of the law and thus most discrimination continues to be subject to a facial rather than an effects test. Women are yet to reap the benefits of the long-term employment relationship that exists between male employees and their employers.[160] Domestic violence against women also remains a problem in Japan (as it is in the United States).

155. Carl F. Goodman, *The Somewhat Less Reluctant Litigant*, 32 L. & Policy Intl. Bus. 769, 799–800 (2001). Although the court ordered payment for the alleged incident, it refused a request that the defendant post an apology.

156. The Fifth Periodic Report by the Government of Japan Under Article 40 paragraph 1 (b) of the International Covenant on Civil and Political Rights (December 2006); www.mofa.go.jp/policy/human/civil_rep6.pdf, discloses that as of March 2004 Japan had only 70 female members in the Diet and only thirty-four or 7.1% of the members of the more important Lower House were females. The same report shows that as of 2003 only one woman chaired a standing committee in the Upper House while none chaired such committees in the Lower House.

157. Hiroshi Nomaki, *Gender Equality in Japan*, (May 16, 2011), http://www.americandailyherald.com/world-news/asia-pacific/item/gender-equality-in-japan.

158. AFP Jiji, *Japan's female bosses near last in Asia*, Japan Times (July 3, 2012), http://www.japantimes.co.jp/text/nn20120703b3.html.

159. Sayoko Kodera, *Implementation of the Convention on the Elimination of All Forms of Discrimination against Women Within Japan*, 39 Japan Annual Intl. L. 149, 169 (1996) [Kodera cites a publication "The World's Women 1995–Trends and Statistics" to the effect that "Japanese women's average wages as 44% of men's in 1980 and 41% in 1990, the lowest percentages among all countries included".].

160. Rene Duignan, *Anthony Iaquinto, Female Managers in Japan: Early Indications of Career Progression*, 20 Women Mgt. Rev. 191 (2005), www.emeraldinsight.com/Insight/ViewContentServlet?Filename=Published/EmeraldFullTextArticle/Articles/0530200304.html.

Women are also disadvantaged when a marriage breaks up. (See Chapter 9) While much is being done, and while it remains the case that what you see in the written law is not what you get in this area of the law, clearly progress is being made in the fight for equality by women, although the gender gap is still very significant with Japan still ranked near the lower end of all countries in terms of gender equality (98 out of 135 countries) and at the low end of OECD developed countries[161], and the fight for equality by other groups in Japanese society such as the Ainu, *Burakumin*, Brazilians of Japanese origin, Okinawans and foreigners continues.[162]

161. Sayuri Daimon, *Gender gap shows scant improvement*, Japan Times (Dec. 23, 2011), http://www.japantimes.co.jp/text/nn20111223f2.html.
162. Daniel P. Aldrich, *Civil Society and Japanese Politics*, (a Review of Three Books) 68 J. Pol. 465–467 (2006).

CHAPTER 9
Family Law and Issues of Modern Science that Affect the Family

§9.01 UNITED STATES

[A] The Common Law and the Status of Wives

The Declaration of Independence was written for men in a male dominated society and refers to men, not as a euphemism for members of the human race, but as males. Thus, while all men are created equal (except for African slaves) no mention is made of the rights of women. European feudal society was also a male dominated society but unlike Japanese feudal society where women had virtually no rights or status, European women had some rights and protections. The desire to secure a male heir may have been the driving force behind King Henry VIII discarding so many wives, but eventually his daughters Mary and Elizabeth became queen in their own right—and a great deal of right they had. No one can deny the power of the first Queen Elizabeth and her role in shaping English history. Henry II had been forced to negotiate with his wife because her property rights in France were of more significance than his own. Nor can the role of Queen Anne or Victoria be disregarded.

English common law recognized that women were entitled to legal rights in property. Married women had dower rights against their deceased husband's property[1]. Still, the law did not grant women the same rights as men and the United States Constitution carried forward this discrimination. Indeed, at the most fundamental level of Western law, the contract, women were typically disadvantaged and lacked the right

1. See, e.g., W. F. Finlason, Reeves, History of the English Law From the Time of the Romans to the End of the Reign of Elizabet at 274, 275. Dower rights could be quite extensive-they allowed the widow the right to income from 1/3 of her deceased husband's real property.

to contract and at the most fundamental level of political rights—the right to vote—women were excluded until passage of the Nineteenth Amendment in 1920.[2]

[B] Family Law as a State Law Issue

Under American federalism, most issues involving family law are issues of state law. Some issues that directly affect the family have been "Constitutionalized" under the rubric of "privacy". Abortion, which had traditionally been a state law matter (and typically outlawed by state law), became a federal issue with the Court's decision in *Roe v. Wade*[3] recognizing a woman's right to an abortion. Over the years federal courts have had to deal with the abortion question and the Congress has also passed legislation dealing with the issue.[4]

Fundamental questions such as marriage, divorce and child custody are matters for state law.[5] Life support and assisted suicide[6] are issues for state law. Oregon and Washington permit assisted suicide because of legislation and the State of Montana permits it because the State's highest court has ruled that punishing euthanasia violates the State's Constitution. Under the Full Faith and Credit clause of the Constitution, once a state has ruled in this area federal issues are presented as to the binding effect of the state action on other States. Recognition of this complex interaction of the effect of one States' actions on other States complicates what might otherwise be seen as a relatively simple issue—the state of domicile or the state where a marriage or divorce takes place has jurisdiction to decide marriage or divorce and custody issues. In recent years this issue has been further complicated by the debate over "same-sex marriage" and the determination of several states and the District of Columbia to allow same-sex marriage.[7] Some states have banned same-sex marriage. Still others, while not permitting same sex marriage recognize such marriage when performed in a permitting

---

2. Former male slaves were given a Constitutionally protected right to vote a half a century earlier through the Fifteenth Amendment.
3. 410 U.S. 113 (1973).
4. In *Gonzales v. Carhart*, 550 U.S. 124 (2007) the Supreme Court upheld the Constitutionality of the Partial Birth Abortion Ban Act of 2003 against a facial challenge while reaffirming a woman's right to an abortion during the first trimester.
5. For a discussion of the history of the domestic relations exception to federal court jurisdiction see *Marshall v. Marshall*, 547 U.S. 293 (2006).
6. *Washington v. Glucksberg*, 521 U.S. 702 (1997).
7. *Goodridge v. Mass. Dept. of Public Health*, 440 Mass. 309 (2003) California adopted a referendum that defined marriage as between a man and a woman. The 9th Circuit held that the referendum violated the 14th Amendment to the U.S. Constitution. *Perry* et al. *v. Brown*, Feb. 7, 2012, http://www.ca9.uscourts.gov/datastore/opinions/2012/02/10/10-16696.pdf. En banc review denied, June 5, 2012, http://www.ca9.uscourts.gov/datastore/general/2012/06/05/1016696ebofinal.pdf. Certiorari will likely be sought. The European Court of Human Rights has held that the question of legality of same-sex marriages was a matter for each country covered by the Human Rights treaty and that the treaty did not guaranty a right to same-sex marriage. The ruling appears to be based on the fact that there is no consensus among the member States on the issue of same-sex marriage. ROBERT WIELAARD and JILL LAWLESS (Associated Press), June 25, 2010, http://www.google.com/hostednews/ap/article/ALeqM5igM8F4LEfcn4EMpHF5tI6O5tV8gAD9GID7300; *European Court rules gay marriage not universal human right, says countries can make own rules*, June 25, 2010,| Associated Press,

State. Opponents of same-sex marriage prevailed on Congress to enact the Defense of Marriage Act (DOMA) defining marriage as the union of one man and one woman, further clouding the full faith and credit debate.[8] Litigation is pending challenging the constitutionality of DOMA.[9] [Recognizing that same-sex marriage is permitted in some American States and some other countries, the Government of Japan has taken steps to allow overseas Japanese who wish to engage in same-sex marriage with foreign nationals (in a country recognizing such marriages) to obtain the necessary Certificate showing that they are not married in Japan.[10] Japan does not permit same-sex marriage. It is unlikely that the Family Registrar would record a same-sex marriage of a Japanese couple married abroad as such marriage would likely be considered to violate both Japan's public policy and Constitution.]

States have come to different conclusions as to whether the child born of posthumous conception (either through use of a deceased husband's sperm or use of embryo's formed prior to the deceased husband's death) is the child of the deceased husband and thus entitled to inheritance and other rights. This issue gets clouded when claim to federal rights is involved (such as survivor's benefits for children under the Social Security System) as the social security eligibility requirements are based on state laws dealing with intestate inheritance. Federal questions are also raised when a federal employee seeks health care coverage for a same-sex spouse.[11]

[C] Marriage, Divorce and Custody of Children

As a general proposition, in the United States marriage is a civil act but the consecration of the marriage in a religious ceremony constitutes marriage. A marriage license may be required by the state and state laws set the required minimum age for marriage and the close family relationships among whom a valid marriage cannot be consummated. Because marriage has both a religious and/or secular nature a valid marriage may arise (a) when there has been a formal religious ceremony by a recognized religious official with authority to consecrate marriage, or (b) when there has been a civil ceremony performed by a government official such as a Justice of the Peace or a town clerk, or (c) in some states, when there has been no religious ceremony but the parties have entered into the contract of marriage. Because marriage is "contractual" in nature, the contract

FOXNews.com, http://www.foxnews.com/world/2010/06/25/european-court-rules-gay-marriage-universal-human-right-says-countries-make/. New York became the sixth state to recognize same-sex marriage in June of 2011 and Maryland followed in 2012.

8. 110 Stat. Section 2419.
9. See, e.g., *Massachusetts v. U.S. Dept, Health and Human Services*, 698 F. Supp. 2d 234 (D. Mass., 2010), aff'd, 1st Circuit, May 31, 2012, http://www.ca1.uscourts.gov/pdf.opinions/10-2204P-01A.pdf.
10. Kyodo News, Ministry clears path to same-sex marriage, Japan Times, Mar. 28, 2009.
11. See, e.g., *Gill v. Office of Personnel Management*, 699 F. Supp. 2d 374 (D. Mass, 2010) affirmed, 1st Cir., May 31, 2012, No. 10-2207 & 10-2214, http://www.ca1.uscourts.gov/pdf.opinions/10-2204P-01A.pdf. Joe Davidson, Obama administration allows health coverage for same-sex spouse, Washington Post, Mar. 26, 2012, http://www.washingtonpost.com/blogs/federal-eye/post/obama-administration-allows-health-coverage-for-same-sex-spouse/2011/04/15/gIQAddI4cS_blog.html.

of marriage may be recognized even if not formalized in writing. This willingness of some States to recognize an informal marriage contract gives rise to the concept of the "common law" marriage, i.e., a marriage by informal contract, which is proven by the actions of the parties living together as husband and wife.

Divorce, on the other hand, is a judicial act that dissolves the pre-existing marriage. As part of the divorce decree the court may determine such issues as division of the marital estate (in community property states the rules for division may differ from the rules in states that do not recognize community property), alimony and where there are children of the marriage the question of custody of the children. Custody orders had historically not been entitled to Full Faith and Credit recognition but under the Uniform Child Custody Jurisdiction Act, a version of which has been adopted by all 50 states, and under the federal Parental Kidnapping Prevention Act, states must, as a general matter, give full faith and credit to the custody orders of courts from other states that had jurisdiction to enter the custody order.[12]

Although state policies concerning the award of custody in divorce cases is a matter for state law, there are discernible patterns to state practice. Thus, while joint custody was relatively infrequent as late as 1970, by 1990 a number of States had adopted a liberal attitude towards granting the divorcing spouses joint legal custody of children of the marriage, while a smaller number of States granted the parties joint physical custody.[13] And, of course, even when joint custody is not awarded many States permit a non-custodial parent to have visitation rights—even including "virtual visitation" (either by way of court decision[14] or statute) through use of computer technology.[15] Custody determinations are typically based on the "best interests of the child" and considerable weight is given to providing custody to custodial parents. The nationality of the disputing parties is not supposed to be a consideration, as nationality typically has no bearing on the child's best interests. Of course, where the parent who is seeking custody comes from a country that has less than friendly relations with the United States parties opposing the request may attempt to create an issue as to whether returning the child to the less than friendly country is in the child's best interest.[16] Joint

12. 28 USC 1738A. The federal statute provides that A court of a State may modify a determination of the custody of the same child made by a court of another State, if–(1) it has jurisdiction to make such a child custody determination; and (2) the court of the other State no longer has jurisdiction, or it has declined to exercise such jurisdiction to modify such determination.

13. Richard Kuhn and John Guidubaldi, Child Custody Policies and Divorce Rates in the U.S., 11th Annual Conference of the Children's Rights Council (Oct. 23–26, 1997). www.angelfire.com/gundam/drmashie/spcrc97.pdf.

14. See, e.g., *Gilbert v. Gilbert*, 2007 ND 66, 730 N.W.2d 833.Virtual visitation is becoming more widely recognized as a way to supplement in-person visitation." http://www.ndcourts.gov/court/opinions/20060306.htm. See, Virtual Visitation, Internet Visitation.org, http://www.internetvisitation.org/web_pages/divorce_cases.html.

15. Ofelia Casillas, *Divorced parents using virtual visitation*, Laptop video conferences help keep families in touch, Chicago Tribune, (Jan. 22, 2010), http://www.chicagotribune.com/news/local/chicago/ct-met-0123-virtual-visitation-20100122,0,6425916.story; See also, *Internet Business Law Services* (Jan 25, 2010), http://www.ibls.com/internet_law_news_portal_view.aspx?s=latestnews&id=2301.

16. *Gonzalez v. Reno*, 212 F.3d 1338 (11th Cir. 2000), rehearing denied, 215 F.3d 1243, cert. denied, 120 S. Ct. 2737 (2000). The Federal Circuit Court specifically ruled that the fact that the parent of the minor child on whose behalf the asylum petition was filed was a resident of communist

custody and visitation rights likely have the effect of furthering the best interests of the child.

The United States is a signatory to the Hague Convention on the Civil Aspects of International Child Abduction, which has as its objective the recognition by signatory countries of the custody orders of other signatory countries and when necessary the return of children who have been improperly removed from a signatory country. In 2010 the Supreme Court of the United States held that a Chilean father's judicially granted *ne exeat* rights effectively gave him custodial rights and thus the removal of the child from Chile violated the Hague Convention and the child should be returned under the terms of the treaty.[17]

[D] Modern Science and Family Law Issues: "Legitimacy", In Vitro Fertilization, Posthumous Conception, Surrogacy, and Death and Dying

Advances in modern science have created new issues in family relations matters and typically these issues are matter for state law. As a consequence states may differ in their approach to the legal issues presented. An example of such modern issue is the question of the so-called Right-to-Die. The Supreme Court refused to recognize a federal Constitutional Right-to-Die in cases coming from California and New York. The matter was left to the determination of the state government.[18] When the state of Oregon passed an assisted suicide statute[19] and the Attorney General of the United States attempted to prevent doctors from prescribing drugs to be used for the purpose of assisting in the suicide, the Supreme Court determined that the Attorney General lacked the authority that he claimed flowed to him under the federal Controlled Substances Act.[20] This determination effectively upheld the legality of the Oregon statute.

[1] General Discussion

[a] "Legitimacy"

When dealing with the issue of distinctions made on the basis of legitimacy versus illegitimacy the Supreme Court has been confronted with an equal protection issue and this in turn implicates the level of scrutiny to which distinctions based on legitimacy and illegitimacy are subject. While the court's jurisprudence in the area has not always

---

Cuba did not in and of itself require that a non-parental party represent the child and the fact that upon return to Cuba the child might be subject to communist "indoctrination" and training did not provide a basis for asylum. See Sean D. Murphy, *Contemporary Practice of the United States Relating to International Law*, 94 Am. J. Intl. L. 516–526 (2000).

17. *Abbott v. Abbott*, No. 08-645, 560 U.S. ___ (2010).
18. *Washington v. Glucksberg*, 521 U.S. 702 (1997).
19. Oregon Death with Dignity Act (ODWDA). Ore. Rev. Stat. §127.800 et seq. (2003).
20. *Gonzales v. Oregon*, 546 U.S. 243 (2006).

been crystal clear,[21] what does seem clear is that a distinction cannot be upheld when the function of the distinction is to punish the "illegitimate" child for the sins of the parent or to attempt to influence the parent's conduct.[22] Nor may an illegitimate be treated less fairly in the interests of protecting the sanctity of marriage.[23] State laws also recognize that discrimination between legitimate and "illegitimate" children should not be permitted. Thus the Uniform Parentage Act provides that "A child born to parents who are not married to each other has the same rights under the law as a child born to parents who are married to each other".[24]

The Supreme Court has recognized that an "illegitimate" child may have more difficulty than a legitimate child in proving that it is in fact a child of the deceased and that such difficulty may, depending on circumstance justify a difference in treatment.[25] The Uniform Parentage Act seeks to avoid this issue by creating presumptions of parentage. Proof issues are also present when a child is born after the father has died. Many States have adopted a presumption in the Uniform Act that if the child is born within 10 months or in some cases 300 days after death of the father the child is presumed to be the child of the father.[26] Where a child is conceived by in vitro procedures during the life of the father, the child is considered an heir even if the father dies before the child is born, as the child would meet the 300 day presumption. Where the child is conceived by in vitro fertilization after the father dies ("in vitro conception") the legal issues are more complex and states differ in their treatment.[27] In vitro conception is treated in more detail in part §9.01[D][1][b] *infra*.

[b] *Assisted Pregnancy and Birth: In Vitro Fertilization and Posthumous Conception*

The Uniform Paternity Act also seeks to deal with issues of assisted pregnancy and birth. The 2000 version of the Act provides that in all cases the donor of sperm (or the donor of an egg) is not to be considered the parent (except of course where the husband is the sperm donor or the woman who delivers is the egg donor). This avoids questions regarding the marital status of the mother. Presumably it states a categorical rule that cannot be waived by the donor and recipient.

Known sperm donors arguing that they are entitled to fatherly parental rights have brought litigation. These cases are determined under state law and, as states have different laws dealing with the issue (some states have not adopted the Uniform Law, others have adopted it with amendments and some adopted earlier versions of the

21. See *Lali v. Lali*, 439 U.S. 259 (1978).
22. See *Lali v. Lali*, 439 U.S. 259 (1978); *Clark v. Jeter*, 486 U.S. 456, 461 (1988)..
23. *Trimble v. Gordon*, 430 U.S. 762, 769 (1977).
24. See the Delaware version of the Act -74 Del. Laws, c. 136, §1.Delaware Laws Title 13, Domestic Relations, Chapter 8 Uniform Parentage Act sections 8-202.
25. *Gomez v. Perez*, 409 U.S. 535 (1973); *Lali v. Lali*, 439 U.S.259 (1978).
26. Uniform Parentage Act 204(a)(2), section 204. Presumption Of Paternity In Context of Marriage.
27. For a discussion of in vitro and surrogacy practices of various countries see, *Third Party Assisted Conception across Cultures* (Blyth & Landau eds., Jessica Kingley Publishers 2004).

law[28]) the rule differs in differing states. Because of the difference in state laws and considering that sperm may be donated in State A, the mother inseminated in State B, the child may have been born in State C, and the child may be raised by its mother in State D, it is obvious that American choice of law ("private international law") rules may be implicated in such litigation. As choice of law is also a state law issue (the Constitution requires some contact of the state whose law is chosen but the threshold for Constitutionality is very low (see Chapter 15)) different state choice of law rules may apply to the same fact pattern arising in different states.

Although the Uniform Act attempts to resolve donor's rights issues, the fact is that only a minority of states has adopted the law. Complications can arise in situations where States require that a contract to give up parental rights must be in writing or where in vitro fertilization paternity laws deal solely with married couples. Courts have reached different decisions. In a New York case[29] the intermediate appeals court held that the known donor who had donated sperm to be used by a lesbian couple was entitled to parental rights along with the mother notwithstanding the assertion that there was an oral agreement that the donor would not claim parental rights.[30] On the other hand, a Pennsylvania court on public policy grounds upheld the oral agreement between the known donor and the mother that the mother would not make paternity claims against the donor.[31] Thus while many states have adopted laws that contain the presumption that a husband who consents to his wife's in vitro fertilization is the father of the child, complications arise when the woman is unmarried and/or where the sperm donor is known[32] and either claims[33] or denies paternity and there is no state statutory law dealing with the situation.[34]

---

28. For a breakdown of the different approaches in varying states as well as a general discussion of the issue see, Helene H. Shapo, *Assisted Reproduction and the Law: Disharmony on a Divisive Social Issue*, 100 Northwestern U. L. Rev. 465, 468 (2006).
29. New York's law deals solely with in vitro fertilization and married couples. See, *Anonymous v. Anonymous*, 302 A.D.2d 378 (N.Y. App. Div. 2d. 2003).
30. *In re Thomas S. v. Robin Y.*, 618 N.Y.S.2d 356 (N.Y. App. Div. 1994).
31. *Ferguson v. McKiernan*, 940 A. 2d. 1236 (PA. 2007), http://www.aopc.org/OpPosting/Supreme/out/J-60-2005mo.pdf; For a discussion of the Pennsylvania decision and the Kansas decision see, Charles W. Adamson, *Assisted Reproductive Techniques: When is Sperm Donor a Dad?*, 8 Whittier J. Child & Family Advoc. 279 (2009).
32. In Australia a known sperm donor's name which had been placed on the birth certificate of the child was removed when the former partner of the child's mother sought to have her name placed on the certificate. There was no contractual undertaking to place his name of the birth certificate. See, Maya Driver, Findlaw UK, Aug. 18, 2011, http://blogs.findlaw.co.uk/solicitor/2011/08/family-law-sperm-donor-is-not-father-in-eyes-of-the-law.html.
33. Claiming paternity may have adverse consequences not anticipated by the known sperm donator–such as liability for support payments. *Curtis v. Prince*, Ohio Court of Appeals (2010) Appeal Denied, 128 Ohio St 3rd 1429 (2011).
34. Some State Courts have held that an absolute bar to asserting paternity (such as the 2000 version of the Uniform Law appears to contain) raises Constitutional questions when the parties have entered into an agreement concerning parental rights. For a general discussion of the subject see, Justice Carol A. Beier & Larkin E. Walsh, *Is What We Want What We Need and Can we Get It In Writing? The Third-wave of Feminism Hits the Beach of Modern Parentage Presumptions*, 39 U. Baltimore L. Forum 26 (2008) https://litigation-essentials.lexisnexis.com/webcd/app?action=DocumentDisplay&crawlid=1&doctype=cite&docid=39+U.+Balt.+L.F.+26&srctype=smi&srcid=3B15&key=f00706c5113f79ffc2878c6dbac9c19a.

Complications also arise when the in vitro conception is posthumous. Here a sperm donor father cannot claim custody or parental rights as he is deceased, but inheritance and federal benefits issues arise. In the benefits arena state law also controls as most benefits cases arise under the Social Security Act that defines "child" for purposes of the benefit in state law terms.[35] Although the states deal with the issue differently[36], certain general principles appear to be developing.[37] Where the state inheritance statutes deal with the issue either by declaring posthumous conception against public policy, prohibiting inheritance of a posthumously conceived child, allowing such inheritance or allowing inheritance with conditions (typically state's that allow apply conditions both temporal—to enhance estate administration and allow for the timely closing of estates—and consensual—requiring consent during the life of the deceased "father donor") courts will follow the state law. Where the law is silent courts must fashion a rule considering the same factors as legislators. Among factors considered by courts are: public policy including ethical considerations,[38] consent of the deceased,[39] best interests of the child, estate administrative considerations, etc. Note however that the issue arises in a financial setting—inheritance or benefits while in Japan (as discussed *infra*) the issue arises in the Family Register context.

The issue of posthumous conception is also of interest to the military establishment since troops sent into battle may lose their life and may wish to provide for posthumous conception through preservation of their sperm. Issues of morale as well as benefits are likely to be called into play. Since the federal government has authority to deal with matters related to the federal military establishment federal legislation to

35. *Astrue v. Capato*, 566 U.S. ___ (2012).

36. For an extensive discussion of the situation (including inheritance rights or lack thereof of posthumously conceived children in the various States of the United States), in the United States, United kingdom, New South Wales, New Zealand and Ontario Canada see, *Posthumously Conceived Children Intestate Succession and Dependants Relief, Manitoba Law Reform Commission* November 2008.

37. A sampling of U.S. cases showing different approaches of State law includes: *Woodward v. Commissioner of Social Security*, 435 Mass. 536 (2002); *Estate of Kolacy*, 753 A.2d 1257 (N.J. Super. Ct. Ch. Div. 2000); *Finley v. Astrue*, 270 S.W. 3.d 849 (Ark., 2008); *Gillett-Netting v. Barnhart*, 371 F.3d 595 (9th Cir., 2004); *Vernoff v. Astrue*, 568 F.3d 1102 (9th Cir. 2009). In *Astrue v. Caputo*, 566 U.S. ___ (2012) the Supreme Court noted that various states have rules for how to deal with posthumously conceived children and noted that time limits are of relevance in state laws.

38. For a discussion of some ethical issues involved in posthumous in vitro fertilization see, McLachlan & Swales, *From the Womb to the Tomb: Issues in Medical Ethics* 251 (Posthumous Insemination and Consent) (Humming Earth 2007).

39. Consent is also the defining characteristic of defining parentage in the latest draft of the American Bar Association's Model Uniform Parentage Act. See, American Bar Association Model Act Governing Assisted Reproductive Technology (February 2008) section 501 (3)(f), 504. http://www.abanet.org/family/committees/artmodelact.pdf; Charles P. Kindregan, Jr., *Clarifying the Law of ART: The New American Bar Association Model Act Governing Assisted Reproductive Technology*, 42 Family L. Q. 203, 215–216 (2008). See also Uniform Parentage Act (2002) section 707, which by negative implication makes a donor who consents in a record to parentage through posthumous assisted reproduction a parent of the child born of such reproduction. The Act has been adopted by a few states. See, Robert Matthew Harper, *Dead Hand Problem: Why New York's Estates, Powers and Trust Law Should be Amended to Treat Posthumously Conceived Children as Decedents' Issue and Descendants*, 21 Quinnipiac Probate L. J. 267, 273 (2008).

deal with the issue could help create a uniform approach for those who serve in the armed forces. It has been argued that when the service member has consented to the removal and banking of semen and has consenting in advance that such semen may be used for posthumous conception, the child born of the process should be considered as part of the military family for purposes of all benefits that military families are typically entitled to[40] and presumably should be allowed to inherit under the service member's Will.[41]

[c] Assisted Pregnancy and Birth: Surrogate Motherhood

Another modern medical advance that has created state law issues relates to surrogate birth. Here again the issue has as a general matter been relegated to the state courts and state law. Before state legislatures became involved in surrogacy contract issues, state courts dealt with such issues on a common law basis. A significant case arose in New Jersey and set the background for later cases and legislation.[42] Surrogate birth not only implicates the state law of contracts and domestic relations but also intersects with state laws dealing with inheritance rights, and legitimacy as well as federal laws dealing with citizenship. Citizenship is not an issue for a child born in the United States who is automatically a United States citizen. Litigation between the surrogate mother and the couple (or individual) hiring her can lead to inconsistent state decisions.[43] The Uniform Paternity Act recognizes the legality of gestational agreements and provides a mechanism to have such agreements judicially validated. While some States have adopted the Act (with modifications) many have not[44]. Some states have passed legislation declaring surrogacy to be against state public policy.

The American debate concerning how to deal with gestational surrogacy has both ethical and legal roots. It is reported that laws regulating surrogacy exist in 17 states and that these laws take different approaches with 10 states allowing surrogacy under conditions including 6 states that limit compensation paid to the surrogate.[45] There is dispute in the ethics community as to whether commercial surrogacy is ethical. On the other hand there is the recognition that the best interests of the child must be

40. Major Maria Doucettperry, *To Be Continued: A Look at Posthumous Reproduction As It Relates to Today's Military*, Department of the Army Pamphlet 27-50-420, May 2008, http://www.loc.gov/rr/frd/Military_Law/pdf/05-2008.pdf, last accessed Sept. 15, 2012.
41. For a discussion of legal issues of the posthumously conceived child and inheritance under the deceased "father's" will see, Kristine S. Knaplund, *Postmortem Conception and a Father's Last Will*, 46 Arizona L. Rev. 91 (2004).
42. *In re Baby M*, 109 N.J. 396, 537 A2d 1227 (1988) reversing 217 N.J. Super. 313, 525 A2d 1128 (1987).
43. See, Stephanie Saul, *21-st Century Babies, Building a Baby with Few Ground Rules*, NY Times (Dec. 12, 2009).
44. See sections 807 and 808 of The Uniform Act.
45. For a discussion of the ethical issues in ART generally see, *Ethical Dilemas in Assisted Reproduction Technologies* (Joseph G. Schenker ed., Walter de Gruyter 2011); for the U.S. and other country legislation see K. Svitnev, Legal Control of Surrogacy–International Perspectives at p. 149 of the same volume. See also, http://www.jurconsult.ru/publications/ethical_dillemas/13_Legal%20control%20of%20surrogacy%20-%20international%20perspectives.pdf.

considered and the view that such child's interests should be protected before the interests of the contracting parties.

Where United States citizenship is claimed for a child born abroad to a surrogate mother federal law as interpreted by the State Department is controlling. The Foreign Affairs Manual (FAM) recognizes the existence of surrogate pregnancy and birth. The FAM deals with the potential circumstances (assuming residency requirements are met) based on genetic characteristics and the genetic relationship of the child to the parents.[46] The nationality of the surrogate is not relevant to the citizenship determination and the surrogate is not treated as the mother.

§9.02 JAPAN

[A] The Feudal Family System of the *Ie*

One of the principle elements of the Japanese feudal system was the *Ie*. The *Ie* encompassed more than simply the samurai class family law system of feudal Japan. The notion of the *Ie* reflected the entire community of the family, its members, its property, its holdings, its responsibilities, its continuation, etc. The *Ie* represented not simply the present generation but the past as well as future generations. The present generation had an obligation to preserve what it had inherited and to pass it along, together with accretions to future generations who in turn had the same obligation going forward. The *Ie* represented a never ending stream of the family relationship, past, present and future.[47]

The head of the household "owned" all of the household property and was granted great powers over other members of the family. He could disinherit members and approved or rejected marriages for family members. He was owed obedience from other members of the family. By rule, inheritance was a system of male primogeniture with the eldest son inheriting the head of household mantle[48] although if the eldest son were deemed incapable of continuing the *Ie* for the benefit of its members, his father could designate a younger son as successor.[49] The *Ie* stressed filial piety and family obligations.

When a woman married she became a member of her husband's *Ie* and generally moved into his family's home. Here she was subordinate to her mother-in-law and in many senses was property of the family unit she had just joined. Upon marriage she was removed from her parent's Family Register and was registered in her husband's Family Register, although such registration was not an essential for the marriage and in many situations, especially in the lower classes, the marriage was simply concluded

46. Foreign Affairs Manual section 1131.4-2, The manual may be found at http://www.state.gov/m/a/dir/regs/fam/.
47. James L. McClain, *A Modern History of Japan*, 90(WW Norton & Company 2002).
48. William Noel, *The Right To Life In Japan* (Routledge, 1997) 60.
49. Anne E. Imamura, *Family Culture*, in *The Cambridge Companion to Modern Japanese Culture* 76, 77 (Yoshio Sugimoto ed., Cambridge University Press 2009).

when the wife moved in with her husband's family.[50] Her marriage had been arranged by her *Ie* and she may not have met her husband until after the wedding had been agreed upon. Her ability to get support from her husband, who himself was subordinate to more powerful members of the family, was limited.[51] Marriage as an institution was viewed by the upper reaches of society as "political" matter not as a personal matter. The Second Tokugawa Shogun had promulgated a rule for the Daimyo houses in 1615 that specified that private considerations were not to be the basis for marriage, while Fifth Tokugawa Shogun's rule prohibited high-ranking Lords from entering into marriage arrangements without first getting approval from the local Magistrate, whose decision in the matter was to be followed.[52]

Women had no right to inherit. A husband could divorce his wife without the necessity for any formal proceedings by simply returning her to her family with a notice that they were divorced. The lot of a woman was not a happy one.[53] While for many Japanese families in the countryside and towns the structure of the family had dramatically changed by the time of the Meiji Restoration, the Meiji government continued the *Ie* and applied it to all classes of society,[54] although under Meiji a woman could inherit the mantle of Head of Household when the family had no son to inherit.[55] Under the newly adopted Civil Code marriage was only legal if registered with the Family Registrar. Many couples continued as they had before the Code- the bride moved in with her husband (more likely with her husband's family) and they took up life together as husband and wife.[56] Such "de facto" marriages were similar to the American common law marriage but without legal effect.

It was on the shoals of Family Law that the Civil Code controversy ultimately doomed the Old Civil Code—based on French Civil Law—and ushered in the New Civil Code based on German Civil Law structure.[57] One of the major goals of the Occupation was to replace the *Ie* family law system—which was seen as supporting the Emperor system where the Emperor was seen as the Head of the Japanese national House—with an American or European vision of the nuclear family based on mutual affection and

50. T. Fueto, *The Discrepancy Between Marriage Law and Mores in Japan*, (Comment) 5 Am. J. Comp. L. 256 (1956).
51. See Ogawa, Overview of the Japanese Family Law System, Focusing on A Historical Survey.
52. John Carey Hall, *Japanese Feudal Law* (University Publications of America, Inc. 1979) (reprint edition) 300.
53. For a discussion of the travail of a married woman in Tokugawa Japan under the *Ie* system see George Sansom, *A History Of Japan, 1615–1867*, 89–90 (Stanford University Press 1963).
54. For a discussion of the *Ie* and how the *Ie* has a lasting effect on Japanese family law see Book Review, Christopher S. Thompson, *Gendai Noson ni okeru Ie to Josei: Shonai Chiho ni Miru Rekishi no Renzoku to Danzetsu (Ie and Women in Modern Rural Society: Continuity and Discontinuity in the History of the Shonai District, Yamagata Prefecture)*, by Nagano Yukiko. Tokyo: Tosui Shobo, 2005, 10 *Social Science Japan Journal* 131–134 (2007).
55. Ogawa, Overview of the Japanese Family Law System, Focusing on A Historical Survey.
56. Comment, *The Discrepancy between Marriage Law and Mores in Japan*, 5 American Journal of Comparative Law 256 (1956).
57. Fujiko Isono, *The Evolution of the Modern Family Law in Japan*, 2 Intl. J. L. & Family 183, 186–189 (1988).

equality. However, it was not until the 1990s that domestic violence was recognized as a societal and individual problem in Japan.[58]

[B] The Family Law System after the Occupation and under the Post War Constitution

One of the objectives of the Occupation of Japan was to dramatically change the status of women and raise them to the same level as men in Japanese society. To accomplish this goal several Constitutional provisions were written both explicitly and implicitly granting women equal treatment with men. Thus Article 13 requires respect for people as individuals, rather than as members of a group. Individual respect is to be given so that men and women are entitled to the same status—equal respect as individuals not as men on one hand and women on the other. Article 14 provides for equality under law for all persons (a sexually inclusive term) and prohibits sex discrimination in political, economic and social matters. As a direct assault on the institution of the *Ie*, Article 24 maintains that the institution of marriage is based on mutual consent of the husband and wife and is premised on equal rights of each spouse. The Constitution requires future family laws to be based on respect for the individuality of each spouse and the fundamental equality of the sexes. Article 26(2) requires equal treatment of boys and girls in basic education. The writers of the Constitution of Japan sought to assure that sex discrimination would be outlawed in Japan and women would enjoy the same rights as men. The Convention on the Elimination of All Forms of Discrimination against Women ratified by Japan in 1985 called for the elimination of all forms of discrimination against women.

[1] Marriage, Divorce and Child Custody

The Occupation's changes in Japan's Constitution dealing with marriage and the family required changes in the Family Law sections of the Civil Code. The *Ie* system was abolished, although the Family Register was maintained—now in the form of a nuclear family rather than the continuous family of the *Ie* system. Marriages, births, divorce are all matters to be recorded in the Family Register.

The Civil Code recognizes marriage as completed when it is registered in the Family Register.[59] It prohibits bigamous marriages,[60] sets completion of the 18th year as the age when a man may marry and the 16th year for a woman,[61] prohibits marriage between certain close relatives, lineal relatives or between an adopted child and a

58. Yukiko Tsunoda, *Legal Response to Domestic Violence in Japan*, in *Japanese Family Law in Comparative Perspective* 165 (Scheiber & Mayali eds., Robbins Collection Publications 2009).
59. Civil Code Article 739. When Japanese nationals marry abroad they are required to notify the responsible Japanese Foreign Ministry official in their location. Article 741. See also Family Register Law Article 41.
60. Civil Code Article 732.
61. Civil Code Article 731.

parent,[62] and recognizes both divorce and annulment.[63] (For the issue of same-sex marriage see part §9.03[A][5] of this Chapter *infra*)

The actual process of getting married is quite simple. No formal marriage ceremony civil or religious is required. In fact, such ceremonies while typically performed are of no legal significance. All that is required is that the parties to the marriage consent to be married, fill out a marriage notification form at the local ward, city or town office, stamp the form with their *inkan* stamp, get two witnesses to witness and file the form with the Family Registrar (typically the ward or town officer). An American marrying a Japanese national would sign the form (not having a *inkan* stamp a signature is utilized) and would need to provide evidence that he/she is not already married—this can be done via an affidavit. A Japanese national need not provide such evidence, the information would already be contained in the Family Register. Upon filing the marriage is complete and the Family Registrar will create a new register for the newly married couple showing the Head of House and family surname (either the husband or wife can be chosen as Head whose surname can be chosen, but in over 95% of cases it is the husband as Head and his surname selected). Foreign spouses cannot be Head and are not directly listed in the new Family Register but can be listed in a comments section.[64]

Marriage in Tokugawa times was contractual in nature, but the contract was not between the marrying parties. Rather it was between the Houses of which the bridal couple was a part.[65] Under the Pre-war Civil Code the respective Houses had to give their consent to the marriage or the parties could be expelled from the House. However, marriage was no longer seen as a "de facto" matter, all "legal" marriages had to be registered.[66] The 1948 revision of the Code while providing that consent of the couple to be married was required continued the pre-existing system under which the marriage was concluded by a notification filed in the Family Register. Nonetheless, the existing system under which parties lived *as if* married without filing the necessary notification continued in immediate Post-Tokugawa Japan.[67]

The ideas underlying divorce in Japan are somewhat inconsistent. On the one hand judicial divorce is based on conceptions of fault; on the other, parties can divorce without judicial involvement, all that is required is consent.

The Civil Code recognizes two types of divorce[68]:

---

62. Civil Code Article 734, 735 and 736.
63. Civil Code Articles 742–749; and Articles 763–771.
64. See, e.g., Vera Mackie, *Family Law and its Others*, in *Japanese Family Law in Comparative Perspective* 139 at 154 (Scheiber & Mayali eds., Robbins Collection Publications 2009).
65. It has been suggested that under the feudal system marriage was neither religious nor contractual but was simply a process wherein the wife was turned over to and became a part of her husband's Ie. Charles Henry Huberich *The Paternal Power in Japanese Law*, 12 Yale L. J. 26 at 29 (1902).
66. For a discussion of marriage (as well as divorce) in Japan See Harald Fuess, *Divorce in Japan, Family, Gender and the State* 1600–2000 (Stanford University Press 2004). See also, Matsushima, *The UN Convention on the Rights of the Child and Controversial Issues in Japanese Family Law and Child Affairs in Families Across Frontiers* 151–163 (Martinus Nijhoff 1996).
67. See Rex Coleman,*Japanese Family Law*, 9 Stamford L. Rev. 132, 132–142 (1956).
68. For a discussion of Japan's dual system for divorce See Harald Fuess, *Divorce in Japan, Family, Gender and the State 1600–2000* at 100–118 (Stanford University Press 2004).

a) *Divorce by agreement of the parties*—the parties are expected to agree not just to divorce but on division of property and custody of children. The Family Court may in the interests of the child change the custody arrangement.[69] If the parties agreeing to divorce cannot agree as to custody or financial arrangements the Family Court may resolve the issues.[70] 90% of all divorces in Japan are achieved through consensual divorce. Of the remaining 10% it is reported that 9% are achieved through Family Court conciliation while the remaining 1% require a judicial decree.[71] While consensual in form many of the 90% are hotly contested out of court at a cost to the wife, who typically seeks the divorce and custody of children and is disadvantaged by the long time it takes to get a judicial divorce.[72] Consensual divorce occurs when the consenting parties file a divorce form with the Family Registrar—the form contains space for the parties to designate which party gets custody of which child. There is neither provision for joint custody nor for both divorced parents to retain parental rights.[73] Because either party may file the consent document containing the *inkan* seal of both parties, fraud in registering consensual divorce is a common problem. While married one party to the unhappy marriage may have access to the seal of the other as well as their own seal making it easy to seal the document and simply file it.[74] In recognition, but not a solution, Family Registrars have put in place a procedure by which a party to a marriage may request that no documents be filed in the Family Register for a limited period of time unless they are first notified. Since 2008 the Registrar must be shown identification papers in order to prevent false notifications[75] but this too is likely to have little effect.

The Civil Code has no mandatory provisions regarding custody or rights of a divorced parent who lacks parental rights and it has been folklore in Japan that a child of a divorced couple is better off not seeing the parent who lacks parental rights.[76] In 2012 the Code was amended, to provide that parents involved in a consensual divorce *should* (but are not required) discuss and seek to resolve the issue of visitation by the

69. Civil Code Article 766. See especially 766 (2) where the Family Court when it is deemed for the benefit of the child may change custody arrangements.
70. Civil Code Articles 766 and 768.
71. John Crouch, *New Reforms Abound at D.C. International Family Courts Conference*, reporting on the lecture by Professor Tomiyuki Ogawa, http://patriot.net/˜crouch/flnc/afc.html. See also, Masayuki Murayama, *Convergence from Opposite Direction? Characteristics of Japanese Divorce Law in Comparative Perspective*, in *Japanese Family Law in Comparative Perspective* tbl. 1 at 72(Scheiber & Mayali ed., Robbins Collection Publications 2008) showing that in 2000 of 264,246 divorces 91.5% were consensual, 7.7% resulted from conciliation and only 0.8% were judicially ordered divorces.
72. Allison Alexy, *Home and Family in Japan*, Chapter 12 (Richard Ronald & Allison Alexy eds., Routledge 2011).
73. Colin P.A. Jones, *In the Best Interests of the Court: What American Lawyers Need To Know About Child Custody and Visitation in Japan*, 8 Asian-P. L. & Policy J. 166, 212 (2007).
74. Masayuki Murayama, *Convergence from Opposite Directions? Characteristics of Japanese Divorce Law in Comparative Perspective*, in *Japanese Family Law in Comparative Persopective* 73 (Scheiber & Mayali eds., Robbins Collection Publications 2009).
75. See, *United Nations Economic and Social Commission for Asia* (Nov. 5, 2010), http://www.unescap.org/stat/cst/2/CST2-INF13.pdf, last accessed Sept. 15, 2012.
76. See Matthew J. McCauley, *Divorce and the /welfare of the Child in Japan*, 20 Pacific Rim Law & Policy Journal 589 (2011).

non-parental rights parent. The amendment also urges the parties to resolve issues dealing with support payments by the non-parental rights parent.[77] It is hoped by some that such provisions although not mandatory will create a new norm under which regular visits with the parent who lacks parental rights will be seen as in the best interests of the child. As the father is typically the parent who gives up parental rights the Civil Code amendment apparently seeks a compromise under which the father will make support payments in exchange for being able to meet regularly with his child. Family courts can award custody and in 2010 custody was forcefully taken from one parent and given to another in over 100 instances. However, the enforcement mechanism for custody awards is weak; there is no special procedure for enforcement; parties must rely on the Civil Enforcement Law that was not designed for family matters and many courts are unwilling to apply it to custody; habeas corpus is also not designed for custody.[78] In part this may reflect Tokugawa ideals where family matters were "personal matters" and not something the Magistrate should concern himself with.

While consensual divorce is valid in Japan, its recognition by States in the United States is problematic, as divorce in the United States requires a judicial determination.[79] There is no Japanese court decree to be recognized via "comity". Japan's accession to the Hague Convention on the Civil Aspects of International child Abduction might cause complications with consensual divorces containing parental rights and visitation provisions as no court order is implicated. Whether accession will lead to amendment that will allow consensual divorce arrangements to be embodied in a consensual court order remains to be seen. The weak domestic enforcement mechanism may similarly render enforcement of orders entered abroad and subject to The Hague Convention weak although separate and more compelling procedures for hand over in Hague cases likely will be applied. Accession might lead to amendment of the law making custody orders more readily enforceable in domestic cases in Japan.[80] Accession may not have a significant affect as loopholes and exceptions being considered in the draft law effectuating accession leave plenty of reason to believe few if any Japanese children will be returned even after accession. No law consistent with accession obligations (a precondition to accession) was enacted before the Lower House disbanded in September 2012.

b) *Judicial divorce*—parties who cannot agree on a divorce may obtain divorce through judicial proceedings.[81] Before judicial divorce can be sought the parties must

77. Yoshiko Kosaka, *Revised code to aid parental visits*, Daily Yomiuri (Aug. 20, 2011), http://www.yomiuri.co.jp/dy/national/T110819005086.htm.
78. *Forced custody transfer orders hit 120 in 2010 / Enforcement unsuccessful in many cases*, The Yomiuri Shimbun (Jan. 10, 2012), http://www.yomiuri.co.jp/dy/national/T120109004533.htm.
79. See *American Consulate in Naha Okinawa*, http://usembassy.state.gov/naha/wwwh2080.html.
80. Although the Constitution provides for habeas corpus (Article 34) it is questionable as to whether this provision provides support for enforcement of custody orders as it is geared to criminal cases and the Supreme Court rules on habeas are quite limited in scope.
81. For a general discussion of divorce in Japan including a discussion of child custody and visitation See, Takao Tanase, *Post-Divorce Laws Governing Parent and Child in Japan* (Sept. 14, 2010), http://travel.state.gov/_res/docs/pdf/tanase_on_visitation_law_in_english.pdf.

attempt conciliation before the Family Court and a high percentage of non-consensual divorce situations are resolved through the conciliation route. Parties may use a private or Family Court conciliation; although to date the vast majority of conciliations are carried out in the Family Court.[82] This does not necessarily mean that the parties to the divorce dispute are in fact reconciled to the conciliated settlement. There are many reasons why a wife may agree to the conciliated result although not in agreement with the result. Although the judicial system finds that conciliation is successful in resolving divorce disputes there is disagreement on this point with some suggesting that conciliation is in fact not effective.[83] Conciliation places pressure on the "weaker" party to the marriage break up, typically the wife who is typically the party seeking divorce (approximately 70% of the time). Since judicial divorce requires "fault" the party seeking divorce bears the burden of showing that grounds for divorce exist. There is no presumptive ground and the court has the final say as to whether a divorce should be granted. The wife may bargain away her "right" to a greater financial award in favor of agreement to divorce. A similar state of affairs existed in the United States in the 1950s before presumptive ground for divorce (e.g., living separately for a period of years) was introduced in several American states. It was a short step from "presumption" to "no fault" based on the idea that unsuccessful marriage should be allowed to be dissolved.[84] Japan may be on a similar, although somewhat slower path. It was only recently that a party "at fault" could obtain a judicial divorce. At the same time Japanese Family Law contains no provisions *requiring* alimony or child support as between the parties (there is a child support allowance that a divorced spouse with parental rights receives from the government) leaving the financial settlement terms up to the parties or the court (or the persuasive power of the conciliators). The relevant Civil Code provision deals with a "division of property" rather a stream of income based on future earnings.[85] Child support can be obtained via a stream of income approach but this is deemed a matter that the divorcing parties should determine

82. Aya Yamada, Divorce Mediation in Japan: Legalization, Privatization and Unification, in JAPANESE FAMILY LAW IN COMPARATIVE PERSPECTIVE (Scheiber and Mayali, Ed., Robbins Collection Publications, 2008) 99. Family Court mediation is undertaken by a panel of three of whom two are lay persons and one a Family Court Judge. Like conciliation of estate cases in Family Court the Judge usually lets the lay conciliators handle the conciliation and only gets involved to advise the lay conciliators.
83. See, Masayuki Murayama, *Convergence from Opposite Direction? Characteristics of Japanese Divorce Law in Comparative Perspective*, in *Japanese Family Law in Comparative Perspective* 78 (Scheiber & Mayali eds., Robbins Collection Publications 2008).
84. For a discussion of the stages in development of divorce law in the United States see, Lawrence W. Friedman, *Legal Culture and Family Law*, in *Japanese Family Law in Comparative Perspective* At 11, 14–18 (Scheiber & Mayali eds., Robbins Collection Publications 2008).
85. Article 768. Under 768 the Code first assumes that the parties will both divorce by consent and provide for a division of property as part of that consensual arrangement. Indeed 768 is part of the first portion of the Code sections dealing with divorce, namely the portion dealing with divorce by agreement. If the parties cannot agree then a request may be made to the court to provide for a "division of property" between them (the request must be made within two years of the consensual divorce of the parties or it is outside the statute of limitations contained in 768). The court then has discretion both as to whether to order a division of property and if so how to divide the property. Under Article 771, in the portion dealing with Judicial Divorce, Article 768 is to be applied mutatis mutandis to judicial divorce.

amongst themselves. To aid in this process there are standardized charts, created in 1999 by the Judges of the Tokyo Family Court, available through the court system that utilize the income of each parent in determining the amount of child support.[86] However, the charts are not binding and factors other than income can be used to moderate the chart amount.

Because the law recognizes that each spouse owns their own property, including property each earned during the marriage, and because the husband is typically the significant breadwinner, the wife is at a financial disadvantage and must argue that her services as housewife are entitled to be considered in the financial settlement. There is evidence that the wife's contribution to the marriage's financial estate is calculated at only somewhere between 20% and 30% of the financial property of the marriage. This provides the backdrop to negotiations leading up to consensual divorce and the financial arrangements agreed to in such divorce as well as the negotiations undertaken in the conciliation proceedings.[87] Although the requirement for conciliation has an adverse effect on the wife it is not sex discrimination under Japanese law (both parties are required to engage in conciliation so in form both sexes are treated equally and to reach agreement both parties must agree so there is formal equality). The requirement for conciliation was a demand made the conservative forces in the pre-war era so that so-called Japanese values (which favored compromise to keep the marriage in place and favored the male in the marriage relationship) rather than law or rights could prevail. The basic foundation of the conciliation system remains the pre-war system with its pre-war favoritism of the male member of the family.

The Civil Code sets forth a number of grounds for divorce, including a catch all for inability of the parties to continue in a married state.[88] But even if one (or more) of the stated reasons for divorce is established the Family Court may refuse to grant a divorce if the court is of the view that the marriage should continue.[89] Divorce by judicial decree involves a long and arduous process requiring that it be shown that the parties cannot get back together again. This in turn means that the parties must be separated for a long period of time—perhaps more than five years—before the court will act.[90]

The Civil Code provides that a child conceived during marriage is presumed to be the child of the husband and that a child born 200 days or more after marriage or less than 300 days after dissolution of a marriage is presumed to be conceived during the marriage (and hence the husband is presumed the father).[91] The Civil Code makes no

86. One can even find a support chart calculator on the web–see, http://www.asahi-net.or.jp/~zi3h-kwrz/lawychspcal.html.
87. Aya Yamada, *Divorce Mediation in Japan: Legalization, Privatization and Unification*, in *Japanese Family Law in Comparative Perspective* 113–114 (Scheiber & Mayali eds., Robbins Collection Publications 2008).
88. Civil Code Article 770.
89. Civil Code Article 770 (2).
90. John Crouch, New Reforms Abound at D.C. International Family Courts Conference, reporting on the lecture by Professor Tomiyuki Ogawa. <patriot.net/˜crouch/flnc/afc.html>. See also, Harald Fuess, *Divorce In Japan, Family, Gender and the State 1600–2000* at 161–166 (Stanford University Press 2004) for a discussion of the "liberalization" of divorce laws in Japan in the 1990s and the inability of politicians in Japan to agree on divorce law reforms.
91. Civil Code Articles 772–791.

provision for modern science's ability to assist in pregnancy or birth and thus has no provisions dealing with surrogacy, biological donors or in vitro fertilization and children born as a consequence of such modern medical procedures.

Although parents have parental rights over their minor children (the code makes no distinction between mothers and fathers in this respect)[92] a parent may lose such parental rights for various reasons including abuse of the parental right or gross misconduct or mismanagement of a child's individual property.[93] A presumption in favor of custody by the mother may be gleaned from the Civil Code provisions that give custody and parental power to the mother (absent an agreement between the parties) if the parents divorce before the child is born.[94] The Family Court may, after divorce, transfer parental power from one parent to another when the interests of the child are served.[95] The 2004 Law for the Prevention of Spousal Violence and the Protection of Victims[96] provides that in cases where spousal violence is feared or where it is feared that custody may be forcefully taken from the custodial parent, a protective order may be obtained prohibiting the other spouse from approaching the child at school or otherwise.[97]

It is estimated that as many as one-third of all marriages in Japan will end up in divorce.[98] There has been a noticeable increase in divorces of older couples as older married woman suffering from so-called "retired husband syndrome"[99] have sought divorce.[100] The plight of older women caught in unhappy marriages—and many marriages among seniors in Japan fall into this category as most Japanese men have devoted their lives to their companies as distinguished from their families—was eased by a law that went into effect in April of 2007 under which a woman can make claim to as much as 50% of her spouse's retirement pension benefits.[101] There was a spike of over 6% in divorces immediately after the effective date.[102] This new statute has arrived at just that point in time when the Japanese baby boomers are scheduled for

92. Civil Code Article 818.
93. Civil Code Articles 834–837.
94. Civil Code Article 819 (3).
95. Civil Code Article 818 (6).
96. Law No. 64 of 2004 amending Law No. 31 of 2001.
97. Law No. 64 of 2004 amending Law No. 31 of 2001, Chapter 4 Article 10. Where the child involved is over the age of fifteen, the Protective Order can only be granted with the child's consent.
98. James M. Raymo, Miho Iwasawa, Larry Bumpass, *Marital Dissolution in Japan: Recent Trends and Patterns*, Demographic Research, Volume 11, Article 14, 395–420, published Dec. 17, 2004, www.demographic-research.org/Volumes/Vol11/14/.
99. See BBC News, *Japan retired divorce rate soars*, http://news.bbc.co.uk/go/pr/fr/-/2/hi/asia-pacific/4741018.stm.
100. See, Masayuki Murayama, *Convergence from Opposite Direction? Characteristics of Japanese Divorce Law in Comparative Perspective*, in *Japanese Family Law in Comparative Perspective* fig. 6 at 90 (Scheiber and Mayali ed., Robbins Collection Publications 2008) showing an increase in the percentage of divorce between couples living together for more than 20 years from 4% in 1950 to 16% in 2005.
101. See BBC News, *Japan retired divorce rate soars* <http://news.bbc.co.uk/go/pr/fr/-/2/hi/asia-pacific/4741018.stm.
102. Blaine Harden, *Learn to be Nice to your Wife, or Pay the Price*, Washington Post A1 (Nov. 26, 2007).

mandatory retirement—the baby boom generation has reached the customary mandatory retirement age of 60 beginning in 2007.[103] The effect of forced retirement of the husband (placing him suddenly in the home he had virtually abandoned during his working life) and both the stress this places on the wife[104] together with the wife's ability to obtain some measure of financial security through divorce may have a significant effect on Japanese society.

§9.03 WHAT YOU SEE MAY NOT BE WHAT YOU GET

[A] Family Law Issues

[1] General Discussion

Adoption of the Post War Constitution required a re-writing the sections of the Civil Code dealing with family law. The *Ie* system was abolished[105] and while the Family Register system was maintained changes were made to abolish the multigenerational Family Register and replace it with a new Family Register upon marriage, which reflected a new nuclear household. Leaving the Family Register in place has resulted in retaining the previous feudal notion of the family as an entity centered on the register; one marries and enters into the Register of the Head of the House (typically the husband's House); one divorces and leaves the House. This has subtle but real consequences as it affects the thought process of judges, mediators, conciliators and family members when dealing with issues such as child custody and/or visitation by a non-custodial parent. The rules of succession were changed to abolish primogeniture and provide that property can be distributed by Will although spouses and children were given reserved portion that cannot be vitiated by Will.[106]

---

103. Yutaka Asao, Outlook *on the Retirement Process of Dankai No Sedai, or the Japanese Baby-Boom Generation, The Japan Institute for Labor Policy and Training,* 4 Japan Lab. Rev. No. 4 at 121, 123 (August, 2007).
104. The wife may have married her husband for better or for worse—but not for lunch!
105. Some remnants of the *Ie* remain as shown by the Supreme Court's decision concerning how to distribute funds received from a third party user of common land in a small Japanese village. As the use of the common can be traced back to feudal times when use was controlled by the various *Ie* Heads of House, it was considered appropriate to distribute funds based on succession as if the succession was to the current Heads of House, although the *Ie* as such has been abolished. See, *Common Funds Distribution case,* Case No. 2004 (Ju) No. 1968, 60 Minshu No. 3, http://www.courts.go.jp/english/judgments/text/2006.03.17-2004.-Ju-.No..1968.html (P.B., Mar. 17, 2006).
106. See Civil Code Articles 890–893. Wills are not as common in Japan as they are in the United States and the American device of a Living Trust is not available. A will can be either Notarized or informal. Notarized wills are prepared by Judicial Scriveners and have an immediate effect on death without the need for a probate proceeding, although heirs may challenge the will in the Family Court. Informal wills need to be certified by the court. In either case the procedure is not the same as an American Probate proceeding although challenges to the will in the Family Court may resemble challenges in a Probate case by raising such issues as whether a will is the Final Will or a superseded will and whether the maker of the will was competent at the time of making the will. Because either a formal (Notarized) or informal (not Notarized) will speaks immediately at death the issue is presented as to whether a named heir may immediately

Inheritance disputes are within the jurisdiction of the Family Court and conciliation is a first step.[107] If agreement cannot be reached the court determines distribution.[108] No distinction is made between male and female spouses or between male and female children or lineal descendants. However a distinction is made between legitimate and "illegitimate" children.[109] Unlike the approach adopted in the United States, the Supreme Court of Japan held distinctions between the inheritance rights of illegitimate and legitimate children could be justified in order to support the sanctity of marriage—the system of marriage by law rather than de facto marriage. Whether this discriminatory treatment of "illegitimate" children is valid after the decision in the *Portion of Nationality Law Unconstitutional Case* is debatable. In the Nationality Law case the Court noted that the child was not to blame for the failure of its parents to marry and could not be treated differently on this basis.[110] This same rationale would seem applicable in the inheritance context, but a Petty Bench of the Supreme Court in a 2009 decision rendered after the Nationality Law decision again upheld the discrimination against "illegitimate" children relying on the Court's earlier decision upholding the discrimination. In July 2010 a different panel of the Supreme Court was presented with the same question and referred the issue to the Grand Bench leading many to believe that the Petty Bench believed that the earlier decision should be reversed.[111] While pending before the Grand Bench the case was settled and the Grand Bench

register real property left to the heir by the will prior to any court proceeding requiring the challenging party to initiate a Family Court proceeding to challenge the registration. The Supreme Court has held that the heir may so immediately register the property without obtaining consents from other heirs. For a criticism of the rule see, Yasuhei & Akiko Taniguchi, *Succession Law and Inheritance Disputes*, in *Japanese Family Law in Comparative Perspective* 132–133 (Harry N. Scheiber & Laurent Mayali ed., Robbins Collection Publications 2009).

107. Conciliation is undertaken by a conciliation committee consisting of 3 persons, 2 of whom are lay persons and one the Family Court Judge. The lay participants are in charge of the conciliation process and if they cannot obtain agreement the Judge will decide the matter. While the statute sets forth the percentages of reserved shares the court may have to decide how to distribute the actual physical and/or real property among the heirs. For a discussion of conciliation before the Family Court in inheritance cases see, Yasuhei &Akiko Taniguchi, *Succession Law and Inheritance Disputes* in *Japanese Family Law in Comparative Perspective* (Harry N. Scheiber & Laurent Mayali eds., Robbins Collection Publications 2009).

108. See, e.g., Kyodo News, *Heirs Kids Not Next in Line High Court Rules*, Japan Times (Feb. 23, 2011), http://search.japantimes.co.jp/cgi-bin/nn20110223a4.html.

109. Article 900 (4) provides for equal treatment among children (or siblings) but an "illegitimate" child is entitled to only 50% of the share reserved for a legitimate child. The Court upheld the discrimination. *"Illegitimate" child Inheritance Case*, 49 Minshu 1789, Case No. 1991 (Ku) No. 143, (G.B. July 5, 1995) http://www.courts.go.jp/english/judgments/text/1995.07.05-1991-Ku-No.143-155301.html.

110. *Portion of Nationality Law Unconstitutional Case*, Case No. 135 (Gyo-Tsu) of 2006, 62 Minshu No. 6, http://www.courts.go.jp/english/judgments/text/2008.06.04-2006.-Gyo-Tsu-.No..135-111255.html (G.B., June 4, 2008).

111. While the case was pending before the Grand Bench another illegitimate inheritance case was appealed to the Osaka High Court. The High Court found the inheritance distinction between legitimate and "illegitimate" children unconstitutional relying on the rationale of the Nationality Act case.

returned the case to the Petty Bench which then dismissed the action because of the settlement.[112]

Although the Occupation sought to abolish the *Ie* system its decision to allow Japan to continue the Family Register system has had the effect of continuing various aspects of the *Ie*. One spouse is Head of House retaining the idea that he (over 90% of couples choose the male) is Head and she subordinate; the wife is listed as a part of the Head of House's household, replicating the feudal notion of the wife entering her husband's House. As has been suggested the, *Ie* while revoked as a matter of law retains staying power in Japan.[113] The system has a psychological effect of perpetuating old notions concerning the House. Thus, there are efforts to keep the Family Register "clean", to make sure there are no entries that would bring "shame" on the family, to not disclose that a child was born out of wedlock. One strategy is for the parents to "marry" prior to birth—this results in the setting up of a new family register for the couple—have the child entered in the new Register (each of the parents will have been removed from their father's Family Register so no notation concerning the child "taints" the grandparent's Register)—and after birth the couple divorces by consent. The wife can then create her own Family Register and either retain her married name (since 1976) or use her maiden name. Other escape mechanisms exist by which the pregnant woman can voluntarily withdraw from her parent's register and create her own register. While this would allow the parents' register to remain clean, it would result in the child being known to be "illegitimate" with both legal and social consequences.[114] These consequences and the efforts of some Japanese nationals to avoid the stigma of an unclean Family Register should be borne in mind when considering the cases in which the Supreme Court of Japan has held that a child born through posthumous in vitro fertilization or surrogacy cannot be entered in the family register of its parent as a "natural child" of its biological parents.[115]

The Civil Code and Family Register law require that both husband and wife utilize the same family name. The effect of the law is that women disproportionately change their name. Many women, especially those who have had a career or a profession prior to marriage, object to the Civil Code's requirement and feel that it adversely affects their career and causes them a loss of "self".[116] Efforts to change the

112. *Illegitimate child Inheritance Case 2*, Case No. 2009 (Ku) No. 1027, Minshu Vol. 65, No. 2 (Sup. Ct. P.B. Mar. 9, 2011), http://www.courts.go.jp/english/judgments/text/2011.03.09-2009.-Ku-.No..1027.html.

113. See, e.g., Atsushi Omura & Hiroto Dogauchi, *Status of Women in the Family: the balance between Autonomy and protection*, 1 U T Soft L. Rev. 86, 89 (2009).

114. See, Karl Jakob Krogness, *The Ideal, the Deficient, and the Illogical Family*, in *Home and Family in Japan* (Richard Ronald and Allison Alexy, Ed., Routledge, 2011) at 65 and in the same volume, Ekaterina Hertog, *I did not know how to tell my parents, so I thought I would have an abortion*, in *Home and Family in Japan* 91 (Richard Ronald & Allison Alexy ed., Routledge 2011). 91;. Rachel Brehm King, *Redefining Motherhood: Discrimination in Legal Parenthood in Japan*, 18 Pacific Rim Law and Policy Journal 189, 203–204 (2009).

115. For a discussion of the relationship between the Family Register system and restrictions on Surrogacy and in vitro conception and birth see, Rachel Brehm King, *Redefining Motherhood: Discrimination in Legal Parenthood in Japan*, 18 P. Rim L. & Policy J. 190 (2009).

116. Tadaki Matsukawa, *The Japanese Family between Tradition and Modernity*, in *The European Family* 139, 146 (Jacques Commaille ed., Kluwer Academic Publishers 1997).

Code through legislative means have been unsuccessful. Recently a litigation strategy arguing that the Code provision is inconsistent with the equality grant in the Constitution, has been adopted.[117] An LDP lawmaker who has campaigned to change the current system and allow women to keep their own surname after marriage recently gave birth to a child conceived via ova transplant; she married her de facto husband by filing notice of marriage with the family registrar; her husband took her surname.

The Family Register Law in Japan makes a distinction between the manner in which legitimate and "illegitimate" children are registered. The Tokyo District Court found such a difference a violation of the right to privacy of the "illegitimate" child.[118] The Ministry of Justice adopted an Ordinance so as to treat legitimate and "illegitimate" children the same for registration purposes.[119] However in 2005 the Tokyo High Court upheld the different treatment of legitimate and "illegitimate" children by the Family Registrar and that determination was affirmed by the Supreme Court on procedural grounds.[120] Adopted children are listed as such in the Family Register and thus are distinguished from biological children. As special adoption (the procedure for adopting young children) is relatively new in Japan such adoption creates questions and assumptions that the child is illegitimate—creating problems for the child and family.

Even a casual observer of the Japanese scene recognizes that complete equality of the sexes both at home and at work does not exist. Article 762 of the Civil Code appears on its face to treat the sexes equally by providing that property acquired by either spouse during marriage remained the property of that spouse. But, since the husband, as the principle breadwinner in the family acquires more property than his wife during their marriage, such provision perpetuates the subordinate status of the wife during marriage and in divorce proceedings. The Supreme Court has upheld this provision.[121]

Non-citizen wives of Japanese men have a particularly difficult time. This issue has become more prominent as the percentage of foreign marriages in Japan has increased from approximately 0.5% in 1970 to almost 5% in 2003—mostly foreign wives.[122] Spouses of Japanese nationals, as a rule, obtain yearly visas to reside in

117. Associated Press, *Women Sue to Keep Surnames in Marriage*, Japan Times (Feb. 16, 2011), http://search.japantimes.co.jp/cgi-bin/nn20110216a8.html; Kyoto News, *Suit Claims Single Surname Rule Contravenes Constitution*, Japan Times (Jan. 7, 2011), http://search.japantimes.co.jp/cgi-bin/nn20110107a8.html.; Justin McCurry, The Guardian, Jan. 11, 2011, *Japanese Marital Surname Law Faces Legal Challenge*, http://www.guardian.co.uk/world/2011/jan/11/japan-marital-surname-law-challenge.

118. *Family Register Right of Privacy and Illegitimacy* case, Case No. 26105 (Wa) of 1999, decided Mar. 2, 2004.

119. A discussion of this change and the role of the court's decision on the change may be found in The Fifth Periodic Report by the Government of Japan Under Article 40 paragraph 1 (b) of the International Covenant on Civil and Political Rights para. 259 (December 2006), www.mofa.go.jp/policy/human/civil_rep6.pdf. last accessed Sept. 16, 2012.

120. *Family Register Right of Privacy and "illegitimate" children Procedural Dismissal case.* The Supreme Court held that the action of the Registrar was not subject to review under the ACLL since no Administrative Order (shobun) was implicated. For a discussion of the doctrine of "shobunsai" see Chapter 17.

121. See Hiroyuki Hata & Go Nakagawa & Takehisa Nakagawa, *Japanese Constitutional Law* 115 (Kluwer Law International 2001), Separate Property Case, 15 Minshu 2047 (Sept. 6, 1961).

122. Gavin Jones & Hsiu-hua Shen, *International marriage in East and Southeast Asia: trends and research emphases*, 12 Citizenship Stud. 9, 11–12 (2008).

Japan. A non-Japanese national spouse who is living separately from her spouse through no fault of her own, may be denied the necessary papers to remain in Japan and may be deported.[123] The fact that the husband was at fault was of no moment as the determination of whether the spouse performed her activities as a spouse (the criteria for the visa) was an objective not a subjective judgment. Such a rule places all non-Japanese spouses of Japanese husbands at a significant disadvantage. It is uncertain if the same decision would follow if the abandoned spouse was caring for children of the marriage. What you see, a Law and Regulation that permits non-Japanese spouses to live in Japan while they are married to a Japanese national, is not what you get—only if the Japanese spouse wishes to allow the non-Japanese spouse to remain in Japan can the spouse remain. It was not until a 2009 Amendment that foreign wives who had good cause to leave the spousal home (such as spousal abuse) were able to retain their spousal visa. [Good cause will likely be interpreted to mean such cause as the courts conclude are consistent with the common sense judgment of the Japanese people. Thus, at least for the reasonable future foreign wives are left somewhat confused as to the meaning of the good cause requirement.]

Under Article 733 of the Civil Code a woman is forbidden to remarry within six months of the dissolution or annulment of her prior marriage. A man has no such restriction. The Supreme Court upheld the Code provision on the ground that its purpose was to prevent paternity disputes.[124] This purpose is supported by part 2 of Article 733, which lifts the six months distinction if the woman gives birth prior to the expiration of six months. The Court conspicuously refrained from discussing the Constitutional challenge simply upholding the Code provision as providing a reasonable basis for the distinction between the sexes.[125] The United States approach would be to require a six-month waiting period for both sexes —assuming any waiting period was considered "reasonable".

[2] Age Discrimination

Japan has no general legislation prohibiting discrimination in the workplace based on age.[126] However in 2007 the Employment Measures Act was amended to prohibit discrimination in initial hiring of new graduates. The law provides exemptions, the

123. *Non-Japanese Spouse Change in Status Determination*, Case No. 46 (Gyo-Hi) of 1999, 56 Minshu (No. 8) at 1823, http://www.courts.go.jp/english/judgments/text/2002.10.17-1999.-Gyo-Hi-.No.46.html (P.B., Oct. 17, 2002). See also Satoshi Minamikata, Marriages Between Japanese and Non-Japanese in Rural Areas in *Families across Frontiers* (Kluwer Law International, 1996), 513–521.
124. *Remarriage Case*, 1563 Hanji 81, 5 December 1995. Article 772 of the Civil Code establishes a presumption that a child conceived by a wife during marriage is the child of the husband.
125. 1563 Hanji 81 (Sup. Ct. 5 December 1995) discussed in Hiroyuki Hata & Go Nakagawa & Takehisa Nakagawa, *Japanese Constitutional Law* (Kluwer Law International 2001). In 1991 the Hiroshima High Court did consider the Constitutional issue and upheld the provision. Yuji Iwasawa, *International Law, Human Rights, and Japanese Law* (Oxford University Press 1998).
126. The Age Discrimination in Employment Act in the United States contains general prohibitions against age discrimination against older workers and, with certain exceptions, prohibits mandatory retirement. See 29 USC sections 621 et seq.

principle of which allows for age based hiring when the employer is hiring new graduates into a "lifetime employment" program, i.e., a program where a long period of time is required for the new graduate to better develop skills.[127] This exemption virtually eliminates the prohibition for major Japanese business (and government) entities that engage in hiring new graduates from University—the core of the future management of the company or government entity. As is true in the sex discrimination area (with certain limited exceptions discussed *supra*), the equality provision does not take into account "effects discrimination" but deals solely with discrimination on its face. This leaves room for employers to set conditions for employment that while they appear age neutral, exclude older workers.

The age 60 has been the typical mandatory retirement age in Japan (statutes allow an employer to set a mandatory retirement age at age 60 or older)[128] since 1986 when legislation mandated that business attempt to bring its retirement age policy into line with the public pension system which paid pensions at age 60. Japan has increased the age at which the national pension is paid to 65. In 2004 the law was changed to mandate that employers continue to provide employment to older employees who wished to continue working past age 60.[129] The law did not require that employers raise their mandatory retirement age to age 65. Employers were given the option of: (a) raising the age to 65; (b) getting rid of mandatory retirement; or (c) providing a scheme for continuation of employment (although not necessarily in the same position or at the same salary and benefits). Most companies have opted for the "continuation" option. Companies took the alternative available to them to negotiate a continuation program with their internal labor union. The union, which represents all workers (most of whom do not fall into the elderly worker category), has no obligation to hold out for terms favoring elderly workers over middle age or younger workers. Continuation programs, in theory designed to benefit older workers, do not provide older workers with the same or even comparable benefits as would an elimination of mandatory retirement or a raising of the mandatory retirement age to 65. Because continuation programs take into account pension payments to workers over the age of 60, the wages that such workers are paid in a continuation plan are significantly lower than the wages earned prior to adoption—estimated to be about 60% of wages prior to attaining age 60.[130] And, because the employer can modify working conditions, job description and set various criteria for eligibility in the program, the program leaves much to be desired

127. For a general discussion of the 2007 Amendment see Ryoko Sakuraba, *The Amendment of the Employment Measure Act: Japanese Anti-age Discrimination Law*, 6 Japan Lab. Rev. 56 (2009). Other permissible basis for age based hiring discrimination are: mandatory retirement programs, statutory age limits (i.e., persons under the age of 18 are prohibited from engaging in certain work activities), affirmative steps to hire those in underrepresented age groups to assure a good flow of workers, hiring older workers to meet other statutory programs, and in the arts and entertainment fields to ensure authenticity of performances.
128. Act Concerning Stabilization of Employment of Older Workers, Article 8, Amended 2004.
129. For a discussion of the retirement age legislation see Noboru Yamashita, Act Concerning Stabilization of Employment of Older Persons, 4 *Japan Labor Review* No. 3, Summer 2007, 71.
130. Noboru Yamashita, *Act Concerning Stabilization of Employment of Older Persons*, 4 Japan Lab. Rev. No. 3, 71 at 88–90 (Summer 2007). Akemi Nakamura, *Back to Square One After a Lifetime of Work*, Japan Times (Mar. 14, 2008).

in achieving its asserted goal of rising the retirement age to 65. The program is consistent with the need to allow younger "lifetime employees" to move into more senior positions—a critical aspect of the "lifetime employment" system. (See Chapters 12 and 13)What you see, i.e., an act to stabilize employment of older workers by harmonizing the national pension system retirement age with retirement in the private sector is not what you get. The Act results in retention of older workers at reduced wages and changed working conditions while preserving Japan's "lifetime employment" system.

Because the amendment to the Employment Measures Act deals solely with *hiring* based on age, other age based employment actions are not covered. Thus, a reduction in force that centers on older employees is not covered by the Act but would be subject to the abusive discharge doctrine discussed in Chapter 12

[3] Visitation and International Child Custody: Spousal Abuse—Presumption of Parentage

"Best interests of the child" is recognized in the Civil Code, but other aspects of the family relationship are entitled to equal if not more weight.[131]

The Japanese Supreme Court has held that where Japanese parents were living separately and the wife was bringing up the child and the father went to the child's nursery school and forcefully took the child from his maternal grandmother in order to obtain custody of the child the actions of the father constituted kidnapping.[132] Similarly it has been held that when a non-Japanese father took his child from a hospital where his separated wife was undergoing treatment in order to take the child back to the Netherlands with him, the taking constituted kidnapping.[133] A Chinese husband whose wife left him in Japan and who then took their two daughters to China where they lived with him was arrested, tried and convicted when years later he returned to Japan.[134] But, these domestic determinations do not appear to be applicable to custody battles between Japanese and non-Japanese parents where the Japanese parent acquires physical custody.

Japan's emergence as a major exporting country has resulted in marriages consummated between a Japanese national and a non-Japanese. A percentage of such

131. Best interests of the child is also a standard provided in the UN Convention on the Rights of the Child: Article 3. This may affect the interpretation of "grave risk" under the Hague Convention on the Civil Aspects of International Child Abduction. See, *Neulinger and Shruk v. Switzerland* (No. 41615/07) Grand Chamber of the European Court of Human Rights, http://www.caselaw.ch/d/div/egmr%206-7-10.pdf.
132. *Parental Kidnapping* case (*Japanese parents*), Case No. 2199(A) of 2004, 59 Keishu, No. 10, http://www.courts.go.jp/english/judgments/text/2005.12.06-2004.-A-.No..2199.html (P.B., Dec. 6, 2005).
133. *Parental Kidnapping* case (*Dutch Father*), Case No. 2002 (A) No. 805, 57 Keishu No. 3, at 371, http://www.courts.go.jp/english/judgments/text/2003.03.18-2002-A-No.805.html (P.B., Mar. 18, 2003).
134. *Double Standard on International Child Abduction*, Mainichi Shimbun reported in Japanese Law Blog, http://japaneselaw.blogspot.com/2009/12/double-standard-on-international-child.html (Dec. 4, 2009).

marriages end in divorce, either in Japan or in another country. In such situations, the customs and expectations of the Japanese parent and the non-Japanese parent may differ. When the Japanese parent has possession of the child in Japan the non-Japanese parent has not been able to obtain custody or even visitation rights. This can have a perverse adverse effect on a Japanese parent whose child is in the custody of a non-Japanese divorced spouse located outside of Japan.[135] The non-Japanese spouse is unlikely to consent to visitation in Japan for fear of forever losing contact with its child.[136]

Visitation was not specifically provided for in the Civil Code until the 2011 amendments that call upon the parents in consensual divorce to take into consideration and resolve questions of visitation and child support. If parents are unable to do so the Family Court can deal with such issues. The amendment may be interpreted to mean that the Family Court should give primacy to the best interests of the child.[137] The Family Court has authority to make custody determinations and this could be interpreted to give it authority to order visitation—in reality visitation may be granted when the parent in physical custody of the child agrees to it, but otherwise the non-Japanese parent will not get visitation rights. The rationale is that the conflict between the parents is "confusing" and unhealthy for the child. Thus it is assumed that the child's interests are protected by denying visitation when the parents cannot agree to visitation, the reality of the best interests of the child as demonstrated by studies conducted outside of Japan notwithstanding.

It may be that visitation although not prohibited is not favored in Japan because of a feeling that the child should not be subjected to the tension and disagreement between parents that are at the root of a divorce.[138] Divorce may be seen as a "selfish" act on the part of parents who, putting their own interests ahead of the interests of their child and their obligation to properly raise their child, simply end their marriage relationship.[139] In such case the party who does not have custody of the child has only himself to blame for his situation. Perhaps the Family Court system and the mediators used by the system are simply not familiar enough with visitation to undertake the task of working out reasonable visitation arrangements. Perhaps the historical basis for family law matters, the *Ie*, affects modern custody decisions. Under the *Ie* system the actual parents had no rights concerning their child—the Head of the House had such

135. Maya Kaneko, Moms here also face custody torment, Japan Times (June 5, 2012), http://www.japantimes.co.jp/text/nn20120605f1.html.
136. See, e.g., *When Families Break Up / Japan – where some parents never see their kids*, Daily Yomiuri (Feb. 5, 2010), http://www.yomiuri.co.jp/dy/national/20100205TDY01301.htm.
137. Law No. 61 of 2011 (June 3, 2011) amending Article 766 of the Civil Code.
138. For the American view that abduction itself harms the child see, *Abbott v. Abbott*, 560 U.S. ___ (2010) See N. Faulkner, *Parental Child Abduction is Child Abuse* (1999), http://www.prevent-abuse-now.com/unreport.htm last accessed Sept. 16, 2012 (See also, Huntington, *Parental Kidnapping: A New Form of Child Abuse* (1982), in *American Prosecutors Research Institute's National Center for Prosecution of Child Abuse, Parental Abduction Project, Investigation and Prosecution of Parental Abduction* (1995).
139. See Mason, Tsuya and Choe, "*The Changing Family In Comparative Perspective*" 35 (University of Hawaii East West Center 1999).

rights.[140] Whatever the reason, it appears that visitation is rarely ordered and even when ordered is for short duration separated by extended periods of time[141].

This assumption is likely to affect the question of how vigorously Japanese courts and the bureaucracy will enforce the Hague Convention on the Civil Aspects of Child Abduction rights should Japan accede to the Convention as it has said it will. It is possible that Japanese Courts will consider that failure to obtain consent from the parent having custody will result in "grave injury" to the child. Grave injury is a loophole in the Hague Convention. So too Japan's focus on the expressed desires of the child may result in denial of Hague Convention rights as children are likely to want to stay with the parent who has custody simply to avoid more trauma and because the child has both lack of understanding to make an informed decision, immaturity, and is likely to have been "brainwashed" by the parent with custody. Although the act of the forcibly taking of a child by one custodial parent from another custodial parent is a crime in Japan, the Japanese government has not assisted foreign authorities in efforts to have such children who have been removed from the custodial parent in the foreign country and brought to Japan returned to the country from which taken or have the offending parent apprehended for the crime committed abroad.[142] This reality is to be compared with United States law where American courts have rejected the appeal of the American parent seeking (typically out of concern for the prospect that they will be deprived of their visitation rights) to prevent the Japanese parent from taking the child to Japan for a temporary period of time.[143] Accession to the Hague Convention on the Civil Aspects of International Child Abduction will not affect pre-accession custody orders and cases. After accession an office in the Ministry of Foreign Affairs is supposed to assist other signatory countries and parents in covered cases.

The difficulties of getting Japan to recognize a foreign custody order or to return a child abducted to Japan in violation of that order as well as the gap between what you see and what you get was highlighted by the U.S. State Department's web posting on this issue wherein the Department noted that although the Japanese Ministry of Justice says that:

> redress in child custody cases is sought through habeas corpus proceedings in the court. There is no preferential treatment based on nationality or gender

140. See, Anne E. Imamura, *Family Culture*, in *The Cambridge Companion to Modern Japanese Culture* 76 et seq. (Yoshio Sugimoto ed., Cambridge University Press 2009). (noting on page 77 that children belonged to the *Ie* not to their mother.)
141. Takao Tanase, *Divorce and the Best Interest of the Child: Disputes Over Visitation and the Japanese Family Courts*, (Matthew J. McCauley trans.) 20 P. Rim L. & Policy J. 563, 563–565 (2011).
142. Japan's refusal to return abducted children when an American court has given custody to a parent in the U.S. prior to abduction has caused some to compare Japan's attitude to abducted children returned to Japan with its demands that North Korea provide information on Japanese children abducted to North Korea years earlier. Japan has rejected the comparison on grounds that child custody should be resolved by the parents while the North Korean matter is state action. See, *Campbell's Hague plea irks North abductee kin*, Japan Times (May 9, 2012), http://www.japantimes.co.jp/text/nn20120509a9.html.
143. See e.g., *Criss v. Kunisada*, No. 19361, Intermediate Court of Appeals, Hawaii, Feb. 5, 1998 and *MacKinnon v. MacKinnon*, 191 N.J. 240, 922 A2d. 1252 (Sup. Ct. N.J., June 11, 2007) Compare *Shady v. Shady*, 858 N.E. 2d 128 (Ct. App., Indiana, Dec. 11, 2006).

the reality is that:

> in cases of international parental child abduction, foreign parents are greatly disadvantaged in Japanese courts, both in terms of obtaining the return of children to the United States, and in achieving any kind of enforceable visitation rights in Japan. The Department of State is not aware of any case in which a child taken from the United States by one parent has been ordered returned to the United States by Japanese courts, even when the left-behind parent has a United States custody decree.[144]

It is reported that in only one case has a non-Japanese mother been successful in obtaining custody from a Japanese father and further that Japan is one of the most difficult countries from which a parent can recover an abducted child.[145]

Japan began to seriously consider joining The Hague Convention on the Civil Aspects of International Child Abduction in 2010 and in the lead up to accession has studied the joint custody system of the United States and other countries and taken steps leading to amendment its domestic law to be consistent with its treaty obligations. Nonetheless, it is questionable whether joining the treaty regime will actually change the prospects for getting children abducted to Japan returned. Proposed legislation would allow a Japanese court to refuse to return a child where (a) spousal abuse might have been involved in the abducting parent's determination to leave. It is possible that if a Japanese national spouse were to claim spousal abuse as the cause for leaving, a Japanese court would not accept the foreign court's determination in the custody proceeding that no such abuse was proved nor question why the spouse did not try the issue of abuse before the foreign court. (b) where the abducting spouse might face criminal prosecution (for the abduction) in the country where the child is to be returned (a likely event since the abduction is likely a criminal act in the country from which the child was abducted). (c) judicial proceedings have not been brought in a short time period (one year is under consideration) that would presumably take into consideration the child's adoption of Japanese society[146] and (d) consideration of the child's view would likely influence a Japanese decision that grave risk would accompany compliance with the foreign court order.[147] [The Convention considers the child's view when the child is old enough to have a view. The Convention applies to children

144. http://travel.state.gov/family/abduction/country/country_501.html.

145. Yasuhiro Okuda, *The United Nations Convention on the Rights of the Child and Japan's International Family Law including Nationality Law*, www.law.usyd.edu.au/anjel/documents/ZJapanR/ZJapanR_15_08_Okuda.pdf. See also, Takahiro Fukada, *Canada, U.S. Nudge Japan to Join Abduction Resolution Framework*, Japan Times (Mar. 15, 2008). In August of 2010 Japan announced that it would likely sign the Hague Convention in 2011 in an effort to resolve international pressure. See, Kyodo News, *Japan to join Hague child-custody treaty in '11*, Japan Times (Aug. 15, 2010), http://search.japantimes.co.jp/cgi-bin/nn20100815a1.html. As of this writing in 2012 Japan has yet to accede and yet to enact necessary domestic legislation. If a Japanese parent absconds with the child in violation of a custody order and returns to the U.S., the parent may be charged with kidnapping. See, Alex Martin, *Japanese Held in U.S. over Child Custody*, Japan Times (Oct. 28, 2011), http://www.japantimes.co.jp/text/nn20111028x3.html.

146. It is not unknown for spouses in a custody case to hide their whereabouts and the whereabouts of the child for extended periods of time.

147. Minoru Matsutani, *Outline of child Custody Bills Approved*, Japan Times (Feb. 7, 2012).

under age 16. In Japan the child's view re: organ donation is relevant when the child is over age 15.] The child's view, while clearly a nod in favor of autonomy for the child, can be inconsistent with the basic concept of best interests of the child on which the Convention is founded and surely goes beyond the grave risk exception. Others have noted that while autonomy allows for a decision to be made at a specific point in time the law recognizes that people change over time—and children especially so. For this reason the law allows a decision by a child to be "trumped" by "wisdom" that is based on accumulated knowledge.[148] Children have yet to accumulate or to digest information and experience accumulated by adults.

In addition to the grave risk loophole, the Japanese courts are unlikely to order return if the abduction took place when the abducting parent had lawful custody of the child. Should this turn out to be the case, preemptive abduction might result. Moreover, as Japan's custody system involves granting one parent parental rights rather than joint custody, it is even possible that Japanese judges might find a joint custody arrangement as involving "grave risk" to the child. These "modifications" or "interpretations" of the treaty regime may disclose an unwillingness to return abducted children when to do so is not in the interest of the abducting Japanese parent.[149]

The Japanese position is not without substance when return would not be in the best interest of the child and a grave risk exists. The European Court of Human Rights used the best interests of the child rationale in a case involving the Hague Convention and The Convention for the Protection of Human Rights and Fundamental Freedoms. The rights of the child under the Convention had to be considered as well as the rights of the two parents. These rights were relevant to a determination of whether the exception of "grave risk" contained in Article 13 of the Hague Convention was applicable. The fact that the abducting parent might be subject to criminal prosecution and possible imprisonment upon return was relevant to the best interests of the child—especially in the unusual facts in the case decided where questions about the father's ability to care for the child on his own were raised and where the divorce and custody order were followed by a second marriage, charges of abuse, divorce, and yet a third marriage by a father with no means of support.[150] The issue, of course, is whether the Japanese judiciary acting under the domestic law would make a searching inquiry that treats the non-Japanese parent fairly or whether it would simply follow past practice and the societal view that the Japanese child would likely suffer grave psychological and other risks if returned to the non-Japanese parent and that it is in the best interest of the child to be with its Japanese parent (especially if that parent is the

148. Charles Foster, *Human Dignity in Bioethics and Law* 115 (Hart Publishing 2011).
149. Kyodo, *Six Nations Press on Hague Treaty*, Japan Times (Nov. 10, 2011).
150. *Neulinger and Shruk v. Switzerland* (No. 41615/07) Grand Chamber of the European Court of Human Rights, http://www.caselaw.ch/d/div/egmr%206-7-10.pdf. The dissenting and concurring opinions in the case pointed to the unusual circumstances in the *Neulinger* case raising the question of whether the case should be used for a general principle where those unusual circumstances are not present.

mother).[151] Japanese Family Courts will have to recognize that the Japanese system of single parent rights should not be applied to determine grave consequences when the joint custody or parental visitation rights have been decided by a foreign court prior to the abduction. On the other hand, accession to the Hague Convention may bring about changes in Japanese domestic law dealing with custody and visitation.

Typically it is a difficult and time-consuming process for the Family Court system to take parental rights away from a custodial parent creating problems for women who leave their husbands alleging abuse and seek shelter outside the family home. Even if it is asserted that the father has abused the child and a child protective agency takes in the child to protect it, the father may be able to assert his custodial rights and reclaim custody.[152] It is possible for the court system in cases deemed emergencies to act quickly. Thus a Family Court expedited procedures and within a day temporarily suspended parental rights so as to enable the child to receive medical treatment needed to save the child's life even though the parents objected.[153] In 2011 the Diet enacted legislation allowing for suspension of parental rights for two years at the request of the child involved as well as certain other relatives including for example the other spouse, a prosecutor or a guardian.[154] The basic thrust of the law is to protect children removed from the home and placed in a shelter (thus granting a wife who leaves her husband and takes refuge in a shelter with the child legal rights to have the child remain in the shelter) as well as children denied needed medical care. Because the change in rights is temporary, the new law should make it easier for Family Courts to act.[155] Child abuse has been recognized as a problem in Japan since 1990. As the problem has become more understood and recognized the number of cases of child abuse reported has steadily risen.[156] In 2010 the number of cases jumped by a reported 28% over the

151. Similarly the domestic Japanese court should make a searching inquiry of abuse charges and not simply accept that abuse exists or existed because the Japanese parent makes such an allegation. The burden of proof establishing such abuse should lie with the party making the allegation.

152. See, Masanao Umezaki & Keiko Kosaka, *Parents, social workers at odds / Law revision boosting officials' power to guard kids sparks conflict*, Daily Yomiuri (Nov. 27, 2009).

153. Kyodo News, *Family Court Moves Fast to get Treatment for Boy*, Japan Times (March 16, 2009). http://search.japantimes.co.jp/cgi-bin/nn20090316a5.html.

154. Guardians may be appointed by the Family Court. Japan's guardian system treats elderly people differently from children. The appointment of guardians for the elderly has been on the rise as the elderly population has grown. There has been an increase in embezzlement cases involving guardians. The Supreme Court, began an investigation in 2011 looking at ways in which the system can be improved so that the assets of wards are better protected. See, *Spotlight on legal guardians / Rising cases of dismissal for misconduct prompt top court review*, Yomiuri Shimbun on line (Sept. 16, 2011), http://www.yomiuri.co.jp/dy/national/T11091 5005203.htm.

155. Kyodo News, *Bill to Suspend Abusive Parent rights gets Ok'd*, Japan Times (Apr. 29, 2011), http://search.japantimes.co.jp/cgi-bin/nn20110429b1.html; Kyodo News, *Abusive Parents Loss of Rights Set*, Japan Times (May 28, 2011), http://search.japantimes.co.jp/cgi-bin/ nn20110528b2.html.

156. Kyodo News, *Reported cases of child abuse have been on the increase for each year since statistics began to be collected in 1990, Record 44,210 child abuse cases logged in '09*, Japan Times (July 29, 2010), http://search.japantimes.co.jp/cgi-bin/nn20100729a3.html.

previous year.[157] The new brain death transplantation law allows donation of organs of children under age 15 who are brain dead but prohibits recognition of brain death for if the deceased child was subject to abuse. Since it is difficult for doctors to determine abuse this provision inhibits use the use of organs from brain dead children. As of mid-2012 only two cases of organ donation by a child under age 15 have been performed.[158]

The first law recognizing spousal abuse as a problem was the 2001 Law for the Prevention of Spousal Violence and the Protection of Victims.[159] The 2001 Law recognizes spousal abuse as a violation of basic human rights and also recognizes that women are typically the victims of an abusive spouse. Spouse is defined to include a current spouse (both de jure (registered) and de facto) or a spouse from whom one is divorced (including a former de facto spouse whose situation has changed so as to be equivalent to a de facto divorce)[160]. The Law creates Spousal Violence Counseling and Support Centers. Although the Law does not require professionals with reason to believe that spousal violence has or is taking place to report such fact, such persons should endeavor to report such facts to either such Centers or the local police.[161] When the police authorities have reason to suspect spousal violence they must endeavor to provide the victim protection.[162] Upon application by a victim the court may grant a protective order that is designed to keep the victim (and the victim's family) and perpetrator separate for six months, to prevent the perpetrators from communicating with the victim by phone or other means or seeking a face to face meeting, from making harassing phone calls, from disclosing certain confidential information and the court may require the perpetrator to leave the family residence for two months from the issuance of the Order.[163] Although the protective order deals with a family matter the District Court rather than the Family Court is given authority to enter such orders.[164] Evidence of abuse and need must be filed with the petition and the victim must include either a notarized statement of facts or information concerning the victim's notification of violence to either the Police or the Counseling and Support Center in order to enable the court to obtain the police or support center report.[165] This last requirement creates problems for the petitioning victim because notarized statements are relatively expensive and visiting the Center and having the Center's report given to the court could implicate privacy interests. The requirement that the perpetrator leave the family residence for a two-month period implies that after two months he may return. The

157. Kyodo, *Reports of child abuse top 50,000 in 2010, a record high*, Japan Times (July 21, 2011), http://search.japantimes.co.jp/cgi-bin/nn20110721a8.html.
158. Kyodo, *The Mainichi*, June 14, 2012, *Japan's 1st child brain death confirmed for organ transplant*, http://mainichi.jp/english/english/newsselect/news/20120614p2g00m0dm096000c.html.
159. Act No. 31 of Apr. 13, 2001.
160. Article1.
161. Article 6. Provisions concerning privacy are waived to permit such disclosure and doctors are given specific direction to endeavor to report such incidents and to provide information to their patient about reporting such incidents.
162. Article 8.
163. Article12.
164. Article11.
165. Article12.

implication is that the woman (the usual victim) must ultimately leave the family residence [leave the House?] to avoid the abuse rather than the abuser [Head of the House?] leaving the residence and the further assumption is that two months is sufficient time for the woman to make new living arrangements.[166] The law supports this implication by providing that an extension of the Order may be obtained when the victim needs additional time beyond the two months to find a suitable living arrangement.[167] This limited time and the requirement that to avoid abuse the abused rather than abuser must leave the home furthers the wife's dependence on her husband and can have a chilling effect on seeking protection orders.

As noted above, like the Uniform Parentage Act Japan's Civil Code contains a presumption that a child born within 300 days of dissolution of a marriage is presumed to be the child of the husband. The presumption may be overcome by facts disclosing a "de facto" divorce, i.e., that the wife and husband had not cohabited for an extended period prior to the divorce decree.[168] On the other hand, it has been held that the same law prohibits the registration of a child born within 300 days of a divorce from being registered as the child of its mother and the husband she married after the divorce and who was her husband at the time of the birth. Public distress over such a ruling led politicians to find a fix by permitting the child to be registered as the child of the husband at the time of birth if the mother submits a doctor's certificate showing that she became pregnant after the divorce from the first husband was finalized. Such a result would still leave those children who were conceived by the second husband and the mother during the time when the wife was waiting for the divorce decree to be finalized as unable to be legitimate children of their biological (and married) parents. If the first husband sued to have the child declared the child of the biological father (second husband) the child's status could be effectively resolved but requiring the divorced wife to go to her estranged first husband creates a complication that is neither appropriate nor available in many cases (especially but not exclusively where the first marriage involved spousal abuse). To deal with this situation the Internal Affairs and Communication Ministry issued guidelines to allow a proxy to be appointed for the child and have the proxy file for in court mediation. In such a case, where the biological father (the second husband) acknowledges paternity the child may then be registered as his child. If the first husband consents to registration of the child in the second husband's family register no mediation is required.[169]

166. See, Yukiko Tsunoda, *Legal Response to Domestic Violence in Japan*, in *Japanese Family Law in Comparative Perspective* 165 (Scheiber & Mayali ed., Robbins Collection Publications 2009).
167. Article18.
168. *No Presumption of Divorced Husband's Parentage* (300 day case), Case No. 1184 of 1968, 23 Minshu No. 6, http://www.courts.go.jp/english/judgments/text/1969.05.29-1968.-O-.No..1184.html (P.B., May 29, 1969).
169. The Yomiuri Shinbun, Sept. 12, 2008 reported that the first child to be registered under the mediation procedure was registered in Kagawa Prefecture.

[4] *In Vitro Fertilization, Posthumous Conception and Surrogacy Issues*[170]

The 300 days rule also has a potential impact on in vitro fertilization cases. Where a husband undergoes medical treatment that can adversely affect his sperm he and his wife may agree to preserve his sperm so that it can be used at a later date for in vitro fertilization of the mother. Typically the question of whether the husband is the father of the child does not arise because the Family Registrar not being aware of the vitro fertilization simply registers the child as the child of the husband.[171] The Japan Society of Obstetrics and Gynecology ("Gynecology Society") has advised members that in vitro fertilization is unethical—although in 2007 the ethical standards were relaxed to allow the in vitro fertilization of a wife of a couple where the husband had had a sex-change operation.[172] Sex change is permitted because Japan recognizes gender identity disorder. After a sex-change operation a person who is not married may change their sex as shown on the Family Register[173], but if the person has a child such change in the Register must await the child's reaching majority (age 20).[174] (Perhaps this is designed to assure that the Family Register is not tainted while the child is in the Register—after age 20 the child is an adult and can form its own Family Register.)Where a husband born a woman but who had a sex-change operation sought to have a child conceived via donated sperm and born to his wife registered as his child the government refused to recognize the child as the child of the sex changed husband.[175] The rationale for the determination was that the husband had no genetic relationship to his wife's child—a rationale that runs contra to court rulings and the Gynecology Society's position regarding a child born to a surrogate mother.[176]

Assuming the husband dies before the sperm is implanted and the sperm is later implanted so that the child is born more than 300 days after the marriage is terminated

---

170. As used herein surrogacy refers to gestational surrogacy, using implantation and no genetic link between the surrogate and the child. "Traditional" surrogacy, where a woman is impregnated by the father so that a child can be born to the father even though the father is not married to the surrogate is not considered as surrogacy herein. Such traditional surrogacy was utilized in ancient times, especially in royal families (including the Japanese royal family) to continue the imperial or kingship line.
171. Lower courts in Japan but not yet the Supreme Court have had to deal with issues arising when the birth mother conceived via artificial insemination using donor sperm and a dispute later arose between the birth mother and her husband. Mayumi Mayeda, *Present State of Reproductive Medicine in Japan–Ethical Issues With a Focus on Those Seen in Court Cases*, 7 BMC Medical Ethics 3 (2006) <www.pubmedcentral.nih.gov/articlerender.fcgi?artid=1481581>.
172. Satoko Uehara, Sex-change man says boy his own, Asahi Shimbun, Jan. 11, 2010; http://www.asahi.com/english/Herald-asahi/TKY201001110053.html.
173. See, Claire Maree, *The Un/State of Lesbian Studies: An Introduction to Lesbian Communities and Contemporary Legislation in Japan*, 21st Century Lesbian Stud., J. Lesbian Stud. 296 (2007).
174. Kyodo News, *Sex-change legal revision enacted*, Japan Times (June 11, 2008), http://search.japantimes.co.jp/cgi-bin/nn20080611a8.html.
175. *Child "illegitimate" due to sex change*, United Press International (Jan. 11, 2010), http://www.upi.com/Odd_News/2010/01/11/Child-illegitimate-due-to-sex-change/UPI-30081263233670/; City's birth challenge linked to sex change, Japan Times, Jan. 11, 2010, http://search.japantimes.co.jp/cgi-bin/nn20100111a2.html. Kyodo, *GID Patient's Bid to be Deemed Legal Dad Nixed*, Japan Times, Jan. 28, 2012, http://www.japantimes.co.jp/text/nn20120128a7.html.
176. The court decision and position of the Society are discussed *infra*.

by the husband's death, is the child the legitimate child of the wife and her deceased husband? The "flip side" of a presumption of legitimacy and fatherhood of a 300 days rule is that if the birth takes place later than 300 days after the marriage is terminated the presumption is against fatherhood and legitimacy. But should such a presumption apply when the biological parents of the child were in fact married and agreed to the in vitro fertilization procedure? This implicates the legal issues surrounding posthumous in vitro conception.

The Takamatsu High Court was presented with such a case and determined that when the father had consented to the in vitro fertilization and when the genetic material used was from the husband and wife the child should be recognized as the legitimate child of the husband and wife and entered as such in the Family Register notwithstanding the 300 days rule. The Japanese government objected to the decision and appealed to the Supreme Court,[177] which reversed the High Court.[178]

The Supreme Court noted that as a general matter a parent-child relationship should be created by "blood". And, in the normal course of events such blood relationship is established through natural birth of the child—whether legitimate or illegitimate. The Court recognized that modern medical science has made it possible to conceive children through methods not contemplated by the Civil Code and the existing legal system. Under such circumstances the Court had to determine what rule to apply to a child conceived after the death of the biological father (the sperm donor). The Court looked to two factors in making its decision.

First, a normal family relationship between the child and the father was not possible. Second, the laws of inheritance were seen as an impediment. A child might have certain inheritance rights vis-à-vis the family of its "father". The Court seemed clear that under the current state of the law a child born to the posthumously conceiving father could not be an heir of the father's family. Although it failed to address the best interests of the child in its decision the Court appeared to recognize that the issue is relevant to any statutory scheme that the Diet might devise. The Court called on the Diet to resolve the issue and devise a system to deal with issues such as inheritance and best interests of the child. The lack of a legislative solution resulted in the Court refusing to recognize the legitimacy of the child. The Supreme Court might have been able to base its decision on failure to prove that the deceased "father" had consented to posthumous conception (leaving the question of whether proof of consent would be sufficient in any event)—but that was not the basis for the decision.

The Court could have dealt with the inheritance problem by simply noting that as the inheritance laws do not deal with the question of inheritance rights of a posthumously conceived child the child has no inheritance rights. This would not have adversely affected the child since holding the child was not the biological father's had

177. Mayumi Mayeda, *Present State of Reproductive Medicine in Japan–Ethical Issues With a Focus on Those Seen in Court Cases*, 7 BMC Medical Ethics 3 (2006), www.pubmedcentral.nih.gov/articlerender.fcgi?artid=1481581.

178. *Posthumous in vitro Fertilization Legitimacy Case*, Case No 1748 (Ju) of 2004, 60 Minshu No. 7, http://www.courts.go.jp/english/judgments/text/2006.09.04-2004.-Ju-.No..1748.html (P.B, Sept. 4, 2006).

the same result.[179] The fatherly custody issue is, of course, insoluble but children conceived in the normal way to a married couple and whose fathers die before they are born are in the same position of being denied fatherly company, custody and support. Yet such children are recognized as the legitimate children of their deceased father. In short, the reasoning of the court appears to be makeweight for its ultimate decision to deny the existence of the parent-child relationship.[180]

Why then does the court deny this relationship? It is suggested that there are three other potential rationales for the decision: (a) Japanese society has not yet reached a consensus as to how to deal with this issue; until such a consensus is reached, the Judicial Branch is not going to change more traditional approaches to the parent-child relationship; or (b) recognizing the child would place the child in the family tree of his father and potentially could affect the father's family and inheritance from members of the family; this in turn creates conundrums that directly impact on the forward looking nature of the old and abolished family *Ie* system and at a more subconscious level the entire question of ancestors; or (c) there is simply no procedure under the Family Register law that would accommodate having a child enter its father's House (the Register) at a time when under the Family Register law the death of the father would have caused the Father to have been stricken from the Register. Unlike the wife who entered the House when the father was alive, it is difficult to imagine a child entering the House of a dead person. On a cultural level there is the question of whether the entire process of in vitro fertilization is itself "unnatural" and more specifically whether the idea of fathering a child after death is "unnatural".[181] While some members of the Court recognized that the child might suffer some damage by not being registered as the natural child of the father they concluded that the damage would be minimal. However this determination either blinks the reality that an "unclean" family register[182] could carry social stigma or recognizes that the necessity of putting the child's birth date in the Register which already contains the father's date of death would lead to the same stigma.

179. This was the approach taken in *Hecht v. Superior Court*, 20 Cal. Rptr. 2.d 275 (Cal. Ct. App. 1993) See, Raymond C. O'Brien, *The Momentum of Posthumous Conception: A Model Act*, 25 J. Contemp. Health L. & Policy 332, 341–344 (2009). see also, Roderick R.M. Paisley, *The Succession Rights of the Unborn Child*, 10 Edinburgh L. Rev. 28, 58 (2006); BBC News, *Blood claims IVF paternity victory* (Feb. 28, 2003); BBC News, *Diane Blood registers sons* (Dec. 1, 2003), http://news.bbc.co.uk/2/hi/uk_news/england/nottinghamshire/3252436.stm.

180. See, John A. Robertson, *Cancer and Fertility: Ethical and Legal Challenges*, 34 J. Natl. Cancer Institute Monograph (2005) arguing that, as a general matter, the risks to the child of having a single parent are not so great as to make consensual posthumous conception unethical. To the same effect see, *Fertility preservation and reproduction in cancer patients, The Ethics Committee of the* Am. *Society for Reproductive Medicine*, 83 Fertility & Sterility 1622–1628 (2005).

181. For a discussion of some ethical issues involved in posthumous in vitro fertilization see, McLachlan & Swales, *From the Womb to the Tomb: Issues in Medical Ethics* (Posthumous Insemination and Consent p.251) (Humming Earth 2007).

182. See, Karl Jacob Krogness, *The Ideal, the deficient, and the illogical family*, in *Home and Family in Japan* (Richard Ronald & Allison Alexy, ed., Routledge 2011); Ekaterina Hertog, *Home and Family in Japan* (Richard Ronald & Allison Alexy eds., Routledge 2011); Rachel Brehm King, *Redefining Motherhood: Discrimination in Legal Parenthood in Japan*, 18 P. Rim L. & Policy J. 190 (2009).

Posthumous in vitro conception and posthumous implantation of embryos create legal questions in both Japan and the United States. In both countries the courts have called upon the duly elected legislative bodies to provide a legislative remedy for dealing with the issue. As the United States is a common law jurisdiction familiar with "judge made law" its courts appear more accommodating to the concept of applying general principles such as consent, choice by the married couple and best interests of the child[183] until the legislature resolves the problem. The Supreme Court of Japan, on the other hand, does not appear willing to apply such principles when doing so may not be consistent with the Court's view of a consensus of society or absent such consensus falling back on old Codes that do not contemplate the issue especially where private ordering through the Gynecology Society provides an answer.[184] The Society also rejects transplantation of an egg from a third party into a woman who wishes to have a child but cannot produce eggs. A group of infertility doctors and clinics in Japan have established the country's first "egg bank",[185] formed their own group, the Japanese Institution for Standardizing Assisted Reproductive Technology (JISART), and created their own standards for when both in vitro fertilization and egg transplantation should be performed. There is evidence that "ova brokerages" have sprung up in Japan and that Japanese women have been going abroad, mainly to the United States, to have someone else's ova fertilized by the Japanese woman's husband and then transplanted into the Japanese woman.[186]

Domestic surrogate pregnancy is rarely an alternative for Japanese spouses. The Ministry of Health, Labor and Welfare called for banning the practice [187] but the Minister of Science and Technology supported the practice in certain situations.[188] The Gynecology Society forbids members from engaging in the practice.

There is at least one doctor in Japan who openly operates a fertility clinic that performs surrogate pregnancies—always utilizing the sperm and egg of a married couple that wishes to have a child but where the wife cannot—for medical reasons—carry the child during pregnancy.[189] In all cases the doctor has used as a surrogate a female relative of the wife or husband. Japanese parents who cannot have

183. See, Christopher A. Scharman, *Not Without My Father: The Legal Status of the Posthumously Conceived Child*, 55 Vanderbilt 100 (2002).
184. The Lancet, Volume 357, Issue 9270, Pages 1774 (J. Watts, *Mixed emotion after first Japanese surrogate birth*).
185. See, *Nation's 1st ova bank to open / 21 fertility clinics to begin asking for volunteer donors by end of year*, Yomiuri Shimbun (Aug. 31, 2008), http://www.accessmylibrary.com/article-1G1-188116293/nation-1st-ova-bank.html.
186. Ova *brokers remain unchecked / No. of births resulting from in vitro fertilization abroad unknown*, The Daily Yomiuri (Apr. 30, 2012), http://www.yomiuri.co.jp/dy/national/T120429002794.htm.
187. The Report on Ideal Reproductive Treatment Using Donor Sperms, Eggs and Embryos, December 2000 of the Ministry of Health, Labor and Welfare's Special Committee on Medical Technology for Reproductive Treatment Assessment Subcommittee for Advanced Medical Care of the Health Science Council (on the website of the Ministry of Health Labor and Welfare, www.mhlw.go.jp/english/wp/other/councils/00/index.html.
188. The Lancet, Volume 357, Issue 9270, Pages 1774 (J. Watts, *Mixed emotion after first Japanese surrogate birth*).
189. See, *Japan's surrogate mothers emerge from shadows*, Reuters (Mar. 12, 2008), http://www.reuters.com/article/2008/03/13/us-japan-surrogate-idUST356552008031 3.

children can travel abroad to engage in assisted pregnancy and birth. When a Japanese wife (who could not carry a child for medical reasons) and her husband donated their egg and sperm and an American surrogate, operating under a lawful U.S. surrogate contract, delivered their child the Family Registrar refused to register the child as their natural child and was upheld by the Supreme Court notwithstanding the parents had obtained a judicial order in the United States declaring them the parents of the child.[190] The Court concluded that the Nevada judgment was not entitled to comity as it was against the public policy of Japan. It relied in part on the presumption in the Civil Code that a woman who gives birth to a child is the child's mother. It recommended that the Japanese couple be allowed to adopt the children, which they did.[191] It is reported that in Japan it is assumed in many cases that an adopted child is in fact an "illegitimate" child—and illegitimacy still carries a stigma.[192] It is not suggested that Japan has to or should recognize the legality of surrogacy contracts (especially commercial surrogacy contracts) or that it cannot punish the Japanese party or parties to such a contract under its domestic law. The child can be protected while the Court remains agnostic as to the moral and ethical questions presented.

The Supreme Court of Japan decision is not inconsistent with the rulings of courts in other countries[193] and was consistent with the views of the government whose Assisted Reproduction Technologies Review Committee report of April 2003 disapproved of surrogate birth.[194] Notwithstanding its decision on the merits, the Supreme Court urged the government to obtain a consensus of Japanese society concerning surrogate birth and then adopt a legal regime reflecting that consensus.[195]

---

190. *Surrogate Birth Child Denied Registration Case*, Case No. 47 of 2006, 61 Minshu No. 2, http://www.courts.go.jp/english/judgments/text/2007.03.23-2006.-Kyo-.No..47.html (P.B., Mar. 23, 2007).
191. Adoption places a blemish on the Family Register. See, Rachel Brehm King, *Redefining Motherhood: Discrimination in Legal Parenthood in Japan*, 18 P. Rim L. & Policy J. 189, 203–204 (2009). As the article points out although there have been amendments to the Family Register law to make it more difficult to discover special adoption, the fact remains that such fact can be ascertained by a determined investigator. See also, Ekaterina Hertog, *Home and Family in Japan*, 102 (Richard Ronald & Allison Alexy eds., Routledge 2011).
192. See, e.g., Fumio Tokotani, *Adoption and Child Welfare in Japanese Law: Has the Special Adoption Law failed?* 33, http://ir.library.osaka-u.ac.jp/metadb/up/LIBOSIPPK/2-3_n.pdf, last accessed Sept. 16, 2012; Karl Jacob Krogness, *The Ideal, the deficient, and the illogical family in Home and Family in Japan*, at 84(Richard Ronald & Allison Alexy eds., Routledge 2011).
193. *France: Surrogacy Ban Affirmed, Associated Press*, New York Times (Apr. 6, 2011), http://www.nytimes.com/2011/04/07/world/europe/07briefs-Surrogacy.html. (France goes further than Japan in refusing to recognize surrogacy–in the Japanese case the court specifically indicated that adoption was permitted but in France adoption of surrogate children by the parents contracting with the surrogate is not allowed.) JILP Forum, *The prohibition of surrogate motherhood in France*, http://nyujilp.com/2012/01/31/the-prohibition-of-surrogate-motherhood-in-france-2/.
194. Mayumi Mayeda, *Present State of Reproductive Medicine in Japan–Ethical Issues With a Focus on Those Seen in Court Cases*, 7 BMC Medical Ethics 3 (2006), www.pubmedcentral.nih.gov/articlerender.fcgi?artid=1481581.
195. Although commercial surrogacy is not permitted in England, twins born in the Ukraine to a surrogate for British parents were allowed into England and the British parents awarded custody so that the children would not be sent to a Ukrainian orphanage. Ben Jones, *High Court Rescues Surrogate Twins from International Custody Limbo*, BioNews (Dec. 14, 2008), http://www.bionews.org.uk/page_13609.asp. Twins born in India to a surrogate using the sperm and

In 2008 (thus after the Supreme Court's decision) the Assisted Reproductive Technologies Review Committee of the Science Council of Japan rendered a report recommending among other things that: surrogate pregnancy be prohibited; that all parties (except the surrogate herself) to commercial surrogate pregnancy (the physician, mediators and couple seeking a child) be subject to penalties exacted by the state; that the surrogate mother be deemed the mother of the child; that the family seeking the surrogate child be permitted to adopt the child; that a clinical study be performed of surrogate pregnancy and that in such event surrogacy be permitted solely for the study but that even in such case the child be deemed the child of the surrogate and not the couple who sought to have a surrogate child and who are the biological donors of all the biological material; and finally that in dealing with the general subject the best interests of the child should be the defining factor.[196] The report would appear to be a conclusion with explanations written to support the conclusion. Perhaps the biggest drawback in the report is its primary and perverse reliance on best interests of the child for both denying the child an immediate relationship with its biological parents as well as creating complications for its future including nationality, educational and social problems.

The report's major problem is that it fails to address the fundamental best interest questions—assuming that all of the rationalization engaged in by the authors was accepted, why is the child's best interest served by denying it such basic attributes as Japanese citizenship or loving parents? Why is the child better off being adopted by its biological parents than being recognized as the "natural" child of its biological parents? The report fails to recognize the reality that the child "cannot be sent back" and that the child should not be punished for the actions of its biological parents in seeking surrogacy. The report and the decisions in the posthumous in vitro fertilization and surrogacy cases fail to deal with the reality of the decisions on the children involved.

In mid-2012 a Study Group made up of members of the LDP drafted legislation that would permit in vitro fertilization whether by means of sperm, ova or fertilized egg. Commercial sperm or egg banks or donations as well as commercial surrogacy would be prohibited. In addition the draft legislation would permit surrogacy when the couple seeking a surrogate cannot conceive for medical reasons and when the Family Court has approved the request for surrogacy.[197] The Study Group would also amend

---

egg of a German couple were denied a German visa for two years before the German government agreed to grant a visa and the Indian Governments agreed to allow the children to go to Germany. *Germany relents, admits twins with Indian surrogate mother*, http://news.monstersandcritics.com/europe/news/article_1558693.php/Germany-relents-admits-twins-with-Indian-surrogate-mother.

196. Assisted Reproductive Technologies Review Committee of the Science Council of Japan, Issues Related to the Assisted Reproductive Technologies Centered on Surrogate Pregnancy—Towards a Social Consensus—(Apr. 8, 2008), http://www.scj.go.jp/ja/info/kohyo/pdf/kohyo-20-t56-1e.pdf (English version) p. 17. For another view see, Marcelo de Alcantara, *Surrogacy in Japan: Legal Implications for Parentage and Citizenship*, 48 Family Ct. Rev. 417 (2010).

197. The use of Family Court pre-authorization would make the Family Court a kind of regulatory agency for surrogacy cases. It is inconsistent with the view of some that Japan's legal system is evolving away from a before the event regulatory system to a post hoc review/damages system.

the Civil Code to provide that the woman giving birth via in vitro fertilization and the woman seeking surrogacy would be the child's mother—and thus presumably the husband of such woman would be presumed the father and therefore the child could be registered in his family register. The details of the proposed legislation are not yet available and are being considered by the Gynecology Society.[198] It is not known how or if the proposed legislation would impact foreign surrogacy or in vitro fertilization as foreign ART that was commercial in nature might be considered to violate Japanese public policy. Non-commercial sperm, egg or surrogacy would likely not be deemed as in violation of public policy if the legislation were approved. The draft legislation is inconsistent with the Report of the Science Council of Japan referred to above.

The importance of the concept of maintaining "blood lines" probably accounts for the fact that domestic surrogate birth mothers in Japan tend to be the mother or sister of the wife seeking to have a child. Keeping the "uterus" in the family retains the bloodline. This leads to elderly women being surrogates for their daughters.[199] In such cases, the birth—surrogate—mother and her husband might register the child and then consent to have their daughter and son-in-law adopt the child under Japan's "special adoption" procedure that irrevocably cuts the ties between the "natural parents" and the "adoptive parents"[200]. Keeping the "uterus in the family" may also make it easier to keep a "clean" Family Register for all concerned.

At least in part, the legal objection to surrogacy (and perhaps to in vitro fertilization) is the legitimate concern that the process dehumanizes the surrogate mother and makes her simply a device or vehicle for reproduction inconsistent with her right to be respected as an individual.[201] This concern also affects the debate about

---

198. *Japan's LDP drafts proposal for conditional approval of surrogate births*, The Mainichi (June 11, 2012), http://mainichi.jp/english/english/newsselect/news/20120611p2a00m0na018000c.html.

199. See Shino Yuasa, *Japanese Woman, 61, Gives Birth to Grandchild from Donated Egg*, Atlanta Journal Constitution (Aug. 21, 2008).

200. Kyodo News, *Surrogate baby awarded normal status*, Japan Times (Apr. 23, 2009), http://search.japantimes.co.jp/rss/nn20090423a7.html. The special adoption law was enacted as an amendment to the Civil Code in 1987 and permits adoption of children under the age of 6 and in special situations between the ages of 6 and 8.

201. *In the Matter of Baby M*, 109 N.J. 396, 537 A.2d 1227 (1988). See, *J.F. v. D.B.*, 116 Ohio St.3d 363 (2007) *IN RE C.K.G., C.A.G., & C.L.G*, http://www.tsc.state.tn.us/OPINIONS/TSC/PDF/054/CKGOpn.pdfsee (2005); see also, *Ethical Dilemas in Assisted Reproduction Technologies* (Joseph G. Schenker ed., Walter de Gruyter 2011); Michael I. Sandel, *Justice* 91–101 (Farrar, Straus & Giroux 2009) for a philosophical approach to surrogacy for pay; Elizabeth Anderson, *Is Woman's Labor a Commodity?*, 19 Phil. & Pub. Affairs 71 (1990); Elizabeth Anderson, *Why Commercial Surrogate Motherhood Unethically Commodifies Women and Children: Reply to McLachlan and Swales*, 8 Health Care Analysis 19 (2000) (arguing that commercial surrogacy contracts are unethical and should be illegal); A.V. Campbell, *Surrogacy, Rights and Duties: A Partial Commentary*, 8 Health Care Analysis 35 (2000); Pamela Laufer-Ukeles, *Approaching Surrogate Motherhood: Reconsidering Difference*, 26 Vermont L. Rev. 407 (2002) arguing against enforceability of surrogacy contracts and arguing for a best interests of the child standard when a dispute arises out of a surrogacy agreement–but distinguishing surrogacy from egg and/or sperm donation). For a *contra* view see, Hugh V. McLachlan & J.K. Swales, *Babies, Child Bearers and Commodification: Anderson, Brazier et al., and the Political Economy of Commercial Surrogate Motherhood*, 8 Health Care Analysis 1 (2000); Hugh V. McLachlan & J.K. Swales, *Surrogate Motherhood, Rights and Duties: A Reply to Campbell*, 9 Health Care Analysis 101 (2001); Hugh V. McLachlan & J.K. Swales, *Exploitation and Commercial Surrogate*

human cloning.[202] The 2001 law dealing with the regulation of human cloning and similar techniques has as its primary purpose the prevention of creating a cloned human being. The Law does not explicitly prohibit human cloning for research that has as its goal therapeutic remedies—so long as the cloned embryo is not transplanted. The government is given authority to expand the scope of therapeutic cloning through issuance or modification of guidelines.[203] Japanese scientists have made significant contributions to animal cloning.[204]

In neither the *Posthumous in vitro Fertilization Legitimacy* case nor the *Surrogate Birth Child Denied Registration* case did the Supreme Court consider and resolve any of the issues that would have been foremost in the thought process of an American court—best interests of the child, the rights of the egg donor and in the in vitro case the right of the gestational parent, the rights of the genetic parents and finally, the rights of the child itself. Indeed, it can be argued that consideration of these issues is supported by the Universal Declaration on Bioethics and Human Rights (2005) which states in part: "The interests and welfare of the individual should have priority over the sole interest of science or society."[205] Instead the Court appears to have been concerned with the issue of private ordering by the relevant medical society and whether there was a consensus in Japanese society concerning the question of in vitro fertilization and posthumous birth or surrogate pregnancy; with familial rights (inheritance) and familial recognition thrown into the mix.

Professor Tanase, in discussing the question of visitation by a non-custodial parent after divorce notes that Japan does not treat children as autonomous beings.[206] It can be argued that in the posthumous in vitro fertilization and surrogacy cases the Court did not treat the children as autonomous beings with legal rights that must be respected by the parties to a custody, surrogacy or registration dispute as well as by the judicial system. As Foster in discussing the nexus between best interests and dignity, has aptly noted best interest requires an "objective" analysis of what is best for reaching full potential.[207] In the case of best interests of the child that would require an objective analysis of what furthers the child's interests—not what furthers the interest of the parent or the norm of the society of which the child is deemed to be a part. The

Motherhood, 7 Human Reproduction & Genetic Ethics 8 (2001); Hugh V. McLachlin, *Defending Commercial Surrogate Motherhood Against Van Niekerk and Van Zyl*, 23 J. Medical Ethics 344 (1997); Denise E. Lascarides, *Note, A Plea for the Enforceability of Gestational Surrogacy Contracts*, 25 Hofstra L. Rev. 1221 (1997). And, Life-Giving Love in an Age of Technology, United States Conference of Catholic Bishops (Nov. 17, 2009), http://www.usccb.org/LifeGivingLove/lifegivinglovedocument.pdf.

202. See, Masahiro Morioka, *The Ethics of Human Cloning and the Sprout of Human Life in Cross Cultural Issues in Bioethics: The Example of Human Cloning* (Roetz ed., Rodopi 2006).

203. Global Policies on Human Cloning, http://www.libraryindex.com/pages/2266/Cloning-GLOBAL-POLICIES-ON-HUMAN-CLONING.html; see also, Wheat & Matthews, World Human Cloning Policies (Japan), http://novae-med.bg-id.com/base1/5.pdf.

204. See http://www.globalchange.com/cloning-of-mouse-frozen-for-16-years-what-next.htm.

205. Universal Declaration on Bioethics and Human Rights (2005), http://www.unesco.org/new/en/social-and-human-sciences/themes/bioethics/bioethics-and-human-rights/.

206. Takeo Tanase, Commu*nity and the Law: A Critical Reassessment of American Liberalism and Japanese Modernity* (Luke Nottage & Leon Wolff trans. & eds. Edward Elgar Publishing Ltd. 2010).

207. Charles Foster, *Human Dignity in Bioethics and Law* 117 (Hart Publishing 2011).

child born as result of surrogacy or from in vitro fertilization (whether posthumous or during the life of the donor) will clearly and objectively best thrive from being treated as the child of its biological parents in the *Surrogate Birth Child Denied Registration case* and the same is true of the child denied registration in the *Posthumous in vitro Fertilization Legitimacy* case. In neither case was such issue resolved by the Court.

Although it is against Japanese public policy to recognize the surrogate birth child as the child of the genetic material donating parents entering into the contract with the surrogate, it appears to be consistent with Japanese public policy to recognize as valid, for purposes of Japan's Welfare Pension Insurance Act, the de facto marriage of an uncle and his niece—at least for purposes of Japan's Welfare Pension Insurance Act[208] notwithstanding the specific prohibition of such a marriage in Civil Code Article 734. It would appear that the real problem with surrogate birth is not that it is inconsistent with the Civil Code (which on deeper analysis it may not be) but rather that the Court is not convinced that the Japanese public has yet accepted surrogacy. And the real reason for accepting the de facto marriage of an uncle and niece, which is clearly inconsistent with the Civil Code, is that such marriages took place and were historically recognized in feudal and pre-war Japan, the issue arose in a rural farming community, and the de facto marriage at issue was consistent with the views of the family and local community.[209]

American law has also faced posthumous in vitro conception and surrogacy issues. Unlike Japan however these issues have involved private litigation (*surrogate v. genetic parents*) or benefits litigation (inheritance or social security) rather than "public law" questions such as registration in a Family Register. States have reached different conclusions both in legislation and in case law. Nonetheless, the trend appears to be one of recognizing the best interests of the child and not punishing the child because of the actions of the adults involved in its conception and birth. (See part §9.01[D] of this Chapter).

[5] Same-sex Relationships

Marriage is "Constitutionalized" in Japan.[210] Article 24 provides that "marriage shall be based only on the mutual consent of both sexes and it shall be maintained through mutual cooperation with the equal rights of husband and wife... "Reference to both

208. *"Common law" Marriage Between Uncle and Niece Case*, Case No. 354 of 2005, 61 Minshu, http://www.courts.go.jp/english/judgments/text/2007.03.08-2005.-Gyo-Hi-.No..354.html (PB Mar. 8, 2007).
209. There was a dissent in the "common law" marriage between uncle and niece case. The dissenting Justice placed his dissent squarely on the fact that the Civil Code specifically prohibited the "marriage" at issue and hence the alleged wife could not be a "spouse" for purposes of the Welfare Pension Insurance Act. It has been suggested that Japanese authorities are reluctant to intervene in matters in rural communities, effectively leaving such communities to be self-regulating. See Catherine Burns, *Sexual Violence and The Law in Japan* at 53 (Routledge Curzon 2005) Surely this case is consistent with such a view.
210. See, Vera Mackie, *Family Law and its Others*, in *Japanese Family Law in Comparative Perspective* 139 at 142–143 (Scheiber & Mayali eds., Robbins Collection Publications 2009); Shigenori Matsui, *The Constitution and the Family in Japan*, in *Japanese Family Law in Comparative Perspective* 33 at 50–51 (Scheiber & Mayali eds., Robbins Collection Publications 2009).

sexes would provide a basis for concluding that two sexes are required for a marriage and thus that same-sex marriage is not recognized by the Constitution. On the other hand, Article 24 does not prohibit same-sex marriage—it clearly was not considered by the drafters as in the 1940s the idea of same-sex marriage as a legal right was not available in either the United States, Japan or generally. On the other hand, Article 24 also refers to enacting laws relating to the family based on recognition of "individual dignity" and most jurisdictions that recognize same-sex marriage do so based on concepts related to dignity of the individual.

The Family Registrar will not accept a document purporting to constitute a same-sex marriage effectively barring de jure same-sex marriage in Japan. This, of course, does not mean that same-sex relationships do not exist in Japan, they do. But such relationships are not legally recognized and there is no equivalent to a same-sex union or some relationship short of marriage that grants same-sex couples the legal rights of spouses.

Some same-sex couples have attempted to bridge the legal divide through use of the adoption laws. Since an adult may through a general as distinguished from a special adoption adopt another adult[211] it is possible for a same-sex partner to adopt his or her younger partner. (A special adoption could not be undertaken as it applies only to children and thus would be the form of adoption used in a surrogacy situation). Such a ruse has the potential for giving the adoptive parent or adoptive child legal rights—most significantly rights to inherit. Through adoption and use of a written notarized Will, a same-sex partner who dies has his/her estate (or at least a portion of the estate) distributed to the other partner either as a child or as a parent.[212] Such procedure is consistent with the use of adoption during the Tokugawa and pre-war period to preserve the *Ie* and is used in modern times to allow a family with no sons to adopt a daughter's husband to continue the family name and pass the family property down to "blood" children and grandchildren.

[6] Death and Dying

The concept of brain death has yet to receive widespread acceptance in Japan[213] and doctors who have engaged in transplants from a brain dead patient have risked

211. Civil Code Article 799 makes Code provisions 738 and 739 applicable to certain adoptions (i.e., those of adults). Article 738 deals with marriage of an adult ward, showing that an adult can be adopted and 739 provides that marriage occurs on filing papers with the Family Registrar. Thus an adult can be adopted easily through the filing of the necessary adoption papers with the Family Registrar. No Family or other Court procedure or approval is required for a general adoption. In a general adoption the "biological" family retains its rights and relationship to the adopted person. Like a consensual divorce, a general adoption can be undone through consent and a filing with the Family Registrar. Special adoption, what in the United States would be the typical adoption, is more complicated and requires Family Court approval.
212. Claire Maree, *Same-Sex Partnerships in Japan: Bypasses and Other Alternatives*, 33 Women's Stud. 541–549, 2004, http://www.hawaii.edu/hivandaids/Same-Sex_Partnerships_in_Japan__Bypasses_and_Other_Alternatives.pdf, last accessed Sept. 16, 2012.
213. Minoru Nakamura, *Privacy: Current Status and Pending Issues in Japan*, NRI Papers No. 131 (2008) at 15–16, http://www.nri.co.jp/english/opinion/papers/2008/pdf/np2008131.pdf, last accessed Sept. 16, 2012.

criminal prosecution.[214] Although the 1997 Organ Transplant Law permitted use of organs from brain dead patients (over the age of 15) who (a) had consented ahead of time to use of their organs and (b) whose family consents to the use, the law was little used and resulted in few donations. Moreover, the Ministry of Health, Labor and Welfare limits the number of medical institutions that have authority to diagnose a person as brain dead limiting the universe of potential donors In 2009 a law was enacted that recognized brain death as death for organ transplantation purposes and permitted (with some restrictions) brain death organ transplants from minors under age 15 with family consent. The consent of the donor need not be in writing as long as the donor had not indicated opposition to organ donation. A preference for use of organs is given to the family of the brain dead donor.[215] Initial results from families that have consented to donation even when the donor had not made a writing consenting to donation is encouraging for those who support donation from persons declared brain dead.[216] However there have been only 2 cases of donation from children under the age of 15.[217]

214. See Akemi Nakamura & Mayumi Negishi, *Japan Struggles with the right-to-die Issue*, Japan Times (Apr. 8, 2006), http://www.japantimes.co.jp/text/nn20060408f1.html. In February of 2004 a Hokkaido doctor who determined that his ninety-year-old patient was brain dead removed life support. The police began an investigation. It was not until August of 2006 that authorities determined not to proceed against the doctor because the patient would have died within a short time frame even if the equipment had not been removed. See *Mercy Killing or Murder? Japan looks at the law*, Medical News Today (June 3, 2004); Valarie J. Vollmar, *Recent Developments in Physician Assisted Suicide* (2006), www.willamette.edu/wucl/pdf/pas/2006-10.pdf, last accessed Sept. 16, 2012.

215. For a brief history and discussion of the law see, Masahiro Morioka, *Brain Death and Transplantation in Japan: Some Remarks on the Proposals for the Revision of Japan's Organ Transplantation Law*, (Oct. 23, 2000 Revised: July 8, 2001, Jun 2003, April 2010) Lifestudie-s.org, http://www.lifestudies.org/specialreport02.html.

216. Among the changes in the Organ Transplant Law is a provision that permits the donor to designate, in a writing, a family member (husband/wife, parent/child) as the organ recipient in preference to others on the organ transplant list. The law came into effect in July 2010. About 40% of the hospitals designated to find brain death were unable to harvest or transplant organs from brain dead children. *Brain death baffles 40% of child hospitals*, The Daily Yomiuri (July 18, 2010), http://www.yomiuri.co.jp/dy/national/T100717002396.htm. The first instance of use of the new law occurred in August 2010. The victim donor died as a result of a traffic accident and his family consented to the designation of brain death and use of the organs even though the donor's intentions were not in writing but had previously orally been communicated to family members. Natsuko Fukue, *Kin agree to donate brain dead man's organs*, Japan Times (Aug. 9, 2010), http://search.japantimes.co.jp/cgi-bin/nn20100809x1.html. As of mid-2012 of the 337 hospitals that are authorized to perform organ transplants, only 42% (144) actually will accept organs for transplant. See, Yuichi Morii & Masayuki Takata, *Key step made in child organ transplants*, Yomiuri Shimbun (June 16, 12), http://www.yomiuri.co.jp/dy/national/T120615004285.htm.

217. Kyodo News, *Brain Death Declared for Organ Donor under 15*, Daily Yomiuri (Apr. 13, 2011), http://www.yomiuri.co.jp/dy/national/T110412006255.htm; see also, *Child Organ Transplants Still Face Hurdles*, Japan Times (Apr. 28, 2011), http://search.japantimes.co.jp/cgi-bin/nn20110428f2.html;.Jiji Press, *Heart transplanted from youngest donor*, Daily Yomiuri (June 16, 2012), http://www.yomiuri.co.jp/dy/national/T120615005307.htm.; *14 children pronounced brain dead in past year did not donate organs despite legal changes*, Mainichi Daily News (July 18, 2011) http://mdn.mainichi.jp/mdnnews/national/archive/news/2011/07/18/20110718p2a00m0na006000c.html.

Transplantation from brain dead patients is particularly important in Japan where transplants from living persons is frowned upon and requires either that the donor and recipient be related or reviews from several organizations before it may proceed making kinship the only viable process. Most transplantation takes place from persons who have died but consented to such transplantation prior to death. Because of the shortage of organs available for transplantation in Japan and the need for organs, scams and ruses to avoid the ethical and legal restrictions are not uncommon. Thus to meet the ethical requirement for a family relationship the ruse of general adoption as discussed in same-sex situations above is sometimes used.[218] It is reported that Japan's crime organizations trade in organs.[219]

The concept of the right-to-die or at least make one's own decision as to whether one should be allowed to die without medical intervention is undergoing scrutiny in Japan. Advance directives although not generally recognized[220] may have an effect when they are in writing, are given contemporaneously with the treatment, and the patient is in acute pain.[221] Physicians who remove patients from life support face the prospect of criminal prosecution even if the patient has allegedly consented.[222] The Ministry of Health, Labor and Welfare has been working on guidelines to deal with the means of obtaining and giving respect to a patient's desires since 2006[223] but to date has only come up with some guides to ethical considerations which do not deal with a doctor's potential criminal or civil liability The Japan Medical Association has not been actively involved noting that the public has not yet reached a consensus on the issue.[224] Cases concerning physician liability for removing life support are contradictory.[225]

---

218. Japanese law recognizes two kinds of adoption. General adoption is based on the need in Tokugawa times to adopt a male heir (typically the husband of a female child of the adopter) in order to continue the House (Ie) through finding a new Head of House to inherit on the adopter's death. Such adoption is of an adult, consensual and takes place by a filing with the Family Registrar. A "special adoption" is a relatively new procedure for the adoption of a child and requires the consent of the Family Court. Special adoption is what is more typically considered adoption in the United States. http://search.japantimes.co.jp/rss/nn2009 0423a7.html.

219. See, e.g., Kyodo, *Ehime hospital in organ trade raid*, Japan Times, June 29, 2011, http://search.japantimes.co.jp/cgi-bin/nn20110629a9.html.

220. Rihito Kimura, *Dynamics and Change of Bioethics in Japan* (Doctoral Thesis, Waseda University Graduate School of Human Sciences, January 2004) 145, 151.

221. *Medical news Today, Mercy Killing or Murder, Japan Looks at the Law* by Masayuki Takata and Junpei Monma, The Yomiuri Shimbun, < www.medicalnewstoday.com/articles/9042.php >.

222. Akemi Nakamura and Mayumi Negishi, *Japan Struggles with the Right-to-die Issue, Japan Times* 8 April (2006), http://www.japantimes.co.jp/text/nn20060408f1.html, last accessed Sept. 16, 2012.

223. See Valarie J. Vollmar, *Recent Developments in Physician Assisted Suicide* (2006), www.willamette.edu/wucl/pdf/pas/2006-10.pdf, last accessed Sept. 16, 2012.

224. Kyodo News, *Death with Dignity, Lawmakers Group Readies Bill for Steps to Remove Life Support*, Japan Times (June 9, 2007).

225. *Dropped Case Changes Terminal Care Debate*, Daily Yomiuri (Dec. 26, 2009). Just two weeks earlier the Supreme Court upheld the conviction of a doctor for removing a breathing tube and then administering a muscle relaxer finding that the doctor's actions caused the patient's death although the patient's family had asked for the tube to be removed. Case Number 2007 (A) No. 585, Keishu Vol. 63, No. 10, http://www.courts.go.jp/english/judgments/text/2009.12.07-2007.-A-.No..585.html (P.B., Dec. 7, 2009).

In January of 2012 the geriatric association in Japan determined that the issue of routine use of feeding tubes in treating terminally ill patients should be reconsidered. This position is consistent with practice in other countries such as the United States[226] but it also may be a response to potential prosecution in the event a tube is inserted and then after time the family determines that it is more humane to permit the elderly patient to die with dignity.[227]

Japanese Law also provides a presumption of death in certain situations where death is not certain—for example the asserted deceased cannot be located. In cases of a disaster or ship sinking and airline crashes the presumption applies after only one year[228]. Under some social benefit laws the presumption comes into play after only three months. The Great East Japan Earthquake and Tsunami prompted the government to make the disaster presumption applicable to such events only three months after the occurrence.[229] Moreover the Civil Code's presumption of simultaneous death will likely also be applied to the Great East Japan Earthquake and Tsunami.[230]

226. Yoko Harihara & Masaru Fujita, *Feeding Tubes Questioned / Society Backs Halting of Insertion through Patients' Stomachs*, Daily Yomiuri, Feb. 4, 2012, http://www.yomiuri.co.jp/dy/national/T120203006287.htm; *Tubes Used Less in U.S., Europe*, Daily Yomiuri (Feb. 4, 2012), http://www.yomiuri.co.jp/dy/national/T120203005704.htm.
227. Yoko Harihara & Masaru Fujita, *Feeding tubes questioned / Society backs halting of insertion through patients' stomachs*, Daily Yomiuri (Feb. 4, 2012), http://www.yomiuri.co.jp/dy/national/T120203006287.htm.
228. Civil Code, Act No. 89 of 1896, Article 30.
229. *Presumption of Dearth to be Hastened*, Yomiuri Shimbun (Apr. 11, 2011), http://www.yomiuri.co.jp/dy/national/T110410002991.htm.
230. Civil Code, Act No. 89 of 1896, Article 32-2.

CHAPTER 10

Article 9: Renunciation of War—Military Power and Responsibility

§10.01 UNITED STATES

[A] Historic Background to the Military Power, Authority and Responsibility

The American Revolution began as an armed conflict between the state of Massachusetts and Great Britain. Massachusetts could not by itself defeat Great Britain and it was the policy of John Adams of Massachusetts (the first Vice President of the United States and its second President) to get help from the other colonies. When he succeeded in getting the other colonies to join the fight an issue arose as to who should command the "national" regular army that, in addition to the various State Militia, would be needed. To bind the confederation of Northern and Southern States, Adams favored a Southern General to be Commander in Chief of the new army. George Washington of Virginia was selected as the Commander in Chief. Washington, in turn, served under the authority of the Continental Congress, which had the responsibility of raising the money needed to prosecute the war. Washington dutifully reported on his activities to the Congress and recognized that he was the servant of the Congress. When the Revolutionary War was successfully concluded, Washington resigned his Commission as Commander in Chief and returned to his farm in Virginia.

The primary function of the central authority established by the Colonies in rebellion was to prosecute a war. Each colony viewed itself as a self-governing body but each could not send its own army into the field nor could each have its own commander for the military forces. A united effort was required. It was this war power or war making authority that created the unity that eventually created the United States. It is not surprising that the Constitution of the United States specifically focuses on the military authority of the new government.

[B] Separation of the Military Power between Congress and the President

Congress is given the power to declare war (Article 1, section 8 clause 11), to raise an Army (Article 1, section 8 clause 12) and Navy (Article 1, section 8 clause 13), to make rules for the governance and regulation of land and sea forces (Article 1, section 8 clause 14), to call up the State Militia (Article 1, section 8 clause 15) and for providing funds for the military forces (Article 1, section 8 clause 12—but funds cannot be provided for more than two years at a time). Of the eighteen enumerated powers of congress, fully one-third are devoted to the military power.

The very first authority given to the president is that he shall be "Commander in Chief of the Army and Navy of the United States, and of the Militia of the several States, when called into the actual service of the United States". (Article 2 section 2 [1]) The idea of creating a united government but not giving that government military power was not a viable option. The distribution of that power within the federal government was divided and has led to controversy. Presidents have tended to take the position that they had the exclusive war making power and that when deemed necessary they could undertake military action without Congressional authorization.

It seems clear that when the country is attacked the president can act before any Congressional authorization. Thus, in connection with the American Civil War, President Lincoln did not wait for Congressional approval to blockade Southern ports at the start of the war and his authority to act as a defensive matter was upheld by the Supreme Court, which indicated that the president was not only authorized to act to defend the United States when attacked but also that he had a duty to act.[1] That presidents have acted in other contexts without Congressional declarations of War is also clear. It has been estimated that between 1798 and 1970 presidents have sent war material and/or troops abroad without Congressional authorization from between 125 to 130 times.[2] Even the War Powers Resolution passed over President Nixon's veto (based on Constitutional objections) permits the president to use military force if the United States has been attacked.[3]

The more complicated questions relate to "preemptive self-defense" and military actions taken abroad that are not in self-defense. The war in Yugoslavia was an example of the problem as was the U.S. support of the "opposition" in Libya. While the issue gives rise to much academic debate, the reality is that the president, on his own, cannot effectively wage a war for any sustained period of time—even the War Powers Resolution gives the president 60 days before he needs Congressional authorization when he sends troops abroad. President Obama sent American warplanes to participate in NATO actions in Libya in 2011 but failed to give the Congress the notice that the War Powers Act calls for. When challenged by a Republican House of Representatives

1. *Prize Cases*, 67 U.S. (2 Black) 635 (1863).
2. Leonard C. Meeker, *The Legality of US Participation in the Defense of Vietnam*, 54 Dept. St. Bull. 474 (1966) reprinted 75 Yale L. J. 1085,1101 (1966); John E. Nowak & Ronald D. Rotunda, *Constitutional Law* (4th ed., West Publishing Co. 1991).
3. 50 U.S.C. sections 1541–1548.

the president presented the argument that as no ground forces were committed to the Libyan operation there were no "hostilities" and since the War Powers act is limited to "hostilities" he was under no obligation to proceed under the law. Those opposed to the president disagreed. What was different about the Libyan adventure was that the president unlike his various predecessors of both parties did not claim the law was unconstitutional.

The president must obtain some form of Congressional authorization because he lacks the power of the purse and if for no other reason must get money from Congress to carry on the military activity. While this may be something short of a war declaration, the fact is the president does not act on his own. And, when the president and Congress jointly act in the military field, the Judicial Branch is not likely to intervene but rather it finds some mechanism—standing, ripeness, political question—to avoid involvement.[4]

[C] War Against Non-state Adversaries

During the American Civil War the Union (Northern) forces and the National government took the position that the Confederacy (Southern States that had left the Union and created their own government) was not a State but rather an illegal confederation in rebellion against the United States. The reality was that there was a vicious war going on, mostly in the territory of the Confederacy. Issues arose as to how to treat those who supported the Confederacy. President Lincoln even went so far as to set aside the Great Writ of Habeas Corpus in his effort to fight the war. The Supreme Court recognized that in light of the war conditions it was permissible to set aside the Writ in territory controlled by the Confederate forces (and thus treat persons in such territory differently from other citizens of the United States) but also found that it was not permissible to set aside the writ in the territory of the Northern or Union forces. In the North government sanctioned courts were still open and available and hence persons arrested in the North were entitled to the benefits of Habeas Corpus.

Two of the most significant cases arising out of the present conflicts against non-State entities and forces are (a) *Hamden v. United States* wherein the Supreme Court found that certain Articles of the Geneva Convention were applicable against the government of the United States and its treatment of captured non-State combatants[5] and *Boumediene v. Bush*[6] where the Court held that non-United States citizens held at the American Guantanamo Naval Base in Cuba were entitled to protection of the writ

---

4. See e.g., *MacArthur v. Clifford*, 393 U.S. 1002 (1968) (cert. denied); *Massachusetts v. Laird*, 400 U.S. 886 (1970) (leave to file complaint denied); *DaCosta v. Laird*, 405 U.S. 979 (1972); *Holtzman v. Schlesinger*, 414 U.S. 1304 (Marshall, Circuit Justice), 1316 (Douglas Circuit Justice), 1321 (Marshall, Circuit Justice) (1973). For a more recent example, see *Campbell v. Clinton*, 203 F.3d 19 (D.C. Cir. 2000) (lack of standing of Congressman–Court finding that Congress has a range of legislative power that it can use to stop a President's ability to make war). For a discussion of the Court's abstinence in the Vietnam War context see Louis Henkin, *"Viet-Nam" in the Courts of the United States: "Political Question"*, 63 Am. J. Intl. L. 284 (1969).
5. *Hamden v. United States*, 548 U.S. 557 (2006).
6. *Boumediene v. Bush*, 553 U.S. 723 (2008).

of habeas corpus. Although the Executive Branch may not have been pleased with the Supreme Court's decisions it has abided by them.

Although a "declaration of war" or some other affirmative Congressional action is not necessary for the president to use power abroad in self-defense and at an initial stage of a conflict, the extent of the president's power to wage war (without Congressional approval) against a non-State adversary (i.e., the war on terrorism) especially where United States citizens may be in the enemy camp or where the "President's action has affects in the United States", raising new issues. It remains to be seen how far the president and the Congress together may go in waging such a war when actions have affect in the United States and on the "rights" of citizens in the United States.

[D] Providing "Material Support" to Terrorist Organizations

The Congress has made it a crime to provide material support to terrorist organizations. This statute was challenged on "void for vagueness" and First Amendment grounds. The Supreme Court in 2010 upheld the law in the face of the challenge and based on the activities that plaintiffs' claimed they wished to enter into.[7] (See, Chapter 7)

§10.02 JAPAN

[A] Historic Background to the Military Power, Authority and Responsibility

Japan's military history is very different. Originally power resided in the Imperial family and a military composed of peasant conscripts. A change in policy and needs resulted in the phasing out of conscription in favor of the hiring of privately trained and armed elite soldiers who became known as Samurai.[8] These private military figures eventually banded together (around the tenth Century) and formed large military bands held together by loyalty and family ties (either actually or constructed). Within the military structure there were the equivalent of military ranks and thus the Samurai were themselves structured in a hierarchical manner and eventually took over the government. Minamoto Yoritomo, the head of the Minamoto clan was given the title of *seii Tai shogun* but the first person to hold the title of shogun from the start to finish of his rule was Yoritomo's son Sanetomo (known historically as the third Kamakura shogun—1203-1219).[9]

The military/civil (as distinguished from Imperial) authority established its government in Kamakura, a small city outside of present day Tokyo. The Kamakura Shogunate ruled Japan from the end of the twelfth century until early fourteenth century. Kamakura was a military government with power residing in the samurai warrior class. When the Kamakura government fell there were abortive efforts by the

7. *Holder v. Humanitarian Law Project*, 561 U.S. ___ (2010), discussed in Chapter 7.
8. Karl Friday, *Once and Future Warriors: The Samurai in Japanese History*, 10 Educ. About Asia 31 (2005).
9. Sanetomo replaced his brother who was the second Kamakura shogun.

Imperial House to regain power; civil society broke down and the country fell into a period of nearly continuous warfare that lasted for over a century (the *sengoku* period). The country was divided into warring camps of local warlords who sought to expand their power at the expense of neighboring warlords.

Japan was reunified through the actions of three figures—Oda Nobunaga, Toyotomi Hideyoshi and Tokugawa Ieyasu. All were military leaders. Ieyasu was the founder of the Tokugawa Shogunate. Like Kamakura, the Tokugawa Shogunate faced its most daunting challenge from a foreign military opponent. This time the "invasion" came not from the Asian continent but from Admiral Perry and his black ships whose armaments were too strong for Tokugawa to resist. By the time Perry arrived the Tokugawa Shogunate had been in power for two and a half centuries and had lost its vitality. The government in Edo gave in to United States demands for trade concessions and soon found it had to cede similar rights to other Western powers and Russia. After a brief civil war initiated by samurai from Western Japan, the Tokugawa were forced to cede power to the new rulers who ruled in the name of the Meiji Emperor.

[B] Separation of the Military Power from Civilian Rule in Meiji Japan

With this military history as a foundation and having to sign unequal and humiliating treaties because of their own lack of military power, the new rulers set about remedying the situation by developing a Western-style military along with the new governmental structure. The basis of the new structure was the Meiji Constitution and it, like the United States Constitution, contained several provisions concerning the military. Under Articles 10–13 the Emperor was in charge of military affairs. He was supreme commander as well as sole administrator of the Army and Navy. He set military officer's salaries and he could declare war and make peace. At first the Japanese looked to the French for a model for their new army. France's loss to Prussia in the Franco-Prussian War caused a rethinking and reorientation towards Prussia. An independent general staff was created in 1878. In 1884 an expansion program for the Army was started and by 1894 the army numbered almost 250,000. The navy, in turn, looked to the British model. By 1894 the Japanese were able to build their own warships and advanced munitions for such ships. Conscription was introduced in 1873 and the military power of Japan began to equal that of other powers.[10]

The Japanese Cabinet was composed of both civilian and military officials. Indeed, it was required that the Cabinet contain representatives of the Army and Navy. These representatives were active duty members of the forces of General, Admiral or other high rank and viewed themselves as responsible solely[11] to the Emperor and not to the Cabinet or civilian government. The Cabinet was required to disband if any

10. Hugh Cortazzi, *The Japanese Achievement: A Short History of Japan & its Culture* 209–212 (Sidgwick & Jackson Great Civilization Series, St. Martin's Press 1990).
11. This doctrine of "independent supreme command" not only frustrated the civilian government but also was disruptive of Japan's efforts during the Second World War There was never a true commander-in-chief, even when Army Commander Tojo was prime minister. James L. McClain, *A Modern History of Japan*, 484(WW Norton & Company 2002).

member resigned and, as a new Cabinet was required to have active military in its membership, the military was given a great deal of power in the government. The Japanese annexed Korea in 1910 after having declared a protectorate in 1905. Japan joined the side of the allies in the First World War and declared war against Germany in 1914.

A series of assassinations organized by military groups, the never ending war in China and an inability of a civilian government to organize itself without aid from the military led to a downfall of civilian government in the 1930s and the formation of what was basically a military controlled government that ruled until the end of the Second World War.

The Occupation viewed Japan as a militaristic State and set as one of its goals the demilitarization of Japan. The draft Constitution that the Americans submitted to the Japanese contained as Article 9 a clause renouncing war and prohibiting Japan from maintaining military forces. Whether General MacArthur suggested Article 9 of the Constitution to the Japanese government or whether Prime Minister Shidehara suggested it has been a subject of some debate.[12] What cannot be seriously debated is that the Occupation was strongly behind the notion of Japanese disarmament and the prohibition of the Japanese to ever again become a military power—that is, until the Korean War and the realization that Japanese help in the Cold War was called for.

§10.03 WHAT YOU SEE MAY NOT BE WHAT YOU GET

[A] Sharing Power Over the Military in the United States

Although the American president is Commander in Chief of the American military forces, his role would appear to be limited. The president cannot declare war, he cannot fund the military, he cannot on his own appoint the senior officers, etc. The Congress would appear to have primary responsibility in regard to matters of War and Peace—it is the Congress that declares war and it is Congress that funds the military. Yet the reality is otherwise. President Truman sent military forces to the Korean conflict without asking for Congressional approval and did not seek a declaration of war. President Reagan committed troops to the invasion of Granada without congressional authorization. President Bush (I) committed American troops to the Gulf War without a Congressional declaration of war (although he did seek congressional support, not as a legal requirement but to strengthen his hand in dealing with the problem at hand).

12. See, Klaus Schlichtmann, *Article Nine in Context–Limitations of National Sovereignty and the Abolition of War in Constitutional Law*, Vol. 23-6-09 Asia-P. J. (June 8, 2009), http://www.japanfocus.org/-Klaus-Schlichtmann/3168,;. Dan Fenno Henderson, *The Constitution of Japan, its First Twenty Years 1947–1967 (U. of Wash. Press, 1968);* Kenzo Takayanagi, *Some Reminiscences of Japan's Commission on the Constitution*, 86–88 quoted in James E. Auer, *Article Nine of Japan's Constitution: from Renunciation of Armed Force "Forever" to the Third Largest Defense Budget in the World*, 53 Law & Cont. Prob. 171, 173–174 (1990); Yasakuni Onuma, *War Guilt, the Peace Constitution and Japan's Role in Global Peace and Security*, International Symposium July 25–28, 1994, Tokyo Japan, Trilateral Perspectives on International Legal Issues: Relevance of Domestic Law and Policy (Transnational Publishers 1996).

President Bush (II) did not seek a declaration of war before committing troops to the Afghanistan and Iraq conflicts. And the Vietnam War had been prosecuted under the Tonkin Gulf resolution—an open ended Congressional resolution but not a declaration of war. Still, Congress is not a passive bystander in matters of war and peace. The president may be able to immediately commit forces to conflict but he cannot maintain them in the field without Congressional support in the way of appropriations and spending measures. President Roosevelt may have seen the German threat to America long before the Congress but he could not proceed until after Japan bombed Pearl Harbor and even then he could not proceed against Germany until that country declared war on the United States four days later.[13] The end of the Vietnam War was foretold by Congressional objections to further funding activities.

It has been said that under the American Constitutional system the president can make war but cannot declare war. However, while the president has the power as Chief Executive and Commander in Chief to commit forces on an emergency basis, the fact remains that the president cannot prosecute a war on his own. Admittedly, it is unlikely that a Congress would refuse to support a president's request for funds once troops have been committed, nonetheless the funding of the war effort remains a congressional prerogative and the president cannot proceed without the necessary funds.

[B] Article 9

[1] Interpretation

[a] Text of Article 9

Japan's Constitution contains a renunciation of war clause that appears deceptively simple and straightforward. Its history is short: General MacArthur[14] had advised his staff that the new Constitution of Japan should contain a provision under which Japan would renounce war as a means of settling disputes even to the extent of protection of its own security and that no Army, Navy or Air Force would ever be authorized by Japan.[15] As submitted to the Japanese the draft Constitution dropped the phrase

13. Congress passed a resolution recognizing that a state of war with Germany existed but did not actually declare war against Germany.
14. There is dispute about whether MacArthur suggested Article 9 or whether the prime minister suggested a renunciation of war clause. It is likely that it was MacArthur's suggestion. Prior to MacArthur's role in the drafting process, a State Department working group drafted instructions concerning the new Constitution, which recognized that a Japanese armed force might be created in the future by limiting the ministers in charge of such a force to civilians with no special access to the Emperor. Theodore McNelly, *The Japanese Constitution: Child of the Cold War*, 74 Pol. Sci. Q. (issue 2) 176, 179–180 (1959).
15. For a discussion of the history of Article 9, see James E. Auer, *Article Nine of Japan's Constitution: From Renunciation of Armed Force 'Forever' to the Third Largest Defense Budget in the World*, 53 L. & Contemp. Probs. 171 (1990); Shotaro Hamura & Eric Shiu, *Renunciation of War as a Universal Principle of Mankind–A Look at the Gulf War and the Japanese Constitution*, 44 Intl. & Comp. L. Q. 426 (1995).

prohibiting Japan from protecting its own security through use of force. As finally adopted the renunciation of war article reads as follows:

> Chapter II. Renunciation of War
>
> Article 9. Aspiring sincerely to an international peace based on justice and order, the Japanese people forever renounce war as a sovereign right of the nation and the threat or use of force as a means of settling international disputes.
>
> 2. In order to accomplish the aim of the preceding paragraph, land, sea, and air forces, as well as other war potential, will never be maintained. The right of belligerency of the state will not be recognized.

Over the years three major themes have evolved dealing with the interpretation of Article 9. The first is terminology, the second is the nature and size of military forces that might be permitted, and the third is the use that might be made of a force organized in conformity with the Article. As originally explained to the Japanese people, Article 9 was a complete prohibition of the establishment of any military force for any purpose. In the early years of the Occupation Japan had no force whatsoever. The Korean War changed the situation. An indigenous Japanese force was required to perform the functions previously provided by the United States military. MacArthur directed Prime Minister Yoshida to create a 75,000-man National Police Reserve (NPR).[16] By April of 1952 the name had changed to the National Safety Force (NSF) and contained both a land and sea component. This name change was followed by a further change in name in August 1952 to the National Safety Agency (NSA) and finally in 1954 to the Japan Defense Agency (JDA). The "forces" under the jurisdiction of the JDA became known as the Self Defense Forces (SDF).In 2006 the Diet enacted legislation changing the Defense Agency into the Ministry of Defense (MOD) and in 2007 a new Cabinet-level, Ministry of Defense, came into existence.

The position of the ruling party of Japan in 1952 was that Article 9 prohibited maintenance of any war potential, whether aggressive or defensive. The forces under the control of the NSA were considered as consistent with the Constitution because they were not "war potential" since neither their equipment nor numbers were sufficient to allow the NSA to conduct modern warfare. A subtle but important switch had been made in Constitutional interpretation. The prohibition against land, air and naval forces was not exclusive—rather, only such forces as were capable of waging modern war were prohibited.

In 1953 a further modification was agreed to between the ruling party and the opposition. Under this modification the defense of Japan against "direct aggression" became part of the mission of the newly renamed Self Defense Force (SDF). The issue now was whether the function of the force was defensive or aggressive. Aggressive military force was prohibited but an effective defensive force was permitted. A build up

16. James L. McClain, *A Modern History of Japan*, 554–555(WW Norton & Company 2002) notes that as early as 1948 the United States considered creation of a Japanese paramilitary force of up to 150,000 members. John W. Dower, *Embracing Defeat* 548 (W.W. Norton & Company 1999) reports that in the early days of the Korean War the United States wanted Japan to create a 300,000 to 350,000-person army.

of the SDF was undertaken, consistent with this new mission statement and interpretation of Article 9. This new stance was confirmed in 1955 when the Cabinet issued a policy statement to the effect that the renunciation of war clause of the Constitution did not prohibit a war of self-defense. While in 1967 the government announced the three non-nuclear principles[17] that Japan officially[18] maintains to this day,[19] reflecting an interpretation of the Constitution that could permit Japan to possess, manufacture and maintain nuclear weapons for self-defense purposes.[20] Indeed, as early as 1957 the government announced in the Diet that Japan had the right to possess nuclear weapons and the powerful Cabinet Legislation Bureau (CLB) opined that if minimally necessary for self-defense purposes the country could possess nuclear weapons[21]. Japanese statute law prohibits the possession of nuclear weapons.[22] In 1994 the Government of Japan had taken the position that the use of nuclear weapons was not a violation of international law.[23] While discussion of attaining its own nuclear deterrent may have lost its status as a taboo subject, it is unlikely that Japan will adopt a go it alone nuclear and/or military posture at any time in the foreseeable future.[24]

In addition to the three non-nuclear principles, Japan has also adopted non-proliferation of military products principles that evolved into an embargo on the sale of military equipment to any country with limited exceptions to allow sale to the United States. Japan and the U.S. have some joint military development programs. One program involves the joint development of anti Missile defenses. In 2011 Japan agreed that the U.S. could sell such jointly developed equipment to other countries (e.g., NATO Member Countries) even though such sale might be inconsistent with the three non-proliferation principles.[25] In addition, Japan is considering lifting such principles

17. Japan will not possess, manufacture or permit nuclear weapons to be brought into Japan. The last of these principles has been a source of dispute since the United States has refused in some cases to advise Japan whether United States ships at U.S. bases in Japan have nuclear weapons on board.
18. It appears that over the years Japan has looked the other way when one of the principles was being challenged by U.S. action in sending ships in Japanese waters that likely had on board nuclear weapons.
19. While Japan outwardly adheres to these sacrosanct three non-nuclear principles, political party leaders have indicated that Japan could become a nuclear power. Japan can be nuclear power: Ozawa, *Japan Times* Apr. 7, 2002, http://www.japantimes.co.jp/text/nn20020407a1.html; *Koizumi Downplays Non-nuclear Policy Quip*, Japan Times (June 2, 2002); *Opposition Seeks Fukuda's Head*, Japan Times (June 4, 2002).
20. James E. Auer, *Article Nine of Japan's Constitution: From Renunciation of Armed Force "Forever" to the Third Largest Defense Budget in the World*, 53 L. & Contemp. Probs. 171 (1990) quotes Prime Minister Kishi as taking the position as early as 1959 that the Constitution did not prohibit Japan from maintaining the minimum amount of nuclear weapons needed to defend Japan.
21. Mike M. Mochizuki, *Japan Tests the Nuclear Taboo*, 14: 2 Nonproliferation Rev. 303, 305 (2007).
22. Atomic Energy Basic Act (Act No.186 of 1955) Article 2 http://www.nsc.go.jp/NSCenglish/documents/laws/1.pdf, last accessed Sept. 16, 2012.
23. *Renunciation of War as a Universal Principle of Mankind–A Look at the Gulf War and the Japanese Constitution*, 44 Int'l and Comp. L. Q. 426, 432 (1995).
24. For a discussion see, Mike M. Mochizuki, *Japan Tests the Nuclear Taboo*, 14: 2 Nonproliferation Rev. 303–328 (2007).
25. *Japan To Allow U.S. To Export New Missile*, Japan Times (May 25, 2011), http://search.japantimes.co.jp/cgi-bin/nn20110525a7.html.

to allow for the sale of military hardware abroad, especially to South East Asian countries (other than China).[26] In late 2011 the Government of Japan partially lifted the arms export ban requiring that exports be limited to defense related materials for humanitarian or peaceful purposes.[27] And in 2012 it extended joint development to the UK, the first country other than the U.S. with whom it will develop military equipment.[28]

Shortly after being elected the DPJ government reiterated its support for the three non-nuclear principles[29] while the Defense Minister stated that in an emergency and when needed for Japan's defense, it might be permissible for the United States to bring nuclear weapons into Japan.[30]

[b] International Peace Keeping Operations and Evolving Views of Self-defense

The 1960 mutual defense treaty with the United States again changed the role of the SDF because it provided for "mutual defense" and thus contained within its terms the assumption that Japan would play a larger role in its own defense. Meanwhile the size of Japan's SDF was increased to meet its new role. In 1965 the government made it clear that the size of the SDF was not limited by the Constitution. In 1976 a limit of 1% of GNP was placed on the defense budget. In 1981 a division of responsibility agreement between Japan and the United States gave Japan greater responsibility to protect the sea and air lanes leading to Japan. Japan took the position that self-defense could require protection for up to 1,000 miles around Japan. In 1986 a five year plan for modernization of the Japanese SDF was undertaken within the 1% limit. By 1987 the 1% limit was scrapped. By 1990 estimates of Japan's defense budget were that it was either the third[31] or fourth[32] largest in the world and Japan's SDF was a high technology fighting force. Since then as other country defense budgets have increased Japan has dropped to a somewhat lower place in the scale.

26. Kyodo, *Give SDF more freedom on guns use abroad: Maehara*, Japan Timers on Line (Sept. 8, 2011), http://search.japantimes.co.jp/cgi-bin/nn20110908x2.html; Yuko Mukai, *Maehara: Review arms export policy / Mentions SDF weapon use in U.S. speech*, Daily Yomiuri (Sept. 9, 2011), http://www.yomiuri.co.jp/dy/national/T110908005663.htm.
27. *Govt decides to ease arms export ban / Way clear for joint intl arms development*, The Yomiuri Shimbun,Yomiuri Shimbun on Line (Dec. 28, 2011), http://www.yomiuri.co.jp/dy/national/T111227003855.htm; *Government Draft Proposal Would Ease Curbs on Arms Export*, Daily Yomiuri (Dec. 14, 2011).
28. *Japan, U.K. to develop defense equipment*, The Yomiuri Shimbun (Apr. 5, 2012), http://www.yomiuri.co.jp/dy/national/T120404005786.htm.
29. Kyodo News, *DPJ stands by no-nuke principles*, Japan Times on Line (Jan. 28, 2010), http://search.japantimes.co.jp/cgi-bin/nn20100128a7.html.
30. Kyodo News, *In-country nukes a crisis option: Okada*, Japan Times (Mar. 18, 2010), http://search.japantimes.co.jp/cgi-bin/nn20100318a3.html.
31. James E. Auer, *Article Nine of Japan's Constitution: From Renunciation of Armed Force "Forever" to the Third Largest Defense Budget in the World*, 53 L. & Contemp. Probs. 171 (1990).
32. Glenn D. Hook & Gavan McCormack, *Japan's Contested Constitution: Documents and Analysis* (Routledge 2001).

In the 1990s Japan was confronted with questions regarding the use that could be made of its Self Defense Forces. The Gulf War presented a problem because Japan is dependent on oil from the Middle East. Yet when the United States requested that Japan send mine sweepers to the area to assist in the conflict, Japan was unable to assist because the CLB had, in the 1960s opined that the Constitution did not permit the use of Japanese forces when Japan's self-defense was not at stake[33] and had not changed its view. Japan contributed large sums to the Gulf War effort but the minesweepers did not arrive until after the fighting was over. Subsequent events in South East Asia were drawing Japan into the world "peace keeping" context. Cambodia's warring parties were coming to agreement and some outside military force, under UN auspices was needed to assist them in maintaining the peace they had agreed to. Japan, as the world's second largest economy and the first largest in Asia was asked to assist.

After much debate, Japan's Diet enacted the Peace Keeping Operations Law (PKO) in June 1992.[34] Under this law the Self Defense Force could be used, in cooperation with the United Nations, to assist in keeping the peace provided certain conditions were met:

(a) sufficient cease-fire arrangements to assure that there was no fighting;
(b) agreement by the parties to Japanese participation;
(c) Japanese neutrality as between the parties to the dispute;
(d) withdrawal of Japanese forces if changed circumstances resulted in any condition not being met; and
(e) while individual members of the Japanese contingent could use their weapons to defend themselves, the contingent as an institutionalized force could not use weaponry.

The PKO law engendered Constitutional debate in Japan. By focusing in on the cooperative nature of the undertaking and the responsibility of the United Nations for the peace keeping, supporters argued that "Japan" was not an active "participant" in the peace keeping operation but rather the operation was a UN operation and Japan was merely cooperating.[35] Japan has since sent PKO forces to other countries:

33. See, Congressional Research Service, The U.S.-Japan Alliance, Jan. 18, 2011, 15.
34. For a discussion of the PKO law and Japan's experience under the law, see *Renunciation of War as a Universal Principle of Mankind–A Look at the Gulf War and the Japanese Constitution*, 44 Int'l and Comp. L. Q. 426, 427–429 (1995); (Draft paper) Shunji Yanai, Law Concerning Cooperation in United Nations Peacekeeping Operations and Other Operations–Japanese PKO Experience, International Symposium 25–28 July 1994, Tokyo, Japan, Trilateral Perspectives on International Legal Issues: Relevance of Domestic Law and Policy 682.
35. For a discussion of the post-Gulf War situation see Yasakuni Onuma, War Guilt, the Peace Constitution and Japan's Role in Global Peace and Security, International Symposium 25–28 July 1994, Tokyo, Japan, Trilateral Perspectives on International Legal Issues: Relevance of Domestic Law and Policy 757, 769–772.

Mozambique,[36]Golan Heights (1996); East Timor (2002); Nepal (2007); Pakistan (floods); Haiti (hurricane damage); South Sudan (2010 and 2012).[37]

The PKO law permits the sending of SDF units abroad as part of a UN peacekeeping mission while the restrictions written into the law are designed to prevent the units deployed from using force and to assure that Japan itself is not seen as a threat to use force.[38] Consequently deployment abroad is typically accompanied by a debate as to what arms the troops deployed may use and whether they can use them to protect other forces who are working side by side with Japanese forces (the answer has typically been no—as this is not defense of Japan and hence not self-defense).

In 2001 the government set out its view on the meaning of Article 9 in a policy statement based on five principles focusing on self-defense and non-possession of aggressive weapons.[39]

Japan has embarked on a Ballistic Missile Defense system whose sole purpose is the defense of Japan and that cannot be used to defend a third party country.[40] The first component of that system was placed on line in March of 2007. North Korea's nuclear test in 2006 had a great impact on Japan and resulted in a strengthening of Japan's already strong defense ties with the United States.[41]

Defense Ministry's statements reiterate that under Article 9 Japan is prohibited from utilizing military force to prevent an attack on a defense partner when Japan is not under attack.[42] This limiting approach to "mutual defense" has created problems in Japan/United States relations[43] and there are calls for its review in Japan.[44]

Japan's concern over Chinese intentions in the South China Sea highlighted by the clash between a Chinese fishing vessel and a Japanese Coast Guard vessel (and subsequent actions by China, which claims the islands involved and which islands are under Japanese administration) has brought about a rethinking of defense policy away

36. Shotaro Hamura & Eric Shiu, *Renunciation of War as a Universal Principle of Mankind–A Look at the Gulf War and the Japanese Constitution*, 44 Intl. & Comp. L. *Quarterly* 426, 427–428 (1995).
37. *Japan troops begin S. Sudan peacekeeping mission with road construction*, Daily Yomiuri (Apr. 3, 2012), http://mdn.mainichi.jp/mdnnews/national/archive/news/2012/04/03/20120403p2g00m0dm048000c.html; *SDF group arrives in South Sudan*, Japan Times (Jan. 17, 2012), http://www.japantimes.co.jp/text/nn20120117a5.html;*Kyodo, GSDF kicks off S. Sudan mission with ceremony*, Japan Times (Jan. 8, 2012), http://www.japantimes.co.jp/text/nn20120108a9.html; *Gov't OKs SDF Unit Dispatch to South Sudan*, Daily Yomiuri (Nov. 2, 2011), http://www.yomiuri.co.jp/dy/national/T111101005009.htm.
38. Hiroyuki Hata & Go Nakagawa & Takehisa Nakagawa, *Japanese Constitutional Law* sec. 402 (Kluwer Law International, 2001).
39. Government View on Purport of Article 9 of Constitution, on the Web through use of the prime minister's web page link to Defense Agency at www.kantei.go.jp/foreign/index-e.html; 2009 White Paper on Defense Policy, http://www.mod.go.jp/e/publ/w_paper/pdf/2009/18Part2_Chapter1_Sec2.pdf, last accessed Sept. 16, 2012.
40. Statement of the Chief Cabinet Secretary, Dec. 19, 2003.
41. Joint Statement May 1, 2007.
42. Japan Ministry of Defense Website, Defense Policy, Fundamental Concepts of National Defense, Basis of Defense Policy, http://www.mod.go.jp/e/publ/w_paper/pdf/2009/18Part2_Chapter1_Sec2.pdf, last accessed Sept. 16, 2012.
43. See, Congressional Research Service, The U.SA.-Japan Alliance, Jan. 18, 2011.
44. *Gov't panel urges Japan to allow collective self-defense*, The Mainichi (July 7, 2012), http://mainichi.jp/english/english/newsselect/news/20120707p2g00m0dm035000c.html.

from static defense forces that can be used on land to more mobile naval forces that can protect Japan's outlying islands. Japan selected an American made stealth fighter jet as its plane of the future notwithstanding the high cost of the fighter coming at a time of stressed budgets and a huge outlay expected as a consequence of the Fukushima earthquake/tsunami/nuclear tragedy.[45] Concern about Chinese intentions has strengthened the hand of those in Japan who believe that a fundamental shift in defense policy should be undertaken moving away from dependence on the Japan/ United States alliance to a more unilateral or autonomous approach that would lead to Japan being in charge of its own defense. This approach however has severe cost implications and in light of the Great East Japan Earthquake and Tsunami funds for such an autonomous venture are unlikely to be obtained. The earthquake and tsunami may result in an even greater reliance by Japan on United States forces for its defense but this in turn may mean an interpretation more in line with United States expectations of support should there be an attack on United States forces.

Japan has one of the most sophisticated military machines and a force in excess of 240,000. It trains as any army would, even to the point of using bombers on simulated runs using live bombs, which are described as a potential defensive weapon.[46] And, its sacrosanct three-non-nuclear principles may have cracks in them.[47] Moreover, although it cannot send troops abroad that does not mean that Japan's government is limited to solely domestic activity. Thus in 2008 it appears that Japan created its first post-war intelligence operation modeled on the American CIA and British MI6.[48]And, in 2009 it launched one of a series of both optical and radar spy satellites.[49] Japan's plan is to have two radar satellites in place by 2013 to complement its existing optical satellites. In December 2011 it successfully launched its first radar satellite.[50] In 2010 as part of the battle against piracy the MSDF opened its first overseas naval base in Djibouti.[51] In December 2011 Japan and India announced that their navies would engage in joint exercises in 2012. And in June 2012 closer militaries ties

---

45. Chico Harlan, *Japan Chooses New Stealth Jet Fighter*, Washington Post A19 (Dec. 14, 2011); *Kyodo, F-35 Looks to be Next Fighter Jet for Japan*, Japan Times (Dec. 14, 2011), *Government to Choose F35 Fighter*, Daily Yomiuri (Dec. 14, 2011), http://www.yomiuri.co.jp/dy/national/T111213005424.htm.
46. See Norimitsu Onishi, *Bomb by Bomb, Japan Sheds Military Restraints*, New York Times (July 23, 2007), www.nytimes.com/2007/07/23/world/asia/23japan.html?pagewanted=print.
47. Richard Halloran, *Sign of Secret U.S.-Japan Pact Found*, New York Times (Dec. 13, 2007) http://query.nytimes.com/gst/fullpage.html?res=9B0DE1DD143DF934A35757C0A961948260.
48. *Japan Building Foreign Spy Service*, The Economic Times (Feb. 21, 2011), http://economictimes.indiatimes.com/news/politics/nation/japan-building-foreign-spy-service-wikileaks/articleshow/7538486.cms, *Cable Leak: Japan Has Spy Agency*, Kyodo News, Japan Times (Feb. 21, 2011), http://search.japantimes.co.jp/cgi-bin/nn20110221x2.html.
49. *Japan Launches Fifth Spy Satellite*, PHYSORG.com (Nov. 28, 2009), http://www.physorg.com/news178615475.html.
50. *Kyodo, H-II Puts New Spy Satellite into Orbit*, Japan Times (Dec. 12, 2011), http://www.japantimes.co.jp/text/nn20111212x1.html; Intelligence Satellite Launched into Orbit, Daily Yomiuri, Dec. 13, 2011, http://www.yomiuri.co.jp/dy/national/T111212005082.htm.
51. Alex Martin, *First overseas military base since WWII to open in Djibouti*, Japan Times (July 2, 2011), http://search.japantimes.co.jp/cgi-bin/nn20110702f2.html; *SDF readies overseas base in Djibouti / 1st outpost abroad to help fight piracy*, Daily Yomiuri (May 29, 2011), http://www.yomiuri.co.jp/dy/national/T110528002667.htm.

between Japan, Australia and the United States were announced that include joint exercises.[52] Similarly there has been consideration of joint naval maneuvers between Japan and South Korea. Although focused on Japan's self-defense these activities represent a further expansion of the role of the MSDF and are likely a response to what is seen in some circles as more aggressive behavior by China.[53] So too the announcement of Japan's participation of joint Philippine / U.S. military exercises appears to be related to concerns about China.[54]

In May of 2008 Japan enacted a new Basic Law on Space that replaced a 1969 unanimously adopted resolution of the Diet that, on its face, left no room for the SDF to use space for any purpose. It is asserted by some that the enactment of the Basic Law was designed, in part, to open the door for use of space for "non-aggressive" self-defense purposes[55] and the Ministry of Defense outline of the law specifically notes "Government must take necessary measures to promote development and use of outer space that contributes to… … … Japan's national security."[56] Japan had used modern satellite technology to gather information prior to the enactment of the Basic Law.[57] Thus, as interpretation of Article 9 changes it is to be expected that definition of such things as peaceful purposes (whether of space or otherwise) will similarly undergo interpretation.

[2] Litigation

Both the existences of the SDF and its uses have been the subject of litigation. The Japanese Supreme Court has never held the SDF in violation of Article 9.[58] There are four principal Supreme Court cases touching on the Article 9 issue discussed below:[59]

52. *Japan, U.S., Australia to boost military ties Kyodo*, Japan Times (June 3, 2012), http://www.japantimes.co.jp/text/nn20120603b3.html.
53. *Japan, India Agree to Boost Maritime Security Cooperation*, Daily Yomiuri (Dec 30, 2011), http://www.yomiuri.co.jp/dy/national/T111229005248.htm;*Kyodo, Japan, India Hike Defense, Economic Ties*, Japan Times (Dec. 30, 2011), http://www.japantimes.co.jp/text/nn20111230a1.html.
54. *Kyodo, SDF to join U.S.-Filipino military drill*, Japan Times (Mar. 5, 2012), http://www.japantimes.co.jp/text/nn20120305a5.html.
55. Maeda Sawako, *Transformation of Japanese Space Policy: From the 'Peaceful Use of space' to 'the Basic Law on Space,'* 44-1-09 Asia-P. J. (Nov. 2, 2009), http://www.japanfocus.org/-Maeda-Sawako/3243.
56. Basic Guidelines for Space Development and Use of Space page 1, http://www.mod.go.jp/e/data/pdf/space_development.pdf, last accessed Sept. 16, 2012.
57. *Japan Launches Fifth Spy Satellite*, PHYSORG.com (Nov. 28, 2009), http://www.physorg.com/news178615475.html.
58. It has been suggested that the reticence of the Supreme Court to clearly define Article 9 has resulted in ceding authority for such definition to the Cabinet Legislation Bureau. See, JPRI Working Paper No. 99 (March 2004) Politics, Security Policy, and Japan's Cabinet Legislation Bureau: Who Elected These Guys, Anyway?* by Richard J. Samuels, http://74.125.93.132/search?q=cache:sUQmQziADgkJ:www.jpri.org/publications/workingpapers/wp99.html+japan+%22cabinet+legislation+bureau%22&cd=2&hl=en&ct=clnk&gl=us.
59. Prior to the establishment of the SDF there was a National Police Reserve. This resulted in litigation challenging the legal authority of the government to create the reserve. In the *National Police Reserve Case*, No. 1952 (Ma) No. 23, 6 Minshu 783 http://www.courts.go.jp/english/judgments/text/1952.10.8-1952.-Ma-.No..23.html (G.B. Aug. 10, 1952), the Court

[a] The Sunakawa Case

The issue of the Constitutionality of the SDF has come up in various ways. In the *Sunakawa* case[60] the issue of Constitutionality was raised as a defense to a criminal charge of destruction of property and interference with a survey performed for the extension of a runway on a United States air force military base in Japan. Defendants had been charged under a criminal law specifically designed to enforce the Administrative Agreement entered into under Article III of the Security Treaty between the United States and Japan. Defendants argued that Article 9 of the Constitution barred the Agreement, and thus there could not be criminal responsibility for their acts. The lower court found the treaty unconstitutional since the stationing of U.S. troops on Japanese soil was "war potential" and thus violated Article 9. On direct appeal the Supreme Court reversed.

The Court applied a "political question" doctrine analysis in holding that it had no jurisdiction in the case.[61] Nonetheless it discussed the merits. On the political question issue the Court based its decision on the highly sensitive political nature of the security Treaty and the treaty's relationship, both as an historic matter and a practical matter—to Japanese sovereignty, i.e., it was part of the San Francisco Accords that gave Japan back its sovereignty.

The Court in discussing the merits agreed that Article 9 renounced war potential but found that this was not inconsistent with the inherent right of self-defense that Japan, along with all sovereign nations possesses. A proper interpretation of Article 9 meant that what was renounced was "aggressive war" and command and control mechanisms over the potential to wage aggressive war. Since Japan did not have command and control over the United States base there was no Constitutional infirmity totally aside from the fact that the forces involved were there for self-defense of Japan.

[b] The Naganuma Case

In the *Naganuma* case, residents of Hokkaido objected to the JDA decision to build a missile base on a forest preserve on Hokkaido near Naganuma. The plaintiffs argued that the decision of the Ministry of Agriculture to withdraw preserve status of the forest would cause them flooding and other damage and sought to overturn the ministry's decision because the base itself was in violation of Article 9. The Supreme Court held that the plaintiffs lacked standing to sue. To have standing the plaintiffs needed a

---

rejected a suit challenging the Reserve on the ground that plaintiffs had failed to establish a concrete legal dispute between specific parties and that it had no power to issue advisory orders. As there was no case or controversy the court dismissed the action.

60. *Sakata v. Japan,* 13 Keishu 3225, Case No. 1959 (A) No. 710, http://www.courts.go.jp/english/judgments/text/1959.12.16-1959-A-No.710.html (G.B., Dec. 16, 1950). See, Kisaburo Yokota, *Political Questions and Judicial Review: A Comparison* 147–148 and Hideo Tanaka (assisted by Malcolm D.H. Smith), *The Japanese Legal System* 709–711 (University of Tokyo Press 1976).

61. The court had previously established the political question doctrine in the *Dissolution of the House of Representatives case,* Case No. 1955 (O) No. 96 http://www.courts.go.jp/english/judgments/text/1955.6.8-1955.-O-No.96.html (G.B. June 8, 1955).

"direct interest" in having the forest declared a reserve and the Court required that they be directly adversely affected by the withdrawal of Forest Preserve status. (See, Chapter 17 for standing in Administrative Law cases) A potential water shortage caused by the cutting of timber and bamboo that would accompany the construction operation would not provide standing since such use followed the withdrawal of forest preserve designation and was not caused by the withdrawal itself. Since they lacked standing,[62] the action was dismissed and the Supreme Court never reached the Constitutional issue.[63]

[c] *The Hyakuri Air Base Case*

At first blush the *Hyakuri Air Base* case[64] appears to be a simple real property case. S sold land to B and had the property registered in B's name. B failed to pay the purchase price so S rescinded his contract with B and resold the land to B-2 and tried to re-register the land in the name of the new owner. B refused to recognize S's right to rescind. S and B-2 sued B to compel a transfer of the registration to S and then to B-2. There was no fact dispute that B had failed to pay and that S sought to resell to B-2 and B-2 was ready and willing to buy. The case becomes complicated because B was the representative of an antiwar anti SDF group, B-2 was the SDF and the property was needed by the government as part of its plan to build an air force base. B argued that S could not rescind because the reason for rescinding was to sell the property to the SDF and such sale was illegal as a violation of Article 9.

It would appear that B is in no position to argue about the subsequent contract between S and SDF. The only question in so far as B is concerned is whether he paid and if he did not than he has no rights and the sale should be rescinded. The Supreme Court so found. It nonetheless dealt with the argument that somehow B acquired rights under Article 9 of the Constitution. As an initial matter the Court held that Article 9 does not create any rights in any private parties because, similar to the social rights provisions of the Constitution,[65] Article 9 is not directly applicable to actions of private parties. Next the court referred to the State's right to contract as well as the right of the seller to contract with whomever it wished—even the State. Finally, the Court concluded that the seller had the right to rescind the first contract for failure to make payment and then had the right to contract with the State if it wished and such contract had no relationship to the first buyer who was simply an interloper at that point.

---

62. *Uno v. Minister of Agriculture, Forestry and Fisheries*, 36 Minshu 1679 (Sup. Ct. P.B., Sept. 9, 1982); For an English language translation see Lawrence W. Beer & Hiroshi Itoh, *The Constitutional Case Law Of Japan, 1970–1990* at 122 (University of Washington Press 1996).
63. Auer's comment that the Court upheld the decision on the grounds that the case did not involve a legal question but "was merely a political issue" may more accurately reflect the court's approach James E. Auer, *Article Nine of Japan's Constitution: From Renunciation of Armed Force "Forever" to the Third Largest Defense Budget in the World*, 53 L. & Contemp. Probs. 171, 182 (1990).
64. *Ishizuka v. Japan*, 43 Minshu 385, Case No. 1982 (O) No. 164 and (O) No. 165, http://www.courts.go.jp/english/judgments/text/1989.6.20-1982.-O-.No..164.and.-O-.No..165.html (P.B. June 20, 1989).
65. See discussion in Chapter 5.

Moreover, contracts between the State and private persons acting for the SDF were not considered by the Japanese public (at least at the time the contract involved had been signed in 1958) as antisocial and/or against public morality. Thus there was no Civil Code Article 90 issue presented.

Article 90

Some commentators treat the *Hyakuri Base* case as a political question decision and, as a practical matter, they may be correct.

[d] The Okinawa Mandamus Case[66]

In order to meet its commitments under the mutual defense treaties with the United States, the government of Japan determined that it needed to expropriate land on Okinawa on which the United States bases were located.[67] To do so the government needed the assistance of the Governor of Okinawa who, for political reasons, was refusing to help. Mandamus was sought to compel the governor to carry out certain directions given to him by the national government. If the governor did not raise Article 9 as a defense, at least Article 9 was considered to be part of the issues that surrounded the case. If the bases were unconstitutional then there would be no public purpose for the expropriation so the legality of the treaties and the bases would appear to be directly involved in the controversy. Indeed, the governor argued that Articles 9 and 13[68] as well as the Preamble of the Constitution guaranteed a right to live in peace and that the proposed expropriation violated Article 29(3) of the Constitution, which limits expropriation to public use purposes. The governor appeared to argue that even though the treaties involved were not in violation of the Constitution, the expropriation of property to conform to the stationing of troops under the treaties was not a public use. The Court took advantage of the governor's uncomfortable position to avoid making a ruling on the Article 9 question and dismissed the suit based on the governor's concession that the treaties involved were not unconstitutional.

Since the *Okinawa Mandamus* Case decision parties opposed to expansion of Japan's military or the U.S. military presence in Japan have sought to challenge the right of the national government to decide on expropriation of land arguing that such decisions should be made by local expropriation councils. The Supreme Court has held that expropriation of land for use in connection with the mutual defense treaty is a national function within the discretion of the prime minister and thus not within the jurisdiction of local councils.[69]

66. Case No. 1996 (Gyo-Tsu) No. 90, http://www.courts.go.jp/english/judgments/text/1996.08.28-1996-Gyo-Tsu-No.90.html (G.B. Aug. 28, 1996).
67. The leases for the bases were expiring and the owner of the land was refusing to renew the leases. The concept was that the government would expropriate the property (paying just compensation) and would then lease the property to the Untied States.
68. Use of Article 13 appears to be a stretch. Article 13 requires that people be treated as individuals and protects life, liberty and pursuit of happiness as long as they do not interfere with public welfare.
69. *Expropriation for US Bases Case*, Cases No. 129 and 141 of 2004, 57 Minshu, http://www.courts.go.jp/english/judgments/text/2003.11.27-2003-O-No..129.and.2003-Ju-No..141.html (P.B., Nov. 27, 2003) Since the creation of the Ministry of Defense this will now be a matter for the discretion of the Defense Minister.

[e] Other Cases

Several pollution cases have been brought against U.S. bases and Japan's actions in connection with U.S. bases. The courts have granted monetary relief against Japan for noise pollution, have granted the U.S. sovereign immunity for its military flights and have refused to enjoin the ongoing activities.[70]

[3] Political Challenges

In addition to judicial challenge the changes in regard to the SDF have not gone politically unchallenged on Constitutional grounds. Two bodies of thought have developed by those who support the expansion of the SDF and its role: (a) the Constitution should be amended to permit a normal military and (b) there is no need to amend the Constitution, which is flexible enough to accommodate the SDF and its changing roles. The second alternative has been followed, probably because it is consistent with public opinion not to change the Renunciation of War Article in the Constitution.[71] Or if amendment is considered appropriate there is no consensus on what that amendment should provide. Nonetheless, the "need" to change Article 9 is seen by some as argument for Constitutional amendment. Former Prime Minister Abe made amendment of the Constitution—primarily to deal with Article 9 and Renunciation of War—a principle part of his program. Abe pushed through a Constitution Referendum Law so that Article 9 might have a chance of being amended to legitimatize the SDF. The DPJ has been unwilling to move forward on Constitutional amendment.

Nonetheless, just as the first Gulf War caused Japan to rethink its policy regarding the SDF and invoke a broader interpretation of the Constitution so too the rise of China as both a military and economic power is causing a rethinking on military policy and Constitutional interpretation in Japan.

[4] Terrorism, Piracy and Potential Nuclear Proliferation

The events of 11 September 2001 brought about a new crisis in connection with the use that could be made of the SDF and the cooperation that could be given to the United States in the war against terrorism. Prime Minister Koizumi was determined that Japan

70. E.g., *Atsugi Base Noise Pollution* case, 47 Minshu 643, Case No. 1987 (O) No. 58, http://www.courts.go.jp/english/judgments/text/1993.2.25-1987.-O-.No..58.html (P.B. Feb. 25, 1993); *Yokoda Air Base* case, 1612 Hanji 101; 953 Hanta 298 (Mar. 14, 1997); Masami Ito, *JPY 3.25 billion Ordered in Yokota Base Noise Suit*, Japan Times (Dec. 1, 2005); *X v. United States*, 56 Minshu 729, Apr. 12, 2002; *Government Ordered to pay JPY 810 million to local residents over ASDF base noise*, Japan Times (July 7, 2002).

71. For a discussion of Article 9 and whether there is a "need" to amend the Constitution or whether Japan's policy of imaginative interpretation is sufficient, see Takahashi, *Comment*, 53 L. & Contemp. Probs. 189-190 (1990); Yoshiro Matsui, *UN Activities for Peace and the Constitution of Japan, International Symposium* 25-28 July 1994, Tokyo, Japan, Trilateral Perspectives on International Legal Issues: Relevance of Domestic Law and Policy 593.

would not be presented with another Gulf War embarrassment. Accordingly the government submitted a new Anti-Terrorism Special Measures Bill to the Diet, enacted in 2001. The law somewhat self-consciously states its purpose in supporting the armed force of another nation (the United States) to be to defeat terrorism and thus carries out the intent of the UN Charter and then provides for the military and humanitarian steps that Japan will be authorized to take. In all cases the Act requires that the activities of Japan cannot constitute either the use of force or the threat to use force. Nonetheless, the Act permits Japan to assist the armed forces of another nation by providing both material and services to such forces. In addition to humanitarian assistance Japan's armed forces may engage in search and rescue missions. And, while there are limitations placed on when they can use them, the forces can be armed and can, under orders, use those arms to protect themselves and in certain situations others under control of the Japanese forces. In 2003 the Diet enacted a series of laws dealing with the SDF. The most important of which is a law that permits the Cabinet to dispatch the SDF, without approval of the Diet, when there exists an emergency situation calling for defensive measures.

The Anti-Terrorism Special Measures law is fundamentally different from previous step-by-step incremental expansion of the meaning of "self-defense". While not exactly permitting a foreign expeditionary force, the law does permit armed Self-Defense Forces to go overseas and undertake air, sea and land operations in support of a military operation led by an ally.[72] It is difficult to find that this new role for Japan is consistent with Article 9 unless one were to interpret Article 9 so broadly as to give it no substance as a rule of positive law—and that may, in fact be the case.[73] When in opposition the DPJ opposed extension of various provisions of the Anti-Terrorism Special Measures law arguing that the law was unconstitutional because the dispatch of troops and provision of aid was not tied to a UN resolution or UN commitment; since coming to power the DPJ government has joined with other nations when the UN has acted. Thus, when the IAEA presented a report to the UN concerning Iran and issues of nuclear weapons proliferation and the UN adopted a resolution concerning such report in the fall of 2011, Japan responded under its Foreign Exchange Law by freezing assets of certain Iranian entities and by including certain Iranian banks within its freeze regime.[74] Because of its dependence on Iranian Oil imports, Japan's actions were measured and did not freeze entities that are involved in the oil trade between Japan and Iran.[75] Japan also maintains freeze orders against Taliban entities and certain other organizations categorized as terrorist organizations. In addition to trade regulations that further international efforts, Japan has trade regulations that are designed to

72. That Japan's actions under the law are to support an ally engaged in a military operation is clear from the Basic Plan adopted to put the law into effect.
73. Although the Supreme Court appears to have gone to great length to avoid making a Constitutional declaration concerning the legality of the Self-Defense Force, it does appear supportive of the determinations of the political branches of the government that Japan requires a military establishment to protect its independence.
74. Press release of December 9, 2011 from Ministry of Economy, Trade and Industry.
75. Japan lobbied the U.S. to be exempt from strong U.S. sanctions that include Iran's oil exports. Daily Yomiuri, *Govt Pressuring U.S. over Iran sanctions*, Dec. 16, 2011, http://www.yomiuri.co.jp/dy/business/T111215004471.htm.

further its own international policy goals. Such regulations primarily focus on and forbid certain trade with North Korea.[76]

Japanese commerce has been affected by the rise of Piracy on the High Seas especially near the Horn of Africa. Japan has authorized MSD armed ships to be dispatched to the area to defend Japanese ships; has opened an marine base near the Horn of Africa; and a special law was passed allowing SDF ships to patrol a portion of the waters off the Horn of Africa to protect both Japanese and other nations' shipping from acts of piracy.

[5] Command and Control

Once it is recognized that Japan can (and indeed does) have significant military forces, the issue arises as to how to control and command such forces. How can the military chain of command and control system be organized in a society that is forever prohibited from having land, sea and air forces? The answer is by legislation. The command and control structure is premised on the primacy of the prime minister and the responsibility of the Minister of Defense, who both must be civilians and are in control of the officer corps. The Japanese government has a Security Council with whom the prime minister must consult in deciding certain basic questions dealing with the SDF. In an emergency situation the prime minister and Cabinet can dispatch the SDF without first seeking Diet approval or even giving the Diet advance notice. The Diet has control over military funding and the defense budget and through legislation determines the organizational structure personnel levels of the SDF.[77]

Article 66 must be considered. Under this Article the prime minister must be a civilian and all Ministers of State must also be civilians. Thus the Cabinet cannot be placed in the position of deadlock that the Army and Navy Ministers forced on Meiji Constitution Cabinets. Although the existence of Article 66 complicates the interpretation of Article 9[78] if there can be no military how can there be military officers—the provision assures civilian control over the military.[79]

76. *Sanctions on North Korea extended 1 yr / Missile launch cited; tougher steps possible*, Daily Yomiuri (Apr. 4, 2012), http://www.yomiuri.co.jp/dy/national/T120403005214.htm. *North Korean Authors Not Entitled to Protection Under Japanese Copyright Law*, Case No. 2009 (Ju) No. 602, 603, Minshu Vol. 65, No. 9 (1st Petty Bench, Dec. 8, 2011) http://www.courts.go.jp/english/judgments/text/2011.12.08-2009.-Ju-.No..602%2C.603.html; *Japan PCs may be linked to crime / Illegally exported computers possibly used in N. Korean cyber-attacks*, Daily Yomiuri (Mar. 13, 2012), http://www.yomiuri.co.jp/dy/national/T120312005409.htm.
77. Hiroyuki Hata & Go Nakagawa & Takehisa Nakagawa, *Japanese Constitutional Law* sec. 407 (Kluwer Law International 2001).
78. Article 66 was inspired by the allied powers and agreed to by MacArthur.
79. It may be that Article 66 was designed to prohibit officers of the Imperial Army and Navy from regaining power by becoming Members of the Cabinet. If that is the rationale, then could a new generation of military officers serve in the Cabinet while on active duty?

[6] Yoshida Doctrine and Non-nuclear Principles in a Changing Neighborhood

Article 9 is central to Japan's view of itself as a pacifist state renouncing war and aggression. Moreover it reflects the Japanese view of itself as a country that because it has suffered a nuclear attack stands as a beacon against nuclear armaments. Article 9 and the need to rebuild Japan after the war led to the Yoshida Doctrine under which Japan has forsaken military advancement and rejected large military budgets in favor of economic advance and riding on the coat tails of and under the American military and nuclear umbrella. From time to time voices are raised in Japan to reject the Yoshida Doctrine in favor of "more equality" with the United States in military matters or in support of Constitutional Amendment to make Japan a more "normal" state in the military arena. To date the Japanese public has rejected such calls and budgetary restraints have limited the government's ability to change direction. Although the DPJ called for more equality with the U.S. on military matters it eventually moderated its stand on moving the American Futenma airbase out of Okinawa[80] although the U.S. compromised on moving some of the American forces to Guam.

Changing conditions in Japan's immediate neighborhood have raised questions as to whether the Japanese should, at a minimum engage in a national debate as to whether to consider nuclear armament. Although not one of the three non-nuclear principles, there has been an unstated fourth principle that Japanese politicians will not publicly discuss the issue of nuclear armament. Sitting across a relatively narrow body of water from two nuclear armed countries with whom it has shaky relations at best is obviously on the minds of Japanese policy makers. Nonetheless it appears that talk of "going it alone" in the defense arena is quite mooted and on the fringe in Japan.[81]

It is suggested that Article 9 and its renunciation of war is central to the Japanese identity and that any rejection of the renunciation of war language in the Constitution would constitute a major reevaluation of how Japan views itself and how it wishes to be perceived by the world at large. Such is not likely to occur. Nor, in the absence of a change in the United States' policy of defending Japan by both nuclear and conventional means, is the Yoshida Doctrine likely to be rejected, especially as Japan rebuilds from the earthquake, tsunami and nuclear disaster at the Fukushima plant and finds itself with an enormous budget deficit. So too, Japan's view of itself as a victim of

---

80. *Okinawa residents have refused to agree to move the base to a more remote spot in the island. The government of Japan has been unable to persuade the local public to relent. Marine Base to Remain in Futenma: U.S.*, Japan Times (Feb. 6, 2012), http://www.japantimes.co.jp/text/nn20120206a1.html. Michael E. O'Hanlon, Director of Research and Senior Fellow, Foreign Policy, 21st Century Defense Initiative and Mike Mochizuki, Professor, The George Washington University, Rethinking Okinawa, Japan Military Relocation, Brookings, Feb. 2, 2012, http://www.brookings.edu/opinions/2012/0204_japan_military_ohanlon.aspx.

81. To the three factors identified by Professor Mochizuki as bulwarks of Japan's non-nuclear policy (identification as a non-nuclear peace state, support of the non-proliferation regime and realism especially as to its relationship with the U.S. (see, Mike M. Mochizuki, *Japan Tests the Nuclear Taboo*, 14: 2 Nonproliferation Rev. 303, 305 (2007)) should be added a fourth, namely Japan's view of itself as a victim in the context of the nuclear attacks on Hiroshima and Nagasaki at the close of the Second World War.

nuclear war and as a non-nuclear nation is a central tenant of Japanese identity that affects views regarding Article 9. Thus while it is possible that at a future date Article 9 will be amended, perhaps to make clear that Japan may have a SDF and retains the right of Self Defense, including the right to enter into truly reciprocal mutual defense arrangements, it is unlikely that that the renunciation of war clause will be fundamentally changed anytime soon.

§10.04 CONSTITUTIONAL TRANSFORMATION AND CONSTITUTIONAL AMENDMENT

However one views the terms of Article 9, it appears clear that what you get is something other than what, at least at first glance—and perhaps even after searing examination—you see. This seeming contradiction between terms and actual practice is a reflection of a more general approach to Constitutional interpretation in Japan—highlighted by Article 9, but not unique to it. "Constitutional transformation" is a concept under which the text of the Constitution remains fixed but the meaning of specific terms in the Constitution are changed from what the text appears to say through a process of interpretation. Under the doctrine, no formal amendment of the Constitution is required as the process of transformation works a change in the Constitution—although the words of the text remain fixed.[82] The idea of Constitutional transformation is not unique to Japanese legal scholars. A few American scholars have suggested that a similar doctrine applies to the United States Constitution[83] at least in connection with the foreign relations powers of government[84]although there appears to be no case that has actually applied the concept and this view is subject to sharp disagreement.

As early as 1973 and continuing until the present, there has been debate in Japan as to whether Article 9 had undergone a Constitutional transformation. It is argued that the first condition of transformation, namely that the provision as written has lost its normative meaning, has been met because an extended period of time has passed

82. See Tomosuke Kasuya, *Constitutional Transformation and the Ninth Article of the Japanese Constitution*, 18 L. Japan 1 (1986) and introductory note thereto written by Paul Stephen Taylor.
83. Bruce A. Ackerman, *We the People: Transformations* (Harvard University Press 1998).
84. It has been suggested that a kind of transformation has transformed the United States Constitution's treaty making power to permit "Congressional/Executive Agreements" although no such power is to be found in the Constitution. Bruce Ackerman & David Golove, *Is NAFTA Constitutional?*, 108 Harvard L. Rev. 799 (1995), contra view expressed, Lawrence H. Tribe, *Taking Text and Structure Seriously: Reflections on Free-Form Method in Constitutional interpretation*, 108 Harvard L. Rev. 1221 (1995). For analogous arguments, see Peter J. Spiro, *Treaties, Executive Agreements, and Constitutional Method*, 79 Texas L. Rev. 961 (2001) ("Constitutional increments"); Major Geoffrey S. Corn, Clinton, *Kosovo and the Final Destruction of the War Powers Resolution*, 42 William & Mary L. Rev. 1149 (2001) ("historical gloss"). These American law reviews discuss issues related to foreign affairs where, because of lack of Constitutional clarity as to the proper assignment of Executive and Congressional responsibility (see Saikrishna B. Prakash & Michael D. Ramsey, *The Executive Power over Foreign Affairs*, 111 Yale L. J. 231 (2001) for a discussion of this problem) there may be reason for new methodologies and Constitutional interpretation.

during which Article 9 has in fact not been used to prohibit Japan from having a military force. Moreover, those who argue for transformation would argue that not only has the written text lost its original meaning but it is not likely that such a meaning can ever be reclaimed. The debate seems to focus more on the second requirement of transformation doctrine namely, that the public has accepted the new meaning of the text as appropriate. Such a requirement would seem critical to transformation as public consent to Constitutional amendment—whether by formal means or by transformation—would appear critical. Here the debaters are more divided—or at least they were more divided in 1986. Nonetheless, it was argued that as of 1986 the process of transformation was almost complete.[85]

While there may be agreement that the SDF is Constitutional there appears to be little agreement as to what use may be made of the SDF. The major political parties appear to agree that when the conditions of the PKO Law are met the SDF can be sent abroad, under the umbrella of the United Nations. But beyond that there appears, at least on the surface, to be little agreement. Even among the conservative elite in the LDP there are conflicting views as to the proper role of the SDF and what is or should be permitted[86] although the party is working towards putting together a unified draft to be considered before the next Lower House election (that must be held in 2013 at the latest).[87] And the view of the Japanese public is not fixed. It is not clear that there is great support for an expanded military as distinguished from civilian disaster relief and crisis management role of the SDF.[88] Serious question exists as to whether transformation should be applied to a Constitution. It is likely that the doctrine can be applied to statutory provisions that have become anachronisms by reason of time and cultural mores and practices. But when Constitutions are involved the rule of transformation is more complicated. Constitutions have as one of their purposes a check on popular beliefs as to what the law ought to be and a check on the power of the government (through court decisions as well as legislative action). It is for this reason that many Constitutions contain amending clauses that require supermajorities for change and have procedures that allow for extended debate. Moreover, as Japanese nominative legal provisions have a restraining effect on policy determinations, even if they do not have an effect of creating judicially enforceable rights, the doctrine if applied to the "rights" provisions of the Constitution or to Article 9 would have the effect of reducing the force of the Rule of Law.

---

85. Tomosuke Kasuya, *Constitutional Transformation and the Ninth Article of the Japanese Constitution*, 18 L. Japan 1 (1986).
86. See, Christian G. Winkler, *The Quest for Japan's New Constitution* (Routledge 2011).
87. *LDP drafts Constitution revisions / 2nd version clarifies right to collective self-defense, emergency provisions*, The Yomiuri Shimbun (Apr. 29, 2012), http://www.yomiuri.co.jp/dy/national/T120428003646.htm.
88. The experience after the Great East Japan Earthquake and Tsunami as well as the Fukushima nuclear disaster is typical. The SDF was on the front line of disaster relief and assistance in trying to cool the nuclear reactors. All meeting with approval of the general public. See, Chico Harlan, *A Pacifist Nation Comes to Depend on the Service of its Troops*, Washington Post A 12, (Apr. 3, 2011).

Japan's Constitution requires both a two-thirds vote of each House of the Diet and a popular referendum (majority vote) for amendment of the Constitution.[89] While the public may support the SDF and its currently interpreted self-defense mission, there is serious question as to whether a proposed amendment could garner either the legislative two-thirds vote or the majority referendum vote required for amendment of the Constitution. According to a survey conducted by the conservative Yomiuri Shimbun in 2011, although 43% of respondents favored amendment of the Constitution, 45% of respondents were opposed to amendment of Article 9 while only 32% wanted Article 9 amended. And while 49% of respondents felt that Japan should exercise collective self-defense, a minority of these supported amendment to achieve this end while a majority favored a new interpretation of the Constitution.[90] To permit "transformation" and hence amendment without following the prescribed procedures would seriously undermine the amendment clause of the Constitution and would strain the Rule of Law. This is especially so when the very provisions that it may be argued were the subject of transformation were the very provisions that the government sought to change—but could not change—by amendment.

Whether or not Constitutional Transformation applies to Article 9 and whether if applicable a transformation has taken place, it seems clear that insofar as Article 9 is concerned what you see is not what you get.

§10.05 CONCLUSION

But merely saying that Article 9 has no substance as a rule of substantive law is not the same as saying the Article has no practical effect. Such a conclusion would be inconsistent with the forces behind Japanese law and legal thinking. The Article may not encompass rights that any citizen or group of citizens may rely on in a judicial setting but (and it is a huge but) the Article sets down a marker informing Japanese policy makers that where the military is concerned they must go slow, they should not proceed on their own, their actions should, at a minimum conform to the views of the international community.[91] Japanese legal principles and rules, while they may not bind the government in a particular situation and may not form the basis of a right on which to base a cause of action, do serve a significant role in molding public opinion and reaching consensus and do act as a restraining force against policy decisions that are not consistent with the consensus view of society.[92]

Article 9 may not mean what it appears to say—namely that Japan is prohibited from maintaining military forces (or at least significant military forces capable of

89. Article 96.
90. *Poll: 43% of voters support making amendments to Constitution*, Yomiuri Shimbun on Line (Sept. 15, 2011), http://www.yomiuri.co.jp/dy/national/T110914006038.htm.
91. If not the entire international community at least that portion of the community that, for the particular event, Japan associates itself with. In the case of the terrorist attacks that would mean the Western powers as represented by the U.S. and EU. But it is conceivable that in an Asian setting that community would not include such Western powers but would be more limited to Asian countries.
92. Haley, *Introduction:* Legal v. Social Controls, 17 L. Japan 1, 5 (1984).

waging an aggressive war)—but that does not change the character of the Constitution. Namely, the Constitution retains its original role as a peace or pacifist Constitution that renounces war and looks to mutual cooperation and negotiation as the means for settling international disputes.[93]

93. Glenn D. Hook & Gavan McCormack, *Japan's Contested Constitution: Documents and Analysis* 13-17 (Routledge 2001) while quite critical of the interpretation of Article 9 that has resulted in a Japanese military force ["State Pacifism Compromised"] nonetheless recognize that the Article has helped shape policy and limited Japan's military role.

CHAPTER 11

Separation of Church and State

§11.01 UNITED STATES

[A] Historic Basis for the American Freedom of Religion Doctrine

The American experience with religious tolerance and religious minorities was framed, in part, by the European experience. The split between the protesters against what they viewed as excesses of the Catholic Church and the established Church that gave rise to the Reformation and the establishment of numerous Protestant Churches had led European countries into religious camps. Governments lined up on one side or the other of the religious (Christian) divide. Protestants in Catholic countries were subjected to state organized and state condoned religious persecution; Catholics in Protestant countries experienced the same persecution. Members of other religious sects in these countries similarly were discriminated against. Religious wars were fought in Europe over a number of centuries.

Many of those discriminated against by government edict or at least government inaction sought a freer environment in which to practice their beliefs. The lands of the New World, untainted by the religious conflicts of Europe seemed a good place to find this freedom.

One of the founding principles of United States Constitutional law was the separation of the government from religious matters. To assure that the new federal government it was creating did not impede religious freedom, the body of the Constitution provides that "no religious Test shall ever be required as a Qualification to any Office or public Trust under the United States".[1] The First Amendment to the Constitution provides, *inter alia*, "Congress shall make no law respecting an establishment of religion, or prohibiting the free exercise thereof".

1. Constitution Article VI. This provision applies only against the newly created government. Nonetheless, through the application of the First Amendment to the States the same result has been reached at the State level. See e.g., *Torcaso v. Watkins*, 367 U.S. 488 (1961).

[B] The Free Exercise Freedom and the Prohibition against Establishment of Religion

The First Amendment contains two complimentary but in some respects contradictory guarantees—(a) free exercise of religion and (b) prohibition against establishment of religion. Establishment may be violated in cases where government action supports religion, but such support may be necessary in some cases to enable people to exercise their right of free exercise. Thus the Supreme Court held that disqualifying persons who refused to work on Saturday from receiving unemployment benefits violated the free exercise clause, although government provided benefits to those whose refusal to work on Saturday resulted in supporting Saturday Sabbath observers.[2] While the free exercise clause has resulted in some contentious litigation—the Court distinguishing between conduct and belief in some cases, especially where the conduct violates of some generally applicable statute[3] the general rule remains that the government cannot burden a person's free exercise of religion unless the burden arises from a policy that is applicable to—and to be effective requires application to—the public at large and is necessary to achieve a particularly important and valid governmental objective. Prohibition of door-to-door religious solicitation without a permit does not meet this test[4] nor does the requirement that all students receive a secondary school education.[5] But it is permissible to require all to pay social security taxes, even if it is alleged that payment of such taxes violates a person's religious beliefs.[6] While the Supreme Court's jurisprudence in the free exercise area is not free of conflicts[7] and has shown a wide split among the Justices on the periphery, the most contentious issues in the separation of Church and State realm lie in the "establishment of religion" cases.

It is clear that neither the states nor the federal government can "establish" a government religion. Moreover, it appears clear that government cannot give monies to religious groups to support their religious activities, although government may exempt religious groups from paying taxes[8] thereby leaving them with more funds to carry out their religious activities. And, because of the stringent standing rules in United States law that prohibit a taxpayer from suing based solely on her standing as a taxpayer, it is possible for a government to allow taxpayers to make the voluntary choice of redirecting some of their tax payments from the public fisc to private educational institutions, including religious schools.[9] The more contentious issues are how far the state can go in taking action involving public institutions that may appear to some to support religion and how far the state may go in providing aid that benefits religious oriented schools in teaching secular subjects and providing education in general. Cases

2. *Sherbert v. Verner*, 374 U.S. 398 (1963).
3. *Employment Division, Oregon v. Smith*, 494 U.S.872 (1990).
4. *Schneider v. New Jersey*, 308 U.S. 147 (1939); *Cantwell v. Connecticut*, 310 U.S. 296 (1940).
5. *Wisconsin v. Yoder*, 406 U.S. 205 (1972). [Amish families entitled to remove their children from secondary school to teach them agrarian life style, which is fundamental to the Amish religion.]
6. *United States v. Lee*, 455 U.S. 252 (1982).
7. See *Gonzales v. O Centro Espirita Beneficente Uniao Do Vegetal*, 546 U.S. 418 (2006).
8. *Walz v. Tax Commission*, 397 U.S. 664 (1970).
9. *Arizona Christian School Tuition Organization v. Winn*, 563 U.S. ___ (2011). [*Flast v. Cohen*, 392 U.S. 83 establishes a narrow exception to the taxpayer standing rule.]

in these areas have produced wide splits among the Justices and no discernible unifying concept.

The starting point for Establishment Cases is *Lemon v. Kurtzman*[10], where the Supreme Court established a three-part test to determine whether a governmental action is valid or whether it ran afoul of the establishment clause. To be valid the action must (a) have a secular purpose, (b) its primary effect must neither advance nor inhibit religion, and (c) it cannot lead to an excessive entanglement of government and religion.[11] Although the Court for a quarter century paid at least lip service to *Lemon* in its establishment cases, the "test" of *Lemon* was more a guide than a test. While *Lemon* may provide a framework for discussion of establishment cases, in its original three-part form it does not appear to be the "rule" currently employed. For example, in *Agostini v. Fenton*,[12] the Court used a somewhat different test to determine whether there had been a violation of the establishment clause wherein only "excessive" entanglement was forbidden and in resolving this question looked to factors similar to those involving effect. The "entanglement" prong of the three-part test became a part of the "primary effect" prong rather than a separate consideration.[13] This shift is particular relevant to students of Japan/United States comparative law as the Supreme Court of Japan has utilized a two-part test seemingly derived from *Lemon*, namely the purpose and effect test.

In *Mitchell v. Helms*,[14] the plurality read *Agostini* as meaning that government neutrality as to recipients of funds and purpose was the key factor, how the institution that received indirect government aid used that aid [computers for use in the classroom] was not a relevant factor. However, a majority of the court (two concurring Justices and three dissenting Justices) disagreed.[15] *Zelman v. Simmons-Harris*[16] upheld a student voucher program notwithstanding that most recipients of vouchers used them to send their children to religious affiliated schools. The five Justice majority utilized a two-part purpose and effect test and held the effect was neutral because the funds were not provided to religious schools but rather to a widely diverse group of parents who made independent choices as to where to send their children to school and thus where to use the voucher funds. The majority opinion never mentions *Lemon*, although one of the Justices in her concurrence applies a two-part (purpose and effect)

---

10. 403 U.S. 602 (1971).
11. The Japanese Supreme Court has adopted a purpose and effect tests although the interpretation of purpose and effect may be different from *Lemon*.
12. 521 U.S. 203 (1997) overruling *Aguilar v. Felton*, 473 U.S. 402 (1985) and *School District of Grand Rapids v. Bull*, 473 U.S. 373 (1985) both decided on the basis of the *Lemon* test. But the criteria to determine effect changed. As to entanglement, only such entanglement as had the effect of advancing or inhibiting religion was prohibited.
13. Justice O'Connor made this point clear in her concurring opinion in *Zelman v. Simmons-Harris*, 536 U.S. 639 (2002) where she noted that in *Agostini* the court had "folded" the entanglement prong of the *Lemon* test into the "primary effect" inquiry.
14. 530 U.S. 793, 836 (2000).
15. See, e.g., *Good News Club v. Milford Central School* 533 U.S. 98 (2001). The court applied free speech content neutrality–the school having opened its premises for a limited public forum could not exclude a religious oriented group because such exclusion was based on the religious message.
16. 536 U.S. 639 (2002).

Lemon analysis. On the other hand, the court in 2005 specifically looked to *Lemon* as providing a framework for decision.[17]

Part of the establishment clause doctrine seeks to prohibit those acts of government that have the effect of supporting religion in the public context and thereby sending a message that religion or the specific religious practice involved is "appropriate"—another part is the doctrine that government cannot coerce people to support religion or engage in religious ceremony. Consequently, requiring students to recite prayers in public schools constitutes a violation of the establishment clause because it constitutes government approval of or support for religion.[18] The posting of symbols of religion in government facilities is also a prohibited endorsement of religion. But some religious symbols also have secular meaning creating questions as to whether their display by government is Constitutional. Both Christmas and Chanukah are religious holidays with secular messages and their symbols can have both religious and secular meaning. The symbols may be displayed when the message conveyed is secular and not religious.[19] In 2005 the Court decided two *Ten Commandments* cases on the same day. In one it prohibited Kentucky from displaying the Ten Commandments in its courthouses and in the other permitted Texas to display the Commandments on the state Capital grounds. While each case was decided by a close five to four vote, the swing vote in the *Texas* case (Justice Breyer) had voted against the Kentucky display. In the *Kentucky* case the majority looked back to its *Lemon* decision and especially the purpose part of the test. Based on the facts it found that Kentucky's purpose in display was not secular as claimed but predominantly religious in nature, and was not neutral on the question of religion. Accordingly it was in violation of the First Amendment.[20]

In the *Texas* case decided the same day, Justice Breyer, found that the purpose was not predominantly religious.[21] Justice Breyer *rejected use as controlling authority of any of the previous tests applied by varying majorities of the Court in the establishment area*—these tests were useful but not compelling. Ultimately the matter was one for legal judgment

While the Supreme Court's establishment jurisprudence is far from clear and while the Court's view on the subject appears to be in flux, the fact remains that it approaches the problem with a general understanding that the Constitution is designed to prohibit government support of religion in general and surely the government cannot support one religion over another. Moreover, government action that endorses religion or has the effect of indoctrination is prohibited. At all events, the fact that most

17. *McCreary County, Kentucky v. ACLU of Kentucky*, 545 U.S. 844 (2005); *Van Orden v. Perry*, 545 U.S. 677 (2005).
18. See e.g., *Engel v. Vitale*, 370 U.S. 421 (1962); *School District v. Schempp*, 374 U.S. 203 (1963). See also, *Wallace v. Jaffree*, 472 U.S. 38 (1985); *Lee v. Weissman*, 505 U.S. 577 (1992); *Sante Fe Independent School District v. Doe*, 530 U.S.290 (2000).
19. *Allegheny County v. Greater Pittsburgh ACLU*, 492 U.S. 573, 579 (1989); *Lynch v. Donnelly*, 465 U.S. at 687–694 (O'Connor J., Concurring). Of course, viewing the same symbols in the same setting different people may receive different messages. Compare concurrence in *Lynch* (secular message) with dissent (religious message).
20. *McCreary County, Kentucky v. ACLU of Kentucky*, 545 U.S. 844 (2005).
21. *Van Orden v. Perry*, 545 U.S. 677 (2005).

Americans are adherents of a Christian faith is of no consequence in the Court's separation of Church and State jurisprudence.

§11.02 JAPAN

[A] An Historic Analysis

Japan's experience with freedom of religion is very different. As an initial matter, the indigenous religion of Japan, Shinto, is not an exclusionary religion. Thus one can practice Shinto but practice another religion at the same time. Thus, many Japanese are both Shinto and Buddhist. This ability to accommodate different religions in an individuals' life meant that Japanese could be both Shinto and Christian—a concept that Westerners found difficult to comprehend.[22]

Like Buddhism, Christianity was an import to Japan. Christianity had arrived in Japan with the Portuguese traders who brought goods but also Catholic Priests with them to the Orient. Unlike Buddhism Christianity was viewed by the early Tokugawa rulers as having a "political" as well as a religious context. To the early unifiers of Japan and the early Tokugawa's, who were struggling to keep a previously divided country together under their rule, there was a duality in Christianity that was inconsistent with political ends. Namely, a dual loyalty—to Rome and Tokyo. In 1587 Tokugawa's predecessor Hideoshi ordered Jesuit Missionaries to leave Japan. In 1614 Tokugawa Ieyasu ordered all Christian Missionaries to leave the country. Again in 1622 Christianity was prohibited and the Tokugawa Shogunate began to execute Christians. The *Buke Shohatto* (Tokugawa Rules for the Daimyo houses) promulgated by the Third Tokugawa Shogun in 1635 again prohibited Christianity in all of Japan.[23] For the approximately two and a half centuries of Tokugawa rule, Japan was virtually closed to the outside world and thus closed to the importation of "Western" religious views. It was not until 1859 that Catholic priests could again visit Edo (later renamed Tokyo) and Protestant priests could also visit Japan. It was not until 1873 that the prohibitions against Christianity were lifted.[24] In any event, it was not a place where government placed great value on religious tolerance or diversity.[25]

With the fall of the Tokugawa Shogunate, the new rulers of Japan sought to solidify the position of the Emperor, in whose name they were governing the country. Religion was one method of carrying out this goal. The new rulers were aided in their quest of Emperor worship—as a means of extending the power of the Emperor—by the neo-Confusion school of thought that had grown up during Tokugawa rule.[26] Meiji

22. At the start of the Meiji Restoration Shinto was preferred over Buddhism and Shinto/Buddhist Temple/Shrines were divided and Buddhist officials and religious leaders persecuted. See Marius B. Jansen, *The Making of Modern Japan* 352–355 (The Belknap Press of Harvard University Press, 2000).
23. John Carey Hall, *Japanese Feudal Law* 296 (University Publications of America, Inc. 1979) (reprint edition).
24. James L. McClain, *A Modern History of Japan*, 270(WW Norton & Company 2002).
25. For a discussion of religious persecution in Japan during the Tokugawa era see Marius B. Jansen, *The Making of Modern Japan*, 75–80(The Belknap Press of Harvard University Press 2000).
26. Christopher A. Ford, *The Indigenization of Constitutionalism in the Japanese Experience*, 28 Case W. Res. J. Intl. L. 3, 9 (1996).

Japan by focusing on the Imperial State and the Japanese family created a new form of Shintoism—State Shintoism with the Emperor as a God figure.[27]

This new State "religion" was used as a rallying call during the difficult times of the Second World War and thus became one of the features of Japan that the Occupation set out to undo in the new Constitution.[28] Article 20 of the new Constitution provides for religious freedom and prohibits the Government from engaging in religious activities. Moreover the Government is not permitted to grant any privileges to any religious group. Individuals cannot be required to take part in any religious activities and, under Article 89 public monies cannot be spent for the benefit of or to aid any religious group.

§11.03 WHAT YOU SEE MAY NOT BE WHAT YOU GET

The interpretation of the First Amendment of the United States Constitution has been far from consistent over the years. Part of the problem lies in the sometimes-contradictory notions of freedom to practice religion and the obligation of the government not to make laws that violate the notion of separation of Church and State. Nonetheless, the Supreme Court has consistently upheld the fundamental principle that the state cannot force people to either exercise religion in general or a specific religion in particular. Nor may government itself support a religion to the exclusion of other religions; nor support religion in general in opposition to those who have no religious belief. Where the great Constitutional disputes in this area arise is when a government policy has an effect that supports religion but whose purpose was to support some secular notion. Such issues are on the fringe not at the heart of the separation doctrine.

Some matters that implicate religion either go unchallenged or are generally considered as simply not involving the First Amendment. The Congress of the United States hires a religious leader who says a prayer to open the sessions of Congress. The president openly attends "prayer breakfasts" and openly attends religious services on a regular basis. The military pays for chaplains of various religions to minister to members of the armed forces. American money carries the motto "In God we trust" and the pledge of allegiance has, for the past half century, within it the notion of the United States as "one nation, under God".[29]

In Japan the matter is more complex. The popular notion of the homogeneity of the populous is consistent with a homogeneous religious experience. Moreover, during the Second World War shrines were government supported and some had special significance associated with militarism and the war effort. A shrine that deifies Japan's World War II dead will have a different meaning to Japanese than to the peoples of the Asian countries occupied by Japan during the war. Hence any shrine that deifies the

27. James L. McClain, *A Modern History of Japan*, 272 (WW Norton & Company 2002).
28. Marius B. Jansen, *The Making of Modern Japan*, 669–671(The Belknap Press of Harvard University Press 2000).
29. In *Elk Grove Unified School District v. Newdow*, 542 U.S. 1 (2004).

war dead may prove to be a "flash point" for the concept of separation of Church and State. In this connection the Yasukuni Shrine in Tokyo is particularly important.

Yasukuni was established in 1869 to honor those who died in the war that created the Meiji Restoration and eventually became a shrine to honor all of Japan's war dead. There are other Shrines in Japan where the war dead are also venerated and deified, especially the Gokoku Shrines, but Yasukuni has become a flash point because of its location in Tokyo, the Meiji Emperor put his special seal of approval on the shrine and its activities by attending ceremonies held at the shrine,[30] and because of revisionist museum.

Today ceremonies are still held at the shrine and separation of Church and State issues arise, as do issues of Japan's relations with its neighbors, when government ministers attend such ceremonies. In some cases the ministers try to obviate the Church-State question by noting that they are appearing in their "personal" as distinguished from their "official" capacity—a distinction not satisfactory to Japan's former colony or neighbors occupied during the Second World War. Sometimes ministers will appear without attempting to hide behind the "personal-official" dichotomy. In any event, appearance at the Shrine is both a domestic political issue and an international issue. Efforts to treat the internment of war dead as a secular issue with a secular location separate from Yasukuni have been unsuccessful. While LDP prime ministers including Prime Minister Koizumi visited the shrine while in office, stoking anti Japanese feeling in neighboring countries, DPJ prime ministers have avoided visiting the Shrine while in office.[31] Yasukuni Shrine figures in the judicial treatment of Church/State doctrine in Japan.

[1] Tsu City Case

Jichinsai is a Shinto religious purification ceremony. When *Tsu City* constructed a new city gymnasium in 1971, the City spent public monies to hire a Shinto Priest to perform the *Jichinsai* ceremony. A city counselor sued, alleging that such expenditure of public funds violated Articles 20 and 89 of the Constitution of Japan. Japan's Supreme Court disagreed.[32]

---

30. James L. McClain, *A Modern History of Japan*, 268 (W.W. Norton & Company 2002); Marius B. Jansen, *The Making of Modern Japan*, 354–355(The Belknap Press of Harvard University Press 2000).
31. *Natsuko Fukue, Cabinet gives Yasukuni a miss*, Japan Times, Aug. 15, 2011, http://search.japantimes.co.jp/cgi-bin/nn20110815x2.html. DPJ Prime Minister Noda had urged Cabinet Ministers not to attend services at Yasukuni Shrine but nonetheless in 2012 some Ministers visited the Shrine. Masami Ito, Two Cabinet ministers visit Yasukuni, 'Private' call by high-ranking DPJ politicians at war-related shrine a blow to Noda's authority, Japan Times, Aug. 16, 2012, http://www.japantimes.co.jp/text/nn20120816a3.html.
32. *Tsu City Ground Purification Case, Kakunaga v, Sekiguchi*, 31 Minshu 533), Case No. 1971 (Gyo-Tsu) No. 69, http://www.courts.go.jp/english/judgments/text/1977.7.13-1971.-Gyo-Tsu-.No..69.html, (G.B. 7/1377). For criticism of the Court's decision see David M. O'Brien, *To Dream of Dreams, Religious Freedom and Constitutional Politics in Postwar Japan* 97 (University of Hawaii Press 1996).

The District Court in Tsu determined that the ground purification ceremony, although performed by Shinto priests, and although it might appear to have religious significance was simply a folk custom of Japan and therefore there was no Constitutional bar to the City's paying for the ceremony. On appeal, the Nagoya High Court found that the payment by the city was in violation of the Constitution's prohibition against state support of religion.

For the Supreme Court the principle issue was whether the purpose and effect of the payment was primarily religious or secular. For "purpose" the Court looked to the subjective intent of the City fathers who had authorized the payment. For "effect" it looked to whether the effect of the actions of the City was to either favor or inhibit religion as such. The Court allowed subjective factors such as the actor's awareness of the religious character of the acts involved play a significant role and concluded that this Shinto rite had, over a period of time, become secularized and thus there was no violation of Church/State doctrine nor a violation of Article 89 for the City to pay the Shinto Priest to perform this Shinto rite.[33]

The two-part test applied by the Court in the *Tsu City* case (purpose and effect) may have been modified by a more nuanced test articulated by the Supreme Court of Japan in 2010 in the *Sunagawa Shrine* case,[34] discussed *infra*, at least in cases where public lands are being used by a religious institution.

[2] Ehime Prefecture Case

The reasoning of the *Tsu City* case was drawn into question in the *Ehime Prefecture* decision.[35] In the *Ehime Prefecture* case, residents of the prefecture sued to recover back public monies paid by officials of the prefecture to the Gokoku Shrine of Ehime Prefecture and to the Yasukuni Shrine in Tokyo For ceremonies to honor the war dead. The Supreme Court of Japan ruled in favor of the residents—but the decision is not as broadly protective of separation of Church and State as may appear at first glance.

The Court begins by taking as a given that it is virtually impossible to completely separate Church and State. Moreover to attempt to do so would not be justified. From this it follows that some degree of Church/State relationship is permissible. The Constitution requires neutrality by the State on religious matters but not abstinence from all connection to religion. With this as predicate it harkens back to its "purpose and effect doctrine" as set out in *Tsu City* and finds that the doctrine is only violated when the State crosses the line between permissible involvement with religion and

33. The court's "purpose and effect" test appears to be derived from the United States Supreme Court's decision in *Lemon v. Kurtzman*, 403 U.S. 602 (1971). However, as the commentators in 18 Waseda Bulletin of Comparative Law 68–70 note, the Court did not adopt all of the three pronged *Lemon* test nor did the Court apply the *Lemon* test the way it would be applied by the United States Supreme Court.
34. *Sunagawa Shrine Case*, Case No. 2007 (Gyo-Tsu) No. 260, http://www.courts.go.jp/english/judgments/text/2010.01.20-2007.-Gyo-Tsu-.No..260.html (G.B., Jan. 20, 2010).
35. *Ehime Prefecture Case*, Case No. 156 of 1992, http://www.courts.go.jp/english/judgments/text/2010.01.20-2007.-Gyo-Tsu-.No..334.html (G.B. Apr. 2, 1997).

impermissible involvement. That line, in turn, is determined by the social and cultural norms of Japanese society.

The term "religious activity" of Article 20(3) must be defined and does not include some religious activity because some religious activity has social or cultural positives benefits. In determining what is prohibited religious activity the Court looks at the activity itself but also considers such subjective factors as intention, purpose and awareness of the religious nature of the activity. Finally, all of these factors have to be considered against the guidepost of the cultural and social norms of Japanese society. In the *Ehime Prefecture Shrine* case the Court found that the offering of certain forms of monetary contributions to the Shrine by the prefecture officials breached the Church/State separation line because the purpose and effect of the offerings led to support or promotion of a specific religious shrine and because they were public contributions publicly acknowledged by signs hung in the Shrine rather than anonymous. As a result, the relationship between the local government and the Yasukuni Shrine and similar shrines venerating the war dead exceeded what was reasonable under social and cultural Japanese norms.

The Court appears to recognize that anonymous contributions paid out of public monies for a "social" as distinguished from a religious purpose are permitted under the Constitution. Indeed, the Court refers to and reaffirms its decision in the *Tsu City* case because in that case the payment was for a rite that had become a social or cultural rite rather than having a religious purpose.

What appears to be the rule arising from the *Tsu City* and the *Ehime Prefecture Shrine* cases is that there is no complete separation of State from Church required by the Japanese Constitution. Rather, only those religious activities that support or inhibit a specific religion and can be deemed as exceeding the cultural and social norms of Japan are prohibited. And, in this context in determining what exceeds these norms the Court must look to the subjective intent and subjective purpose of the public officials involved as well as the views of the majority of Japanese about those activities. The contributions were not for the secular purpose of honoring the war dead because there were other ways for the public officials to console the bereaved families without supporting a specific religion. Such an interpretation would likely have surprised the American drafters of Japan's Constitution, as it was their intent to separate the social and cultural norms supporting Shinto from permissible government action. The Court's failure to look at purpose and effect from the point of view of a disinterested observer rather than applying subjective views of the government actors leaves open potential for government support of religious activity. In any event, "purpose and effect" in Japan has a different meaning than "purpose and effect" in the United States and that to an American lawyer viewing purpose and effect what you see may not be what you get.

[3] Sunagawa Shrine Case[36]

In 1953 a resident of Sunagawa (a municipality in Hokkaido) gave a piece of land as a gift to the city. This piece as well as several other pieces either donated to the City or purchased by the city became the site of a Shinto shrine. The shrine used the land without making any rental or other payments to the city. Local residents sued arguing that the provision of free use of city owned property for a religious shrine violated the Constitutional separation of Church and State. The Supreme Court held that placement of the shrine in city property without payment to the city was the equivalent of giving public property to a religious body which is inconsistent with the Constitution. In addition, the Court noted that the city's actions could lead citizens to believe that the city administration favored the particular sect that the shrine was associated with. This publicly singling out of a single religion for special treatment was similar to the support given to a specific sect by a governmental unit in the *Ehime Prefecture case.*

In rendering its decision, the Supreme Court utilized a test somewhat different from the purpose and effect test used in the *Ehime Prefecture* and *Tsu City cases.* In *Sunagawa* the Court rather than making a purpose and effect analysis used public opinion, the way in which the facility was being used, the character of the facility and the context in which the right to use the land free of charge arose. The *Sunagawa Shrine case* and *Tsu City* share important characteristics. In both cases the Court looked to public opinion—in *Tsu City* the view of workers who worked on the gymnasium project was reflective of public opinion as was the general view that such ground breaking ceremonies should be held to assist worker safety while in *Sunagawa* public opinion was found to believe that the city supported the shrine as well as used to try to find a solution that would not cause city residents who used the shrine difficulty in practicing their religious beliefs. Although the Court continued to treat the issue of Church/State separation as one involving an analysis that must take into account culturally acceptable standards and societal norms, it also referred to such matters as the nature of facilities donated to the religious body and the rationale of the public body when allowing the use of the property for a shrine. It is possible that the Court's reference to the public body's rationale is a restatement of purpose and effect, focusing specifically on the purpose of the public body. Here those standards were breached when a specific shrine was given specific benefits and the general public was left with the impression that the city administration favored that specific religious body. However the Court did not order that the shrine be removed from the public property—rather it sent the case back to the lower court to fashion a solution that while meeting the separation doctrine would allow the shrine to remain on the city owned property. Among the options that the Court mentioned for the lower court to consider was a sale of the property to the shrine or a lease agreement under which the shrine would pay rent for the privilege of using the property.

36. *Sunagawa Shrine Case,* Case No. 2007 (Gyo-Tsu) No. 260, http://www.courts.go.jp/english/judgments/text/2010.01.20-2007.-Gyo-Tsu-.No..260.html (G.B., Jan. 20, 2010).

In a related case decided on the same day the Supreme Court upheld an outright gift.[37] In determining that gift or lease of the land to the religious organization for use as a shrine was Constitutional the Court took account of the comingling of Church and State during the Meiji Period and the law enacted after the war pursuant to which public lands occupied by shrines were *sold or gifted* to religious organizations in order to separate the religious function from government and thus achieve a separation of Church and State. In effect the current solution was a continuation of such program.

This history may better explain the action of the Court than the reference to hardship caused to community members who have used the shrine for religious purposes. The Court appears to use a balancing test similar to the circumstance decision of Administrative Law (Chapter 17) to allow the Shrine to remain on public property and the Shrine adherents to continue to obtain a benefit, although the adherents must now pay for that benefit (unless the Shrine is gifted to them—but even in such case they must pay the upkeep and continuing expenses)—while adherents of a different belief are not afforded the same benefit (i.e., other religious bodies are not permitted to use public property even if they pay a rental and certainly not permitted to use land at the same location).[38]

In the *Tomihira Shrine case* the Court finds the post-war law under which shrine properties that had been operated by the State during the Meiji Period were granted to organizations to separate the Church and State are the equivalent of or at least consistent with the local ordinance in the *Tomihara* case.

The Supreme Court of the United States also has problems dealing with the issue of whether certain activity on government land violates the First Amendment's Freedom of Religion and Establishment clauses and remains sharply divided on the appropriate test and standards in such a case although there appears to be agreement that the government should not act so as to be seen as supporting a specific religion. As in Japan, efforts to avoid the Establishment clause issue by transferring land on which a religious symbol stands to a private party has spawned litigation and confusing opinions by the Justices.[39]

37. *Tomihira Shrine Case,* Case No. 2007 (Gyo-Tsu) No. 334, http://www.courts.go.jp/english/judgments/text/2010.01.20-2007.-Gyo-Tsu-.No..334.html (G.B., Jan. 20, 2010).

38. After the Supreme Court's decision an agreement was reached between the Shrine organization and the City whereby certain changes were made in the signage and name of the structure and certain land was returned to the city, and the remainder leased to the Shrine organization (at a rental of 35,000 Yen or approximately $400 per annum). A means for clearly designating which property was city property and which was leased to the Shrine for its use was implemented. Suit was brought challenging the new arrangement arguing that in substance no change had been made. The Supreme Court held that this new arrangement was substantially in accord with its prior decision and did not violate the Constitution. *Sunaga Shrine Rental Constitutional Case,* 2011 (Gyo-Tsu) No.122, Minshu Vol.66, No.2 (P.B., Feb. 16, 2012). http://www.courts.go.jp/english/judgments/text/2012.02.16-2011.-Gyo-Tsu-.No.122.html.

39. See, *Salazar v. Buono,* 559 U.S. ___ (2010).

[4] *Miscellaneous Cases*

Some cases appear easy. Thus, in the *Jehovah's Witness* case[40] a Jehovah's Witness student who refused to participate in kendo at school could not be expelled because to do so would be to punish his religious beliefs and thus interfere with his right to practice his religion. An individual has a right to make personal decisions based on the individual's religious beliefs. Thus a doctor who refused to recognize the clearly expressed view of a Jehovah's Witness that she did not wish to have a blood transfusion was responsible in damages for the giving of the transfusion—even if the transfusion was necessary as a medical matter to save the patient's life. The patient's right to decide not to have a transfusion for religious reasons must be respected by the doctor.[41]

Others are more difficult. In the *Omihachiman City/Shiga Prefecture* case, the High Court found large expenditures by public authorities for ceremonies at Shinto shrines for good harvests gave the impression that the government was supporting the Shinto religion.[42]

More interesting are cases involving the Shinto ceremonies undertaken when the present Emperor ascended the throne. As part of the ascension certain ceremonies were held at a Shinto shrine and the entire ascension had a great deal of Shinto symbolism and ceremony associated with it. The Tokyo Municipal government donated substantial sums to help defray costs of some ascension celebrations and ceremonies. Tokyo citizens sued alleging a violation of Articles 20(3) and 89. Although the Tokyo District Court recognized that there were many Shinto elements in the ceremonies the court rejected the Constitutional challenge finding that the ceremonies and celebrations had a secular aspect—namely the Emperor's ascension as a Constitutional officer—and that they conformed to Japanese culture. The payments by the city were viewed as secular in nature and not as support or endorsement of Shintoism to the exclusion or detriment of other religions.[43]

While ceremonies associated with the Emperor's ascension may be secular in nature (even though they involve some Shinto elements), the same probably cannot be said for visits to the Yasukuni Shrine by government officials. In August of 2001 then Prime Minister Koizumi visited the Yasukuni Shrine. A group of Japanese citizens instituted suit claiming that as the prime minister arrived at the shrine in a government vehicle and signed the guest book as Prime Minister of Japan he attended in an official

---

40. 50 Minshu 13-469, 1564 Hanji 3 Case No. 1995 (Gyo-Tsu) No. 74, http://www.courts.go.jp/english/judgments/text/1996.3.8-1995.-Gyo-Tsu-.No..74.html (P.B., Mar. 8, 1996).
41. *Blood Transfusion case, Takeda v. State*, Case (o) No. 1081 and No. 1082 of 1998, http://www.courts.go.jp/english/judgments/text/2000.02.29-1998.-O-.No..1081.and.1998.-O-.No..1082.html (P.B., Feb. 29, 2000).
42. 1671 Hanji 19 (Dec. 15, 1998).
43. *Heisei Emperor Ascension case*, 1673 Hanji 3, 1003 Hanta 89 (24 March 1999). A similar case was dismissed by the Osaka High Court. in an unpublished opinion of 9 March 1995. In the Osaka case the High Court questioned the Constitutionality of the expenses. David M. O'Brien, *To Dream of Dreams, Religious Freedom and Constitutional Politics in Postwar Japan* 203–209 (University of Hawaii Press 1996).

capacity and that the distinction of *personal v. official* is illusory[44] Other similar suits were brought for subsequent visits. The Supreme Court in 2006 refused to specifically rule whether such visits were inconsistent with Japan's Constitution it held that plaintiffs were not entitled to monetary damages for psychological injury allegedly caused by the prime minister's visits.[45] It has been reported that the memoirs of the Director of the Imperial Household Agency during Emperor Hirohito's reign disclosed that the former Emperor disapproved of the enshrinement of war criminals at the Shrine and refused to visit the Shrine after such enshrinements. The present Emperor has not visited the Shrine after his accession to the throne.[46] One wonders if the *Yasukuni Shrine* cases dealing with visits by the prime minister really involve the question of separation of Church and State and Freedom of Religion. American presidents attend church services on a regular basis without any litigation asserting a violation of the First Amendment. Presidents and prime ministers are entitled to religious freedom and thus are entitled to attend religious services of the religion they hold to or at churches, synagogues, temples, shrines or mosques they choose. One sees no law suits challenging the right of the prime minister or members of the Cabinet to attend services at Buddhist Temples or at Shinto Shrines not associated with the Second World War or the military. Yasukuni is special because of its enshrinement of deceased Japanese military personnel, including some Class A war criminals and because of its museum. What you see may not be what you get in the sense that Freedom of Religion and Separation of Church and State cases involving Yasukuni are really not about either Religion, Separation nor about fear of a resurgence of State Shinto. They are about the Second World War, Japan's relations with its Asian neighbors, and the enshrinement of Class "A" war criminals. The objection is not that the prime minister attends a Shinto Shrine or a Shinto Ceremony—it is that he attends this specific Shinto Shrine with its specific relationship to the war, revisionist history and Japan's closest neighbors.

In the *Aum Shinrikyo Dissolution of a Religious Corporation case*[47] the Court upheld the dissolution order requiring the dissolution and liquidation of assets of the Aum Shinrikyo religious corporation. The leader of the religious group and several of his followers were convicted of the saran gas attack in the Tokyo subway system that took many lives and caused both injuries and panic. In addition several members of the group were convicted in the killing of a lawyer and his family who had opposed the

44. For a general discussion of two case studies involving freedom of religion and "State Shinto" see David Forfar, *Individuals against the State? The Politics of Opposition to the Re-emergence of State Shinto, in* Roger Goodman & Ian Neary, *Case Studies on Human Rights in Japan 245* (Japan Library 1996; Curzon Press 2003).
45. Teruki Tsunemoto, *Commentary on Important Legal Precedents for 2006: Trends in Constitutional Law Cases*, 9 Asian-P. L.& Policy J. 213, 225 (2008); Martin Fackler, *Japan's Top Court Rejects Suit to Bar Shrine Visits*, International Herald Tribune (June 29, 2006), www.iht.com/articles/2006/06/23/news/shrine.php.
46. *Emperor Turns 73, Avoids Shrine Topic*, Japan Times (Dec. 24, 2006), http://search.japantimes.co.jp/cgi-bin/nn20061224a6.html.
47. *Aum Shinrikyo Dissolution of a Religious Corporation case*, Case No. 1996 (ku) 8, 50 Minshu No.1, at 199, http://www.courts.go.jp/english/judgments/text/1996.01.30-1996.-ku-.8.html (P.B., Jan. 30, 1996).

religious group. The Court found that liquidation of the assets of the group was not a direct action against the group and was not a violation of the freedom of religion clauses of the Constitution. Moreover, freedom of religion was not a limitless right but could be restricted in appropriate, albeit rare, cases. In this case, taking into account the actions of the group and the fact that believers could still believe as they wished and even hold ceremonies, the balance of *public interest v. the rights of the believers* was in favor of dissolution.

[5] Enshrinement Case

The *Gokoku Enshrinement* case[48] presents a somewhat different aspect of the Church-State doctrine. In this case the wife of a deceased member of the SDF sued both the Gokoku Shrine and the government alleging a violation of the separation of Church/State doctrine. The wife was a Christian. The deceased husband's family was Buddhist, although he appears not to have had any significant religious belief. The deceased was killed in a traffic accident while a member of the SDF. He was accorded Buddhist funeral rites and his wife was given his ashes. She, in turn left some ashes with her father-in-law and placed the other part in a Christian Church where, each year, she attended memorial services for her husband.

The local Veterans Association in the area where the father-in-law lived petitioned the shrine to have the husband enshrined as a member of the SDF at the Gokoku shrine—a shrine for Japanese war dead. The wife objected because of her religious beliefs. The Veterans Association continued with the enshrinement and the Shrine performed the necessary services to enshrine the deceased. The wife sued both the government and the shrine. The court rejected the case against the government on the grounds that the Veterans Association was a private group and the SDF had played no role in the enshrinement. The enshrinement complained about was an act of the shrine—a private party and not a governmental act.

In considering the case against the shrine the "indirect" applicability of the Constitution under Article 90 of the Civil Code was considered. (See Chapter 3) In considering whether Article 20 was violated the Court was concerned with the competing religious beliefs and feelings of the deceased's father and wife. On the one hand the wife argued that her religious beliefs were infringed by the enshrinement. On the other, enshrinement was consistent with the desires of the father and indeed consistent with the general views of the local community. In other words, it was the wife's insistence on her Christian beliefs that were out of step with the majority community's Shinto/Buddhist [and nationalistic] beliefs. In this context the wife's beliefs could not be given primacy.

The key issue was whether in weighing the competing interests of the wife, the Shrine and the deceased's family and community the wife could show that her personal right to beliefs and practices were being disadvantaged by the enshrinement. Failure to

48. *Gokoku Enshrinement*, Case No. (0) 902 of 1982, *Japan v. Nakaya*, 42 Minshu 277, http://www.courts.go.jp/english/judgments/text/1988.06.01-1982-O-No.902.html (G.B. June 1, 1988).

show that her freedom to practice her religion was being adversely affected resulted in dismissal of her claim. Enshrinement as such was viewed as not adversely affecting anyone's legal rights and enshrinement did not require the wife to either attend ceremonies at the Shrine or otherwise act in a way that was inconsistent with her personal religious beliefs.

The *Gokoku Enshrinement* case implicates the intersection of two cultural/social imperatives in Japan, aside from the Church-State religious question. On the one hand there is the question of how to treat the war dead including those who died in the Second World War and those who have given their lives while members of the SDF. This implicates legal questions about the Constitutionality of the SDF and its proper role and questions concerning how the society should treat those who die while in its "military" service. These fundamental issues affecting Japanese society and the view taken of Japanese history have nothing to do with Mrs. Nakaya's religious beliefs and only tangentially implicate the Church-State religion question. The second issue relates to the proper respect to be given to the extended family of the deceased. Here there were conflicting questions of how to pay respects and thus the Court was confronted with a conflict between a spouse and the deceased's parents and community. In historical terms there was a strong argument that the family, as represented by the parents, had the greater claim.[49] On the other hand, the more recent views of the significance of the nuclear family (and especially the equality of the wife) would appear to favor the right of the wife over those of the parents. It may well be that, as the concurring opinion in the case appears to indicate, in this contest between individual rights of the wife and communal rights of the village and extended family, the individual rights must give way to tradition and cultural values that are generally accepted in the community.

Not only the rights of the parents but also the rights of the local community of which Takafumi Nakaya was a part must be considered. The enshrinement case placed the widow in opposition to the local community, in opposition to her in-laws and in opposition to what most Japanese would consider to be the socially acceptable norms of society. As such, the values of the group from which her husband came, (and from which the Justices on the Supreme Court also came) rather than the widow's individual beliefs, were given prominence by the Court.[50] In philosophical terms the enshrinement enhanced the "good" of the community of which Takafumi Nakaya was a part—this was more significant than the asserted individual right of his spouse.

A similar decision was rendered in late 2011 when the Supreme Court rejected a lawsuit filed by Koreans who objected to their relatives having been enshrined at the Yasukuni Shrine for their relative's service to the Japanese military during the Second World War when Korea was a colony of Japan. The Court rejected claims against the shrine noting that the enshrinement itself was a religious function of the Shrine and not

49. See discussion concerning the *Ie* in Chapter 9.
50. See John Owen Haley, *The Spirit of Japanese Law* 199 (University of Georgia Press 1998). For a more recent case discussing the importance of and effect of community acceptance on the law see "common law" *Marriage between Uncle and Niece* case, Case No. 354 of 2005, 61 Minshu (Sup. Ct., PB 8 March 2007). Available in English through the website of the Supreme Court of Japan.

a governmental function. As in the Gokoku case the government had provided the Shrine with records that enabled them to make the enshrinement but such action was not considered as religious in nature and not subject to the prohibition of commingling Church and State in the Constitution.[51]

[6] Conclusion

The Japanese Supreme Court appears to be searching for a practical solution to the problems presented by Japan's past and the fact that many in Japan view Shinto and Buddhism as part of the indigenous culture and social fabric. Consistent with the intent of the American writers of the Japanese Constitution and consistent with the liberalism represented by that Constitution the Court appears to have drawn a bright line that prohibits government action—and even private action—that prevents those who are not Shinto/Buddhist from practicing their own religious beliefs free from intimidation or other disadvantages. Moreover, significant public contributions to religious institutions, whether it be free public lands or monetary contributions, that carry with them the acknowledgment that the Shrine is receiving government assistance is forbidden Incidental government support of Shinto/Buddhist establishments or beliefs could be permissible as long as such support conformed to the Court's view of reasonable limits consistent with Japan's social and cultural norms. While such a view may be consistent with the religious views of most Japanese citizens, it does not appear to protect the minority Christian community in Japan. On the other hand, in determining what the Constitution means it may be relevant to acknowledge the first imperative of the Freedom of Religion clause may have been political—removing the Emperor's status as a God—rather than religious—although it has been reported that after promulgating the Constitution as required by the Occupation, the Emperor attended special ceremonies at Shinto Shrines designed to allow him to advise his ancestors of his actions.[52]

51. (*Korean Enshrinement at Yasukuni Case*) Kyodo, *Top Court Nixes Korean Suit Against Yasukuni Enshrinement*, Japan Times (Dec. 3, 2011), http://www.japantimes.co.jp/text/nn20111203a8.html.
52. James L. McClain, *A Modern History of Japan*, 540–542 (WW Norton & Company 2002).

CHAPTER 12
Contracts

§12.01 UNITED STATES

The concept of contracts is a fundamental building block of United States law. It exerts a strong influence on Western society.

Contract and the binding nature of contract have religious as well as societal roots in Western law. Canon law recognized contracts as binding and enforceable. Failure to carry out one's contractual commitments was a breach that had religious consequences. In time, failure to live up to one's contractual obligations acquired a moral component and such failure was considered immoral.

Western societal and governmental systems have a contractual base. Western feudalism was grounded in contract. There were rights and obligations flowing between the nobility and there were rights and obligations flowing between the noble class and the peasant class. Contracts to sell land and other contracts that were not under seal were originally not subject to trial in the King's courts. However, once the writ of assumpsit making oral agreements subject to litigation in the King's Court was available, contract cases could be tried in the King's court. (See Chapter 1)

With the enlightenment came notions of a "social contract" based, in part on natural law. The Declaration of Independence with its rights based foundation deals with the relationship between the colonies and the King as one where each side has rights and obligations—a contractual base. The Constitution is, basically, a contract negotiated between the States and later adopted by the people through their vote and acceptance thereof. New States entering the Union adopted the contract and became parties thereto. Breach of the contract could form the basis for a suit that was tried in the courts of the new government. The issue of whether a contracting party could leave the contractual relationship was a legal question. As there was no clause in the Constitution dealing with the issue and as there was no neutral forum acceptable to all to resolve the question, it was resolved through battle (Civil War) rather than the more civilized methods of resolving questions—litigation. Some Constitutions of federations actually provide for contracting States to withdraw from the contractual arrangement within a period of time or else be deemed to have accepted an obligation to never withdraw. Singapore chose to withdraw from the Malaysian "contract" and form its own sovereignty. Social contract ideas have been referred to by both political and moral philosophers in the West.

Intimate social relations are seen as contractual in nature. Marriage is a contract. Religion recognizes traditional marriage as a contractual undertaking—in some religions the contract cannot be renounced through divorce but the contract can be set aside (annulled) for breach of the basic requirements of contracts—knowing consent. Fraud is a basis for annulment because fraud "sets aside" or annuls the contract and makes it as if there were no contract to begin with. This, of course, requires some special rules for children of an annulled marriage. King Henry VIII and the Catholic Church had a "contract" dispute that led to Henry's adoption of reformation views and creation of the Anglican Church to avoid the jurisdiction of Rome over the contract matter. Once his own Church relieved him of his "contractual" obligations he was free to marry again. Secular society also views marriage as a contract and thus those defenses against the existence of a contract, such as fraud in the inducement, apply to marriage and make marriage dissolvable for failure to meet contract law requirements. Because of their contractual nature, some States do not even require either religious or civil ceremony to validate a marriage and recognize so-called "common law" marriages. Once entered into the parties to the contract have rights vis-à-vis each other and these rights may be enforced in a court.

Contract fits nicely into the "enlightenment" and works easily for a society based on rights and belief in individual autonomy. As long as I have the capacity to voluntarily enter into a contract, I am permitted to make a contract, which then forms the rules that govern my relations with the other contracting party. Because contract is a matter of free will, I have several "choices" that I can voluntarily exercise in a contract relationship. First, is the choice as to whether and with whom I will contract. As a general rule I can make that choice freely—if I do not wish to do business with X I can decide not to contract with X and instead do my business with Y.[1] Second, is the choice of my relationship with Y once we have decided to contract. Here we can agree to the rules that will govern our relationship. If we expect a dispute we can decide to go to arbitration or decide that the court in New York should resolve the matter. It is our choice.[2] If we decide the price of bicycles should be USD 100 it will be USD 100 even if my financial advisor suggests I can get the bicycles from Z for USD 95. Contract is a matter of free will. But once X and I decide that he will sell and I will buy the bicycles for USD 100 (and consideration is given) we are bound to follow through on that agreement. If either of us breaches, the essential nature of contract is that the other may seek court enforcement either by compulsion (in the case of specific performance) or

1. For public policy reasons such freedom of contract may be limited. Thus Labor Laws, recognizing the unequal power of the employer and a single employee, may require that employers contract with a union. Anti-discrimination laws may prohibit the freedom to contract to engage in unlawful discrimination.
2. *Stolt-Nielsen S.A. v. Animalfeeds, International*, 559 U.S. ___ (2010).

by money damages to satisfy the loss suffered by breach. Of course, parties may agree to limit their obligations, such as by including war exclusion or natural disaster clauses, or a limitation of liability clause.

Thus contract expresses a statement of concurring wills. To be binding the parties must be able to have the necessary wills. Accordingly there are rules in all states governing such matters as capacity to form a will—insane persons and minors are incapable of forming a will the law will recognize as voluntary and thus their attempts to contract are void or voidable. Similarly, there are some fundamental mistakes that make a common joinder of will impossible—X is selling a cow and A thinks he is buying a horse. This fundamental mistake may void the contract. Or X offers to sell what is represented to be an authentic piece of baseball memorabilia and A agrees to buy it. However, X has knowingly misled A as X manufactured the article in his basement and made it appear like the real thing. There has been no joinder of the minds and A can back out of the deal. Of course, if X is simply mistaken and A is on guard to protect himself then *caveat emptor*—let the buyer beware—may enter the picture and the contract may be binding.

As a contract represents a joinder of wills, disputes may arise as to what the parties intended and contract interpretation may be called for. This may be the function of a jury trial in the United States.

Contract law was not originally a part of the jurisdiction of the Common Law Courts in England. It was not until the writ of assumpsit that the common law courts could effectively deal with contract law. Up till that time "lesser" judicial bodies, such as "pie powder courts", handled contract disputes. In these bodies merchants created the law merchant. But once in the common law courts, contract law was made through the eyes of lawyers and judges who were dealing with "dysfunctional", that is to say "contracts gone bad" problems. From these failures the law of contract developed and as a consequence lawyers in the United States write contracts to deal with contract relations that go bad. The "rules" of contract are designed in great measure to assure a victory once one is in the courtroom. As contract became a subject for common law courts prior to the American Revolution, parties to a contract dispute of over USD 20 have a Constitutional right to a jury trial.

American society views itself as having a minimal interest in contracts because the contract is the province of the contracting parties. Societal interest is represented by certain minimal social norms that cannot be "voluntarily" given away or that must be followed in the contract decision. Thus contracts that are against good morals are void—such as a contract for prostitution or gambling contracts in states where prostitution and gambling are illegal or the contract to sell illegal drugs or contracts with a usurious rate of interest. But, the term good morals is narrowly construed so that it is not a violation of good morals if one party has better negotiating skills than another or better information. Absent a statutory requirement there is no general moral responsibility to advise the other negotiating party about matters that are equally available to both parties, although perhaps not noticed by the other party. Contracts in violation of substantive law provisions are void and unenforceable, e.g., an agreement in restraint of trade. But contracts against good morals are a very small percentage of actual contracts and such public policy objectives are typically spelled out in legislation or court decisions so parties know in advance what they may or may not contract about. Also, basic civil rights issues cannot be contracted away. X cannot decide not to sell his house to A because of A's religion or ethnic background or race. These are social values that the law does not allow X to bypass. Racial or religious covenants in deeds are unenforceable because against public policy. The number of categories involved is relatively small and represents basic social values set out in laws such as the equal housing legislation or EEO Act. As a general rule the common law has no "roving" good morals concept applicable to contracting. Although the Uniform Commercial Code imposes a good faith duty in performance and enforcement on parties who have already entered into a contract.[3]

Finally, there are some situations where the respective power of the parties is so disproportionate that the law will either prohibit certain types of contracts between the parties (a labor agreement under which an applicant agrees not to join a union) or will grant one side (the weaker side) an opportunity to withdraw in a relatively short period (three days to decide to withdraw from a home improvement contract where the improvement may result in a lien on the property and potentially ultimate dispossession of the homeowner). Special rules apply to contracts between large business entities and consumers to protect the consumer who is viewed as at a disadvantage in the contractual relationship. Again, limited categories are typically set out in a statute or in court decisions. Under American law once these hurdles have been overcome, the agreement between the parties is their "law"—it binds them to do what they have agreed to do and the courts are available to deal with failure to carry out the agreement. If the parties are worried about changed circumstances—the price of a raw material component could rise and make the seller's agreed price unprofitable—they should provide for that contingency in their contract.[4]

Modern contracting questions have arisen in connection with the rise of computer software and purchases over the Internet. Here rules are "in formation". However the issues are framed in typical contract terms. What is being debated is how one proves that there has been or has not been a meeting of wills.

Contract law is a matter of state law and the rules for making an American contract are short and simple. As a general rule a contract needs an offer by one party, an acceptance of the offer by a second party—a conditional acceptance is not an acceptance but a counteroffer with the condition now a part of the offer. Finally the common law incorporates into the requirement of consideration—something to bind the contract. A horse, a hawk, a robe or even a pepper corn as an early court put it may serve as consideration. A promise to do something may be consideration for a contract.

3. UCC Articles 1-203 "Every contract or duty within this Act imposes an obligation of good faith in its performance or enforcement."
4. Although a treaty question (although some might argue that the essence of treaty obligations is contract as treaties are considered contracts between the treaty parties)-the comment of the 8th Circuit in *Mille Lacs Band of Chippewa Indians v. Minnesota*, 124 F.3d 904, 934 (8th Cir. 1997) is instructive: "Despite the 160 years that have passed since the signing of the Treaty, it remains good law. One of the hallmarks of our Constitutional system is respect for the law, regardless of changed circumstances or the inevitable passage of time." But changed circumstances and the context in which the parties find themselves are important components of Japanese law.

If parties who can have a meeting of the minds do these three things and if the contract does not violate public policy and if there are no special circumstances that compel protection of one side from the other (lawyer/client) and no statute requiring some formality that has not been met (such as a writing required by a Statute of Frauds) and there is no mistake that avoids the contract or fraud that avoids it, the parties, as a general rule have a deal. And failure to follow the terms of the deal leads to judicial enforcement of the deal or damages.

Because of problems of proof (the concern that a jury could be easily misled as to whether in fact a contract had actually been entered into) some types of contracts must be in writing. This "statute against frauds" concept exists in all states but the types of contracts that are covered by the statute differ as the public policy objectives of the states differ. Similarly, the jury determination concept is at the root of the American Parole Evidence rule under which the signed contract represents the deal of the parties and evidence of agreements outside the contract cannot be introduced to modify or change the contract.

The idea that contracts are binding, that parties are morally as well as legally obligated to carry out their contractual commitments is so strong in the United States that it finds voice in the Constitution. Article 1, section 10 provides that "No state shall [...] pass any [...] Law impairing the Obligation of Contracts".[5] Article 6 provides that "All Debts contracted and Engagements entered into, before the Adoption of the Constitution, shall be as valid against the United States under this Constitution, as under the Confederation". In other words, contracts entered into by the predecessor government bound the new government.

§12.02 JAPAN

Contracts were not unknown in feudal Japan but neither were they common or the preferred method of dealing. Agreements—understandings that were not enforced by the power of the state—were far more common. One reason for this distinction was that the greater part of the population of feudal Japan lived in villages and the authorities—either the central Shogunate authority or the local daimyo authority—relegated village affairs to resolution within the village. Thus, disputes were to be resolved internally not externally and dispute over the meaning or breach of most "agreements" could thus not be enforced in the embryonic "legal" system that was developing. Even if a claim of breach could be brought to the Daimyo or Shogun's Magistrate—such as an alleged breach in an agreement between members of different villages (a diversity case)—so-called "money suits" were required to go to conciliation not "litigation".[6] (See Chapter 14)

5. In Federalist Paper No. 44 it was argued that laws impairing contract obligations violate both principles of sound government and the basic social contract that governed the relations of private parties. See Federalist No. 44, in Jacob E. Cooke, *The Federalist* 301 (Wesleyan University Press 1961).
6. Dan Fenno Henderson, *Village "Contracts" In Tokugawa Japan* 18–19, 29 (University of Washington Press 1975).

Although the "right" to get enforcement of the agreement (or damages in lieu of enforcement) by the governing authority (an essential element in the definition of a contract) was missing in the case of most feudal agreements, agreements continued to exist. Agreements were not meaningless, in that village authority enforced them. Wise men, councils, and headmen were used to mediate and conciliate disputes over agreements.[7] If a party was recalcitrant and refused a compromise position there was always the option of expulsion from the village or ostracism.

Of significance is the "non-binding" nature of the agreements referred to. Non-binding in the sense that there was no State or government mandated enforcement mechanism. The prevailing enforcement mechanism was a form of consensus arrived at through a process of negotiation—which is what conciliation and mediation really involves. The "binding" nature of agreements was more in the form of some loose understanding of interpersonal trust, not a "Rule of Law" or the moral imperative associated with Western religious ideas associated with contract.

The different nature of Japanese and European feudalism also had a profound effect on the "binding" nature of contracts.[8] While in Europe the bargain between and among the classes was viewed as contractual in nature and enforceable by religious doctrine or supernatural beliefs in the power of the oaths that bound the parties or mutual undertakings, in Japan feudalism had a different basis. Concepts of religious covenant were not available and the supernatural power of oaths was not part of the culture. Roman law ideas about mutual obligations were not a source that could apply. Accordingly the idea of a contract was not available. Family ties and kinship ideals became the "glue" that bound the parties to their feudal obligations. Confucian values—with their emphasis on duties owed by superiors and subordinates—held the parties to their obligations. But the idea of a binding covenant or contract was not available.

Moreover, Tokugawa society was rigidly structured on class lines. Samurai were prohibited from being merchants. Merchants could not bring claims against samurai to the Daimyo or Shogun's "court". Agreements across "class" lines were simply unenforceable except to the extent that the more powerful party agreed to enforce the agreement. In such a setting, it is probable that agreements represented what the more powerful party was prepared to do and the weaker party could only hope that the more powerful party would honor his obligation. It is thus easy to speculate that the average person would view contract as a means by which the more powerful could assert its will on the less powerful. The idea that contracts represented a means for social superiors or stronger parties to work their will on weaker parties continued into the

7. George Sansom, *A History of Japan, 1615–1867*, 101 (Stanford University Press, 1966); James L. McClain, *A Modern History of Japan* 100 (W. W. Norton & Company, 2002); John O. Haley, *Authority Without Power: Law and the Japanese Paradox* 51 et seq. (Oxford University Press 1991) Magistrates and Mura.

8. For a comparison of Western and Japanese feudalism see John O. Haley, *Authority without Power: Law and the Japanese Paradox* 37–38 (Oxford University Press 1991).

Meiji era.[9] This is not a good foundation on which to build a binding contract law theory.

§12.03 WHAT YOU SEE MAY NOT BE WHAT YOU GET

With the legal reforms of the Meiji Restoration, Japan adopted a Civil Code that followed European contract theory. As a general rule Japan follows the concept of freedom of contract.[10] Parties who lack capacity, such as minors and incompetents,[11] cannot contract unless special conditions set forth in the Code, such as obtaining the consent of a legal representative, are met. Freedom to contract is established by the Code's declaration that so long as they do not violate laws that protect the public interest, parties are free to contract in derogation of statute law.[12] However, as Japanese law recognizes two types of laws and ordinances—those that are mandatory, where a contract cannot contradict the mandatory law, and those that are optional, where a contract can override the optional legal provision—it is necessary to make the optional/mandatory conclusion before you can determine if the contract overrides the law or ordinance. Frequently mandatory provisions protect the weaker party in a contractual relationship, such as a consumer in a consumer contract. Moreover, as all contracts are subject to the good faith and abuse of rights doctrines set out in the Civil Code, all contract provisions as well as negotiations are subjected to these provisions.

Under the Code a contract is formed by the expressed will of the contracting parties through the mechanism of an offer and acceptance. The common law concept of consideration is not a part of Japanese law. Unlike United States law, an offer that has no time stated for its durability cannot be withdrawn at any time but remains open for a reasonable period of time.[13] An offer may specify a period for acceptance. In such case the offer remains open for that period and cannot be withdrawn during that period. A contract is formed when the acceptance is sent—although if a period for acceptance is included in the offer then the contract is formed when the acceptance is received prior to such date, thereby shifting the burden of establishing timely receipt onto the accepting party—or, in the case of electronic consumer contracts, when the electronic acceptance (such as email, fax, etc.) is received.[14] The acceptance of an offer with conditions is considered as a rejection and the making of a counteroffer.[15] Third

9. See Eiichi Hoshino, *The Contemporary Contract*, 5 L. Japan 1 (John O. Haley trans.) (1972–paper written in 1966) applying this theory to the state of contracts in Japan in the 1960s).
10. The Supreme Court has even relied on the freedom of contract concept to reject a suit wherein an applicant for a position lied on his application form and later was fired during the probationary period as a consequence. *Mitsubishi Jushi K.K. v. Takano*, 27 Minshu 1536 Case No. 1968 (O) No. 932, http://www.courts.go.jp/english/judgments/text/1973.12.12-1968-O-No.932.html (G.B. Jan. 12, 1973).
11. Civil Code Articles 4–20.
12. Civil Code Article 91.
13. Civil Code Article 524.
14. Civil Code Article 526. Article 4, Act on Special Provisions of the Civil Code Concerning Electronic Consumer Contracts, Act No. 95 of 2001, as amended.
15. Civil Code Article 528.

party beneficiary contracts are permissible and enforceable by the beneficiary.[16] Beginning in 2007 certain contracts entered into by the government of Japan must take into account environmental factors such as green house gasses.[17]

Since contracts are based on joint meeting of common wills, fundamental mistake as well as fraud can void a contract. Innocent third parties may however have rights that can be enforced even if the contract is considered void between the contracting parties.[18] And, although a contract may be void as between the contracting parties, where one of said parties acted wrongfully and received the benefit of the contract the doctrine of "unjust enrichment" may require that party to pay damages as if the contract had been violated.

Japanese law permits the parties to a contract to choose the law that will govern the contract and choice of law provisions (Chapter 15) are usually included in international contract.[19] Parties may choose that foreign law that will govern their contract. Where a governing law is not chosen the law of the place with the most significant relationship controls, although there are special rules for consumer and labor contracts.[20] In a labor agreement it is deemed that the place where the labor is performed has the most significant relationship and in a real estate transaction it is likely that the law of the place of the location of the reality will govern. Selection of the governing law may have significant consequences. On July 1, 2008 Japan signed the United Nations Convention on Contracts for the International Sale of Goods effective as of August 1, 2009.[21] Prior to accession, there were several non-Japanese court and arbitration decisions applying the Convention when the State whose law was chosen had signed the Convention.[22]

Parties may also agree to arbitration in place of litigation to resolve disputes.[23] This is particularly significant as both Japan and the United States are parties to the New York Convention of 1958 and that the Convention is construed in Japan as having the effect of domestic law.[24] Moreover, the Arbitration Act of 2003[25] contains

16. Civil Code Articles 537, 538.
17. *Environmental-Conscious Contract Law* Enacted; http://www.japanfs.org/en/pages/026784.html.
18. Civil Code Article 96 (3).
19. Act Concerning the General Rules of Application of Laws, Law No. 10 of 1898 as amended 21 June 2006, Article 9. For an English translation see, Kent Anderson & Yasuhiro Okuda, *A Translation of Japan's Private International Law: Act Concerning the General Rules of Application of Laws*, 8 Asian-P. L.& Policy J. (Fall 2006). See, Chapter 15 herein.
20. Law No. 10 of 1898 Amended June 21, 2006 Articles 7, 8, 11, 12. See, Kent Anderson & Yasuhiro Okuda, *Translation of Japan's Private International Law: Act on the General Rules of Application of Laws*, 8 Asian-P. L.& Policy J. 138 (2006).
21. http://www.mofa.go.jp/announce/announce/2008/7/1181058_1030.html.
22. Hiroo Sono, *Contract Law Harmonization And Non-Contracting States: The Case of the CISG*, Modern Law for Global Commerce, Congress to celebrate the fortieth annual session of UNCITRAL, www.uncitral.org/pdf/english/congress/Sono_hiroo.pdf. Vienna (July 9–12, 2007).
23. *Ringling Brothers Arbitration decision*, Case No. 1994 (0) No. 1848, http://www.courts.go.jp/english/judgments/text/1997.09.04-1994-O-No.1848.html (P.B. Sept. 4, 1977).
24. *Arbitration Agreement Enforced Case*, Case No. 3851 (wa) of 1998, Yokohama District Court, Aug. 25, 1999 (enforcing an arbitration award between a Japanese and Chinese company).
25. Act No. 138 of 2003 effective Mar. 1, 2004.

provisions consistent with the Convention. Japanese courts enforce arbitral awards under the Convention. As a general rule, parties may also agree to the litigation forum for resolution of disputes.[26] A 2011 change in the Civil Procedure Code specifically allows the parties to a contract to decide in writing the forum for resolution of any dispute concerning performance of the contract. Where no forum selection has been made but the parties have determined in the contract whose law is to govern the contract and that law provides for the appropriate forum, the court will apply the forum selected by the law chosen.[27]

Although parties are free to make their own contracts, standard form contracts are a regular part of Japanese contracting practices. Japan recognizes that situations exist where the bargaining power of the parties is not equal and many special laws provide relief to the weaker party in such situations. Illustrations are residential leases and consumer contracts. Some contracts may require administrative agency approval or parties may seek "administrative guidance" as to the propriety of contract terms.[28]

Contract assumes mutual obligations. Each side has some obligation to perform. The Civil Code has a separate Book on Obligations and the rules therein apply when a party to a contract fails to perform his obligation. The rules are quite specific in many respects. Articles 412–426 deal with defaults. Article 416 allows for ordinary damages for failure to perform a contractual obligation. If unusual circumstances were either foreseen by the parties or should have been foreseen, a damage claim including loss based on those unusual circumstances is permitted. Such damages are, however, difficult to prove.[29]

The Civil Code contains nine articles dealing with the subject of rescission of a contract.[30] When rescission is exercised, interest must be paid on any money to be refunded.[31] The Civil Code is replete with provisions that disclose the binding effect of contracts under Japanese law. Yet there is dispute as to how binding a contract really is in Japan.

Although writing is not required to bind most contracts in Japan, there is a popular perception that writing, or some down payment, is required before an agreeing party is obligated to perform.[32] Indeed, the statutory requirement of writing is rare. [The 2008 Labor Contract Law does not require a labor contract to be in writing but recommends such writing.] It may appear in cases such as the purchase and sale of

26. See *Forum Selection case*, Case No. 1970 (0) No. 297, http://www.courts.go.jp/english/judgments/text/1975.11.28-1970-O-No.297.html (P.B. Nov. 28, 1975). See also, *Kawasaki* 561 U.S. ___ (2010).
27. A question arises as to whether the forum chosen by a law that is selected under Japanese principles of conflict of laws should be used where the parties have not selected a forum.
28. See Higashi Tanikawa, *Business Transactions Law in Hideo Tanaka* (assisted by Malcolm D.H. Smith), *The Japanese Legal System* 132 (University of Tokyo Press 1976).
29. The new Code of Civil Procedure contains a provision designed to make such damages easier to assess, but it is questionable whether the new Code will result in liberalization of the rule. See Chapter 14.
30. Civil Code Articles 540–548.
31. Civil Code Article 545 (2).
32. Takeyoshi Kawashima, *The Legal Consciousness of Contract in Japan*, 7 L. Japan 1 (1974). Civil Code Article 446(2) requires that guarantee contracts must be in writing.

agricultural land, where writing is required because approval of administrative authority is called for, but Japan (which does not have a jury system) has no need for a "Statute Against Frauds" and thus does not have the written requirement of many American states. Writings may be required because of the substantive law provisions of special statutes. And, writing may be required because as a practical matter it may not be possible to prove the existence of a contract, should a dispute arise, without a written contract. Of course, if the parties have agreed that no contract exists until a writing is agreed to between them, then a written contract is required—although the duty of good faith may make a party who withdraws from negotiations without good cause before a writing is signed liable for the expense damages suffered by the other side in the reasonable belief that negotiations had reached such a stage that a written agreement would be entered into.

In addition, the giving of a deposit or other consideration is not required for a contract. All that is required is the offer and consent meeting of the minds. But the fact remains that while the Civil Code may not require writing, writing may in fact be required. If it is the custom of the industry to put a contract in writing then an oral agreement will likely not be recognized. Where the custom is to deal on an oral basis then an oral agreement will be recognized. Where the custom is to give a deposit to bind a contract, a deposit may be required.[33] Where a commercial relationship between merchants who have regularly dealt with each other is involved, an offer to contract in connection with that business may be accepted by silence.[34]

The "good faith" obligations of parties to a contract come into play even before the contract is entered into. Good faith applies at the negotiation stage so that each party owes a duty of care to act in such a way as to not cause damage to the other party. Thus, if a party knows that it will be impossible for the contract to be performed (such as a contract for a sale of a property that no longer exists—e.g., a ship that has sunk) but nonetheless proceeds as if the contract can be carried out, such party may be liable for expenses incurred by the other party acting in good faith and in the reasonable belief the property can be delivered and the contract performed. Similarly, where the parties have completed most steps in the contract negotiation and one party in bad faith determines to end negotiations, it may be responsible for the costs incurred by the other party in reasonable reliance on the belief that a contract would be consummated. In 2011 the Supreme Court held that when a credit cooperative solicited an investment from parties without telling them of the precarious state of the cooperative's finances and the cooperative later went bankrupt, the investors had a tort cause of action based

---

33. Compare the *Aji-no-moto soybean case* where the court found as a fact that the custom was not to put large soybean contracts in writing and applied that rule to an oral contract between Japanese businesses engaged in an international transaction, with *Suehiro Shoji case* where the court found that it was customary to put large real estate contracts in writing and bind them with a deposit. This custom had to be given weight and in doing so the court held that absent the writing and deposit there was no contract. See Veronica L. Taylor, *Continuing Transactions and persistent Myths: Contracts in Contemporary Japan*, 19 Melbourne U. L. Rev. 352, 368–369 (1993).
34. Commercial Code Article 509.

on the breach of good faith in negotiations.[35] So too a party with superior knowledge, such as professionals (lawyer, doctor, etc.) or specialists (stock brokers, banks, etc.) has an obligation to provide necessary explanations to the other contracting party so as not to take advantage of such superior knowledge to the detriment of the "weaker" party.

Custom plays a special role in Japanese law, especially commercial law and that includes law that relates to commercial and continuing relationship contracts.[36] In the hierarchy of laws in Japan, the most specific law applies first and when there is no provision in that law the next most specific is looked to. In the commercial setting, the hierarchy is somewhat modified in that the Commercial Code is very specific in requiring that when a commercial matter is involved and there is no provision in the Commercial Code, before going to the Civil Code to find the applicable law commercial customary law is to be used.[37] Moreover the Civil Code itself provides that where a custom exists that is contrary to provisions of law that are not designed to protect the public interest the custom has precedence over the statute law.[38] Custom is not only at work in determining whether a contract exists and what the parties may agree to, but custom is also relevant to the interpretation of the contract. This is especially true where the contracting parties have had prior business relationships or where they belong to a common business association or where there are other common aspects to their business so that a customary interpretation is generally known. Unless the parties to a commercial contract specifically provide that a mutually understood customary practice will not be the rule for their contract the custom will apply.

The giving of a deposit, while it may satisfy the general perception that a contract exists, may actually lessen the obligations of buyer and seller. Article 557, dealing with sales contracts allows parties to a sale where a deposit has been given to repudiate the contract upon forfeiture of the deposit (if the buyer rescinds) or return of the deposit plus an equal sum (if the seller repudiates).[39]

Japanese law recognizes the rights of parties to set off one obligation against another and the two obligations need not have any relation to each other, other than the parties to the obligations.[40] However, a party may not assert a tort claim and then use that assertion to set off the claim against a debt owed.[41] Nor may a creditor acquire a claim and use that claim as a set off to funds in its possession when it acquired the claim after the funds in its possession had become the subject of a judicial attachment. A creditor (such as a bank) that has a debtor's funds in its possession prior to a judicial

35. *Good Faith Required in Negotiations Case*, Case No. 2008 (Ju) No. 1940, Minshu Vol. 65, No. 3, (Sup. Ct., PB Apr. 22, 2011) http://www.courts.go.jp/english/judgments/text/2011.04.22-2008.-Ju-.No..1940.html.
36. Takao Tanase, *Global Markets and the Evolution of Law in China and Japan*, 27 Michigan J. Intl. L. 873, 888 (2006).
37. Commercial Code Article 1.
38. Civil Code Article 92.
39. If a party has commenced performance under the contract repudiation by forfeiture or double payment is not effective. Civil Code Article 557.
40. Civil Code Article 505.
41. Civil Code Article 509.

attachment may set off a debt which it held prior to the attachment, even if the set off occurs after a judicial attachment has been ordered.[42]

In Japan signatures are typically not used. Rather, "*inkan* stamps" registered in a public office are utilized in place of written signatures. This can lead to "forgery" type situations that are not encountered in the United States. In the United States if a bank pays out money on deposit to a party that forges the depositor's signature the bank is responsible, even if it used good care in analyzing the signature. It is a case of the bank not abiding by its contractual obligation to pay the depositor's money to the depositor or to those who the depositor (by his signature) has authorized payment. But in Japan the bank is authorized to pay out based on the presentation of the bank pass book and the *inkan* stamp of the depositor. Assuming a third party has come into possession of both the book and the stamp, that third party can present both to the bank and make a withdrawal. The bank is not responsible for having paid the wrong party as long as the bank has not engaged in negligence. Negligence would arise if the bank had failed to advise its depositor (when the account was opened) that monies could be withdrawn upon presentation of the passbook and the *inkan* stamped withdrawal form. Depositors are typically advised to keep their bankbook and *inkan* in separate places.

Guaranty contracts in Japan differ from such contracts in the United States. While in both countries the party holding the guaranty can proceed against the guarantor when the prime debtor has failed to make payment, in Japan the guarantor can refuse to pay when the debtor has the resources to make payment and execution against such resources is relatively easy. In other words the guarantor can force the debtor to proceed against the prime debtor to recover before proceeding against the guarantor. As a consequence guaranty obligations are not primary obligations but only secondary obligations that can be proceeded against only after the primary obligor is unable to pay. These special attributes may be attributable to the fact that guaranty obligations may sometimes come into being because of the activities of organized crime organizations. To further protect guarantors, guaranty contracts must be in writing. Guarantees of revolving credits are only valid for a limited period of time and must state the maximum amount of the sum guaranteed.[43]

If the parties to an agreement come from the same group or are members of the same industrial or institutional "family" then an agreement that would not be seen as binding as between strangers may be viewed as binding but not so much as a matter of law as of conscience. Such a view of group association and affiliation is hard to separate from the feudal notions of obligations running between parties and the need to maintain harmony by performing according to your agreement (whether legally obligated to or not). Yet there is an anomaly to requiring a deposit to bind a contract when in fact the giving of a deposit confirms that the parties may disown the contractual obligation, as long as the disowning party is willing to pay for default.

---

42. *Set off permitted after rehabilitation commenced,* Case No. 2010 (Ju) No. 16, Minshu Vol. 65, No. 9, http://www.courts.go.jp/english/judgments/text/2011.12.15-2010.-Ju-.No..16.html (P.B., Dec. 15, 2011).
43. Civil Code Articles 446 and 465-2 through 465-5 dealing with guarantee of revolving loans.

Until relatively recently it was said that the general idea that contracts are binding is not held in high regard in Japan regardless of what the Civil Code may provide.[44] The view that contracts were relatively unimportant and need not be followed was based on several premises e.g., contracts were not consistent with the Japanese character, they were inconsistent with the social relationships between Japanese, they were unnecessary and reflected a lack of trust between the parties, they represented domination by one party over another and perpetuated feudal dominance in certain arenas; they were inconsistent with the Japanese value of indirectness and harmony, etc. But, it may be that the view had less cultural justification than institutional justification. And, while the nature of contracts in Japan is changing and the binding nature of contracts is becoming more evident, to the extent that some of the institutional basis remain the binding effect of contracts may still be in some doubt.

Of course, it may be that contracts in Japan are just as binding as contracts in the United States but (1) contracts are designed to take account of changing circumstances and thus they will be flexible to deal with changed circumstances, (2) contracts dealing with continuing relationships may have special "good faith" obligations attached even when unstated, (3) the law favors consumers in consumer contracts, and (4) the means of enforcement are different.

[A] Contracts Take Account of Changing Circumstances

The good faith obligation of parties to a contract (and the provisions of Civil Code Articles 1, 90 and 91) can have much broader meaning than an American lawyer would think looking at American notions of good faith and freedom to contract. For example, in exclusive distributorship agreements a clause giving the principal authority to terminate without cause may be in violation of good faith and unenforceable. Even where an agent or a distributor has violated the agreement, termination is not permitted unless the violation is considered material, and this is true even if the agreement allows for such termination. On the other hand a non-exclusive distributorship agreement can be terminated without cause but reasonable notice must be given, whether or not the contract so provides.[45] Thus, substantive contract law makes Japanese contracts more flexible than American contracts.[46]

The requirements of Civil Code Article 1 requiring that the exercise of rights conform to principles of good faith and fairness and prohibiting an abuse of rights are given broad effect by Japanese courts and are part of every Japanese contract.[47] These

44. Eiichi Hoshino, *The Contemporary Contract*, 5 Law in Japan 1, 44 (translated by John O. Haley) (1972–paper written in 1966).
45. Takeshi Kikuchi, *Agency And Distributorship Agreements In Japan*, sec. 2.10 Termination (found in 3 International Agency).
46. U.S. law contains statutory provisions (some at the State level and some at the National level) that protect distributors and franchisees in certain fields and give rise to a cause of action when the statutes terms are not followed.. *Mac's Shell Service, Inc. v. Shell Oil Products Co.*, 559 U.S. ___ (2010).
47. Note that the Japanese Constitution also prohibits an abuse of the rights granted therein. See Chapter 3.

requirements give rise to the Japanese doctrine of changed circumstances as providing relief from failure to perform a contract as written. Changed circumstances must be distinguished from the Civil Code defense of impossibility of performance discussed below. In general a change of circumstance that occurred after the contract was entered into and that was not foreseen and is not a product of either fault or negligence by the party seeking relief may provide relief if requiring performance is so onerous (but not impossible) that it constitutes an abuse of right.

A major drafting difference between United States and Japanese contracts relates to matters not covered in the contract or issues that can arise in the future. American contracts tend to follow the lead of the Parole Evidence Rule and provide that the contract is the entire agreement, leaving the parties to negotiate a new contract to deal with a changed circumstance or leave the agreement as it is and possibly debate the issue before a court. A typical "entire agreement clause" would provide that "this agreement sets forth the entire agreement and understanding of the parties; no modifications, supplements or amendments shall be effective for any purpose unless in writing signed by all parties". The purpose of such a clause is to bind the parties to the terms of the written agreement and not allow for changes unless the change is itself a new contractual undertaking. The contract is fixed at the time it is made and its terms are the terms that are contained in the document and none others.

Japanese contracts are not bound by a parole evidence concept. Thus, documents and agreements outside the contract such as those entered into at the time of contracting or during negotiations can be used to both determine what the contract means and to prove the existence of a contract. Similarly, conduct undertaken after the entry into force of the contract may be used to determine the intent of the parties and the obligations undertaken.

Also, a Japanese contract would likely contain a "mutual cooperation and resolution" clause. This is a contractual obligation for the parties to meet and attempt to find a good faith solution to problems or to changed circumstances. Such a clause would typically require the parties to behave in a cooperative manner and to act in mutual cooperation, and to make efforts to promote their mutual benefit by promoting the relationship between them. It would require that if disputes or misunderstandings arise the parties should consult in a cooperative manner and in good faith to resolve such disagreements or misunderstandings. These Japanese style clauses represent the intent to continue an ongoing relationship in good faith rather than a take it or leave approach that relies on rights negotiated at an earlier time in different circumstances. These clauses do not literally affect the binding nature of the contract but they do affect the definiteness of the contract—Japanese contracts are thus less definite and more flexible. And the clauses have real meaning and real effect. The good faith obligation to seek a negotiated settlement means that the parties must attempt, in good faith, to resolve the issue fairly. Only after such efforts have failed can it be said that there exists an issue that might go to court.[48]

48. Tsuyoshi Kinoshita, *Legal System and Legal culture in Japanese Law*, 44 Comp. L. Rev. 25, 162 (2010).

The significance of changed circumstances is illustrated by the measure of damages allowed in a Japanese contract case. Utilizing the *Hadley v. Baxendale*[49] rule under which damages which are foreseeable may be taken into account in an award, the Japanese twist on *Baxendale* is to apply the question of foreseeable not necessarily at the time the contract was entered into (the Hadley/British rule) but rather to sometimes apply foreseeability as of the time of the breach.[50] While at first the shift in time of foreseeable may seem small, upon examination it is seen that it is a fundamental shift away from a basic contract principle, namely that the parties through their agreement define the terms of their relationship. When foreseeable moves from the time of the agreement to the time of the breach, what has happened is that the party's agreement has been modified by the damages rule. Risk is no longer allocated based on the facts known or knowable at the time of contracting but now risk is allocated on an unknowable set of facts that are not and cannot be taken into account in the contract.

Japanese law also recognizes that impossibility of performance is a defense to a claim for damages for failure to perform—when the failure is not the responsibility of the defaulting party.[51] One cannot rely on its own caused impossibility to acquire a defense. The definition of impossibility follows the general nature of much of Japanese law in that it is to be determined by the common sense of the community—in this case the commercial common sense since this is a commercial transaction. This standard leaves the definition somewhat "fuzzy" and gives the courts latitude to take into account the realities of the situation. Responsibility is determined without regard to intent—so that the party claiming relief will be denied relief if at fault even if the fault was not intentional but was simply negligent or even neither intentional nor negligent but a result of its action or inaction nonetheless. The party seeking relief bears the burden of showing that it was not responsible for the default. When performance is only partially impossible the question of performance of the part that can be performed is based on an analysis of how important the impossible portion is to the purpose of the contract. If the purpose of the contract cannot be attained even if the part that can be performed is performed then the entirety of the contract is deemed impossible. Japanese law recognizes *force majeure* as a defense to contract non-performance. Impossibility and changed circumstances must be considered together as changed circumstances may make performance impossible and as a party may not be able to establish impossibility but may still be relieved of liability because of changed circumstances. In either event, when the impossibility or changed circumstance is foreseeable at the time of contracting and can be resolved by the contract, the party who seeks relief may be denied relief on the theory that it should have contemplated

foreseeability @ time of breach

---

49. 9 Exch 341 (1854). See Civil Code Article 416.
50. Hisakazu Hirosi, *Some Thoughts on 'Japanese' Contract Law*, www.kclc.or.jp/english/sympo/EUDialogue/hirose.htm. For a discussion of "proportionality" and of "foreseeability" see Y. Nomi, *Proportionality in Tort and Contract Law*, Public Lecture delivered at Utrecht University, 1996. www.j.u-tokyo.ac.jp/~nomi/ENGLISH/proportionality.html also in Modern Trends in Tort Law, Hondius (ed.), (Kluwer Law International 1999).
51. Civil Code 415 (1). The Civil Code is worded in the positive-making a party responsible for its failure to perform unless there is impossibility not the fault of the failing party. By negative implication this makes impossibility a defense. See also Article 536 of the Civil Code dealing with Sales.

the circumstances and provided for them in the contract. Again, the rule is sufficiently flexible for the court to take into account realities in reaching an appropriate determination. Thus the changed circumstance may be foreseeable but the extent of the change not foreseeable and thus there may be basis for utilization of the changed circumstance doctrine.

In the more "modern" post-war era, Japan has become a major exporting country and many of its companies are among the world's leaders in international trade. International business is transacted on a "Western" (one might even say American) contractual model. As this model has been applied to international agreements, Japanese business has come to apply the model at home as well. Japanese international contractual undertakings can be as complicated and "lawyered" as any United States contract. It remains true that some Japanese entities when contracting in Japan continue to use, in many cases, the short form type incomplete lack of full detail Japanese contract. And, Japanese businessmen prefer the old style contract.[52] But Japanese businessmen may not reflect the view of the Japanese lawyer community. Consider that Japanese company law departments are not staffed by licensed lawyers but rather by businessmen (who probably graduated from a *hogakubu* faculty), and it may explain why "internally drafted" contracts are less "Americanized" than contracts written by American lawyers. Still, contracts are becoming more detailed in Japan.

[B] Contracts Dealing with Continuing Relationships May Have Special "Good Faith" Obligations Attached

Typical among the contracts that have judicially defined "good faith" obligations that protect the "weaker" party to a continuing relationship contract are the employment contract, leasehold, and the distributorship agreement.[53] In each of these situations the courts have developed a line of cases that limit the authority of the landlord, the manufacturer and the employer under the good faith obligation of Article 1 of the Civil Code. The new legislative approach to providing consumers with protections is consistent with the approach of "leveling the playing field" between the stronger (manufacturer or retailer) and weaker (consumer) party to a contract.

The efforts of the Judicial Branch to create a legal doctrine favoring the "lower-status class" in its conflict with the "upper classes" evidence the persistence of hierarchical and status elements that characterized Tokugawa Japan in modern Japanese society. Thus, tenants are favored over landlords, employees over employers, franchisees over franchisors and distributors over manufacturers, thus leveling the divide between them. Modern legislation integrates this theme by providing consumers with protection against business.[54]

---

52. Robert C. Christopher, *The Japanese Mind: The Goliath Explained* (Simon and Shuster 1983).
53. For a succinct analysis of Japanese court doctrine in these areas see J. Mark Ramsayer, *Book Review of Japanese contract and Anti-Trust Law: A sociological and Comparative Study* by Willem M. Visser "T" Hooft, 31 J. *Japanese Studies* 421 at 423–424 (2005).
54. Carl F. Goodman, *The Evolving Law of Document Production in Japanese Civil Procedure: Context, Culture, and Community*, 33 Brooklyn J. Intl. L. 125, 178 (2007).

Whether the Japanese lifetime employment system (See Chapter 13) is a product of a political settlement of labor problems arising after the Second World War,[55] or a product of law making by a Japanese judiciary intent on favoring the weaker employees against the stronger employer,[56] or an outgrowth of Weimer Republic Labor Law transplanted in Japan,[57] or a product of a sense of justice present in Japanese society,[58] the reality is that the system is supported by judicial decision making that restricts the employer's right to terminate full time career employees.[59] In a 1975 judgment the Supreme Court was confronted with an employee's dismissal from the union that had a union shop agreement with the employer. If the dismissal from the union was proper so too was the dismissal from employment, but by the same token if it was improper so too was dismissal from employment. The Court set out the standard for proper dismissal—the rationale for dismissal must be proper when viewed objectively and it must meet the commonly accepted view of society.[60] More recently the judiciary has even extended some rights to fixed term and part time employees who have been with the employer for a number of years.[61] Of course, the extension of lifetime employment benefits to career employees is not a one-way street. Lifetime employees have an obligation to sacrifice various aspects of their life for the benefit of the company to which they are tied. And, the use of lifetime employment for core employees by major companies means that there is virtually no market for mid-level management labor in Japan. Accordingly choosing the company to go to at graduation is critical as the ability to move to another company later in life is almost non-existent. In a sense, lifetime employment ties both the employer to its employees and the employees to their employer.

The judicial underpinning of the lifetime employment system is based on the abuse of rights doctrine contained in Civil Code Article 1. Using this doctrine the courts changed the character of what was essentially an employment at will employment agreement between employer and employee into an agreement that the employer could not break if its action was viewed by the courts as an abuse of the employer's right to terminate. To be valid, an employer had to have just cause for termination which in turn required that the termination be both socially acceptable and reasonable under the circumstances. Even when an employer is faced with economic problems that in the United States would lead to downsizing and forced layoffs, Japanese courts might find

55. Ronald J. Gilson & Mark J. Roe, *Lifetime Employment: Labor Peace and the Evolution of Japanese Corporate Governance*, 99 Columbia L. Rev. 508, 516–523 (1999).
56. Daniel Foote, *Judicial Creation of Norms in Japanese Labor Law: Activism in the Service of–Stability?*, 43 UCLA L. Rev. 635 (1996).
57. David Kettler & Charles T. Tackney, *Light from a Dead Sun: The Japanese Lifetime Employment System and Weimar Labor Law*, 19 Comp. Lab. L. & Pol. J. 1 (1997).
58. Takao Tanase, *Global Markets and the Evolution of Law in China and Japan*, 27 Michigan J. Intl. L. 873, 884 (2006).
59. Curtis J. Milhaupt, A *Relational Theory of Japanese Corporate Governance: Contract, Culture, and the Rule of Law*, 37 Harvard Intl. L. J. 3, 44 (1996).
60. *Japan Salt* case, Case No. 499 (O) of 1968, 29 Minshu No. 4 at 456, http://www.courts.go.jp/english/judgments/text/1975.4.25-1968.-O-.No..499.html (P.B., Apr. 25, 1975).
61. Takashi Araki, *Labor And Employment Law in Japan* 34–36 (Japan Institute of Labor 2002); see also, Shinya Ouchi, *The Actual Legal Problems on Labor Contract in Japanese Labor Law*, 36 Kobe U. L. Rev. 1, 8 (2002).

such actions unreasonable. Typically the employer must show (a) that it has a business necessity for the termination, (b) that downsizing was a "last resort" and that it took remedial steps in an effort to avoid a downsizing such as reducing management salary and benefits, reduced the size of its incoming employee class, cut back on overtime, etc., (c) that it selected the employees to be terminated through an objectively reasonable methodology and (d) the employer met in advance with the employee union or representative (or if there is none with the employee) to discuss the downsizing and reasons for downsizing.[62] The 1990s, when the Japanese economy was under stress, may have served to moderate some of the judicial rules. Thus, the Tokyo District Court has attempted to modify (not do away with) some of the requirements of the abusive dismissal doctrine so that economically warranted downsizing was subject to the four test analysis described but that the four tests were not hard and fast rules but rather simply factors to be considered in determining whether downsizing met the reasonableness and socially acceptable standard.[63] Should the lifetime employment system be modified as a consequence of other changes in Japanese society then it is likely that the courts will react. It has been suggested that more recently Japanese courts are looking to more classical contract doctrines and less to the abusive dismissal doctrine.[64] This may be true of the Tokyo District Court in some labor situations but it is unlikely that, absent a major change in the closed market for lateral transfers between companies, the rule will be significantly modified. Even where a company has declared bankruptcy it is significantly more difficult for the bankrupt Japanese entity to discharge employees than it is for an American company in bankruptcy.[65]

Japanese labor law applies to employment contracts for labor in Japan and while the basic choice of law rules in Japan permit parties to choose the law to govern their contract relations this rule does not apply to such employment contracts. Rather when the employment is in Japan it is presumed that Japan is the place that has the most significant relationship with the contract and thus Japanese law governs the labor contract. This special status for employment contracts recognizes the special place of employment in the constellation of communities to which Japanese belong. The corporate enterprise has, in many respects, replaced the feudal *Ie* family system as a central community for Japanese employees.[66] Lay off thus has a social as well as an economic impact as such laid off workers are effectively excluded from a pivotal

62. Takashi Araki, *Labor and Employment Law in Japan*, 24–28 (Japan Institute of Labor 2002); ILO Country Summary (Japan) www.ilo.org/public/english/dialogue/ifpdial/info/termination/countries/japan.htm by Angelika Muller (updated Mar. 15, 2007).
63. For a discussion of the four criteria / four factor debate see, Takashi Araki, *The Widening Gap between Standard and Non-Standard Employees and the Role of Labor Law in Japan*, 8 J. L. & Pol. 3, 5–6 (University of Tokyo 2011).
64. Willem M. Visser "T Hooft, *Japanese Contract and Anti-Trust Law: A Sociological And Comparative Study* 187 (2002).
65. Compare the efforts of JAL to reduce employment while in bankruptcy with the efforts of GM. JAL Belatedly Addresses Big Job Cuts, Shoichi Shirahaze and Masataka Morita, Asahi Shimbun, Nov. 17, 2010, http://www.yomiuri.co.jp/dy/business/T101116005661.htm.
66. See, Imamura, *Family Culture* in *The Cambridge Companion to Modern Japanese Culture* 76 et. seq., 80 (Yoshio Sugimoto ed., Cambridge University Press 2009).

community of which they were and of which they see themselves as members. Such exclusion from a significant community is not to be lightly undertaken and hence requires legal protection against arbitrary action by employers. Similarly when an employee reaches mandatory retirement age and must leave his company the break is not simply economic but is social as well. Many Japanese companies have programs for former employees that help to let them see themselves as still part of the corporate family just in a different capacity—i.e., as retiree rather than employee.

The judicial doctrine of abusive dismissal received statutory recognition in 2004 when the Labor Standards Law was amended to include a provision dealing with abusive dismissal.[67] That the judiciary will continue to be the major engine for interpreting abuse of rights in the labor context regardless of the statute is obvious from the fact that the statute itself was a compromise arrived at after labor and management forces could not agree to compromise their respective positions regarding how the statute should be drawn. Both agreed the rule should be embodied in legislation but rather than agree on what the legislation should say they simply codified the existing case law.[68] The Labor Contract Law went into effect in the spring of 2008.[69] It too is likely to have little effect on the judge made law especially as it requires an objectively rational reason for an employer to terminate a core (standard or lifetime) employee—the equivalent of the abusive dismissal rule. If the action taken is deemed by the courts not to comply with the general consensus of society that it was reasonable, the termination will not be permitted. The Labor Contract Law provisions dealing with termination of employment are fundamentally a codification of the pre-existing judicial precedents and the 2004 Labor Standards Law provisions that were themselves dependent on the precedents.[70] Where a fixed term labor contract is involved, the law forbids dismissal prior to the end of the term unless there is a compelling reason for the dismissal—it is likely that this means the employer must show that dismissal cannot be avoided in the circumstances.[71] Moreover, provision in

67. Labour Standards Law Article 18-2. The legislation merely adopts a rule that social norms require a dismissal to be based on objectively reasonable grounds and that a dismissal that fails to meet this standard is abusive and thus invalid. The exact parameters of what is objectively reasonable are not set out in the law, which was designed to codify the existing case law. However, the Tokyo District Court had, prior to the legislation, rendered a series of decisions cutting back on the traditional four point requirements set out in the text above. Thus, the exact parameters of the existing case law are not settled. In any event, the statutory language is sufficiently flexible to allow the courts to continue to make and modify the law concerning abusive dismissal. For a discussion see Ryo Kambayashi, *Review of Kaiko Hosei wo Kangaeru: Hogaku to Keizaigaku no Shiten* (Examining Dismissal Law: From the Perspective of Legal and Economic Studies), (Fumio Ohtake, Shinya Ouchi & Ryuichi Yamakawa eds.), 4 Japan Labor Review 70 (2004).
68. Takashi Araki, *Changing Employment Practices, Corporate Governance, and the Role of Labor Law in Japan*, 28 Comp. Lab. L. & Policy J. 251, 272–273 (2007).
69. Act No. 128 of 2007.
70. See, Ryuichi Yamakawa, *The Enactment of the Labor Contract Act: Its Significance and Future Issues*, 6 Japan Lab. Rev. 4 (2010) and 27 Waseda Bull. Comp. L. 79–85, Developments in 2007, http://www.waseda.jp/hiken/jp/public/bulletin/pdf/27/079-085.pdf, for a general discussion of the Labor Contract Act.
71. The Labor Contract Law deals with work rules, which in many instances deal with matter that in the United States would be part of the contract itself. In this sense, work rules are deemed part of the Labor Contract and while an employer may unilaterally change work rules it may

a fixed term contract that permits dismissal without unavoidable circumstances before the end of the term is invalid. The PTA (Part Time Act) enacted in 2007 provides part time workers with some additional protections.

The PTA does not resolve questions raised by the increase in part time workers. Rather the Act applies to workers who work fewer hours than full time workers (also called regular workers) and provides little in the way of actionable rights, being mostly a law that calls on employers to endeavor to achieve certain goals when dealing with part timers. Part timers are entitled to information about such matters as wages (including whether or not they will be entitled to increases in wages), bonus payments (in Japan the winter bonus is typically quite large when compared to monthly salary and is considered by many employees as a part of their wages) and whether they have retirement benefits and if so what those benefits are, in addition to such matters as are required by the Labor Standards Act (contract term, overtime requirements, hours of work, vacation, etc.). Where part timers or contract workers share certain characteristics with regular (or full time) workers, then part timers should be considered as persons who should be treated as regular workers and as such, treatment different from that accorded regular workers in a wide variety of working conditions (such as wages and benefits) is prohibited—but nonetheless part timers (also called temporary workers and sometimes "freeters") are laid off sooner than life time employees and with less protection from the courts.[72] The shared characteristics are: similar duties and responsibilities, for all intents and purposes there is no time limitation on employment (thus where part timers have had numerous renewals of their part time contract they are in essence no longer contract workers but regular workers) and the potential for change in job duties and responsibility is the same as for regular workers. Unfortunately, the percentage of contract or part timers who can meet these criteria is quite small—estimated at between 4% and 5%.[73] Where part timers fail to meet the above three characteristics the Act called on employers to endeavor to treat such workers as equally as possible with regular workers but was amended in 2012 so that no unreasonable difference in the working conditions between part timers and core

only do so when it has informed the employee of the change and the change is reasonable (this is consistent with the Supreme Court's decision in the *Shuhoku Bus* case (Dec. 25, 1968)—see, Yasuo Suwa, *Relation of Collective Agreement to Rules of Employment*, (4. Special Legal Effect of Work Rules based upon Judge-made Law), http://www.jil.go.jp/jil/bulletin/year/1993/vol32-03/05.htm) and when it has been explained to the union or if there is no union to the employees. Provisions in a labor contract that are less favorable to an employee than the work rules are invalid and the more favorable work rule applies. Reasonableness is based on a balancing test that balances the effect of the work rule on the employee against the business necessity of the change as well as the content of the rule change and other relevant circumstances. A reasonable change meeting the above conditions is binding on all employees, including those who disagree with the change. Where a labor union has agreed to the rule change there is dispute as to how much weight should be given to the union's agreement in determining reasonableness.

72. See, Yuri Kageyama, *Japan Times "Temp" Protests Warp Face of Egalitarian Japan Inc., Fallout from Firing Contract Workers Underlines Dangers of New Culture of Convenience*, Feb. 27, 2009, http://www.japantimes.co.jp/text/nb20090227f1.html.

73. Akemi Nakamura, *Reforms offer little promise for part-timers–Companies expected to balk at proposals for providing equal treatment*, Japan Times, Apr. 15, 2007, http://search.japantimes.co.jp/cgi-bin/nn20070405f1.html.

employees will be allowed. Unreasonable will likely be interpreted by the courts. This is not the same as requiring equal treatment, but rather is a kind of loose fair treatment based on circumstances type of obligation.[74] What is perhaps most significant for such part timers is the requirement that employers design systems that enable them to offer contract workers or part timers full time or regular worker status and in a Bill enacted in August 2012 part time workers were given the option of moving to regular status after five years (the law is effective in 2013 and the five year clock runs from the effective date.[75] The Executive Branch's response was a short time bonus program that provided subsidies to large employers who transferred "freeters" into core or lifetime employee positions.[76]

The post-war real estate market and shortage of rental housing placed the landlord in a far superior position to the tenant. Forced eviction left a tenant in a position of having no place to live. The courts adopted a rule that afforded protection to the tenant by prohibiting the landlord from evicting tenants while at the same time allowing for a reasonable increase in rent payable to the landlord. These rules applied whether or not there was a fixed termination date in the lease.[77] Although these judge made rules have served to protect tenant interests they have had a significant effect on the rental market in Japan and may be, in part, responsible for the fact that most Japanese apartments are quite small by American standards (landlords are unlikely to want to tie up space when they cannot force tenants out and thereby get the full market value of their property) and that there is almost no single family rental market in Japan (even Japanese executives sent abroad by their company for several years are hesitant to rent their homes while away for fear that they will be unable to evict the tenant and move back in once they return).

Distributorship agreements also involve a continuing relationship between unequal parties. Here the distributor is typically at a disadvantage to the manufacturer of the product to be distributed. (Although in international distributorships where a foreign firm is seeking to distribute its product in Japan through a Japanese distributorship network, because of the nature of the Japanese distributorship system the "stronger" party is likely to be the Japanese distributor.) Here too the courts have formulated rules that center on the abuse of rights doctrine and forbid precipitous action by the manufacturer when actions short of termination of the distributorship agreement can be used. This is especially true in situations involving exclusive distributorships where the distributor has expended time, effort and money supporting

74. Professor Araki referred to the original Act as requiring a "balanced treatment" rather than an "equal" treatment and such balanced treatment involves a procedural duty of explanation. Takashi Araki, *The Widening Gap between Standard and Non-Standard Employees and the Role of Labor Law in Japan*, 8 Journal of law and Politics 3,16 (University of Tokyo 2011). It is likely that the new law provides somewhat greater rights to part timers.

75. Kyodo, Japan Times, Aur. 4, 2012, *Diet revises labor contract law*, http://www.japantimes.co.jp/text/nn20120804b4.html.

76. *State to pay firms hiring "freeters"*, The Japan Times Weekly on Line, http://www.japantimes.co.jp/weekly/news/nn2008/nn20081025a2.htm.

77. See Yukio Noguchi, *Land Problems and Policies in Japan; Structural Aspects*, in *Land Issues In Japan: A Policy Failure?* 26 (John O. Haley & Kozo Yamamura eds., Society for Japanese Studies 1992); John Owen Haley, *The Spirit of Japanese Law* 140–147 (Univ. of Georgia Press 1998).

the manufacturer's brand. In applying the abuse of rights doctrine to distributorship agreements courts will likely look to the motivation of the terminating manufacturer and whether that motivation is objectively reasonable and secondly whether the terminating manufacturer gave the terminated distributor timely notice of termination so as to enable the distributor to take appropriate action to buffer the effect of the termination.[78]

Whether the issue is employment, tenancy or distributorship the continuing relationship contract creates a tension between the legal principles of freedom of contract and abuse of rights. An analysis of the employment agreement situation shows that courts are requiring the employer to show that there are circumstances that require it to take the strong action of dismissal—even when the company is in financial trouble it must basically show that lay off is unavoidable. This same concept of unavoidability applies in the distributorship arena where a manufacturer terminating an exclusive distributorship agreement that has no fixed period but which has been in existence for a period of time must show that there are circumstances that make such termination unavoidable; even when the agreement has a fixed termination date, when the parties have extended the agreement over time the courts may treat the agreement as if it was of indeterminate duration and require a showing of necessity before termination or refusal to renew will be permitted. Nonetheless, there are some cases where the court will apply the terms of the contract demonstrating the tension between the freedom of contract and abuse of rights doctrines.[79] In effect, the competing doctrines give the courts the opportunity to look at the facts and determine the law to apply depending on the "just" decision that is required in the case (much as the Tokugawa Magistrate would seek to find a "just" decision to the matter before him). Thus, when a distributor has made substantial investments and/or has played a substantial role in advertising or popularizing the manufacturer's brand it is less likely that a court will adopt a freedom of contract approach than is the case where the distributor has been a passive player in the marketing of the brand. So too, by having competing doctrines to rely on the court can carve out a middle course (as some cases have done) of permitting termination but providing an extended notice period before the termination becomes effective or providing compensation to the terminated distributor. [This flexibility also makes it easier for the court to bring about a reasonable settlement between the parties as the court can freely move between the doctrines in pressuring the parties to be "reasonable" in reaching a compromise. It also means that when interpreting contract terms agreed to in advance by the parties the court may conclude that what you see may not be what you get.]

The similarity between the judicial approach to employment relationships and distributorships is said to be based on the continuing relationship doctrine; and indeed both involve continuing relationships. It is also said to rely on the status relationships of power between the parties and the need to level the playing field so that the weaker

78. See *Servo Kinetics Inc. v. Tokyo Precision Instruments Co., Ltd*, No. 05-2741 (6th Cir., Jan. 30, 2007). http://www.ca6.uscourts.gov/opinions.pdf/07a0048p-06.pdf.

79. Willem M. Visser T Hooft, *Japanese Contract And Anti-Trust Law: A Sociological And Comparative Study* 27-38 (Routledgecurzon, 2002).

employee is favored over the stronger employer and the weaker distributor over the stronger manufacturer. There is however another factor that unites these areas—namely the closed markets in which they operate. The lifetime employment system supports a weak (virtually non-existent) market for the sale of services by a mid-level executive (indeed any non-entry level employee seeking a career position) and the peculiarities of the distributorship system similarly severely restricts the ability of the distributor to move from one manufacturer to another. In such a closed market setting the law should and does provide protection to the party who might find itself suddenly thrust into the cold. In such a case it is reasonable for the courts to require that termination of employment or distributorship is unavoidable.

[C] Consumer Contracts

Japan's Consumer Contract Law[80] is specifically designed to protect consumers in contracting with businesses. The law is based on an assumption that business has more and better information than consumers and consequently consumers are at a disadvantage when negotiating with business[81] and recognition of the fact that the business entity typically prepares the contract with no negotiations between the parties. Consumers who have entered into contracts may nonetheless rescind those contracts when the business with whom they have contracted has made misrepresentations (whether intentional or not) or has failed to point out negative aspects of the deal (when noting positive aspects of the deal) or when the business has refused to either leave a consumer's place of residence (or business) or has refused to let the consumer leave the business establishment until the contract was signed.[82] The Law also prohibits certain clauses that limit the liability of a business in a consumer contract and prohibits certain liquidated damages clauses that exceed the typical damages allowed for breach or that provides for interest on unpaid sums at a rate in excess of the rate set forth in the Law.[83] [Japanese contract law generally permits the use of liquidated damages clauses.] The Law specifically includes the good faith and abuse of rights concepts of Article 1 of the Civil Code and provides that clauses in a contract that are one-sided and violate Article 1 are void.[84]

80. Law No. 61 of 2000, amended by Law No. 56 of 2006. For a general discussion of the Consumer Contract law see, Masahiko Takizawa, *Consumer Protection in Japanese Contract Law*, 37 Hitotsubashi J. L. & Pol. 31 (2009).
81. Consumer Contract Law Article 1. The Report of the Consumer Policy Committee, Social Policy Council (January 1999) makes it clear that the purpose of the law is to level the playing field between the superior party (business) and the less informed party (consumer). To do so, the intent of the law is to relieve consumers from decisions made under the influence of high pressure sales tactics, misrepresentations and acts inconsistent with the good faith requirements of law in general. www5.cao.go.jp/99/c/19990128c-keiyaku-e.html, last accessed Sept. 16, 2012.
82. Consumer Contract Law Article 4. The right to rescind expires in five years to act but in many cases expires in six months. Some types of contracts, such as some covered by the Companies Law and the securities laws are exempt from the rescission provisions of the Law.
83. Consumer Contract Law Articles 8 and 9.
84. Consumer Contract Law Article 10.

In addition to granting consumers special rights in the Consumer Contract Law, consumers are given special rights under the Arbitration Law of 2003. A consumer who is not a claimant in an arbitration proceeding is entitled to cancel an arbitration agreement that is part of a consumer contract.[85] In addition, when the business initiates arbitration a notice must be sent to the consumer party advising of the consumer's right to cancel the arbitration agreement. And, failure of the consumer to respond to such notice shall constitute an "opt-out" and cancellation of the arbitration agreement.[86]

Further, the Civil Procedure Code was amended in 2010 to give Japanese courts special jurisdictional authority in cases brought by consumers against a business entity, including a foreign business entity that either sold goods in Japan or sold goods to a Japanese consumer who then brought the goods into Japan. Thus, a Japanese Court can claim jurisdiction over an American merchant who sold a product to a Japanese consumer in the United States which product was brought into Japan by the consumer who then claimed a breach of contract (such as that the product failed to work properly or otherwise caused the consumer damage). All the consumer need prove for jurisdictional purposes is that it is a consumer and a resident of Japan. As long as the consumer was a domiciliary of Japan at the time of the filing of the suit or at the time of the conclusion of the contract the court has jurisdiction, although the law permits the court to reject jurisdiction on fairness grounds.[87]

[D] Means of Enforcement Are Different

Some institutional factors affect the definiteness and/or binding effect of contracts in Japan.

Article 90 of the Civil Code makes void a juristic act that is contrary to public order and good morals. This general good morals provision is in Book 1 of the Civil Code and thus affects all of the types of contracts provided for in later Books of the Code. A broad interpretation of the provision allows courts to set aside contract provisions that are contrary to the general view of the Japanese public as that view is understood by the court. This creates some insecurity and indefiniteness as to contract clauses that might be "stretching the envelope" in areas as yet undermined. Moreover, there exists a general good faith obligation for contracts which requires that there be fair dealings among the parties. What might have been fair at the time the contract was written might not be fair at a future date. Fairness must be considered in context. In such situation the contract will have to be re-written, either by negotiation and

85. For a very different approach under U.S. law see, *Compucredit Corp. v. Greenwood*, 565 U.S. ____ (2012).

86. Arbitration Law, Law No. 138 of 2003, Supplementary Provisions Article 3.

87. Civil Procedure Code Articles 3-4, 2010 Amendment. The court might still dismiss the suit on the basis of Articles 3-9 which allows for dismissal if the court finds special circumstances that inhibit fairness by requiring the defendant to defend the suit in Japan. Although it is likely that a court would dismiss a suit based on purchase of a product in a foreign country that is then brought back to Japan such as by a tourist, a Japanese Court faced with a damages suit based on a contract for air transportation and a subsequent crash of the airplane abroad causing severe injury or death to Japanese nationals might retain such jurisdiction as the impetus for the law was such a situation where the court held it had no jurisdiction.

agreement or failing this by the court before which the issue may be brought, to recreate the fair dealing situation.

As a general matter, American lawyers draft a contract looking at the ultimate decider of issues—the court (or jury). In such situation, drafting is guided by determinations of what a judge or jury is likely to find when a claim for breach is presented. To the business person (either in the United States or Japan) the guiding principal is likely to be different. Business people are more concerned with getting the job done and more concerned with a successful dealing—and hopefully future deals—than with assumptions of failure and resort to court. Thus, it is likely that they will approach the contract with a different frame of mind. The operative assumption is not failure but success. In such a situation it is reasonable to draft an agreement with less emphasis on what happens when we fail.

The institutional difficulties of obtaining effective and timely relief before a Japanese court can affect the binding nature of a contract. After all, the defining nature of contract is that it can and will be enforced by a court either through specific performance or damages. To the extent that there are structural barriers to litigation seeking relief from breach, the contract itself becomes less enforceable. The work of the Law Reform Council thus may have an effect on the binding nature of Japanese contracts. As the Council's work helps to establish the Rule of Law concept throughout Japanese legal communities, it will reinforce the binding nature of contract. But as Japanese law does not contain the elements of the common law doctrines of "equity" such as punishment by way of contempt for a failure to follow a court injunction, parties may breach contractual undertakings—even those that are judicially determined to be binding—when they feel that other imperatives are more compelling than the judicial decision. In such cases the injured party may be left with a damage claim but not the benefit of required performance.[88]

Japanese contractual relations may be enforced by extra-judicial mechanisms. Many Japanese contracts are between separate companies that are tied together in some formal or informal manner. Sister companies in a keiretsu organization immediately come to mind, but there are other more informal relations developed over the years and bound by personal as well as professional friendships. In such situations detailed Americanized contracts do not appear necessary and probably are not. Long-term relationships, especially successful long-term relationships, are less susceptible to detailed contracts than are incidental dealings.

Reputation is an important factor in business relationships (and personal relationships) in Japan. A loss of reputation as a consequence of lack of understanding in a situation that requires a contract modification may be more damaging to the recalcitrant party than foregoing the profit that could be generated by literal interpretation of the contract. This kind of informal sanction for failure to renegotiate when renegotiation is called for can be more important than a specific term requiring change A in the event of condition B occurring. This is especially true when it may not be possible to anticipate all the changed circumstances that might arise.

88. See, e.g., Kyodo News, *No Charges for Prince Hotels in Teacher, Injunction Snub*, Japan Times, July 3, 2010, http://search.japantimes.co.jp/cgi-bin/nn20100703a5.html.

Mediation and conciliation remain powerful tools to resolve disputes, including contract disputes. Since courts may require the parties to mediate as part of the litigation, it may make sense to avoid the litigation cost (and embarrassment) and seek mediation before a situation gets out of hand. Whether the mediator/conciliator is a court or a third person selected by the parties, it is likely that the mediator/conciliator would suggest the parties take reasonable account of the changed circumstances and compromise their differences.

These factors do not make contracts less "binding" but they make contractual terms more susceptible to reinterpretation and make contracts less definite—even contracts with seemingly definite terms.

While Japanese contract law appears on its face to represent the same kind of Rule of Law structure as American law, and while Japanese contracting practices may be coming closer to American practice, the fact remains that what you see may not be what you get. Attitudes towards contracts in the two countries are different and as a consequence the reality of contractual relations is different. Although one may disagree as to the causes of the different Japanese perspective on contract, it is probably true that regardless of the formal law and the provisions of the Civil Code, Japanese (as a rule) do not consider informal oral agreements to be binding unless there is a community or group identification that would require performance; partial written agreements that fail to meet the requirements for a complete detailed contractual obligation are considered binding; compromise and mediation rather than the rule ordered detailed provisions of the Code and the adjudicatory system the Code appears to support, are the preferred methods used to resolve disputes; and even though every contract in a series of agreements is a separate agreement giving rise to separate rights and obligations, Japanese parties will tend to look at the gestalt of the relationship and agreements in determining a fair resolution.[89]

Perhaps the most significant factor at work in understanding Japanese contract law is the utilization by contracting parties, the courts and mediators of the good faith and abuse of rights provisions of the Civil Code. Good faith and prohibition against the abuse of rights doctrine permeates Japanese contract law. Good faith and abuse of rights notions apply to the negotiation as well as the final contract, require explanation to avoid misrepresentation, underlie theories of mitigating damages, prohibit nullification for violations that are not significant (even if the contract otherwise might allow for nullification), require reasonable notice when a contract may provide otherwise, assist in interpretation of terms—sometimes to the point where the interpretation finally arrived at is not what the parties mutually intended when they entered into the contract but instead represents a revision of the contract, operate to place the contractual obligations of parties into the norms expected of the parties by the society

---

89. Hiroshi Wagatsuma & Arthur Rosett, *Cultural Attitudes Towards Contract Law: Japan and the United States Compared*, 2 UCLA Pac. Basin L.J. 76–77 (1983).

and underlie the duty to renegotiate, in good faith, when there are changed circumstances[90] or when the situation calls for renegotiation. Good faith and abuse of rights doctrine require that the law of the contract be understood in the context in which the parties find themselves. In this regard Japanese contract law is binding but the meaning of the contract can change over the term of the contract. Moreover, it allows the parties to the contract to leave unsaid many things that good faith will take care of. This kind of "relativism" or context determining element may be unsettling to American lawyers but it lies at the heart of much Japanese law. As the playing field (the rights and obligations laid out in the contract) may change as circumstances change, one can say what you see is what you get when you look at the contract but how you interpret what you see may be different at different times and under different circumstances.[91]

In the recent meltdown of the sub-prime mortgage market in the United States it has been suggested that lending institutions and/or mortgage brokers bear at least some responsibility for placing mortgages with people who could not reasonably be expected to pay off the escalating mortgage rates. It is also suggested that the complexity of the escalations taken together with the "teaser" quality of the initial rates were partially responsible for the "mortgage mess". Suggestions have been made ranging from statutory moratoriums on foreclosure to private bank consortium voluntarily agreed moratoriums on interest rate increases. Perhaps an abuse of right approach might serve to allocate responsibility more equitably. Should the facts disclose that the initial lender failed to adequately consider the financial condition of the borrower or the value of the home, the abuse of rights concept might result in requiring a scale back of accelerating interest or a moratorium on foreclosure. Should a bundler of mortgage loans (or the loan rating agency) be shown to have failed to adequately disclose the risk involved in purchasing a bundle of "secured loans" then part of that risk could be allocated to the bundler or agency and spread more evenly than by leaving it solely with the investor. In any event, the abuse of right doctrine might "level the playing field" between the sophisticated bundler of loans and less sophisticated investors and/or between more sophisticated bankers/mortgage brokers and less sophisticated home purchasers. With the field leveled, it might be easier to reach settlements that eventually are in the interests of both lenders and purchasers—and the economy as a whole.

90. John O. Haley, *Rethinking Contract Practice and Law in Japan*, 1 J. East Asia & Int'l L. 47, 61–62 (2008) (discussing Japanese contracts and the doctrines of impossibility and /changed circumstances).

91. For an interesting discussion of the effect of social norms on contract law see Kazuaki Sono, *Private Law over the Past Half Century*, 26 L. Japan 59 (2000).

CHAPTER 13
Corporate Matters

§13.01 UNITED STATES

The Spanish Conquistadors colonized South America. They brought with them the economic system of Spain, a system based on class distinction and huge wealth for some with lower social and economic status for the mass. This economic philosophy infected South American society and still has an impact on the economic and social systems of the former Spanish colonies. The fact that South America was "Spanish" while North America was "British" affects the differences between the continents to this day.

North America was settled by Great Britain. Here, the change over from feudal society to a modern economic system based on small farmers owning their own lands and small businesses making their own way in society was more advanced than in Spain. British colonists were not Conquistadors but rather were settlers who sought to become small farmers and in the North American continent they could achieve this desire—especially as they displaced the native population and took over their lands. With American victory in the Revolutionary War many of the former British troops determined to remain in the New World and they too sought status as small farmers or business owners. A decentralized highly competitive capitalistic economic system was developing with little or no direct government involvement.

Successful businesses required low-wage workers and the flood of new immigrants that came to the Northern Colonies and then the Northern States met this need. In the South, slaves were imported to meet the labor requirements of large plantation farms.[1] To some extent the plantation system in the South was similar to the Conquistador system established in South America. But the North was the dominant industrial force in the new United States and a *lassie faire* system was the dominant

1. There was slavery in the North, but it was in the South that slavery became the foundation of both the economic and social systems.

economic system of the North and became the dominant system of the country with the North's victory in the Civil War. In addition to low-wage labor, business required capital for growth and with acceptance of national bank legislation, low interest loans to supplement capital infusions made economic expansion possible.

By the mid nineteenth century the United States was emerging as a world economic power and was beginning to flex its economic (and political) muscle on the international scene. With the incorporation of large parts of what had been Mexico into the now continental country, the muscle was exercised abroad and in international trade. Like the other Western powers, the United States participated in the imperialistic expansion of the West into Asia. It was, after all, Commodore Perry whose "black ships" "opened up" Japan to the West and America assumed a dominant role in the consular jurisdiction agreements with Tokugawa Japan.

The national government in the United States aided industrial development through such mechanisms as the national bank and easy credit, an immigration policy that accommodated new immigrants, and by fostering competition and taking a hands-off attitude to business practices. The Constitutional framework for fostering economic development was the Commerce Clause, which prohibited the various States from enacting legislation that burdened interstate commerce and thereby created one national trading and economic community throughout the United States. From time to time economic crisis caused the national government to enact reforms based on its Commerce Clause powers. By the start of the twentieth century reformers saw the need for the government to act to restrain the power of large economic forces. An anti-monopoly law was passed to limit the power of monopoly at the start of the new century. Social reforms also affected business practices, but the basic economic philosophy was one of allowing industry to develop itself without government involvement in individual companies or industries.

For the most part, business law was and remains a function of state law. The creation of corporations is a matter of state law and issues of corporate governance are, as a general matter, subjects of state law. The laws of the state where the corporation is incorporated typically govern the internal affairs of a corporation, such as the powers of the Board of Directors or the timing of annual meetings, etc. The rules governing the relationship between corporate directors and the shareholders, such as rules concerning the fiduciary obligations of directors and officers, the rules prohibiting directors and officers from taking corporate opportunities away from the corporation and unto themselves, etc. are similarly matter for state law. Of course federal Constitutional law impacts corporations and it has been held that corporations have First Amendment free speech rights.[2] Also, corporations may be parties to litigation and federal law defines the state in which a corporation is resident for purposes of federal court diversity jurisdiction. It has been held that the state of residence is the state where the corporation has its headquarters as long as that is the location that can be viewed as the "nerve center" for the corporation where officers direct, control and coordinate the corporation's activities.[3]

2. *Citizens United v. Federal Election Commission*, 558 U.S. ___ (2010).
3. *Hertz v. Friend*, 559 U.S. ___ (2010).

Major national economic reform legislation was enacted in the Unit following the Great Depression of the 1930s. Again, national government inv was kept to a minimum and the major vehicle of reform was seen as "transpa national securities markets. Companies with publicly traded securities (as well as capital markets) were required to have accounting practices that supposedly told the economic facts that made the operations of the trading of equities or bonds in such markets reliable. Most of the requirements of the Securities and Exchange Act deal with public information and transparency. The national government itself, while it might exercise a watchdog function over reporting obligations, was not an instrument for the development of particular industries or particular companies. Of course, government subsidies did help to build the infrastructure industries such as the railroads and later the airlines and of course, government building of the interstate highway system made the trucking industry a possibility.

The role of the national government is limited by the Constitution's limited power philosophy. The national government has only such powers as are given to it by the Constitution. Thus, in dealing with economic matters, the national government's role is limited by the powers given to the national government by the Commerce Clause and its taxing powers. Over the years the Judicial Branch has interpreted the Commerce Clause to broadly expand the national government's power. Thus, national farm policy is established under the Commerce Clause, the regulation of securities markets are covered by the commerce clause, federal equal employment opportunity legislation has been upheld under a broad interpretation of the Commerce Clause, etc. In recent years the Supreme Court has been nibbling at the edges of the expansive interpretation of the Commerce Clause to limit the further expansion of commerce clause doctrine. Similarly, the court has been expanding Eleventh Amendment state immunity jurisprudence to limit the applicability of the private right of action contained in certain laws. At the close of its 2011 Term the Supreme Court upheld the Health Care Reform Act but five Justices found that it could not be upheld on Commerce Clause grounds.[4]

§13.02 JAPAN

Japan's industrial history is very different. Pre-Meiji Japan was feudal but not of the Conquistador variety. Modern business enterprises had begun to grow pre-Meiji but not to the same extent as in the industrialized West. When Japan was "opened up," Japanese leaders realized that Japan was far behind the West in industrial development and the government established a program to catch up just as it had established a program to Westernize the military, the legal system and other aspects of society. As a consequence Japan has more of a history of government involvement in industrial development, guidance and assistance than the United States. Moreover, efforts to quickly industrialize may have been responsible for the centralization of economic power in tightly linked industrial organizations—zaibatsu—as the government turned

4. *National Federation of Independent Business v. Sebelius*, 567 U.S. ___ (2012).

to these groups and provided them with economic inducements, subsidies and benefits for quickly developing industries looked on with favor by the government.

The creation of a modern economic system was done under the framework of the new "legal" system being established. Thus, the Commercial Code was the vehicle for establishing the types of business organizations that could be created and the internal organization and controls utilized in such organizations. The German Commercial Code provided for three basic types of business entities—partnerships, limited partnerships and joint stock companies. As a consequence the Commercial Code of Japan provided for these three types of business organization. Only later did Germany create a fourth type of entity—the limited liability company and only later (and outside the Commercial Code—the Limited Liability Company Act) was this type of entity recognized in Japanese law.

The zaibatsu organizations were a major aspect of the pre-war Japanese economy. The American Occupation viewed the zaibatsu organizations as a major cause of the War and as a consequence the Occupation set out to dismantle and forbid creation of future zaibatsu. To this end the holding company structure was prohibited.

The dismemberment of the zaibatsu organizations[5] only partially achieved the result sought by the Occupation.[6] In place of the family controlled zaibatsu, Japan's economy created the cross-holding corporate keiretsu organization.[7] Like the zaibatsu, the keiretsu is involved in many business enterprises, is a vertically integrated organization with close ties between member companies. Rather than a holding company structure, the keiretsu (and many companies outside the keiretsu structure) is held together by cross stock ownership between member companies. Typically a keiretsu has a bank or other major financial organization at the top of the organization chart. An insurance company will also be typically involved in the keiretsu. The bank and insurance company own shares in member companies and act as the financial resource of the organization. Member companies own shares in the bank, the insurance company and in each other thus centralizing control of the organization.

Typically a keiretsu will have a trading company in its organization, will be vertically integrated in connection with the supply of raw materials and component parts to its manufacturing members, will control distribution for the member companies, and will purchase each other's products outside the manufacturing arena in order to keep profits within the organization. It is claimed that as each entity in the keiretsu has an interest in the success of each other entity in the group, such an organization results in better quality control, faster inventory turnover and generally a better economic environment for member companies. On the other hand, the existence of

5. For a discussion of the breakup of the Zaibatsu family organizations see John W. Dower, *Embracing Defeat* 529–533 (W. W. Norton & Company 1999).
6. Although family control and holding company control of the zaibatsu were abolished, the initial plan to dismember over 1,000 companies was scaled back and less than 30 were actually dismantled. Among these were the Mitsubishi and Mitsui zaibatsu organizations. Marius B. Jansen, *The Making Of Modern Japan* 686–688 (The Belknap Press of Harvard University Press 2000).
7. For a discussion of the rise of keiretsu organizations in place of the pre-war and war time zeibatsu see James L. McClain, *A Modern History of Japan* 576–578 (W. W. Norton & Company 2002); John W. Dower, *Embracing Defeat* 545 (W. W. Norton & Company 1999).

such a tightly knit organization makes it difficult for competitors of members of the keiretsu to compete for business with other keiretsu members. Thus it is claimed that parts suppliers cannot compete for the manufacturer's business against keiretsu parts suppliers even if the outside competitor has a lower price and/or a superior product. In such case the keiretsu may actually be a hindrance to efficient economic operation by supporting inefficient members at a cost to other members of the group. Keiretsu banks may find it difficult—even impossible to cut off funding to inefficient members, thereby creating bad loan problems for the bank and adversely effecting not simply the economy of the keiretsu organization but the national economy as well.

Although the holding company was abolished under the Occupation, recent amendments to Japanese corporate law have allowed for the creation of holding companies.[8]

The Occupation also attempted to introduce into Japan American concepts of corporate democracy. Thus, although the Civil Code and the Criminal Code were not subjected to major re-writing by the Occupation the Commercial Code provisions dealing with corporate entities (stock companies) was.

§13.03 WHAT YOU SEE MAY NOT BE WHAT YOU GET

[A] Corporate Structure

Business organization in Japan parallels such organization in the United States in many ways. There are partnerships—both general and limited—and there are "corporations" both closed (known as a limited liability company) and open (the stock company).[9] The limited liability company is a form of stock company whose shareholders are small in number and where alienability of shares is limited to other stockholding members unless permission to sell outside the group is given by the other shareholders. As in the United States, the stock company is favored for its limited liability features and in general can be equated both organizationally and in its significance to the national economy with the American corporation. For ease of reference such stock companies are hereinafter referred to by the term "corporation." There are small and "large corporations"[10] and, as large corporations are the main vehicles for international commerce, the discussion herein relates to large corporations.

The extended recession in Japan in the 1990s heralded numerous changes in Japanese corporate law and corporate governance. A spate of amendments to Japanese

8. Antimonopoly and Fair Trade Maintenance Act Law. No. 54 of 1947, *translation available at* http://www.jftc.go.jp/en/legislation_guidelines/ama/amended_ama09/index.html, last accessed Sept. 16, 2012; Andrew H. Thorson & Frank Siegfanz, *The 1997 Deregulation of Japan's Holding Companies*, 8 *Pacific Rim Law & Policy Journal* 261 (1999).
9. Companies Law Article 2 (1); Old Commercial Code Chapter 4.
10. Companies Law Article 2 (6) defines a large corporation as a stock company having a paid in capital of JPY 500 million or more or liabilities of JPY 20 billion or more. In 2002 the law was amended to permit such large corporations to adopt the corporation with committees structure—in 2005 it was further amended to permit such structure for all corporations choosing to adopt.

Corporate law was enacted at the turn of the century. More recently these provisions as well as the older sections of the Commercial Code have been brought together under a new Companies Law.[11] Under the present Companies Law, two corporate structures are permitted[12] the classical Japanese corporation (a company with statutory auditors) wherein the board consists of insiders who have spent their lifetime employment with the company and are the heads of its various divisions and businesses and a "Board of Directors" structure with a "board with committees" system (typically called a "Company with Committees") where "outside" directors serve along with the company insiders and where American style officers run the business under the monitoring of the board and Committees. Both are discussed. Although much heralded, the new structure is still not frequently used.

Both structures are based on a corporate charter called the Articles of Incorporation[13] and are theoretically governed by the shareholder's meeting[14] which elects and has the power to remove the governing body— the Board of Directors.[15] As is true of American corporations, Japanese corporations may, if permitted by the Articles of Incorporation, issue different classes of shares. Shares may be owned in joint names, but in such case (as a general rule) the shareholders must designate one party who has the authority to exercise the rights of stock ownership. Corporations may have either cumulative voting or non-cumulative voting, although in Japan the presumption is in favor of cumulative voting unless the Articles of Incorporation prohibit it.[16] Typically the Articles prohibit cumulative voting.[17] Shareholders may own voting or non-voting shares. Both preferred and common shares may have non-voting status. However, shares with limited voting rights are limited to one-half of the total shares issued. The Articles of Incorporation may permit stock with special voting rights as to various matters. Such stock may provide that resolutions as to such matters must obtain both a majority vote of all shareholders and a majority vote of such class of stock. The issuance of par value stock has been eliminated.[18]

A company can issue unit shares (there may be many shares in the unit) which are limited to a single vote.[19] Shareholders who own less than a full unit lose the right to vote and are not entitled to receive certain corporate communications such as notice of the date of the annual meeting nor a right to attend. While the unit share system leads to administrative convenience for the corporation, it has a negative effect on

11. Law No. 86 of 2005. See, Japanese Law Translation web site, http://www.japaneselawtranslation.go.jp/?re=02.
12. Companies Law Article 2 definitions; compare Companies Law Article 2 (9) and 2 (12).
13. Companies Law Book 2—Stock Corporations, section 2; see also Articles 95–101.
14. Companies Law Articles 295 et seq.
15. Companies Law Article 329, see also Article 347.
16. Companies Law Article 108. Companies Law Article 106. Companies Law Article 342.
17. cfa institute centre for financial market integrity, Independent Non-Executive Directors, p. 36 noting countries in Asai using cumulative voting but not including Japan. http://www.scribd.com/doc/34003705/Independent-Non Executive-Directors#page=44, last accessed Sept. 16, 2012.
18. Companies Law Book 2 Chapter 2 Shares.
19. Companies Law Article 308.

"corporate democracy" and places control of corporate matters in the hands of large shareholders who can afford to own share units and exercise the rights of shareholders.

The committees structure firm has three committees; the audit committee, the appointments committee and a compensation committee. Each committee must have at least three members and a majority of members of each committee must be Outside Directors, although the Chair of the Committee need not be an outside director. In addition the corporation *must* adopt an officer structure with at least one officer having the authority that a Representative Director under the classical system possesses (referred to as a "Representative Executive Officer," but more familiar in American terms as the CEO), namely the ability to bind the company in relations with third parties. [Since 2002 companies operating with the classical system may also adopt an executive structure with officers similar to American companies and many have, including calling the representative director the company CEO—this is referred to as a hybrid model.] Committees have been delegated the functions that correspond to their name and the Companies Law does not contain any provision allowing the board as a whole to reverse or change a decision of the committee—even if the Board also has a majority of Outside Directors. The function of the Board as a whole is to monitor the activities of the managers of the business, including the "CEO."

Treasury stock is permitted but cannot be voted by the corporation.[20] Provisions for treasury stock were liberalized for closed corporations in 2002—prior to the amendments all corporations were required to issue at least 25% of authorized shares. Closed corporations are no longer bound by this requirement and in addition may increase the number of authorized shares to four times their issued and outstanding shares.[21] As a general matter, all members of a class of stock must be treated equally.[22] This equality requirement may be interpreted broadly so that a shareholder engaging in a hostile takeover may be treated differently (although technically fairly) to thwart the takeover. Since 2002 a corporation may issue tracking stock tied to either performance of subsidiaries or to lines of business. A shareholders meeting must be held at least annually, although meetings can be held more frequently.[23] Proxy voting is permitted.[24]

As a general rule, resolutions at a shareholders meeting are determined by majority vote although resolutions that have a fundamental effect on the company may require a supermajority vote.[25] The Companies Law permits the corporation through its Articles of Incorporation to make changes in the general quorum requirements[26] and

20. Companies Law Articles 400, 155 and 308.
21. This change was made to permit closed corporations to have greater flexibility in arranging financing.
22. Companies Law Articles 108 and 109.
23. Companies Law Article 296. Article 296 (2) permits the holding of a special shareholders meeting whenever it is considered necessary.
24. Companies Law Article 310.
25. Companies Law Article 309.
26. All corporations are required to have Articles of Incorporation. Companies Law Articles 26-31. Articles of Incorporation may be amended. The general meeting of shareholders may, as a general rule, amend the Articles. Companies Law Article 466. Certain types of amendment may

voting percentage requirements for various types of activities.[27] A director is liable to the company for neglect of duties, and certain failures that cause damages to the company are presumed to involve neglect.[28] Where a company proposes to forgive a liability due to the company by a director, the general shareholders meeting must approve the action.[29] Directors are appointed for a term not to exceed two years, (in a Company with Committees directors are elected for a one year term) although the Articles of Incorporation may provide a shorter period. As a general rule directors pass resolutions by a majority vote, although the Articles of Incorporation may require supermajorities on special issues. Proxy voting is not permitted at board meetings.

Directors may not compete with their corporation and may not take to themselves corporate opportunities unless the Board is notified in advance and gives its consent—consenting directors may, if there is damage to the company be held responsible for granting consent.[30] Directors have an obligation to advise the shareholders (or where there is a statutory auditor the statutory auditor) concerning exceptional matters that could cause significant losses to the company. Except where the transaction is in the normal course of trade (such as a director of an electronics company buying a product manufactured by the company), directors may not engage in transactions with their company unless the Board of Directors is advised of the transaction and agrees to it.[31] A director who engages in a transaction forbidden by Article 356 and causes a loss to his company is guilty of breach of his "fiduciary" duty to the corporation whether his actions were either intentional or simply negligent.[32] Shareholders owning 3% or more of shares who have reason to believe that certain irregularities have occurred (e.g., violations of laws, or violations of the certificate of incorporation, etc.) may petition the court to appoint an inspector to look into the matter. Board members who agree to a self-dealing transaction may be held personally liable and are treated as if they personally performed the transaction that they have agreed to if the transaction is to the disadvantage of the corporation.

Corporations are juridical persons and thus may perform the functions of a juridical person such as contracting and are subject to rules relating to competency so that it may not perform functions that are *ultra vires* or otherwise outside the scope of the corporate charter. As a general rule, charters are given a broad interpretation so as to permit the corporation to carry out its basic business purposes. The corporate veil may be pierced to place personal liability on controlling shareholders or certain corporate officers when to do so will protect creditors or is necessary to carry out

require special provisions in addition to a determination of the general meeting of shareholders. See e.g., Companies Law Articles 110, 111, 426 (5) regarding limiting liability of directors after the fact. Companies Law Article 309 (1).

27. Companies Law Article 309 (2).
28. Companies Law Article 423.
29. Companies Law Article 424.
30. Companies Law Article 332. Companies Law Article 369. Companies Law Articles 356 and 423.
31. Companies Law Article 357. Companies Law Articles 356 and 365.
32. Companies Law Article 355, 428. Companies Law Article 423. Companies Law Article 358. *Director's Liability Case,* Case No. 1998 (O) No. 920) 54 Minshu 2619. http://www.courts.go.jp/english/judgments/text/2000.10.20-1998.-O-.No.920.html (P.B. Oct. 20, 2000).

legislation *and* the corporate formalities or structure has not been recognized by the controlling shareholder or Director.[33]

Recently corporations were permitted to grant stock options to directors and employees, to officers and employees of subsidiaries as well as the parent company, to professionals (accountants and legal counsel), to financial institutions and a catch all provision allows issuance to any person (if deemed necessary), subject to shareholder approval. "Free floating" warrants to purchase stock at a fixed price can be issued and traded without relationship to other securities. Options can be issued to purchase the full amount of authorized but unissued shares. The option may not be unlimited in time but can have an unstated time period for exercise.

Board members have an obligation to faithfully perform their duties on behalf of the corporation. A company with statutory auditors may also have a Board of Directors that appoints the Representative Director (or directors) who has the authority to represent the company both in judicial proceedings and otherwise and has the duty to manage the business[34] and typically takes a title similar to that of an officer in American corporations (the hybrid model). Where more than one Representative Director is appointed, the board may require that Representative Directors act jointly although if there is no such provision each may separately represent the company.[35] While not providing for officers as such, the Commercial Code did provide that where a director has been given a title that would identify him as a Representative Director, third parties could, in good faith rely on his ability to represent the company. Such titles included President, Vice-President, Senior Managing Director and Managing Director.[36] These provisions were carried over to the new Companies Law.

Corporations that adopt the new Committee structure may appoint American style officers, may act through the committees rather than the entire board and do not need to appoint statutory auditors.[37] This is designed to give the company greater flexibility, to enable it to operate more efficiently and through the requirement that there be Outside Directors with oversight responsibilities provide a check on the activities of the corporate insiders on the board and management.[38]

Statutory auditors are appointed by the general shareholders meeting and are subject to most provisions relating to directors. The statutory auditor, in addition to financial audit responsibilities has a duty to audit the management functions of the company and audit the performance of the duties imposed on directors. Statutory auditors can discharge outside auditors,[39] are required to attend and express opinions at board meetings[40] and are jointly and severally liable to the corporation for neglect of

33. Kraakam, et al, *The Anatomy of Corporate Law: A Comparative and Functional Approach* 94 (Oxford University Press 2004); Corporate Law Tools Project Art. 6.2 p.9 http://198.170.85.29/Corp-law-tools-Japan-Cotty-Vivant-for-Ruggie-28-Sep-2009.pdf, last accessed Sept. 16, 2012.
34. Companies Law Article 356. Companies Law Article 362. Companies Law Article 363.
35. Companies Law Article 349.
36. Old Commercial Code Article 262.
37. Companies Law Articles 326, 327, 328.
38. Companies Law Articles 400 et seq.
39. Companies Law Article 347. Companies Law Article 381 Companies Law Article 340. Old Commercial Code Article 274.
40. Companies Law Article 383.

duty,[41] may not hold another position with the company such as a director or employee and may not hire or discharge company employees. Large corporations that are not using the Company with Committees structure must appoint a Board of Statutory Auditors of at least three members whose term is four years and at least 50% of a Board of Auditors must be "outside auditors."[42]

Shareholders present at the general shareholders meeting may ask questions of directors and auditors provided the subject of the question is relevant to the matters being discussed at the meeting. Unless response would be seriously damaging to the general interests of shareholders or would require investigation, directors and statutory auditors are required to respond and give appropriate explanations of actions questioned.[43] Corporate democracy is based on the theory that the shareholders, through their powers at the shareholders meeting, are in control of the company and that the directors have a fiduciary responsibility to the company thus assuring good governance. The Supreme Court of Japan has held that under Article 254-3 of the Old Commercial Code and Article 644 of the Civil Code, a director has a fiduciary type duty to the corporation.[44] In theory, the Board of Directors as an institution is responsible for company management and the Board as an institution can assert its authority when a single member or group of board members acts outside their duties. The reality is different—what you see is not what you get.

In the United States where shares of large companies are widely traded and thus widely held and where corporate directors and officers tend to have large shareholdings (perhaps as a result of lucrative stock option plans), individual shareholders typically have little to say about corporate management. An entrenched board can control proxy voting and thus maintain control while shareholders have inability to organize sufficiently to take on management. Where large institutions such as pension funds hold a significant number of a company's shares, trustees of the funds may organize to achieve management changes. This can serve as a vehicle for corporate democracy. The staffing of boards with "Independent Directors," i.e., directors who are neither managers nor employees of the corporation but are totally independent of the management structure, to insure corporate democracy nay be compromised as Directors tend to support the managers who appointed them and can probably appoint

41. In the *Daiwa Bank case* the court did not hold all directors liable and did not hold that directors who were liable were jointly and severally liable. Rather it apportioned liability between directors held responsible and absolved other directors. In the final settlement of the case, plaintiffs took a substantial reduction in damages awarded but insisted that all directors pay a portion of the damages. Companies Law Article 335.

42. Companies Law Article 336. For a discussion of the 1993 amendments to the Commercial Code see Ken-ichi Yoshimoto, *1993 Company Law on the Supervisory System and Corporate Governance in Japan*, 41 Osaka U. L. Rev. 23 (1993). Companies Law Articles 381–390 deal with statutory auditors and Boards of Statutory Auditors and their responsibilities and duties.

43. Companies Law Article 314.

44. *The Nomura Securities Compensation of losses case*, Case No. 1996 (O) 270, http://www.courts.go.jp/english/judgments/text/2000.07.07-1996-O-No.270.html (Sup. Ct. P.B. July 7, 2000). Justice Tahara has noted that Directors of a corporation have both a duty of care as a prudent manager and a duty of loyalty. *Directors Duty Case*, Case No. 2006 (A) No. 2057, Keishu Vol. 63, No. 9, http://www.courts.go.jp/english/judgments/text/2009.11.09-2006.-A-.No..2057-163245.html (P.B., Nov. 9, 2009).

successors; director's fees have become significant, directors have been granted stock options similar to those granted to senior officers of the company, giving them the same interests and temptations that may affect the judgment of officers. The Independent Director is seen as a critical corporate democracy, good management, insuring mechanism. For this reason, Independent Directors are supposed to be in charge of audit committees and management remuneration committees. Evidence exists that Independent Directors standing alone are not a sufficient governance mechanism to oversee management accountability.[45]

There are other mechanisms in addition to proxy contests available in United States law that help to keep directors focused on the good management of the corporation, such as takeover and tender offer mechanisms that theoretically cause management to maximize profits to ward off "hostile raiders." Directors and/or officers who have violated their fiduciary duties may be subject to derivative lawsuits brought on a contingent fee basis. Where appropriate, class actions on behalf of investors and against directors and officers may be pursued. Congress has tightened the rules for such actions because of perceived abuses. The Securities and Exchange Commission rules (for publicly traded companies) require periodic filings of reports concerning various matters including financial reports and changes in the business that could affect shareholders significantly. In addition to review of these reports by staff of the Commission, these reports are analyzed by financial analysts and derivative lawsuit lawyers and are available as evidence in derivative or class action cases.

Nonetheless, as events disclose there are serious flaws in the United States system.

In Japan as well, what you see when you look at the corporate democracy management provisions of the law may not be what you get. Here the reasons are different than in the United States and the corporate democracy problems for individual shareholders may be greater than in the United States. Cross-shareholdings have been the common practice in Japan.[46] Moreover, a "lead bank" and an insurance company that holds shares in its customers are also typical lenders to the company. Many shares of a publicly traded company are held by related or "friendly" interests depriving a "hostile raider" of opportunity to obtain enough shares to displace management. The interconnected shareholdings and business relations between the cross-shareholding companies may mean that considerations other than simply the economics of the company at issue are involved in decision making as to corporate management.

---

45. See, *Corporate Governance in Japan: Institutional Change and Organizational Diversity* 42–43 (Aoki, Jackson, Miyajima ed., Oxford University Press 2007)..
46. Antimonopoly Law Article 9-2 limits the shareholdings of large non-financial corporations but does not prohibit all such holdings. Moreover, the section contains several exceptions, including an exception for a business to be undertaken abroad and an exception for companies exempted by Cabinet Order or where permitted by the Fair Trade Commission. Financial companies are generally restricted to a 5% ownership (10% for insurance companies). Antimonopoly Law Article 11. Exceptions are available, such as when stock in excess of 5% has been acquired by the foreclosure of a lien or where the Fair Trade Commission authorized acquisition in advance.

On the other hand, while individual stockholders in a Japanese company may traditionally have had little to say about corporate governance matters, the concentration of stockholdings in the hands of a few investor and creditor banks, insurance companies and related companies, gave these shareholders an important voice in governance matters. Corporate governance can be exercised through these relationships.[47] To the extent that interests of large shareholders parallel those of small shareholders there may be greater democracy aspects to the Japanese corporation.[48] To the extent that interests of shareholder/creditor/business "partner" differ from the interests of individual investor shareholders, the Japanese shareholder is at a distinct disadvantage to the United States shareholder. The corporate executive may be more responsive to large shareholder commentary in Japan than in the United States.[49]

Unlike the United States, Japanese corporations have few Outside Directors. Most publicly traded companies rarely have more than one "Independent Director" and most have no Outside Directors. The board of a company with statutory auditors consists of the senior managers of the company who are responsible for various parts of the company's business. Rather than overseeing the management of the various departments, the board is composed of the managers of the various departments. As a consequence the board has less of an overseeing responsibility.[50]

In addition, not all board members are equal. Representative Directors are obviously more powerful than other directors. Senior board members are more powerful than juniors. A committee of the president, vice-president and managing directors acting as a kind of Executive Committee, (*jomukai*) may make most important decisions and the board as an institution then rubber stamps approval. This makes the board as an institution and board members individually less responsible and less diligent for overseeing activities of the company.

Nor have Statutory Auditors protected the interests of the company as the Code intends. Previously most statutory auditors were former employees and/or managers of the company. Although no longer holding such positions, they had loyalty responsibilities to the senior managers with whom and/or for whom they may have worked while with the company in its management structure. Moreover, although selected by the shareholders meeting auditors were, in reality, appointed by the company president. This significantly affected their "independence." In 2002, the law was amended to provide that outside statutory auditors must never have been employees or directors of the company, although statutory auditors of a subsidiary company may have previously worked for the parent company. At the same time, the term of office of the outside statutory auditor was increased from three years to four years.

---

47. For an interesting discussion of relationship of large creditors to large shareholders in Japanese companies and its effect on corporate governance see Stephen D. Prowse, *The Structure of Corporate Ownership in Japan*, 47 J. Finance 1121 (1992).
48. See Curtis J. Milhaupt, *A Rational Theory of Japanese Corporate Governance: Contract, Culture and the Rule of Law*, 37 Harvard Intl. L. J. 3 (1996).
49. For an interesting discussion of how corporate success or failure affects Japanese executives see J. Mark Ramseyer, *Columbian Cartel Launches Bid for Japanese Firms*, 102 Yale L. J. 2005 (1993).
50. Companies Law Article 363 (2) Companies Law Article 362 (2). *Tasks for the Corporate TSE*, Japan Times (Nov. 2, 2001).

[B] Corporation with Committees

To permit a more "Americanized" style of management the Corporation with Committees model was authorized. It remains to be seen how many companies will adopt the newly permitted system. The number to date is still quite small and the number of companies newly creating such committee system is declining. Most companies operate under the old-statutory auditor model.

As of July 2011 it was estimated that 65% of companies listed on the first section of the Tokyo Stock Exchange (the highest number and ratio of companies with foreign shareholders are the first section TSE companies and the companies with foreign shareholders are the most likely to have either the company with committee model or Outside Directors[51]) still had no independent directors and that the average number of independent directors in companies was less than two per company[52] and that of the Nikkei 300 companies 40% still had no independent directors—although the increase in outside directors of Nikkei companies in the past several years has been impressive. Still the average number of such outside directors at these companies remains low. Of the first section TSE companies that had outside directors, the average number of such directors per corporation was also approximately two but this represented an increase of only 0.1% from the average of 1.9% in 2004—89% of directors in these major companies are inside directors.[53] Of all TSE listed companies in 2011 over 95% still utilize the statutory auditor model and the number of companies with committees slightly declined between 2008 and 2011.[54] The 2011 disclosures concerning concealment of matters at a TSE listed company by its president and alleged complicity by its director's rekindled interest at the government level of reexamination of Japanese corporate governance policies and legal requirements[55] but corporate management beat back such efforts.[56]

It is important to distinguish the American concept of the "independent" director to the Japanese concept of the "outside" director. Outside directors need not be independent—for example, in an organization of related companies the outside directors may be directors of related companies such as suppliers or distributors or

51. Tokyo Stock Exchange Listed Companies, White Paper on Corporate Governance (2011), http://www.tse.or.jp/rules/cg/white-paper/b7gje60000005ob1-att/b7gje6000001m8gl.pdf last accessed Sept. 16, 2012.
52. Kazuaki Nagata, *Corporate Japan: Woeful Lack of Outside Directors*, Japan Times (Jan. 17, 2012), http://www.japantimes.co.jp/text/nn20120117i1.html.
53. Japan Association of Corporate Directors, 2011 Survey on Corporate Governance of Listed Corporations, http://www.jacd.jp/e/reports/pdf/111004_01reports.pdf. last accessed Sept. 16, 2012.
54. Tokyo Stock Exchange Listed Companies, White Paper on Corporate Governance (2011), at p. 15 chart 14, http://www.tse.or.jp/rules/cg/white-paper/b7gje60000005ob1-att/b7gje6000001m8gl.pdf last accessed Sept. 16, 12.
55. Yoshihisa Mizukami, *Govt., DPJ eye steps to watch firms / Scandal at Olympus raises issues of internal, external controls of activities*, Daily Yomiuri (Nov. 27, 2011), http://www.yomiuri.co.jp/dy/national/T111126003386.htm. It is interesting to note that the company involved was one of those that had Outside Directors (3 of the 15 directors) on its Board.
56. *Companies let off hook over outside board directors*, Yomiuri Shimbun (July 19, 2012), http://www.yomiuri.co.jp/dy/national/T120718005347.htm.

sister companies in a related group. The interests of outside directors and inside managers may in fact be identical.

Rising to the level of a board member in the classical structure and in the committee structure is seen as a part of normal progression of valued company employees. In some companies there may be directors who entered the company at the director level after serving a lifetime career as a government bureaucrat ("descent from heaven") who is an outside director. When a regulator has become an outside director as a result of descent from heaven the government regulator is likely to "delegate" some regulatory functions to the company itself since an outside director who was formerly a senior official of the regulator is on the scene and aware of the agency's functions, policies and is an easy conduit for "guidance" by the regulator. (See Chapter 17) This may have been the reason why there was no official guideline to nuclear power companies as to what action to take in the event of a prolonged loss of power at a nuclear plant—the problem that resulted in the Fukushima nuclear disaster of 2011.[57] Moreover this outside director was likely the mentor of the current official in charge of regulating the company and thus can influence the agency. In addition, companies also send their employees to work in Administrative Agencies and this "two-way street" eases guidance from the agency to the company.[58] Consequently: (a) Boards tend to be the product of inbreeding as most board members have never served in any other company leading to parochial thinking about management [Even new outside directors are likely to be lifetime career employees of related or affiliated companies having the same mind set as the inside directors.] This serves to limit the number of outside ideas and new ways of doing things that are permitted into the management structure. This may account for the reliance that some companies place on outside management consultants when dealing with new problems or trying to resolve issues that do not seem to be responsive to traditional ways of doing things. (b) Non-outside board members owe their positions to the senior members of the board for whom they worked when employees and for whom they continue to consider themselves working as board members. The most powerful of these senior board members is the representative director CEO who, while theoretically subject to control by the board, controls the board.[59]

[C] Mandatory Retirement and "Independence" of Board Members

Japanese mandatory retirement policies also affect power relationships and board politics. Most Japanese companies have a mandatory retirement policy for both employees and board members. (See, Chapter 9) Typically employees are required to

57. Kyodo, *Watchdog let utilities justify omitting nuclear plant power supply safety steps*, Japan Times (June 6, 2012), http://www.japantimes.co.jp/text/nn20120606a3.html reporting that the nuclear watchdog agency allowed the electric utilities to write portions of the guidelines omitting consideration of a sustained power loss.

58. Walter Hatch, *Regionalizing the State: Japanese Administrative and Financial Guidance for Asia*, 5 Soc. Sci. Japan J. 197, 181–182 (2002) referring to the two-way street as swopping hostages.

59. Companies Law Articles 362, 363.

retire at an earlier age than board members who are required to retire at an earlier age than managing directors who are required to retire at an earlier age than senior managing directors. For an employee the objective is to become a board member and then managing director and senior managing director thereby obtaining status, other financial benefits and postpones mandatory retirement. The president makes all such decisions.

The president may have great power over the economic future of the retiring board members who may be granted executive positions in a company subsidiary (with a later mandatory retirement age) or granted consulting contracts. The president may even have the power to determine the amount of the severance package given to retiring board members. As severance packages for board members can be quite large, this strengthens the hand of the president in dealing with the board.[60]

There are some matters where the board must act as a board: sale or purchase of significant assets; appointment or discharge of certain "important" employees; significant borrowings[61] by the company; and creation or abolition of branch offices or other important parts of the corporate organization,[62] although amendment permits creation of a special committee to more quickly sell, buy or use significant assets as security for borrowing. Considering the loyalty obligations of junior directors as well as the power of senior directors, this requirement likely has little substantive effect on operations of most corporate boards, except to delay decisions. The law was amended to permit large corporations to create a special committee to deal with significant assets. Such committee, which must contain at least three directors, can be given power to act.

[D] Derivative Lawsuit

Japanese law does provide the mechanism of the derivative lawsuit to assist in supervising the responsibilities and duties of the corporation's board and officers, whether a classical or committee structured corporation. A written request that the company sue a director or auditor must be made by a shareholder who has continuously owned shares for at least six months; the company has 60 days in which to bring such an action, although this time may be shortened if there is a risk of irreparable

60. It is reported that in the financial scandal involving a major company in late 2012 the Board failed to supervise in part because directors approved actions the president wanted since he had authority over their pay and promotions (See, *"Extreme Sectionalism" Blinded Olympus Board*, Asahi Shimbun (Dec. 8, 2012), http://ajw.asahi.com/article/behind_news/social_affairs/AJ201112070049) as well as loyalty concerns (see, *Panel Urges Legal Action in Damning Olympus Report*, Reuters, Asahi Shimbun (Dec 6, 2012), http://ajw.asahi.com/article/behind_news/social_affairs/AJ201112060083.
61. What constitutes an important employee was not defined in the Code. How much debt is required to make the borrowing significant was not defined in the Code.
62. Old Commercial Code Article 260 (2). In The *Definition of Article 260 (2) case*, Case No. 1993 (O) 595, 48 Minshu 1, http://www.courts.go.jp/english/judgments/text/1994.1.20-1993.-O-.No.595.html (P.B. Jan. 20, 1994) the Supreme Court found that although the assets sold constituted only 1.6% of the book value of assets, the market price was unknown and thus sale at market might have a significant effect on assets and the P&L of the company. Thus the transaction was not an ordinary business transaction and might be considered as a disposal of significant assets under Article 260(2).

injury to the company.[63] Failure to bring the action permits the shareholder to sue on behalf of the company.[64] Where the company makes a prima facie case of bad faith filing the court may order the plaintiff to provide security to cover the costs of suit.[65] Unlike the United States, there is no legal requirement that the derivative plaintiff establish that it is an appropriate representative of the company's shareholders.[66] Jurisdiction is in the District Court where the company has its principal office.[67] A successful plaintiff is entitled to court ordered "reasonable" attorney's fees (which may or may not reflect the actual fees charged by counsel). An unsuccessful plaintiff is only responsible for the company's expenses if the court finds the action was brought in bad faith.[68] Until the mid-1990s the derivative action was not an effective vehicle for policing corporate management. The court filing fees for a derivative suit rose as the size of the damages claimed increased. In 1993 the filing fee for a derivative suit was capped at JPY 8,300 [at a rate of USD 1 = JPY 100 this would be a cost of USD 83]. There has been an increase in both the number of amount of damages sought in derivative litigation.[69]

The largest and most significant derivative judgment was rendered in 2000 when the shareholders of Daiwa Bank won a District Court recovery in excess of USD 775 million against certain directors who failed in their duty to properly monitor the affairs of the Bank's New York office.[70] The court applied a negligence standard but it is likely the court was motivated by the fact that the directors were aware there was a violation of American law by the New York office. The case was settled on appeal with damages dramatically reduced to JPY 250 million or approximately USD 2.1 million.[71]

Thereafter the law was amended to permit corporations to limit the recovery in derivative lawsuits where the actions of the directors involved were neither intentional

63. Companies Law Article 847 (1) (5).
64. Companies Law Article 847 (3).
65. Companies Law Article 847 (7) (8).
66. Companies Law Article 847 (7) (8).
67. Companies Law Article 848.
68. Companies Law Article 852.
69. This reform to the Commercial Code is another instance where Japan responded to foreign complaints about its legal system. The costs of derivative lawsuits were a subject of the Japan/U.S. Strategic Initiative talks. In addition to reducing the filing fees for a derivative suit, the amendments in 1993 also gave shareholders greater access to corporate records. Carl F. Goodman, *The Somewhat Less Reluctant Litigant: Japan's Changing View Towards Civil Litigation*, 32 L. & Policy Intl. Bus. 769, 798 (2001).
70. For a discussion of the *Daiwa Bank case* as of 2001 see Carl F. Goodman, *The Somewhat Less Reluctant Litigant: Japan's Changing View Towards Civil Litigation*, 32 Law & Policy in International Business 769, 798 (2001); for a discussion of the Daiwa Bank problem see Mitsuru Misawa, *Daiwa Bank Scandal in New York: Its Causes, Significance. And Lessons in the International Society*, 29 Vanderbilt J. Transnatl. L. 1023 (1996).
71. Bruce E. Aronson, *Reconsidering the importance of law in Japanese Corporate Governance: Evidence from the* Daiwa Bank Shareholder Derivative *case*, 36 Cornell Intl. L. J. 11, 42 (2003). Aronson notes various factors that led to such a sharp reduction in the damages among which was concern that the Daiwa Bank would restructure and create a holding company with the Bank as a subsidiary and the Bank's former shareholders as shareholders in the parent holding company. Under this structure the plaintiffs would no longer be shareholders in the bank and thus might lose their status as shareholders eligible to bring a derivative suit. (see note 130 on 42) The New Companies Law specifically resolves this issue by providing that in such situation the shareholder may continue as a plaintiff in the derivative suit. Companies Law Article 851.

misconduct nor gross errors of judgment. Directors' liability may be limited to six-year compensation for Representative Directors, four-year compensation for other directors who are not outside directors and two-year compensation for outside directors.[72] Outside directors may enter into agreements limiting their liability in derivative litigation to a specified amount.[73] 73% of outside directors have such limited liability agreements.[74] The limitation of liability provisions must be incorporated in the certificate of incorporation or approved by a general meeting of shareholders and in a corporation with committees, the proposal to limit liability must be approved by each member of the audit committee; and in a classical system company each statutory auditor must approve it.[75] It is likely that this has limited the potential prophylactic effect of derivative litigation. Another fallout of the *Daiwa* case was the dramatic increase in the number of companies purchasing D&O insurance for their directors.

The Daiwa case may have had a significant effect on corporate governance in Japan. The lower court had held that directors were liable because they had failed to have in place a system for assuring that employees were not acting illegally. After the Daiwa case many companies adopted internal control and compliance systems to try to protect against illegal activities and today corporations must have in place internal control systems and compliance programs to assure that Directors, Officers, and employees do not engage in illegal acts or acts that are outside the corporate charter.[76] J-SOX (the Japanese version of the American Sarbanes Oxley law) requires the establishment of internal control systems, (including information retention systems regarding information about how and whether directors are properly carrying out their duties) compliance programs and audits of such programs by outside corporate auditors. Companies must have in place risk management systems.[77] Where a company has engaged in price fixing or other cartel activities it can be argued that risk management and internal control and compliance systems should have disclosed such information and such failure may give rise to shareholder derivative litigation alleging violation of J-SOX. Similarly, failure of directors to quickly apply for the Japan FTC's leniency program can result in substantially higher fines if the FTC takes action against the cartel scheme. Such failure to try to be the first applicant (getting the greatest discount on damages) may also give rise to derivative litigation.

Although derivative lawsuits are easier to bring such suits are not easy to win. Japanese directors are entitled to defend on theories similar to the business judgment

72. Companies Law Article 425.
73. Companies Law Article 427. For a discussion of the relationship of the amendment with the 'desire' to get people to serve as outside directors see Motomi Hashimoto, Commercial Code Revisions: Promoting the Evolution of Japanese Companies, Nomura Research Institute, NRI Papers, No. 48, May 1, 2002.
74. TSE-Listed Companies, White Paper on Corporate Governance 2011, p. 28.
75. Companies Law Article 425 (3) (2). Companies Law Article 425 (3) (1).
76. *Eleven Misunderstandings about the Internal Control Report System*, Financial Services Agency publication, http://www.fsa.go.jp/en/news/2008/20080408/01.pdf, last accessed Sept. 16, 2012.
77. For a discussion see, Yoshiaki Miyasako, *Compliance Programs in Internal Control Systems and the Response of Japan, the United States and Europe*, 7 J. L. & Pol. 67 (University of Tokyo) (2010).

rule in the United States and are not responsible for mere errors of judgment. In the *Nomura Securities Compensation of Losses* case[78] the Court held that the fact that directors acted in violation of an applicable statutes was not sufficient to award damages against the directors.[79] To be liable the directors also had to intentionally or negligently violate the law. In the *Nomura* case the directors considered whether compensating for losses violated the Securities Law (and concluded correctly that it did not violate the law as it existed at the time) but did not think of the Anti-monopoly Law as being an issue. The FTC did not take a position that compensating for security losses was an unfair practice until after the payments had been made.[80] And, the directors had received Administrative Guidance from the Ministry of Finance that led them to conclude that compensation arrangements were acceptable. Accordingly, the directors were not considered negligent and the derivative suit was dismissed.[81]

Evidence to prove a derivative suit is difficult to get. The Supreme Court has held that notwithstanding a derivative suit is brought for the benefit of the corporation; a derivative suit plaintiff is not entitled to production of self-use documents created for the exclusive use of the corporation.[82] (See Chapter 14)The corporation may intervene to assist the defense of the directors.[83]

While derivative suits can be brought against parent company directors, as the parent controls its subsidiaries, suit against the executives and boards of subsidiaries is difficult to pursue although legislative change may allow such suits where the parent owns a significant percentage of the subsidiary.[84]

---

78. The Nomura Securities Compensation of Losses case, Case No. 1996 (O) 270, http://www.courts.go.jp/english/judgments/text/2000.07.07-1996-O-No.270.html (P.B. Jul. 7, 2000).
79. Old Commercial Code Article 266 (in effect at the time of the litigation) lists actions for which a director is liable to the corporation. One such item listed is performing an act that violates a statute. The Court found that causing the corporation to violate the Antimonopoly law was a violation of Article 266. For a discussion of director liability to third parties who deal with their corporation (and for a discussion of relationship between Board Members) see Robert W. Dziubla, *Enforcing Corporate Responsibility: Japanese Corporate Directors' Liability to Third Parties for Failure to Supervise*, 18 L. Japan 55 (1986).
80. The Fair Trade Commission found that the compensating of customers for losses suffered was part of a plan to retain the investment banking business of the customer and was an unfair method of soliciting customers in violation of Article 19 of the Antimonopoly Law. Article 19 is a general provision that prohibits unfair trade practices.
81. Bruce E. Aronson, *Reconsidering the Importance of Law in Japanese Corporate Governance: Evidence from the Daiwa Bank Shareholder Derivative Case*, 36 Cornell International Law Journal 11, 32 n. 92 (2003).
82. In the *Derivative Lawsuit, Self-use document case*, Case No. 1999 (Kyo) No.35, 54 Minshu 2709http://www.courts.go.jp/english/judgments/text/2000.12.14-1999.-Kyo-.No..35.html (P.B. Dec. 14, 2000).
83. *Derivative Lawsuit intervention case*, Case No. 2000 (Kyo) No. 17, 55 Minshu 30, http://www.courts.go.jp/english/judgments/text/2001.01.30-2000.-Kyo-.No.17.html (P.B. Jan. 30, 2001).
84. Kyodo, *Corporate law change eyed for investor suits*, Japan Times (Nov. 24, 2011), http://www.japantimes.co.jp/text/nn20111124a2.html.

[E] The Effect of the Lost Decade on Corporate Structure and Governance

Japan's cross shareholding system is under attack. Failures by some of Japan's insurance companies have required these companies to sell their portfolio of securities reducing the number of shares in "friendly hands" while economic troubles at Japan's banks have led banks to sell securities in companies for which they are the main bank. Legislation limiting shareholdings that a bank may keep on its books caused banks to sell some shares diluting cross shareholding. Foreign (especially American) investment funds and hedge funds have as a result acquired large shareholdings. In 2010 it was determined that the number of cross shareholdings in Japan had declined to the lowest point since the early 1990s[85] although the trend has moderated as companies seek protection against hostile bids.[86]

This is to be expected as cross-shareholdings were always seen as a protection against hostile takeovers[87] and even as the percentage of cross-shareholdings declined Japanese managers of companies that considered themselves vulnerable to a hostile takeover refrained from taking action that would encourage cross shareholders such as their lead bank to unwind their friendly stock interest.[88] Nonetheless foreign ownership of Japanese stock exchange listed companies has climbed to 28%[89] from a mere 8% in 1995 and 19% in 2000[90] and it is these foreign owners who are most forceful in attempts to change Japanese corporate practices in an effort to, if not maximize at least, increase shareholder interests and values.

---

85. *Cross Shareholdings Lowest since 1992; Banks Lead Sell off*, Japan Times (Nov. 27, 2010), http://search.japantimes.co.jp/cgi-bin/nb20101127n1.html.
86. Tomoko Yamazaki & Takahiko Hyuga, *Hedge Funds Shed Japan Holdings*, International Herald Tribune/Bloomberg News (Nov. 26, 2007); Kyodo News, *Cross-shareholding sees first rise since '90s*, The Japan Times (Sept. 2, 2007); see also, e.g., *Nippon Steel Others to Boost Cross-shareholdings*, Dow Jones (Dec. 19, 2007), Hiroyuki, *Regulator Approves Japanese Steel Merger*, Wall Street Journal, Dec. 14, 2011, http://online.wsj.com/article/SB10001424052970204844504577097881939278546.html. See also, *Corporate Governance in Japan: Institutional Change and Organizational Diversity* 42 (Aoki, Jackson, Miyajima ed., Oxford University Press 2007).
87. See, Yakult president opposed to Danone's stake increase, Ymiuri Shimbun (June 8, 2012), http://www.yomiuri.co.jp/dy/business/T120607004454.htm indicating that Yokult's President was preparing for a bid for shares by soliciting more friendly shareholders and calling of "client" companies to buy shares to beat back a potential unfriendly bid to increase shares by a French company owning 20% of Yakult.
88. For example, companies that are in danger of hostile takeover tend to keep their cross shareholding relationship with financial institutions and refrain from selling their cross shareholding in bank lenders notwithstanding the economic considerations for such sales. Hideaki Miyajima & Fumiaki Kuoki, *The Unwinding of Cross Shareholdings in Japan*, in *Corporate Governance in Japan: Institutional Change and Organizational Diversity* 97–98 (Aoki, Jackson, Miyajima eds., Oxford University Press 2007).
89. Hugh Patrick, *Japan's Economy: The Idiosyncratic Recovery Continues, Center on Japanese Economy and Business Working Paper Series*, Columbia University, 15 (August 2007).
90. Bruce E. Aronson, *Reconsidering the importance of law in Japanese Corporate Governance: Evidence from the* Daiwa Bank Shareholder Derivative *Case*, 36 *Cornell International Law Journal* 11, 16 n. 20.

Some Japanese companies are restructuring their Board of Directors to reflect a more "Americanized" board[91] by reducing the number of board members and making senior managers non-board "officers" responsible to a slimmed down board. The board in turn is given greater supervisory responsibility and less day-to-day management responsibilities. Such changes are consistent with the "Company with Committees" model.[92] As noted previously some classically structured companies are even bringing in a few outside directors to serve on their Board of Directors. Even the prohibition against holding companies, adopted in response to Occupation efforts to dismantle the zaibatsu organizations, has been set aside[93] in a drive to permit ease of decision making so that Japanese companies can become more competitive.[94] The economic malaise in Japan has resulted in experimentation in corporate governance.[95] However, it also appears that with concern about hostile takeovers, especially from American hedge funds, Corporate Japan is sliding back to older, more comfortable ways and patterns.

Both the Japanese and American model of corporate governance as set out in the written law envision a corporate structure wherein ownership and management are separated. While that model is imperfect in monitoring management of the American corporation it was virtually meaningless in the Japanese setting where most shares were not traded in the market, where there exist main bank and other financial institution relationships that differ significantly from the American financing system and where cross stock ownership has been the predominant factor in corporate relationships. As a consequence the shareholders meeting in Japan has proven itself to be an "inconvenience" to be limited in time and scope by resolving issues in advance between cross stock holding "partners." Similarly the mechanism of the derivative lawsuit to achieve monitoring of directors and managers has proven weak because of lack of sufficient incentives to make such suits "profitable." This new structural approach was adopted in years in which the American economy appeared strong. However, events such as accounting irregularities at several large companies, the criminal conviction (later reversed) of a major accounting firm,[96] the financial crisis at

91. The shift toward American style management and movement towards reliance on 'Outside Directors' to assure good management is a sharp contrast to the thinking in the early 1990s when Japan's economy was riding high and the United States was just recovering from recession. For a discussion of corporate governance and Japanese management techniques based on main bank and cross ownership relations as seen through the rosy lens of the early 1990s economy, see Ronald J. Gilson & Mark J. Roe, *Understanding the Japanese Keiretsu: Overlaps between Corporate Governance and Industrial Organization*, 102 Yale L. J. 871 (1993).
92. Companies Law Article 400.
93. Article 9 of the Antimonopoly Law was amended in 1997 to permit holding companies in circumstances where they did not excessively concentrate economic power. To maintain some control over holding companies, they are required to file annual statements with the Fair Trade Commission if the company's assets exceed a monetary minimum that can be raised by the Cabinet without further legislative action.
94. For an interesting discussion of present practices and efforts to by pass Commercial Code restrictions on corporations see Sachiko Hirao, *Staging a Comeback—Mired in Bureaucracy—Business Law Changes Just Scratch the Surface*, The Japan Times (Mar. 8, 2001).
95. See e.g., Akema Nakamura, *Firms Fear Losing Global Race—Postwar Corporate Model Shed in Quest for Success*, Japan Times, (Apr. 5, 2001).
96. The conviction was later reversed but not before the firm went out of business. *Arthur Anderson LLP v. United States*, 544 U.S. 696 (2005).

American banks, reported "hedging losses" in the billions at a major bank, questions about a potential disconnect between corporate management on the one hand and stockholders on the other disclose that there are severe problems with the United States corporate governance model. The New York Stock exchange sought to restore investor confidence through new listing requirements[97] and the SEC adopted new rules to deal with accounting and other corporate governance issues[98] and Congress enacted the Sarbanes-Oxley Act. As a consequence of the financial crisis of the second half of the first decade of the twenty-first Century, the Dodd/Frank Law was enacted.

The legislative approach[99] calls (*inter alia*) for an independent accounting oversight board,[100] certification of accuracy of financial reports by the CFO and CEO of the company,[101] recoupment from CEOs and CFOs of certain bonuses or equity based compensation received based on restated financial reports, prohibiting sales of securities in the company by officers and directors during any period when there is a similar prohibition applied to company pension fund participants,[102] increasing criminal penalties for corporate fraud,[103] authorizing the SEC to disqualify certain persons from serving as corporate directors and/or officers,[104] extending the statute of limitations in corporate fraud cases to the longer of two years from discovery or five years of the fraud,[105] providing corporate whistleblowers both an administrative and civil action remedy for alleged retaliation,[106] etc. The shakeout continues with the Dodd-Frank legislation and a new regulator with consumer interests. Question is raised whether the

97. The New York Stock Exchange has proposed, *inter alia*, that companies that are listed and that wish to be listed on the exchange take steps to increase the role of Independent Directors in corporate governance by requiring that Boards of Directors of listed companies have a majority of Independent Directors and that Independent Directors be the only directors on audit committees as well as compensation and nominating committees. For a discussion of the NYSE proposals (see Bulletin issued by the NYSE on 13 June 2002) and for follow up on the proposals see the website for the NYSE at www.nyse.com.
98. See SEC Press Release of 20 June 2002.
99. See Sarbanes-Oxley Act of 1992. Enacted into law, July 2002.
100. Sections 101–109. The Supreme Court held that the provisions of the law that restricted the ability of the SEC to remove the Board Members at will coupled with the President's inability to remove members of the SEC except for cause was unconstitutional. *Free Enterprise Fund v. Public Company Accounting Oversight Board*, 561 U.S. ___ (2010) slip opinion p. 14–15.
101. Section 302.
102. Section 306.
103. See e.g., sections 820, 805, 807, 901–906.
104. Section 1105.
105. Section 804.
106. Section 806.

American model is a good model for Japan to be emulating.[107] This has not been lost on Japanese decision makers.[108]

Japan's new corporate governance structure was incorporated into a legal structure that does not reflect the reality of the shareholding relationships between Japanese entities or the Japanese corporate culture. The new "Americanized" structure appears not to reflect the reality of the relationships that exist in the Japanese corporation. Perhaps this is the reason so few Japanese corporations have chosen to adopt the new company with committee model. This new structure appears to be designed to deal with an American style corporate philosophy—maximizing profits—while the corporate philosophy in Japan has additional goals. If the corporate law fails to reflect the reality of corporate governance and philosophy, what you see is likely to be not what you get. That is, in fact, the situation.

The lack of funding for new capital investments that accompanied the "lost decade" resulted in changes in the law permitting more and greater direct foreign investment in Japan such as Wal-Mart's purchase of an interest in the Japanese retailer Seiyu. Under the deal Wal-Mart obtained the right to ultimately increase its interest to 66.7%[109] from which Wal-Mart could and did force out the minority so that in June 2008 Seiyu became a wholly owned subsidiary of Wal-Mart. Seiyu took advantage of changes in Japanese law permitting the use of options and relaxing the requirements for issuing new shares. Flexibility in the rules governing options and the creation of free floating warrants make mergers and acquisitions easier to finance. Triangular mergers that utilize the stock of a foreign acquiring parent as consideration for the shares of the target company are permitted under the new Companies Law. As a legal matter, the mechanism for an active Merger and Acquisition market exists in Japan. Such active market exists for friendly mergers but not for hostile takeovers, especially hostile attempts by foreign acquirers.

Along with greater access to ownership opportunities, the economic malaise had made some failing Japanese companies more responsive to both foreign management techniques and foreign managers. The Wal-Mart/Seiyu deal assumed an influx of Wal-Mart managers to assist Seiyu's recovery; the dramatic turnaround of Nissan Motors after management responsibility was given to a Renault executive did not go unnoticed.

---

107. Even the role of the SEC in bringing and then settling cases against major banks charged with involvement in the mortgage securitization financing schemes used in the lead up to the foreclosure mess has been the subject of criticism, in this case by a Federal Judge charged with determining whether such settlements were fair and reasonable in the public interest. See, Peter J. Henning, *Behind Rakoff's Rejection of Citigroup Settlement*, New York Times (Nov. 28, 2011), http://dealbook.nytimes.com/2011/11/28/behind-judge-rakoffs-rejection-of-s-e-c-citigroup-settlement/.

108. For a strong attack on the American Shareholder model and the complicity of Independent Directors and Management see, Simon Caulkin, *Corporate Apocalypse, Management Today*, January 2009, http://www.managementtoday.co.uk/news/870435, last accessed Sept. 16, 2012.

109. See *Seiyu Shareholders go for Wal-Mart Deal*, Japan Times (May 24, 2002).

[F] So-Called Sokaiya

Corporate governance in Japan cannot be discussed without some discussion of the "*sokaiya*" phenomenon. Japanese corporations appear to fear stockholders meetings, although the corporation, through cross stockholdings and proxies, typically has the needed votes to deal with any issue. To avoid "confusion" at stockholders meetings, most Japanese companies adopted a policy of holding their meetings on the same day and at the same time[110] making it impossible for shareholders to attend more than one meeting. Although the practice of holding meetings on exactly the same day is diminishing, meetings are clustered within a one week period of each other. In part, this clustering is brought about by the requirement that the annual meeting be held within 90 days of the close of the fiscal year, which for most Japanese companies is March 31.[111] As companies tend to hold the annual meeting as late as possible after the close of the year, late June is the peak season for holding annual meetings. To avoid questions Japanese companies have, in the past, paid shareholders to either not raise issues or to support the company if contentious issues are raised, or both. Criminal elements have purchased shares and then advised companies that they would raise embarrassing questions at the annual meeting. In essence money is then extorted from the company in exchange for an agreement not to raise such issues or to create disruption if others raise such issues. So-called "*sokaiya*" gangster elements have been a staple of Japanese corporate governance for many years. To avoid the *sokaiya* phenomenon, the law was amended to contain a specific prohibition against payment to such *sokaiya*.[112] If such a payment is made, both the party receiving the payment and the company employee, director, auditor, or other management official responsible for making the payment are guilty of a crime.[113] Notwithstanding the carryover of this provision when the Companies Law was adopted, the practice of payments to *sokaiya* continues in Japan.[114]

110. In 1995, approximately 96% of companies listed on the Tokyo Stock Exchange held their annual meeting on the same day. By 2002 the percentage had dropped to 76.5%. *Japan Times* 14 June 2002 76.5% of Listed Companies to Hold Annual Meeting 6/27.
111. The Tokyo Stock Exchange reports that 75.8% of companies listed on the exchange close their books at the end of March. Also the TSE reports that 61.6% of such companies held their meetings on the same peak day. The TSE did not report what percentage of companies grouped their meetings on the next highest day. TSE-Listed Companies White Paper on Corporate Governance 2009, http://www.tse.or.jp/rules/cg/white-paper/b7gje60000005ob1-att/b7gje6000001m8gl.pdf, last accessed Sept. 16, 2012.
112. For a discussion of sokaiya and their effect on shareholders meetings see Akio Takeuchi, (Russell E. Colwell trans.) *Shareholders' Meetings under the Revised Commercial Code*, 20 L. Japan 173 183–186 (1987). Companies Law Article 120; Commercial Code Article 497.
113. Commercial Code Article 497.
114. For an interesting discussion of sokaiya as a vehicle of corporate democracy see Mark D. West, *Information, Institutions, and Extortion in Japan and the United States: Making Sense of Sokaiya Racketeers*, 93 N.W. U. L. Rev. 767 (1999).

[G] Stakeholder Concerns Other than Shareholder Concerns

The maximizing of profits for the benefit of shareholders (an American idea) is not the prime motivating force behind a Japanese corporation: (a) those corporations that are part of a keiretsu organization may have institutional concerns that override their individual profit concerns. A parts manufacturing arm may forgo profit to assist a sister company that uses those parts in a finished product; (b) Assuring future payment of debt and interest on debt may carry a higher priority than distribution of profits to shareholders when large shareholders are also the large creditors of the corporation; (c) Concern for personnel, in an institution whose directors and officers graduated to that status from lifetime employment in the organization, may predominate over shareholder interests.

This concern for personnel is especially important in an environment that considers loyalty—that can be measured in lifetime employment, which reflects employee loyalty to the corporation and corporation loyalty to the employee—a virtue. This concept of loyalty is recognized in the Whistleblowers Protection Act (WPA) effective April 1, 2006. At first glance whistle blowing would appear to be an act of extreme disloyalty. But in Japan, following a series of scandals involving wrongdoing by corporations that were brought to light by whistleblowers, both the public and companies came to recognize that whistle blowing could in fact result in benefits to the corporate employer by protecting it from the consequences of the wrongful act. The WPA seeks to bring together the loyalty obligation of the employee with the best interests of the employer by allowing employees to blow the whistle inside the company when the employee believes that an event that is reportable (i.e., criminal act or violation of laws and regulations) has occurred so that corrective action can be taken. Even if the whistle blower is wrong in belief that there has been a violation the whistle blower is protected, when blowing the whistle in house, although the law contains no specific mechanism for such protection.[115] A major shortcoming of the law is that a whistle blower who claims retaliation must be an employee to sue the company, meaning that if the company retaliates the employee must suffer in his retaliated against position while the litigation, which can take years, proceeds through the court system. Whistle blowers can only go outside the organization when they have more evidence of wrongdoing than simple belief. Thus to go to a government authority with jurisdiction to handle the matter the whistle blower must have reasonable grounds to believe that a violation has occurred—this typically requires some documentary evidence on which to base the belief of wrongdoing. The whistle blower who goes to entities outside the employer and government is not protected if it turns out that the belief is erroneous and is not protected if the whistle blower goes to a competing entity. Where the employer has established an internal procedure for reporting events covered by the WPA the employee must first utilize the internal mechanism. In essence the thrust of the law is to have matters reported in-house so they can be taken care of

115. AP, *Whistle-blower defeats Japan Inc. for first time*, Japan Times (July 1, 2012), http://www.japantimes.co.jp/text/nn20120701a2.html.

in house.[116] Exception to the requirement to report in-house is made when a company sets up an outside whistle blower mechanism at an independent third party such as a law firm or auditing firm. In such case the employee may either blow the whistle in-house or use the company authorized out-house mechanism. In this way the loyalty obligation is met and both the employer and employee can be comfortable in the disclosure.[117] It is not unusual for companies to use the risk management department or similar organizational unit required by J-SOX as the place where internal whistle-blowers are to bring their beliefs, concerns and evidence.

The American practice of drastically cutting employee rolls to increase profitability has, until recently, been looked on as a practice not to be followed in Japan, and is still frowned on by the public, government, corporate boards and the courts. Thus, while American companies came out of the recession of the early 1990s relatively quickly and as "leaner and meaner" competitors with less employees and higher productivity, Japanese companies that did not follow a more "hostile" approach to employee rolls were not been able to cut costs as dramatically and have not been able to come out of recession as strongly or quickly (or perhaps even at all.) Companies have turned to less confrontational means of reducing the core employee pool, such as reduced hiring of full time lifetime core employees and greater use of part-time, contract or non-core employees.

The institution of lifetime employment remains an important part of Japanese business (although the number of employees who fall into the lifetime employee category has declined)[118] and places different priorities on Japanese managers than the pure profit motive of American managers.[119] The structure of Japanese stock ownership also affects the relationship of stockholders to the corporation.

Along with stock values affecting capital pressure, banks were under pressure because of bad loan problems. The desire to avoid writing off large bad loans or to take large reserves for bad loans (especially as capital is already strained by the market declines in stock values—placing pressure on balance sheets and capital) along with the refusal of main banks to allow their corporate "sister" companies to fail, led some banks to continue funding failing companies in which they have a large stock interest. Lending to such failing institutions had the effect of allowing the lending bank to be paid interest on its previous loans by having its loan recycled as interest payment

116. Hideo Mitzutani, *Whistleblower Protection Act*, 4 Japan Lab. Rev. No. 3 95 (2007).
117. In the aftermath of the Great East Japan Earthquake and Tsunami and the Fukushima nuclear tragedy an employee of an electric power company blew the whistle on company practices designed to skew public opinion about leaving power plants operating by going outside the company to Prefectural Assembly member. See, Kyodo, *Insider blew whistle on Kyushu Electric TV stunt*, Japan Times (July 10, 2011), http://search.japantimes.co.jp/cgi-bin/nn20110710a1.html.
118. Caslav Pejovic, *Japanese Corporate Governance: Behind Legal Norms*, pages 26–27 http://www.law.utoronto.ca/documents/conferences2/IACCL10-Pejovic.pdf, last accessed Sept. 16, 12.
119. See Corporate Governance Principles—A Japanese View, *Corporate Governance Forum of Japan*, 7 Corporate Governance 208, 211 (1999) distinguishing between the single focus (shareholder return) of American corporations and the 'social harmony' multi focus of Japanese (and to some extent European) corporations that includes values of employees as well as shareholders.

and returned in part to the bank. This "ever greening" process, reminiscent of a Ponzi scheme, had a positive effect on bank balance sheets. The result was continued lending to corporations that were unable to repay higher and higher loans and an accelerating negative effect on capital available for potentially profitable new businesses. Calls for banks to write off bad debts and to allow failing debtors to fail had been made by numerous economists but until the Koizumi administration had been heeded more by government rhetoric than by action on the ground. Indeed there is evidence of government complicity in the "ever green" process.[120] The Koizumi administration did however take steps to ameliorate the bad debt crisis and together with the accounting reforms discussed below make balance sheets more transparent.

Japanese accounting rules that did not require consolidation of accounting statements led some companies to hide their true condition by placing failing operations in unconsolidated subsidiaries so that the parent company could report a relatively good (and "clean") financial statement while the losses of the enterprise built up in its subsidiary. Publicly traded companies must now use consolidated balance sheets and profit and loss statements (and also mark to market accounting). New provisions give relevant ministries the authority to define accounting principles so as to make accounting statements more transparent and bring about uniformity between accounting practices under the Code and the Securities Exchange Law. Companies may use electronic files for corporate records and financial statements need not be published in paper copy in newspapers, but can be displayed through the company's home page on its website.

The Japanese government's policy of spending to support the economy resulted in large deficit financing and has caused credit agencies to question the debt ratings of Japanese government bonds. [Japan's credit rating was reduced in early 2011.] These actions have resulted in a number of economic reform proposals and some economic reform action. The Financial Services Agency in 2012 required banks to report the number of employees who were paid salaries and bonuses that exceeded those paid to bank board members—the theory is to limit relationships that encourage unacceptable risk taking for personal gain.[121] Most significantly, real steps have been taken to have banks write off bad debts and limit lending to failing operations. The cross ownership phenomenon and the main bank system lengthened the economic malaise that Japan was in since the collapse of the bubble economy in the 1990s until the early twenty-first century. But at the same time it buffered the effect of that decline as corporations and government support of corporations became the safety net for lifetime employees. The downturn created by the Great East Japan Earthquake and Tsunami may once again force consideration of corporate reform.

Cross ownership and main bank relations affect the ability of foreign enterprise to compete in Japan at both the retail and the industrial level. The distribution system in

---

120. Dan W. Puchniak, *Perverse Main Bank Rescue in the Lost Decade: Proof That Unique Institutional Incentives Drive Japanese Corporate Governance* 16 Pac. Rim L. & Pol'y J. 13 (2007).

121. Minoro Matsutani, *FSA seeks disclosure on bank salaries*, Japan Times (Feb. 7, 2012), http://www.japantimes.co.jp/text/nb20120207a1.html.

Japan is substantially more complicated and multi-level than is true in the United States. Distribution companies deal with retailers with whom they have relationships that include funding when times get tough and reduction of profits at the distribution level when necessary to keep retailers and other distributors in the distribution chain alive. Distributors may take back product that does not sell quickly in retail establishments and the producer may take the product back from the distributor. Unlike the United States where a manufacturer may deal with several distributors at the first level and these distributors may deal with retailers, in Japan there are several levels of distribution: a first level distribution company (perhaps a subsidiary or a cross-shareholding "sister" company) that deals with a second level company that will deal with a third level of distribution, etc. There are more levels in distribution than in the United States. This additional distribution cost must be borne by the consumer. In bad economic times there are more levels that can take a little less profit and thus even out the burden that might fall on the retailer alone. Because of relationships in the distribution chain it is difficult for a new enterprise—and that includes a new foreign enterprise to break into the market since it cannot obtain adequate distribution arrangements.

Since cross ownership companies wish to make their owned related companies more profitable there is a natural tendency to buy from within the group or to make arrangements that maximize the group's purchasing power with a company that will in turn buy its needs from group members. Such arrangements inhibit competition from outsiders, especially from outsiders who are foreign entities. The existence of cross stock ownership and keiretsu organization inhibits competition and stifles dynamic international trade into Japan. Such problems have led to disputes between Japan, the United States and other Japanese trading partners, who have argued that such cross ownership relationships are a form of unfair trade barrier.[122] On the other hand, the economic malaise in Japan created opportunities for foreign investors. One of the changes brought about in 2002 was legislation overturning previous laws that required foreign companies that regularly did business in Japan to have a branch office in Japan. Now such companies can conduct such business without a branch as long as their financial statements are publicly disclosed in Japan.

[H] Insider Trading and Anti-trust Prohibitions

One of the reforms insisted on by the Occupation was legislation similar to the United States Securities and Exchange Law to prevent the improper trading of securities by insiders. The Japanese Securities and Exchange Law of 1948 contains an anti-fraud provision that is similar to the U.S. Securities Act and is designed to prevent fraud in the trading of securities. The law was amended in 1988 to strengthen its anti-insider

122. For a discussion of this issue (and of the keiretsu organization in general) see Gregory K. Bader, The *Keiretsu Distribution System of Japan: Its Steadfast Existence Despite Heightened Foreign and Domestic Pressure for Dissolution*' 27 Cornell Intl. L. J. 365 (1994); see also Marius B. Jansen, *The Making of Modern Japan* 756 (The Belknap Press of Harvard University Press 2000).

trading features by including both reporting requirements and criminal penalties. Under these amendments corporate insiders (and persons receiving tips from insiders) who have obtained material information as a consequence of their relationship to the corporation may not trade securities listed on an exchange on the basis of that information until the information has been made publicly available.[123] Although the law replicates in many respects Rule 10-b 5 of the United States Securities and Exchange Commission, question has been raised as to whether the amended law has achieved its objectives.[124] Nonetheless, people have been arrested in Japan for alleged prohibited inside trading[125], corporate executives have been discharged for such activities[126] and government officials have been charged with insider trading.[127] Although charged, the usual punishment is a fine and the fines are usually small, especially in relation to the profits realized.[128] The Supreme Court of Japan in 1999 gave a broad interpretation of the Securities and Exchange law to find a violation when a corporate auditor and legal counsel to a traded company purchased shares of the company based on insider information that a representative director of the company had concluded that a merger should be completed.[129] But, significantly, the law does not prohibit brokerage firms from leaking inside information. A scandal in mid-2012 and the subsequent loss of new issue business by Japanese brokerages has brought about demands for change to prohibit such practices.[130]

Japanese law prohibits certain short swing trades by insiders and permits corporations to recover profits if such trades are discovered. The Supreme Court turned back a challenge to such law based on Article 29 of the Constitution, which protects property rights.[131] While profits may be recovered and while insider traders may be fined for their activities and receive suspended prison sentences, it is extremely rare for an inside trader to actually be sent to prison. The *Livedoor* case, discussed below, is a rare exception—and may be based less on insider trading than on the fact that the principal sentenced was on the verge of changing important aspects of Japanese corporate culture that neither the government, the courts and perhaps the public were yet prepared to accept.

---

123. For a discussion of the 1988 amendments and the reasons for those amendments see Tomoko Akashi, (Note), *Regulation of Insider Trading in Japan*, 89 Columbia L. Rev. 1296 (1989).
124. See Mitsuri Misawa, *Daiwa Bank Scandal in New York: Its Causes, Significance, and Lessons in the International Society*, 29 Vanderbilt J. Transnatl. L. 1023, 1039–1048 (1996) questioning whether the Japanese rules against insider trading are effective.
125. *Accountant Arrested over Insider Trading*, Japan Times (Feb. 21, 2001).
126. *Kenematsu Insider Trading Probe*, Japan Times (June 16, 2001).
127. Kyodo, *METI Bigwig Nabbed in Insider Trading in Wife's Name*, Japan Times (Jan. 13, 2012), http://www.japantimes.co.jp/text/nn20120113a2.html.
128. See, AFP Fuji, *Probe spotlights Japan's culture of insider trading*, Japan Times (June 12, 2012), http://www.japantimes.co.jp/text/nn20120612f3.html, reporting fines of about USD 1,500 and a recent suggestion by the regulator that a company be fined JPY 130,000 in an insider transaction where the alleged profit was JPY 60,000,000.
129. *Insider Trading case*, Case No. 1998 (A) Nos. 1146, 1229 (Sup. Ct. P.B. 10 June 1999).
130. Mia Tahara Stubbs, *Japan to tighten insider trading law*, Reuters (June 26, 2012), http://www.reuters.com/article/2012/06/26/japan-insider-okubo-ifr-idUSL6E8HQ76H20120626.
131. *Court Rules for Companies on Short-term Transactions*, Japan Times (Feb. 14, 2002) (Short Swing Profits case).

The Japanese Anti-Trust laws are heavily indebted to the United States law from which they are borrowed. Yet, keiretsu organizations continue to exist and there is no doubt but that cartel arrangements have been either formally or tacitly accepted by the Japanese Government in the past when it was determined that it was in the interests of the society to do so.[132] How could such relationships and anticompetitive conduct exist in light of the anti-trust law? It is a question of what you see not being what you get. Although recent changes in both the anti-trust law and the activities of the FTC demonstrate a heightened regard for competition and the advantages of competition and a much more active FTC pursuing anti cartel cases with vigor as well as engaging in active review of merger cases and demanding divestitures when necessary to protect competition.

In January 2010 amendments to Japan's 1947 Anti-monopoly law went into effect, strengthening penalty provisions in the law and strengthening the enforcement authority of the Japan FTC. This amendment created a greater enforcement policy than had previously existed and prevents private monopolization that excludes entry into the market—thus affecting such matters as mergers that have the effect of monopolizing the market and excluding entry—and correspondingly prohibits a company with a dominant market position from improperly using its power to unfairly bargain with others. Cartels are now being more closely scrutinized for illegality and bid rigging (especially rigging that affects public contracting or the lives of ordinary citizens) is more vigorously prosecuted. The powers of the FTC have been expanded so that the JFTC can itself carry out inspections on site and even conduct searches in a criminal investigation. Fines have been increased, especially for recidivists and ringleader companies in cartels. Although plea-bargaining is not permitted in the Japanese criminal justice system, the JFTC has followed the lead of the United States and other countries in adopting a leniency program designed to get companies to come forward and report cartel like activities and price fixing schemes. Up to five members of the cartel can apply for reduced fines on a sliding scale that rewards initial applications for leniency more favorably than later applications (where more than one cartel member is part of a single group of companies, joint application may be made by the related companies).[133] The leniency system has in fact brought forth a significant increase in

132. When it is not considered in the interests of society to permit such cartel arrangements the Japanese Fair Trade Commission may investigate and bring proceedings. Review of Japanese FTC determinations is in a High Court. The Japanese FTC may waive or reduce fines for companies that report cartel activities on a voluntary basis. See, Kyodo, *Parts maker Denso bids for leniency over cartel violation*, Japan Times (July 22, 2011), http://search.japantimes.co.jp/cgi-bin/nb20110722a2.html.

133. See, http://www.jftc.go.jp/en/policy_enforcement/leniency_program/about_leniency.pdf for a discussion of the leniency program.

reports of price fixing activities[134] and more enforcement including more cease and desist orders[135] by the FTC but still enforcement is limited.[136]

The merger rules under the new law are more consistent with international standards and like other regimes call for pre-merger notification to the FTC and pre-closing review, based on revenues of the companies involved rather than the previous regime that concerned itself with asset values. The notification thresholds are the same for domestic and international mergers.[137]

[I] Corporate Culture and Labor Relations

Large Japanese corporations tend to have a uniform corporate culture. The business year begins April 1 (as is the start of the school year) and most new hires begin work on April 1. This may change as Tokyo University and several other schools in early 2012 began politicking to change the school year to begin in the autumn as is the situation in the West. Hiring at the management-training level is typically related to the university attended by the applicant—Japanese universities are vertically structured and, for example, graduates of the Faculty of Law of Tokyo University have an easier time getting hired than the graduates of less prestigious schools. Most starting salaries are the same and at least for the early years promotion is based on seniority and salaries remain the same or virtually the same for everyone in the same hiring class.

The personnel department in a Japanese company plays a more significant role in the corporation than in the United States and is responsible for training, tracking and

134. Paul Schoff & Andy Matthews, *Cartels: Overview, 2011The Asia-Pacific Antitrust Review*, Global Competition Rev. 9, 10 (2011) The web site of the JFTC shows 85 applications for leniency in fiscal 2009 and 131 applications in fiscal 2010. http://www.jftc.go.jp/en/pressreleases/uploads/110613Enforcement%20Status.pdf, last accessed Sept. 16, 2012. Not only has the leniency program brought forward more information but it has also resulted in larger cases being brought. The web site discloses that between 2008 and 2010 anti cartel cases involved such important fields as vinyl chloride pipes, optical fiber cable, electric wire and galvanized steel sheets.

135. Cease and desist orders were a feature of the 2005 amendment to the law. A cease and desist order can be challenged in a review proceeding before the FTC and an adverse decision by the Commission can be challenged by suit in the Tokyo High Court under a substantial evidence test. Objections have been raised to the use of cease and desist orders on separation of function grounds that have sometimes also been raised to administrative proceedings before a deciding agency in the United States. Additionally objections to the restrictive rules regarding disclosure of evidence in the hands of the agency representatives are similar to criticisms made to the restrictive rules affecting prosecutor disclosure of evidence. A drive to require more disclosure is underway in the FTC procedure arena. Parties to a FTC proceeding do not have a right to counsel at the proceedings and questions as to whether the attorney client privilege applies when counsel advises the respondent are implicated by the failure of recognition of a right to counsel. Whether to change the system is a subject of dispute in Japan that was not addressed directly in the 2010 amendments. Mitsuo Matsushita, *Reforming the Enforcement of the Japanese Antimonopoly Law*, 41 Loyola U. Chicago L. J. 521 (2010).

136. *FTC panel dismisses claim of JASRAC music monopoly*, Daily Yomiuri (Feb. 9, 2012), http://www.yomiuri.co.jp/dy/business/T120208006100.htm.

137. See, e.g., *Japan: Amendment of the Anti-Monopoly Act of Japan and Its Impact on Mergers and Acquisitions*, Jones Day (Oct. 8, 2009), http://www.mondaq.com/article.asp?articleid=87354; David A. Higbee, *Merger Control: Overview in The Asia-Pacific Antitrust Review*, Global Competition Rev. 9 (2011).

selecting those who are expected to rise to high positions in the company. The head of the personnel department will probably advance to the board. Most large companies have advanced management-training programs and tend to train their executives in -house rather than relying on training in university graduate schools. These training programs have favored male employees and a two-track career system has arisen in which male employees are trained for executive advancement while female employees are disadvantaged. With amendment of the Equal Opportunity Law such systems were supposed to break down but as a practical matter such systems have proven quite resistant to change. Many companies still view it as their role to hire female employees who are viewed as good wives for male employees and many Japanese men find their wives at the company where they work.(See Chapter 8)

Lifetime employment for full time core employees has been a staple of large company employment policies. However these programs are for full time core employees and many employees at companies are not full time and some full timers may be contract workers, not core lifetime employees. Most women employees may not have full time career status and in a slow economy they may be the first to be laid off. As employment statistics tend to be based on full time employment, this practice skews the unemployment rate. Recent economic troubles are beginning to affect the lifetime employment system but the system is very resistant to change, in part because lifetime employment is supported by judge-made law that makes it very difficult for employers to discharge lifetime employees—even in the face of financial difficulties for the company. (See Chapter 12)

Japan has a national health insurance system that is organized around employment and workers receive their national insurance as part of their employment package. Personal income taxes are progressive and can reach high percentages—but for most workers the withholding system pays the tax due and there may be no obligation to file a tax return as taxes are calculated by the taxing authority based on salary and at the end of the tax year an employee may receive a small tax bill or refund. Of course businesses, including individual operated businesses, have tax reporting and paying obligations, as do independent professionals such as lawyers.

Union membership and collective bargaining are a Constitutional right along with the right to work and choose one's own occupation.[138] During the Occupation the union movement threatened a general strike causing a shift in Occupation policy reducing union power.[139] While Japan has a national labor organization representing unions, most unions are "enterprise unions" organized on a company or plant basis including all workers of the company both blue and white collar and office and factory workers but excluding part-time workers.[140] Many times the leadership of the union

138. Constitution Articles 22, 27 and 28.

139. For a discussion of labor policy under the American Occupation and the ban on the general strike, see Theodore Cohen, *Remaking Japan: The American Occupation As New Deal Part IV*, 185-300 (The Free Press 1987).

140. Because of the increase in part-time workers in Japan as part of industry's effort to provide itself with flexibility that is missing because of its inability to lay off core employees, there has been some movement in Japan for unions to accept in their ranks part-time workers. But, as the interests of part-timers and core employees are fundamentally different it remains to be seen

either was or is involved in the active management of the company. Union relations in Japan tend to be much less confrontational than in the United States and strikes are a relatively unusual feature of Japanese labor relations. In part this is related to management's view of its workers as an asset of the company, in part it is related to a "paternalistic" attitude towards workers by management, in part it is related to worker's attitudes toward "their" company and in part it is related to the concept of lifetime employment for core workers and the reality that company managers rose from the ranks as corporate employees and many were not just company union members but union leaders. Employees tend to want their company to be successful—this is also an aspect of lifetime employment and strikes do not help the prospects of a company. Employees have a greater say on production matters than is true in the United States. Individual workers and groups of workers are more involved in decision making on the factory floor in Japan. In many ways the employer/employee relationship of modern Japan replaces the old family system of feudal Japan.[141] As workers in a lifetime employment system are dependent for personal success on the success of their company they tend to work long hours and are extremely loyal to their company. This has created a social problem related to death caused by overwork.[142] Similarly, workers have job security and the company needs some mechanism to give workers the incentive to improve productivity—the annual bonus, a significant part of worker's compensation is designed for this purpose.

The corollary to a lifetime employment system is the lack of a market for mid-level employee talent. With companies committed to training their own employees to move up the corporate ladder, there is no place for lateral hires and no market for such hires. Courts recognizing the dilemma are not likely to change the protections given to lifetime employees—even if this places the employer in jeopardy and reduces competitiveness.

---

whether this movement will have significant effect on labor relations in Japan. See, International Trade Union Confederation, *2007 Annual Survey of violations of trade union rights—Japan*, June 9, 2007, available at: http://www.unhcr.org/refworld/docid/4c52ca27c.html.

141. Tsuyoshi Kinoshita, *Legal System and Legal Culture in Japanese law*, 44 Comp. L. Rev. 25, 110 (2010). Richard Ronald & Allison Alexy, *Continuity and Change in Japanese Homes and Families*, in *Home and Family in Japan* 1, 8(Richard Ronald & Allison Alexy eds., Routledge 2011) noting that the family "metaphor" was used for the company and mimicked in many ways the feudal and pre-war *Ie* concept of the family. See also, Ross Mouer, *Work Culture*, in *The Cambridge Companion to Modern Japanese Culture* 113 at 125 (Yoshio Sugimoto ed., Cambridge University Press 2009).

142. Death from overwork is known as *karoushi*. The Industrial Safety and Health Act was amended to provide protection to employees in an effort to reduce overwork death and illness. See Fumiko Obata, *Bill For the Partial Amendment of the Industrial Safety and Health Act and Other Related Acts*, 4 Japan Lab. Rev. No. 3, 53 (2007). The Supreme Court has held that the Local Government Employees' Accident Compensation Fund must pay compensation when an employee committed suicide because of harassment on the job brought about by the assertive nature of the employer suicide. *Power Harassment case*, Supreme Court Second Petty Bench (Feb. 22, 2012), *Woman wins power harassment court battle over husband's suicide*, Mainichi Daily News (Feb. 23, 2012), http://mdn.mainichi.jp/mdnnews/news/20120223p2a00m0na002000c.html. The Fukushima Nuclear Tragedy also resulted in claims for *karoushi*. Kyodo News, *Overwork death recognized for worker at Fukushima plant* (Feb. 24, 2012), http://english.kyodonews.jp/news/2012/02/143646.html.

The barrier to downsizing because of the loss of lifetime employee jobs is being breached as lifetime employment itself is being challenged—not by abolition of the system but by a reduction in the number of core employees covered by the system. This in turn has led to greater use of contract and part-time workers (by 2006 part-timers were over 20% of the work force and the great majority of part-timers are women), for work that traditionally was performed by core (lifetime) workers.[143] The courts and later the Cabinet and the Diet—have reacted to this increase. (See Chapter 12).

Most retired workers get employment after retirement with a company lower on the vertical status matrix. Retired salarymen operate many of Japan's small retail stores that are part of the nationwide social safety net. Efforts to replace them with large more competitive retail operations create both economic and political issues.

[J] Hostile Takeover Attempts and Defenses

The arena of merger and acquisition through hostile takeovers is an illustration of corporate law that fails to reflect corporate and societal culture and values. When the legislation permitting such M&A devices as triangular mergers was pending in the Diet opposition was voiced that these devices would make hostile takeovers by American companies more easily obtainable. Consequently the M&A liberalizing provisions were delayed a year to allow Japanese companies to put takeover defense mechanisms in place. Typically these measures call for disclosure to the Board prior to any large purchase of company stock or prior to any tender or other takeover device so that the Board can questions of the prospective acquirer to determine whether the takeover is good for the company and adequately inform shareholders and in some cases to take measures to protect shareholder interests. Even if no measures have been authorized prior to a takeover attempt, a target of a takeover may call a meeting of the shareholders and place before them a special resolution amending the certificate of incorporation by adopting an anti-takeover defense.

[1] Delaware Law

Poison pill and other takeover defenses are an established aspect of Delaware Law. The leading Delaware case is *Unocal v. Mesa*[144] holding that directors owe both a duty of care and a duty of loyalty to the shareholders and, as a general matter the actions of the directors when confronted with an unsolicited takeover proposal were protected by the presumption in Delaware's business judgment rule. Because of their duty to become informed directors may rely on the advice of expert professionals retained by the Board; the duty of loyalty requires acting solely in the best interests of the company and

143. For a discussion of the new Part-Time Work Act see Michiyo Morozumi, *Balanced Treatment and Bans on Discrimination—Significance and Issues of the Revised Part-Time Work Act*, 6 Japan Lab. Rev. 39 (2009) and Takashi Araki, *The Widening Gap between Standard and non-Standard Employees and the Role of Labor Law in Japan*, 8 J. L. & Pol. 3 (University of Tokyo 2011).

144. 493 A.2d 496 (Del. Sup. Ct., 1985).

its shareholders not in the interest of other parties, such as the board itself, incumbent officers or a subgroup of shareholders. The business judgment rule presumption will, as a general matter, provide protection to the board members if they are later sued as long as they have not acted in bad faith, their decision was made in good faith and is rationally related to a benefit running to the shareholders[145] and was made in a situation where the duty of loyalty was followed.

Where there are facts indicating that the duty of loyalty may not have been followed, the Directors must meet a standard of review more stringent than the business judgment rule presumption. In such a case the Delaware Court will apply an "entire fairness" standard in reviewing the actions of the Board.[146]

As a result, when a board is composed of a majority of independent directors and has taken and followed the advice of expert professionals, the decision of the board is more likely to be subject to the business judgment rule presumption than if insiders dominate the board or the board did not take and rely on professional expert advice.[147]

However, when the directors take an anti-takeover defensive measure, such as by invoking the terms of a poison pill or other takeover defense, there is the danger that the board has a conflict of interest because of the interest of the board members in retaining their position on the company's board. This potential caused the Delaware Supreme Court in *Unocal* to apply a heightened standard of review when a board activates a takeover defense mechanism. Thus the board members had the burden of showing that the purpose of the activation of the poison pill was to benefit the company and its shareholders and not to perpetuate the board in office.

In a later decision, the Supreme Court of Delaware held that when sale of the company was inevitable or when the board determined to seek a sale of the company to defeat the takeover attempt or where a breakup of the company was inevitable, the function of the board was not to defeat the takeover but was to achieve as high a price per share for the shareholders as possible.[148] In such situations the board was essentially holding an auction the purpose of which was to achieve the highest price for the shareholders. The *Unocal* and *Revlon* decisions have evolved but the basic premise that directors have a fiduciary duty remains, i.e., directors have an obligation to act in the interest of the company and the shareholders and may not remain passive and action should be proportional to the threat posed and should benefit shareholders.[149]

---

145. *Revlon, Inc. v. MacAndrews & Forbes Holdings*, 506 A. 2d 173 (Del. Sup. Ct., 1986) ("while concern for various corporate constituencies is proper when addressing a takeover threat, that principle is limited by the requirement that there be some rationally related benefit accruing to the stockholders.").
146. *Selectica, Inc. v. Versata Enterprises, Inc.* (Del Court of Chancery, 2010).
147. Delaware courts apply a different standard to alleged breach of duty of care and alleged breach of duty of loyalty because while it is sometimes possible under Delaware law to exculpate directors from liability for a breach of duty of care by way of a Certificate of Incorporation provision, such exculpation does not apply to asserted breach of loyalty claims. *Lyondell Chemical v. Ryan* (Apr. 16, 2009 Sup. Ct. Del. 2009).
148. *Revlon, Inc. v. MacAndrews & Forbes Holdings*, 506 A. 2d 173 (Del. Sup. Ct., 1986).
149. See, e.g., *Unitrim Inc. v. American General*, 651 A.2d 1361 (Del. Sup., 1995); *Paramount v. QVC.*, 637 A.2d 34 (De. Sup. 1994); *Omnicare Inc. NCS Healthcare*, 818 A.2d 914 (Del. Sup. 2003) *Lyondell Chemical v. Ryan*, Del. Sup. Ct., Apr. 16, 2009); *Gantler v. Stephens*, 965 A.2d

Under Delaware law the purpose of a takeover defense mechanism is to prevent harm to the corporation and the shareholders and to maximize the value of any takeover price so as to benefit shareholders. In *Unocal* the Delaware Court noted that one purpose of the takeover defense in that case was to protect the corporation from the threat of greenmail—the payment of a premium price to a single shareholder not shared with other shareholders in order to get the shareholder to sell its shares and thus withdraw the hostile takeover bid.

There is evidence that United States companies are less likely to have takeover defense mechanisms in place today than they were 10 years ago and evidence that when utilized takeover defenses in the U.S. typically do not defeat takeovers but result in greater recovery for the selling shareholders.

[2] Takeover Defenses in Japanese Law

There appears to be a divide between METI, whose goal appears to be to more closely follow the Delaware takeover defense model and recognizes the duty of the board to become informed about the takeover proposal and take a proactive role in advising shareholders as well as the purpose of defense mechanisms to benefit shareholders and that hostile takeovers may serve a valid governance function, and the Judicial Branch, whose goal is as yet unclear but appears to favor an approach that leaves it to shareholders (with no or little responsibility on the board to become educated about the takeover bid or to educate the shareholders) to decide how to defend against a hostile takeover, at least when the takeover defense prevents a foreign entity from acquiring a Japanese firm.

[a] Early "Hostile Actions" by Foreign Funds

In 2003 Steel Partners, an American hedge fund that has been active in acquiring positions in Japanese companies and has taken steps to unlock stockholder value in such companies through hostile moves, made a tender offer for a Japanese company in which it held a significant but clearly minority position. The target company held large reserves and paid an annual dividend of JPN 14 per annum. To fend off the hostile move by Steel Partners the target raised its dividend to JPN 200 per annum. This drove up the price of the stock and the takeover failed but Steel Partners and all other shareholders received a significantly higher dividend and a higher share price when they sold out their position. Having once succeeded in raising stock price and return to shareholders (including itself) Steel Partners made a hostile tender bid for the shares of another company similarly situated. The target followed the same script with the same

695 (Del. Sup. Ct. 2009). Poison pills are a form of takeover defense that may be used consistent with the basic idea that their use is designed for the benefit of the company and its shareholders. *Moran v. Household International*, 500 A.2d 1346 (De. Sup., 1985). *Moran*, like *Unocal* and *Revlon* has spawned its own jurisprudence concerning use of poison pills and restrictions.

result. After the takeover threat went away the increased dividend was brought back down. Presumably the share price also came down to reflect the new (old) reality.

[b] Livedoor and Nippon Broadcasting System (NBS)

The *Livedoor/Nippon Broadcasting System (NBS)* case never reached the Supreme Court nor was it the first case to involve the question of whether an issuance of shares for a price lower than market was allowable in a hostile takeover scenario. Under the Companies Law (and before that the Commercial Code) a company can issue new shares in order to raise needed funds and may also determine whether to solicit the purchase of those shares from existing shareholders (pre-emptive rights) or to seek funds from a third party. The board may have an obligation to explain its actions if the price per share is less than market value (after consideration of dilution).[150] An existing shareholder may sue to prevent the issuance of the new shares if issuance is inconsistent with existing law or if the issue price is considered significantly unfair to the company or if the issuance is otherwise very unfair.[151] If a company issues shares at an extremely low price and the purpose of the issuance is to keep the current management in office by diluting the ownership of an objecting shareholder, then issuance can be considered as being extremely unfair and can be enjoined by a court. If directors have a good business reason for the issuance, such as to raise capital or bind a new business relationship or to create a joint venture that is deemed to be profitable, then the issuance may be accepted by the court and the new shares may be issued.

In the 1980s a "primary purpose" test was adopted by courts to deal with the issuance of new shares to friendly shareholders to fend off a potential hostile threat to management.[152] If the primary purpose of the issuance was to raise capital then the issuance was permissible even if it had the effect of shielding incumbent management from a threat; if the primary purpose was to perpetuate management in office then the issuance was not permissible. The *Livedoor* case may be explained as a case where management could not show that its primary purpose was acceptable indeed, the facts of the case indicate that the only purpose of management in issuing warrants for additional stock (fully 140% more stock) was to perpetuate itself.

Livedoor was an upstart Internet company begun by a young Tokyo University dropout who had created a significant Internet player. NBS was an established media company that was part of a family of companies including Fuji Television (Fuji TV). Livedoor seeing an opportunity to take advantage of the complicated cross ownership between NBS and Fuji TV and a gap in the securities laws surreptitiously purchased a large block of NBS shares through an after-hours trading network run by the Tokyo

150. See, e.g., Companies Law Article 199.
151. Companies Law Article 210.
152. See, Minoru Tokumoto, *The role of the Japanese Courts in Hostile Takeovers*, 27 L. Japan 1 (2001) as pointed out the Japanese courts did not view the issue from the perspective of a hostile takeover defense but rather as a Commercial Code issue regarding the proper issuance of shares. (pages 4–5).

Stock Exchange and through the purchase acquired a significant interest in NBS.[153] It then sought to acquire control over the Fuji TV group and launched what NBS considered a hostile takeover. Management adopted a stock warrants program under which Fuji TV (its affiliate) would be granted warrants (at no cost) for stock in the parent NBS and through exercise of the warrants would sufficiently dilute Livedoor's holdings so that the hostile effort would fail. Livedoor sued. Both the District Court and Tokyo High Court ruled in Livedoor's favor. The court found that the effort by NBS was designed solely to preserve the position of the entrenched management of NBS and had no beneficial corporate or shareholder purpose.[154] The Tokyo High Court also held that a company could adopt a takeover defense to protect itself against an "abusive acquirer," that was defined as, for example, (a) a "greenmailer," (b) a company engaged in a "scorched earth" policy whereby core assets of the target would be sold for the benefit of the acquirer, (c) a "leveraged buyout" whereby the acquirer would use the target's assets to pay for the purchase, and (d) assets would be used by the acquirer for "price manipulation" or to declare dividends benefiting the acquirer. NBS and Livedoor eventually settled—but only after NBS continued defensive action by "leasing" away voting rights that Livedoor thought that it had acquired as a consequence of the complicated relationship between Fuji TV and NBS. Under the terms of the settlement Livedoor did not obtain control—NBS purchased a large stake in Livedoor and paid Livedoor a profit for the shares.

The Livedoor/NBS/Fuji TV contest was a major news story in Japan. Livedoor's non-conformist founder/major shareholder was a media sensation and ran (unsuccessfully) for the Diet after Prime Minister Koizumi dissolved the Lower House after losing the vote for his Postal Service Reform proposal in the Upper House. Livedoor's attempt to take control of an old established conforming Japanese entity excited the bureaucracy's interest differently. The Finance Ministry opposed the effort to take over NBS; conservative politicians in the LDP objected. The fact that Livedoor had apparently acted either in concert with or was sharing information with a Japanese fund that was seen variously as a corporate green mailer or a corporate shareholder advocate that had

153. At the time, although the Securities Laws required a mandatory tender offer for an acquirer that acquired a 1/3 or more interest in the target, the law contained an exemption for shares acquired on an Exchange. There existed a question as to whether Livedoor was covered by the exemption and whether purchases through the trading network were an exchange purchase. In 2006 legislation (Act No. 65 of 2006 and Act No. 66 of 2006) resolved the question by covering all acquisitions of over 1/3 whether through an exchange or otherwise. The Law also applies to the acquisition of more than a 10% interest in a company during a three month period and prohibits the acquisition of more than 10% of shares in a seven day period. The new Financial Instruments and Exchange Law also extends the Tender Offer Period from 20 to 60 calendar days to 20 to 60 business days, allows the tendering party to withdraw the tender if the target exercises a takeover defense mechanism, and requires the offeror to purchase all shares tendered if it acquires more than a 2/3 interest in the target. Financial Services Agency Newsletter, November 2006, http://www.fsa.go.jp/en/newsletter/2006/11b.html. The 2/3 "watermark" is significant because under the Companies Law certain significant corporate actions require an affirmative vote of 2/3 of the voting shares. Since an acquirer of 2/3 can achieve this level on its own (and force out the minority) it was considered appropriate to allow the minority 1/3 shareholders to sell out as part of the Tender Offer process.

154. *Livedoor High Court Case*, Case No. 429 (ra) of 2005, Tokyo High Court, Mar. 23, 2005, Hanrei Jiho No. 1899.

bought NBS shares and threatened to vote for Livedoor's takeover further riled the establishment. A criminal investigation followed. Both Livedoor's founder and the founder of the fund were indicted and convicted. Both were given criminal sentences that were not suspended (in *Livedoor's* case two and a half years and in the fund manager's case two years). On appeal the fund manager's sentence was suspended.[155] The prison term for Livedoor's founder and the fund manager's conviction were affirmed by the Supreme Court.[156] Livedoor's founder was ordered to pay damages in excess of JPY 7 billion in a civil suit brought by investors in Livedoor.[157] Livedoor was ruined, its founder was ruined, the fund dissolved and its founder was financially ruined. NBS emerged unscathed with its conservative management intact.

Activities such as those by Steel Partners and Livedoor had been taken without any significant government guidance as to what board action to defend against hostile takeover activity was and what was not permitted. To bring order to the hostile takeover field, METI (and the Ministry of Justice) devised takeover guidelines in 2005 that were designed to provide companies with a roadmap for appropriate defenses that could be put in place *prior* to a hostile offer. These guidelines appear to track Delaware law in allowing takeover defenses and also in rejecting efforts by management to perpetuate itself in office. The METI guidelines are based on three principles: (a) protecting corporate value for the shareholders rather than protecting corporate management; (b) informing shareholders of plans and taking the shareholder's consensus into account; and (c) the measures should be necessary and reasonable to protect corporate value. In addition METI adopted the Delaware Law's approach of giving weight to the opinion of "independent directors" and outside experts as to the need to utilize and the appropriateness of a takeover defense measure. But the METI guides of 2005 were carefully worded so that corporate value was defined broader than simply shareholder value and included matters that contribute to the interests of shareholders so that matters other than simply direct shareholder interests may be a proper reason for a defense.[158] Many companies took advantage of the one year grace period before the triangular merger provisions of Japanese Law went into effect and put in place takeover defense plans. Another 200 companies passed plans at their June 2007 annual meeting.[159] More have done so since the *Steel Partners/Bull Dog* litigation referred to below. Unlike Delaware plans that generally have had the effect of

155. *Japan: Fund Manager Convicted of Insider Trading, but Prison Sentence Suspended*, Securities Docket, (Feb. 9, 2009), http://www.securitiesdocket.com/2009/02/09/japan-fund-manager-convicted-of-insider-trading-but-prison-sentence-suspended/; Setsuko Kamiya, *Muakami's Sentence Suspended*, Japan Times, (Feb. 4, 2009); http://search.japantimes.co.jp/cgi-bin/nn20090204a1.html.
156. Kyodo News, *Inside trader's appeal rejected*, Japan Times (June 9, 2011), http://search.japantimes.co.jp/cgi-bin/nn20110609b1.html.
157. *Japan's ex-IT mogul told to pay damages in Livedoor scam*, Physorg.com (May 21, 2009), http://www.physorg.com/news162107752.html; Kyodo News, *Shareholders win suit for Livedoor damages*, Japan Times (May 22, 2009), http://search.japantimes.co.jp/cgi-bin/nn20090522a5.html.
158. Guidelines Regarding Takeover Defense for the Purposes of Protection and Enhancement of Corporate Value and Shareholders' Common Interests, May 27, 2005.
159. Hugh Patrick, *Japan's Economy: The Idiosyncratic Recovery Continues, Center on Japanese Economy and Business Working Paper Series* (Columbia University August 2007).

increasing the cost of a takeover thereby benefiting shareholders, Japanese plans appear to have had the effect of perpetuating management, even at a significant cost to shareholders. It appears that those worried that the effect of the new legislation would lead to American acquisition of Japanese entities need not have worried.[160]

[c] Steel Partners and Bull Dog[161]

Livedoor's success in the courts is to be compared with the effort of Steel Partners (an American investment fund) to launch a hostile takeover of the Bull Dog sauce company. Steel Partners sought to buy control of Bull Dog, a condiment and sauce company. Bull Dog resisted and *after* the hostile attempt was started put in place a takeover defense that was overwhelmingly approved by shareholders at the company's annual meeting. The purpose of the plan was to thwart Steel Partners by diluting Steel Partners' ownership interest through purchase of most of Steel Partners' shares at a significant premium to the pre-tender offer market price. Notwithstanding that the price offered for the stock by Steel Partners contained a very significant premium over market and represented something more than three times Bull Dog's prior year earnings the shareholders overwhelming approved the takeover defense plan.

Unlike *Livedoor/Fuji TV*, in *Bull Dog* the defense was not instituted by board action but was instituted through a resolution of the shareholders at the company's annual meeting, whose timing came soon after the hostile bid by Steel Partners. This is a significant difference and may have significant effect on the development of hostile takeover defense law and serves to distinguish the *Bull-Dog* case from the *Livedoor* case. Incumbent management proposed the plan to the shareholders. This raises the question of what is the appropriate level of review to be undertaken by the court of such an incumbent management referral. This issue was not discussed in the decision in the *Steel Partners/Bull Dog* case.

Under the plan Steel Partner would receive cash from Bull Dog while other shareholders received additional stock thereby diluting its interest from 10% to approximately 3%. The cash price was determined by using the price that Steel Partners had initially offered to pay shareholders in its hostile offer. Steel Partners sued. The Tokyo District and High Courts ruled in Bull Dog's favor. The District Court's decision was primarily based on the fact that the takeover defense was adopted by the general shareholders' meeting and placed reliance on the principle that it is the shareholders who should decide the fate of the company. The High Court found that the hostile bid met its test for an "abusive acquisition" set out in the *Livedoor* case.

In finding the actions of Steel Partners abusive the High Court did not focus on any specific act but rather characterized Steel Partners as not interested in long-term

160. At the end of 2010 Steel Partners sold off its interest in Japanese brewer Sapporo after it failed to change the management of the company. See, James Simms, *Steel Partners' Early Sapporo Gift*, Wall Street Journal, Heard on the Street (Dec. 19, 2010), http://online.wsj.com/article/SB10001424052748704034804576025093638774576.html.
161. *Steel Partners/Bull Dog case*, case No. 2007 (Kyo) No.30, Minshu Vol. 61 No.5, http://www.courts.go.jp/english/judgments/text/2007.08.07-2007.-Kyo-.No.30.html, (P.B., Aug. 7, 2007).

gains but in short and medium term returns to shareholders and specifically that as a fund Steel Partners had a fiduciary duty *to its* shareholders or fund members to *maximize its* profits. While characterized as abusive the actions of Steel Partners appear to be quite normal for a hostile takeover and reflect the general notion that shareholders are entitled to maximize their investment returns. It would appear that the High Court viewed Steel Partners' takeover bid with disfavor in part because Steel Partners had failed to give the Bull Dog Board a business plan that would disclose Steel Partners' plans to revitalize the company and increase profits. Such failure likely raised suspicion by both the Bull Dog shareholders and the High Court that Steel Partners had "abusive" plans for the company if it succeeded in its takeover bid. Steel Partners appealed to the Supreme Court, which affirmed but on grounds different from the High Court and closer to the District Court.[162]

The Supreme Court held that the obligation to treat all stockholders of the same class equally does not apply when there is a possibility that the acts of a stockholder will result in the demise of the company or adversely affect company values so as to affect negatively the company's future—such as through the hostile takeover that Steel Partners had launched. The Supreme Court did not discuss the significant premium that was contained in the Steel Partners bid nor did it consider whether the directors might have negotiated with Steel Partners or some third party to increase the tender offer price. Most notably *the court did not consider whether the board's recommended takeover defense would adversely affect shareholder values and negatively affect the future prospects of Bull Dog.* A payment to buy out a single 10% shareholder for three to four times the company's last year's profits might have raised some concern that the best interests of the shareholders were not served by the takeover defense.

The Supreme Court held that where the value of the company or the profits of the company are endangered by a hostile takeover bid the company can respond in a manner that treats the hostile bidder differently from other shareholders in an effort to protect corporate value and profits. The hostile bidder in such a situation must however be treated fairly and reasonably. But how did these factors play into Steel Partners' bid? The Court appears to not have directly answered that question—rather it found the following factors determinative: (a) Steel Partners was getting proper value (the price was based on Steel Partner's tender price) even if it was not getting shares like the other shareholders, (b) the poison pill had been placed before the shareholders and they had overwhelmingly approved the pill, and (c) Steel Partners had been given an opportunity to be heard on its plan by the other shareholders in the company. [The Court's approach is quite different from the Guidelines approach. For example, there is no discussion of or exploration of the obligation of the directors to see if a deal could be structured that would increase shareholder value, there is no discussion or consideration of the question of how to unlock shareholder value or whether the defensive measures were in fact necessary or proportional to the threat.] The Supreme Court specifically failed to comment on the harsh language the High Court had used in describing the efforts of Steel Partners as abusive leaving open the possibility that it

162. For a discussion of the three court decisions see, Sadakazu Osaki, *The Bull-Dog Sauce Takeover Defense*, 10 Nomura Capital Mkt. Rev. No. 3.

agreed that maximizing medium term profits over long-term profits and generating returns for shareholders over other values is "abusive."

The Supreme Court opinion appears to be primarily based on the overwhelming vote (more than 80%, which constitutes more than 90% of all shareholders except Steel Partners which owned over 10%) that the poison pill plan received at the annual meeting. While on its face a clear victory for corporate democracy by allowing the shareholders to determine whether to put the defense in place, the decision raises corporate democracy questions.[163]

First, if the matter is to be left to shareholders, then a vote on the tender offer would likely achieve the same result, namely rejection of the tender offer, and by a more appropriate shareholder body. Because of the time lag between the recording date for shareholder eligibility to vote and the date of the actual vote, it is possible that many shareholders who voted might have sold out when shares in Bull Dog rose as a consequence of the announcement of the hostile offer. Having reaped their profit, these former shareholders might vote against the takeover for reasons unrelated to corporate democracy, including the desire to see the tender defeated so that they could buy back in once the share price declined to levels before the offer (and indeed lower than the pre-offer price since the windfall payment to Steel Partners to defeat their bid would cause, and in fact did cause the shares to decline below the pre-offer price). Leaving determination of the tender to those shareholders who could tender, namely present shareholders might well be more democratic. Indeed shareholders who purchased Bull Dog shares between the date of the announced tender and the date of the annual meeting in anticipation of the tender premium were unable to vote at the annual meeting. In addition if Bull Dog had unit shares smaller shareholders would not have been permitted to vote at the meeting.

Second, the approval of Bull Dog's post-offer actions could be viewed as support for legalized greenmail. In effect, the company simply bought out Steel Partners' position (or most of its position) at a price well above the market price. In essence Steel

163. The Supreme Court's reliance on shareholder vote in *Steel Partners/Bull Dog* in not unique. Rather the Supreme Court has also placed great reliance on shareholder votes in cases involving a "friendly merger." Under the Companies Act (Article 806) a dissenting stockholder in a company being merged or consolidated into a new company may demand a buy out of its shares at a "fair price." To determine price, one factor to be considered is the ratio at which shares of the merging companies were converted into shares of the new company. This share ratio is agreed to by vote at the shareholders meetings approving the consolidation. When a dissenting shareholder objected the Court determined, in a case where there was no synergy that added extra value to shares of the newly consolidated company and no prior shareholding relationship between the merging companies, both that a) the starting point (and unless there were unusual factors the ending point) in determining fair value was the market price of the shares (although as the concurring opinion points out the market participants may have incomplete information as to the true or objective value of the shares) and b) that the share ratio agreed to by the shareholders after receiving adequate information from the company was, except for unusual circumstances, to be respected because it was an objective decision of the shareholders as to the proper ratio. The Supreme Court also assumes that the Directors of the company acted in the interests of their shareholders. *Fair Price Determination in Corporate Consolidation Case,* Case Number 2011 (Kyo) No. 21 and No. 22, Minshu Vol. 66, No. 2 (Sup. Ct., 2nd Petty Bench, Feb. 29, 2012). http://www.courts.go.jp/english/judgments/text/2012.02.29-2011.-Kyo-.No..21.and.No..22.html.

Partners received what a green mailer might have hoped to receive. The District Court conclusion that greenmail was not involved because Steel Partners did not intend to sell back its shares to Bull Dog shows that Steel Partners was not a greenmailer. But this misses the point. Greenmail is greenmail whether sought by the hostile bidder or forced on the hostile bidder by the incumbent board and/or a majority of the shareholders through the takeover defense. Presumably the Supreme Court was not concerned about whether the defensive measure was fair to the shareholders other than Steel Partners since such holders had overwhelming voted for the defense and thus had no complaint. It may be that the Supreme Court, aware that greenmail has been used in the past to ward off hostile stockholders, simply has accepted the practice and thus felt no need to comment about it.[164]

Third, the plan deprived non-approving shareholders of the ability to sell their shares to Steel Partners at a premium price. Why are those who object not entitled to have the board provide all shareholders with an objective analysis of whether the defense or the bid is in the best interest of shareholders? Years after the takeover was defeated, Bull Dog stock had not achieved the market value it had prior to the initial Steel Partners offer taking into account the dilution of the shares through the four for one stock split. Of course, if sufficient shareholders had rejected the Steel Partners tender without a takeover defense put in place the objecting shareholders could not complain—but so too they would not have to suffer the loss occasioned by the payment of a premium to Steel Partners.[165] It may well be that the real basis for the Supreme Court's decision in *Steel Partners/Bull Dog* is the Court's application of a communitarian philosophy of law under which the view of the community of shareholders (even if not unanimous) binds the few "out of step" members of the community who object to the generally accepted view of the community and thus overrides their assertion of "rights."[166]

Question exists as to whether Steel Partners was a potential abusive acquirer, as found by the High Court, or a maximizer of corporate values by seeking to replace what might have been incompetent management while maximizing profits for shareholders through payment of the market price plus a significant premium. The Supreme Court appears convinced—based on what evidence and what arguments we are only to guess—that the takeover defense, which had been devised by and suggested by incumbent management, was not intended to perpetuate in office the current entrenched management. Considering the high premium paid to Steel Partners and the

164. For the view that green mail was used extensively in the past see, Dan W. Puchniak, *Delusions of Hostility: The Marginal Role of Hostile Takeovers in Japanese Corporate Governance Remains Unchanged*, ZJAPANR / J.JAPAN.L, Nr. / No. 28 89 at p. 96 (2009), http://sydney.edu.au/law/anjel/documents/2010/DelusionsofHostility.pdf.

165. Delaware Law contains a doctrine of shareholder approval as ratifying acts of directors. However, such doctrine only applies to situations where shareholder approval of the so-called ratified act is not statutorily required. A change in the certificate of incorporation, the action taken by the shareholders in the *Steel Partners/Bulldog case* requires shareholder approval. *Gantler v. Stephens,* 965 A. 2d 695 (Del. Sup. Ct. 2009).

166. Communitarianism and Japanese Law is discussed in greater detail in Chapter 18.

failure of Bull Dog several years later to achieve a stock value of even 50% of what it paid to Steel Partners[167] this conclusion is questionable.

[3] The Lack of "Equity" Jurisdiction and "Equity" Rules in Japan

The Delaware law applicable to duties as well as the "fiduciary" responsibilities of corporate directors has been created in the Chancery Court of Delaware and upon appeal to the unified Supreme Court of Delaware. The Chancery Court has "equity" jurisdiction and directors of corporations owe an equity duty as fiduciaries to the stockholders of the corporation. The significance of the law of equity on corporate directors' actions was highlighted in the Delaware Supreme Court's decision in *Schnell v. Chris-Craft*[168] in which the court enjoined the advancement of the date of the corporation's annual meeting notwithstanding the directors acted lawfully, they acted in violation of equity. Directors' equitable fiduciary duties include the duty of care and the duty of loyalty referred to above in the subsection on Delaware law.

Japanese law is based on Civil Law that has no division between "Law" and "Equity." As a consequence, while Japanese company directors owe a *form* of fiduciary duty of care to the company based on the Civil Code, significant question exists as to whether the directors of a Japanese company owe the equivalent of an American fiduciary type duty of care and a duty of loyalty to shareholders. This distinction between legal systems and legal concepts may explain why the decisions in cases such as *Livedoor* and *Steel Partners/Bull Dog* do not encompass the ideas that would be uppermost in the mind of American lawyers and would form the basis for the decisions of Delaware courts dealing with cases alleging director misconduct by breach of fiduciary duties to shareholders. While many younger Japanese law professors and some younger judges are advocating that American style fiduciary duties should be placed on directors of Japanese companies it is not clear that either the Supreme Court or the legal community in general is prepared to take that step.[169]

As a consequence of the lack of "equity jurisprudence" decisions such as *Livedoor* and *Bull Dog* focus on the legal (i.e., Companies Law and/or Civil Code) rights of the parties to the litigation. In *Bull Dog* that means whether Steel Partners was treated in accord with the Companies Law but does not include whether shareholders were treated fairly by the directors when the directors recommended the Certificate of Incorporation amendment adopting the takeover defense. Under the Companies Law a shareholder (including Steel Partners) is entitled to equal treatment with other shareholders of the same class and a shareholder may seek an injunction to prevent

167. http://www.reuters.com/finance/stocks/keyDevelopments?rpc=66&symbol=2804.T&timestamp=20080515020000, last accessed Sept. 16, 2012.
168. *Schnell v. Chris-Craft Industries*, 285 A2d 437 (Sup. Ct. Del., 1971).
169. See, Minoru Tokumoto, *The Role of the Japanese Courts in Hostile Takeovers*, 27 L. Japan 1 (2001) noting that Japanese scholars had argued that the issue of conflict of interest and burden of proof were issues that should have been considered by Japanese courts that adopted the primary purpose test in the 1980s. Thus the issue of potential conflict of interest and thus burden of proof—the linchpins of *Unocal*—were not unknown when the Supreme court rendered its *Steel Partners/Bulldog case* decision.

directors from issuing shares if the issuance violates law or is unfair. Thus the Court in *Steel Partners v. Bull Dog* is required to deal with these "legal" questions but not equitable fiduciary duty questions and concepts. Since the duty of loyalty found in Delaware equity jurisprudence is not a part of the Companies Law,[170] there is no discussion of that duty in the court's decision. The court in Japan is concerned with whether directors are acting in the interests of the company and less interested in whether they are acting in the interests of the shareholders there can be a difference between the two, especially in the context of a Japanese company where interests of stakeholders other than shareholders may predominate; where stakeholders are also directors; and where non-economic considerations may play a role not implicated in either American corporate governance or American corporate law.

[4] METI Reaction to Recent Events

METI's guidelines had adopted a Delaware style approach to hostile takeover defenses.[171] That was not the approach taken in either the *Livedoor* or *Steel Partners/Bull Dog* cases. METI saw the *Bull Dog* case as a potentially damaging precedent that could adversely affect capital inflows. METI convened a study group to consider takeover defenses—the Corporate Governance Study Group that rendered reports in 2008 dealing with corporate value and hostile takeover defense measures and a final report in 2009 dealing with independent directors.

In its Report of June 2008[172] the Study Group recognized the appropriateness of poison pills adopted after a hostile tender offer had been made and gave greater weight to shareholder rather than board of directors adoption of a poison pill than did the original 2005 Guidelines. But the Report also rejected the idea that it was appropriate to pay hostile bidder compensation for withdrawing its offer or for rejection of its bid. Greenmail or the potential for greenmail was rejected. The Report rejected the approach taken in the Bull Dog takeover defense.

The 2008 Corporate Value Report places on directors the responsibility of dealing with a hostile takeover in a manner that while it may not replace the American notion of enhancing shareholder value recognizes the common interests of the shareholders. The directors have a responsibility to guide shareholders and cannot simply leave the ultimate decision to the shareholders meeting without significant and fair input by the

170. Of course, under the Companies Law Directors owe many loyalty duties to the Corporation—such as the duty not to compete with the company or take for themselves a corporate opportunity. And the general Civil Code requirements of fair dealing and not abusing power apply to corporate directors. But to date this is different from an adoption of the elastic and flexible equity jurisprudence that underlies the Delaware cases and the American Directors' fiduciary duty to shareholders.

171. For a discussion of the case law in Delaware and its parallel in the METI Guidelines see, Jacobs, *Implementing Japan's New Anti-Takeover Defense Guidelines Part I Some Lessons from Delaware's Experience*, 2 NYU J. L. & Bus. 323 (2006).

172. http://www.meti.go.jp/english/report/data/080630TakeoverDefenseMeasures.pdf, last accessed Sept. 16, 2012.

directors.[173] Again, the Report departs from the decision of the Supreme Court in Steel *Partners/Bull Dog*. While the Court focused on fairness to the hostile bidder, METI focused on the duty of directors to all shareholders, including and most importantly holders other than the hostile bidder. It seems clear that it is the intent of the Report to moderate the Supreme Court's approach and to place greater responsibility on the directors when a hostile bid has been made and to avoid the payment of what might be viewed as greenmail, whether consistent with the Supreme Court's *Bull Dog* decision or otherwise.

The 2008 report sees hostile takeovers as potentially useful in disciplining boards of directors and places great weight on enhancing shareholder values while reducing (but not completely rejecting) concerns for other stakeholders in the company. METI favors requiring directors who have received a bid critically analyze it and if it has potential to benefit shareholders to negotiate to get the best price for shareholders.[174] BUT, it is a Report not a legislative measure and does not have the force and effect of law. Nonetheless, it is both likely to have some effect on corporate as well as judicial action as relates to takeover defenses and unlikely to stop both the return to more extensive use of cross-shareholdings to protect against hostile takeover bids and the use of other tactics by entrenched management to ward off hostile bids.[175]

[K] What You See May Not Be What You Get in the Corporate Governance / Takeover Defense Area

What you see may not be what you get in the hostile takeover/poison pill area. The corporate law has been amended to permit both cash out mergers and triangular mergers—both mechanisms that should make it easier for parties to engage in hostile takeover activity. Hostile takeovers are recognized as a method for requiring managers to act in the shareholder's interests (although there is controversy as to whether corporate governance (except for information flow and transparency) has any effect on

173. This approach is consistent with the 2006 Financial Instruments and Exchange Law which places a responsibility on the company to make a "position statement report" on a potential acquisition. See, FSA Newsletter, November 2006, http://www.fsa.go.jp/en/newsletter/2006/11b.html.

174. It has been said that the original purpose of "poison pills" was to give Boards sufficient time to enable Boards and shareholders to analyze the offer and make a reasoned s\decision—not to entrench management or reject out of hand all takeover attempts. See, *Poison Pills in France, Japan, the U.S. and Canada* 13 Institutional Shareholder Services (2007), http://www.complianceweek.com/s/documents/PoisonPillPrimer.pdf. METI's approach appears to be to carry out this objective.

175. See, e.g., Press Release from Steel Partners, http://www.spjsf.jp/pdf/080708-sapporo_e.pdf. For a discussion of the Corporate Value Report see, e.g., *Recent Developments in Takeover Defense Discussions in Japan*, Jones Day, September 2008, http://www.jonesday.com/newsknowledge/publicationdetail.aspx?publication=5461; Shintaro Takai, *Hostile Takeover Defensive Measures*, IFLR Global Practice Service (Dec. 1, 2008), http://www.iflr.com/Article/2075192/Hostile-takeover-defensive-measures.html; Luke Nottage, *The Politics of Japan's New Takeovers Guidelines* East Asia Forum, Aug. 31, 2008, http://www.eastasiaforum.org/2008/08/31/the-politics -of-japans-new-takeovers-guidelines/, last accessed Sept. 16, 2012.

company performance.[176] The law permits takeover defenses adopted by shareholder vote prior to the commencement of a hostile takeover. The corporate law requires equality of shareholders as a general matter. Actions by a board that are designed to keep entrenched management in place in face of a hostile takeover are not permitted and are abusive tactics by management. Yet hostile takeovers, whether by foreign or domestic companies are virtually always defeated by management[177] although in 2008 Steel Partners was able to oust the management of Aderans (a wig maker) and in 2009 was able to elect a majority of the Board of Directors of Aderans, over the objection of a domestic Japanese buy-out fund[178] but has been unable to bring Aderans into profitability. On the other hand, friendly mergers, management buy outs and friendly cross-shareholding arrangements (typically among Japanese companies) are on the rise in Japan.[179] Management is required to pay a fair price for the shares in a buyout as shareholders are entitled to fair compensation.[180] METI has issued Guidelines concerning MBO pricing that requires management to give shareholders sufficient information for them to make an informed decision as to the proposed buyout. In addition management must provide shareholders a third party valuation report.

The *Bull Dog* decision has likely strengthened managements' desire to have a stable group of long-term, related shareholders, to protect the company from hostile "outsiders," i.e., friendly cross-shareholdings.[181]

176. See, e.g., Sanford M. Jacoby, *Foreign Investors and Corporate*, in *Corporate Governance and Managerial Reform in Japan* at fn. 4, 99–100, and 120–121 (Whittaker and Deakin ed., Oxford University Press 2009).

177. Takahiko Hyuga, *DaVinci Drops Takeover Attempt in Japan*, International Herald Tribune, Bloomberg News (July 24, 2007); Oji Paper puts Hokuetsu tender to rest, *Failure of takeover bid could prompt a shakeout in the industry*, International Herald Tribune (Aug. 29, 2006).

178. Tomoko Yamazaki & Akiko Ikeda, *Aderans, Citizen Jump After Steel Partners-Led Revolt* (Update3), Bloomberg.com (May 30, 2008), http://www.bloomberg.com/apps/news?pid=20601101&sid=abYFrvQsLmGQ; Tomoko Yamazaki and Komaki Ito, *Steel Partners Wins Aderans Board Vote*, Blocking Bid, Bloomberg.com, May 28, 2009, http://www.bloomberg.com/apps/news?pid=20601101&sid=a2mT3zJULeoA&refer=japan; Junko Fujita, *Aderans shareholders back Steel board proposal*, Rueters (May 28, 2009), http://www.forbes.com/feeds/afx/2009/05/28/afx6473639.html.

179. See, Dan W. Puchniak, *Delusions of Hostility: The Marginal Role of Hostile Takeovers in Japanese Corporate Governance Remains Unchanged*, http://www.law.usyd.edu.au/anjel/documents/2010/DelusionsofHostility.pdf; Dan W. Puchniak, *The Efficiency of Friendliness: Japanese Corporate Governance Succeeds without Hostile Takeovers*, 5 Berkeley Bus. L.J. 195 (2008).

180. Supreme Court of Japan decision of May 29, 2009 in case involving buy out of minority shares in Rex Holdings. In the *Rex Holdings case* the management changed accounting practices and consequently wrote down forecast earnings prior to the squeeze out offer. This resulted in a decline in the share price. The Court required that rather than using the price at or about the time of the squeeze out offer, management should be required to use a price based on the average share price for the six month period prior to the offer plus a premium. Since Rex Guidelines issued by METI's Corporate Value Study Group have been amended to take account of the decision and to protect shareholders from the inherent conflict of interest involved when management is making a buyout of shareholders.

181. See, Curtiss J. Milhaupt, *Bull-Dog Sauce for the Japanese Soul? Courts, Corporations, and Communities - A Comment on Haley's View of Japanese Law*, 8 Wash. U. Global Stud. L. Rev. 345 (2009), http://law.wustl.edu/WUGSLR/Issues/Volume8_2/milhaupt.pdf.;see also, Zenichi Shishido, Changes in Japanese Corporate Law and Governance: Revisiting the Convergence Debate, UC Berkeley, Berkeley Program in Law and Economics 10 (2004)(reporting on the use

The Japanese FTC has adopted new guidelines making it easier for Japanese companies to merge by changing the market share criteria from a domestic Japanese market to a worldwide market.[182] Where the parent of the surviving company in a triangular merger is non-Japanese the Financial Products and Exchange Law requires (assuming certain financial thresholds are met) a registration statement be filed prior to the merger as the delivery of the shares is to be treated as if it were a sale of securities. And, the non-Japanese company will be subjected to continuous reporting requirements because shares will have been delivered to Japanese shareholders.[183] These provisions are justified on the theory that they are needed to protect Japanese shareholders who do not need such protections when the parent of the survivor is Japanese because they already have similar protections under Japanese law. The requirements create additional burden for a non-Japanese company that wishes to acquire a Japanese entity through a triangular merger.

Japan's new corporate law was designed to permit a more Americanized system for corporate management—BUT unlike American corporate law Japanese firms utilizing the new committee system need not engage "independent directors," it is sufficient if "outside directors" are used. And, other typical mechanisms that U.S. law uses to check management—threat of derivative litigation and hostile takeovers that displace management—appear as very weak reeds in the arsenal of corporate reformers.

Why then do some in Japan see hostile takeovers by American firms as a threat?[184] The answer may lie in corporate culture. The American takeover company sees values for shareholders that are not realized—the focus is on value and shareholders. But Japan's corporations have other stakeholders, one of the most important of which is the lifetime employees.[185] In Japan the entrenched management represents the employees of the company—past, present and future[186] (shades of the family *Ie*)—and by staying in place it preserves the lifetime employment system. Holding on to earnings so that in bad days the company can retain its core work staff rather than declaring a large dividend may not be in the best interests of the current shareholders but it does protect other stakeholders. The problem with adopting the American

of stock buy back plans to purchase shares that were held by friendly shareholders who are compelled by economic circumstances to sell their shares) http://www.escholarship.org/uc/item/9376480h;jsessionid=213FE3E5671FC9174D0C82BAD1ED9D93.

182. *FTC to Ease Rules to Spur Mergers*, Japan Times (Feb. 1, 2007); see also, Kyodo News, *Mitsukoshi Isetan Shareholders OK Megamerger*, Japan Times (Nov. 21, 2007).

183. *FTC to Ease Rules to Spur Mergers*, Japan Times (Feb. 1, 2007); see also, *Mitsukoshi Isetan Shareholders OK Megamerger*, Japan Times, Kyodo News, 21 November 2007.

184. Kaho Shimizu, *Move on Sapporo Double-Edged, Steel Partners—Foreign Raider or Catalyst for Shakeup?*, The Japan Times (Feb. 27, 2007).

185. See, e.g., William Sun, Jim Stewart and David Pollard, *Corporate Governance and the Global Financial Crisis International Perspectives* 11 (Cambridge University Press 2011).

186. See Takashi Araki, *Changing Employment Practices, Corporate Governance, and the Role of Labor Law in Japan*, 28 Comp. Lab. L. & Policy J. 251, 270 (2007) disclosing that 28% of top management in companies surveyed had not only been members of the company's union but had been leaders of the union. As Araki notes labor relations in Japan are essentially a discussion between present and former union leaders.

approach is that it fails to take into consideration the Japanese culture and values.[187] The result is, of course, that while on paper the approach may look like the American corporate law what you get is something quite different. Indeed serious question exists as to why recent stockholders such as American funds that bought into Japanese companies during and after the "lost decade" of the 1990s are "entitled" to the cash hordes built up over years of reduced dividends by stakeholders such as cross-shareholding business partners and employees who accepted reduced wages or bonuses to permit the stockpiling of reserves precisely to provide a cushion or sinking fund that could be used to support the stakeholder interests in the company in difficult times. Perhaps recognition of this question underlies the failure of virtually all (if not all) attempted hostile takeovers in Japan by American funds.

The same may be said for the new "Americanized" company with committees structure. On its face the inclusion of outside directors on the board parallels the use of independent directors by American companies but outside directors are not necessarily independent. It is independence that allows American courts to give some degree of deference to the actions of boards. The few outside directors that are on boards are likely to be inadequately briefed and have little effect on company decision making.[188] Yet it is likely that Japanese courts will give more deference to actions taken by boards with outside directors than boards without. The 2008 Corporate Value Study Group Report suggests that boards dealing with a hostile takeover offer should establish a special committee to review the offer and that such committee should be "mainly" composed of "independent, outside directors."[189]

In its Final Report (2009), the Corporate Governance Study Group dealt with the difference between the American independent director and the Japanese "outside directors" and concluded that while "independence" assisted in the protection of minority shareholders the failure of independent directors to have the same knowledge base as some "outside directors" could adversely affect minority shareholder interests; the Study Group recommended a structure that contains at least one independent director but did not endorse changing outside directors with independent directors.[190]

187. The relationship of core or lifetime employees and their company is a two-way street. Thus retirees as well as current employees are stakeholders of the company and share loyalty to the company. Recently TEPCO retirees reacting to the Fukushima nuclear disaster voluntarily agreed to a reduction in their pension benefits in order to assist the economics of the company—an action not likely in the case of retirees of a United States company. See, Kyodo, *Tepco retirees endorse pension cuts*, Japan Times (June 6, 2012), http://www.japantimes.co.jp/text/nn20120606b3.html.

188. See Hugh Patrick, *Japan's Economy: The Idiosyncratic Recovery Continues, Center on Japanese Economy and Business Working Paper Series* (Columbia University August 2007) noting that a number of firms have one or two outside directors but that such directors have little independent power and are not well-briefed (14). Nonetheless, initial studies indicate that companies with outside directors perform better than those with the classic Japanese structure. Bebenroth & Donghao, *Performance Impact at the Board Level*, 6 Asian Bus. & Mgt. 303-326 (2007).

189. For a discussion of the concepts of "inside," "outside" and "independent directors" under Delaware Law see, *Selectica Inc. Versata Enterprises*, No. 4241-VCN 2010 WL 703062 (Del Ch. Feb. 26, 2010).

190. An English language version of the Final Report of the Corporate Governance Study Group June 17, 2009, may be found on the web at http://www.meti.go.jp/english/report/downloadfiles/

The Study Group also concluded that even where there is a board of statutory auditors, companies should, on a voluntary basis but not as a requirement, introduce the outside or independent director model to its governance structure. Greater transparency as to the corporate governance structure was also recommended. But, significantly the Study Group recommended that no legislative changes were required in corporate governance and that the financial exchanges should set their own rules for corporate governance for listed companies. Now that the holding company structure is again permitted, some Japanese companies have adopted the practice of structuring the Holding Company on the company with committees' model and structuring the operating companies on the classical Japanese company model with statutory auditors.

Japanese law concerning hostile takeovers is in a process of evolution *Steel Partners/Bull Dog* leaves many aspects of takeover defenses, even those voted on by shareholders, unresolved. Moreover, the division of opinion between the "hard law" of *Steel Partners/Bull Dog* and the "soft law" of the METI (and MOJ) Guidelines and Study Group report must be rationalized or resolved.

For managers of the Japanese company the corporate structure is of little importance as they are the product of lifetime employment systems and see their role as one which perpetuates the lifetime system for the core employment group. The Audit Committee does not significantly improve corporate governance and suffers from many of the infirmities of the statutory auditor system when it comes to governance. While companies have adopted the hybrid structure of "Executive Officers" and while this hybrid has had the effect of making boards of directors somewhat smaller and has quickened the pace of decision making thus making Japanese companies somewhat more able to respond more quickly, the governance aspects have not significantly changed. Boards are still dominated by inside managers—whether of classically structured companies or companies with committees—outside directors are not required to be independent. Statutory auditors and audit committees may still only recommend and lack the hire and fire authority. Anecdotal reports indicate that little has changed in the governance area with the introduction of company with committees structure.[191] Further, the initial "rush" to become a company with committees has slowed to a trickle and few companies have taken the plunge to restructure on the company with committees model.

Derivative lawsuits may be easier and cheaper to bring than in the past but the prospect of plaintiffs being required to post security for costs, the inability to access corporate documents that likely would contain relevant evidence and limitation of liability provisions that limit damages recoverable in a derivative case and the "bad

200906cgst.pdf, last accessed Sept. 16, 2012. This recommendation is to be compared with the Asian Corporate Governance Association (ACGA) White Paper on Japan (2008), which recommends that Japanese companies should have a minimum of 3 "independent" directors, eventually rising to at least 50% of the Board and that all Committees, but especially the Audit Committee, should be chaired by an Independent Director. http://www.acga-asia.org/public/files/Japan%20WP_%20May2008.pdf, last accessed Sept. 16, 2012.

191. John Buchanan & Simon Deakin, *In the Shadow of Corporate Governance Reform: Change and Continuity in Managerial Practice at Listed Companies in Japan*, in *Corporate Governance and Managerial Reform in Japan* 43 (Whittaker & Deakin, eds. Oxford University Press 2009).

reputation" of such suits amongst some judges inhibit the bringing of such suits. It remains that to be successful a derivative plaintiff must, as a practical matter, show illegal conduct by the defendant—a difficult standard to meet.[192]

Hostile takeovers, while allowed, are restricted by takeover defense mechanisms which, combined with the fact that most hostile takeover attempts emanate from foreign shareholders, typically make such attempts futile—although the corporate "raider" may well profit from the exercise while investor ("public") shareholders in general appear to be the losers in the long run. Although it appears that METI would like to see a change so that hostile takeovers can perform a corporate governance function much as they supposedly do in the U.S.,[193] METI still recognizes the "other than shareholder values" that are inherent in "corporate value" and in any event METI's guidelines and reports lack legally controlling weight. The Supreme Court in *Steel Partners/Bull Dog* showed itself much more willing to permit shareholders to pay off a raider than would METI. And the April 27, 2009, Second Research on "Management Visions and Ethics "report of the Japan Productivity Center indicates that while Japanese manager's sought to improve profitability, returning such profits to shareholders was far down the list of company priorities (13.2%) while improving employee satisfaction was at 63.7%.[194] Companies still consider the interests of stakeholders before the interests of shareholders.[195] Nor does the Supreme Court's decision in *Bull*

192. The most recent large derivative action is a suit against former officers and directors of Olympus for hiding losses over a period of years. Suit was instituted both by the company against officials and also by stockholders. *Olympus shareholders lodge $2.9mn damages suit*, The Times of India, Economic Times, (Jan. 24, 12), http://economictimes.indiatimes.com/news/international-business/olympus-shareholders-lodge-2-9mn-damages-suit/articleshow/11613949.cms.
193. METI is not always consistent in its approach. For example, when the British Hedge Fund TCI (Children's Investment Fund) attempted a takeover of electric company Electric Power Development (J-Power) METI joined forces with the Ministry of Finance in invoking provisions of the Foreign Exchange and Trade Law to prevent TIC from acquiring up to 20% interest in the company. The apparent rationale was that a change in management could adversely affect the continuous supply of power to consumers and might have an effect on Japan's nuclear policy since the company operated nuclear electric power plants. TCI later failed in its proxy attempt to get J-Power shareholders to agree to a significant dividend increase (although the company itself raised its dividend—less than the amount TCI sought) as well as to add three "outside directors" to the board (it was agreed that one outside director would be appointed) and to limit cross shareholdings in the company. Justin McCurry, *TCI's J-Power Bid Fails*, Guardian.com (June 28, 2008), http://www.guardian.co.uk/business/2008/jun/26/tci.jpower.japan.
194. Japan Productivity Center, Second Research on "Management Visions and Ethics Apr. 27, 2009 Chart 3, http://www.jpc-net.jp/eng/research/2009_03.html The three top priorities were increasing profits, customers and employees.
195. TSE-Listed Companies, White Paper on Corporate Governance 2009, p. 68, http://www.tse.or.jp/english/rules/cg/white_paper09.pdf. Similarly, Nippon Keidanren (the premier industry organization) sees stakeholder interests as at least as important as stockholder interests in the company and governance of the company. See, *Towards Better Corporate Governance* (Interim Discussion Paper on Key Issues) Apr. 14, 2009, http://www.keidanren.or.jp/english/policy/2009/038.pdf. The 2011 White Paper noted that the number of takeover defense plans had leveled off, that companies considered relations with stakeholders including but not limited to stockholders as a prime company value and that on balance companies considered relations with other stakeholders as equal to relations with stockholders. The same report showed that there was a slight decline in the number of TSE listed companies that utilized the Company with Committees model and that only 43 of the 1,669 TSE First section TSE companies used the

Dog preclude the need to take into account stakeholder interests other than simply "investment" or "financial" shareholder interests.

Stock options are however more in vogue in Japan and the number of companies utilizing options as part of senior executive's pay packages is growing. Yet this aspect of corporate governance may be the weakest in terms of bettering governance and improving performance as options may have the effect of increasing risk to obtain short-term benefits.

Where a sea change has taken place is in the area of transparency and stockholder communications. Change in borrowing patterns (away from main bank lenders and towards borrowing on public markets through bond financing) and accompanying accounting rules now require Japanese firms to consolidate their financial statements so that bad debts or loss generating operations can no longer be squirreled away in some obscure subsidiary leaving the parent company with a "clean" balance sheet. Moreover, the increase in foreign investors and a decrease in main bank influence resulted in a burgeoning of Investor Relations departments in major Japanese companies and a greater flow of information to stockholders and markets in general. J-SOX also required more and more accurate reporting by listed companies.

While corporate governance was seen as linked to American rebound from the recession at the end of the First President Bush's Presidency, there is no evidence that such is in fact the case. And breakdown in governance—especially the American model of governance is seen by some as responsible for the banking crisis of the late first decade of the twenty-first Century and the resulting worldwide contraction spawned by such crisis.[196] At the same time, it is not clear that there is a consensus in Japan that the stakeholder model of the Japanese corporation should give way to a more "stockholder value" model notwithstanding METI's apparent efforts to move industry in this direction. Japanese executives continue to see their firms as having obligations to the traditional stakeholder interests.[197] Japanese shareholders may not share a stockholder

---

committee model. Of companies using the Statutory Auditor model only 1% had a majority of outside directors on the board while only less than 9% had 1/3 of the Board composed of outside directors. The average number of outside directors for all listed companies is still less than1. TSE-Listed Companies, White Paper on Corporate Governance 2011, http://www.tse.or.jp/rules/cg/white-paper/b7gje60000005ob1-att/b7gje6000001m8gl.pdf; See also, TSE-Listed Companies, White Paper on Corporate Governance 2011, http://www.tse.or.jp/rules/cg/white-paper/b7gje60000005ob1-att/b7gje6000001m8gl.pdf, last accessed Sept. 16, 2012.

196. See, e.g., William Sun, Jim Stewart & David Pollard, *Corporate Governance and the Global Financial Crisis International Perspectives* (Cambridge University Press, 2011) taking the "third view" that the crisis was at least in part attributable to a failure of corporate governance—meaning the American corporate governance model (see. E.g., pages 5–12); and in the same volume, Thomas Clarke, *Corporate Governance Causes of the Global Financial Crisis* page 28 etc.

197. Compare, Takeshi Inagami, *Managers and Corporate Governance Reform in Japan: Restoring Self-Confidence or Shareholder Revolution, George Olcott, Whose Company Is It? Changing CEO Ideology in Japan* and Takashi Araki, *Changes in Japan's Practice Dependent Stakeholder Model and Employee-Centered Corporate Governance with Ronald Dore, Japan's Conversion to Investor Capitalism*, in *Corporate Governance and Managerial Reform in Japan* (Whittaker & Deakin, eds., Oxford University Press 2009). Even Dore acknowledges that Managers of Japanese entities (other than financial firms) do not see themselves as serving stockholder only interests but rather see the firm as a community enterprise with other stakeholder interests to be considered (see, "and what do managers think" at pages 153–155).

as investor as distinguished from stakeholder mentality. Nonetheless, there is some empirical evidence that the "outside director" model used by some Japanese corporations has had a positive effect on monitoring management and the greater the proportion of outside directors to total directors the greater the monitoring effect.[198]

198.), Chunyan Liu, Jianlei Liu & Konari Uchida, *Do Independent Boards Effectively Monitor Management? Evidence from Japan During the Financial Crisis* at ch. 10, 188 etc. in William Sun, Jim Stewart & David Pollard, *Corporate Governance and the Global Financial Crisis International Perspectives* (Cambridge University Press 2011),.

CHAPTER 14
Civil Litigation

§14.01 UNITED STATES

When the Duke of Normandy won the Battle of Hastings (1066) and declared himself the King of England the Duke faced two problems—both of which required some military force. First, he refused to acknowledge that his new conquest (England) was subject to French rule. This put him in conflict with the French king and required that he keep a significant military force in Normandy to protect his French holdings. Second, the new king of England needed to solidify and expand his power over his new realm. This required a military force. But the forces at his disposal (and at the disposal of his heirs) were not sufficient to rule such a large holding. Another mechanism for control was required. The English kings used the law and especially the law as dispensed by their traveling judges to extend their rule. The traveling judges were an extension of the "King's Court" and dispensed the king's justice.[1] It was by virtue of the circuit law courts that the "King's writ" (the document that placed the matter before the King's court) was extended throughout the kingdom. The matters covered by writs expanded over time (especially as a consequence of the Black Death) and accordingly the jurisdiction of the King's common law courts expanded. Litigation became an important element in the governing structure. Most law making was done "on the spot" through judge's decisions and later determinations of the Assize and then the jury, which could be appealed to a higher and centrally located law court (on the basis of the factual record made before the lower court judge). Lower court judges were required to follow the decisions and reasoning of this higher court whose decisions were published. The common law system, as we know it today took form. When they came to the Colonies, the Colonists viewed themselves as English until the shooting started in

1. It is no accident that the same word, court, is used to describe the English law court and the king's royal court. In Japan, the word for the place where justice is dispensed (the American court) has no relationship whatsoever to the word used to describe the Imperial 'Court'.

New England. The Colonists brought with them the view that litigation was not something to be shunned—rather it was an integral part of the governing system.

While obviously much too simplistic, the above discussion helps to make the main point of concern here—litigation, and the procedures of litigation such as the jury, has played a significant role in the governance system of the United States from the beginning.

§14.02 JAPAN

Litigation in Japan has a much different history. In Tokugawa Japan there was the beginning of an adversary private dispute system but litigation was not a right but a privilege limited to disputes between members of the same class and permitted to villagers only when the village leadership approved (which was rare). Neither village elders nor local Daimyo were anxious to have local matters aired in front of government officials. As there were no "rights" as recognized in Western law there was no right to have the matter considered and many types of matters were either not considered at all or there were times when certain types of complaints were no longer considered. Legal rules' as such did not come into play and cases were handled on an ad hoc and on a matter of grace basis. No body of precedent governing disposition of disputes developed (although in the later Tokugawa period there was an effort to begin compiling rulings for use in similar cases but such efforts were limited to Magistrates and copies of decisions in cases were not readily available to others outside the Magistrate group). Instead the office tried to determine what was appropriate in the circumstances of each case. Although a determination could be made by the office, attempts were made to get the parties to agree to a solution recommended by the office—a kind of in-court conciliation.

Neither Tokugawa nor Daimyo officials were interested in civil disputes as their primary concerns related to getting the rice revenue demanded from villages and maintaining the social status order.

Conciliation was utilized to resolve various problems. Conciliation could be called for either before any formal "complaint" was filed, after the "complaint" was filed with the authorities but before it was formally accepted or after it was accepted and a response called for. For disputes between villagers of the same village or town residents residing in the same local area of the town, local village or town officials might act as conciliator. Where the dispute was between persons from different villages or portions of a town, an outsider needed to be used as conciliator and the Daimyo or Shogunate official could assist in getting a conciliator. As was true in feudal England local inns became quite adept at assisting parties who had filed formal "complaints" and these inns could be used in the conciliation process. Conciliation became a favored method of resolving disputes.[2]

2. For a discussion of 'litigation' under Tokugawa law see Yoshiro Hiramatsu, *Tokugawa Law* (Dan Fenno Henderson trans.), 14 L. Japan 1, 37–38 (1981). For the view that conciliation was

Many of these same arguments used to favor conciliation over litigation in Tokugawa Japan, such as placing practical solution ahead of legalistic solutions, restoration of harmony over contentious dispute resolution, efficiency, etc. are used to favor conciliation in modern Japan. Shogunate officials considered parent/child disputes and master/servant disputes as inappropriate for handling. These were matters to be resolved internally between the parties.[3] Even in disputes between members of the same class, the respective status of the parties affected the determination of the matter. To the extent there was law, its purpose was not so much to order individual relationships, as it was to order the relationships between status groups and preserve Tokugawa power. Most interpersonal problems were left to the parties themselves to resolve without the aid of the central authorities. When litigation reached a Magistrate the Magistrate attempted to get the parties to compromise and settle the dispute.

But even the few Shogunate official procedures that existed were unavailable to most Japanese. These rules generally applied in transactions or situations involving residents of towns or merchants. For village matters, most issues were determined internally. Village matters tended to be resolved through mediation or conciliation without the help of the central or local government. Japan remained an agricultural country where most people (80%) lived in their village, worked in their village and did not stray far from their village into the nineteenth century. In the village, compromise, conciliation, mediation, group pressure and respected elders resolved disputes, not litigation.

§14.03 WHAT YOU SEE MAY NOT BE WHAT YOU GET

In the United States law enforcement is viewed as a joint effort by individuals and government officials. Accordingly much American legislation contains within it or has been interpreted as containing a right to sue clause under which an individual (or entity) that has suffered injury as a consequence of a violation of the law may sue for money damages (and in some cases injunctive relief) for the violation of law. Such suits relieve the government of the necessity of investigating such alleged violation and then acting on the results of the investigation. In essence, many United States laws make the citizenry "private Attorneys General" with power to enforce the laws through litigation. Civil tort actions are used to enforce laws that may not have specific right to sue provisions.

an outgrowth of purely Japanese way of dealing with disputes even before the Tokugawa period see, Tsuyohshi Kinoshita, *Legal System and Legal Culture in Japanese Law*, 44 Comp. L. Rev. 25, 87–88 (2010).

3. Echoes of this Tokugawa approach can be found in the distinction made between North Korea's abduction of Japanese citizens and abduction to Japan by Japanese mothers of children whose custody was given to American fathers. The North Korean abduction was by a foreign State but the abduction by a mother was a matter that should be decided by the parents. *Campbell's Hague plea irks North abductee kin*, Japan Times (May 9, 2012), http://www.japantimes.co.jp/text/nn20120509a9.html. This of course, totally disregards the role of the court that made the custody order.

In Japan law enforcement is viewed as a government function.[4] Thus most legislation does not grant the citizenry the right to sue to enforce the law. Moreover, most legislation is drafted in what appears to be hortatory terms leaving it up to government officials to determine what should be enforced and how to enforce the law. Nonetheless recently producers of films have initiated a program to sue persons who sell copied versions of such films relying on Japan's copyright laws. The stated purpose of such suits is to enforce the producers' copyright by subjecting violators to big damage awards.[5]

Even when courts have created new causes of action in favor of private parties, the government in Japan has tended to act to close off the private litigation avenue.[6] A notable exception is the Supreme Court's decisions allowing consumers a cause of action for recovery of money paid to finance companies that charged usurious rates.

Where the government fails to address an issue, rather than litigate parties are more likely to engage in direct action, demonstration, contained violence or civil disobedience with litigation used to publicize an issue by bringing it to the attention of the public. The objective is not so much to get the court to change the policy as to get the issue before the public so that policy makers will be forced to deal with the issue and perhaps change policy. Japanese courts aid this process by sometimes deciding a case by retaining the status quo but nonetheless suggesting government action to mold public understanding and legislation to resolve the issue. When this occurs the government will often act.[7]

The litigation system in the United States may be viewed as a means for redistributing wealth or a risk sharing insurance program with the manufacturing sector of society seen as the "insurance company" in that it spreads the risk of injury among all its customers (by raising the price of its product by the value of the "insurance premium"). Japanese products liability law and judicial decisions dealing with products liability does not serve this function.

---

4. For a general discussion of the subject see Hideo Tanaka & Akio Takeuchi, The Role of Private Persons in the Enforcement of law: A Comparative Study of Japanese and American Law, 7 L. Japan 34, 36 (1974); see also Frank K. Upham, *Law And Social Change In Postwar Japan* (Harvard University Press 1987) for a discussion of how litigation has been used in Japan by private parties, in some circumstances, to effect social change.
5. Kaoriko Okuda, *Huge Lawsuits Seek to Deter Sellers of Pirated DVD's*, Asahi Shimbun (Oct. 1, 2011), http://www.asahi.com/english/TKY201109300366.html. As the article notes, the police have also been involved in enforcing the copyrights implicated in the suits. Japan's Copyright Law does not have a "fair use" defense as does the U.S. law. However, copying for personal or private use is permitted. Teruo Doi, *Availability of then "Fair Use" Defense under the Copyright Act of Japan*, 57 J. Copyright Soc. 631 (2010). In early 2012 the Tokyo District court enjoined publication of a travel guide because it contained copyright material used without permission of the writer. *Court order halts publication of guidebook over copyright violations*, Mainichi Daily News (Feb. 16, 2012), http://mdn.mainichi.jp/mdnnews/news/20120216p2a00m0na016000c.html.
6. See, Joseph W.S. Davis, *Dispute Resolution In Japan* 127 (Kluwer Law International 1996); Frank K. Upham, *Law and Social Change In Postwar Japan* (Harvard University Press 1987).
7. The use of litigation as a means of affecting public policy even if success is not considered likely is not unique to Japan. See, Sharyn L. Roach Anleu, *Law and Social Change* 126–133 (2d ed., Sage Publications 2010).

The litigation system in the United States is used by elements of the public to create new rules of law in areas where the Legislative Branch is either unable or unwilling to act. Constitutional Law centered around the so-called right to privacy finds expression in cases like *Roe v. Wade* and more recently in the same sex marriage arena.[8] The Japanese Supreme Court does not serve this function. In the American system the plaintiff hopes to win and thereby create a legal doctrine with the effect of a rule of law. In Japan the litigant does not expect to win (and is surprised in the few cases of litigation success, such as the *Minamata disease* case) but seeks to bring the issue into public view in an attempt to create a consensus in favor of the litigant's position. This attitude may be changing as a consequence of the Great East Japan Earthquake and Tsunami and the subsequent Fukushima Nuclear Disaster which has sparked a number of lawsuits around Japan in which local residents seek to prevent the reopening of ageing nuclear facilities based on safety concerns.

In Japan the resort to the legal system is considered as a last resort. Prior to litigation the parties will have made sincere efforts to resolve their differences short of litigation. This attempt to salvage a relationship is probably the reason why most litigation in Japan is automobile accident litigation that typically involves strangers. Nonetheless, the court, the lawyers and ultimately the parties are affected by the general thrust of relationship breakdowns—there is a dynamic that seeks to restore harmony between them even if not a formal relationship. So too, the dynamic of legal fees in Japan pushes the lawyers to support compromise as fees are fixed (not hourly).

One does not have to agree with the myth that Japanese are reluctant litigants[9] to accept the idea that once litigation has begun the role of the judge, the lawyers and even the parties in Japan is to find a solution that recreates a "live and let live" atmosphere between the parties.[10] Whether one agrees or disagrees with the psychological explanations offered by some for the less frequent use of litigation in Japan than in the United States,[11] the fact remains that the attempt to find harmony strikes a chord with the participants in Japanese litigation.[12]

It has also been suggested that there is less litigation in Japan because the parties tend to know what to expect from the law (a variation of the Ramseyer analysis that the litigation system works in Japan because parties can reasonably determine the result of litigation and thus have no need to actually litigate but can settle disputes in the

8. *Goodridge v. Mass. Dept. of Public Health,* 440 Mass. 309 (2003);.
9. John O. Haley, *The Myth of the Reluctant Litigant,* 4 J. Japanese Stud. 359 (1978).
10. This idea has deep roots in Japanese history and may account for the rise of samurai power and the decline of civil power in Kamakura Japan. See, Karl Friday, *Once and Future Warriors: The Samurai in Japanese History,* 10 Education About Asia 31, 35–36 (2005).
11. Yosiyuki Noda, Nihon-Jin No Seikaku Tosono Ho-Kannen (The Character of the Japanese People and their Conception of Law) reprinted in Hideo Tanaka (assisted by Malcolm D.H. Smith), *The Japanese Legal System* 295–310 (University of Tokyo Press 1976).
12. See, Sharyn L. Roach Anleu, *Law and Social Change* 121–123 (2d ed., Sage Publications 2010) for a discussion of the *cultural v. structural arguments* and the potential effect of culture on structural arrangements.

shadow of the litigation result). Knowing what their legal obligations will lead to they can resolve disputes before they reach the point of litigation.[13]

The fable "each lost one" has meaning among Japanese lawyers, legal philosophers and judges.[14] In the fable a local Lord resolves a dispute between two samurai over three gold coins by donating one coin of his own and distributed two coins to each of the samurai—thus each lost one.[15] The Lord (as judge) found a solution that all can live with (with honor), rather than making a determination based on rights/obligations or other concepts that are legalistic. The fable establishes the priority of an amicable resolution over strict "legal" rules.[16]

Similarly, the concept of apology as a social lubricant that can obviate the need for litigation plays a significant role in Japanese society.[17] The willingness to make a sincere apology can reduce the need for litigation by making the wronged party emotionally whole. And, the refusal to make apology, even in the face of willingness to make monetary compensation, may result in litigation.[18] Settlement may be postponed

---

13. Takehiro Ohya, *On the Scarcity of Civil Litigation in Japan: Two Different Approaches and More*, 49 Acta Juridica Hungarica 340 (2008) (discussing the various theories for why Japan's litigation rate is lower than other developed countries).
14. Although not mentioning the fable by name, Takeo Tanase, a leading figure in Japanese legal philosophy distills the two essential points of the fable in his essay on Invoking Law as Narrative (Chapter 2 in *Community and the Law: a Critical Reassessment of American Liberalism and Japanese Modernity* (Luke Nottage & Leon Wolff trans. & eds., Edward Elgar Publishing Ltd. 2010). First, rather than being bound by the rule of law, interpersonal relationships, including disputes, should be handled so that persons control law rather than have law rule. The Lord's understanding of the feelings of the two samurai and his rejection of a "legal" solution to the problem in favor of a solution that allows the feelings of the participants to be understood and reconciled is paramount to the tale. This notion of rejection of the "legal" answer in favor of a contextual or communally accepted answer also appears in Chapter 3 of Tanase where it is argued that while law is supposed to be universal it may not be appropriate because of the circumstances of the situation (page 51). Second, all participants to the dispute, the parties as well as their lawyers and the judge have an obligation to put themselves in the position of the other in order to find a solution that is favorable to all—whatever the law as an abstract proposition may require. This can be achieved by understand where each party is coming from and devising a compromise that satisfactorily resolves the matter.
15. For other statements of the Japanese hostility to 'law based/ winner vs. loser' resolution of disputes based on culture and a need to retain harmony see Richard Parker, *Law Language, and the Individual in Japan and the United States*, 7 Wisconsin Intl. L. J. 179, 179–180 (1988).
16. Tsuyohshi Kinoshita, *Legal System and Legal Culture in Japanese Law*, 44 Comp. L. Rev. 25, 92 (2010).
17. See generally, Hiroshi Wagatsuma & Arthur Rosett, *The Implications of Apology: Law and Culture in Japan and the United States*, 20 L. & Soc. Rev. 461 (1986).
18. For the role of failure to acknowledge wrong doing and refusal to make apology in the Minamata disease case see Frank K. Upham, *Law And Social Change In Postwar Japan* (Harvard University Press 1987); See also, Robert C. Christopher, *The Japanese Mind* 166 (Simon and Shuster 1983) implying that a contrite apology by Chisso might have resolved the case at a much earlier stage. Although the company was found responsible, it took a significantly longer time for the government's responsibility to be established through litigation. *Government's failure to Enforce Water Quality Laws in Minamata Disease Episode Leads to Government Liability case*, Case No. 2001(O)Nos. 1194 and 1196, and 2001(Ju)Nos. 1172 and 1174, 58 Minshu No. 7, (P.B., Oct. 15, 2004). In 2010 the government accepted a court suggested settlement with unrecognized Minamata disease victims. *State accepts Minamata settlement*, The Asahi Shimbun (Mar. 20, 2010).

or rejected if the defendant is not prepared to apologize.[19] The giving of and acceptance of a sincere apology as part of the resolution of litigation goes a long way to restore social harmony[20] and may be an essential element in a negotiated settlement.[21] Failure to apologize can affect the amount of damages awarded in a case just as failure to accept a sincere apology may reduce the financial damages awarded.[22]

Nor does one have to accept the "social/cultural"[23] or the Confucian approach[24] to dispute settlement to accept that the notion of the judge acting to bring about a harmonious resolution of the problem brought to the court. Influenced as she is by myths in the culture and by the parable of "each lost one" and similar sociological underpinnings, it is to be expected that the court in Japan will attempt to find a resolution or push the parties to a resolution that will, if not recreate a harmony that never existed in the first place, at least not present the parties with an outcome that makes one of them more uncomfortable than is necessary to achieve peace.

One need not accept the myth that Japanese are reluctant litigants to recognize that if the Government accepts the myth, or even if it rejects the myth but seeks to perpetuate the underlying values of the myth (sameness, the Japanese society as family, rejection of conflict in favor of compromise, etc.), it will structure the legal system and substantive law to obtain the end results of the myth. Namely, less litigation to begin with and compromise and settlement in the event litigation is instituted. Thus Japanese administrative statutes typically lack a right to sue provision as do other statutes creating rights such as the Equal Opportunity Law. Injunction, which is an inherent part of the American judge's portfolio of remedies is only permitted pursuant to statutory grant in Japan's civil law system and there are few statutes granting an injunction right and courts are reluctant (although not completely unwilling) to find a right to injunction in a substantive statute that has no stated remedy. When substantive law is modified to allow a right to sue then litigation on the

19. In 2011 the plaintiff's in a mass tort suit against the government accepted a settlement but only if the government would offer them an apology in addition to monetary compensation. Kyodo News, *Hepatitis B Suffers OK Plan to Settle Suit*, Japan Times (Jan. 23, 2011), http://search.japantimes.co.jp/cgi-bin/nn20110123a4.html.
20. This Japanese attitude towards apology is to be compared with the American practice of penalizing the doctor who apologizes, even in those states that have 'apology laws'. See Marlynn Wei, *Doctors, Apologies, and the Law: An Analysis and Critique of Apology Laws*, Yale Law School Student Scholarship Series, Year 2006 Paper 30.
21. See Eric A. Feldman, *The Ritual Of Rights in Japan, Law, Society and Health Policy* 127–128 (Cambridge University Press 2000)..
22. The failure of the Governor of Osaka to apologize for his alleged sexual harassment of a campaign worker resulted in the plaintiff raising the amount of damages she sought in the case. Tolbert, *Japan Official Is Cited for Harassment*, Washington Post (Dec. 14, 1999) at A. 31. When the Governor continued to refuse to accept responsibility for his actions, criminal proceedings were instituted. The Governor then resigned.
23. For a discussion of the social-cultural approach and the role of 'harmony' in dispute resolution see Takeyoshi Kawashima, Dispute Resolution in Contemporary Japan, found in Arthur Taylor von Mehren *Law in Japan* 41, 43–44 (Harvard University Press 1963).
24. For a discussion of the Confucian approach based on the Confucian value of harmony see Kenzo Takayanagi, *A Century of Innovation: The Development of Japanese Law, 1868–1961*, in Arthur Taylor von Mehren, *Law in Japan* 5, 39 (Harvard University Press 1963).

basis of such new or modified substantive law increases.[25] The values that underlie the myth form part of the structure of the "ethics" courses taught in school. The Judiciary opposed the creation of a jury trial system in Japan by relying on precisely the sociological/cultural arguments that underlie what Professor Haley called the Myth of the Reluctant Litigant.[26] If the ultimate goal of those deciding cases is not to find a clear cut winner and not to impose a solution on a clear cut loser, then it can be said that the function of the system is to restore harmony—if not between the parties at least in society in general.

Japanese High Courts do not have to trouble themselves with the precedent setting value of their decisions. The matter is more complicated for the Supreme Court. But even here, decisions do not have the stare decisis effect of a common law judgment[27] and by the time the case gets to the Supreme Court it seems clear that there must be an ultimate winner and loser. Even here decisions can be written in such a way as to make each party somewhat happy with the conclusion. Restoration of harmony influences the parties as well. Traditional norms affect us all and in Japan harmony and group identity and group unity is a strong norm.[28]

Of course there are cases of principle that cannot be settled either because one side or the other is intransigent, and the search for harmony does not mean that Japanese people are reluctant to litigate for cultural reasons, rather the point is that once litigation is started there is a great emphasis on "putting the pieces back together"; to make the parties as whole as can be expected without either having to concede loss on all points and with each able to find something of comfort in the resolution.

Japanese law permits a process for conciliation as part and parcel of adversary litigation. A party may file an application for conciliation with a court before instituting a lawsuit. If the defendant agrees then conciliation before the court is held. If the defendant disagrees the matter is at an end. A party may also request conciliation during the course of a trial or the court on its own motion may decide that conciliation is appropriate. The court forms a conciliation committee (at least one member will be a judge) and the litigation is placed on hold. This committee has significant

---

25. The dramatic spikes in litigation in 2007 and 2009 are likely directly related to the Supreme Court of Japan decisions in 2006 and 2008 dealing with protection of consumers from money lenders and opening judicial remedies to consumers who overpaid interest and then redefined the manner in which interest was calculated to result in more overpayment situations. See, *Consumer Lending Interest Rate cases*, Case No. 2003 (Ju) No. 1653, Minshu Vol. 60, No. 1 (Sup. Ct. Jan. 24, 2006); Case No. 2004 (Ju) No. 1518, Minshu Vol. 60, No. 1 (P.B., Jan. 13, 2006); Case No. 2006 (Ju) No. 2268, Minshu Vol. 62, No. 1 (P.B., Jan. 18, 2008).
26. Hiroshi Fukurai, *The Rebirth of Japan's Petit Quasi-Jury and Grand Jury Systems: A Cross-National Analysis of Legal Consciousness and the Lay Participatory Experience in Japan and the U.S.* 40 Cornell Intl. L. J. 315, 332–333 (2007), http://organizations.lawschool.cornell.edu/ilj/issues/40.2/CIN202.pdf.
27. See Chapter 5 discussion of the lack of effect (to date) of the Grand Bench decision in the *Portion of Nationality Law Unconstitutional Case* on the issue of inheritance rights of "illegitimate" children.
28. Hiroshi Wagatsuma & Arthur Rosett, *Cultural Attitudes Toward Contract Law: Japan and the United States Compared*, 2 UCLA Pacific L. Basin L. J. 76, 85 (1983). Harmony has even been invoked as a part of good manners and a means to both avoid auto accidents and vandalism. See, Joshua Hotaka Roth, *Heartfelt Driving: Discourses on Manners, Safety, and Emotion in Japan's Era of Mass Motorization*, 71 J. Asian Stud.171 (2012).

authority—it will hear the position of the parties; may also investigate the matter on its own; can call witnesses and ask to see documents; and can maintain the status quo until resolution of the matter. If the committee cannot bring the parties to an amicable resolution[29] it may meet with the judge handling the case and express views about how the matter should be resolved.[30] This can be a powerful device as the court may then propose a tentative decision in the case and the parties have two weeks to file objections or accept the decision. As there is no trial by jury, the tentative decision lets each side know in advance what decision they may expect if settlement is not achieved.[31] Even when the parties do not seek conciliation before the court, the court may, and typically will, recommend a settlement.

A suggestion regarding the appropriate terms of settlement by the very judge who is both fact finder and law determiner exerts a strong influence on settlement.[32]

While United States judges would like to see the parties before them settle the case (and while most cases in the United States are in fact settled), failure to bring about a settlement is not viewed by the judge as a personal failure. In Japan judges view it as their duty to bring about party negotiated settlements.

The restoration of harmony as a goal of the judicial system is consistent with the view that the legal system in Japan lacks strong sanctioning mechanisms and thus there is weak enforcement of the law through formal means.[33] The system need not have the power to enforce its orders when the parties have "voluntarily" resolved their dispute. Compelling settlement to restore harmony appears inconsistent with the American approach that extols predictability as a virtue stronger than harmony.[34]

---

29. In some cases the parties may be convinced to agree in advance to follow the recommendations of the committee. In such case the process more closely resembles arbitration and the decision of the committee becomes the decision of the court. Arbitration is generally not favored in Japan because like litigation there is a binding decision made by the arbitrator(s). Koji Shindo, *Settlement of Disputes over Securities Transactions*, 14 Hastings Intl. & Comp. L. Rev.399, 402 (1991).
30. While United States courts may recommend conciliation to parties and upon agreement may appoint a conciliator, such conciliation is shrouded in secrecy so that the judge, who will be trying the case, is not made privy to the views of the parties, the offers made and rejected or the thoughts of the conciliator as to who was obstinate and who helpful.
31. For a discussion of compromise procedures see Iwasaki, Reconciliation of Commercial Disputes in Japan, www.gsid.nagoyau.ac.jp/project/apec/lawdb/japan/dispute/adr-en.html; See generally Yasunobu Sato, *Commercial Dispute Processing and Japan* ch. 8 (Kluwer Law International 2001).
32. For a discussion of the judge's role in bringing about settlement see Shunko Muto, *Concerning Trial Leadership in Civil Litigation: Focusing on the Judge's Inquiry and Compromise*, 12 L. Japan 23, 24 (1979).
33. See generally, John Owen Haley, *Authority without Power: Law and The Japanese Paradox* (1991).
34. See Harold See, *The Judiciary and Dispute Resolution in Japan*, 10 Florida St. U. L. Rev. 339, 367 (1982).

[A] Access to the Judicial System[35]

United States courts and Japanese courts are available to virtually anyone who has a claim that they wish to have litigated. But that does not mean the courts are equally available in the United States and Japan. In the United States there is in fact easy access to the courts. Courts are ubiquitous. Federal District Courts in each state and State Courts in every county in every state as well as in every city and large town and many villages. The same may not be said of Japan. Although there are over 400 Summary Courts in Japan their jurisdiction is limited to small claim cases. These courts are similar to United States State Small Claims Courts. The increase in the court's jurisdiction to JPY 1.4 million is surely a good step in making the courthouse more accessible. In many outlying areas there is no readily available court in the region and potential litigants must travel long distances to file a lawsuit.

The United States has a large body of judges to handle cases. There are over 28,000 trial judges and quasi-judicial officers at the State Court level in the United States as well as more than 600 active duty federal district judges (who are aided by senior judges who still handle cases) compared to approximately 3,500 judges in Japan (of whom more than 800 serve in the Summary Court).[36] This small number of judges not only makes access to the courts more difficult than in the United States but it also results in greater backlog causing delay that may result in people determining that it is not worthwhile seeking a judicial remedy. Consistent with the recommendations of the Law Reform Council the judiciary has been adding about 50 judges a year over the past few years.

Access to lawyers is relatively easy in the United States as law schools churn out lawyers by the thousands every year. State Bar examiners appear to have adopted a policy under which approximately 60% of all applicants pass the bar examination. There are enough lawyers so that it is profitable for lawyers to devote at least a portion of their time to handling cases on a contingent fee basis.

In Japan, as discussed in Chapter 4 herein the number of lawyers is dramatically lower and as most lawyers are to be found in Tokyo and Osaka, there are few lawyers in the smaller cities of Japan and in many communities there are no lawyers. Legal fees in Japan are relatively high and, there are few if any lawyers willing to take contingent fee cases.[37] Exceptions to this rule include (a) "politically" charged cases and (b) cases against local authorities or against third parties who improperly received monies from local authorities[38], and (c) derivative lawsuits against corporations by shareholders. Many Japanese lawyers consider it their duty to represent the underprivileged or those

---

35. For a discussion of the effect of limited accessibility to the judicial system in Japan on litigation in Japan see Carl F. Goodman, *The Somewhat Less Reluctant Litigant: Japan's Changing View Towards Civil Litigation*, 32 Law and Policy in International Business 769, 790–791 (2001).

36. The Supreme Court of Japan reports that in 2009 there were 2737 full and assistant Judges and 806 summary court judges. Supreme Court Website, Overview of the Judicial System, http://www.courts.go.jp/english/system/system.html (accessed Feb. 2012).

37. Contingent fees are not 'illegal' in Japan as they are in certain other countries that consider them a form of champerty. While not illegal, there are still few contingent fee cases.

38. The Local Autonomy Law permits private citizens to request an audit of funds spent by the local government authority and in some cases to sue to recover back monies improperly paid

who have been harmed by the society. In the case of a local inhabitant suit, if the local authority recovers monies as a result of such suit the local inhabitant is entitled to recover from the authority reasonable attorney's fees (not to exceed the amount paid by the inhabitant). Such fees are many times calculated and paid on a contingent fee basis.[39] The New Code of Civil Procedure introduced the Preparation for Oral Argument procedure that permits lawyers to participate in some procedures by telecommunication and has reduced some costs.

Filing fees in the United States are relatively low and are not based on the prayed for recovery. In Japan the filing fee is typically based on the amount of damages sought. This may cause an otherwise worthy, but not very wealthy, plaintiff to decide to forgo suit because the "entry fee" is simply too high and it may cause plaintiffs to reduce the damages claimed because the fee is too high. As lawyers' fees are also tied to the amount of damages sought, reducing damages becomes an economic proposition. Both Japan and the United States follow the "American Rule" under which the losing party in litigation is not, as a general matter, required to pay the legal fees of the winning party. In many situations where citizens are granted a right to sue the government, American fee shifting statutes requires a losing government entity to pay the fees of the prevailing party plaintiff.[40] In Japan, legal fees are supposed to be part of a successful plaintiff's damage award in tort cases but the amount awarded for such fees is typically significantly less than the actual fees.

The restrictions on access to the courts in Japan have an effect of limiting the number of cases brought each year. This effect is surely a burden for the number of people who might otherwise wish to institute litigation. Recent changes, changes in substantive and procedural law, have had the effect of ameliorating some of these burdens and have (especially the substantive law changes) increasing the number of cases filed.

While access to the formal legal system is restricted in Japan, Alternative Dispute Resolution (ADR) mechanisms are ubiquitous and, as the courts decide that either the government or private parties are responsible in various situations new ADR mechanisms are created to siphon off cases that would otherwise go into the formal legal system. Thus, where the government is found responsible for failing to act in a situation that may bring forth thousands of claimants, it is likely that an administrative remedy will be provided to eliminate or at least reduce the number of cases brought for relief. Similarly when the courts begin to allow suits for damages, such as in the big four pollution cases, automobile accident cases or the recent upsurge in medical malpractice cases, ADR mechanisms to resolve these disputes outside the court, either

---

by the authority to third parties or to sue the local mayor or council for improperly paying out monies. See, Local Autonomy Act, Article 242-2 (local inhabitants suit).

39. See, e.g., *Local Inhabitant Suit Attorney Fee Calculation Case*, Case No. 2007 (Ju) No. 2069, 63 Minshu No. 4 (P.B., Apr. 23, 2009) setting out the basis for determining the amount of fee recoverable for such a successful suit The proper fee is the amount that is both reasonable and fair based on socially accepted standards (undefined).

40. A prevailing party means the party ultimately successful in the litigation. Thus, where a plaintiff prevailed at a preliminary injunction stage but ultimately lost the case, the plaintiff was not a prevailing party. *Sole v. Wyner*, 551 U.S., 127 S. Ct. 2188 (2007).

sponsored by the government or by private parties, take root. Thus as malpractice suits have multiplied the Japanese government has begun to explore a non-fault mechanism to provide relief outside of court.[41]

[B] Civil Procedure

[1] United States

Civil procedure in the United States differs from state to state and between states and the federal court system. Nonetheless there are certain common features: basic Constitutional requirements of notice and fair opportunity to be heard; pleadings to get issues raised with the court; relatively broad discovery devices to ascertain the facts; trial by jury in cases at common law; an "on the record" form of appeal; and a post-trial mechanism to assist in locating assets so that a successful litigant can recover on its judgment.

Jurisdictions in the United States basically adopted a notice of claim pleading procedure to inform the opposition party of the basis for the claim against it and provide a means to set forth its defenses to the claim made restricted to a complaint, an answer and in some case a counterclaim, which may call for a reply.[42] Pleadings are not intended to be a litany of the ultimate facts in the case nor designed to set forth the documents and facts that plaintiff will rely on.[43] More recently the Supreme Court has indicated that a more fact oriented pleading may be required in some situations[44] but the Court has not jettisoned the "notice" nature of United States pleading, rather more detail may relate to the nature of the lawsuit and concern that before extensive discovery is undertaken the plaintiff should plead sufficient facts to show that a basis for litigation actually exists. In complex litigation courts may be looking for appropriate "filters" just as requiring a real fact issue when deciding a summary judgment motion may be a filter before a time consuming trial takes place. It is unlikely that the *Twombly/Iqbal* standard will be interpreted by lower courts or expanded by the

41. See, Kyodo, *Automatic Redress Plan Mulled for Victims of Medical Malpractice*, Japan Times (July 10, 2011), http://search.japantimes.co.jp/cgi-bin/nn20110710a5.html.
42. A counterclaim and reply are really just a complaint and answer but the parties are reversed. The counterclaim is a complaint by a defendant directed toward a plaintiff and the reply is the plaintiff's answer to the counterclaim.
43. 'Federal Rule of Civil Procedure 8(a)(2) requires only "a short and plain statement of the claim showing that the leader is entitled to relief."
44. See, *Bell Atlantic Corp. v. Twombly*, 550 U.S. 544 (2007); *Ashcroft v. Iqbal*, 129 S. Ct. 1937 (2009) For the view that taken together *Twombly* and *Iqbal* herald the creation of a new "plausibility" standard requiring a modicum of proof at the pleading stage see, Dodson, *Comparative Convergence in Pleading Standards*, 158 U. of PA L. Rev. 441 (2010); Dodson, *Federal Pleading and State Presuit Discovery*, 14 Lewis & Clark L. Rev. 43 (2010). More recently the Court has reemphasized that this is a pleading requirement and does not require fact pleading—the facts can be discovered during the discovery process. See, *Matrixx Initiatives Inc. v. Siacusano*, 563 U.S. ___ (2011).

Supreme Court to mean the same thing as civil law fact pleading although the full extent of the decisions remains to be seen.[45]

While it is commonly said that a function of the complaint and answer is to narrow the issues in a case, it is unlikely that these documents achieve that objective in many cases. Although notice pleading is the norm in federal courts, it has been recognized that such liberal pleading rules can lead to frivolous litigation initiated for the purpose of "extorting" a settlement rather than pay the costs of defense. To guard against this perceived abuse the Congress can and has acted to require more specific pleadings in some situations.[46] Congress has the power to require specific pleading and the court will adhere to Congressional intent in interpreting such a specific pleading statute.[47] The complaint is typically required to be served on the defendant within the jurisdiction of the court or if not served personally in the jurisdiction there must be some other "contacts" that the defendant has with the jurisdiction to make it fair for the defendant to be forced to litigate in that jurisdiction. (See Chapter 15).

The "pleading stage" is over relatively quickly and the parties move to the gathering of evidence or discovery stage that can and typically does take a substantial period of time, extending into years in many cases. Discovery is directly linked to trial by jury as the case must be tried quickly without delays so the jury of ordinary people can go back to their ordinary lives quickly. For this to occur, all of the evidence must be gathered in advance. Discovery serves two purposes: first, it permits this evidence gathering function to take place before the trial begins and second, it allows the parties, through their attorneys, to discover evidence that is not in a party's possession.

Discovery is a lawyer-to-lawyer procedure with the court becoming involved only when the parties (through their lawyers) are unable to resolve the issue.[48] Discovery rules in the United States are quite liberal— indeed the most liberal in the world. Discovery can be used to obtain a tactical advantage over another party. The federal court system has adopted rules designed to limit the discovery that a party may take by such devices as limiting to eight hours on one day the time permitted for taking testimony from a witness and by restricting the number of interrogatory questions that can be asked.[49]

More recently the advent of "e-discovery," the discovery of computer-generated documents has placed a great burden on litigants as thousands of emails located on hundreds of computer drives may be implicated and there is an obligation to preserve documents and computer records once litigation is anticipated or it is reasonable to anticipate that litigation may come. The court has authority to issue sanctions against

---

45. See, Hon TS Ellis & Nitin Shah, *Iqbal, Twombly and What Comes Next, A Suggested Impeprical Approach,* 114 Penn Statim 64 (2010), http://www.pennstatelawreview.org/114/114%20Penn%20Statim%2064.pdf.
46. See, Private Securities Litigation Reform Act of 1995, 15 U.S.C. 78u-49b)(2).
47. *Tellabs Inc. v. Makor Issues and Rights Ltd.*, 551 U.S. 308 (2007).
48. See FRCP Part V, Disclosures and Discovery, Rules 26–37.
49. In addition Congress has prohibited class actions in certain security fraud situations in order to deal with perceived abuses, including perceived discovery abuses. See *Merrill Lynch v. Dabit*, 547 U.S. 71 (2006).

a party that fails to live up to its preservation of documents obligation.[50] To carry out their "hold" obligations companies, governments and institutions have put into effect "litigation hold" guidelines for employees that come into effect as soon as litigation is reasonably anticipated or foreseen.[51] Since parties to American litigation may include foreign companies (such as Japanese entities) or may involve foreign offices of American companies, these non-destruction obligations may affect documents located outside the United States. Discovery is allowed of the parties themselves. Corporate officers of a corporate party as well as of third persons with knowledge of potentially relevant facts and experts who may be called to testify at trial may be required to give oral testimony in a lawyer's office before trial. After the discovery stage is completed either or both parties may move for summary judgment—this is a request that the court order that no trial is needed as the facts are clear and based on the clear facts one or the other party would have to win at trial. This motion may be used to obtain judgment as to all claims made in a case or as to some of the claims made.

When the discovery stage is completed (and typically after motions for summary judgment, if any, are resolved) the court will meet with the lawyers for the parties at a "pre-trial" conference where the procedures to be used at trial will be resolved. It is at this stage that the factual issues are narrowed to what is truly in dispute, the witnesses who will appear at trial are identified along with the documents each side intends to use, and the time for the trial is estimated. Following pre-trial there is the actual trial, which proceeds on the basis of oral testimony given in open court on a question and answer basis, before a judge or in front of a jury. During the course of the trial the judge acts as a neutral arbiter, maintaining order in the court and ruling on objections the parties may make to offers of evidence put forward by the other side.[52] The parties, through their lawyers are responsible for producing the relevant evidence in the case and are responsible for questioning the evidence produced by the other side such as through the cross-examination of witnesses. When the evidence presentation stage of the case ends, the judge advises the jury as to the legal rules it must apply in reaching its decision. The jury will adjourn to a closed room and in private will meet for as long

50. FRCP Rule 37. See also, *Chambers v. NASCO,* 501 U.S. 32 (1991). For litigation involving sanctions for failure to properly place a "hold" on document destruction activities, including electronic documents, and the types of steps to be taken when electronic discovery is likely to be involved (including written litigation "holds") see, *Zubulake v. USB Warburg*, 220 FRD 212 (SDNY, 2003) and 229 FRD 422 (SDNY, 2004) and *Pension Committee of the University of Montreal Pension Plan v. Banc of America Securities,* Amended Order Case No. 05-cv-9016 (SDNY, Jan. 15, 2010). Whether the standards set in the Southern District of New York applies more generally remains to be seen. See also, John M. Barkett, Zubulake Revisited: Pension Committee and the Duty to Preserve, February 26, 2010 ABA Litigation News, http://www.abanet.org/litigation/litigationnews/trial_skills/pension-committee-zubulake-ediscovery.html.

51. See, e.g., *State of Rhode Island*, Litigation Hold Policy (Oct. 19, 2010), http://www.hr.ri.gov/documents/Policies%20&%20Communications/Litigation%20Hold%20Policy_10-10-19.pdf; *What to do When you Receive a "Litigation Hold" Notice*, University of Washington, http://www.washington.edu/admin/ago/litigationhold.pdf, last accessed Sept. 16, 2012.

52. Since many cases are tried to a jury rather than to professional judges the United States has detailed rules of evidence designed to prevent the jury from being misled by evidence that is not relevant or reliable (e.g., hearsay) or which may unduly excite emotion rather than reasoned judgment.

as is required to determine who the winner is and who the loser, or if they are divided on the question to decide that they cannot decide the case, in which situation the case may be rescheduled for a trial before another jury.

Unsuccessful parties may appeal to a higher court from a judgment rendered by the trial level court, but such appeal is on the record made in the court below and new evidence will not be permitted to be introduced. Appeals are based on legal points or challenges to rulings made during the course of the trial by the judge.

[2] Japan

In Japan the procedure is fundamentally different. The Code of Civil Procedure calls upon courts to see that civil cases are handled fairly and in good faith.[53] The Supreme Court of Japan has utilized this statutory grant to require that something akin to a "due process" right to be heard applies in civil litigation.[54]

The plaintiff begins the case by filing a complaint with a court that has jurisdiction over the subject matter and over the parties. Because it is a unitary state, Japanese District Courts are not courts of limited jurisdiction as are American Federal District Courts. Japan has recently jettisoned its previous rulings following the absolute theory of sovereign immunity and has adopted the restrictive theory of immunity for foreign States[55] under which immunity is denied for commercial activities. (Jurisdiction is discussed in Chapter 15)

The Japanese complaint has a broader function than the American complaint and should contain ultimate facts and the facts and evidence required to prove the ultimate facts.[56] This fact pleading requirement is typical of civil law jurisdictions and has its genesis in the German Code of Civil procedure. Neither conclusory allegations nor mere allegations of ultimate fact are sufficient because they do not educate the judge as to the real facts of the matter and do not form a basis for the judge to begin the process of "confirming" what are the true issues and true facts in the case. Japanese pleading serves the purpose of educating the judge as to the basis in fact and law for the claim.[57]

53. Code of Civil procedure Article 2.
54. See *Notice and Opportunity to Respond to Appeal Required case*, Case No. 2010 (Ku) No. 1088, Minshu Vol. 65, No. 3 (P.B., Apr. 13, 2011), http://www.courts.go.jp/english/judgments/text/2011.04.13-2010.-Ku-.No..1088.html. In the referred to case the due process violation was failure to give appellee notice and an opportunity to respond to appellant's petition for review.
55. *Restricted Theory of sovereign Immunity case, Tokyo Sanyo Trading Corporation v. Republic of Pakistan*, Case No. 2003 Ju 1231, 60 Minshu No. 6, http://www.courts.go.jp/english/judgments/text/2006.07.21-2003.-Ju-.No..1231.html (P.B. July 21, 2006). In 2009 Japan adopted a law on Civil Jurisdiction against Foreign States (Act on the Civil Jurisdiction of Japan over Foreign States, Act No. 24 of 2009, effective Apr. 1, 2010) following the restrictive theory of immunity.
56. Rule 53 (1). An English language translation of the Rules of Civil Procedure (CCP) may be found in Yasuhei Taniguchi, Pauline C. Reich, Hiroto Miyake, *Civil Procedure In Japan* (Juris Publishing 2000).
57. This educating of the court function separates even the new "plausibility" pleading requirement and non-conclusory allegation requirements of recent Supreme Court of the United States cases from the Japanese pleading requirement. The new plausibility and non-conclusory allegation rules that are emerging may serve a useful notice and gatekeeper function—closing

Moreover, the court reviews the complaint before it is served on the defendant and it may be returned to the plaintiff for correction and if not corrected, the complaint may be dismissed even before it is ever served.[58] When approved by the court, the court serves the complaint.

Failure to correct a complaint may not reflect a disregard for the court. A plaintiff may fail to correct simply because the plaintiff does not have available the evidence that must be submitted with the complaint. As there are no "discovery" tools available to such a "plaintiff in waiting," it may simply be impossible to file a complaint—even though the plaintiff may have a valid claim. The court sets a date for an initial hearing and the parties are summoned to appear. At this initial hearing the process of defining and narrowing the dispute is started. This process ("clarification") extends over several hearings and the court may call for a "preliminary" hearing to assist in the issue defining process.[59] At either the initial hearing (called a "plenary hearing") or at a "preparatory plenary hearing" the court may require the parties to present evidence.[60] Under a procedure codified in the 1996 a "Preparation for 'Oral Argument'," stage may be used and is today the preferred procedure. This preparation stage is designed to achieve most of the functions of the Oral Argument (another name for the Plenary Proceeding) stage but is considered as *preparatory* to the plenary stage so that it may be held in private rather than in a public forum. The relative privacy enables the parties to more quickly come to a settlement than under the older procedure. Many of the fact-finding procedures of the Oral Argument or Plenary Proceeding stage are handled in the more informal preparation stage.

The 1996 Code also introduced a new Inquiry Procedure (designed after the American Interrogatory) wherein the parties may make inquiry of the opposing party in an effort to obtain evidence and parties may request written answers to the questions asked.[61] Inquiry cannot be made that is unduly expensive or time consuming to respond to; or where the answer would cause the respondent embarrassment; opinions cannot be sought. While a party may inquire, there is no corresponding duty to respond![62] The Inquiry process is little used and when used rarely produces significant

---

the courthouse door to cases where there is not enough evidence to warrant discovery and not enough reason to believe that a cause of action exists to open the process of the court to the plaintiff. But the function is not the education of the court (as decider of the fact, law and case).

58. CCP 137, 140. Under Rule 56 the presiding judge may have the clerk require the correction to the complaint.
59. CCP Articles 164–167.
60. For a discussion of the issue narrowing process and a discussion of civil procedure in Japan see Goodman, *Justice and Civil Procedure in Japan* (Oceana 2004).
61. CCP Article 163.
62. For a discussion of the changes made in the 1996 new Code of Civil Procedure see Yasuhei Taniguchi, *The 1996 Code of Civil Procedure of Japan—A Procedure for the Coming Century?*, 45 Am. J. Comp. L. 767, 779 (1997); Takeshi Kojima, *Japanese Civil Procedure in Comparative Law*, 46 Kansas L. Rev. 687 (1998).

answers.[63] "Inquiry" can be used by a potential plaintiff. The pre-filing Inquiry may be used to demonstrate a claimant is serious.

After Preparation for Oral Argument a plenary hearing (Oral Argument) is initiated. The real hope of the new procedure is that the case will be settled at the preparation stage or if not settled the issues will have been narrowed so that the Oral Argument stage is quickly resolved. If a party frustrates this purpose by failing to identify evidence or issues at an early stage, it will be required to explain its failure. While the court has authority under certain circumstances to refuse to later consider matters not identified early in the proceeding,[64] such refusal is not common. At the preparation stage, the court may make evidentiary rulings, such as excluding evidence at the plenary hearing but the formal submission of witness testimony and admission of documents into evidence takes place at the Plenary Hearing.

While the terms preliminary plenary, preparation for oral argument and plenary hearing have a singular sound to them the fact is that such hearings include several sessions and may last months or even years. As the preparation stage (and Oral Argument stage) constitutes a series of meetings and consultations between the parties and the judge and continues over an extended period of time, the court may "request" or "suggest" production of documents "during the trial" rather than as a pre-trial matter as in the United States, However, Japanese "production" rules are much more restrictive than "discovery" in the United States. There are no depositions and documents while subject to an order to produce are not subject to what American lawyers would call discovery as the requesting party must know of the existence of the document before it can ask the court to request production. Production under the new Code is somewhat broader than previously but it is still quite restrictive and the sanctions available against an unwilling third person are relatively light.

Eventually the plenary hearing (Oral Argument or trial) stage is reached and here the judge, again, plays a major role. The presiding judge controls the hearing and may allow or prohibit persons from making statements at the hearing;[65] question parties and witnesses; order the production of evidence and documents either on request or *sua sponte*, and may order expert witness testimony or report.[66] A party may object but the ultimate decision on such matters as order of witnesses, order of questioning of witnesses, introduction of documents, whether a witness may be called, etc. belongs to the court. A party seeking production is required to specify both the document sought and the person in possession of the document;[67] the substance of the document, the

63. Carl F. Goodman, *Japan's New Civil Procedure Code: Has it Fostered a Rule of Law Dispute Resolution Mechanism?*, 29 Brooklyn J. Intl. L. 511 (2004); Yasunori Honma, *The Tendency of the Recent Reforms of the Japanese Code of Civil Procedure*, 49 Acta Juridica Hungarica, 318, 322-324 (2008).
64. CCP Article 157.
65. CCP Article 148.
66. CCP Articles 149-151.
67. Documents identified as part of a party's case in its complaint or response are automatically required to be produced. But any document that does not assist a party will not be listed in these documents. Of course, the real objective of 'discovery' is the location of documents that do not assist the party in possession of the documents.

reasons for requesting its production, and the facts that are to be proven by the document must also be laid out in the request.[68]

Without knowing what the document says it is extremely difficult to provide this information. The Code permits the requester to set out material that enables the holder of the document to identify the same in cases where it is unusually difficult to specifically identify the document or the person in possession thereof.[69] The court may review the document requested *in camera* and the court may call for the redacting of portions of the document. While the new Code somewhat liberalizes document production, the basic issue of what documents may be required to be produced remains. The writers of the new Code were confronted with a problem in that there were two opposing positions on document production. The first group sought to keep production narrow (this group consisted of interests that viewed themselves as likely defendants, i.e., major companies) and a second group wanted liberal document discovery similar to, but not as broad reaching, as in the United States (this group saw itself as representing potential plaintiffs). No compromise appears to have been workable between the groups. As a consequence the new Code contains the provisions of the old Code plus a new fourth section on discovery, which appears on its face, to represent a significant victory for the second group. The first three sections represent the old law on document production under which documents a party itself refers to must be disclosed, documents that a party has a right to demand possession of under some provision of substantive law must be produced and documents that are prepared for the benefit of the party requesting the document or which documents the relationship between the parties must be produced (so-called "benefit" or "relationship" documents). The fourth category broadly reads as a catchall apparently designed to cover any other documents[70] except three categories of documents: (i) where the privilege against self-incrimination is involved[71]; (ii) where a privileged communication or a protected secret would be divulged,[72] and (iii) where the document sought was created for the sole use of the party in possession of the document ("self-use documents"). It is this third exception that has the potential to swallow the otherwise broadly worded production rule.

Prior to the amendment of the Code, some Japanese courts had broadly interpreted the "relationship" or "benefit" category of documents in an effort to make more documents subject to the production rule. Other judges, in an effort to cabin or limit this expansive doctrine had devised a document exception rule under which "self-use" documents were excluded from discovery. Thus a document created by a party exclusively for its own use and not disclosed to others was not subject to document production. This limitation is extremely limiting to potential plaintiffs. Although the new Code appears to be a broad acceptance of the notion that all relevant documents should be disclosed, this exception appears to make the most damaging of documents

68. CCP Article 221.
69. CCP Article 222.
70. CCP Article 220 (iv).
71. Not only the privilege of the holder of the document but also the privilege of certain close relatives is protected. CCP Article 196.
72. See CCP Article 197.

unavailable to a plaintiff. Although it has been suggested that the new Code should severely narrow the definition of self-use documents[73] such does not yet appear to be the case.

The Supreme Court has held that a document prepared by a bank and to be used for internal decision making as part of a loan application process is a self-use document. Such documents need not be produced in litigation, even where it is claimed the bank improperly made the loan because it was aware that the plaintiff could not afford the loan and would not be able to repay the loan.[74] To require such documents to be produced would interfere with the frank discussion of views within the bank and would violate the privacy rights of the bank.[75] Similarly the Court has held that a derivative lawsuit plaintiff suing the directors of a credit union is not entitled to production of loan documents because the decision making documents are self-use documents made solely for the use of the credit union.[76] The Supreme Court has modified but not abolished the Fuji Bank rule.[77] Thus, if the bank involved has failed and gone out of business (its assets were acquired by the Japanese equivalent of the Federal Deposit Insurance Corporation or its designee for the purposes of collection) and thus was no longer making any loans, the decision making document could be ordered produced.

For a viable going concern (Fuji Bank) there is a need for open communications and open expression of opinion. The *Fuji Bank* rule thus protects the company's decision making process *(ringisho)* by keeping documents used in that process confidential and not subject to production. For a defunct company there is no need for open lines of communications as there is no longer a decision making process to protect.[78]

The significance of protection of the decision making process is exemplified in the Supreme Court's decision allowing production of a document prepared by a company for distribution to its branch offices explaining a decision made by management at the home office. The document was prepared by the company for its internal self-use and

73. Toshiro M. Mochizuki, B*aby Steps or Giant Leap: Expanded Access to Documentary Evidence under the New Japanese Code of Civil Procedure*, 40 Harvard Intl. L. J. 285 (1999). Mochizuki acknowledges that his view is contra to the view expressed by the Justice Ministry and the Judicial Branch when the new Code was promulgated.

74. The facts of the *Fuji Bank case* are eerily familiar to the 'subprime mortgage crisis' in the United States. In Japan there exists a cause of action when the lender makes a loan that it should have known the borrower could not pay back. This liability arises from the abuse of rights doctrine in the Civil Code Articles 1 and 90—by demanding repaying in such a situation the bank would be abusing its right to repayment.

75. See *Fuji Bank v. Maida*, Case No. 2 of 1999, http://www.courts.go.jp/english/judgments/text/1999.11.12-1999-kyo-No.2.html (P.B.,11/ 1/99).

76. *Derivative Lawsuit Self-use Document* case, Case No. 1999 (Kyo) No. 35, 54 Minshu 2709 (Sup. Ct. P.B. 14 December 2000).

77. For a discussion of recent developments in the document production area and a cultural rationale for the Supreme Court's rule see Carl F. Goodman, *The Evolving Law of Document Production in Japanese Civil Procedure: Context, Culture, and Community*, 33 Brooklyn J. Intl. L. 125 (2007).

78. See *Bank in Liquidation Document Production Case*, Case No. 15 of 2001, 55 Minshu 1411, http://www.courts.go.jp/english/judgments/text/2001.12.07-2001-Kyo-No.15.html (P.B., Dec. 7, 2001).

did not go outside the confines of the company. Hence it met all of the statutory terms for a self-use document. Moreover, it would appear that production of the document would interfere with the open communication between the head office and branches and thus would constitute the necessary harm to the company. Nonetheless the Court ordered the document produced. The document was considered as informational and most significantly it was not a decision making document of the company.[79] Production of the document would not adversely affect the decision making processes of the company. Together with the redacting authority of the judge this raises the possibility that the Court may eventually hold that the facts recited in a document may be subject to production while the decision making aspects of the document are protected.

The Supreme Court has also held that where a company went into bankruptcy and a secured lender to that company sued the bankrupt's main bank alleging that prior to the bankruptcy the bank was aware of the precarious position of the borrower but nonetheless misled the secured lender as to the support the bank would provide the bankrupt, the secured lender was entitled to production of various bank records relating to the bankrupt[80] Including financial records given by the bankrupt to the bank prior to the bankruptcy under a pledge of secrecy. The Court held that as the bankrupt company would be required to produce those documents, the bank was required to produce them and could not hide behind a pledge it had made to the bankrupt. Financial analysis that utilized methodologies that were not sufficiently novel or secret as to be treated as trade secrets could also be obtained under a balancing test. Whether this indicates that in the future the Court will apply a balancing test in production cases similar to the balancing test used in determining privilege claims remains to be seen. Finally, the Supreme Court refused to review the lower court's use of in camera inspection of the records involved finding that such procedure was not a question of law and thus not subject to review on appeal to the Supreme Court. This later ruling may be a green light to lower courts to make more use of the in camera review procedure in document production requests.

The Court has taken a broad view of what documents fell into the category of documents that a party has a right to demand possession of and thus was entitled to production of in litigation. There need not be a specific statutory provision granting a party a right to possession.[81]

Special although generally similar rules apply to production of government documents. Documents that would disclose a government secret, harm national security, prejudice the government in negotiations with foreign powers or with an International Organization, be against the public interest to produce or would damage the government's ability to perform a public function need not be produced. Special

79. *Communication to Branch Office Ordered Produced* case, Case No. 39 of 2005, 60 Minshu No. 2, http://www.courts.go.jp/english/judgments/text/2006.02.17-2005.-Kyo-.No..39.html (P.B., Feb. 17, 2006).
80. *Production of Bank Records Case*, Case No. 2008 (Kyo) No. 18, 62 Minshu No. 10, http://www.courts.go.jp/english/judgments/text/2008.11.25-2008.-Kyo-.No..18.html (P.B., Nov. 25, 2008).
81. *Debt Payment Records Produced to Borrower* case, Case No. 965 of 2004, 59 Minshu No. 6, http://www.courts.go.jp/english/judgments/text/2005.07.19-2004.-Ju-.No..965.html (P.B., July 19, 2005).

procedures are established whereby the government's position is entitled to be heard by the court before any order of production can be entered against the government.[82] Where the government is in possession of "private secret documents" that are given to the government under conditions of confidentiality and a third person asks that the government be required to produce those documents the documents are considered to be government secret documents and the limitations against production set forth above come into play. The Supreme Court has held that a portion of a Labor Investigation report dealing with an industrial accident that contained secrets dealing with the government's decision making process and the opinion of government bureaucrats dealing with that decision making is exempt from production as production would harm the ability of the government to perform its functions. Note that the reasoning is similar to *Fuji Bank*—in essence production of this part of the report would hinder government decision making by exposing its internal decision making process to public view. The Court treated the government decision making process documents the same as it would private company decision making documents. But the case also involved a part of the report that contained what can be termed private secrets, i.e., material garnered from the company and its employees during the investigation. As to these the Court found that while they now were to be treated as government secrets they did not fall within any of the restricting categories because the Labor Law required that the company and its executives/employees cooperate with the government. Thus ordering production of this part of the report would not harm the government's ability to carry out its functions in the future. Had the documents been voluntarily produced by the employer without a requirement that they be produced, they would have remained secret because production might convince other companies in the future not to produce documents voluntarily.[83]

Where a party has been ordered to produce a document and refuses to do so the court may make findings adverse to the party that refuses to produce and those findings may be the basis for a judgment against that party. Such sanction is unlikely and will be utilized only in rare and severe situations. Where a third person fails to produce a requested document the power of the court is limited to the leveling of a non-penal fine not to exceed JPY 200,000

The Civil Procedure Code appears to provide that as a general matter trials should take place at a relatively quick pace with continuous testimony of parties and witnesses.[84] But what you see is not what you get. The backlog of cases and the needs of other parties make it rare that a court can actually take a great deal of testimony or other evidence at a single session. As a result the "trial" phase of the case, like the clarification phase, extends over several sessions, each of which may take place several weeks after the preceding session. Although, recently there is a greater emphasis on

82. Code of Civil Procedure, Article 223.
83. *Child Worker Injury Labor Report Production case*, Case No. 11 of 2005, 59 Minshu No. 8, http://www.courts.go.jp/english/judgments/text/2005.10.14-2005.-Kyo-.No..11.html (P.B., Oct. 14, 2005).
84. CCP 182.

taking direct and cross-examination at the same session and taking testimony of several witnesses on the same day.

Witnesses are to be examined in the same order as would be the case in the United States and the Code and rules contemplate questioning by the lawyers for the parties. Again, what you see is not what you get. Japanese lawyers are not as active as American lawyers in examining witnesses and the Code and Rules allow the questioning of witnesses by the court.[85] The court may even change the order of witness questioning.[86] This allows the judge to initiate questioning and permit the parties to question after the court has finished. Witnesses may not be asked insulting or embarrassing questions, leading questions, duplicative inquiries, and irrelevant questions, matter of opinion or questions that seek information the witness is not familiar with.[87] Witnesses, who refuse to testify after being ordered to do so, may be subjected to a small non-penal fine.[88] Unless ordered otherwise by the court, witnesses are examined prior to parties.[89] Examination of parties is similar to examination of other witnesses[90] although party testimony is not favored.

Witnesses and parties are entitled to rely on certain privileges in addition to the privilege against self-incrimination of the witness or certain family members.[91] Since a witness can neither be asked questions about which he lacks personal knowledge nor embarrassing questions, problems may be presented when litigating against a company. Lower ranking company officials may be found to lack knowledge because they are unfamiliar with the "whole picture" of company involvement while higher ranking officials may be excused from answering since disclosure of damaging information against one's own company may be very embarrassing.

Like the United States Japan has been wrestling with the issue of whether and to what extent a news reporter has a privilege against disclosing sources. This subject is covered in Chapter 7. Japan has no hearsay rule in civil cases (there is a hearsay rule in criminal cases but it has little effect). Even if a witness does not appear for his cross-examination the direct examination will not be excluded (although the judge may determine to give it no weight). Finally, great weight is given to written evidence and the pleadings and briefs of the parties. The reality is that there are few live witnesses at a Japanese civil trial. A court may decide not to take evidence on an issue because it is considered unnecessary.[92]

The Occupation made changes in the Japanese Code of Civil Procedure in an attempt to recreate an American style adversary procedure in Japan.[93] Thus, many of the Code and Rule provisions appear to contemplate an American style procedure. For example, the immunity rules were narrowed to abolish the refusal to testify against

85. 202 (1); See also, Rules 113.
86. CCP 202 (2).
87. Rule 115.
88. CCP 192, 200.
89. CCP 207.
90. CCP 210.
91. CCP Articles 196, 197.
92. CCP Article 181.
93. Alfred C. Oppler, *Law Reform in Occupied Japan* 130–134 (Princeton University Press 1976).

employers[94] but judges interpret the rules consistent with Japanese notions of the essentially group identification between employer and employee that makes permitting such derogatory or unfavorable testimony too embarrassing to be permitted.

At first blush, a reading of the Code sets out a procedure that seems familiar to the American lawyer. But what you see may not be what you get. Code provisions may have been removed and a new style procedure may have been introduced, but the judge retains her primary role in proceedings and concepts of loyalty are still given primacy through rulings of the court. Court cases are much more concerned with narrowing the scope of the questions that must be answered to resolve the matter and in the process trying to get an agreed to settlement or if that is not possible assure that the party that ought to win in fact wins. The greater part of the judicial procedure is taken up with this issue of fact identifying and clarifying. While the Code appears to countenance broad production of documents, the self-use limitation (even as modified) makes the reality quite different. While any person may be called as a witness, the concern that a senior executive not be placed in the embarrassing position of testifying against his own company and the concern that such a witness not be required to disclose confidences that are kept confidential within the company restricts actual examination. While judges have sanctioning powers in some situations they are rarely used and in other situations the court lacks authority to sanction, such as refusals to answer Inquiries. And, because trials are to the court without a jury, rules of evidence and objections on evidentiary grounds are not significant players in the Japanese trial. The court determines what documents will be produced and what weight to give them; the court determines what witnesses will be heard (although the parties are in charge of suggesting witnesses so the old rule that a judge could call a witness ex officio has been changed) and what witnesses will be permitted to testify about; the court determines whether the parties will be examined and if so about what issues; the court determines the order of proof and the order of examination of witnesses; and the court ultimately makes the factual findings and legal conclusions in a matter.

[3] Remedy and Finality

While an American trial and the procedures for the trial appear designed to assist the plaintiff, Japanese procedure appears designed to protect the defendant (although this is changing to reflect the Law Reform Council's recommendations that Japan adopt a more "rule of law" ordered society). This is consistent with the differing functions assigned to the litigation system in each country. So too the decision and remedy phase of the case reflects different societal value judgments about litigation.

In the United States, if the weight of the evidence favors the plaintiff then plaintiff wins even if there is significant evidence to support the defendant. Preponderance is simply 50%+ in favor of the winning party. It is a much more lenient standard for a plaintiff to meet than the beyond a reasonable doubt standard that is required in a criminal case in the United States. In assessing damages, the jury is free to determine

94. See *Ibid*, 134.

for itself the economic as well as emotional costs suffered by the plaintiff. In certain types of cases the jury may award punitive damages, that while considered a civil penalty are designed to enforce the law by civilly punishing a defendant whose conduct has been particularly reprehensible. [On the other hand, punitive damages have a penalty aspect to them that could be considered as making them "penal" and thus not proper vehicles for comity.][95] Judges in the United States retain the power to set aside a damage award in some situations and have the power to reduce an unreasonably high damage award—both punitive and compensatory. Nonetheless, the "base" from which the judge starts in deciding whether and if so to what extent to reduce a damage award is the jury's determination or verdict.

As a general rule, a losing party in the United States has one right of appeal. But appeal is on the record and new evidence cannot be taken on appeal or new issues raised that were not raised in the trial court. Facts found by a jury are entitled to controlling weight unless clearly contrary to the evidence. Facts found by a judge without a jury are not so binding but are entitled to great deference because the trial court is in the best position to make credibility determinations. Only a losing party can appeal and the party that appeals may be required to buy an insurance policy to assure that if it loses the appeal it will pay the damages awarded.

Once a judgment is final the winning plaintiff may take steps to collect on its judgment. Typically the judgment is given to a government officer (a sheriff) to collect and the state becomes a significant partner with the plaintiff in recovering the damages awarded. In addition, there are extensive discovery procedures available to a winning plaintiff to assist in locating assets.

In Japan the system is different. Typically the court will take the matter under advisement and then will advise the parties when the judgment will be issued. Although the Code establishes two months after trial as a benchmark for decision, judges may disregard the two-month rule when circumstances require.[96] The decision is issued in open court. A more "free form" evaluation of evidence is undertaken.[97] The court must be convinced that the plaintiff has met its burden of proof—a higher standard than preponderance. The stringency of the standard has caused judges and legislators to shift the burden of proof in certain types of cases;[98] the most noteworthy

95. The Supreme Court of Japan has refused to extend comity to a punitive damages award rendered by a California court. *Punitive Damages* case, Case No. 1993 (O) No. 1762 (Sup. Ct. P.B. July 11, 1997) See Dan Fenno Henderson, *Comparative Law in the Japanese Courts: Punitive Damages*, 24 L. Japan 98, 103 (1991) for a criticism of the District Court's determination that was upheld on appeal. Although punitive damage awards are not entitled to comity in Japan, an award requiring the losing party to pay 100% of the attorney fees of the winning party is not against public policy as long as the fees awarded do not exceed the actual attorney's fees paid. *Comity Granted to Attorney Fees*, Case No. 19, 994 (O) No. 1838 (Sup. Ct. P.B. 28 April 1998).

96. CCP Article 251.

97. CCP Article 247.

98. E.g., *Burden of Proof, Unanticipated Accident Case*, Case No. 1206 (Ju) of 2005, 60 Minshu No. 5 (Sup. Ct. 1 June 2006). See *Auto Damage Deliberate or Accidental, Burden of Proof on Insurer Top Court* Japan Times, (June 2, 2006).

of which were the so-called *big four pollution* cases[99] where the court redefined and shifted the burden of proof so that the plaintiffs could be successful. In reaching its monetary award, the Japanese court is controlled by different factors than is an American court: (a) damages are viewed as compensation for injury and are typically much lower than in the United States. This is true even when a court may decide that a plaintiff is entitled to damages for emotional suffering caused by the defendant;[100] (b) Japan has no "collateral source" rule such as exists in the United States.[101] This tends to reduce damage awards and limits plaintiffs to recovery of actual out of pocket damages suffered and not compensated for;[102] (c) Judges in Japan are aware of what their colleagues are awarding in similar cases and will tend to follow the established pattern. Schedules for damages in certain types of personal injury cases (principally auto accident, and more recently medical malpractice) are available for use by judges, lawyers and parties. One spin off of this practice is that it is easier for the parties to estimate recovery and thus easier to bring about settlements without the need for trial.

Japanese courts have adopted a rule of proportionality under which a portion of the damages may be placed on the shoulders of the plaintiff.[103] Such a proportionality rule is the comparative negligence rule familiar to American lawyers. But in Japan the proportionality rule may extend beyond comparing the negligence of the tortfeasor and the victim. Where a victim's family member is also partially at fault (so that there would be liability on the part of both the family member and the third person tortfeasor) that family member's contributory negligence may be applied against the victim.[104] For public policy reasons this rule was not applied to reduce damages in a death from overwork case where it was argued the family should have kept the worker home from work.[105]

---

99. *Yokkaichi Air Pollution* case, 1972, *Kumamoto Minamata Disease* case, 1973, *Niigata Minamata Disease* case, 1971, *Itai-ltai Disease Case*, 1971.
100. In the medical malpractice area see, Eric Feldman, *Law, Society and Medical Malpractice Litigation in Japan*, 8 Wash. U. Global Stud. L. Rev. 257 (2009).
101. Under the collateral source rule a plaintiff may recover full damages even though the plaintiff recovered back some of the damage suffered from a third party such as an insurance company. See e.g., *Halek v. United States*, 178 F.3d 481 (7th Cir. 1999). Parties may, by contract, modify the rule. See e.g., *Sereboff v. Mid Atlantic Medical Services*, 547 U.S. 356 (2006).
102. See, e.g., *Calculation of Damages in Auto Accident Case*, Case No. 2008 (Ju) 494, 64 Minshu No. 6, http://www.courts.go.jp/english/judgments/text/2010.09.13-2008.-Ju-.No..494%2C.495.html (P.B., Sept. 13, 2010). Where the tort that underlies the cause of action is considered a heinous act, such as loan sharking, which is both illegal and a violation of public policy, the tortfeasor will not be able to recover back from the borrower the benefit the borrower derived from the loan. *Unjust Enrichment Denied as Set Off in Loan Sharking Case*, Case No. 569 (Ju) 2007, 62 Minshu No. 6, http://www.courts.go.jp/english/judgments/text/2008.06.10-2007.-Ju-.No..569.html (P.B., June 10, 2008).
103. *Proportional Damages Case*, Case No. 1094 (O) of 1988, 46 Minshu No. 4 at 400, http://www.courts.go.jp/english/judgments/text/1992.6.25-1988.-O-.No.1094.html (P.B., June 25, 1992).
104. Y. Nomi, *Proportionality in Tort and Contract Law Public Lecture held at Utrecht University Dutch-Japanese Law Symposium*, 1996.
105. *Death from Overwork Damages case*, Case No. 217 and 218 of 1998, 54 Minshu 1155, http://www.courts.go.jp/english/judgments/text/2000.03.24-1998.-o-.nos.217%2C.218.html (P.B., Mar. 24, 2000).

Damages are also limited by the fact that there are no class action damage suits in Japan. Thus, small claimants are not prone to bring what would in the United States be big cases on behalf of a class of small plaintiffs. Japan has a "representative action" procedure under which a number of plaintiffs may join together and name one to litigate the matter on behalf of all. Unlike a class action which includes all members of the class except those who "opt out" the Representative Action involves an "opt in" procedure where parties who wish to may have their names added as plaintiff.[106] Recent changes allow certified consumer groups to bring injunctive type actions to prevent false and deceptive claims.[107] However such groups cannot bring monetary damages actions. It is reported that as of May 2010 only seven such cases had been brought in Japan.[108]

Punitive damages are not permitted in the Japanese system and a Japanese court will not give comity to an American punitive damages award as such an award violates Japanese public policy. Although punitive in character, a judgment entered by an American Court under Federal Rule 37 as a sanction for failure to make discovery is not a violation of Japanese public policy and does not exceed the compensatory damages sought in the lawsuit.[109] Further, although Japanese courts may award damages for future losses, they may do so only if the damages were foreseeable[110] a difficult standard to prove.[111] Recent changes in the Code are designed to make proof of such damages easier.[112]

As Japan has moved from a country with low technology industries that thrive on inventions made in other countries to a high tech society with intellectual property

106. See Goodman, *The Somewhat Less Reluctant Litigant: Japan's Changing View Towards Civil Litigation*, 32 *Law and Policy in International Business* 769, 794 (2001). The Supreme Court of Japan has held that it is appropriate to add together the damages sought by each plaintiff member of the representative action to determine whether the case is properly filed in the District Court. Although each claim asserted was less than JPY 1.4 Million, the jurisdictional limit for Summary Court cases the total of all claims exceeded said JPY 1.4 Million and thus the case was properly filed in the District Court. See *Aggregation of claims in Representative Action Permitted for jurisdictional Amount Purposes Case*, case No. 2011 (Kyo) No. 4, Minshu Vol. 65, No. 4, http://www.courts.go.jp/english/judgments/text/2011.05.18-2011.-Kyo-.No..4.html (P.B., May 18, 2011).

107. This procedure parallels European practice. For a discussion of EU practice see, Towards a Coherent European Approach to Collective Redress, Commission Staff Working Document (Feb. 4, 2011), http://ec.europa.eu/dgs/health_consumer/dgs_consultations/ca/docs/cr_consultation_paper_en.pdf.

108. Comparative Consumer Law Blog, *Japanese Consumer Law* para. 15, http://tmuramot.wordpress.com/confusion-of-the-concept-between-fiduciary-duty-and-suitability-rule/. (May 15, 2010) This failure is also evident in the German experience and for a similar reason. In Germany monetary damages are possible but the money does not go to the damaged consumers, instead it is paid to the government. Accordingly there is little incentive for the certified organizations to sue. http://ec.europa.eu/consumers/redress_cons/collective_redress_en.htm#Studies.

109. *Tada v. Sakurai*, et al., Case No. 35 (Wa) of 1997, Mito District Court, Oct. 29, 1999, Hanrei Taimuzu No. 1034:270.

110. The Japanese rule for contract damages is based on the foreseeable test of *Hadley v. Baxendale*, 9 Exch 341 (1854), discussed in Chapter 12).

111. For a general discussion of the inadequacy of damages in Japan see Joseph W.S. Davis, *Dispute Resolution In Japan* ch. 12 (Kluwer Law International 1996).

112. CCP Article 248.

assets that need protection, the Intellectual Property laws have been modified to provide for greater damages awards, easier methodologies for establishing damages and easier access to documents in an Intellectual Property case.[113] Towards the end of 2011 Japan, the United States and the EU countries (among others) entered into a multilateral agreement designed to improve enforcement of intellectual property rights that calls for establishing criminal penalties for copying and selling pirated material in digital format.[114] Changes have been made in an effort to provide a measure of protection to a plaintiff from having to disclose its own trade secrets when filing a case claiming a violation of Japan's Unfair Competition Prevention Law ("UCPL"), a statutory protection of trade secrets. The amendment allows the court to hold closed door proceedings to safeguard a party's trade secrets and specifically provides for the availability of protective orders to keep secrets secret all in an effort to protect secrets once litigation is started.[115] The court may close the proceedings and may require the opposition party (allowed to be present in order to defend itself) to maintain secrecy.[116] The court may also limit the availability of the court record.[117] While it is believed by some that the present system protects trade secret holders so that they may bring misappropriation litigation,[118] enforcement must be by way of criminal action. Thus, a putative plaintiff must take into consideration the various factors that might influence a prosecutor's decision as to whether or not to seek criminal penalties when a protective order has been violated. The 2003 amendments to the Unfair Competition Law that created criminal sanctions in some cases of infringement of trade secrets and the 2005 amendments strengthening criminal sanctions for violation of the trade secrets provisions of the law might have a positive effect on prosecutor discretion to charge for a violation of a court issued protective order.[119] But, Japanese courts are, as

113. See e.g., Patent Law sections 102–105, 105*bis* and 105*ter*. Unfair Competition Prevention Law, Act No.47 of 1993 as amended Act No. 55 of 2006 (Effective Jan. 1, 2006) Article 4 (Damages).
114. See, Kyodo, *Multilateral Pact Inked to Target Bootlegging*, Japan Times (Oct. 1, 2011), http://search.japantimes.co.jp/cgi-bin/nn20111001x2.html. Japan has an active market for rental of videos and music where royalties may not be paid to the artists whose works are rented. Whether this pact will affect such industry remains to be seen.
115. See, Tatsubumi Sato, *Protection of Trade Secrets in Japan*, http://www.ip.courts.go.jp/documents/pdf/thesis/060928_29_1.pdf. Judge Sato notes that the definition of a trade secret in Japan is a three part test the information must be (1) commercially useful (and of a business of technical nature); (2) must not be publicly known or publicly available [the ability to acquire the information through reverse engineering does not make the information publicly available as the cost to reverse engineer could be prohibitive, but actually acquiring the information by reverse engineering might meet the publicly available standard); and (3) steps must be taken by the party claiming a secret to keep the information secret.
116. Act No.47 of 1993 as amended Act No. 55 of 2006 Article 10 (Protective Orders), Article 13 (in camera presentation of testimony).
117. Act No.47 of 1993 as amended Act No. 55 of 2006 Article 12.
118. Dario A. Machleidt, *Japanese Trade Secret Protection: Litigants Can Feel Secure Bringing Misappropriation Claims in Japanese Courts*, 15 CASRIP Newsletter (Winter/Spring 2008), http://www.law.washington.edu/Casrip/Newsletter/default.aspx?year=2008&article=newsv15i1TradeSecret.
119. For a discussion of the 2005 criminal law amendments to the Unfair Competition Law see, Yoshikazu Iwase & Wakako Sekiyama, *The Latest Amendments to the Japanese Unfair Competition Prevention Law*, http://www.jp-ta.jp/pdf/committee/005/JTA/11b.pdf, last accessed Sept. 16, 2012.

a general rule, reluctant to enforce their orders in litigation with strong sanctions. The UCPL specifically allows a court that issued a protective order to rescind the order.[120] Undoubtedly the present system is better than the pre-2005 situation. Nonetheless, trade secret litigation is not likely to be as aggressively pursued in Japan as in the United States.[121]

Once a plaintiff has won at the trial level in Japan the plaintiff has not yet won. This may seem contradictory but what you see is not what you get. The trial level is really only a "preliminary trial" level in the sense that a losing party may appeal to the High Court. On appeal in Japan the parties may introduce new evidence and even can advance new theories not raised below.[122] In a sense, this first level appeal is merely a continuation of the trial.[123]

Even after a plaintiff has finally obtained a final judgment, there is no assurance of payment. Japan does not have a supplementary proceeding procedure to assist a party in locating assets of the defendant. While efforts have been made to make collection more likely, the Judicial Reform Council found this an area requiring reform.[124]

On its face the Japanese civil procedure system appears to resemble, and thus one would expect it to function as, an American style civil procedure system. What you see may not be what you get. Putting aside the differences between the Japanese and American trial, more fundamental differences relate to: (i) the willingness of the trial court to render a decision in favor of one and against the other party, and (ii) the ultimate relief that can typically be obtained through the use of the judicial process.

120. Act No.47 of 1993 as amended Act No. 55 of 2006 (Effective Jan. 1, 2006) Article 11 (rescission of protective order).

121. Both Japanese prosecutors and courts are also likely to take into account the fact that the 2005 amendments and protection of trade secrets in general were a result of international efforts rather than indigenous developments in Japan. Japan's agreement to the TRIPS Agreement resulted in charges that Japan was failing to live up to its TRIPS obligations by not protecting trade secrets. The 2005 amendments were designed to quiet the international complaints.

122. Presumably the efforts to limit the raising of new evidence and new issues after the 'preliminary plenary session' or the 'preparation session' should limit the raising of new issues and contentions at the appeal level. However, if the party seeking to do so can satisfactorily explain why it did not raise the issue earlier (an easy standard to meet), the court will allow the new materials to be considered and new issues to be raised.

123. Although the Supreme Court is not supposed to accept new evidence in criminal cases as well as in civil cases, the reality is that prosecutors may supplement the record even after the High Court has entered its judgment and the supplemented record may then form the basis for the Supreme Court's decision. *Supplement of Record After Second Level Appeal decided is Evidence Before Supreme Court*, Case No. 2011 (A) No. 469, Keishu Vol. 65, No. 7 (2nd Petty Bench, Oct. 26, 2011), http://www.courts.go.jp/english/judgments/text/2011.10.26-2011.-A-.No..469.html. Whether the Supreme Court would consider such evidence in a civil case is unknown.

124. Recommendations of the Justice System Reform Council—For a Justice System to Support Japan in the twenty-first century, June 12, 2001 The Justice System Reform Council, www.kantai.go.jp/foreign/2001/0612report.html.

[4] Role of the Public

The United States judicial system is "publicly driven." The public is viewed as an important, perhaps the most important, part of the law enforcement mechanism. Not only does the public decide what cases to bring and when to bring them, the public actively participates in the decision of cases through service on the jury. This public participation is not available in Japan. There is no civil jury.[125] The system does not favor public involvement in law enforcement that is viewed as a function of the government bureaucracy.[126]

Nonetheless, changes in Japanese procedure and substantive law have resulted in a greater number of Japanese availing themselves of the judicial system than in the past. This development has shown itself most dramatically in those areas where plaintiffs feel morally outraged by the conduct of the opposite party, where legislative changes have skewed the cost/benefit analysis so that the benefits of litigation may far outweigh the cost, where the consensus of society has shifted to favor making a defendant responsible for its improper acts and where the court system has created a new cause of action.

The consensus of society has recently shifted away from considering medical doctors and their decisions immune from liability.[127] Slowly but perceptively the Japanese courts have begun the process of adopting an "informed consent" doctrine in Japanese law and shifting away from physician dominance to patient discretion in treatment.[128] Medical malpractice suits are on the rise in Japan.[129] And, as the consensus of society has shifted in other areas, such as sex discrimination and the responsibility of employers for the death of their employees as a consequence of overwork, the measure of damages has increased.

---

125. While Japan has re-introduced public participation in criminal cases through the Saiban'in mixed panel system (See Chapter 16) no such effort is being pursued in civil cases.
126. Hideo Tanaka & Akio Takeuchi, *The Role of Private Persons in the Enforcement of Law: A Comparative Study of Japanese and American Law*, 7 L. Japan 34 (1974).
127. Medical malpractice is also professional negligence—a crime and doctors have been prosecuted for matters that in the United States would be treated as civil rather than criminal liability. See, Robert B. LeFlar, *"Unnatural Deaths," Criminal Sanctions, and Medical Quality Improvement in Japan*, 9 Yale J. Health, Pol'y L. & Ethics 1 (2009); Kyodo, *Automatic redress plan mulled for victims of medical malpractice*, Japan Times (July 10, 2011), http://search.japantimes.co.jp/cgi-bin/nn20110710a5.html.
128. See, *Informed Consent Case*, 1011 Hanji 54, 447 Hanta 78 (Sup. Ct., June 19, 1981); Yutaka Tejima, *Recent Developments Concerning a Doctor's Legal Duty of Explanation after Medical Treatment in Japan*, 40 Kobe U. L. Rev. 87 (2006);.Yutaka Tejima, *Recent Developments in the Informed Consent Law in Japan*, 36 Kobe U. L. Rev.45, 48 (2002); Barron T. Oda, *An Alternative Perspective to Battling the Bulge: The Social and Legal Fallout to Japan's Anti-Obesity Legislation*,12 Asian-P. L. & Policy J. 249 (2010); Minoru Nakamura, *Privacy: Current Status and Pending Issues in Japan*, NRI Papers No. 131 (2008) at 15, http://www.nri.co.jp/english/opinion/papers/2008/pdf/np2008131.pdf.
129. Barron T. Oda, *An Alternative Perspective to Battling the Bulge: The Social and Legal Fallout to Japan's Anti-Obesity Legislation*,12 Asian-P. L. & Policy J. 249 (2010); Eric Feldman, *Law, Society and Medical Malpractice Litigation in Japan*, 8 Wash. U. Global Stud. L. Rev. 257 (2009); Shogo Sasao, et al, *Medical Malpractice Litigation in Gastroenterological Practice in Japan: A 22-Yr Review of Civil Court Cases*, 101 Am. J. of Gastroenterology 1951 (2006).

There have been a string of tort cases brought against the Japanese government for complicity in medical malpractice decisions. These cases started with litigation charging that the government improperly permitted use of HIV tainted blood, have extended to cases involving government failure to act decisively in the Mad Cow disease arena, improper treatment of victims of Hanson's disease and in connection with donated blood and hepatitis.[130] All of these cases involved outrage at government complicity and refusal to recognize its responsibility. In each case the courts determined that the government had acted wrongly and damages were awarded to the plaintiffs. The government thereafter established procedures to provide similar relief to victims who had not joined in the lawsuits.[131]

Although the number of lawyers in Japan has risen in recent years there does not appear to have been a corresponding rise in legal malpractice suits. Reason for the low number of legal malpractice suits may be because the judge in Japanese litigation takes an active role in cases and thus may remedy malpractice before it can rise to the level of something actionable; because the standard for success in such suits is high; and because damages are limited to those that clearly relate to and were caused by the malpractice.[132]

[5] Alternative Dispute Resolution and Other Extra-Judicial Remedies

One of the major objectives of the Occupation was to strengthen the Japanese legal system and the independence of the courts so that Japanese would utilize the courts for dispute resolution. Prior to the Occupation the normal means of resolving disputes was by way of conciliation. This was viewed as "anti-democratic." Nonetheless, in postwar Japan ADR mechanisms are highly valued and used. This is to be expected in a country that takes its history seriously and in Japan history points in the direction of ADR.

Today virtually all "family matters" including divorce or issues related to divorce that cannot be resolved by consent of the parties in the first instance must go through

130. See e.g., Akemi Nakamura, *'Late Settlement Little Solace,' Hepatitis disaster another warning ignored*, Japan Times (Dec. 5, 2007). In 2011 the government settled a suit brought by sufferers of Hepatitis B who had contracted the disease as a consequence of the shared use of needles in group vaccinations. Among other things the agreement called for an apology on the part of the government which was given by the Prime Minister, Kan. Kyodo, *Plaintiffs in hep. B suit settle with state*, Japan Times (June 25, 2011), http://search.japantimes.co.jp/cgi-bin/nn20110625a7.html.

131. The government has been slow to act in the vaccine area. Natsuko Fukue, *Polio shot sheds light on vaccine lag, System, bureaucratic cowardice work against new drug approvals*, Japan /times on Line (Jan. 12, 2012), http://www.japantimes.co.jp/text/nn20120112f1.html. It may be that the government has failed to license new vaccines because there are no Japanese manufacturers of the vaccine while there are Japanese manufacturers of older less effective vaccines. Public pressure caused the government approved the importation vaccines. Jiji, Kyodo, *Inacctivated Polio vaccines to get OK*, Japan Times (Apr. 21, 2012), http://www.japantimes.co.jp/text/nn20120421a9.html.

132. For a discussion of legal malpractice suits in Japan see, Kyoko Ishida, *Ethics and Regulations of Legal Service Providers in Japan* 164–180 (vdm Verlag, Dr. Muller 2011).

mediation before a litigation can be undertaken.[133] In typical tort areas, the government or private industry has established claims resolution procedures outside the court system. One of the basic elements of making out-of-court resolution effective is the Japanese practice of standardizing recovery. Parties knowing the probable outcome of a successful litigation may gear their settlement negotiations to the range previously established.

Although most litigation in Japan involves automobile accidents, most automobile accident cases are amicably resolved without resort to the courts. This is achieved through a combination of government and private methods that have the effect of limiting fact disputes (all accidents must, by virtue of the Road Traffic Act, be immediately reported to the police who make an immediate investigation, which usually results in an agreed statement of facts as to the accident); and resolving questions of comparative negligence through a standardized classification system and publishing damages table both developed by the Tokyo District Court (a similar table has been prepared for medical malpractice). Even if the matter cannot be resolved through negotiation, other mediation devices are available to resolve the matter short of litigation. The Traffic Accident Dispute Resolution Center, established by insurance companies, with offices in major cities throughout Japan is a respected mediator of traffic accident cases. While its determinations are not binding, insurance companies will, as a general rule, accept its decisions. Accident victims can either accept the decision or choose the litigation alternative. Between negotiation and mediation it is suggested that less than 1% of all traffic accidents lead to court initiated litigation.[134] Similarly there are private mechanisms available to resolve disputes arising from medical malpractice.[135] ADR is available in such diverse areas as environmental hazards[136] and product failure, etc.[137] Non-legal disputes may also be resolved through ADR available through the Civil Liberties Bureau.[138] Even in areas where the courts have been utilized to establish liability, the government has moved in to create alternative forums to take the matter out of the hands of the court system—HIV[139] government responsibility for the mistreatment of Hanson's Disease

133. For a discussion of the history of conciliation in divorce cases and the adverse effect of the requirement of conciliation on women in Japan see, Masayuki Murayama, *Convergence from Opposite Direction? Characteristics of Japanese Divorce Law in Comparative Perspective*, in *Japanese Family Law in Comparative Perspective* 61 (Scheiber and Mayali, ed., Robbins Collection Publications 2008).

134. See Takao Tanase, *The Management of Disputes: Automobile Accident Compensation in Japan*, 24 L. & Soc. Rev. 651 (1990).

135. *Out-of-court mediation offered for malpractice*, The Yomiuri Shimbun (Sept. 10, 2008).

136. Eric Feldman, *Law, Society and Medical Malpractice Litigation in Japan*, 8 Wash. U. Global Stud. L. Rev. 257, 278 et seq. (2009) for a discussion of methods adopted by the Japanese government to resolve tort cases in non-judicial settings and the rising tide of use of the courts to resolve tort damages cases as a consequence of recent governmental efforts to make litigation more accessible and public consciousness.

137. See J. Mark Ramseyer, *Products Liability Through Private Ordering: Notes on a Japanese Experiment*, 144 U. Pennsylvania L. Rev. 1823 (1996).

138. See Joel Rosch, *Institutionalizing Mediation: The Evolution of the Civil Liberties Bureau in Japan*, 21 L. & Soc. Rev. 243 (1987).

139. The HIV case was pending for years when the court suggested a settlement. The parties then negotiated concerning the settlement and the parties advised the court as to changes they

and hepatitis patients—Minamata Disease and more recently, preempting litigation the government was quick to adopt a compensation system for victims of the 3/11/11 Great East Japan Earthquake and Tsunami and Fukushima tragedies.

The government views ADR as a preferred method of resolving disputes that might otherwise be referred to courts. Legislation may create an ADR remedy rather than a judicial remedy. The new Labor Court is essentially an ADR mechanism and was instituted in substantial part because of an increase in the number of individual labor disputes being initiated in court.[140]

Conciliation is not simply a means to avoid litigation of "personal" or "individualized" disputes. Conciliation has a broader context in Japan and is used to resolve disputes between interest groups, between the government and groups, as well as between individuals.[141]

It is estimated that fully 30% of all litigations in Japan are resolved through the process of in-court compromise (*soshojo no wakai*).[142]

The Japanese system of appeals, the weak system for execution on judgments rendered by a court and the ability of the judge to act as mediator by indicating to the parties what decision might be expected, all favor settlement rather than judicial decision. ADR is not the only extra-judicial means utilized to resolve disputes. It is reported that bill collectors in major Japanese cities may use the threat of violence and even violence itself to collect on outstanding loans. This is, of course, criminal conduct but it nonetheless is apparently seen as an acceptable alternative to resort to the judicial system.[143] Similarly, *sokaiya* racketeers, while technically illegal and sometimes prosecuted along with the companies that pay them off, have been described as a surrogate for effective shareholder litigation to enforce corporate governance standards.[144]

Controlled limited violence is a methodology that also appears to be acceptable—under the appropriate circumstances—in resolving what American's would view as a legal issue to be resolved by the courts. This is not as startling as it may appear at first glance. If the function of a judicial system is to resolve disputes in a civilized non-violent manner, and if the judicial system either lacks effective sanctions

---

thought advisable to the proposed settlement. A second court proposed settlement was forthcoming which, while it did not go as far as the plaintiffs' desired met many of their conditions. The case was settled. See Eric A Feldman, *The Ritual of Rights in Japan, Law, Society and Health Policy* 121–128 (Cambridge University Press 2000).

140. Ryuichi Yamakawa, *The Enactment of the Labor Contract Act: Its Significance and Future Issues*, 6 Japan Lab. Rev. 4, 5 (2010).

141. Frank K. Upham, *Visions of Justice in Postwar Japan: A Preliminary Inquiry*, L. E. & W. 145, 161–162 (Waseda University Press 1988).

142. See Judge Tetsuya Obuchi, *Role of the Court in the Process of Informal Dispute Resolution in Japan: Traditional and Modern Aspects, With Special Emphasis on In-Court Compromise*, 20 L. Japan 74 (1987); Iwasaki, Reconciliation of Commercial Disputes in Japan, www.gsid.nagoya-.ac.jp/project/apec/lawdb/japan/dispute/adr-en.html; For a discussion of in-court mediation and conciliation in commercial disputes. See Yasunobu Sato, *Commercial Dispute Processing and Japan* 285–301 (Kluwer Law International 2001).

143. Takeyoshi Kawashima, *Dispute Resolution in Contemporary Japan, found in A. von Mehren*, L. Japan 41, 48–49 (1963 ed.).

144. Mark D. West, *Information, Institutions, and Extortion in Japan and the United States, 'Making Sense of Sokaiya Racketeers,'* 93 N.W. U. L. Rev. 767, 783 (1999).

to carry out this goal or is not understood by the general public as available to carry out this goal, then organized, structured and controlled violence—undertaken as a last resort—may be seen as an acceptable alternative.

This is not to suggest that violence is always or even predominantly or even frequently resorted to, to resolve a fundamentally legal issue. Rather, it is an extreme method used in extreme cases where the judicial system and other means of "civil" non-violent resolution have failed or are viewed as inadequate.[145] In such cases, restrained violence appears acceptable as a means of assisting in the dispute resolution process and may also serve as a safety value to release pressure felt by victims who appear to have no other way of being heard.[146] Where pressure builds and violence is not resorted to plaintiffs in Japan may mobilize protests to support their litigation as was done in the AIDS tainted blood litigation.[147]

[6] Judicial Reform

Special legislation was passed by the United States Congress and signed by the president to shield a manufacturer of a small, inexpensive but essential part of heart pacemakers from liability if the part malfunctioned. The manufacturer had threatened to stop production because profits on the part were a small part of the company's income and the risk to its bottom line of liability suits was simply too high. After a flood of lawsuits and several large damage awards, the primary manufacturer of breast implants filed for bankruptcy. As part of the bankruptcy filing the company entered into a global settlement of breast implant litigation. The latest scientific studies indicate that there is no connection between the bankrupt company's product and the complaints of woman who had implants. No other company was prepared to face the litigation risks involved and women who might otherwise want implants could not find the product or doctors willing to perform the surgery in the United States. Breast cancer survivors were left with few choices for implantation. States that settled with the tobacco companies and achieved a windfall in revenues now find themselves in financial problems because their anti-smoking campaigns have reduced tobacco sales and thus state revenues from the settlement.[148] It would appear that the United States

145. For a discussion of the role of controlled violence in the Minamata Disease case see Frank K. Upham, *Litigation and Moral Consciousness in Japan An Interpretive Analysis of Four Japanese Pollution Suits*, 10 L. & Soc. Rev. 579 (1976).
146. *In the Asahikawa Proficiency Test Case, Japan v. Sato* et al., 30 Keishu 615 (Sup. Ct. G.B. 21 May 1976) school teachers who opposed the use of standardized proficiency tests not only refused to give the tests but assaulted local education officials who were trying to administer the test as well as the local school principal. For an English language translation of the case see Lawrence W. Beer & Hiroshi Itoh, *The Constitutional Case Law of Japan, 1970 through 1990* at 230 (University of Washington Press 1996).
147. See Eric A. Feldman, *The Ritual of Rights In Japan, Law, Society And Health Policy* 123 (Cambridge University Press 2000).
148. Compare the active role of the tobacco litigation in the United States in the changing of public policy with the lack of role played by litigation in Japan's approach to the issue of smoking and health. See Eric A. Feldman, *The Culture of Legal Change: A Case Study of Tobacco Control in Twenty-First Century Japan*, 27 Michigan J. Intl. L. 1,48–49 (2006). In 2012 the government of Japan announced efforts to cut the smoking rate in half (to approximately 10%) by 2013. *Govt.*

might have received more than it bargained for from its litigation system. Many business groups urge judicial reform to correct what they consider to be an imbalance in the tort system. Trial lawyers, flush with multimillion dollar fee awards from the tobacco litigation spend freely to permit "injured parties to be made whole." The American public benefits by having some of the safest, or at least well-tested, pharmaceutical drugs but suffers because the time to get drugs to market is alleged to be too long and many drug companies are afraid to manufacture vaccines because the known side effects to a few could wipe out the firm. As a consequence, each year there are fewer vaccine manufacturers and supplies are chronically short. In the war against bio-terrorism, the United States found itself woefully short of vaccine manufacturing capability.[149] What you see a legal system that supposedly puts the individual consumer first and protects her through private litigation enforcement is not necessarily what you get.

In Japan, reform of the legal system has become a major policy goal. Many of the Reforms suggested by the Law Reform Council have been legislatively adopted in the attempt to make Japan more of a Rule of Law society and the Code changes made in 1996 are more litigation friendly. Some have suggested that preliminary data shows that this accounts for an increase in litigation[150] although the matter is unclear.

The number of new cases increased in the period between 1996 (when the new Civil Procedure Code was adopted) and 1998 (when it came into effect). Clearly this increase cannot be attributed to the New Code. Moreover, between 2002 and 2005 the number of cases filed *declined* before rising again in 2006—but still below the 2002 level. 2003 appears to have been a high-water mark. However, the number of new cases spiked in 2007 and then spiked again in 2009, before falling back in 2010.

At the same time the number of judges (excluding summary court judges) steadily increased.[151] It is likely that the jump in new cases between 2006 and 2007 was brought about by the Supreme Court's consumer loan interest cases that provided significant relief that consumers could pursue in court (the Supreme Court decisions are clustered in 2006 and 2008).[152] Further, the number of new cases filed *declined* during the decade 1996—2005 even though the number of new lawyers increased, the number of judges increased and the New Civil Procedure Code reforms had been put in place.

Aims to Reduce Smoking Rate to Around 10%, Daily Mainichi on Line,1(Jan. 23, 2012), http://mdn.mainichi.jp/mdnnews/national/archive/news/2012/01/23/20120123p2g00m0dm071000c.html.

149. A1–Severe Vaccine Shortages Termed 'Unprecedented,' Washington Post (Apr. 20, 2002).
150. Tom Ginsberg & Glenn Hoetker, *The Unreluctant Litigant? An Empirical Analysis of Japan's Turn to Litigation*, 35 J. Leg. Stud. 31 (2006).
151. The web site of the Supreme Court gives the number of 2739 for 2009 but it is likely that the difference is accounted for by using *end of year v. start of year* numbers or using the *Japanese year v. the American year* numbers. In any event the increase appears to be 50 judges per year.
152. See e.g., *Consumer Lending Interest Rate cases*, Case No. 2003 (Ju) No. 1653, Minshu Vol. 60, No. 1, http://www.courts.go.jp/english/judgments/text/2006.01.24-2003.-Ju-.No..1653.html (P.B., Jan. 24, 2006); Case No. 2004 (Ju) No. 1518, Minshu Vol. 60, No. 1, http://www.courts.go.jp/english/judgments/text/2006.01.13-2004.-Ju-.No..1518.html (P.B., Jan. 13, 2006); Case No. 2006 (Ju) No. 2268, Minshu Vol. 62, No. 1, http://www.courts.go.jp/english/judgments/text/2008.01.18-2006.-Ju-.No..2268-112248.html (P.B., Jan. 18, 2008).

This does not mean that lowering the barriers to litigation has been unsuccessful in generating awareness of the law as a medium for dispute resolution. During the same period steps have been taken in Japan to take out of the legal system but put in the ADR system cases that previously had been heard by the courts. While the number of cases filed tells us how many cases were filed it does not tell us how many cases would have been filed if other dispute resolution steps had not been initiated that mirror the legal process or make resort to the courts unnecessary.

CHAPTER 15
Conflict of Laws

§15.01 UNITED STATES

[A] Federation Form of Government Applying a Common Law System

In the United States the study of conflict of laws, also known as choice of law and in civil law societies as private international law, typically involves three separate but related topics: (a) jurisdiction—whether the court before whom the action is pending has authority over the defendant in the lawsuit; (b) choice of law should the forum court apply its own law to the case at hand or the law of a different jurisdiction; (c) recognition—once a judgment has been entered by the forum court should or must a foreign court give recognition to such judgment and enforce the judgment rendered. Because the United States is a federation of semi-sovereign states issues of jurisdiction, choice of law and recognition can arise in either of two circumstances: (a) where the question implicates sister-states or (b) where the question implicates a nation state foreign to the United States. Although each semi-sovereign state of the United States has authority to determine the scope of the jurisdiction of its own courts, that authority is limited by the Constitutional requirement that the litigants before the court must be given Due Process. Thus an action brought in a New York court against a California resident relating to events that occurred in California and that have no relation to New York raises serious due process questions. The same questions arise if the suit were brought not against a California resident but against a Japanese resident.

Jurisdiction, in the sense of power over the defendant or over the "thing" being litigated, may be territorial in nature. Originally in the U.S. such power existed if the things or the defendant was located within the territorial authority of the court seeking to exercise power. Location of a thing, such as real property, is relatively simple; so too physical location of the defendant in the territory of the court when the suit is initiated gives the court authority or power over the defendant—but even defendants who are not physically present when suit is instituted may be considered as present when their relationship with the forum state makes such consideration reasonable. A person domiciled in a State who is temporarily absent from his place of domicile has sufficient relationship with the territory of the court to enable the court to assert jurisdiction over her. This "general jurisdiction" over the defendant is not related to the claims set forth in the action but is based on duties flowing from and to the domiciliary and the state of domicile. Such general jurisdiction also exists as to corporations who are "domiciled" within the state.

Under the Due Process Clause minimum standards of fairness apply to jurisdictional questions.[1] Through a series of decisions the Court has "Constitutionalized" the question of jurisdiction. United States ideas concerning jurisdiction over the defendant fall into two categories: (a) Questions of general jurisdiction—namely, situations where a court can take authority over any suit brought against the defendant regardless of the nature of the dispute. Thus a corporation that has "continuous and systemic" contact with the forum state may be sued in that state even though the events or circumstances giving rise to the lawsuit all are unrelated to the forum state.[2] (b) Questions of "specific" jurisdiction relate to the facts and circumstances of the case and according to *International Shoe* and its progeny specific jurisdiction is limited to cases that have the necessary minimum contacts with the forum that make assertion of jurisdiction not unfair to the defendant. Where a defendant "purposefully avails itself of the privilege of conducting activities within the forum State, thus invoking the benefits and protections of its laws" the state courts may, consistent with Due Process, exercise authority over the defendant for the transaction involved.[3] The issue of what conduct is sufficient to meet the purposefully avails test remains a subject of litigation in the United States. In *Worldwide Volkswagen v. Woodson*[4] the court held, in a products liability case, that merely because it was foreseeable by a seller of a product that was not sold or purchased in the forum state that the product would be used in that state was not sufficient to allow the seller to be sued in that state. Even if a party does not purposefully avail itself of conducting activities in the forum it may be subject to forum jurisdiction if, for example, there is a substantial connection to the forum and defendant voluntarily accepted the benefits of a relationship that was centered in the forum.[5] As long as a State meets the requirements of due process it may assert its jurisdiction over out of state defendants but that means it must meet the fairness test of *International Shoe* and its progeny.

Having Constitutionalized the issue of jurisdiction, the Supreme Court has left the issue both confusing and complex. The outer limits of jurisdictional fairness are not clear and the area is still the subject of Constitutional litigation. At the end of its 2010 term, the Supreme Court distinguished general from specific jurisdiction by noting:

1. See *International Shoe Co. v. Washington*, 326 U.S. 310 (1945) establishing the requirement of minimum contacts required before a State court may assert jurisdiction over a non-state entity.
2. *Perkins v. Benguet Consolidated Mining Co.*, 342 U.S. 437, 447–448 (1952).
3. *Hanson v. Denckla*, 357 U.S. 235, 253 (1958).
4. 444 U.S. 286 (1980).
5. *Burger King Corp. v. Rudzewicz*, 471 U.S. 462 (1985).

> A court may assert general jurisdiction over foreign (sister-state or foreign-country) corporations to hear any and all claims against them when their affiliations with the State are so "continuous and systematic" as to render them essentially at home in the forum State. See *International Shoe*, 326 U.S., at 317. Specific jurisdiction, on the other hand, depends on an "affiliatio[n] between the forum and the underlying controversy," principally, activity or an occurrence that takes place in the forum State and is therefore subject to the State's regulation. von Mehren & Trautman, Jurisdiction to Adjudicate: A Suggested Analysis, 79 Harv. L. Rev. 1121, 1136 (1966) (hereinafter von Mehren & Trautman); see Brilmayer et al., A General Look at General Jurisdiction, 66 Texas L. Rev. 721, 782 (1988) (hereinafter Brilmayer). In contrast to general, all-purpose jurisdiction, specific jurisdiction is confined to adjudication of "issues deriving from, or connected with, the very controversy that establishes jurisdiction." von Mehren & Trautman 1136.[6]

In the case mentioned the Court held that "Because the episode-in-suit, the bus accident, occurred in France, and the tire alleged to have caused the accident was manufactured and sold abroad, North Carolina courts lacked specific jurisdiction to adjudicate the controversy." In other words there was not sufficient contact by the defendant (Turkish tire manufacturer) and the State of North Carolina to permit North Carolina to require the defendant to come all the way to North Carolina from Turkey to defend itself in the lawsuit.

Jurisdiction may also exist when a party consents to jurisdiction of the court such as by appearing and defending the action brought against it (without reserving jurisdictional objections). Consent can also be obtained in advance such as through a forum selection clause in a contract through which an out of state (or out of country party) agrees in advance to the authority of the specified forum to decide disputes arising out alleged breach of the contract.

Like jurisdiction, recognition of domestic (sister-state) judgments is a matter of United States Constitutional law. The full faith and credit clause of the Constitution provides that:

> Full Faith and Credit shall be given in each State to the public Acts, Records, and judicial Proceedings of every other State. And the Congress may by general Laws prescribe the Manner in which such Acts, Records and Proceedings shall be proved, and the Effect thereof.

While there is some dispute as to how far the Congress can go in providing by general laws the effect to be given to the categories of acts to which full faith and credit is required (e.g., can Congress through the Defense of Marriage Act (DOMA) limit the full faith and credit that is normally given to marriage that is lawful under a sister-state law so as to not require full faith and credit to same sex marriage?), there is no dispute that money judgments rendered in one state must be recognized in a sister-state even if the cause of action on which the judgment is rendered is considered unlawful in the second state.[7] The mechanisms of enforcement of judgments do not travel with the judgment from state to state.

---

6. *Goodyear Dunlop Tires Operations S.A. v. Brown*. 564 U.S. ___ (2011).
7. *Baker v. General Motors Corp.*, 522 U.S. 222 (1998).

The Constitutional requirement that states recognize the preclusive effect of sister-state judgments even when the state's strongly held public policy views are opposed to the judgment does not apply to foreign country judgments. When the judgment of a foreign country is implicated then, in the absence of a treaty, all that can be sought is "comity" and while the various states have rejected the previously held view that reciprocity is required before comity should be given to a foreign country judgment, states are free and do apply the public policy exception to comity when dealing with foreign country judgments.

Unlike both jurisdiction and recognition, choice of law determination is not constitutionalized (with a very narrow and limited due process exception).[8] In almost all cases a state court can determine for itself whose law to apply.[9] It is only when the law chosen is so far removed from the fact situation and/or parties that due process may be invoked to reverse the selection. The consequence is that there is no "United States choice of law" rule—there are many state choice of law rules and these rules may and in many cases do differ from each other—even when the states involved claim to be applying the same rule.

The determination of which country's or state's law to apply has been undergoing a transformation in the United States and elsewhere. Initially the various states applied relatively uniform rules that emphasized the place of injury in a tort case and the place of contracting (for the formalities of contract) or place of breach in a contract case. But these rules while seemingly easy to apply were considered by some as arbitrary and as they were based on territoriality concepts were challenged as failing to reach the more basic questions such as whether a particular jurisdiction has a greater interest than another jurisdiction in having its law applied or whether the facts of the case indicate that one law should predominate over another. Interest analysis and policy goals as well as which state has the most significant relationship with the litigation became mechanisms for challenging the territorial based rules that had been adopted in the First Restatement of Conflict of Laws. The challenge brought forth significant changes in conflicts rules by way of court decisions beginning in the 1960s. Eventually a Restatement Second of Conflicts of Laws was adopted that adopted for torts a more relationship based test rather than a territorial test. Under the Restatement Second, in tort cases the local law of the jurisdiction with the most significant relationship to the events and parties is to be utilized[10]; while in contract cases the law of the jurisdiction selected by the parties if there is one and if not the law of the jurisdiction with the most significant relationship to the transaction and parties is to be utilized.[11] Some states have adopted the Restatement rules, some have adopted some

8. *Phillips Petroleum v. Shutts*, 472 U.S. 797 (1985).
9. *Allstate Insurance v. Hague*, 449 U.S. 302 (1981).
10. Restatement Second, Conflict of Laws section 145. In determining the state with the most significant contacts the Restatement directs the court to consider needs of the national and international systems, the forum's policies, policies and interests of other states with an interest in the matter, justified expectations of the parties, policies underlying the legal area being dealt with, ease in finding and applying the selected law as well as certainty, predictability and uniformity of result.
11. Restatement Second, Conflict of Laws section 188.

but not all, some have rejected the Restatement and some while accepting have interpreted the Restatement differently than other states.

§15.02 JAPAN

Japan is a unitary state and thus jurisdiction over the person rules that might be applicable between sister-states in a federal union are not applicable. In international transactions or events that cross international borders there needs to be some rule as to when a court in Japan has authority over non-Japanese residents. Similarly as a major exporting country and the world's third largest economy Japan needs some mechanism for determining and allowing those who deal with Japan to determine whose law will govern a particular transaction or a tort that occurs outside Japan but has consequences inside Japan.

As in the United States jurisdiction over a defendant or "thing" is territorial. Thus a thing located in Japan can be the subject of an action in rem and a domiciliary of Japan is subject to the jurisdiction of the Japanese courts. Jurisdiction may be based on consent either after a suit is initiated or prior thereto through a contract clause giving the Japanese courts authority. As a general rule, the District Court has general jurisdiction with limited exceptions such as for domestic relations or family law matters where the Family Court has subject matter jurisdiction and certain intellectual property cases where the Tokyo and Osaka District Courts and High Courts have special jurisdiction grants. Where a claim is made that a case has been brought in an inappropriate District Court the argument is one that resembles a venue rather than a jurisdiction argument in the United States. Jurisdiction arguments typically arise in international dispute cases where the question is whether a court in Japan can adjudicate a matter where the defendant is from another country; in intellectual property cases that are transnational in character; and in cases where it is argued that the seizure of property in Japan is an adequate basis for a general jurisdiction over a non-resident defendant.

The Code of Civil Procedure was initially written without great consideration for international disputes and the jurisdiction provisions were designed for domestic cases. Japanese courts stepped into the vacuum surrounding transnational disputes and adopted a rule based on fairness, impartiality and timely resolution by the court.[12] In addition the court adopted rules that were similar to (but not identical) to rules used

12. *Malaysian Airline System v. Michiko Goto*, 35 Minshu 1224, http://www.courts.go.jp/english/judgments/text/1981.10.16-1980-O-No.130.html (P.B., Oct. 16, 1981); *KK Tsuburaya Production v. Sompote Saengduenchai*, District Court (Tokyo), Jan. 28, 1999. Matsuo, *Jurisdiction in Transnational Cases in Japan*, 23 International Lawyer 6 (1978). For a discussion of Japan's rules relating to jurisdiction of international cases prior to the 2011 amendment to the Civil Procedure Code discussed *infra* see, Goodman, *Justice and Civil Procedure in Japan* 246–247 (Oceana Publications Inc. 2004). See also, *Nihon System Wear Co. Ltd. v. Kensuke Koo*, Tokyo High Court, Judgment, March 24, 1999; H.J. (1700) 41 (2000), http://www.tomeika.jur.kyushu-u.ac.jp/intl/jailpdf/Tokyo%20High%20Court,%20Judgment,%20March%2024%201999.pdf applying the fairness concept and permitting suit in Japan.

by United States courts when dealing with forum non-convenience dismissals.[13] Effective April 1, 2012 Japan partially amended the Civil Procedure Code by incorporating in the Code provisions dealing with international jurisdiction

Among the significant changes and/or clarifications made by the new Act are provisions that make it clear that Japanese courts have jurisdiction over: any individual domiciled (meaning under Japanese concepts having your principle place of abode) in Japan (regardless of nationality) as well as any Japanese national who resides in a foreign country and has jurisdictional immunity in said country (thus Ambassadors and others subject to diplomatic immunity abroad may be sued in Japan); and any legal person (e.g., a corporation) that has its principal place of business in Japan or absent a principle place of business has an agent domiciled in Japan that is responsible for its business affairs (Article 3-2); an action based on failure to perform a contract where the contract specifies or selects a law that specifies that Japan is the place of contractual performance or where the suit is on a bill or note where payment is to be made in Japan (Article 3-2 (i)(ii)); an action relating to the carrying out of business in Japan and the defendant (including both individuals and companies/corporations) engages in business in Japan on a regular basis (Article 3-2 (iii)); an action in tort where the act causing harm occurred in Japan or where the injury occurred in Japan, unless it was unforeseeable that harm would occur in Japan (Article 3-2 (viii)); an action relating to real property located in Japan (Article 3-2 (xi). The law also contains specific provisions dealing with consumer contracts and employment relations and contains provisions that grant Japanese courts exclusive jurisdiction for certain matters such as internal corporate matters, and cases dealing with the effect of registration on intellectual property rights that arise out of registration of such right in Japan (Article 3-5). The Act makes it clear that parties have the right to decide for themselves where a claim shall be litigated (choice of forum clauses are permitted when in writing and relate to specified legal relationships[14]) (Article 3-7) but the parties may not choose a foreign forum when the matter is within the exclusive authority of the Japanese courts nor chose a Japanese forum when the matter is within the exclusive jurisdiction of a foreign court (Article 3-10). Finally the Act has a catch all escape clause under which a Japanese court may refuse to accept jurisdiction when there are special circumstances such that acceptance would be unfair to the parties or create an unfair burden on the defendant or would create a burden on the efficient conduct of the proceedings (Articles 3-9).

Japan's choice of law rules are determined by statute. So too its jurisdiction and recognition rules are based on statute although the jurisdiction over foreign entities rules were originally judge made.

---

13. Public factors considered in the United Stats such as those affecting juries are not relevant in Japan.
14. The Law makes no provision for breach of a choice of forum provision through suit brought in a non-selected forum. Whether such a suit subjects the suing party to a breach of contract action is subject to dispute. For a discussion (and the view that such a suit would support and enhance party autonomy) see, Koji Takahashi, *Damages for a Breach of a Choice-of-Court Agreement: Remaining Issues*, 11 Yearbook Private Intl. L. 73 (2009).

Choice of laws initially followed the First Restatement approach but the amended choice of law statute applies interest analysis and most relevant contacts ideas also found in the Second Restatement.

§15.03 WHAT YOU SEE MAY NOT BE WHAT YOU GET

[A] United States

[1] Jurisdiction

Ever since the Supreme Court's decision in *International Shoe*, it is said that the touchstone for jurisdiction is fairness. The various states that have adopted "long arm" statutes permitting their courts to adjudicate cases where there is sufficient contact with the forum have done so because the contacts such as invoking the benefits and protections of the forum law make it fair to require the defendant to appear and defend itself in the forum court. Nonetheless, the United States permits exorbitant jurisdiction claims based on transient presence in the state or "tag" jurisdiction even where it can be argued persuasively that it is unfair to require the defendant to defend itself in the forum. Tag jurisdiction occurs when the defendant has been served (typically touched or tagged) with the necessary process to initiate litigation in the territory of the forum court. The fact that the defendant may be merely traveling through the forum, even may never have intended to enter the forum is not relevant. If the process touches the defendant in the territory of the forum there is a basis for jurisdiction. The Supreme Court has approved "tag" jurisdiction for historic reasons the tag of the summons substitutes for arrest by the sheriff who physically brought the defendant to the court in ancient England. The area over which the court had authority extended as far as the authority of the sheriff making the arrest. Modern court systems define the geographic authority of the court and the summons can be delivered anywhere within the authority of the court or the authority of the State in which the court sits. For a federal court Congress may provide nationwide authority. Modern pleading rules do not require that a summons be delivered within the state as long as it is fair for the defendant to defend within the state and the means of service are sufficient to provide the defendant with notice of the suit and the requirement to defend.[15] It is obvious that in many cases it is fair for a defendant who has been tagged to appear for example, if the defendant resides within the state—but it is also obvious that in some cases (such as an airline traveler whose plane is forced to land because of weather[16]) it is unfair to require the defendant to appear and defend. Nonetheless the Supreme Court in

15. Prior to *International Shoe* the prevailing rule was that jurisdiction could only be obtained by service on the defendant within the jurisdiction of the court. *Pennoyer v. Neff*, 95 U.S. 714 (1878).
16. See, *Grace v. MacArthur*, 170 F. Supp. 442 (ED Ark. 1959) for an exorbitant application of exorbitant tag jurisdiction to an airline passenger while in a plane overflying the court's jurisdiction.

Burnham v. Superior Court[17] gave Constitutional approval to "tag" service and jurisdiction.[18] This exorbitant jurisdiction by the United States has been the subject of criticism both at home and abroad and rightly so.

Moreover, by constitutionalizing the question of jurisdiction as a Due Process issue the Supreme Court has created a quagmire and confusion in the jurisdiction arena. One important area of confusion relates to the "stream of commerce" doctrine. In *Goodyear Dunlop v. Brown* Justice Ginsberg for the Court noted that under *International Shoe* the commission of even a single act in the jurisdiction that gives rise to a controversy may be sufficient to require the company committing the single act to respond in the state where the act occurred— but the commission of that act (or even a series of acts) is not sufficient to require the company respond when the injury is not caused by the act unless general jurisdiction over the defendant exists. Put simply, does a company subject itself to the jurisdiction of other states (and or countries) when it places goods in the stream of commerce that brings those goods to the state or country that seeks to exercise jurisdiction over the company for damage or injury caused by such goods? In *Goodyear* the court did not need to address the issue as the tires that failed and caused injury were never imported into the United States and the accident occurred outside the United States. The fact that other tires of the same type manufactured by the defendant had been imported and thus reached the forum state via the stream of commerce was not relevant.

In 2011 the Court was also presented with the stream of commerce argument in *McIntyre v. Nicastro*.[19] The defendant manufactured machinery that it attempted to sell in the United States by attending sales conferences *but none in the State of New Jersey* where four of its machines eventually wound up. One of those machines (manufactured in England where McIntyre is located) was alleged to be responsible for plaintiff's injury. Plaintiff sued McIntyre in New Jersey where the injury occurred. Justice Kennedy writing for a plurality of the Court (four Justices) noted that the stream of commerce issue had caused great confusion He set forth the two views as to how to apply the stream of commerce metaphor: sovereignty and a fairness approach. Justice Kennedy adopted the sovereignty approach. While McIntyre might have had sufficient contacts with the United States as a country to subject itself to United States jurisdiction, the issue before the court was whether a New Jersey court had jurisdiction and to meet that test McIntyre needed to subject itself to New Jersey, which it had not done. Federalism played a key role in the Court's decision.

Justices Breyer and Alito concurred in the decision but limited their concurrence to reliance on prior precedent and did not go as far as Justice Kennedy would have gone. For them it was sufficient that the Court had never held that a single act of selling a machine that was brought into a state and there caused injury was sufficient to conclude that the manufacturer sent its product into the stream of commerce.

17. 495 U.S. 604 (1990).
18. *Burnham* involved an "interstate" dispute in a domestic relations case. Whether an exception will someday be carved out for tag jurisdiction over a foreign defendant merely transient in the forum remains to be seen.
19. 564 U.S. ___ (2011).

Something more than merely selling a single product out of state that is then brought into the forum state is required before jurisdiction can be asserted by the forum. What that something is was left for a future decision. The law in the area remains unsettled with no majority as to how to apply the jurisdiction rules to modern means of commerce and the stream of commerce.

One area where fairness appears to have held sway is in the area of "quasi in rem" jurisdiction. The issue here is whether a jurisdiction may seize property of the defendant in order to obtain jurisdiction over the defendant, at least to the value of the seized property, when the property seized has no relationship to the claim being litigated. In *Shaffer v. Heitner*,[20] the Court held, based on fairness analysis, that jurisdiction was improper in such a case. The presence of defendant's property in the state standing by itself is not a sufficient basis for the court to assert jurisdiction over the defendant nor is it a sufficient basis for saying that it is fair for the defendant to have to come to the jurisdiction to defend its interest in the property when the action is not related to the property.

[2] Choice of Law

It needs to be emphasized that the Restatement Second of Conflict of Laws is not a restatement of the existing law of the United States. Because choice of law is a common law question for all states (with the exception of Louisiana that because of its civil law heritage has a Conflict of Law code) and is subject to little Constitutional or federal preemption analysis, each state has the right to decide for itself what choice of law rule it wishes to utilize. The Restatement, while carrying weight is nether law nor statute nor binding. For example, in the tort area some States have chosen to adopt the approach of the Restatement Second (most significant relationship), but others have continued to apply the Restatement First (place of injury), while others have adopted different approaches such as California's comparative impairment test or application of the best law or even an approach that honestly states that it favors the plaintiff. Even for those states adopting the Restatement Second approach the flexibility of the factors to be considered is such that many times a reader of opinions is left with the feeling that the court decided the case as it chose and then made the factors fit its decision. The lack of uniformity and clarity has caused some academics to suggest that it is time for a third restatement while others have responded that the problem is not restating but genuine dispute as to the proper rules.

There is greater clarity and consistency in the contract area where by far the general rule recognizes the value and importance of party autonomy and allows the parties great latitude in deciding for themselves whose law will govern their contractual relations. The parties can decide not just law but also forum—although a decision to apply the law of a particular state does not mean that the courts of that state have been chosen as the appropriate forum and choice of a particular state court system as the appropriate forum does not mean the parties have selected that state's internal law

20. 433 U.S. 186 (1977).

as the law to be applied —the forum will likely apply its own choice of law rules (or the law selected by the parties if they have made such a selection) to determine whose law should be applied. Choice of forum and choice of law autonomy has special significance and binding effect in international contracting where the parties are presumed to have selected either or both the forum and governing law in order to carry out their goal of having a defined and understood agreement, breach of which would be governed by a defined and understood legal regime.[21]

[3] Recognition

There is greater (but not complete) clarity in the recognition area. Here it seems clear that a sister-state money judgment must be given the same effect in the second state as it would have in the rendering state. Where lack of clarity exists it is how to apply a law such as the Defense of Marriage Act as it applies to acts of government. On the one side there are arguments that the Constitution grants the Congress authority to limit full faith and credit by general laws (what is a general law?) and thus DOMA controls—on the other there is the argument that failure to recognize same sex marriage is itself a Constitutional violation so that DOMA is itself in violation of the Constitution and thus can play no role in the Full Faith and Credit debate.

Judgments rendered by courts in foreign countries are entitled to such recognition as the various states provide through comity. Here the rules are also relatively clear—exceptions can be made in specific areas such as tax and criminal judgments—but most states allow comity when the originating court had jurisdiction, provided due process and there is no public policy exception to granting comity. The old notion of reciprocity has been abandoned.

[B] Japan

[1] Jurisdiction

The 2011 Act amending the Civil Procedure Code to define those transnational cases that can be brought in Japanese courts is a step forward in defining what suits may be subject to Japanese jurisdiction. The law adopts in great part the fairness doctrine previously established by the Japanese courts. However, it is not clear whether what you see in the Code amendments and the theory of fairness will be what you get. For example, there is no provision in the law dealing with what are known as "mirror image" lawsuits. Such suits exist when a party sues a Japanese entity abroad only to find that such entity responds by filing suit in Japan seeking a declaration that it has no liability for the situation sued on abroad.[22] Such suits have been brought in Japan and have been litigated to success against the foreign party. Even if the foreign party obtains

21. In *Kawasaki Kisen Kaisha Ltd. V. Regal-Beloit Corp*, 561 U.S. ___ (2010).
22. See, Takeo Sawaki, *Recognition and Enforcement of Foreign Judgments in Japan*, 23 Intl. Law. 29, 34–35 (1989). See also, Hideyuki Kobayashi & Yoshimasa Furuta, *Products Liability Act and Transnational Litigation in Japan*, 34 Texas Intl. L. J. 93, 116 (1999).

a judgment in its first filed suit abroad it will not be able to obtain execution of its judgment in Japan because the Japanese court's decision in the mirror suit will preclude recognition of the foreign judgment.[23] The mirror image suit is not precluded by the provisions of Article 3-10 of the new Act although that would have been the logical place to deal with such litigation. Whether the failure to deal with mirror image suits was based on an inability to form a consensus on how to deal with such cases or whether it was determined that it was not in the interests of Japanese business entities to preclude such mirror image suits is unclear. A doctrine based on fairness would have precluded mirror image suits when the first suit is brought in a forum that has jurisdiction, provides the Japanese defendant with due process and where litigation in such forum is not unfair within the meaning of such cases as *International Shoe* or *Malaysian Airlines*.

The Act contains several provisions that give Japanese courts an excessive jurisdiction. Under Article 3-3 (iii) an action can be brought in Japan to recover money damages through the seizure of a debt located in Japan. Since a debt is deemed to follow the debtor this means that suit can be brought in Japan by seizing a foreign party's claim against a Japanese national even though the foreign party has never entered Japan or the transaction being sued on has no nexus with Japan and even though the debt has no relationship to the claim being sued on. This type of action was rejected in *Shaffer v. Heitner*[24] on fairness grounds. Even if seizure could form the basis for jurisdiction, Article 3-3 (iii) does not limit the court's in personam jurisdiction based on seizure to the value of the assets seized. Seizure of an asset worth USD 1,000 could form the basis for jurisdiction over the defendant for a suit involving millions of dollars in damages. It is likely that this excessive jurisdictional grant was intentional and borrowed from German statute law. The German Federal Supreme Court in a case where neither party to the suit had a connection with Germany except for the seized asset saw this rule as excessive. But the court did not find that the jurisdiction asserted was excessive where one party (e.g., the plaintiff) was a German national. As a consequence of limits on jurisdiction contained in the Brussels Convention and European Union regulations, German courts cannot base jurisdiction solely on the residence or nationality of the plaintiff in a suit against another EU company or domiciliary. Fairness is compromised by Article 3-3.

So too, an excessive jurisdiction may exist where consumer contracts are implicated. Article 3-4 provides that an action may be brought in Japan by a consumer if the consumer was a Japanese domiciliary either at the time of filing the action or at the time of concluding the consumer contract. If the consumer was a Japanese tourist who made a purchase while abroad the wording of Article 3-4 would appear to grant a Japanese court jurisdiction over the foreign seller notwithstanding the seller had no nexus with Japan. While the provision is consistent with Japanese law's protection of the weaker consumer against the more powerful manufacturer or seller, it hardly seems

23. For a discussion of mirror suits (called parallel actions) see, Clermont, *A Global Law of Jurisdiction and Judgments: Views from the United States and Japan*, 37 Cornell L.J. 1, 19–20 (2004).
24. 433 U.S. 186 (1977).

fair to require a foreign entity that had no nexus with Japan to defend a suit in Japan simply because the purchaser of its product was Japanese. Article 3-3 allows for jurisdiction by Japanese courts when a defendant does business in Japan even though the defendant has no established place of business in Japan. "Does business" would seem to include companies that sell product into Japan by way of the internet or other forms of electronic commerce. The Article appears limited to claims based on the business done in Japan. This was a question that the concurring Justices in *McIntyre v. Nicastro* reserved for another day.

Article 3-3's expanded tort jurisdiction raises fairness questions. It appears to cast on the foreign defendant the burden of showing that harm occurring inside Japan caused by an act outside Japan was unforeseeable rather than casting on the Japanese plaintiff the burden of showing that harm inside Japan was foreseeable. As a consequence jurisdiction would appear to be presumed and the foreign defendant would have the burden of coming to Japan to establish lack of jurisdiction. This hardly seems a fair allocation of burden of proof and jurisdiction to establish jurisdiction. A broad interpretation to permit jurisdiction cannot be discounted since one purpose of the law was to deal with the frustration felt by Japanese families of persons who died when a foreign airliner on a flight between two foreign cities crashed killing Japanese passengers who had bought their tickets abroad. As the airline knew (or could have known) that it had Japanese passengers aboard it would seem reasonable to argue that it was not unforeseeable that harm would be caused in Japan by a crash of the plane outside Japan. But it does not seem fair to require a foreign airline that does not do business in Japan and has no nexus with Japanese territory to come to Japan to defend itself for an accident that occurred outside Japan simply because a Japanese national bought a ticket outside Japan to travel on the airline outside Japan to a place outside Japan.

All of these problems may be resolved through the judicial application of the special circumstances doctrine set out in Article 3-9 that allows the court when it has jurisdiction to reject jurisdiction (in whole or in part) when it concludes that there are special circumstances that render the retention of jurisdiction unfair to the parties, to the defendant, or where the proper and efficient handling of the case would be adversely affected by retaining jurisdiction. Prior to the enactment of the new jurisdictional provisions the Supreme Court of Japan had dismissed, on fairness grounds, a suit brought in Japan based on a contract signed in Germany for the distribution of product in Germany and where German law was selected as the governing law. The court noted that the defendant had no reason to believe that it would be held answerable in a Japanese court.[25] On the other hand, over reliance on Article 3-9 would leave the law where it was prior to the enactment of the new statute and would leave parties to guess concerning fairness. One purpose of the law was to provide greater transparency and that would call for a limited approach to the special circumstances doctrine.

25. *Special Circumstances to Deny International Jurisdiction case,* Case No. 1993 (O) No. 1660, http://www.courts.go.jp/english/judgments/text/1997.11.11-1993-O-No.1660.html. (P.B., Nov. 11, 1997).

[2] Choice of Law

In 2006 the Diet passed an updated Act on Application of Laws.[26] This new version of the choice of laws statute like the conflicts revolution in the United States (and the Choice of Laws rules adopted by the European Union) threw off many of the sovereignty based notions of choice of law in favor of more nuanced ideas based on party autonomy (such as for choice of law in contracts—with exceptions to protect weaker parties such as consumers or workers) or significance of parties or events. Article 7 dealing with Juristic Acts sets forth the general rule of party autonomy so that the law chosen by the parties shall govern both the rules relating to formation as well as effect of a juristic act (such as a contract) and parties are given specific authority to change the law that shall apply when doing so does not adversely affect a third party (Article 9). [Similarly the new law dealing with jurisdiction allows for party autonomy in selecting either Japanese or foreign forum to resolve disputes—provided the chosen forum is legally and actually able to deal with the dispute.] Only when the parties have failed to make a choice does the default rule—most closely connected place—come into play (Article 8). This replaces the former rule that applied the law of the place of execution of the contract[27] and is consistent with the current trend in the United States (and the European Union) to eschew territoriality for a more nuanced and rational rule. In determining the place with the closest connection the statute provides guidance by looking at the habitual residence of the party that is required to make performance and applying that place as having the closest connection—if the performing party has a business establishment that is related to the performance then the law of the place of the establishment has the closest connection and if there are more than one such establishment the law of the place where the principal establishment is located is selected (Article 8(2)). Where an immovable, such as real property, is the subject of the juristic act then the law of the place where the immovable is located is presumed to be the most closely connected law. And where a party is called upon to do the juristic act the law of that party's residence or place of business, where the act is related to the business, is given priority (Article 8(2) and (3)).

The general rule for tort liability and damages is the place of the injury unless such place was unforeseeable—when the law of the place of the tortuous act applies (Article 17). However this rule is modified by Article 20 which sets out a general rule of the law of the place with which the events and/or parties are most closely connected. Most closely connected appears to reflect a view similar to although not identical to the Restatement Second of Conflicts of Law. It is to be expected that the courts will define when a place is most closely connected to the parties or events. Whether that will lead to as much confusion in Japanese conflict of law determinations as exist in the United

26. An English language translation by Professors Kent Andersen and Yasuhiro Okuda may be found on the web at http://blog.hawaii.edu/aplpj/files/2011/11/APLPJ_08.1_anderson.pdf, last accessed Sept. 17, 2012. Another English language translation, by Masato Dogauchi, may be found at http://www.tomeika.jur.kyushu-u.ac.jp/intl/private/tsusokuho.pdf, last accessed Sept. 17 2012.
27. See, e.g., New Conflict of Law Rules in Japan—Watch out on international transactions, http://www.intershores.org/upload/article/full/437/1.pdf.

States is questionable as Japan's unitary system with a Secretariat training new judges will likely rationalize judicial decisions into a more rule based doctrine than is true in the fragmented American system of semi-sovereign states. Party autonomy may even apply to torts —since torts are generally not predicted in advance such autonomy comes into play only after the act constituting the tort has occurred (Article 21). Tort rules are modified in the international context so that foreign law that would apply does not apply if the acts governed by such foreign law would not be considered as tortuous under Japanese law. This appears to be a public policy exception that demands that Japanese law govern such matters as liability and recovery when Japanese law would not define the acts as a tort (Article 22(1)). Moreover, even if the acts would be recognized as tortuous under Japanese law, Japanese law controls such matters as damages or remedy in general (Article 22(2)). Though there are special rules for defamation (place of the residence of the injured person) and product liability (place where the product was delivered to the injured party but if that place was not foreseeable the place where the manufacturer of the product has its principle place of business) (Articles 17 and 18) these rules are also governed by the public policy under which a tort recognized in a foreign country but not recognized in Japan is not to be considered a tort.

Consumer contracts and labor contracts are also subject to special choice of law rules that favor the law of the consumer's residence (Article 11) and the place where the labor is performed (Article 12). The law recognizes that there may in fact be no one place where the labor is performed—i.e., where a person is hired to perform labor in several different places none of which can be viewed as the habitual place of performance. The concept of habitual performance is part of the EU Rules and is supported by the Restatement Second section 169. It has been suggested that notwithstanding the lack of the specific term habitual, the Japanese conflict statute should be interpreted similarly to the U.S. Restatement or the EU rules[28] and such a rule makes sense and is consistent with the intent of the new choice of law statute. Where there is no such habitual place then the statute grants a presumption in favor of the law of the place where the business that engaged the employee is located. Because the rule is presumptive only the potential for choice of law determinations based on some other theory is possible and like the U.S. law there may eventually be a potential for determination based on other factors (and perhaps the court's selection of law that leads to the determination favored by the judges, as happens in many cases in the United States). Although the employment contract provision of the law contains the concept of party autonomy, Japanese law in general favors the weaker party in various relationships including employment and thus the choice of law statute recognizes the need to protect the employee who may not be able to effectively negotiate about choice of law. If the contract selects a law other than the place where the employment is most closely connected, the employee may nonetheless choose to have the mandatory rules of law of the place most closely connected to the labor applied (Article 12(1)). For

28. Ryuichi Yamakawa, *Transnational Dimension of Japanese Labor and Employment Laws: New Choice of Law Rules and Determination of Geographical Reach*, 31 Comp. Lab. L. & Policy J. 347, 353–354 (2010).

public policy reasons and protection of employees some mandatory rules such as Japanese minimum wage, maximum hour, overtime pay and health and safety laws likely cannot be superseded by party autonomy if the labor is performed in Japan. Japan's Labor Standards Law has many provisions that are likely of this character and some that are likely not. Where the law both provides a standard of conduct and a private enforcement mechanism through the judicial system a good argument can be made that when labor is performed in Japan the provision that is enforceable by suit is controlling. Future cases will make clear which sections of the law will be considered outside autonomy. The case law in Japan that limits an employer's right to discharge employees based on the abuse of rights doctrine as discussed in Chapters 12 and 13 is fundamental to Japanese law and as such should also be considered beyond party autonomy. So too the United States Wage and Hour Laws, as well as the Equal Employment Opportunity Act should be considered mandatory law (where the labor is performed in the United States) that is not subject to party autonomy although Japan has no general anti-discrimination law. Question exists as to whether Japan's law relating to covenants not to compete can be waived through party autonomy- indeed it is not clear what the rule is in dealing with such covenants in Japan[29] (state practices vary widely).[30] How Article 42 (the public policy exception) applies to party autonomy where a law other than Japan is chosen in a covenant not to compete remains to be seen. Japan's Constitution has a clause granting all persons the right "to choose his occupation to the extent that it does not interfere with the public welfare." A covenant not to compete can be said to restrict the right to choose an occupation. The United States law on the subject is also in dispute as different states apply different conflict of law rules to covenants not to compete and the law is less than clear as to how public policy affects such agreements and choice of law questions.

With exceptions for some family law matters, (the statute devotes section 5, Articles 24–35, 25% of the entire statute, to family law matters), Japanese law recognizes the concept of *renvoi* to the extent that where a foreign law is to be applied and the conflict of law rules of that place would apply Japanese law then Japanese law should be applied by the Japanese court (Article 41). The statute does not appear to contemplate a situation where the foreign law would apply a third country's law. Article 42 contains a general public policy exception pursuant to which a foreign law that violates Japanese public policy is not to apply.

Rights in rem to both moveable and immovable property are governed by the law of the situs. Situs law also applies to rights that arise as a consequence of registration (Article 13). This choice of law rule should be considered together with the special and exclusive jurisdiction rules under which an action challenging registration is exclusively within the jurisdiction of Japanese courts and where actions challenging or asserting either the existence or effect of intellectual property rights that arise out of registration in Japan are within the exclusive jurisdiction of the Japanese courts. (This rule does not apply to actions asserting infringement of a patent or copyright as such

29. *Ibid.*, 347, 363–365.
30. See, e.g., Gillian Lester & Elizabeth Ryan, *Choice of Law and Employee Restrictive Covenants: An American Perspective*, 31 Comp. Lab. L. & Pol'y J. 389 (2010).

suites are not based on the registration of the right but on whether the right has been infringed).

[3] Recognition

As a unitary state Japan has no need for a full faith and credit clause and no such clause is found in the Japanese Constitution. Issues of recognition arise in connection with foreign country judgments. Japan's statutory provisions for recognition set forth a four part test—(i) jurisdiction by the foreign court (and lack of exclusive jurisdiction in a Japanese court); (ii) proper service of process on the defendant or actual participation by the defendant in the initial action; (iii) reciprocity of recognition of Japanese judgments by the country whose judgment is involved[31]; and finally (iv) the judgment does not violate the public policy of Japan. Japan will not recognize a judgment that is inconsistent with a valid Japanese judgment.

Jurisdiction issues can arise when the foreign court applies an exorbitant jurisdiction not recognized by Japanese law. Thus the United States acceptance of "tag jurisdiction" may create recognition problems if tag jurisdiction was the only basis for jurisdiction. Proper service implicates the various views of courts in the United States regarding Japan's accession to the Hague Convention on service. (Some courts hold that mail service is permitted because Japan did not object to a provision allowing informal delivery of documents. Others find Japan's objection to two provisions that allow informal service of documents controlling. The later argument is consistent with Japan's intention and domestic law. The first relies on sloppy draftsmanship and a strained interpretation under which delivery and service are synonymous). It seems clear that Japan will and indeed should apply its own interpretation of its accession document and that failure to follow the formal rules of service laid down in the Hague Convention will result in refusal to recognize the United States judgment. Reciprocity does not mean exactly the same recognition but means a substantive reciprocity—this is a general rule followed by many countries. The most interesting factor is public policy.

The public policy exception to recognition includes both substantive and procedural public policy rules. Failure to follow Japanese requirements that lawyers coming to Japan in connection with certain aspects of a foreign litigation, such as the interviewing or the deposition of witnesses, obtain a special visa may result in a public policy exception to recognition. Substantive public policy was the basis for rejecting punitive damage awards and family law judgments that are contrary to Japanese policy such as the recognition of the biological parents as the natural parents of a child born to a surrogate mother.[32] (Chapter 9) Whether Japan's anticipated accession to the Hague Convention on the Civil Aspects of International Child Abduction will result in greater recognition of child custody awards in international divorce cases remains to be

31. Since execution of judgments in the U.S. is fundamentally a State law matter the Japanese court will look for reciprocity to the law of the state where the judgment was entered.
32. *Surrogate Birth Child Denied Registration* case, Case No. 47 of 2006, 61 Minshu No. 2 (Sup. Ct. 2nd Petty Bench, 23 March 2007).

seen.[33] Broad application of the Convention's "grave risk" loophole to recognition could lead to what you see not being what you get.[34]

33. See, Tanase, *Hague Convention Ratification and Post-Divorce Parent-Child Law*, http://www.yomiuri.co.jp/adv/chuo/dy/opinion/20120611.htm, last accessed Sept. 17, 2012.
34. This subject is discussed in Chapter 9.

CHAPTER 16

Criminal Law

§16.01 UNITED STATES

The Framers of the American Constitution were personally familiar with criminal law issues—they were all subjects of the British crown and all in rebellion against that crown. John Adams and John Hancock were nearly arrested for treason and had they been the issue of their guilt or innocence would probably have depended on criminal procedural protections if tried in England they would undoubtedly have been found guilty whereas if tried to a jury in Massachusetts they would have been found not guilty. Procedural protection for the accused was something all rebellious colonialists could identify with.

Yet the original draft of the Constitution contains little in the way of such protections except for the granting of a right to criminal trial by jury in the state where the crime was committed,[1] requiring that treason be proven by testimony of two persons (or by confession in open court), and providing that the writ of habeas corpus cannot be suspended except in cases of rebellion or invasion.[2] Bills of Attainder and ex post facto criminal laws were also prohibited. The original Constitution contained no Bill of Rights and leaders such as Alexander Hamilton supported the omission.[3] The public saw the matter differently, fearing federal government involvement in criminal cases. To obtain public consent it was agreed that a Bill of Rights would be added by way of amendment.

Many of the rights contained in the Bill of Rights are criminal procedure rights. As originally drafted these rights were applicable against the federal government but not

1. Constitution Article 3. Where the crime was not committed in any State the trial must be held in such place as Congress directs.
2. Constitution Article 1 section 9. In such cases the writ may only be suspended in places where hostilities make access to the civil courts impossible. *Ex Parte Milligan*, 71 U.S. ___ (4 Wall.) 2 (1866).
3. See Federalist Paper No. 84 (28 May 1788).

against the States. The Fourteenth Amendment and the Supreme Court's later incorporation doctrine have made most of these rights applicable at both the federal and state level. As a consequence, while substantive criminal law remains a matter (in the main) of state law, the procedural protections granted to defendants are, for the most part, federal and thus fairly uniform.[4] The principle procedural protections offered by the Constitution (aside from the jury trial right) are: right to counsel, privilege against self-incrimination, prohibition of unreasonable search and seizure and a right to a speedy trial. The principle method of enforcing these rights is to prevent the state from gaining an advantage from violating a right and thereby to deter future Constitutional violations—the exclusionary rule.[5] The exclusionary rule also applies to the fruits of illegally obtained evidence (subject to exceptions such as the independent source / inevitable discovery doctrine[6] and the good faith exception[7])—is the principle means for enforcing these Constitutional rights. The exclusionary rule began as a rule of procedure in federal courts[8] and was not applied to the States until 1961 when the court in *Mapp v. Ohio*[9] made it a rule of Constitutional law.

Miranda v. Arizona[10] decided in 1966 applied the right to counsel and the Fifth Amendment's privilege against self-incrimination to require that suspects in custody must be warned that they has a right to silence, any statement made could be used against them and that they have a right to counsel[11] and if the suspect cannot afford counsel one will be appointed. Such warning was found essential to carry out the mandate of the Fifth Amendment. While a suspect can waive the Fifth Amendment right, only a knowing waiver is acceptable and a knowing waiver can only be obtained if the suspect is advised of the right to silence and the right to counsel. Once a suspect indicates a desire to speak with counsel questioning must end. Similarly once the suspect indicates that he/she does not wish to be questioned, questioning must end. Once counsel is requested counsel has a right to be present if the suspect consents to be questioned and future interrogation sessions including interrogation about crimes other than those for which the suspect was arrested, may not be held unless counsel is present and consents.[12] The right to end questioning by claiming *Miranda* rights must be made "unambiguously" and that failure to make such an unambiguous claim

4. States may, of course, provide additional protections and State Constitutional provisions may be interpreted by state courts to provide rights not contained in the federal Constitution.
5. *Davis v. United States*, 564 U.S. ___ (2010) "That rule—the exclusionary rule—is a 'prudential' doctrine, *Pennsylvania Bd. of Probation and Parole v. Scott*, 524 U.S. 357, 363 (1998), ... The rule's sole purpose, we have repeatedly held, is to deter future Fourth Amendment violations. .... Where suppression fails to yield 'appreciable deterrence,' exclusion is 'clearly ... unwarranted.' *Janis, supra*, at 454."
6. See e.g., *Nix v. Williams*, 467 U.S. 431 (1984); *Segura v. United States*, 468 U.S. 796 (1984); *Murray v. United States*, 487 U.S. 533 (1988).
7. See e.g., *Illinois v. Krull*, 480 U.S. 340 (1987).
8. *Weeks v. United States*, 232 U.S. 383 (1914); *Wolf v. Colorado*, 338 U.S. 25 (1949).
9. 367 U.S. 643 (1961).
10. 384 U.S. 436 (1966).
11. Depriving a defendant of counsel of his choice when he has retained counsel and is not indigent is a violation of the Sixth Amendment and a conviction obtained under such circumstances was reversed. *United States v. Gonzales-Lopez*, 548 U.S. 140, 126 S. Ct. 2557 (2006).
12. *Arizona v. Roberson*, 486 U.S. 675 (1988).

renders answers admissible as evidence when the prosecution shows that the suspect was given and understood his *Miranda* rights and did not unambiguously claim such rights.[13] During this questioning session "Police are not required to again warn suspects from time to time." *Miranda* is limited by a narrow definition of custody that is determined by the circumstances and whether the person interrogated reasonably believed there was freedom to leave the place of questioning.[14] While confessions obtained without *Miranda* warnings are excluded from evidence, some of the fruits of the confession may be admissible[15]admissions made in violation of *Miranda* may be used to impeach a defendant if he/she takes the stand,[16] and there is a "public safety" exception to *Miranda*.[17] The basic aspects of *Miranda* have become part of American law and culture.[18] The fruits of a coerced confession are not admissible in evidence and are subject to an exclusionary rule. Closely related to *Miranda* is the Constitutional requirement that a person arrested must be quickly presented to a Magistrate. A confession obtained from a suspect even if voluntary will be suppressed if presentment was not timely made. As a general rule, presentment is to be made within six hours of arrest or from the time taken into custody.[19]

Police have a right to approach people in public and ask them questions and even ask for permission to search, as long as the person approached may refuse and may terminate the inquiry at any point. Police may seek truly voluntary cooperation. In asking for cooperation the police do not have to advise the person approached that she has a right to refuse to permit a search and failure to give such advice does not create a presumption that the search is unlawful.[20] The fundamental issue is whether there exists coercion.[21] Police may also engage in warrantless searches of persons out of prison on parole when there is a condition to parole that permits warrantless searches on the rationale that a person out on parole is still in the custody of the prison system and his agreement to be set free of incarceration includes an agreement to allow such searches without warrants or even probable cause.[22]

---

13. *Berghuis v. Thompkins*, 560 U.S. ___ (2010).
14. *Howes v. Fields*, 565 U.S. ___ (2012) holding that a person imprisoned and questioned while serving his sentence is not in "custody" for Miranda purposes if he is free to leave the questioning session and return to his cell.
15. *Michigan v. Tucker*, 417 U.S. 433 (1974); *Oregon v. Elstad*, 470 U.S. 298 (1985).
16. *Harris v. New York*, 401 U.S. 222 (1971); *Oregon v. Haas*, 420 U.S. 714 (1975).
17. *New York v. Quarles*, 467 U.S. 649 (1984).
18. In *Dickerson v. United States*, 530 U.S. 428 (2000) the Supreme Court held that *Miranda* was constitutionally based and that a federal statute in contradiction to *Miranda* was unconstitutional.
19. The Supreme Court has said "In a world without *McNabb-Mallory*, federal agents would be free to question suspects for extended periods before bringing them out in the open, and we have always known what custodial secrecy leads to.... "[C]ustodial police interrogation, by its very nature, isolates and pressures the individual," *Dickerson*, 530 U.S., at 435. There is mounting empirical evidence that these pressures can induce a frighteningly high percentage of people to confess to crimes they never committed, see, e.g., Drizin & Leo, The Problem of False Confessions in the Post-DNA World, 82 N. C. L. Rev. 891, 906–907 (2004)...." *Corley v. United States*, 556 U.S. 303 (2009).
20. *United States v. Drayton*, 536 U.S. 194 (2002).
21. *Florida v. Bostick*, 501 U.S. 429 (1991).
22. *United States v. Jones*, 565 U.S. ___ (2012); *Samson v. California*, 547 U.S. 843 (2006).

Police may set up checkpoints to stop motorists when the purpose is limited, specific and not to enforce the criminal laws such as to intercept illegal aliens,[23] check for sobriety[24] and check on driver's licenses so that unlicensed drivers can be removed from the roads.[25] But a checkpoint program that has as its primary purpose the discovery of criminal activity is, as a general matter, unconstitutional. Exceptions can be made where there exists a special need such as border patrol or public safety, as exemplified by stop (without suspicion) programs at airports.[26] Police may also enter a residence without a warrant when it is reasonable (applying an objective test of reasonableness) to do so to protect an inhabitant or to render assistance.[27]

Miranda and *Mapp* and the Fourth Amendment exclusionary rule are the staples of American criminal procedural protections. The exclusionary rule,[28] the right to silence and the right to counsel both before and during any interrogation session are considered as essential in making the Constitutional protections effective.

When the Occupation considered criminal law protections they naturally looked to the American experience and replicated the Fourth Amendment's right against unreasonable searches,[29] the Fifth Amendment's privilege against self-incrimination[30] and the Sixth Amendment's right to counsel[31] and speedy and public trial by an impartial fact finder.[32] When the Japanese Constitution was promulgated the Court had yet to decide that the exclusionary rule was a Constitutional rule—*Wolf* holding that the rule was not a Constitutional requirement was decided in 1949 —*Mapp* overturned this ruling 12 years later,[33] and the *Miranda* holding was still some 19 years away.

United States criminal law is dominated by concerns over procedural rights of the accused—both before and during trial. Yet most cases never reach the trial stage because they are determined without a trial in a plea bargain arrangement wherein the defendant admits guilt in exchange for a reduced charge and a consequent reduced sentence.[34] In bargaining, alleged abuse of procedural rights is used by defense counsel to assist in getting the best deal for the defendant in exchange for waiver of the right to trial by jury, the right to confront witnesses, and the right to remain silent and not be a witness against oneself.

---

23. *U.S. v. Martinez-Fuerte*, 428 U.S. 543 (1976).
24. *Michigan v. Sitz*, 496 U.S. 444 (1990).
25. *Delaware v. Prouse*, 440 U.S. 648 (1979).
26. *Indianapolis v. Edmond*, 531 U.S. 32 (2000).
27. *Brigham City v. Stuart*, 547 U.S.398 (2006).
28. When knock and announce is required to execute a warrant and the officers fail to follow the rule the evidence obtained in the search is not subject to the exclusionary rule because knock and announce is designed to protect inhabitants of the premises and to protect property that might otherwise be destroyed. Exclusion is not required to vindicate these interests. *Hudson v. Michigan*, 547 U.S. 586 (2006).
29. Article 35.
30. Article 38.
31. Articles 34 and 37(3).
32. Article 37(1). In the United States Constitution the right is to a speedy trial before an impartial jury but as Japan has no jury trial the right is to such a trial before an impartial tribunal.
33. The 'fruit of the poisonous tree' doctrine applied in Federal Courts long before 1947. See e.g., *Silverthorne Lumber Co. v. United States*, 251 U.S. 385 (1920).
34. *Missouri v. Frye*, 566 U.S. ____ (2012). ("Ninety-seven percent of federal convictions and ninety-four percent of state convictions are the result of guilty pleas.")

United States criminal law appears to have as its function both a punitive and a protective aspect. Punitive in the respect that punishment of the offender is a goal of the system;[35] protective in the sense that (a) warehousing criminals takes them off the streets and thus theoretically protects the public from future criminal acts by these persons[36] and (b) punishment may deter others from committing crimes.[37] While it is sometimes said that rehabilitation is part of the goal of the system,[38] if it is a goal it appears to be secondary at best.[39] Compensation of the victim of crime is not a goal of the system[40]that is a goal of the civil litigation system.

§16.02 JAPAN

Japanese criminal law in Tokugawa Japan was fundamentally different from Criminal Law in feudal England or the American colonies. The criminal prescripts—such as they were—were based on Confucian notions of morality and like the household codes of the local lords, were contained in instructions to officials rather than in "legal codes." Because they were "internal" instructions to the Shogun's officials, they were not generally published and were not generally known to the population. There were different rules and different punishments based on social class and within class, family standing. Few, if any, procedural protections existed.

Criminal procedure in Tokugawa Japan can be viewed as having two steps: (1) investigation and (2) decision. The first step was designed to obtain the necessary elements for the second. The decisional stage can be viewed as the "trial" although it hardly resembles a modern trial, either Japanese or American.

Confession was the mainstay of criminal procedure in Tokugawa Japan. As a general rule, confession was needed to convict (in stage 2) (there were some exceptions but as a practical matter confession was required.) Both the investigation and "trial" was based on confession. Physical evidence was used as an investigatory technique to obtain confession and might be used at "trial" but the confession was supreme. There was no right to silence and suspects were questioned before and after arrest. Refusal to confess could result in different levels of torture being used to obtain a confession. Torture was a last resort (since the rules for torture required a witness to the procedure there was no realistic way to hide the legal use of torture). Investigative officials developed techniques for getting witnesses to confess short of actual use of torture including the threat of torture and the willingness to have the confession prove

35. *Kelly v. Robinson*, 479 U.S. 36 (1986).
36. *Lopez v. Davis*, 531 U.S. 230, 240 (2001).
37. See *Gregg v. Georgia*, 428 U.S. 153, 183 (1976).
38. *Kelly v. Robinson*, 479 U.S. 36 (1986).
39. See Sentencing Reform Act of 1984, 18 U.S.C. 3553(a)(2) listing purposes of sentencing and not mentioning 'rehabilitation' although it is likely that Congress hoped that training and treatment would lead to rehabilitation. The failure to use the term rehabilitation was intentional. See Christopher Mascharka, *Mandatory Minimum Sentences: Exemplifying the Law of Unintended Consequences*, 28 Florida St. U. L. Rev. 935, 940 n. 37 (2001).The Supreme Court has said that when a defendant is subject to resentencing the court should properly take into account his current situation and extent of rehabilitation. *Pepper v. United States*, 562 U.S. ___ (2011).
40. *Kelly v. Robinson*, 479 U.S. 36, 53 (1986).

a minor crime when in reality a major crime had been committed, so that a lesser punishment was exacted.

In addition to public officials, the authorities utilized the services of private parties (*maekashi*) who discovered crimes and criminals and questioned suspects and assisted in determining where suspects should be held prior to "trial." These *maekashi* developed into unsavory figures themselves taking bribes, using extortion, and selling their services to creditors who had difficulty collecting debts.[41]

The "trial" was a procedure in front of a higher level official who was given the defendant's confession and had the defendant admit to the confession by placing his seal on the confession. The function of the procedure was essentially to verify the confession although sometimes some other evidence was taken. If a defendant refused to seal the confession the typical response was to send the matter back for torture until the defendant was more compliant. This procedure was separate from the "sentencing" procedure, which (except for crimes where the sentence was exclusively based on the crime committed and thus no special process was required) was held at a different time and before a different official. To "convict" no evidence in addition to or to corroborate a confession was required.[42]

Substantive criminal law was the shogun's law (although the Daimyo were delegated certain criminal law powers) and recognized status and class. The feudal/class quality of the law resulted in permitted conduct that would strike one today as outrageous. Thus if a commoner insulted a samurai, the samurai was permitted to defend his honor—even to the extent of killing the offending commoner. [To protect against abuse of this power witnesses were required to show that there had been an insult.] In addition, if properly registered a samurai could seek vengeance against other samurai.[43] Status also applied to interfamilial relationships and to superior/inferior relationships, such as servant and master. One's various status relationships determined one's status obligations, ethical and moral obligations and these in turn defined one's "legal" obligations. These status obligations took precedence over formal written "legal" obligations. The penal law was used to enforce status obligations.[44]

Such a criminal law system was not likely to obtain Western understanding and as part of the drive to remove Western consular jurisdiction an effort was undertaken to write a Criminal Code. At first the Meiji government turned to China for a model. The first true Japanese criminal code was prepared in 1869 and then amended in 1873. A Chinese model was not going to get the Western powers to return sovereignty to Japan and the Meiji rulers looked further west for a criminal law system.

---

41. In some ways these *maekashi* appear to be the predecessors of some *Boryokudan* (Yakuza) activities in modern Japan.
42. For a discussion of the criminal justice system in feudal Japan see Yoshiro Hiramatsu, *Summary of Tokugawa Criminal Justice,* (Daniel H. Foote summarized & trans.), 22 L. Japan 105 (1989); see also Yoshiro Hiramatsu, *Tokugawa Law* (Dan Fenno Henderson trans.), 14 L. Japan 1 (1981).
43. See Marius B. Jansen, *The Making of Modern Japan* 60 (The Belknap Press of Harvard University Press 2000).
44. Yoshiro Hiramatsu, *Tokugawa Law* (Dan Fenno Henderson trans.), 14 L. Japan 1, 40–42 (1981).

The Criminal Code of 1880 was based on a French model. Although the Code only lasted a few years—being replaced in 1907—it established principles that remain ingrained in Japanese law. Criminal law could not be secret law. The great principle of *nulla crimen sine lege*— that there cannot be a crime without a law was established. Class distinctions were dropped and the criminal law applied to all equally. The concept of *mens rea* was adopted. To be guilty of a crime there must be criminal intent.[45] Application of *mens rea* meant that each person was guilty for her own crime and not for the crimes of others. Collective responsibility, a staple of the Tokugawa criminal system was abolished and with it rejection of the American notion of criminal conspiracy under which one member of a crime organization can be held responsible for acts of other members of the same organization. This general rejection of conspiracy continues today and complicates Japanese efforts to deal with organized crime, including efforts to deal with Yakuza organizations.[46] The Japanese police estimate that in 2007 organized crime organizations had approximately 84,000 members.[47] Conspiracy was one of the charges leveled at the Class A War Criminals tried in the Allied International Military Tribunal during the Occupation and this may account in part for some of the conservative opposition to the acceptance of conspiracy as a standalone crime.

In 2000 Japan signed the U N Convention against Transnational Crime that calls for signatories to enact conspiracy laws to deal with transnational criminal conspiracies. In accord with its treaty obligations the government submitted a conspiracy law to the Diet four times. The Japanese public objected and in June 2006 the government withdrew its efforts to create a criminal conspiracy law.[48] Although conspiracy as understood under American law is generally rejected, Japanese law makes the joint

---

45. Penal Law Article 38 (1). Japanese Law Translation, http://www.japaneselaw translation.go.jp/law/detail/?ft=2&re=02&dn=1&yo=Penal+Code&ky=&page=1.
46. In 1999, as part of an attempt to control Yakuza organized crime organizations, the Punishment for Organizational Crime and Control of Proceeds of Crime Act was enacted. This law increased the penalty of those engaged in 'organizational crime' and money laundering. The law did not criminalize organized crime or crime families and has been criticized for failing to deal effectively with the organized crime problem in Japan. See Nobuhito Yoshinaka, *New Legislation against 'Organizational Crime' in Japan*, Bull. Intl. Soc. Soc. Defense & Humane Criminal Policy (1999). Local governments have taken steps to try to protect the local population from infiltration by organized crime figures by adopting Ordinances that prohibit organized crime figures from purchasing homes in certain residential neighborhoods. See, *Yakuza Face Hyogo Zone Bans*, Japan Times (Oct. 7, 2010), http://search.japantimes.co.jp/cgi-bin/nn20101007b1.html. And some communities have brought injunction suits to prevent crime organizations from locating their headquarters in the community—especially when another crime organization has established a headquarters in the same neighborhood.
47. Police of Japan, 2009, 20.
48. *JCJ Awards Tokyo Shimbun for Stories on Conspiracy Bill*, Japan Times, July 28, 2006,. For a discussion of the Criminal Conspiracy Bills proposed to meet Japan's Treaty Obligations see, Chris Coulson, Student Author, *Criminal Conspiracy Law in Japan*, 28 Michigan J. Intl. L. 863 (2007).

commission of a crime by two or more joint principals a crime[49] and in rare cases, such as in its election laws, makes conspiracy a crime.[50]

In 2011 the Diet enacted legislation that makes creation or distribution of computer virus criminal activity and makes it a crime to send certain email messages with pornographic images attached. The law was enacted to meet commitments under the Convention against Cybercrime. There is debate in legal circles in Japan as to whether the law violates the Constitutional protection of all forms of communication.[51] Prior to the law's enactment, criminal prosecutors needed to prove that downloading of a virus had damaged property as distinguished from merely temporarily causing computers to not properly function.[52]

The Criminal Code was re-written in 1995 to use more modern language and some substantive changes were made such as taking account crimes that may be committed through use of modern technology.[53]

The 1907 law as grammatically modified in 1995 is the basic Criminal Code in existence today. The Occupation made few changes in the Criminal Code[54] although the sections dealing with crimes against the Imperial family had to be dropped and changes had to be made to crimes that applied solely against women but not men (e.g., adultery by a women had been punishable but not adultery by a husband, unless the female partner was married) as well as crimes that inhibited the new freedoms that were embodied in the new Constitution. Nonetheless the basic structure of the Penal Code of 1907 remains the basic Criminal Code in Japan today. This Code was more aligned with the German concepts of criminal law than was the prior French based Code and replaced the strict rules of punishment based on the crime committed with more flexible rules to be administered by the court. Rehabilitation rather than punishment became the goal of the criminal law. This emphasis on rehabilitation remains a mainstay of Japanese criminal law today.

---

49. Penal Code Article 60. *Joint Principals Crime Case*, Case No. 2007 (A) No. 1580, 63 Keishu No. 5, http://www.courts.go.jp/english/judgments/text/2009.06.30-2007.-A-.No..1580.html (P.B., June 30, 2009); *Joint Principal Need Not be Charged Case*, Case No. 2009 (A) No. 291, Keishu Vol. 63, No. http://www.courts.go.jp/english/judgments/text/2009.07.21-2009.-A-.No..291.html 6, (P.B., July 21, 2009). Inducing someone to commit a crime or failing to stop someone from committing a crime when there is a duty to prevent the commission of the crime may be a crime in and of itself. *Passengers Get Prison Terms in Drunk Driving Case*, The Yomiuri Shimbun (Feb. 15, 2011), http://www.yomiuri.co.jp/dy/national/T11021400 5481.htm.
50. A political office holder may be denied the right to run for office because of the activities of associates engaging in unlawful campaign funding operations. This form of "guilt by association" is considered important to protect the political system. See, *Ex-DPJ Lawmaker Hit with 5-year Poll Ban*, Japan Times Jan. 27, 2011), http://search.japantimes.co.jp/cgi-bin/nn201101 27a7.html.
51. Kyoto News, *Domestic Cybercrime Bill Passed*, Japan Times (June 18, 2011), http://search.japantimes.co.jp/cgi-bin/nn20110618a3.html; Legislation criminalizing viruses passed, Yomiuri Shimbun, June 18, 2011, http://www.yomiuri.co.jp/dy/national/T110617004744.htm.
52. *Heavy sentence given to creator of 'ika-tako' virus*, The Yomiuri Shimbun (July 22, 2011), http://www.yomiuri.co.jp/dy/national/T110720005908.htm.
53. Amongst the changes made was the dropping of the provision for special punishment for crimes against an ancestor that had previously been held unconstitutional in the *Patricide* case.
54. A Penal Code revision was made in 1947 under the influence of the Occupation but it was not a major change.

Meiji criminal procedure followed the French civil law model. It was an "inquest" under the control of the judge. The ability of the accused to have legal representation was recognized, although the accused's lawyer sat at a lower level than the public prosecutor (procurator) who sat at the same level as the judges. The adversary system that characterizes common law jurisdictions was not utilized and initially the jury system was non-existent.

Under the French system, procurators worked under the guidance of magistrates and were a part of the judicial system. The magistrate along with the procurator conducted extensive investigations into alleged criminal conduct and only after this judicial officer was convinced that a crime had been committed would a defendant be indicted. As a consequence, the "trial," which took place before another judicial officer was more in the nature of an appeal than an initial trial and the issue for the defendant became whether he/she could convince the court to overturn the previous magisterial decision.[55]

Japan did adopt, on an optional basis, a form of jury system in the 1920s.[56] Under the Jury Law of 1923 a petit jury of 12 persons could try a criminal case, if a defendant requested. This jury had no authority to find the defendant either guilty or not guilty. Its sole function was to answer factual inquiries put to it by the court. Answers were advisory. The court could not make a verdict contrary to the jury's findings; it could discharge the jury and re-try the defendant before a new jury. Making the jury finding binding (as in the U.S.) was considered unfair. Determinations by the jury did not require a unanimous vote, a vote of 7 of the 12 jurors was sufficient. If a judge did accept the jury's findings the defendant had no right to appeal except for certain alleged procedural errors. As a consequence of its failures to protect defendants, many defendants concluded that their best interest did not lie with a jury and the practice died out. The Jury Law was suspended in 1943 and there is no right to trial by jury.[57]

The Judicial Reform Council, under pressure from the *Bengoshi* Bar, recommended a form of jury system in certain serious criminal cases. The Judicial Secretariat opposed and lobbied against introduction of the American style jury, arguing in part that lay jurors might well convict the innocent and release the guilty. The Secretariat saw no reason for change in a system that it felt worked well. Notwithstanding studies

55. Many common law—adversary procedure—advocates retain this criticism of the French inquisition criminal process.
56. See, Anna Dobrovolskaia, *The Jury System in Pre-War Japan An Annotated Translation of "The Jury Guidebook*, 9 Asian-P. L. & Poly J. 231 (2008), http://www.hawaii.edu/aplpj/articles/APLPJ_09.2_dobrovolskaia.pdf.
57. During the Occupation of Okinawa, the American authority instituted a jury system but few cases were tried to the jury and this system also atrophied. Anna Dobrovolskaia, *An All-Laymen Jury System Instead of the Lay Assessor* (Saiban-in) *System for Japan? Anglo-American-Style Jury Trials in Okinawa under the U.S. Occupation*, http://www.law.usyd.edu.au/anjel/documents/ZJapanR/ZJapanR24/ZJapanR24_09_Dobrovolskaia.pdf, last accessed Sept. 17, 201212. For the view that the experience of serving on a jury trial in Okinawa affected the recent debate in Japan and contributed to the reform that brought in a mixed lay/professional panel see Hiroshi Fukurai, *The Rebirth of Japan's Petit Quasi-Jury and Grand Jury Systems: A Cross-National Analysis of Legal Consciousness and the Lay Participatory Experience in Japan and the U.S.*, 40 Cornell Intl. L.J. 315, 333 (2007), http://organizations.lawschool.cornell.edu/ilj/issues/40.2/CIN202.pdf.

showing that in European countries (Germany, France and Italy) lay jurors had little if any effect on the determination when mixed lay/professional judge panels decided criminal cases,[58] a compromise was reached in which a Germanized form of mixed court consisting of both lay and professional judges would hear a limited category of serious crime cases. The new mixed lay/professional *saiban'in* system went into effect in 2009[59] and survived challenges to its Constitutionality.[60] As anticipated the use of mixed panels has not changed the fate of those charged as such panels convicted over 99% of defendants tried before the panels.[61] This percentage is consistent with the conviction rate in a trial before a judge. Although trial is before a mixed lay/professional judge panel, the appeal from a panel decision goes to a High Court composed entirely of professional judges. Whether the prosecutor or a convicted defendant takes the appeal, the appeal panel need not give determinative weight to the determination of the lay judges on the initial trial panel[62] although in the first case where an acquittal was reversed by the High Court the Supreme Court reinstated the original not guilty verdict holding that in an appeal from a mixed panel decision the High Court may reverse fact findings only when it determines that there is strong evidence that the original acquittal was irrational; the High Court must explain why the panel determination was irrational and inconsistent with common sense; and review

58. Walter Perron, *Lay Participation in Germany*, 72 Intl. Rev. Penal L. 181, 193 (2001) www.cairn.be/load_pdf.php?ID_ARTICLE=RIDP_721_0181; Markus Dirk Dubber, *American Plea Bargains, German Lay Judges, and the Crisis of Criminal Procedure*, 49 Stanford L. Rev. 547, 565 (1997); Joseph J. Kodner, *Re-Introducing Lay Participation to Japanese Criminal Cases: An Awkward Yet Necessary Step*, 2 Wash. U. Global Stud. L. Rev. 231, 246–249 (2003). The utility of lay judges has been questioned in part because of the view that they rarely affect decisions. See Yue Ma, *Lay Participation in Criminal Trials: A Comparative Perspective*, 8 Intl. Criminal Justice Rev. 74 (1998). Similarly, the experience of Russian lay judges was that they infrequently disagreed with professional judges on the panel and when they did they even less frequently prevailed in changing the judgment. Stefan Machura, *Fairness, Justice, and Legitimacy: Experiences of People's Judges in South Russia*, 25 L. & Policy 123, 141 (2003).

59. For a translation of the Saiban'in Law see, Kent Anderson & Emma Saint, *Japan's Quasi Jury (Saiban-in) Law: An Annotated Translation of the Action Concerning Participation of Lay Assessors in Criminal Trials*, 6 Asian-P. L. & Pol'y J. 233 (2005).

60. *Lay Judge System Constitutional Case*, Case No. 2010 (A) No. 1196, Keishu Vol. 65, No. 8 (P.B., Nov. 16, 2001), http://www.courts.go.jp/english/judgments/text/2011.11.16-2010.-A-.No..1196.html; Kyodo, *Lay Judge System OK: Top Court*, Japan Times (Nov. 18, 2011), http://www.japantimes.co.jp/text/nn20111118a6.html and *Lay Judge System Constitutional Case*, Case No. 2010 (A) No. 1299, Keishu Vol. 66, No. 1 (P.B., Jan. 13, 2012) http://www.courts.go.jp/english/judgments/text/2012.01.13-2010.-A-.No..1299.html).

61. See, e.g., Setsuko Kamiya, *Lay judges convict 99%; few shirk duty*, Japan Times (Aug 2, 2011), http://search.japantimes.co.jp/cgi-bin/nn20110802f2.html. While the conviction rate remains constant, lay judges are apparently more willing to accept explanations for why passengers stopped at Japan's borders with illicit drugs are in possession of such drugs. This has caused the Japanese customs authorities to consider taping the process at which such drugs are located in passenger's possession. Kyodo, *Customs may tape drug busts at airports*, Japan Times (Aug. 21, 2011), http://search.japantimes.co.jp/cgi-bin/nn20110821a2.html.

62. In the United States one reason why it is difficult to overturn a decision of a District Court in either a civil or criminal case is the weight that the appeal court must give to finding of the jury. As has been noted by others, the more separate lay jurors are from professional jurors and a procedure that protects the sanctity of the jury's verdict (at least a not guilty verdict) by making it difficult to overturn on appeal, the more juries can act as a restraint on other branches of the government. Richard Lempert, *The Internationalization of Lay Legal Decision-Making*, 40 Cornell Intl. L.J. 477, 483 (2007).

by the High Court should not be de novo but deference should be given to the mixed panel's findings.[63] It is likely that this ruling will be seen by High Courts as a "green light" to affirm acquittals made by mixed panels (and perhaps as a caution light to prosecutors considering such appeals). The decision may be read as advising High Courts to pay greater respect for trial court acquittals in general.

The inquest nature of a Japanese trial did not conform to the views of criminal justice held by the American Occupation. The 1948 Criminal Procedure Code incorporates the American criminal law notions of due process, adversary trial and protection of the rights of the accused.

Japan has a juvenile justice system; juvenile offender cases are heard in the Family Court. The juvenile justice system was modeled on the American system. Like the United States, Japan has had recurring problems of more violent crimes by juveniles—although there is some evidence that the perception of increased juvenile crime in Japan is not consistent with reality.[64] Like the United States, Japan has moved to reduce the age of juvenile offenders in order to subject "older juveniles" to the regular court system. The minimum age at which teenagers can be charged as adults has been reduced to 14 from 16.[65]

§16.03 WHAT YOU SEE MAY NOT BE WHAT YOU GET

[A] General Comment

The fundamental differences between the Japanese and United States criminal justice systems relate to procedural justice. These differences are affected by three principal factors:

[1] Procedural Fairness versus. Substantive Justice

The United States system has procedural fairness at its core. The individual suspect or defendant has procedural rights that must be protected and, as a general rule the United States law means what it says as to such protections. Where the system fails is primarily in those areas where, for socio-economic reasons the end result of the system casts doubt on the efficacy of the protection. In Japan the focus is on substantive justice—the guilty should be convicted. Such an approach has less to do with rights, laws and formal rules than it does with the defendant's guilt. In this regard, what you see in Japan in the way of Constitutional rights and statutory rules may not be what

---

63. *Deference to be given to Mixed Panel's findings case*, Case No. 2011 (A) No. 757, Keishu Vol. 66, No. 2, http://www.courts.go.jp/english/judgments/text/2012.02.13-2011.-A-.No..757.html (P.B., Feb. 13, 2012).
64. See, e.g., Masami Ito, *Minors in own category but never Above the Law*, Japan Times, Jan. 5, 2010.
65. *More Teens Face Charges under Harsher Law*, The Japan Times (Apr. 1, 2002). Not only may prosecutors treat younger juveniles as adults, but also the revised Juvenile Law requires that teenagers over age sixteen who commit intentional murder must be referred to prosecutors for prosecution as adults.

actually is at work in the system at least as those rights and rules are viewed through an American lens that has ingrained on it American procedural values.

[2] Objectives of the System: Punishment versus. Rehabilitation

The American system is influenced by puritanical values that lead the system to goals of apprehension (within the constraints of procedural rules) and punishment of those who commit crimes. In this way American's obtain and bring criminals to "justice." In pursuance of these goals the United States system has mandatory sentences for some crimes and long sentences for others. It is not unfair to say that the system is punitive—let the punishment fit the crime.[66] In Japan the objective of the system is rehabilitation of the offender not punishment. In fact, out of recognition that removing a person from a generally acceptable support system that values societal norms and placing the offender in a population of anti-social individuals leads to more anti-social conduct and is counterproductive to rehabilitation, the Japanese system tries to keep the offender out of prison. All levels of the criminal justice system seek to avoid incarceration. The goal is to keep the individual in the general society where family, friends, group, etc. can assist in rehabilitation. Thus, police, prosecutor, judge, and when it must be used the prison system, have as their objective the offender's rehabilitation. Rehabilitation comes, not from blaming others but from recognition of one's own failings, a taking of responsibility for one's own actions, and a desire to change. As a result great emphasis is placed on confession, remorse, apology, restitution, etc. These factors and the accused's willingness to accept them is a central feature of the Japanese criminal justice system. Although, recent concern over victim's rights and political considerations resulting from the public's perception and fear of crime has resulted in somewhat longer prison sentences than in the past.[67]

[3] Respect versus. Mistrust of Officialdom

As a generalized matter, the public in Japan has respect for and trust of public officials, although the failure of the government in connection with the Great East Japan Earthquake and Tsunami and the Fukushima Disaster has strained that respect. The general public (but not the criminal defense bar) is more willing to accept the decisions of police, prosecutors and judges—although this is changing as a consequence of a number of high profile cases involving coerced confessions and prosecutorial misconduct. In the United States there is less trust of officialdom and efforts are made to cabin official power and minimize the role of public officials. Thus procedural rules backed

66. Although the punishment should fit the crime, the circumstance of the defendant may be taken into consideration when sentencing. This may result in a reduction of sentence. In some cases the statute requires a mandatory sentence e.g., Armed Career Criminal Act (ACCA), 18 U.S.C. §924(e).. *Sykes v. United States*, 564 U.S. ____ (2011).

67. *Long-term prisoners doubled over decade*, The Yomiuri Shimbun (Jan. 1, 2010); see also, Jonathan David Marshall, *Democratizing the Law in Japan*, in *Routledge Handbook of Japanese Politics* 92, 99 (Alisa Gaunder ed.).

up by prophylactic measures (the exclusionary rule) are in place to control police and prosecutorial power. Professional lawyers in an adversary procedure and laypersons, in the form of the jury, are utilized to marginalize the role of the judge.

In addition, the Japanese criminal justice system relies on the Japanese community to both prevent crime and to rehabilitate those who have strayed from the values of the community.[68] Only those who cannot be rehabilitated are excluded from the community by imprisonment. Those who find themselves excluded from the general Japanese community may take refuge in the Japanese criminal community, i.e., the Yakuza.

The consequences for the accused are: (a) if you did not do the crime and are willing to take the risk that failure to persuade the jury of your innocence will lead to jail time, you are better off in the United States system. (b) If you did do the crime and do not want to serve the time but are willing to show contrition, you are better off in the Japanese system. (c) If you did not do the crime you likely will nonetheless be convicted in Japan if the authorities think you committed the crime but your penalty will likely be substantially less than in the United States for a similar crime. As for the public, Japan has less crime than the United States although the crime rate has risen from the mid-1990s,[69] crime has become a concern for the general public,[70] and crime and fighting crime have become a political issue in Japan just as being tough on crime has been a political issue in the United States.[71] Moreover, there is a growing concern about recidivism,[72] (which is on the rise)[73] although Japan has less repeat offenders than the United States. Whether Japan's lower crime rate and lower recidivism rate is a result of its approach to criminal justice, its employment system, its record keeping or other factors is not certain.

[B] United States

As a general matter, what you see is what you get from American Criminal Law and Procedure. Perhaps the biggest areas where practice fails to follow what many consider to be the written law are: (i) double jeopardy; (ii) plea-bargaining; (iii) bail; and (iv)

68. Rick Skwiot, *Cooperative Communities Reduce Crime, Washington University,* St. Louis Magazine (Fall 2009), http://magazine.wustl.edu/Fall09/John%20Owen%20Haley.html (Fall, 2009), last accessed Sept. 17, 2012; John O. Haley, *A Spiral of Success, Community support is key to restorative justice in Japan,* The Ecology of Justice, In Context # 38 (Spring 1994), http://www.context.org/ICLIB/IC38/Haley.htm, last accessed Sept. 17, 2012.
69. Dag Leonardsen, *Crime in Japan: Paradise Lost?* 7 J. Scandinavian Stud. Criminology & Crime Prevention 185 (2006).
70. Martin Fackler, *Fearing Crime, Japanese Wear the Hiding Place,* New York Times (Oct. 20, 2007); *Rising Crime in Japan,* The Economist (Oct. 23, 2003), www.economist.com/displaystory.cfm?story_id=2156625.
71. David T. Johnson, *The Vanishing Killer: Japan's Postwar Homicide Decline,* 9 Soc. Sci. Japan J. 73, 74 (2005).
72. Jun Hongo, *Recidivism Rate Reaches an All Time High in 2006,* Japan Times (Nov. 7, 2007); *Reducing recidivism key to cutting overall crime,* The Yomiuri Shimbun (Nov. 15, 2007), www.yomiuri.co.jp/dy/editorial/20071115TDY04305.htm.
73. See, *White paper: 40% of crimes involve past offenders,* Yomiuri Shimbun (Nov. 12, 2011), http://www.yomiuri.co.jp/dy/national/T111111006148.htm.

right to counsel. The American concept of double jeopardy prohibits a prosecutor from taking an appeal and also prohibits a prosecutor from retrying a defendant who has been found not guilty of a crime.[74] During the Civil Rights Revolution of the 1960s State Court juries in the South found many white defendants accused of committing crimes against African-Americans not guilty of the charges. Federal prosecutors charged the same defendants with federal crimes arising out of the same acts that had been at the base of the state charges. Defendants argued that the prohibition against double jeopardy prevented such second trial. The Supreme Court, finding that the state and federal governments were separate sovereigns and finding that the concept of double jeopardy applied to each sovereign separately found no Constitutional violation. Federal charges after state acquittal continue to be part of the Justice Department's arsenal to protect the civil rights of minorities. While protecting the victim's civil rights, questions are raised as to whether this "splitting of judicial hairs" adequately takes into account the rights of the accused.

Plea-bargaining is at the heart of the American criminal justice system. Under the system the prosecutor gets a conviction without the costs of a trial and the defendant gets a lesser sentence. As part of many plea-bargains the defendant agrees to provide evidence against third persons who may have been involved in the criminal enterprise. [In some cases the prosecutor may provide the defendant with immunity in exchange for testimony.] Plea-bargains save time and expense.[75] Those who support the concept argue that as the bargain is based on the free expression of the defendant's will there are no issues raised as to propriety of the system. Those who disagree point out the different leverage each side has in the bargain situation the prosecutor does not have to worry that she will spend time in jail and further, the expense of prosecution is a government expense. On the defendant's side is both the fear of a long sentence plus the expense of the defense.[76] For a middle class defendant, a criminal trial could mortgage the house; take money put aside for the education of the children, ruin plans for retirement, etc. A not guilty defendant might plead guilty, simply to avoid the expense of a trial especially if the prosecutor agrees to reduce the crime charged to a crime where the defendant probably will not have to serve any jail time. It is true that reputation may be at stake and it is true that the defendant might be not guilty but it is also true that there are children to be concerned about, a family's economic future to consider, etc. By pleading guilty to a charge the defendant gives up several Constitutional guarantees—the right to a trial by jury, the Fifth Amendment right against

74. Even if a defendant has not been found not guilty, double jeopardy may prohibit retrial. Such cases could arise where a jury has been impaneled (jeopardy applies) but during the course of trial a mistrial is declared because of a prosecution motion. If a jury cannot reach a decision then a new trial can be had and it is not considered a violation of the double jeopardy rule. But, where a jury cannot reach a decision as to certain charges but has found the defendant not guilty of other charges whose facts are essential to prove charges on which the jury deadlocked, the prosecutor may not retry the charges on which the jury could not reach a decision. *Yeager v. United States*, 557 U.S 110. (June 18, 2009).

75. *United States v. Ruiz*, 536 U.S. 622 (2002); *Santobello v. New York*, 404 U.S. 257 (1971).

76. For criticism of the United States plea-bargaining system and suggestion that the German system, which forbids plea bargaining is preferable see John H. Langbein, *Land without Plea Bargaining: How they Germans Do It*, 78 Michigan L. Rev. 204 (1979).

self-incrimination, the right to confront witnesses and the right to receive from the prosecution exculpatory evidence.[77] The Government has no need to establish defendant's guilt beyond a reasonable doubt and there need not be any evidence to corroborate the defendant's plea. Because plea-bargaining waives Constitutional rights, the foundation of the plea bargain system is a knowing and voluntary waiver of those rights.[78] A court may, in some cases (where there is evidence of guilt other than the defendant's plea) accept a voluntary guilty plea even when the defendant proclaims innocence.[79]

Because plea-bargaining is so prevalent in the United States criminal justice system (90% or more of federal criminal cases are resolved by plea bargaining)[80] and because as a consequence of the plea agreement the defendant waives substantial Constitutionally guaranteed rights, it may be questioned whether what you see when you look at such rights is what most criminal defendant's ultimately get. Nonetheless, when it comes to the investigative stage of the criminal process the accused does, as a general matter get what the written law appears to require.

The right to bail is a Constitutional right. Bail may be denied in certain cases, such as when there is risk of flight or where protection of the public may make bail inappropriate. The bail system is subject to criticism in its actual workings and its effect on the economically disadvantaged. While the wealthy may be able to post bail, those with limited economic means cannot afford even modest bail. The consequence is that the present system operates to the disadvantage of the poor and has both a disparate economic and racial impact.

Those who can afford counsel and hire their own counsel have a much greater chance of success at a criminal trial than defendants who are represented by public defenders. While indigents are given publicly supported counsel and while the right adheres early in the criminal process, the publicly supported system results in back logs for overworked defenders and in many cases ineffective representation. This failure has spawned litigation (currently pending)[81] challenging the system at state and local levels seeking greater funding for counsel for the indigent based the Supreme Court's determination in *Gideon v. Wainwright.*[82]

---

77. In *United States v. Ruiz*, 536 U.S. 622 (2002).
78. *Brady v. United States*, 397 U.S. 742 (1970); *McMann v. Richardson*, 397 U.S. 759 (1970); *Parker v. North Carolina*, 397 U.S. 790 (1970).
79. *North Carolina v. Alford*, 400 U.S. 25 (1970).
80. *United States v. Ruiz,*, 536 U.S. 622 (2002). For a discussion of statistics demonstrating how plea-bargaining dominates the criminal justice system in the United States, see Judge Earl G. Penrod, *The Guilty Plea Process in Indiana: A Proposal to Strengthen the Diminishing Factual Basis Requirement*, 34 Indiana L. Rev. 1127, 1130–1131 (2001).
81. *Kimberly Hurrell-Harring v. The State of New York*, See, Warner Norcross & Judd, MSC Order: *Duncan v. State of Michigan*, http://www.jdsupra.com/post/documentViewer.aspx?fid=bf173a64-7846-432f-9d0b-5e77f2c8efc6. See Aicia Bannon, *Michigan Victory on Right to Counsel Shifts Spotlight Back to New York, Brennan Center for Justice*, New York University, School of Law (May 4, 2010), http://www.brennancenter.org/blog/archives/michigan_victory_on_right_to_counsel_shifts_spotlight_back_to_new_york/. http://www.courts.state.ny.us/ctapps/decisions/2010/may10/66opn10.pdf.
82. 372 U.S. 335 (1963).

[C] Japan

[1] Substantive Criminal Law

Four basic principles of criminal law can be gleaned from the history of Japan's criminal law. First, to be a crime there must be some form of legislation making the act a crime. This, in turn, adopts the concept that there can be no ex post facto criminal statutes. Moreover, since crimes must be listed in statutes, the American doctrine of "void for vagueness" should be applicable to Japanese law[83] but there appears to be no case applying it to strike down a criminal statute. Second, equality before the law is part of Japanese criminal law. Third, there is individual responsibility for criminal actions and the individual responsible must have formed a criminal intent to be guilty (in some cases a form of negligence, e.g., professional negligence, can substitute for criminal intent). Guilt by association or guilt based on someone else's conduct will not, as a general rule,[84] suffice under Japanese law. The crime of conspiracy standing alone is virtually unknown in Japan, although where one party "conspires" in the sense of getting another to commit a crime for him, both are guilty of a crime.[85] Fourth, when convicted of a crime, the court must consider the question of rehabilitation in assessing the correct penalty. In assessing a penalty the court should also take into account its ability to suspend sentence.

Japan does countenance "aider and abettor" criminal responsibility. The "instigator" is subject to the same punishment as the person committing the crime. Where one instigates another to commit a crime and acts are taken to perform the crime but the crime is never brought to fruition, there is, as a general rule, no crime.[86] A person who has committed and been convicted of committing a crime in Japan has not only brought shame on himself but also has brought shame on his family. Family members may feel obligated to "take responsibility" for the anti-social acts of their own.[87]

To coincide with the definition of a crime and to be against the law, the starting point is the written statute law. This is particularly so in light of the overriding principle of *nulla crimen sine lege*. As an initial matter there is the question "what is a law?" Under the Constitution the Diet is the sole law-making institution. Local public entities: (a) may make regulations concerning organization and operation of the entity as

83. For the U.S. approach see, *Skilling v. United States*, slip opinion p. 38, 561 U.S. ___ (2010). For the view that the Court has upheld criminal and other statutes that are too vague to be sustained. See, dissent of Justice Scalia in *Sykes v. United States*, 564 U.S. ____ (2011). Void for vagueness concepts apply to regulatory action. *FCC v. Fox Television Stations Inc.*, 567 U.S. ___ (2012).
84. Election laws in Japan are an exception See, *Nullified Politician Loses Appeal law*, Japan Times (Mar. 13, 1997), http://search.japantimes.co.jp/cgi-bin/nn19970313a5.html.
85. *Conspiracy case*, Case No. 1954 (A) No. 1056 12 Keishu 1718, http://www.courts.go.jp/english/judgments/text/1958.05.28-1954.-A-.No..1056.html (P.G., May 28, 1958); Penal Code Article 61.
86. An exception is made where a law specifically defines instigating certain activity a crime, such as is the case with the Subversive Activities Prevention Law.
87. Not only family members but also others in a position of authority may feel responsible for the acts of subordinates. See Charles R. Fenwick, *Culture, Philosophy and Crime: The Japanese Experience*, 9 Intl. J. Comp. & Applied Criminal Justice 67, 73 (Spring, 1985).

established by law,[88] (b) and while local entities shall hold public elections for local public office,[89] (c) and whereas local entities have the right to manage their property and affairs;[90] and (d) cannot be discriminated against in national legislation unless they consent (after a public vote),[91] the Local Autonomy Act permits local entities to impose criminal penalties of as much as two years in prison and a fine of as much as JPY 1 million for violations of local ordinances. This is Constitutional on the theory that local assemblies and governors are elected and thus the ordinances should be considered as laws and not simply administrative regulations.[92] Cabinet Orders may only contain criminal penalties if the Diet has passed legislation authorizing such penalties. The punishment for crimes must be established in legislation. Criminality by analogy is not permitted but courts are free to liberally interpret the criminal statutes perhaps giving the same result.[93]

Article 39 of the Constitution prohibits ex post facto criminal laws and bars the infliction of a harsher penalty on a defendant than was in effect at the time the crime was committed; where law sets a more lenient penalty after a crime has been committed, the more lenient penalty applies.[94]

The concept of criminal intent is under attack in modern Japan. Many recent administrative and public safety and health statutes have adopted a no-fault absolute liability standard of criminality. Also, the concept of negligence, which may form the necessary intent,[95] appears inconsistent with the idea that to be guilty not only must the act be guilty but so too must the mind. Nonetheless, there remains a very strong feeling in Japanese legal circles, both among the bar and the judiciary, that to be guilty of a crime the defendant must have intended to commit a wrong. Japan recognizes the defense of insanity. The definition is remarkably similar to the *McNaughton* rule followed in whole or in part by many states in the United States[96] and requires that a defendant not be able to distinguish between right and wrong.[97] Japanese criminal law follows, as a general rule, the principle of territoriality although some, few, crimes have extraterritorial application.[98]

---

88. Constitution Article 92.
89. Constitution Article 93.
90. Constitution Article 94.
91. Constitution Article 95.
92. Hiroyuki Hata & Go Nakagawa & Takehisa Nakagawa, *Japanese Constitutional Law* (Kluwer Law International 2001) section 163 citing 16 Keishu 577 (Sup. Ct., G.B., 30 May 1962).
93. Hiroshi Oda, *Japanese Law* 418 (Oxford University Press 1999); Shigemitsu Dando, *Basic Concepts in and Temporal and Territorial Limits on the Application of the Penal Law of Japan*, 9 New York University School L. Intl. & Comp. L. Rev. 237, 245-246 (B. J. George, Jr. translation, 1988).
94. Penal Code Article 6. See B.J. George, Jr., *Rights of the Criminally Accused*, 53 L. & Contemp. Probs. 71, 80 (1990).
95. See Penal Code Articles 209, 210 and 211. For a discussion of the role of criminal negligence in the medical field see, Robert B. LeFlar, *"Unnatural Deaths," Criminal Sanctions, and Medical Quality Improvement in Japan*, 9 Yale Journal Health, Pol'y L. and Ethics 1, 16 et seq. (2009).
96. *Clark v. Arizona*, 548 U.S. 735 (2006).
97. Shigemitsu Dando, *The Criminal Law Of Japan: The General Part* 143-144 (B. J. George trans., Rothman & Co. 1997).
98. The criminal law recognizes traditional extraterritorial crimes such as those committed on Japanese flag ships, or airplanes; those that have a significant domestic effect on government

The concept of relativism, also called contextualism when applied to the question of rights, has a role to play in Japanese criminal law. By looking at rights in the context of relationships, rights may be found to be less meaningful than would appear in isolation. Similarly by looking at conduct and criminal statutes in relation to what the society expects, criminal statutes may have broader meaning than the mere words would suggest. As a result, sometimes a criminal law provision may be interpreted so that it appears to apply to situations that are 180 degrees removed from the intent of the drafters.[99] In such a situation, what you see is not what you get.

[2] Procedural Law

It is in the area of Criminal Procedure that Japan's legal system saw its greatest postwar changes. These changes reflected American values of due process and rights of the criminally accused. The Japanese Constitution contains numerous provisions that are almost identical to protections contained in the United States Constitution. Yet the values to be protected in the two societies differ. The United States, an individual oriented society, views the function of criminal procedure as a protection of the rights of the criminally accused. To protect the rights of the accused, society may be asked to pay the price of allowing criminals to go free. The United States system focuses on procedural justice to protect society—including those accused but not guilty.

Japan, on the other hand, is a group-oriented society where the rights of the few may have to be sacrificed (or at least limited) to protect the public welfare of the greater society.[100] Constitutional protections of individual rights must be interpreted in a way that is consistent with the greater good of the society. Here the objective is not to assure that the rights of the criminally accused are protected but rather to assure "substantive justice" in the sense that those who have committed crimes are found guilty.

To carry out this philosophy the judiciary has interpreted the Constitution in a way that is very different from what you see in from an American prospective. This section discusses only a few of the ways in which the Japanese legal system has interpreted Constitutional and statutory rights provisions so as to make them unrecognizable to a modern American reader.[101]

Before discussing specific Constitutional rights, it is necessary to keep in mind: (a) statistics show that the Japanese solve an extraordinarily high percentage of crimes (although as discussed below the statistics may be inaccurate and crime solving has

---

such as forgery of public documents or counterfeiting Japanese currency; of broader application are some crimes committed abroad by Japanese nationals and some committed by Japanese civil servants. To these should be added crimes committed abroad that violate Japanese treaty obligations. See Kensuke Itoh, *The 1987 Penal Code and Other Special Criminal Laws Amendments Law: A Response to the Two U.N. Conventions Against International Terrorism*, 32 Japanese Annual Intl. L. 18 (1989).

99. Robert C. Christopher, *The Japanese Mind: The Goliath Explained* 168 (Simon & Schuster 1983).

100. Japan is not alone in this approach. See, *R. v. Sinclair*, 2010 SCC 35 (Supreme Court of Canada, 2010).

101. Tsuyoshi Kinoshita, *Legal System and Legal Culture in Japanese law*, 44 Comparative L. Rev. 25, 135 (2010).

suffered in recent years); (b) 99.9% of all defendants who go to trial are convicted; (c) the length of a defendant's sentence, indeed the question of whether the defendant will serve any time at all (most sentences in Japan are suspended) is affected by: (i) the defendant's ability to be rehabilitated and confession and repentance are the first steps to rehabilitation and (ii) the government's policy objectives that may be furthered by a jail sentence; (d) there is no plea-bargaining in Japan and all felony criminal cases that are brought must go to trial; (e) there is no formal exclusionary rule in Japan so illegally obtained evidence may be used at a criminal trial unless the judge feels the circumstances warrant prohibiting use by the prosecutor[102] although judges do have the authority to exclude illegally obtained evidence they virtually never do so if by doing so they will permit a guilty person to go free; (f) the function of the trial in Japan appears to be very different from the function of trial in the United States—this places primacy in criminal justice in the investigatory stage of a case, and investigation is an inquisition function handled by the police and prosecutors and finally, (g) there is a new criminal trial process involving mixed lay and professional judge panels for the trial of certain types of criminal cases.

The various participants in a Japanese criminal proceeding are: the police; prosecutor; defense counsel; judge; and defendant.

[3] Police

Unlike the United States, policing in Japan is a national government function The Occupation unsuccessfully attempted to localize the police by providing for local police departments. Police are part of a national civil service. Local police ride bicycles and walk patrols so that they are closer to the public they are to serve; talk to shop owners and residents; and conduct twice-yearly residential surveys of the neighborhood talking to residents about employment, family members, property ownership, etc. Members of the community are willing to talk to the police and share information. Each community has a local "police box" (*koban*) that acts as a neighborhood substation. The *koban* is informed when new people move into the neighborhood or when business moves in or out of the neighborhood.

The *koban* assists visitors to the neighborhood. Japanese neighborhoods are not organized in the grid pattern familiar to most Americans. Nor do postal addresses follow the pattern of most Western countries, namely, a street name and a numbered house on the street. Instead, most streets do not have names and each neighborhood has a name (e.g., Naka-ku or central district). Each square block in the neighborhood has a number (e.g., 8 Naka-ku is block 8 in the Naka-ku district) and each building on all four sides of the block has a number (e.g., 8-3 Naka-ku means block 8 building number 3 in the Naka-ku district). Since there are several square blocks in the neighborhood, block 8 could be immediately across the street from block 3. If block 8 is at the perimeter of the neighborhood one or two of its sides is not even across from

102. Compare, *Illegally Obtained Evidence* case, case No. 1976 (A) No. 865, 32 Keishu 1672, http://www.courts.go.jp/english/judgments/text/1978.09.07-1976.-A-.No..865.html (P.B., Sept. 7, 1978) with *Arizona v. Gant*, 556 U.S. ___ (2009).

a Naka-ku address. Finding a location in a big city can be a difficult task. What the visitor does is search out the local *koban* where a friendly, helpful police officer will produce a map of the district and show the newcomer precisely how to get to the building sought while asking for the visitor's name, business in the neighborhood and who is being visited. As a consequence, the police have a reasonably good idea who is in the area and why.

The Police Duty Law[103] obligates the police to investigate crimes and gives the police certain authority to meet this obligation. The police have the right to stop and question persons whom the police believe have information about criminal activity.[104] Persons stopped have an obligation to try to assist the police in their investigations. Police may stop groups of people who may have information. While such stopping may infringe on the temporary freedom of the individual or the group, such minor restriction is warranted by the public's right to be protected from criminals and the police officer's duty to carry out his obligation under the Police Duty Law.[105] In the United States, police stop and pat down authority is narrower and restricted to reasonable suspicion. Police in Japan may stop and question persons when it is believed they may be about to commit a crime to prevent a crime from taking place. At least in the case where a weapon was used in a crime, the police may search possessions of persons not arrested but under suspicion and being questioned, even though no warrant has been obtained and even though the suspect refused to give permission for a search and even though there is time to obtain a warrant, because such a search is consistent with the police officer's duty under the law to solve crimes.[106] If a "pat down" leads to seizure of evidence without a warrant such evidence may still be used at trial because (a) the obligation to obtain a warrant is subject to a balancing test and weighed against the public's right to be free of crime, and (b) if the situation is not egregious illegally obtained evidence is admissible.[107] In the United States a balancing test considering the defendant's right versus the "need to prevent perjury and to assure the integrity of the trial process is sometimes used in search and seizure and right to counsel situations."[108] But the right of the police to do their duty or the right of public to be free of crime is not weighed in the balance.

While the Supreme Court of Japan will sometimes find that evidence should have been excluded at a trial such instances are rare, typically do not allow the defendant to walk free and rarely involve organized crime figures[109] who are unlikely to have evidence suppressed.[110]

---

103. The Police Duty Law Article 2 makes the police responsible for protecting persons and property as well as investigating crimes and arresting suspects. Police are also responsible for traffic control.
104. Police Duty Law Article 2 (2).
105. *Stop and question case, Japan v. Boku*, 38 Keishu 295 (Sup. Ct. Feb. 13, 1984).
106. For a discussion of police techniques and the use of the Police Duty Law see William B. Cleary, *Criminal Investigation in Japan*, 26 California W. L. Rev. 723 (1989).
107. *Illegally Obtained Evidence* case, Case No. 1976 (A) No. 865, 32 Keishu 1672, http://www.courts.go.jp/english/judgments/text/1978.09.07-1976.-A-.No..865.html (P.B. Sept. 7, 1978).
108. *Stone v. Powell*, 428 U.S. 465, 488 (1976) quoted in *Kansas v. Ventris*, 556 U.S. 58 (2009).
109. *Urine Sample Suppression* case, Case No. 167 (A) of 2001, 57 Keishu No. 2, 121, http://www.courts.go.jp/english/judgments/text/2003.02.14-2001.-A-.No..1678.html (P.B., Feb. 14, 2003)

Most investigation results in the identification of a suspect. Once the police focus on a suspect they want to question the suspect at the police station. A police officer (or a prosecutor) may ask a suspect to voluntarily submit to questioning and the Code of Criminal Procedure grants such a suspect the right to refuse to submit to questioning or the right to terminate questioning at any time. Most suspects not only do appear but also have little if any opportunity to leave once they have appeared. The police examination may go on for hours at a time under conditions that are reminiscent of a 1920s Hollywood film. Although there are limits on the amount of time the police may hold a suspect who has been arrested there are no limits on the time that a non-arrested suspect may be subjected to questioning. In fact, the police can and do use a great deal of power to retain a suspect who has voluntarily appeared even to the extent of using physical force in some cases to keep the suspect in the police station.

[a] *Discretionary Justice Function*

The police also have a discretionary justice function. The police, operating under standards established by Japanese prosecutors, have authority to close simple cases or cases involving petty offenses (*bizai shobun*).[111] It is estimated that anywhere from 20% to 40% of all suspects arrested by the police are released under this authority.[112] Many of these cases are resolved through negotiation between the victim and the suspect in which restitution is made, the suspect admits his responsibility, shows remorse, apologizes and accepts the need to change and not commit future crimes. The suspect will write an appropriate letter of apology and contrition that will be kept in the police station but not be made part of any official file. Efforts are made to avoid arrest in minor cases.[113] If the suspect is a juvenile, the parents may be made parties to the process and reminded of their responsibility of supervision. Many criminal suspects are given a "second bite at the apple" on the theory that once having been caught and having gone through the process of rehabilitation they will not commit future crimes. This quasi-judicial function is an important part of policing in Japan as the arrest of a suspect can have a devastating effect. It is also useful in getting suspects to voluntarily

Where police failed to show a warrant, had no warrant, there was time to obtain a warrant and lied to the court during the trial about the circumstances of the search—the evidence was excluded but the defendant was convicted of a related crime based on evidence obtained under a warrant issued based on the suppressed evidence.

110. *Search of naked suspect case,* Case No. 1164 (A) of 1999, 57 Keishu No. 5, 620, http://www.courts.go.jp/english/judgments/text/2003.05.26-1999-A-No.1164.html (P.B., Mar 26, 2003) Compare *Los Angeles County v. Rettele,* 550 U.S. 609 (2007).
111. Code of Criminal Procedure Article 246. See Nobuyoshi Araki, *The Flow of Criminal Cases in the Japanese Criminal Justice System,* 31 Crime & Delinquency 601, 609–610 (1985) for a description of the prosecutor's role in police determinations under bizai shobun; see also, David T. Johnson, *The Japanese Way of Justice: Prosecuting Crime in Japan* (Oxford University Press 2002).
112. See John Owen Haley, *Authority without Power* 126 (Oxford University Press 1991); Daniel H. Foote, The Benevolent Paternalism of Japanese Criminal Justice, 80 *California* L. Rev. 317, 342 (1992).
113. Kevin T. Favreau, *Japanese Offender Rehabilitation—A Viable Alternative?,* 14 New England J. Criminal & Civil Confinement 331, 333 (1988).

agree to accompany police to the station rather than insisting on arrest. Where an arrest is affected, the police may, in controlled circumstances, show and use their weapons.[114] If the police determine that the suspect should be turned over to the prosecutor this must be done within 48 hours of an arrest.[115] Prior to turn over the police are in charge of the investigation; the suspect is held in police cells under police supervision and interrogated.[116] After turn over suspects remain in the same holding cell located at a police facility (sometimes called a "substitute prison" or *daiyo kangoku*) where the suspect is easily available to the prosecutor and not accorded the protections afforded by an independent prison system. The substitute prison system has its genesis in the shortage of prisons at the time the original Prison Law was passed in Japan in 1908.[117] As most confessions (including most false confessions) are obtained while suspects are held in substitute prisons, the *daiyo kangoku* system is intimately related to the issue of interrogation and confession in Japan. The international community and the JFBA have criticized this system because it places the suspect in the control of the very authority that is conducting the investigation into the crime and that is seeking to gain a confession from the suspect. The suspect who may be questioned for a 23 day period is, during this time, dependent on the interrogating officials for such essential things as food, sanitation, recreation and exercise, etc. To date the government has refused to accede to international and Bar Association pressure to abolish the system.[118]

[b] Crime Statistics

[i] Homicide and the Lack of Autopsies

Statistics show that the Japanese police solve a very high percentage of serious crimes. But statistics do not tell the entire story and may not tell an accurate story.[119] There is good reason to believe that statistics on foreigner committed crime and crime against women are especially inaccurate,[120] and police have an inducement to overstate clearance rates to enhance performance records. Although the clearance rate for crimes

114. See B.J. George Jr., *Rights of the Criminally Accused*, 53 Law & Contemporary Problems 71 (1990) for a discussion of when the police may display and use weapons.
115. Code of Criminal Procedure Article 203.
116. See Toshikuni Murai, *Pre-trial Detention and the Problems of Confinement*, 23 L. Japan 85, 87 (1990) (Frank Bennet Jr. trans.).
117. Setsuo Miyazawa, *Policing In Japan: A Study On Making Crime* 9 (Frank G. Bennett, Jr. & John O. Haley trans. State University of New York Press 1992).
118. Compare *Maryland v. Shatzer*, 559 U.S. ___ (2010).
119. The questionable reliability of crime statistics is not limited to Japan. See, William K. Rashbaum, *Retired Officers Raise Questions on Crime Data*, New York Times (Feb. 6, 2010).
120. Catherine Burns, *Sexual Violence and the Law in Japan* at 44–53 (Routledge Curzon 2005); Apichai W. Shipper, *Criminals or Victims? The Politics of Illegal Foreigners in Japan*, 31 J. Japanese Stud. 299, 306–313 (2005). See also, David T. Johnson, *Justice System Reform in Japan: Where are the Police and Why Does it Matter*, February 2004 Horitsy Jiho on the Web at www.law.usyd.edu.au/anjel/documents/ResearchPublications/Johnson2004_JusticeSystemReform.pdf, last accessed Sept. 17, 2012. For a critical view of Japanese criminal statistics see Andrew Finch, *Criminal Statistics in Japan: The White Paper on Crime*, Hanzai Hakusho & Hanzai Tokeisho, 3 Soc. Sci. Japan J. 237, 242 (2000).

may look impressive, the rate has been dropping steadily since the start of the late 1980s.[121] By 2004 the police clearance rate for some serious crimes had dropped from 80% to less than 50% in a five-year period. The police may have overstated the 80% clearance rate.[122] If criminal acts are not reported as crimes or are treated as natural rather than criminal events, the failure to solve the crime will never find its way into crime statistics. This may in fact affect the rate of criminal homicides in Japan.

In 2005 there were almost 1,400 homicides reported in Japan and a reported clearance (solution) rate of some 96.6% (96.8% in 2006). But, the coroner service that the Occupation introduced to Japan has been allowed to atrophy and autopsies are rarely performed. It is estimated that of suspicious deaths occurring in Tokyo in 2000 only 20.5% were investigated by a medical examiner performing an autopsy. Tokyo is a major city with a Medical Examiner's Office. Medical Examiner's offices exist in a few other major cities (Yokohama, Nagoya, Kobe and Osaka) and in some localities local Universities have forensic departments. But such departments are few and far between and have limited staff and perform few autopsies.[123] Many of Japan's smaller cities and towns simply have no Medical Examiner. In such locations there are virtually no autopsies performed.[124] Without an active autopsy system Japanese police are likely to deem suspicious deaths as suicides if the death has the tell-tale signs of suicide such as the use of charcoal briquettes and stoves at the scene—but it is easy enough for criminals to place these items at the scene to cover their tracks. This affects the clearance rate of homicides and likely increases the number of homicides by allowing murderers to commit additional murders.[125] Without an autopsy prosecutors are unlikely to prosecute.[126] Recommendations to increase autopsies have not brought results.[127] In 2011 autopsies were performed for only 11% of cases where police were in control of the body—but because most deaths do not involve police possession of the body—e.g., where death occurs in a hospital and the hospital reports the death as not involving criminality—the percentage of autopsies is actually lower than 11%.[128] The National Police Agency recognizes the difficulties police face because of the lack of sufficient number of coroners and has suggested a tripling of the medical examiners;

121. Dag Leonardsen, *Crime in Japan: Paradise Lost?*, 7 Journal of Scandinavian Studies in Criminology and Crime Prevention 185 (2006).
122. David T. Johnson, *Justice System Reform in Japan: Where are the Police and Why Does it Matter*, February 2004 Horitsy Jiho on the Web at www.law.usyd.edu.au/anjel/documents/ResearchPublications/Johnson2004_JusticeSystemReform.pdf, last accessed Sept. 17, 2012.
123. Natsuko Fukue, *Autopsy report: too few deaths examined*, Japan Times (Mar. 17, 2010), http://search.japantimes.co.jp/cgi-bin/nn20100317f1.html.
124. David T. Johnson, *Justice System Reform in Japan: Where are the Police and Why Does it Matter*, February 2004 Horitsy Jiho on the Web at www.law.usyd.edu.au/anjel/documents/ResearchPublications/Johnson2004_JusticeSystemReform.pdf.
125. Natsuko Fukue, *Low autopsy rate seen abetting murderers*, Japan Times (May 8, 2012), http://www.japantimes.co.jp/text/nn20120508f2.html.
126. Makoto Murayama & Shinichiro Ito, *Are people getting away with murder?*, Daily Yomiuri (Feb 7, 2010), http://www.yomiuri.co.jp/dy/national/20100207TDY03103.htm.
127. Kyodo, *Police plan to increase autopsies*, Japan Times (July 27, 2011), http://search.japantimes.co.jp/cgi-bin/nn20110727a7.html; *Lower House Committee to Seek Doubling of Autopsies*, Yomiuri Shimbun on Line (Aug. 28, 2008).
128. Kyodo, *Police win power to conduct forced autopsies*, Japan Times (June 16, 2012), http://www.japantimes.co.jp/text/nn20120616a8.html.

even if tripled the service would consist of only 653 coroners, far short of the number required.[129] A law allowing police to compel an autopsy was enacted in 2012.[130] If death occurs in a hospital it is the responsibility of the doctors to prepare a Medical Death Certificate with cause of death and doctors are also required to advise the police if they believe the death is unusual—caused by criminality.[131] Doctors are hesitant to report suspicious deaths for a variety of reasons, including patient confidentiality, concern about a criminal gross negligence charge against the medical facility (or the reporting doctor), etc.[132]

When the death occurs outside a hospital the police prepare the Death Certificate. It is the function of the police to determine whether the victim died as a result of a homicide, a suicide or natural causes.[133] But the police have an interest in under reporting homicides to perpetuate the "feel good" feeling of the Japanese public and under reporting dramatically increases the statistical significance of homicides solved. That some homicides go unreported seems clear.[134] Several high profile deaths have been declared suicides with little or no examination, including deaths of a Cabinet minister by hanging; and a financial advisor (with knife wounds on his body).[135] There is no suggestion that these reported suicides were anything but suicides; rather the point is that in none of these cases were the deaths subjected to a coroner's examination and autopsy nor a thorough police investigation. It is reported that autopsies were performed in a mere 4.4% of cases deemed to be suicides in the year 2009.[136] Japan has an extraordinarily high suicide rate.[137] How many of these suicides are actually unreported, unsolved homicides is not known.[138]

129. Kyodo News, *NPA Urges Coroner Ranks Tripled*, Japan Times (July 15, 2010), http://search.japantimes.co.jp/cgi-bin/nn20100715x2.html.

130. Kyodo, *Police win power to conduct forced autopsies*, Japan Times (June 16, 2012), http://www.japantimes.co.jp/text/nn20120616a8.html.

131. Medical Practice Law, Law No. 201 of 1948, Article 21. While the duty to report is clear, their exists confusion as to the cases that trigger the reporting requirement. See, Robert B. LeFlar, *"Unnatural Deaths," Criminal Sanctions, and Medical Quality Improvement in Japan*, 9 Yale Journal Health, Pol'y L. and Ethics 1 (2009); Eric Feldman, *Law, Society and Medical Malpractice Litigation in Japan*, 8 Wash. U. Global Stud. L. Rev. 257 (2009); H Ikegaya, K Kawai, Y Kikuchi, K Yoshida, *Does informed consent exempt Japanese doctors from reporting therapeutic deaths?*, 32 J. Medical Ethics 114–116 (2006); L. Jay Starkey & Shoichi Maeda, *Doctor as criminal: reporting of patient deaths to the police and criminal prosecution of healthcare providers in Japan*, http://www.biomedcentral.com/1472-6963/10/53.

132. Robert B. LeFlar, *"Unnatural Deaths," Criminal Sanctions, and Medical Quality Improvement in Japan*, 9 Yale Journal Health, Pol'y L. and Ethics 1 (2009).

133. J. Sean Curtin, *Suicide in Japan: Part Four—Determining Suicide as the Cause of Death, Japanese Institute of Global Communications*, http://www.glocom.org/special_topics/social_trends/20040113_trends_s66/index.html, last accessed Sept. 17, 2012.

134. *Ex-stable master's prison term reduced*, Japan Times (Apr. 6, 2010), http://search.japantimes.co.jp/cgi-bin/nn20100406a2.html.

135. Bruce Wallace, *Japan's Police See no Evil*, Los Angeles Times (Nov. 9, 2007); Bruce Wallace, *Some Claim Japanese Police Discouraging Autopsies*, Herald Tribune 12A (Nov. 10, 2007). Blaine Harden, *Brutal Beating Death Exposes Sumo's Dark Side*, Washington Post (Mar. 10, 2008).

136. *Autopsies done in only 4% of suicides*, The Yomiuri Shimbun (July 19, 2010), http://www.yomiuri.co.jp/dy/national/T100718001606.htm.

[c] *The Problem of False Confessions*

Additionally, most cases that are "solved" are resolved through a suspect's confession. But there exists in Japan and also in the United States[139] a serious question involving false confessions leading to convictions of the innocent.[140] Once the police (and prosecutor) latch onto a suspect and believe they have caught the guilty party it is almost inevitable that the suspect will confess, whether guilty or innocent. The pressure on police, much of which is self-generated, to obtain a confession is fierce and leads to the use of questionable techniques.[141]

False confessions have become a public issue in Japan as a result of several news worthy cases in which convicted "murderers" were later found to be not guilty as a consequence of DNA tests notwithstanding their confession. Even prisoners on death row who had confessed have been released and granted new trial at which they were found not guilty.[142] False confessions were one of the prime factors in the growing trend in the United States to fully record police interrogation of suspects. Whether the problem of false confession in Japan will result in the recording of full police/

---

137. See, Mizuho Aoki, *Suicides top 30,000 for 14th straight year*, Japan /Times on Line (Jan. 12, 2012), http://www.japantimes.co.jp/text/nn20120112a2.html; Kyodo News, *Suicide, depression toll on economy ¥2.7 trillion*, Japan Times (Sept. 7, 2010), http://search.japantimes.co.jp/cgi-bin/nn20100907x3.html. *Suicides by students hit a record high of over 1,000 in 2011*. Yomiuri Shimbun (Mar. 10, 2012), *Record high for youth suicide / Suicide rates among students increased nearly 11% last year*, http://www.yomiuri.co.jp/dy/national/T120309006954.htm.
138. For a critical view of Japanese criminal statistics see Andrew Finch, *Criminal Statistics in Japan: The White Paper on Crime*, Hanzai Hakusho & Hanzai Tokeisho, 3 Soc. Sci. Japan J. 237, 242 (2000). Japanese crime statistics are not uniform in how they define homicide. Thus, robbery resulting in homicide may be reported as robbery but not homicide, just as a violent assault that results in death may be reported as bodily injury but not homicide.
139. See, Richard A. Leo, Steven A. Drizin, Peter J. Neufeld, Bradley R. Hall & Amy Vatner, *Bringing Reliability Back in: False Confessions and Legal Safeguards in the 21st Century* (University of San Francisco Law Research Paper No. 2009-04), Wisconsin L. Rev. 479 (2006). Amongst other things the authors suggest that to make confessions more reliable the entire custodial interrogation should be recorded (p. 486). In the United States the trend is towards recording custodial interrogations. Ian Herbert, *The Psychology and Power of False Confessions*, 22 APS Observer, Dec. 2009, http://www.psychologicalscience.org/observer/getArticle.cfm?id=2590, last accessed Sept. 17, 2012.
140. Colin P. A, Jones, *Prospects for Citizen Participation in Criminal Trials in Japan, 'Book Review of Takashi Murata, Saiban'in Seido (The Lay Judge System),'* 15 Pacific Rim L. & Policy J. 363, 364 (2006).
141. *Interrogation Abuse, Not Criminal*, United Press International, (Nov. 23, 2007), www.upi.com/NewsTrack/Quirks/2007/11/23/claim_interrogation_abusive_not_criminal/1680/; Setsuo Miyazawa, *Policing in Japan: A Study on Making Crime* 165-167, 171-178 (Frank G. Bennett, Jr. & John O. Haley trans., State University of New York Press 1992).
142. *Fukawa Incident Case Acquittal May Stir Reforms*, Japan Times (Mar. 15, 2011), http://search.japantimes.co.jp/cgi-bin/nn20110315f1.html. *Court Acquits Pair after Serving Decades in Jail*, Japan Times (May 25, 2011), http://search.japantimes.co.jp/cgi-bin/nn20110525a2.html.

prosecutor interrogation of suspects remains to be seen[143] although full recording of suspects arrested by Special Investigation Units has begun and may lead to greater use of full recording. The introduction into evidence of a secret recording of interrogation by one of Ichiro Ozawa's aides disclosing that the interrogator had filed an inaccurate report of the interrogation session will also likely lead to greater use of full recordings,[144] and in fact the prosecutor service has determined to record voluntary interviews undertaken after a Prosecution Review Commission has determined that an indictment should have issued.[145]

Prosecutor misconduct in certain high profile cases has led to a change in practice in 10 district prosecutor offices where full recording of interrogations in cases involving mentally disabled suspects and suspects in cases initiated by Special Investigation Units has begun. In February 2012 full recordings were made in 28 cases handled by such units while partial recordings (likely the portion where the suspect confesses to committing the crime) were made in 39 cases.[146] It is hoped by advocates of full recording of interrogations that this experimental process will eventually result in full recordings in all cases.[147] In the first case where full interrogation procedures were recorded the defendant was found guilty.[148]

False confession may be an especially difficult problem for non-Japanese suspects because of language difficulties and the potential for misunderstanding of both the language and custom. The JFBA has created a note book entitled "Suspect's Notes" with instructions in English, Korean and Chinese that is to be used by foreign suspects to record various matters occurring during their interrogation in the hope that such Notes will be allowed in evidence in cases where false confession and/or abusive interrogation practices are alleged. Suspects should record on a daily basis such things as whether the interrogation was recorded, was an interpreter present, could the suspect understand the interpreter, whether the interrogator prepared a written statement, whether the suspect was given a chance to review and change the statement and whether the statement accurately reflected the suspect's answers to questions.[149]

143. For a prediction that it will see, David T. Johnson, *You Don't Need a Weather Man to Know Which Way the Wind Blows: Lessons from the United States and South Korea for Recording Interrogations in Japan*, 24 Ritsumeikan L. Rev. 13 (2007).
144. Editorial, *Prosecutors' changing attitude*, Japan Times (Apr. 28, 2012), http://www.japantimes.co.jp/text/ed20120428a2.html reporting where special investigation units made arrests full interrogation recordings were made in 40% and that results were changing prosecutor attitudes about full recordings.
145. See, Jiji, *Voluntary questioning in reopened cases to be recorded by prosecutors*, Japan Times (June 25, 2012), http://www.japantimes.co.jp/text/nn20120625a3.html.
146. Jiji Press, *Interrogations /filmed in 97% of Major Cases*, Daily Yomiuri (Apr. 7, 2012), http://www.yomiuri.co.jp/dy/national/T120406004353.htm. see also, Editorial, *Prosecutors' changing attitude*, Japan Times (Apr. 28, 2012), http://www.japantimes.co.jp/text/ed20120428a2.html.
147. *Editorial Reform of Prosecution*, Japan Times (Aug. 2, 2011).
148. Kyodo, *Videotaped scammer jailed*, Japan Times (Feb. 25, 2012), http://www.japantimes.co.jp/text/nn20120225a4.html.
149. Notebooks made for foreign suspects, Japan Times, Sept. 22, 2011, http://www.japantimes.co.jp/text/nn20110922b6.html..

Considering the problem of false confession,[150] it seems clear that the clearance rate overstates the actual resolution of criminal investigations. And, if suicide is considered as a homicide (it is after all the taking of a human life) then Japan's homicide rate rather than ranking at the low end of the scale is actually one of the highest in the developed world.[151]

The reported clearance rate for homicide is significantly higher than the clearance rate for other felonies. For example, in 2004 the clearance rate was: robberies—50.3%; arson—69.6%; and rape—64.5%. But for extortion, a crime that is likely associated with organized crime activity the clearance rate was only 41%. These clearance rates cast doubt on the reliability of the homicide rate.

The Japanese public has grown less confident in its police. The International Crime Survey (2000) discloses that Japan was among the countries that gave its police the lowest marks for performance. Japan was also in the lowest category of countries for victim support.[152] At the same time the report placed Japan among those countries (including for example Finland and Switzerland) with the lowest level of criminal victimization.[153] Crime rates hit a high in 2002 but have been declining ever since.[154] There may be a perception (reality) that the police are unaccountable to either the public or the judicial system and that the police are inefficient. Surely reports of police corruption[155] and the disclosure of cases being reversed because of false confessions cannot help the reputation of the police.[156]

---

150. In early 2012 the Supreme Court of Japan upheld determinations of the High and District Courts that a defendant was not guilty despite his confession (later recanted) to the crime. *Top court acquits man charged with murder, arson but says he was likely culprit*, The Mainichi Daily News (Feb. 26, 2012), http://mdn.mainichi.jp/mdnnews/news/20120225p2a00m0na012000c.html.
151. David T. Johnson, *The Vanishing Killer: Japan's Postwar Homicide Decline*, 9 Social Science Japan Journal 73, 74 (2005).
152. Kesteren, J.N. van, Mayhew, P. & Nieuwbeerta, P. *Criminal Victimisation in Seventeen Industrialised Countries: Key-findings from the 2000 international Crime Victims Survey.* (The Hague, Ministry of Justice, WODC 2000), www.unicri.it/wwd/analysis/icvs/pdf_files/key 2000i/index.htm.
153. Events following the Great East Japan Earthquake and Tsunami, including the evacuation of a 20Km ring around the Fukushima 1 Nuclear Plant as a consequence of the nuclear disaster at the plant reveal that there is crime and victimization in Japan. While immediately after the disaster there was little looting or crime, once the evacuation had taken hold and the area was virtually empty thieves returned to the area where they stole money from ATM and robbed vacated houses. *Thieves raid evacuation areas / Unguarded ATMs robbed of 684 million yen; empty homes violated*, The Yomiuri Shimbun, Daily Yomiuri (July 16, 2011), http://www.yomiuri.co.jp/dy/national/T110715004927.htm.
154. Kyodo, *Fewest Crimes in 30 Years Seen in 2011*, Japan Times (Jan. 14, 2012), http://www.japantimes.co.jp/text/nn20120114b2.html.
155. J. Sean Curtin, *Attitudes towards the Police in Contemporary Japan—Part Three: Scandals Undermine Public Confidence in the Police*, Japanese Inst. Global Comm. (Sept. 21, 2004), www.glocom.org/special_topics/social_trends/20040921_trends_s86/index.html.
156. David T. Johnson, *Justice System Reform in Japan: Where are the Police and Why Does it Matter*, February 2004 Horitsy Jiho on the Web at www.law.usyd.edu.au/anjel/documents/ResearchPublications/Johnson2004_JusticeSystemReform.pdf, last accessed Sept. 17, 2012.

[d] Arrest

Although the Constitution limits arrests without warrants to cases where the suspect is caught in the commission of the crime,[157] the Code of Criminal Procedure allows the police or prosecutor a broader authority. Arrest without warrant is permitted where the suspect flees from the police, there is an emergency and there is sufficient reason to suspect the person involved committed a serious crime or where the arrested person is armed, in possession of stolen property or is in possession of evidence of the crime.[158] On their face, the Code provisions appear to be inconsistent with Article 33 of the Constitution but the majority view appears to be that the more far-reaching Code is Constitutional.[159] The United States Constitution is not as specific as the Japanese Constitution and does not require a warrant for all arrests. The touchstone is reasonableness.[160]

[4] Prosecutor

Prosecutors in Japan are part of a national civil service. The decision to become a prosecutor is made at the Legal Research and Training Institute. It is a career decision and prosecutors rarely (unless they have reached an end to their prosecutorial career) engage in private practice. Criminal defense lawyers, in turn, rarely become prosecutors. [This is different the United States where most defense lawyers were prosecutors and most senior prosecutors had spent some time as defense lawyers.] The consequences of this system are many, including a sense of *esprit de corps* among prosecutors that is not matched in the United States, an "inbreeding" of philosophy as to the role and function of the prosecutor, and an inability for prosecutors and defense counsel to share experiences and thus see an issue from both a prosecutorial and defense prospective. The result is difficulty in achieving consensus on proposed changes in the criminal justice system and an inability to find common ground for discussion.

[a] Independence and Protections against Wrongful Prosecution

The bureaucratic system allows for built in safeguards that are not present in the American system where most senior prosecutors tend to be political figures either elected or appointed. The line between politics and proper administration of justice is subject to debate. In 2007, the Attorney General of the United States was forced from office, in part because of an alleged scandal in the removal of United States Attorneys who serve at the pleasure of the President. A significant number of Senators took the position that removal either for failure to or because of prosecution of political figures

157. Constitution Article 33.
158. Code of Criminal Procedure 210–212.
159. Hiroyuki Hata & Go Nakagawa & Takehisa Nakagawa, *Japanese Constitutional Law* sec. 306 (Kluwer Law International 2001).
160. See *Atwater v. City of Lago Vista*, 533 U.S. 924 (2001).

so impeded justice that it warranted removal of the Attorney General.[161] So too the election of local District Attorneys may inject politics into American criminal procedure.[162]

In the United States cases are looked at on an individual basis and there is little organizational structure that requires consistency in treatment.[163] The bureaucratic nature of the Japanese prosecutorial service and the role that consensus decision making plays in making important decisions assures that the charging decision will receive internal review and the judgment of senior officials in the prosecutorial service.[164] The perceived need to treat cases consistently so that, although each case is analyzed on a standalone basis, no one case is handled so differently from other cases that an appearance of favoritism or punishment appears, means that all cases are measured against their peer cases.[165] Until recently the Japanese public apparently has had almost complete confidence in Japanese prosecutorial decisions.[166] A scandal in 2010 involving the doctoring of a computer disc date by a prosecutor handling the prosecution of an official of a Ministry and the alleged efforts of higher ups to cover up his acts has raised serious questions about the handling of cases by some prosecutors, especially those handling high profile cases.[167] The prosecutor[168] and two supervisors

161. See e.g., Steven Lee Myers & Philip Shenon, *Embattled Attorney General Resigns*, New York Times (Aug. 27, 2007); Philip Shenon, *Panel Rebuffs White House Privilege Claim*, New York Times (Nov. 30, 2007).
162. The *Duke Lacrosse Rape* case See e.g., Duff Wilson & David Barstow, *All Charges Dropped in Duke Case*, New York Times (Apr. 12, 2007) and Duff Wilson, *Prosecutor in Duke Rape Case is Suspended*, New York Times (June 20, 2007). In the United States prosecutors have absolute immunity from money damages actions based on their determinations. In Japan the government can be sued not only for misconduct by the prosecutor but also by a defendant who has been found not guilty.
163. Because of the federal nature of criminal prosecution different standards might apply in different States. And, there is evidence that even the FBI and the Justice Department have not been quick to advise defense counsel of exculpatory evidence. See, *Defendants left unaware of flaws found in cases—Problems with Forensic Evidence—After Review, Justice Dept. only told Prosecutors*, Washington Post, Apr. 17, 2012, A1.
164. See Kent Anderson, *The Japanese Way of Justice: An Up-close Look at Japan's Jack McCoy*, A Review of *The Japanese Way of Justice: prosecuting Crime in Japan* by David T. Johnson, 4 Asia-P. L. & Policy J. 169, 174–175 (2003).
165. For a discussion of the prosecuting decision making process in Japan see David T. Johnson, *The Japanese Way of Justice: Prosecuting Crime in Japan* 154–161, 165–178 (Oxford University Press 2002); see also, Motoo Noguchi, *Criminal Justice in Asia and Japan and the International Criminal Court*, 6 Intl. Criminal L. Rev. 585, 594 (2006).
166. Hiroshi Fukurai, *The Rebirth of Japan's Petit Quasi-Jury and Grand Jury Systems: A Cross-National Analysis of Legal Consciousness and the Lay Participatory Experience in Japan and the U.S.*, 40 Cornell Intl. L.J. 315, 340 (2007), http://organizations.lawschool.cornell.edu/ilj/issues/40.2/CIN202.pdf.
167. See, Takahiro Fukada, *Prosecutor offices flawed: experts, systemic woes must be repaired before debacles taint legal system*, Japan Times (Oct. 2, 2010), http://search.japantimes.co.jp/cgi-bin/nn20101002f1.html, see also, Takayuki Ojima & Kensaku Fujiwara, *Entire prosecution system needs drastic reform*, Daily Yomiuri (Oct. 4, 2010), http://www.yomiuri.co.jp/dy/national/T101003002200.htm.
168. *Former senior prosecutors indicted for cover-up*, NHK World English, http://www.nhk.or.jp/daily/english/21_21.html.

were convicted.[169] The incident resulted in calls for new rules to protect the integrity of digital data evidence,[170] and resulted in the appointment of an independent panel to suggest reforms in the prosecutor service.[171] Prosecutorial misconduct in the case of DPJ leader Ozawa has heightened concern about the handling of high profile cases by Special Investigation Units. Prosecutors feel a need to perform successfully both to solve crimes and obtain promotion.

As part of the Meiji legal reforms, the office of public prosecutor was established in 1872 based on the French inquisition model. The public prosecutor was a position in the Ministry of Justice and was equal in rank and sat at the same level as a judge. By 1916 the prosecutor was able to conduct investigations on his own. By the 1930s they became powerful figures in the Ministry of Justice and even had authority to pass on the promotion of judges. The Occupation sought to make the criminal justice system more adversarial, reduce the power of the prosecutor and make the office similar to the American prosecutor.[172]

It remains the case that the Procurator General is very independent of the Ministry of Justice[173] who neither appoints nor may discharge but can reprimand the Procurator General.[174] In at least one instance the prime minister intervened to prevent a prosecution and the Minister of Justice resigned.[175] The Prosecutor General may not be ordered to take any action or refuse to take action by the ministry and is typically a career prosecutor who has risen through the ranks. The ministry may set forth general enforcement policy but cannot intervene in any specific case.

The national prosecutor service is divided into District Offices (cases before the District Courts), High Prosecutor Offices (cases in the High Courts) and the Supreme Prosecutors Office (cases before the Supreme Court). Local prosecutor offices handle cases before the Summary Courts. Prosecutors are rotated to different geographic areas on a regular basis. Young prosecutors are given substantial discretion in handling cases

169. *Prosecutor Jailed over Tampering*, Japan Times (Apr. 12, 2011), http://search.japantimes.co.jp/cgi-bin/nn20110412x3.html;Kyodo News, *Prosecutor Who Cheated Gets 1 1/2 Years*, Japan Times (Apr. 13, 2011), http://search.japantimes.co.jp/cgi-bin/nn20110413a2.html.

170. *Lax rules on evidence led to prosecutor's crime*, The Yomiuri Shimbun (Oct. 18, 2010), http://www.yomiuri.co.jp/dy/national/T101017002109.htm.

171. Principal among concerns is the use of special investigative groups in the prosecutor's office that investigate high profile cases. See, Kyodo News, *Independent Panel to Reform Prosecutors*, Japan Times (Nov. 5, 2010), http://search.japantimes.co.jp/cgi-bin/nn20101105a3.html.

172. Alfred C. Oppler, *Legal Reform In Occupied Japan* 104 (Princeton University Press 1976).

173. See B.J. George Jr., *Discretionary Authority of Public Prosecutors in Japan*, 17 L. Japan 42, 50 (1984). See 45–47 for a general discussion of the independence of the public prosecutor's office.

174. There is only one case of such reprimand and when the former Minister of Justice stated that he considered using his authority in connection with the failure to indict a member of the Special Prosecutor Unit who had inaccurately reported on his interrogation of an aide to Ichiro Ozawa and such inaccurate report was sent to the PRC, the former Minister was criticized by some in both the ruling DPJ and opposition LDP. *Politicians up in arms over Ogawa's remarks*, The Yomiuri Shimbun (June 21, 2012), http://www.yomiuri.co.jp/dy/national/T120620005081.htm.

175. See *Ministry to Reprimand Top Prosecutor over Underling's Gangland Dealings*, Japan Times (May 31, 2002). See also Richard Boyd, *The Rule of Law or Law as Instrument of Rule in Law and Development in East and Southeast Asia* 167–168 (Antons, ed., Routledge Curzon 2003).

assigned to them, although all decisions to refuse to prosecute must be approved by a superior.

[b] *Investigation Function*

Once the police turn the suspect over, the prosecutor is in charge of the case. However, many times suspects continue to be held at jails in the police station for interrogation by the prosecutor and where it easier for prosecutors to obtain confessions.[176] The prosecutor has one day before he must either release the suspect or appear before a judicial officer and request an additional 10 day period to hold the suspect while investigation continues.[177] Although the Code of Criminal Procedure provides that the judge shall deny the request if no reason exists for continued detention,[178] such requests are routinely granted.[179] Prosecutors almost always ask for additional time.[180] The prosecutor may apply once more for an additional 10 day holding period. It is reported that prosecutors make such additional request in more than one-third of cases and that requests are also virtually always granted.[181] After this 23 day period the prosecutor must release the suspect; file an indictment; or arrest the suspect for a different crime and restart the 23 day clock (*bekken taiho*). The process can, and has been, repeated several times so that it is possible to hold a suspect in "investigatory custody" for a substantial period of time under the *bekken taiho* model.[182] Although each new arrest is based on a new charge the suspect is continually questioned about the most serious crime of which suspected. (The first arrests are usually for more minor offenses.)

---

176. Yuji Iwasawa, *International Law Human Rights and Japanese Law* (Clarendon Press 1998) The use of substitute prisons is a major issue among human rights advocates in Japan.. Japan has come under international criticism for its use of substitute prisons and its focus of extracting confessions from suspects. Toshikuni Murai, *Pretrial Detention and the Problem of Confinement* (Frank Bennet Jr. trans.), 23 L. Japan 85 (1990).
177. Code of Criminal Procedure Article 208.
178. Code of Criminal Procedure Articles 206 and 207.
179. In 2008 the rate of approval of such requests was 93.1% with some crimes having a 98% or 99% rate of granting such requests. Homicide, robbery, fraud, rape arson, controlled substance violations and violations of the immigration laws are among crimes with a 98 to 99% rate of granting additional time. http://hakusyo1.moj.go.jp/en/58/image/image/h002002002001h.jpg, last accessed Sept. 17, 2012.
180. For a discussion of Japan's interpretation of what the Occupation thought was a replication of the American privilege against self-incrimination and the steps taken by prosecutors and police to obtain confessions, see Daniel H. Foote, *Confessions and the Right to Silence in Japan*, 21 Georgia J. Intl. & Comp. L.415 (1991).
181. Daniel H. Foote, *Confessions and the Right to Silence in Japan*, 21 Georgia Journal of International and Comparative Law 415 (1991).
182. An illustration of use of Bekken Taiho is the notorious Hawker killing case where the police had a suspect but allowed him to escape. After more than 2 1/2 years on the run the suspect was captured and charged with abandoning the body of Ms. Hawker. He was held for 23 days (Nov. 10–Dec. 2) and then indicted for the abandonment and immediately rearrested for murder. Within the next 23 day period the suspect confessed to the killing, although denying any intent to murder. *Ichihashi Confesses to Hawker's Slaying*, Japan Times (Dec. 24, 2009), http://search.japantimes.co.jp/cgi-bin/nn20091224a1.html. See also, Jake Adelstein, *Tokyo Vice An American Reporter on the Police Beat in Japan* 103 (Pantheon Books 2009) noting that it was standard operating procedure in homicide cases to arrest for a minor crime but interrogate about the murder.

Because *bekken taiho* warrants are routinely authorized and granted,[183] these protections appear more theoretical than real. One recently enacted protection has some significance. This is the requirement that at the hearing to determine whether to continue detention the suspect be advised of the right to counsel and if indigent that counsel be appointed.[184] Although not as encompassing as a rule that would grant the right to counsel at the time of arrest (or even better at the time when taken into custody) this is a step in the right direction.

Although *bekken taiho* appears to be a clear means of avoiding Constitutional and statutory protections granted to the suspect, it has been upheld.[185] An open question exists as to whether it is Constitutional to hold a defendant on a new charge when there is evidence of subterfuge, with no intent to prosecute on the new charge. Since it is unlikely that a Japanese judge will exclude a confession if to do so would mean that a defendant whom the judge believes is guilty would be set free, there is little prosecutorial down side to abuse of the *bekken taiho* process.[186]

The Japanese Constitution does contain an exclusionary rule for confessions obtained after prolonged arrest or detention,[187] but this provision does not lead to the exclusion of confessions obtained after long detention under *bekken taiho* because such detention is lawful. Lawful detention cannot form the basis for a claim that the detention was prolonged under Article 38.[188]

[c] Quasi-Judicial Function

Prosecutors in the Japanese system find themselves playing three roles in connection with criminal justice. First, they are part of the inquest type investigation system. Prosecutors view it as their role to obtain a confession in every case. Second, they are "adversaries" of the defense counsel in an adversary system looking "trial" held after investigation is completed. To emphasize the adversary role of the prosecutor and his supposedly equal status with the defense counsel, the prosecutor no longer sits on a level with the judge but sits at the same level as defense counsel. Third, the prosecutor plays a "quasi-judicial" role determining whether to whether to prosecute, "suspend prosecution" or drop the charges. In exercising this role the prosecutor takes into

---

183. See Masaki Koyama, *Prosecuting—Japanese Style*, New L. J. 1269 (Sept. 20, 1991,; Nobuyoshi Araki, *The Flow of Criminal Cases in the Japanese Criminal Justice System, 31* Crime and Delinquency, 601, 613 (1985).
184. CCP 37 (2).
185. *Bekkon Taiho* Case, *Hirasawa v. Japan*, 9 Keishu 663 (Sup. Ct. G.B. 6 June 1955).
186. Daniel H. Foote, *Confessions and the Right to Silence in Japan*, 21 Georgia Journal of International and Comparative Law 415, 444 (1991); David T. Johnson, *The Japanese Way of Justice: Prosecuting Crime in Japan* 265 (Oxford University Press, 2002).
187. Constitution Article 38 (2).
188. Arguments have been raised that Japan's system of arrest and questioning of suspects violates the International Convention on Civil and Political Rights. The government of Japan maintains that its system is in conformity with the Convention and points out that under Japanese law a suspect must be brought before a judge within seventy-two hours of arrest and that further detention of suspects is subject to judicial approval. Yuji Iwasawa, *International Law Human Rights and Japanese Law* 264–270 (Clarendon Press 1998).

account the rehabilitation of the defendant and his return to harmony with the society.[189]

[d] Prosecution Review Commissions ("PRC")

Like prosecutors in the United States, the Japanese prosecutor may determine not to proceed to indictment and let the accused go free. Unlike the United States where the prosecutor may need a Grand Jury indictment before bringing a serious crime case,[190] the prosecutor in Japan may need the consent of the community when he determines *not to prosecute*. At the Occupation's urging the Diet enacted the Inquest of Prosecution, Law[191] that created the Prosecution Review Commission ("PRC"), which has authority to undertake an inquest into the reasons why a prosecutor has failed to indict.[192] The PRC can check the prosecutor when there is a determination not to prosecute but a prosecution cannot be demanded against a Minister of State unless the prime minister agrees.

These review commissions are made up of 11 citizens selected by lot from among eligible voters. There are slightly more than 150 Review Commissions spread over Japan. Members serve six months; up to half the members are replaced every three months. Members undertake investigations initiated by or on behalf of victims of crimes or on its own motion. The Commission may question witnesses and prosecutors and may obtain expert advice. As originally formulated the Commission did not have the power to order a prosecutor to indict but could only cause the prosecutor to take a second look at its decision. Commissions were rarely used or if used rarely resulted in indictment.[193]

The Law was substantially modified in 2009 to give the Commission authority to force the prosecution of cases if the PRC twice decides that prosecution was appropriate. In such case the court appoints a private attorney to prosecute the case. To date PRC's have caused indictment in five cases (a high ranking police official,[194] officials of

189. David T. Johnson, *The Japanese Way of Justice: Prosecuting Crime in Japan* 182–192 (Oxford University Press, 2002).
190. See, *Rehberg v. Paulk*, 566 U.S. ____ (2012).
191. This position was a compromise. The Occupation wanted to limit the authority of career prosecutors by making them elected officials or by adoption of a Grand Jury procedure similar to the U.S.. When Japanese officials objected the Review Commission option was adopted.
192. Alfred C. Oppler, *Law Reform in Occupied Japan* 105–106 (Princeton University Press 1976).
193. For a discussion of PRCs prior to the 2004 revision see Mark D. West, *Prosecution Review Commissions: Japan's Answer to the Problem of Prosecutorial Discretion*, 92 Columbia L. Rev. 684 (1992). It is estimated than in the period 1948 through amendment of the law in 2009 the PRC recommended indictment in only 1.5% of cases considered. See, Setsuko Kamiya, *Inquest Bodies give Public a Voice*, Japan Times (Sept. 21, 2010). For a discussion of the PRC prior to amendment, the amendment process and the amended law see, Hiroshi Fukurai, *The Rebirth of Japan's Petit Quasi-Jury and Grand Jury Systems: A Cross-National Analysis of Legal Consciousness and the Lay Participatory Experience in Japan and the U.S.*, 40 Cornell Intl. L.J. 315, 323–328 (2007), http://organizations.lawschool.cornell.edu/ilj/issues/40.2/CIN202.pdf.
194. *Inquest panel: Charge cop in fatal Akashi crush*, Japan Times (Jan. 29, 2010), http://search.japantimes.co.jp/cgi-bin/nn20100129a5.html.

a railroad company[195], an investment firm official[196] (who was found not guilty but the prosecuting lawyers have appealed), a Chinese ship Captain (who could not be served so the case was dismissed), and a major political party leader (Ichiro Ozawa, who was acquitted, the case is on appeal).[197] The indictment of Ozawa by virtue of the PRC threw Japanese politics into confusion. Thus the action of 11 lay persons caused a tidal wave of problems for the DPJ. It had been predicted that change in the law governing PRCs' risked prosecution of political figures that might not be justified.[198] Prosecution under the PRC process raises serious questions regarding the rights of the accused. The setbacks for the PRC process highlight the damage to innocents that can flow from an unregulated process where non-professionals are in charge and where there is no judicial review of the decision to indict except for a criminal trial.[199]

[e] Discretion Re: Refusal to Prosecute and Suspension of Prosecution—Production of Exculpatory Evidence

On the judicial front, courts have generally upheld (subject to the amended PRC process) the unbridled right of the prosecutor not to prosecute a suspect This power is significant since prosecutors indict only about 7% of all cases sent to them.[200]

Some lower courts, in particularly egregious cases, have overturned criminal convictions finding "prosecutorial misconduct" but, the Supreme Court has not accepted this position. The most famous example of such a case is the *Kawamoto* case arising out of the *Minamata* disease tragedy. In the *Minamata Pollution* case, some of the victims of *Minamata* disease refused to seek judicial relief and instead took direct action in the form of violent daily attacks against a barrier built by the Chisso company to protect its offices and employees. During these attacks incidents of assault and battery occurred. The battles continued until a resolution of the judicial case, which

195. One executive of the company was charged by the prosecutors—his trial ended with a not guilty verdict by the District Court that the prosecutors have decided not to appeal. Kyodo, *JR West ex-chief's crash acquittal to be finalized*, Japan Times (Jan. 26, 2012), http://www.japantimes.co.jp/text/nn20120126a7.html The trial of those charged as a consequence of the PRC is not yet completed but the decision of the District Court likely will affect that determination. *Ex-JR chief acquitted over '05 derailment / Court rules accident was unforeseeable*, The Yomiuri Shimbun (Jan. 12, 2012), http://www.yomiuri.co.jp/dy/national/T120111006712.htm.
196. *Inquest panel indicts alleged swindler*, Japan Times (July 19, 2010), http://search.japantimes.co.jp/cgi-bin/nn20100719a3.html.
197. *Attorneys for prosecution to appeal Ozawa acquittal* The Mainichi (May 9, 2012); *Minoru Matsutani and Natsuko Fukue, Ozawa faces appeal over his acquittal*, Japan Times (May 9, 2012), http://www.japantimes.co.jp/.
198. Jonathan David Marshall, *Democratizing the Law in Japan, Routledge Handbook of Japanese Politics* 92, 98, 100 (Alisa Gaunder, Ed., 2011).
199. In addition to the PRC procedure there is another procedure under which for specifically listed crimes a victim may petition a court to appoint a *Bengoshi* prosecutor. The court may grant or deny the petition. Code of Criminal Procedure (Law No. 131 of 1948, as amended) Article 262, 266, et seq., Because of the limits on the type of cases for which the process is applicable the reality is that requests for prosecution under this provision is rarely made and even rarer are the cases where the court appoints a prosecutor.
200. White Paper on /crime 2009, section 3 Disposition in Public Prosecutors Offices, http://hakusyo1.moj.go.jp/en/58/nfm/n_58_2_2_2_3_0.html.

found in favor of the victims and brought about a settlement of all claims. Kawamoto, a leader of the direct action group was indicted for his actions in an assault and battery on the Chisso security forces.

Kawamoto urged the court to dismiss the indictment on the grounds of abuse of prosecutorial discretion. On appeal of the District Court's conviction the High Court dismissed the indictment for prosecutorial misconduct. The Supreme Court both reversed and did not reverse all at the same time. The Court rejected the High Court's arguments in total. Prosecutorial misconduct could not be used as a basis for dismissing the indictment. On the other hand as there was no longer any need to prosecute or punish, the High Court's dismissal was affirmed. There does not appear to be any "doctrinal basis" for this decision. The *Kawamoto* decision appears to be a case of what you see may not be what you get.[201]

In addition to the power to decline prosecution, a Japanese prosecutor has a power unknown in United States law. This is the power of "suspending" a prosecution. In applying his discretion to suspend prosecution the prosecutor is engaged in a quasi-judicial function. A decision to suspend prosecution is considered as and recognized as a determination that the accused committed the crime; the accused is guilty but not charged. This determination becomes a part of the prosecutor's file and can have consequences, especially if the accused is accused of a new crime. Suspension of prosecution as a formal process can trace its history to 1909 when, it appeared in the official criminal statistics alongside statistics for non-prosecution of cases.[202]

The significance of the power to "suspend prosecution" is grounded in the facts that: (a) virtually all criminal cases tried by the prosecutor end in a conviction of the defendant (in 2004 there were 837,528 criminal trials, defendants were found not guilty in only 94 cases with another 657 cases dismissed after trial had begun. Thus the conviction rate was in excess of 99% for all cases charged and 99.9% for cases that went to verdict of the court;[203] in 2006 the 99.9% conviction rate held steady as only 82

201. For a discussion of the *Kawamoto* case see Frank K. Upham, *Law And Social Chance In Postwar Japan* (Harvard University Press 1987). The Supreme Court reaffirmed its *Kawamoto* determination that selective prosecution is not a basis for finding prosecutorial misconduct in (*Selective Prosecution Case*) *Japan v. Fukumoto*, 1006 Hanji 22 (Sup. Ct. 26 June 1981) reversing the Hiroshima High Court's decision finding selective prosecution and overturning the indictment in a case where the prosecutor indicted only one side in a bribery scandal.

202. Shigemitsu Dando, *System of Discretionary Prosecution in Japan*, 18 Am. J. Comp. L. 518 (1970); for other discussions of prosecutorial discretion and suspension of prosecution see Marcia E. Goodman, *The Exercise and Control of Prosecutorial Discretion in Japan*, 5 UCLA Pacific Basin L. J. 16 (1986); Daniel H. Foote, *Prosecutorial Discretion in Japan: A Response*, 5 UCLA Pacific Basin L. J. 96 (1986); Haley, *Authority Without Power: Law And The* Japanese *Paradox, Policemen and Prosecutors, Crime without Punishment* (Oxford University Press 1991).

203. Motoo Noguchi, *Criminal Justice in Asia and Japan and the International Criminal Court*, 6 Intl. Criminal L. Rev. 585, 594 (2006). For ordinary crimes the conviction rate is actually higher as it is reported that most acquittals are in medical negligence cases. Robert B. LeFlar, *"Unnatural Deaths," Criminal Sanctions, and Medical Quality Improvement in Japan*, 9 Yale Journal Health, Pol'y L. and Ethics 1, 17 (2009). The in excess of 99% conviction rate also applies to cases tried before the new Mixed Lay / Professional Judge Panels. Setsuko Kamiya, *Lay judges convict 99%; few shirk duty*, Japan Times (Aug. 2, 2011), http://search.japan times.co.jp/cgi-bin/nn20110802f2.html.

defendants were found not guilty out of 738,240 criminal trials[204] and the same held true in 2008 where only 84 not guilty verdicts were rendered).[205] Nor do those convicted fare any better on appeal. Of a total of 9,343 appeals in 2006 only 20 defendants were found not guilty. On the other hand, of the 36 cases in which prosecutors filed appeals 25 defendants had their not guilty verdicts reversed.[206] (b) the public is aware of the high conviction rate, which carries with it the general understanding that if the prosecutor had determined to prosecute a case the defendant would have been found guilty; (c) when the prosecutor announces that the defendant is guilty but the prosecutor has determined to suspend prosecution as an act of grace, everyone "knows" that the defendant is guilty. An analysis of the above statement reveals two things about whether what you see is what you get in Japanese law insofar as the prosecutor is concerned. First, what you see in the written statutes, Constitution and procedure Code is that the role of the prosecutor is to be an adversary who charges and then tries the defendant before an impartial judge who in turn determines guilt or innocence of the defendant. Because the prosecutor wins virtually all cases brought to trial, it is understood that the decision to try a defendant is tantamount to a determination of guilt and a trial that is not about guilt or innocence but is in the nature of "judicial review" of the prosecutor's determination. What you get is a guilty determination when the prosecutor decides the defendant is guilty. Later in this chapter the criminal trial process and the role of the judge are examined, but in examining the role of the prosecutor it should be understood that success in virtually every case brought before the court supports the view that the prosecutor's role has changed from one of party in an adversary system to that of decision-maker in an inquisition system (since the determination of whether to prosecute is made as part of the inquisition investigative stage of the case). Whereas in the United States the jury and due process rules and Constitutional protections of the rights of the accused stand between the power of the State to punish and the individual defendant (assuming no plea bargain), in Japan the prosecutor is the firewall between her employer and the accused.[207] Suspension of prosecution supports this argument because the quasi-judicial determination of guilt but leniency (through failure to prosecute) is made by the prosecutor rather than an independent court.[208]

Prosecutors in Japan frequently determine that they will suspend prosecution. In 1998 the Japanese Ministry of Justice reported that of approximately two and a half million criminal cases, 25.8% (or over 600,000 cases) were disposed of through

204. White Paper on Crimes 2007, p. 65.
205. White Paper on Crime 2009 Table 2-3-11, http://hakusyo1.moj.go.jp/en/58/image/image/h002003001001h.jpg.
206. White Paper on Crimes 2007, p. 69.
207. For the view that this inhibits democratization of the criminal justice system in Japan see, Jonathan David Marshall, *Democratizing the Law in Japan*, 92, 98 (Routledge Handbook of Japanese Politics (Alisa Gaunder, Ed.).
208. For an analysis of the role of defense counsel and prosecutors in Japan, see David A. Suess, *Paternalism versus Pugnacity: The Right to Counsel in Japan and the United States*, 72 Indiana L. J. 291 (1996).

suspension of prosecution.[209] Included in such cases are matters that are considered as serious crimes such as theft and even homicide.[210] The White Paper on Crime (2007) shows that from 1997 through 2006 the percentage of cases in which prosecutors refused to prosecute was never less than 90% of which suspension of prosecution declined from 78.2% in 1997 to 60.9% in 2006 while lack of evidence rose from 14.4% in 1997 to 30.4% in 2006.[211] In 2007, suspension of prosecution accounted for 63% of cases not prosecuted while lack of evidence accounted for 27%.[212]

A suspect who has been granted suspended prosecution is no longer prosecuted for the crime involved but the fact of suspension remains as part of the prosecutor's files. Should the suspect be arrested again, it is unlikely (but not impossible) that suspension will follow. In other words, like suspects released by the police under *bizai shobun*, suspects released by the prosecutor under its suspension of prosecution authority are given a second bite at the apple. The prosecutor's decision to suspend prosecution is governed by Article 248 of the Code of Criminal Procedure[213] and internal procurator policies written down in the Prosecutor's Manual.[214] Local prosecutor's offices may have their own policies to supplement the Manual. The determination is not subject to judicial review and the Manual is not considered as a rule that must be followed by the prosecutor.

Suspension of prosecution is an important weapon in the fight against crime in Japan. The prosecutor is attempting to restore the defendant to a state of harmony with and return the accused to society. Rehabilitation is the goal of suspension. To return to society the accused must demonstrate rehabilitation through contrition, apology, restitution, remorse, and acceptance of responsibility. If the prosecutor feels that there is likelihood that the defendant will commit additional crimes, suspension is not called for. Letters from family, from an employer, from a respected community member attesting to the defendant's understanding and agreement to change, letters demonstrating employment and a good work ethic are important factors in the decision. The views of the victim is also very important and it is important to get written confirmation of the victim's acceptance of defendant's apology and the victim's agreement to a

209. The statistics can be found on the website for the Ministry of Justice, www.moj.go.jp/English/index.html. under Public Prosecutor.
210. For an analysis of earlier but more detailed statistics on suspension of prosecution see Table 6-3 in John Owen Haley, *Authority without Power* 127 (Oxford University Press 1991); Daniel H. Foote, *The Benevolent Paternalism of Japanese Criminal Justice*, 80 California L. Rev. 317, 350 (1992); Masaki Koyama, *Prosecuting—Japanese Style*, New L. J. 1268 (Sept. 20, 1991); Nobuyoshi Araki, *The Flow of Criminal Cases in the Japanese Criminal Justice System*, 31 Crime & Delinquency, 601, 617 tbl. 2 (1985); Mark D. West, *Prosecution Review Commissions: Japan's Answer to the Problem of Prosecutorial Discretion*, 92 Columbia L. Rev. 684 (1992).
211. White Paper on Crimes 2007, p.63 charts 2-2-3-2 and 2-2-3-3.
212. White Paper on /crime 2008, p. 60 chart 2-2-3-3.
213. Under Article 248 prosecutorial discretion exists not to prosecute when the prosecutor decides prosecution is not necessary. Statutory factors to be considered include personal factors such as the offender's age and character, factors related to the crime such as its seriousness as well as factors subsequent to the crime.
214. The factors to be considered in a determination to suspend prosecution as written in the manual may be found in Marcia E. Goodman, *The Exercise and Control of Prosecutorial Discretion in Japan*, 5 UCLA Pacific Basin L. J. 16, 26 n. 44 (1986).

suspension of prosecution. Having a good family or other support system that will watch the defendant to assure future crimes will not be committed is also significant.

Because suspension is tantamount to conviction it can have serious effects on the defendant, the defendant's family and defendant's opportunity to rise in the corporate ladder, although it does not rise to the same level of social "outcast" status as a formal conviction. Facing the virtual certainty of conviction should the prosecutor decide to proceed to trial, the defendant wants the suspension remedy.

The factors that influence a prosecutor to suspend prosecution are the very factors that point to defendant's guilt. Thus a defendant, who refuses to accept responsibility, or who refuses to pay restitution, is unlikely to get a favorable suspension determination, etc. The defendant must concede wrongdoing to be excused from wrongdoing.

Ingrained biases as well as the perceived need to resolve cases so that the public will feel safe can and in some cases appear to affect the decision to prosecute. Crimes against women are an example of an area where it appears that a male dominated prosecutorial service fails to appreciate the seriousness of the offense,[215] may fail to prosecute cases that should be prosecuted and may pressure victims to accept compensation in lieu of criminal prosecution.[216] Domestic violence cases and rape are particular areas of the law where the Japanese prosecutor's service (and judiciary) needs to be more sensitive.[217] And when such cases are prosecuted it remains a serious question as to whether the prosecutors' office asks for serious enough penalties to either dissuade future offenses or to satisfy the need for justice on the part of victims. Japan's judiciary also needs to take sexual offenses against women more seriously—in 2009 the Supreme Court of Japan set a very high standard of proof for conviction in cases of sexual groping on Japan's subway system.[218] It is unlikely that women who have been groped on a crowded train will have pictures or other corroborating evidence of such crimes although the transit authorities are attempting to devise methods of using cameras to diminish the groping problem.[219] Japan's "Spousal Violence Prevention Law"[220] defines spousal violence as including both physical and psychological violence.[221] The law was amended in 2007[222] and spouses, relatives, children, family members and others close to the victim may obtain protective orders

215. Catherine Burns, *Sexual Violence and the Law in Japan* 55-61 (Routledge Curzon 2005).

216. David T. Johnson, *The Japanese Way of Justice: Prosecuting Crime in Japan*, 206-209 (Oxford University Press 2002).

217. Concluding Observations of the Human Rights Committee (para. 30) (Nov. 19, 1998); www.mofa.go.jp/policy/human/civil_ccpr.html.

218. Kyodo News, *Top Court Issues Groping Acquittal*, Japan Times (Apr. 16, 2009).

219. BBC News, *Anti-groping Cameras Set for Tokyo Train Line* (Dec. 15, 2009), http://news.bbc.co.uk/2/hi/8413780.stm.

220. Law for The Prevention of Spousal Violence and the Protection of Victims, Law No. 64 of 2004-amending Law No 31 of 2001. See summary of report of the Committee of Specialists on Violence against Women On the Implementation of the spousal Violence Prevention Law (2007) on the Hurights Osaka website at www.hurights.or.jp/news/0703/b08_e.html, last accessed Sept. 17, 2012.

221. Chapter 1, Article 1.

222. Report Identifies Challenges in Prevention of Domestic Violence after Law Reform, www.hurights.or.jp/news/0703/b08_e.html, last accessed Sep 17, 2012..

against a potentially violent spouse, in cases of fear of physical violence, threats, and intimidation (including phone and other electronic intimidation).[223] Violation of a Protective Order granted under the law is punishable by up to a year in prison and a fine of JPY 1 million.[224] Police, after notice of potential spousal violence, shall "endeavor" to take actions to prevent the spousal violence.[225] After a failure to protect in 2012 resulting in death police have been more sensitive to and more active in protection. A newspaper survey conducted in late 2011 concluded that 33% of married women had been the subject of spousal abuse, either physical or psychological.[226]

The felt need to resolve cases so that the public both feels safe and confident may lead police and prosecutors to shortcut investigations, rush to judgment, compel innocent people to confess and secrete exculpatory evidence. The problem of false confessions is discussed in section §16.03[C][3][c] "The Problem of False Confessions" herein. The Supreme Prosecutor's Office's ethical code provides prosecutors have a duty to avoid convicting the innocent. But what you see may not be what you get. It is reported that the High Prosecutor's Office in Tokyo has taken the position that it is not a violation of the Code for prosecutors to fail to follow up evidence that would prove defendant is not guilty or make available to the defense evidence that is inconsistent with the prosecutors' theory of defendant's guilt.[227]

The prosecutor's refusal to provide defense counsel with exculpatory evidence has become a major issue in Japan. The production of evidence issue has been affected by the Saiban'in mixed lay / professional judge trial system under which some cases are tried before a nine person Panel composed of six Lay persons and three Professional judges. To speed up such trials by narrowing the evidence to be presented a pre-trial conference procedure was adopted. Such procedure is required in Saiban'in cases and is discretionary with the court in other criminal cases. At such conference prosecutors must provide defense counsel evidence the prosecutor intends to introduce at trial and counsel for the defendant may request and the court may order the prosecution to produce other evidence in the prosecutor's possession that might assist the defense.[228] Amongst the categories of evidence that must be produced at pre-trial conference are physical evidence and reports of analysis of evidence by forensic experts. By comparing these items it should be possible for defense attorneys to determine whether forensic tests were performed on physical evidence—such as whether DNA testing of hairs, saliva, bodily fluids, etc. were performed and if so whether the samples matched

223. Chapter 4, Article 10; See, Stop the Violence, pamphlet issued by the Gender Equality Bureau, http://www.gender.go.jp/e-vaw/book/images/pdf/stoptheviolence.pdf, last accessed Sep 17, 2012.
224. Chapter 6, Article 29. The law also provides that a party who knowingly makes a false statement in a petition for a protective order is subject to a fine of up to JPY 100,000.
225. Chapter 3, Article 8.
226. *Survey, 33% of Married Women are Victims of Domestic Abuse*, Daily Yomiuri (Apr. 22, 2012), http://www.yomiuri.co.jp/dy/national/T120421003045.htm.
227. Minoru Matsutani, *Mainali case exposes flaws, bias in judicial system*, Japan Times (June 13, 2012), http://www.japantimes.co.jp/text/nn20120613x2.html.
228. Japanese Law Translation, Code of Criminal Procedure Article 316-20Cod20, http://www.japaneselawtranslation.go.jp/law/detail/?printID=&ft=2&re=02&dn=1&yo=code+of+criminal+procedure&x=37&y=13&ky=&page=1&vm=02.

the defendant. This has resulted in efforts by defense counsel to obtain such evidence in pre-2005 cases and in cases not subject to mandatory pre-trial conference. Some such efforts have been successful. An informal voluntary organization of former lay judges has presented recommendations to the judicial system recommending that all evidence in possession of the prosecutor be made available to defense counsel and that the lay judges be informed as to the pre-trial events that narrowed the scope of the evidence and arguments to be presented at trial.[229]

As in the false confession cases several defendants found guilty have now been found not guilty on new trial or are awaiting rulings from the court system as to whether a new trial (with a likely not guilty result) will be granted. One of the most egregious cases involves a foreign national convicted of murder by a High Court after being found not guilty by the District Court. The Supreme Court affirmed the conviction. Years later as a consequence of a new trial motion and request for evidence under the new rule, the defense discovered saliva, semen and hairs had been found at the scene. This evidence had been withheld from the defense attorney and the court at the initial trial, although on appeal the prosecutors had argued that there was no basis for believing that anyone other than the defendant was present at the crime scene.[230] New DNA tests were performed that confirmed the existence of a second party.[231] The defendant was granted a new trial and released from prison and deported for a visa violation.[232] In another case the defendant was found guilty and sentenced to death based on the slimmest of circumstantial evidence. The Supreme Court reversed and ordered a new trial.[233] The District Court found the defendant not guilty.[234] The prosecutor office has decided to appeal the not guilty verdict.[235] Whether the Supreme Court's decision will lead prosecutors to more forcefully obtain confessions— or whether the prosecutor will decide not to prosecute based on weak circumstantial evidence but a belief in guilt remains to be determined.

Whether cases such as the above will lead to a demand for prosecutors in all cases to turn over exculpatory evidence and whether such a rule will be adopted in Japan

229. Setsuko Kamiya, *Lay judges present ideas to make system better*, Japan Times (Jan. 21, 2012), http://www.japantimes.co.jp/text/nn20120121f2.html.
230. *New facts may affect retrial / Discovery may also spur debate over disclosure of evidence*, Yomiuri Shimbun (Sept. 5, 2011), http://www.yomiuri.co.jp/dy/national/T110904003736.htm.
231. *DNA evidence again points to 2nd man in Mainali case*, Daily Yomiuri (Mar. 7, 2012), http://www.yomiuri.co.jp/dy/national/T120306005456.htm.
232. Minoru Matsutani, *Mainali granted retrial, is let out of prison, DNA evidence of another man looks set to clear Nepalese*, Japan Times (June 7, 2012), http://www.japantimes.co.jp/text/nn20120607x1.html.
233. *Guilty verdict based on circumstantial evidence only permitted where fact proving guilt cannot be reasonably explained except for guilt*, Case No. 2007 (A) No. 80, Keishu Vol. 64, No. 3 http://www.courts.go.jp/english/judgments/text/2010.04.27-2007.-A-.No..80.html (P.B., Apr. 27, 2010).
234. Kyodo, *Osaka court clears inmate on death row: Retrial faults evidence in double-killing of relatives*, Japan Times (Mar. 16, 2012), http://www.japantimes.co.jp/text/nn20120316a1.html.
235. Kotaro Kodama & Mari Sugiura, *Prosecutors' 99% winning rate being shaken / Judges no longer take assertions of guilt at face value; circumstantial evidence held in lower regard*, Daily Yomiuri (Apr. 12, 2012), http://www.yomiuri.co.jp/dy/national/T120411005382.htm.

also remains to be seen. If so, this will be one of the unanticipated positive results of the Saiban'in system. Whether the Supreme Court's decision in the circumstantial evidence case will cause District and High Court Judges to more realistically examine evidence and act as a neutral protector of the Rule of Law rather than (as is too often the case) a "rubber stamp" for the prosecutor also remains to be seen.

[5] Defense Counsel

Unlike the American defense counsel, the Japanese counsel is not a significant player at the investigation phase of the case. Investigation is basically an inquest function of the police and the prosecutor. The defense counsel is "outside the loop." That does not mean that the defense counsel is not involved in attempting to represent his client before an indictment is handed down. It can be argued that the defense counsel's most important job takes place at this stage since if indictment means conviction the idea is to prevent the defendant from being indicted. Counsel's role is to influence the decision making process to achieve suspension of prosecution.

During the investigative phase of the case, the defense counsel is creating a file to persuade the prosecutor that suspension is appropriate. Defense counsel meets the victim, arranges for the payment of restitution, the giving of an appropriate apology and obtains a letter accepting apology and forgiving the defendant and expressing satisfaction if the defendant is not prosecuted. Counsel will obtain letters of reference and may obtain "guarantors" of future good conduct. In short, the defense counsel will treat the prosecutor as the decision-maker in the criminal process and will work towards convincing that decision-maker that suspension is appropriate.

Because contrition, apology and acceptance of responsibility are very important factors in the suspension decision, defense counsel will urge his client to acknowledge and accept guilt. Unlike the United States where silence is generally the client's best defense, Japanese defense counsel knows that silence complicates the suspension of prosecution decision. It can be reasonably argued that at this stage the role of defense counsel is not to attempt to prove that the client is not guilty but rather to assist the prosecutor by convincing the defendant to confess.[236]

In 99% of cases criminal defendants confess and the confession is admissible in evidence. If the client recants or if the client refuses to confess counsel's job is to try to establish that the confession is not reliable and thus should not be given any weight. Since the prosecution's case is typically based primarily on documents, defense counsel does not have to be a skilled cross-examiner—and most are not. Defense counsel may call witnesses to attempt to disprove the truth of the confession and to disprove the prosecution's case, but once the defendant is in the dock, defense counsel is unlikely to get an acquittal.

236. For an interesting view that defense counsel's 'legitimating function' in the criminal justice system and for a discussion of the role of defense counsel in Japan see David A. Suess, *Paternalism versus Pugnacity: The Right to Counsel in Japan and the United States*, 72 Indiana L. J. 291 320–323 (1996).

Because defense counsel is probably looking at a guilty verdict, the role of counsel becomes convincing the judge to give a lenient sentence. This complicates a strong defense at trial because leniency may depend on the willingness of the defendant to accept responsibility and acknowledge wrongdoing.[237] There is no bifurcated sentencing stage to the case. Both the prosecutor and the defense counsel have the right to suggest a sentence to the court. It is at sentencing, the suspension of prosecution stage (before a trial) and appeal stage that defense counsel performs most work.

[6] Judge and Trial

In theory and according to the written law, the judge is the neutral arbiter who determines whether warrants should be issued, whether searches are appropriate and at trial whether the defendant is guilty or innocent and finally if guilty what penalty should be applied. In reality, warrants are virtually always issued when requested and in many cases, operating under the Police Duty Law, police can proceed without a warrant. Here the role of the judge at the criminal trial and the role of the criminal trial in the criminal justice system are examined.

The District Court is the principal court of original jurisdiction in criminal cases. Exceptions are insurrection, which must be tried in the High Court, certain adult cases involving juveniles and juvenile justice cases, which are tried in the Family Court and crimes where the sole sentence is limited to a fine or very short-term detention that are tried in the Summary Court. Where the penalty for a crime involves a fine and the prosecutor and defendant agree, cases may be tried under a summary proceeding in District Court. This proceeding is an *in camera* procedure (the defendant does not even have to be present) and the maximum penalty that can be assessed is a fine of JPY 200,000 (at a rate of JPY 100 to USD 1, this is USD 2,000). In summary proceedings there are no witnesses and the court reviews the prosecutor's file and recommended sentence. Although the Constitution requires that all criminal trials be held in public, summary proceedings are permitted because the defendant has consented. In 1982, summary procedure accounted for more than 50% of all cases referred to the prosecutor.[238] In 2006 a new Speedy Trial Procedure was instituted for cases involving minor infractions where evidence appears clear and the defendant consents to a speedy trial. Trial is supposed to be completed in one day and a verdict immediately entered. If a prison sentence is imposed it must be suspended.[239]

Prior to the Occupation, Japanese criminal trials followed a European inquest model. The prosecutor put together its case in a written form and presented the dossier

---

237. *Counsel's Disregard of Client Recantation Not Misconduct, Case No. 2172 of 2004*, 59 Keishu No. 9, http://www.courts.go.jp/english/judgments/text/2005.11.29-2004.-A-.No..2172.html (P.B., Nov. 29, 2005). In summation the attorney contradicted the client's recantation but the Supreme Court found that acceptable as council was making the best effort for the client even though the summation undercut the client's defense.
238. Nobuyoshi Araki, *The Flow of Criminal Cases in the Japanese Criminal Justice System*, 31 Crime & Delinquency, 601, 617 tbl. 3 (1985).
239. White Paper on Crime, 2007 p.260.

to the court. The trial was primarily based on this dossier and the judge's decision was based on the facts set out in the dossier. There was virtually no witness testimony—except perhaps for statements by the defendant. The Occupation sought to create an American style trial. The criminal procedure law was amended to achieve this goal. Thus, the Japanese trial, on paper, resembles a typical American trial in many respects. But what you see may not be what you get.

The Japanese trial is fundamentally different from the American trial. Not only are the procedures different, but also it can be argued that the function of the trial is different. Whereas in the United States the function of the trial is to determine whether the defendant is guilty or innocent (or at least not guilty), it can reasonably be argued that the function of the Japanese trial (the situation may be different in the Saiban'in trial) is review the prosecutor's determination that the defendant is guilty.[240]

What you see is not what you get. Why is there this difference?[241]

The objective of the Japanese criminal trial is to see that substantive justice is done—even if procedural "niceties" have not been followed a guilty defendant should not go free. For example, where the prosecution failed to submit a critical document in evidence the Supreme Court nonetheless upheld the defendant's conviction because after trial the document was made a part of the record sent up to the Supreme Court. The nature of the Supreme Court as a court that does not take new evidence was disregarded.[242] In an American trial the objective is to require that the prosecution prove its case beyond a reasonable doubt and if it fails to release the defendant.

Second, Judges are aware of the discretionary decisions made by the police and prosecutors and are aware that the only cases coming to trial are those where the prosecutor is convinced of the guilt of the defendant and further, is convinced that this is not an appropriate case for suspension.

Third, by the time a case gets to trial the investigatory function has yielded confession (in 99% of cases), written police reports, physical evidence, written expert reports, and written witness statements much of which was obtained as a consequence of the confession. The trial of a case that is not tried to the Saiban'in Panel takes on more of the character of a trial by dossier with little evidence adduced in court.

Fourth, emphasis on guilt or innocence could upset the needs of the defendant (to be rehabilitated) and society (to have defendant rehabilitated) by unduly focusing on technical arguments that stand in the way of acceptance of responsibility—the first step in rehabilitation.

At the heart of the difference between trial practice and trial reality are the relationships between the above four factors. Each works to support the other in

240. Ryuichi Hirano, *Diagnosis of the Current Code of Criminal Procedure* (Daniel H. Foote trans.), 22 L. Japan 129, (1989); for a similar view see David A. Suess, *'Paternalism versus Pugnacity': The Right to Counsel in Japan and the United States*, 72 Indiana L. J. 291 (1996).
241. For a discussion of the diminishing role of defense counsel and the court in criminal cases in Japan and the expansion of the role of the prosecutor see Lawrence Repeta, *The International Covenant on Civil and Political Rights and Human Rights Law in Japan*, 20 L. Japan 1 (1987).
242. *Supplement of Record After Second Level Appeal decided is Evidence Before Supreme Court*, Case No. 2011 (A) No. 469, Keishu Vol. 65, No. 7), http://www.courts.go.jp/english/judgments/text/2011.10.26-2011.-A-.No..469.html (P.B., Oct. 26, 2011).

eventually resulting in a trial that may well be validating the prosecutor's determination that the defendant is guilty rather than determining whether in fact the defendant is guilty. The ability of prosecutors to obtain confessions in almost all cases brought to trial[243] support the idea that all defendants prosecuted are in fact guilty. This is also true for Saiban'in trials where only the penalty phase is involved. The Judges probably gives greater weight to the evidence presented by the prosecutor than to the evidence adduced by the defendant.[244]

Although the beyond a reasonable doubt standard should apply the Judge is typically more understanding of the prosecution and may require less proof to meet the standard. The definition of reasonable doubt has undergone some modification in recent cases. Thus in 2007 a Petty Bench of the Supreme Court held reasonable doubt was overcome by common sense.[245] While in 2010 a different Petty Bench decided that when circumstantial evidence is used to prove guilt reasonable doubt may be overcome only when there is a fact that cannot reasonably be explained other than if the defendant is guilty.[246] The Court was of the view that it was simply explaining the opinion in the earlier decision and thus did not need to submit its decision to the Grand Bench.

The high regard in which prosecutors are generally held by judges, knowledge that a large number of cases have been washed out of the system through discretionary action by police and prosecutors, the fact that prosecutors do not indict unless they have a high degree of confidence in the guilt of the defendant recasts the burden of proof to the defendant. The use of written evidence, which has the advantage of speeding up a trial but the disadvantage of not permitting evidence to be adduced in open court, dramatically changes the nature of the trial when there is no mixed panel. The credibility of the written record is enhanced by the actions of High Courts that do not give deference to the trial judge's fact finding.[247] This may be in the process of change in mixed panel cases where the High Court must now give deference to the

243. There may be a bit of a 'chicken or egg' issue here in that without a confession the prosecutor may decide not to go to trial. Therefore in cases where there is no confession there will likely be no trial while in cases that go to trial there will always be a confession. In any event, prosecutors have various means available to them to obtain confessions and they usually get what they want.

244. See Daniel H. Foote, *The Benevolent Paternalism of Japanese Criminal Justice*, 80 California L. Rev. 317, 371 (1992).

245. See, *Reasonable Doubt Defined Case 2*, Case No., 2007 (A) No. 398, 61Keishu, No. 7, http://www.courts.go.jp/english/judgments/text/2007.10.16-2007.-A-.No..398.html (1st P.B. Oct. 16, 2007) http://www.courts.go.jp/english/judgments/text/2010.04.27-2007.-A-.No..80.html.

246. *Reasonable Doubt Defined Case 1*, Case No. 2007 (A) 80, 64 Keishu No. 3, http://www.courts.go.jp/english/judgments/text/2010.04.27-2007.-A-.No..80.html (3rd P.B. Apr. 27, 2010). This later decision may have been influenced by the fact that there was evidence that defendant's confession was coerced through the use of physical force. The concurring opinion of Justice Tahara points to evidence of such abuse when it suggests that on remand the lower court should not give credence to the confession.

247. The disconnect between the written law and reality is highlighted by Hiroshi Oda, *Japanese Law* 428–429 (Oxford University Press 1999) where Professor Oda states on the one hand that the trial is adversarial in nature and on the other immediately thereafter Oda recognizes that this is not how the system works. For an example of the confrontation rule in the United States in a criminal setting see *Crauford v. Washington*, 541 U.S. 36 (2004); *Davis v. Washington*, 547 U.S. 813 (2006).

Saiban'in Panel's determination.[248] Since the Supreme Court's decision the rate of High Court reversals of mixed panel determinations has dropped from 6.4% to 5.1%.[249] The prosecutor service will likely look for a case that gives them a chance to have the Grand Bench review the 2010 *Reasonable Doubt Defined Case* and the *Deference to be given to Mixed Panel's findings case.*

The introduction of the mixed lay / professional judge system for certain major crimes may also elevate procedural "niceties." In a recent capital case the defendant's fingerprints were found at the scene of a murder but the prosecution failed to properly document its examination of the crime scene and also failed to find fingerprints on the murder weapon. In addition the prosecution's asserted motive for the crime—robbery—was inconsistent with the fact that valuables and money were left at the crime scene. Without a confession, the mixed panel acquitted the defendant causing some to believe that the lay jurors were demanding that the presumption of innocence be recognized and that the prosecution prove its case beyond a reasonable doubt. In Saiban'in cases more testimony by police investigators and defendants as well as more dramatic photographic evidence are utilized and mixed panel trials are taking longer than originally anticipated. The trial lasted 40 days, long even for a U.S. jury trial.[250]

The Constitutional requirement that the government be responsible for unlawful acts of public servants may have an unintended consequence in criminal cases. If the defendant is found not guilty the defendant is entitled to damages from the government. On the other hand, if the defendant is found guilty but given no jail time the government is not liable. Japanese Judges are not unaware of this consequence.

The judge [unlike civil cases that are typically tried to a panel of three judges, most criminal cases are tried before a single judge] has an important role to play in determining whether a defendant's confession is reliable. A defendant cannot be convicted on the basis of the confession alone but there must be corroborating evidence,[251] although the confession of another party may be used to corroborate the confession of the defendant.[252] Unlike the United States where a court may be asked to

248. *Deference to be given to Mixed Panel's findings case*, Case No. 2011 (A) No. 757, Keishu Vol. 66, No. 2, http://www.courts.go.jp/english/judgments/text/2012.02.13-2011.-A-.No..757.html (1st Petty Bench, Feb. 13, 2012); *Top court urges high court to respect citizens' viewpoints, scraps acquittal overturn*, Mainichi Daily News (Feb. 14, 2012), http://mdn.mainichi.jp/perspectives/news/20120214p2a00m0na020000c.html.

249. *Lay judge trial rulings see fewer reversals*, The Yomiuri Shimbun (May 21, 2012), http://www.yomiuri.co.jp/dy/national/T120520003043.htm. The statistics do not disclose what percentage of acquittals as distinguished from guilty verdicts are included in the appeal figures although it is likely that almost if not all cases reversed were acquittals as the High Courts generally affirm convictions.

250. See, *Gallows Sought, But in a First, Lay Judges Acquit*, Japan Times (Dec. 10, 2010), http://search.japantimes.co.jp/cgi-bin/nn20101210x1.html. *The defendant was found not guilty First Acquittal in Lay Judge Capital Trial*, Yomiuri Shimbun (Dec. 11, 2010), http://www.yomiuri.co.jp/dy/national/T101210005389.htm; *Innocent Until Proven Guilty*, The Yomiuri Shimbun (Dec. 11, 2010), http://www.yomiuri.co.jp/dy/national/T101210005286.htm.

251. Constitution Article 38 (3) Code of Criminal Procedure Article 319.

252. *Conspiracy* case, Case No. 1954 (A) No. 1056) 12 Keishu 1718, http://www.courts.go.jp/english/judgments/text/1958.05.28-1954.-A-.No..1056.html (G.B., 28 May 1958).

determine if a confession is *coerced*, in Japan the focus is on whether the confession is *reliable*.

It remains to be seen whether the recent decisions requiring deference to Saiban'in determinations and making the prosecution's burden of proof more meaningful will change the attitude of District and High Court judges.

[a] Sentencing Consideration

Where the judge plays her most significant role is (a) in confirming the prosecutor's judgment by rendering a guilty verdict and (b) by passing sentence on the defendant. Japanese judges have great discretion in the sentencing decision including whether to suspend sentence in favor of probation. Even where the statute appears to contain a mandatory minimum sentence, the court has power to reduce that sentence by as much as half. Neither the minimum sentence nor the maximum sentence provided in a penal statute appears to provide much guidance as to the actual sentence that will be meted out.[253] In the *Patricide* case, the Supreme Court acknowledged that statutory penalties were rarely imposed and that in most cases the court reduced the penalty.[254] In mixed panel cases it is the panel that determines the sentence—panels appear to be rendering somewhat harsher sentences than would a professional judge, especially in cases involving sexual assaults—not the result anticipated and sought by *Bengoshi*.

For defendants who have not been imprisoned recently, the Penal Law permits suspension of sentences of three years or less.[255] This provision added to the ability of the court to reduce minimum sentences[256] and considering that most minimum sentences are short, renders suspended sentences the rule.[257] In 2004, of all the guilty verdicts rendered in Japan only 2% of defendants did not have their sentences suspended.[258] An offender may even have more than one sentence suspended.[259] Those sentences that are not suspended are typically of short duration, meaning two years or less and hardly ever, except in truly outrageous cases, more than five years.[260] [The death penalty is discussed in part (b) below.] In 2008 only 2.6% of all sentences

253. Haruo Abe, *The accused and Society: Therapeutic and Preventative Aspects of Criminal Justice in Japan* (Assisted by B.J. George, Jr.) in Arthur Taylor Von Mehren, *Law in Japan* 324, 333–334 (Harvard University Press 1963).
254. The *Patricide* case, *Aizawa v. Japan*, 27 Keishu 3 at 265 Case No. 1970 (A) No. 1310, http://www.courts.go.jp/english/judgments/text/1973.04.04-1970-A-No.1310.html (G.B. Apr. 4, 1973).
255. Penal Code Article 25.
256. Penal Code Article 68.
257. Daniel H. Foote, *The Benevolent Paternalism of Japanese Criminal Justice*, 80 California L. Rev. 317, 351, 353–354. (1992); Haley, *Authority without Power: Law and The Japanese Paradox* 128 (Oxford University Press 1991).
258. Motoo Noguchi, *Criminal Justice in Asia and Japan and the International Criminal Court*, 6 Intl. Criminal L. Rev. 585, 596 (2006).
259. Penal Code Article 25 (2). In cases where a suspended sentence was given and the offender was under supervision when committing a second crime, suspension of the second sentence is not permitted.
260. Daniel H. Foote, *The Benevolent Paternalism of Japanese Criminal Justice*, 80 California L. Rev. 317, 355 (1992); Haley, *Authority without Power: Law and the Japanese Paradox* 128 (1991).

for imprisonment extended five years while 3.9% were for six months or less.[261] On the other hand, more than 80% of defendants tried in District Court were in detention at the time of trial and less than 15% were out on bail.[262] Even when bail is granted the high cost of bail has rendered it unavailable to most defendants. The JFBA is attempting to establish its own bail resources but requires approval from the Supreme Court before doing so.[263] Bail is typically denied on the ground that the defendant might destroy evidence or attempt to escape. There is reason to believe that the real reason is that the prosecutor wants to keep the defendant in custody throughout the trial—perhaps because the prosecutor knows that the defendant even if convicted is unlikely to spend significant time post-trial in confinement. The introduction of the saiban'in mixed lay/professional judge trial has apparently had the unexpected effect of increasing the number of defendants who are granted bail in mixed trial cases. But even here bail is the exception not the rule.[264]

The power of the court in sentencing is used to rehabilitate where possible, not to punish.[265] The Ministry of Justice has stated that the Penal and Detention Facilities Act of (2007) has as its purpose rehabilitation and integration of convicted criminals into society.[266] Nonetheless the 2005 Act for the Partial Amendment of the Penal Code provided for longer sentences for various crimes and longer sentences for such crimes, especially rape are being assessed.[267]

Whether rehabilitation rather than punishment is a goal sought because Japanese myths about homogeneity and group identification,[268] or whether it is simply a reflection of the lack of "power" in Japanese law and society,[269] or whether it is a reflection of paternalism in Japan's criminal justice system,[270] or whether it is a reflection of

261. While Paper on Crime 2009 Table 2-3-2-2, http://hakusyo1.moj.go.jp/en/58/image/image/h002003002002h.jpg.
262. White Paper on Crime 2007, p. 72 Table 2-3-3-1; While Paper on Crime 2009 Table 2-3-3-1, http://hakusyo1.moj.go.jp/en/58/image/image/h002003003001h.jpg.
263. Kyodo, *Lawyers Co-op to Provide Bail Bond Aid*, Japan Times (Dec. 2, 2011), http://www.japantimes.co.jp/text/nn20111202x1.html.
264. *75% of defendants get bail in lay judge trials*, Yomiuri Shimbun (May 25, 2010), http://www.yomiuri.co.jp/dy/national/20100525TDY02T09.htm (the 75% referred to is not the percentage of defendants who get bail but rather the % of defendants in mixed/lay cases who get bail after application (i.e., 43 of 57 defendants who applied for bail—of the total of 444 defendants tried before the mixed panels only these 43 or only 10%, received bail).
265. In the United States there are situations where maximum sentences can be increased such as when a crime is a 'hate crime'. In such case the facts that support increasing the sentence must be proven 'beyond a reasonable doubt' to the jury. *Apprendi v. New Jersey*, 529 U.S. 1002 (2000); *Cunningham v. California*, 549 U.S. 270 (2007). In addition there are sentencing guidelines in the federal court system. Courts may deviate from the guidelines. See *United States v. Booker*, 543 U.S. 220 (2005); *Kimbrough v. United States*, No. 06-6330 (Dec. 10, 2007). The appeals court must use a standard that is deferential to the District Court. *Gall v. United States*, 552 U.S. 38(2007).
266. White Paper on Crime 2007, p. 91.
267. White Paper on Crime 2007, 337–338.
268. See V. Lee Hamilton & Joseph Sanders, *Punishment and the Individual in the United States and Japan*, 22 L. & Soc. Rev. 301 (1988).
269. John Owen Haley, *Authority without Power: Law and the Japanese Paradox* (Oxford University Press, 1991).
270. Daniel H. Foote, *The Benevolent Paternalism of Japanese Criminal Justice*, 80 California L. Rev. 317 (1992).

Japan's policy of providing a more "individualized justice,"[271] or simply a philosophical approach that leads to the conclusion that prison time creates hardened criminals while compassion leads to rehabilitation, the fact is that most Japanese convicted defendants do not go to prison and of those few who do, they do not spend much time inside prison walls.

In making a sentencing determination, the judge uses factors similar to those used by the prosecutor in determining whether to suspend prosecution. Sentencing is not a separate procedure in Japan. Since the contrite, repentant, apologetic, remorseful defendant who acknowledges his guilt is likely to receive a suspended or short sentence, the system provides inducements to the defendant to confess sins and accept mild punishment.

[b] Crimes that Violate Government Policies Concerning Japanese Values

While sentencing may be lenient as a general matter, where the defendant has engaged in conduct that conflicts with essential Japanese values and government policy (as distinguished from personal crime or crimes that do not go to the heart of government and societal value)[272] and where such conduct is so notorious that it may in fact result in a change in values or policy, the defendant may have a severe price to pay. Thus, in the *Livedoor* situation discussed in Chapter 13 the founder of Livedoor was given a prison term (not suspended) and the fund manager who supported him was given a sentence only suspended via appeal. In both cases the object of the crime was a hostile takeover that had been opposed by the government.[273] The fact is that until the Internet executive's sentence, white collar insider traders received suspended sentences[274] and even today receive token fines for insider trading.[275] In fact insider trading is common and brokers who release inside information are not subject to criminal prosecution.[276]

---

271. Haruo Abe, *The accused and Society: Therapeutic and Preventative Aspects of Criminal Justice in Japan* (assisted by B.J. George, Jr.) in Arthur Taylor Von Mehren, *Law in Japan* 324, 329 (Harvard University Press 1963).
272. For the view that the strongest punishments are meted out to those who violate the most important norms of society, especially action that disrupts the existing wealth structure see, John O. Haley, *Comment, Law and Culture in China and Japan: A Framework for Analysis*, 27 Michigan J. Intl. L. 895, 899 (2006).
273. See Yuri Kageyama, *Japanese Court Sentences Fund Manager, Associated Press* (July 18, 2007); Jun Hongo, *Murakami given two-year sentence NBS share buy ruled inside trade*, Japan Times (July 20, 2007); Justin McCurry, *Japanese Activist Shareholder Jailed for Insider Trading*, Guardian Unlimited (July 19, 2007).
274. See e.g., *A Japan 'old boy' falls Insider deals trip up ex-Seibu leader*, International Herald Tribune, Oct. 27, 2005—the defendant was sentenced to a fine of JPY 5 million and had his prison sentence suspended. The two-year unsuspended sentence of the Internet entrepreneur should also be compared with the suspended sentence given the criminals responsible for the theft of approximately 4.5 million records containing private personal information. In the personal records theft case, subscribers sued and an Osaka District Court in May 2006 ordered the company that had failed in its duty of care as to the records to pay JPY 5,000 damages for mental distress caused by the leak as well as JPY 1,000 for attorney's fees (totaling approximately USD 55 to each plaintiff).
275. See, AFP Fuji, *Probe spotlights Japan's culture of insider trading*, Japan Times (June 12, 2012), http://www.japantimes.co.jp/text/nn20120612f3.html reporting that convictions for insider

[c] *Repeat Offenders and the Death Penalty*

Hardened criminals may receive longer sentences (not suspended) as they have demonstrated an inability to be rehabilitated. But even here sentences do not approach those handed out in United States courtrooms. Concern about crime rates and recidivism has resulted in legislation increasing the maximum penalty for various serious offenses. And more recently longer sentences have been imposed for homicide, robbery and rape.[277] Japan has instituted programs to try to rehabilitate sexual offenders and reduce recidivism in sexual crimes[278] but of those sent to prison for rape in 2000 38.5% were repeat offenders (of those sent to prison for robbery 39.1% committed crimes within 10 years of serving their sentence).[279]

Concern about recidivism has some basis in fact as reports show that approximately 30% of all criminal defendants commit approximately 60% of all crimes and repeat offenders commit more than 50% of all intimidation, extortion, physical violence, and controlled substance offenses—all offenses related to activities of organized crime groups.[280]

Even defendants convicted of some homicides may expect leniency in sentencing, although the death penalty still exists in Japan and is used, notwithstanding Article 36 of the Constitution, which prohibits cruel punishments.[281] [The United States, which has a similar Constitutional prohibition also permits the death penalty, but the Supreme Court has held that some crimes do not qualify for the death penalty[282] (it has generally been assumed that the death penalty is only permissible when there is a death involved in the crime being punished (except for crimes such as terrorism), although not all states followed this assumption.[283]) The Supreme Court has also held that the death penalty could not be applied to insane[284] or mentally retarded prisoners.[285]]

---

trading are "few and far between" and that fines levied for such misconduct are in the neighborhood of only USD 1,500.

276. Bloomberg, *Insider trading to be crime: DPJ*, Japan times (July 21, 2012), http://www.japantimes.co.jp/text/nb20120721n1.html.
277. White Paper on /crime 2007, p. 338 although rape sentences of over 5 years fell from 35.8% in 2006 to 10% in 2008. White Paper on Crime 2009, Appendix 2-4 Sentencing of death penalty and imprisonment with or without work in district courts by type of offense (2008), http://hakusyo1.moj.go.jp/en/58/image/image/h008002004-1h.jpg.
278. White Paper on Crime 2007, p. 358.
279. Kyodo News, *Rapist, Robbers have 40% Recidivisim Rate per Decade*, Japan Times (Nov. 12, 2010), http://search.japantimes.co.jp/cgi-bin/nn20101112x3.html.
280. White Paper on Crime, 2007, 278-278 (Table 7-2-2-1); see also, Kyodo News, *Recidivism Rate at Record High in '08*, Japan Times Nov. 14, 2009.
281. See Hanrerishi II, No.3, 191 (Sup. Ct. G.B. 12 March 1948) for an English language translation see John M. Maki, *Court and Constitution in Japan* 156 (University of Washington Press 1964). When the death penalty is executed, the only procedure allowed by the Penal Code is hanging. See *Japan v. Ichikawa*, 15 Keishu 1106 (Sup. Ct. G.B. 19 April 1961); Penal Code Article 11 (1).
282. For example, rape does not qualify. *Coker v. Georgia*, 433 U.S. 584 (1977).
283. *Kennedy v. Louisiana*, 554 U.S. ___ (2008) ("As it relates to crimes against individuals, though, the death penalty should not be expanded to instances where the victim's life was not taken." The Court did not state a rule for crimes not against persons such as "treason, espionage, terrorism, and drug kingpin activity, which are offenses against the State.")
284. *Ford v. Wainwright*, 477 U.S. 399 (1986).
285. *Atkins v. Virginia*, 536 U.S. 304 2002).

The Supreme Court of Japan has established several criteria for death penalty cases that focus on the nature of the crime, the number of victims, the extent of cruelty, the age and criminal record of the defendant, as well as the impact of the crime on society. In addition, events occurring after the crime may be considered to determine whether there is a basis for leniency.[286] The death penalty cannot be assessed to a person under the age of 18 at the time the crime was committed.[287] In 2004 14 death sentences were rendered in Japan[288] but the number jumped to 46 in 2007,[289] falling back to five in 2008.[290] At least seven death row inmates or persons serving life imprisonment have been set free years after conviction after courts concluded that their confessions were false. In 2011 there were no executions in Japan but in 2012 there were five. There are at the time of this writing 130 inmates on death row.[291]

Of the 48 cases decided by Saiban'in mixed panels through March 2011 in which a death penalty could have been imposed, life imprisonment was determined appropriate in 43 cases and the death penalty handed down in 5 cases.[292] By the end of 2011 mixed panels had handed down death penalties in 12 cases. The JFBA has suggested the law be amended to require a unanimous verdict of the entire panel before the death penalty can be assessed.[293]

As in the United States, the Death Penalty raises collateral cruel and unusual punishment issues. In the United States the issue has surfaced in the method used to carry out the death penalty.[294] In Japan the issue is related to the timing of the penalty and the conditions on death row. Prisoners in both the United States and Japan spend a considerable time in prison before being executed. In the United States the time is related to the appeal process; in Japan it may be related to: (a) The Minister of Justice must sign the warrant for carrying out the penalty and some Ministers do not wish to

286. *Death Penalty Criteria* case, Case No. 1981 (A) No. 1505, 37 Keishu 609, http://www.courts.go.jp/english/judgments/text/1983.7.8-1981-A-No.1505.html (P.B., Jul. 8, 1983). In this case the defendant was nineteen at the time of the crimes. This alone was insufficient to deny the death penalty. The Supreme Court remanded the case to the District Court to consider the proper penalty in light of the factors set out.

287. Mayumi Negishi & Kaho Shimizu, *Top Court Sends Case Back, Saying Consider Death Penalty Anew*, Japan Times (June 21, 2006).

288. Motoo Noguchi, *Criminal Justice in Asia and Japan and the International Criminal Court*, 6 International Criminal L. Rev. 585, 596 (2006).

289. Associated Press, *Paper: Japan Condemns 44 to Death in 06*, Washington Post.com, www.washingtonpost.com/wp-dyn/content/article/2006/12/31/AR2006123100366_pf.html; *46 Sentenced to Death in 2007*, Japan Times (Jan. 14, 2008).

290. White Paper on Crime 2009, Appendix 2-4 Sentencing of death penalty and imprisonment with or without work in district courts by type of offense (2008), http://hakusyo1.moj.go.jp/en/58/image/image/h008002004-1h.jpg.

291. *2 inmates executed*, Ymiuri Shimbun (Aug. 4, 2012), http://www.yomiuri.co.jp/dy/national/T120803005475.htm.

292. During the same period mixed panels found the defendant guilty in 99.8% of cases—showing that the new system has not resulted in a higher acquittal rate than the old system, a result predicted based on experience of other civil law countries with mixed panels in criminal cases. See, *Lay Judge Conviction Rate 99.8% so Far*, Japan Times (May 22, 2011).

293. Keijo Hirano, *Lay Judge Death Sentences Must be Unanimous: JFBA*, Japan Times (Mar. 25, 2012). http://www.japantimes.co.jp/text/nn20120325a5.html; Diet Group to Propose Only Unanimous Death Sentences, Feb. 16, 2011 The Yomiuri Shimbun, http://www.yomiuri.co.jp/dy/national/T110215006053.htm.

294. *Baze v. Rees*, 553 U.S. 35 (2008) (not unconstitutional).

be personally responsible for the death of the convict[295], and (b) concern that the convict has not committed the crime. In Japan neither the convict nor family knows when the death penalty will be carried out. The convict is typically given a few hours notice that the sentence is to be carried out, and, while on death row has little contact with the outside world except for infrequently allowed visits from family and defense counsel,[296] is segregated from other prisoners and is in virtual solitary confinement -causing international criticism.[297] In 2007, for the first time the Ministry of Justice publicly announced the names of inmates who had been put to death hoping that such transparency might quell objections to its secrecy policy. But, as the public announcement *after* hanging does not deal with the fundamental issues of notice to the inmate and treatment of inmates while awaiting execution, it is unlikely to have much effect.[298]

Japan has no life without parole sentence. However, those sentenced to life imprisonment rarely get parole and those who are paroled have typically served sentences in excess of 20 years.[299] Some in Japan have suggested that in mixed panel cases there should be a penalty of life without parole permitted.[300] In the United States the Supreme Court has held that a statute that provides for mandatory sentence of life without parole is unconstitutional when applied to a juvenile under the age of 18 at the time of committing the offense.[301]

[d] Foreign Prisoners

Foreign prisoners have a particularly difficult time in the Japanese prison system where differences in language and customs make life more difficult for them. Both Japan and the United States are parties to the Convention on the Transfer of Sentenced Persons[302]

295. The views of the Minister of Justice are very important to death row inmates. Dai Adachi and Hiroshi Tajima, *1 year passes with no death-row executions / Justice minister shows unwillingness to sign orders, draws fire for 'Overstepping authority,'* The Daily Yomiuri, Aug. 2, 2011, http://www.yomiuri.co.jp/dy/national/T110801005012.htm.
296. David T. Johnson, *Japan's Secretive Death Penalty Policy: Contours, Origins, Justifications and Meanings*, 7 Asian-P. L. & Policy J. 62 (Issue 2, Summer 2006); Melissa Clark, *Caught Between Hope and Despair: An Analysis of the Japanese Criminal Justice System*, 31 Denver J. Intl. L. & Policy 525, 545–546 (2003); Howard W. French, *Secrecy of Japan's Executions is Criticized as Unduly Cruel*, New York Times (June 30, 2002); Ed Pilkington, *Sentenced to Death for Crimes They Did Not Commit: The Men Who Lived to Tell the Tale*, The Guardian (Nov. 14, 2007).
297. See e.g., 1227 Concluding Observations of the Human Rights Committee Paras. 20, 21 (Nov. 19, 1998); www.mofa.go.jp/policy/human/civil_ccpr.html.
298. Jun Hongo, *Three Hanged and Named in Ministry First: Disclosures end secrecy policy on executions*, Japan Times (Dec. 8, 2007), http://search.japantimes.co.jp/cgi-bin/nn20071208a1.html.
299. White Paper on Crimes 2007, p. 96 Table 2-5-1-3.
300. See, e.g., Setsuko Kamiya, *Life without parole finding support in Diet*, Japan Times (July 18, 2008), http://www.japantimes.co.jp/text/nn20080718f1.html.
301. *Miller v. Alabama*, 567 U.S. ___ (2012); *Roper v. Simmons*, 543 U.S. 551 (2005) held the death penalty unconstitutional when applied to juveniles under age of 18 at the time the crime was committed. The Court had previously held in *Graham v. Florida*, 560 U.S. ___ (2010) that life without parole violates the Eighth Amendment when imposed on juvenile offenders in cases that did not involve homicide.
302. http://conventions.coe.int/Treaty/Commun/QueVoulezVous.asp?NT=112&CM=8&CL=ENG.

under which convicted prisoners may be repatriated to their home country to serve their sentence. The issue of repatriation is discretionary with the convicting government.[303] Inmates have been transferred to Japan from the United States and from Japan to the United States.[304]

Japan has taken some steps to try to alleviate the problems of foreign prisoners. Thus, some prisons have an international section (Fuchu and Osaka prison) where foreign prisoners can receive visits from and converse with friends or family in their native language, provided a translator is present. So too, prisoners may send and receive mail in their native language—after they have been translated so that the content is revealed to prison authorities. Where for religious reasons prisoners have special dietary requirements these may be met by the prison system.[305]

[7] Defendant

The defendant is a critical part of the criminal justice system and is expected to participate in the investigation (by answering interrogation) and while he may have a right to silence at trial it is not unusual for a court to inquire as to the defendant's response to a matter. It is expected that the defendant will respond, although the defendant may refuse to answer, invoking his Article 38 privilege. It is likely that a judge would hold such refusal to answer against the defendant. If a defendant testifies, the presiding judge or any other participant in the trial (prosecutor, defense counsel, if there is a panel other judges, in a mixed panel lay judges, a co-defendant) may question the defendant.

The defendant has a right to represent himself at trial. The defendant has the right to make the last statement at the trial.

More significantly, the case is about the rehabilitation of the defendant, placing the defendant at the center of the proceedings.

[D] Constitutional Guarantees and Protections Afforded the Criminal Suspect and Accused

As the investigative stage is the critical stage in the criminal process, the rights of the accused at this stage are particularly relevant. The Constitution provides rights that are familiar to Americans. The right to counsel, the right not to be a witness against oneself, the right to be free from unreasonable search and seizure, the right to a speedy trial, etc. While the rights as written may seem familiar, what you see [with eyes accustomed to American interpretation of these rights] may not be what you get.

303. See explanatory report on the Convention at http://conventions.coe.int/Treaty/en/Reports/Html/112.htm.
304. White Paper on Crime 2007 p. 116.
305. See, Information for Prison Inmates, Japan Federation of Bar Associations, http://www.nichibenren.or.jp/en/meetings/year/2004/20040409.html; http://www.nichibenren.or.jp/library/ja/legal_aid/on-duty_lawyer/data/jukeisha_en.pdf, last accessed Sept. 17, 012.

[1] *Confession and False Confession*[306]

The *Mainichi Daily News* of Sunday February 18, 2001 carries a story entitled Police Continue Grilling [suspect name] Over Murder of British Airways Stewardess. The case was notorious and of great public interest. It was reported that interrogation sessions lasted late into the night and that the suspect was sleep deprived and psychologically and physically exhausted as the prosecutors attempted to get him to confess. Because the suspect refused to confess the prosecutor has no choice but to keep up the pressure. It is tough work but it is apparently the only choice the prosecutor felt he had.[307]

Pity the poor prosecutor. It's rough but psychological pressure; all night questioning sessions, etc. were the only option available. What is a poor prosecutor to do if the suspect will not cooperate and give the confession called for?

It is said that confession is good for the soul, and it may be true. But is it good for the suspect? Japanese prosecutors armed with both an adversarial and quasi-judicial role and having as one of their duties the rehabilitation of the criminal would unqualifiedly say yes because the criminal can only be rehabilitated by acknowledging the wrong. Judges would agree and defense counsel will probably advise the suspect that confession is good because the odds are that the defendant will ultimately confess and be convicted. An early and contrite remorseful confession may even lead to suspension of prosecution and in all events it is an arrow in counsel's quiver when he argues for a suspended or reduced sentence.

Confessions in Japan typically take the form of summaries (prepared by the investigator) of the statements made by the suspect. With the introduction of the partial recording the prosecutor will have the suspect repeat his confession (and the voluntary nature of the confession) for the recording device. The confession is a statement against interest and not subject to the hearsay rule. Confessions are admissible unless the judge concludes that the confession is unreliable or was not given voluntarily. But "voluntarily" excludes the state of mind of the suspect and focuses on whether the conditions under which given reach a level that the judge finds unconscionable. Confessions of persons believed guilty by the judge are unlikely to be excluded if to do so would allow a guilty person to go free. Judges may express their disapproval of prosecution methods by excluding confessions of guilty defendants but finding sufficient other evidence to prove guilt.

It is rare to indict and go to trial in a case where there is no confession. It is the duty of the prosecutor to get a confession from a criminal who has committed the

---

306. False confessions are also a serious issue in the United States. See, Richard A. Leo, Steven A. Drizin, Peter J. Neufeld, Bradley R. Hall & Amy Vatner, *Bringing Reliability Back in: False Confessions and Legal Safeguards in the 21st Century* (University of San Francisco Law Research Paper No. 2009-04), Wisconsin L. Rev. 479, 528–535 (2006). Amongst other things the authors suggest that to make confessions more reliable the entire custodial interrogation should be recorded (p. 486). In the United States the trend is towards recording custodial interrogations.
307. Face of the Weeklies, *Mainichi Daily News*, Mainichi Interactive Feb. 18, 2001 found at www.mainichi.co.jp/english/waiwai/face/face.html.

crime. One can surely feel sympathy for the poor prosecutor in the case reported above. [What about the poor accused?].

With the advent of the new saiban'in mixed lay/professional judge panel for certain serious crimes system, the issue of confessions and their use at trial has become a significant issue in Japan. Some police and prosecutors instituted an internal system under which interrogations are be viewed (and heard) by superiors to assure that proper procedures were followed. Internal rules now prohibit interrogation after midnight and for sessions that last more than eight hours, permission of a supervising official is required but such long sessions are not prohibited).[308]

Reports of high profile cases have brought the issue of false confessions to the attention of the Japanese public and government. In 2008 the then opposition DPJ sponsored legislation to require that interrogations be recorded. In May 2011 the first acknowledged taping of an entire interrogation session was undertaken in Tokyo. The problem of false confessions and recent efforts regarding recording of interrogations is discussed in section §16.03[C][3][c] of this Chapter.[309]

It is likely that Japan, will slowly but nonetheless eventually adopt a full recording process, at least for serious cases that might be tried to a mixed lay/professional panel.[310] The practice of recording only the portion of the session at which the prosecutor gives its single notice that the suspect need not incriminate himself and then the record of the confession[311] (given several days later) is unlikely to affect the false confession rate and unlikely to gain support once lay jurors get to understand that the "pressure" aspects of the interrogation are being hidden from them by the prosecutors and police officials.

[2] Right to Counsel

Article 34 of the Japanese Constitution gives those arrested or detained an "immediate" privilege of counsel) and all "accused" have a right to counsel. To an American lawyer, it might appear that those in custody have at least some *Miranda* rights. What you see is not what you get. The Article 37 right to have counsel appointed does not adhere to suspects but only to those indicted.[312] Prior to indictment the police and the prosecutor

308. United Nations Office at Geneva Press Release, Human Rights Committee Considers Report of Japan, Oct. 16, 2008, http://www.unog.ch/80256EDD006B9C2E/(httpNewsByYear_en)/85D3C531C1EC5655C12574E400539DF0.
309. For the increased use of recordings and changing attitudes of prosecutors to support recording in the United States see, California Commission on the Fair Administration of Justice, http://www.ccfaj.org/documents/reports/false/official/falconfrep.pdf; Report on the Electronic Recording of Police Interrogations, http://www.nycla.org/publications/revisedvideotapereport.pdf.
310. David T. Johnson, *You Don't Need a Weather Man to Know Which Way the Wind Blows: Lessons from the United States and South Korea for Recording Interrogations in Japan*, 24 Ritsumeikan L. Rev. 13 (2007).
311. See, Silvia Croydon, *The Impact of quasi-jury introduction on transparency of suspect interrogations in Japan*, 8 J. L. & Pol. 92 (University of Tokyo 2011).
312. See *Right to Counsel (No coerced confession) Case X and Five Others v. Japan*, Case No. 1993 (0) No. 1189 (Sup. Ct. G.B. 24 March 1999). The official Japanese language version of the Constitution uses the term criminal defendant (keiji hik.okunin). In light of the history of the

have plenty of time to interrogate suspects. It is during this investigatory stage that the defendant's fate is determined and it is during this stage that the defendant is most in need of counsel.[313] Confessions obtained during extended lawful detention are not considered coerced and are not subject to the exclusionary rule of Article 38.

A suspect with sufficient resources may take hire counsel. To provide additional legal advice to suspects, the JFBA adopted a plan in 1990 under which all criminal suspects can receive one hour of free consultation advice from counsel after arrest.[314] It is estimated that prior to the 2006 amendment to the Code of Criminal Procedure providing suspects in felony cases who request it an opportunity to meet with defense counsel prior to indictment, less than 20% of suspects retained counsel at the pre-indictment stage of a proceeding.[315] In 2006 the Japan Legal Support Center was established within the Ministry of Justice. In certain limited situations the Center, which is taking over the program initiated by the Bar Association, may be able to provide some suspects with limited legal advice even before indictment. However, as most Japanese *bengoshi* are located in major cities, the unavailability of counsel in rural districts remains.

In 2006 the Code of Criminal Procedure was amended to permit the court to appoint counsel for suspects for whom a detention order (i.e., the 10 day extension of custody before indictment) has been issued in cases involving the death penalty, life imprisonment or crimes punishable by imprisonment for three years or more.[316] The amendment has limited practical effect or importance. While the figures compiled by the Judicial Secretariat indicate an over 90% use of defense counsel by those accused (both before and after the amendment), the figures are not very helpful. First, the figures contain data for cases at the High Court but by the time a criminal case reaches the High Court the defendant has long since been accused and has "graduated" from suspect to accused (and likely convicted) status. Moreover, prior to the 2006 amendment the Secretariat reported the same usage. The illustration used by the Secretariat in its explanation of the criminal procedure shows that the suspect was *not* afforded counsel at the initial stages of the investigation —by the time counsel was requested the suspect had already admitted the killing. Only after admission was a detention order sought with the judge, who after reading the charges and advising the suspect of his right to remain silent, asked the defendant if he wanted to comment on the charges—rather than appointing counsel and then after counsel had a chance to discuss the matter with his client asking whether the defendant wished to comment.[317]

Constitution, the English language version is regarded by many as 'semi-official'. Yuji Iwasawa, *International Law Human Rights And Japanese Law* 273 (Clarendon Press 1998).

313. *Kansas v. Ventris*, 556 U.S. ___ (Apr. 29, 2009).
314. *Ibid.*
315. Yuji Iwasawa, *International Law Human Rights and Japanese Law* 271 (Clarendon Press 1998).
316. CCP Article 37-2.
317. Supreme Court of Japan, Outline of Criminal Justice in Japan, http://www.courts.go.jp/english/proceedings/criminal_justice.html#2_2_a. In the illustration the suspect was arrested on June 5 and questioned by the police and prosecutor before being referred to a Judge on June 8. By this time he had admitted the critical facts of the case (he threatened the deceased with a knife and that knife wound up in the deceased's chest). Only after having received this evidence was the deceased advised that he had a right to counsel.

The amendment does not deal with initial custody, i.e., the three day period during which the police and prosecutor can interrogate the suspect to determine whether to ask for a detention order. The JFBA has noted that the amendment is of little value and that what is needed is a suspect's right to counsel at the time of arrest, i.e., when the suspect is first placed in custody.[318]

If the suspect exercises the privilege and retains counsel (or counsel is appointed after the detention hearing the ability of counsel to adequately assist the client during the investigative stage is limited: counsel cannot attend interrogation sessions which cannot be stopped, the prosecutor determines when and for how long counsel and client can confer,[319] and as noted earlier the ability to suppress a confession is severely limited. "Lawyering up" is unheard of. Although defendants have the right to court appointed counsel, defendants can lose that right when they abuse the procedural rights granted to them[320] and abuse counsel[321]

The Code appears to restrict the prosecutor's authority to restrict meetings with counsel ("designation power") by limiting it so as not to improperly prevent the defendant from preparing a defense. But what you see may not be what you get. This restriction may be more apparent than real. It has been held that the Code was violated when a prosecutor allowed a suspect only two or three minutes to meet with counsel because such limited time did not allow for preparation of a defense.[322] Nonetheless, more than two minutes may also not be enough time to prepare a defense or a strategy for how to deal with police or prosecutorial investigation and questioning.

The designation power was a compromise made by the Occupation. The prosecutor utilizes it to limit counsel's access to the client. The prosecutor may determine that designation is proper in certain types of cases. The type of crimes that the power extends to includes all cases of bribery, dealing in illicit drugs, election law violations and complex cases. The prosecutor may also apply the designation power to specific suspects.[323] In such cases the defense counsel must apply for a time, date, etc. to meet the client. Under current practices, counsel may apply by telephone or other electronic means and may even get permission orally. Since 1992 meetings are permitted on Saturdays. The prosecutor will not permit a meeting if to do so will "interfere" with the

318. Japan Federation of Bar Associations, Jan. 22, 2010, at pages 8 and 9, http://www.ccprcentre.org/doc/HRC/Japan/JFBA_Japan94.pdf.

319. Code of Criminal Procedure Article 39(3). See Atsushi Nagashima, *The Accused and Society: The Administration of Criminal Justice in Japan, found,* in Arthur Taylor von Mehren, *Law in Japan* 305–306 (Harvard University Press 1963); Hiroyuki Hata & Go Nakagawa & Takehisa Nakagawa, *Japanese Constitutional Law* sec. 315(Kluwer Law International 2001).

320. Rules of Criminal Procedure Article 1 (2).

321. *Defense Counsel Rejection* case, *Ogawa,* et al. *v. Japan,* 33 Keishu 416, http://www.courts.go.jp/english/judgments/text/1979.07.24-1976-A-No.798.html (P.B.7/ 2/79).

322. *Prosecutor Designation case (Too Little Time), Hongo v. Japan,* 7 Keishu 1474 (. P.B., July 10, 1953) quoted in Atsushi Nagashima, 'The Accused and Society: The Administration of Criminal Justice in Japan,' 306 found in Arthur Taylor von Mehren *Law In Japan* (Harvard University Press 1963).

323. Because prosecutors use internal communications to officers in charge of the facility where suspects are being held they are not 'dispositions' within the meaning of the Administrative Case Litigation Law they are not subject to judicial review (see Chapter 17). Counsel may apply to the courts for revocation of a specific designation decision affecting a specific client under Article 39(3) of the Code.

investigation.[324] Interference is a broad term and prosecutors use it to prevent meetings if the meeting could adversely affect the flow of the investigation and stand in the way of the prosecutor obtaining a confession.[325]

The most common form of objection to use of the designation power is a damage action against the prosecutor. The extent of the limits on prosecutors is uncertain but the Supreme Court has given some guidance as to its thinking[326] by setting forth situations in which designation was appropriate. Such situations include (a) actual ongoing interrogation; (b) attendance at crime scenes; and (c) where interrogation is about to start based on a pre-existing interrogation schedule.[327]

There is plenty of room for a prosecutor to argue about the meaning of a scheduled interview and an ongoing interview. Since a "warning" that the suspect need not answer any questions against his will need be given only once at the start of an interview and not at later sessions, is the interrogation over a period of days a single ongoing interrogation even if there are no questions being asked at the time counsel requests a meeting with the client? And, if interviews are scheduled to go on non-stop for several days, is the scheduled interview coextensive with the period when questioning may take place?

Of particular interest is the Court's recognition of the importance of interrogation of the suspect to both the general public and the criminal justice process. This importance must be balanced against the suspect's Constitutional right to counsel. The fact that the right to counsel is Constitutional in nature gives it no precedence over investigation by the prosecutor because the prosecutor also has a Constitutional right to investigate.

In 2000, the Supreme Court permitted an action for damages to be brought under the State Redress Law when a lawyer appeared immediately after arrest and requested to meet with his client but was not permitted to meet until the next day. It was improper for the police officer to let the lawyer wait for over an hour without discussing the designation of time, etc. when it was possible to allow the consultation without interfering with the investigation.[328]

---

324. *Prosecutor Designation* case, *Sugiyama v. Osaka Prefecture*, 32 Minshu 820 (Sup. Ct. 10 July 1978).
325. For a discussion of the designation power of the prosecutor and a discussion of the *Sugiyama* case see Jean Choi DeSombre, *Comparing the Notions of the Japanese and the U.S. Criminal Justice System: An Examination of Pretrial Rights of the Criminally Accused in Japan and the United States*, 14 UCLA Pacific Basin L. Rev. 103 (1995).
326. *Defense Counsel Meeting Postponed to Allow Questioning* case, *Asai* case, 45 Minshu 919 (Sup. Ct. May 10, 1991).
327. *Right to Counsel (No coerced confession)* case, *X and Five Other v. Japan*, Judgment of Mar. 24, 1999 Case No. 1993 (0) no. 1189 (Sup. Ct. G.B. Mar. 24, 1999).
328. *Prosecutor Designation case (Meeting should have been allowed)*, Case No. 1995 (0) No. 105, 54 Minshu 1653, http://www.courts.go.jp/english/judgments/text/2000.06.13-1995.-O-.No.. 105.html (Sup. Ct. P.B. June 13, 2000). It is unclear whether the judgment was based on the Court's view of the failure of the officer to allow the counsel and client to have a brief meeting or whether the Court was reacting to lack of courtesy shown to counsel by making him wait for over an hour after making his request before the police officer would discuss the matter with him.

Permitted meetings are typically short—under half an hour. Confessions obtained after a client was improperly denied a right to meet with counsel or was granted too short a time will not be excluded from the case unless the confession is unreliable or exclusion will have no effect on the decision. For the prosecutor there is little if any down side in utilizing the designation power in a way that assists in obtaining a confession.

The privilege of counsel applies to obtaining the advice of counsel and the assistance of counsel but not to the assistance of counsel during interrogation sessions. As a consequence the only persons present during interrogation are the accused and the prosecutor, highlighting the need for full recording of interrogations.

[3] "No Person Shall Be Compelled to Testify against Himself"[329]

This Constitutional protection would seem reasonably clear. A suspect and an accused are both persons and thus are entitled to the Constitutional right no to be compelled to testify against himself. Is this a case where "what you see *is* what you get?" Hardly.

Although all would agree that a person cannot be compelled to testify against himself, the provision says nothing about the authority of the police/prosecutor (or even the judge) to question a suspect. Further the provision says nothing about the suspect's right to make a voluntary statement. Here then are two potential avenues for obtaining a confession from an otherwise unwilling suspect.

The Code of Criminal Procedure requires that the police, upon arrest give the suspect an opportunity to explain himself. Thus the police should offer somewhat contradictory advice to the arrestee—you have a right not to answer any questions against your will and what is your position as to the suspicions we have about you. If the police happen to forget to give the first piece of advice, a confession is still admissible as evidence.[330]

The suspect's right is a right not to answer any questions against his will, not to silence. If the police can get him to change his will, then his answers to questions are not in violation of the Constitution. In attempting to get the suspect to change his will and decide to "cooperate," police and prosecutors may question the suspect.

Unlike American procedure where once a suspect asserts a Constitutional right not to answer questions the authorities must (a) stop questioning and (b) not begin new questioning sessions, Japanese procedure neither compels the cessation of questioning nor does it prohibit future interrogation sessions. The obligation to advise the suspect that he does not need to answer any questions against his will is a one-time obligation. Although the Occupation attempted to give the suspect an absolute right to refuse to be questioned, the Japanese interpretation is to the effect that the suspect has an obligation to submit to questioning.[331]

---

329. Article 38, Constitution. Hiroyuki Hata & Go Nakagawa & Takehisa Nakagawa, *Japanese Constitutional Law* sec. 316 (Kluwer Law International 2001).
330. *Failure to Warn of Self Incrimination Rights case, Kaneyasu v. Japan,* (Sup. Ct. 28 March 1952).
331. For an interesting discussion of the disagreement between the American and Japanese texts of the Code of Criminal Procedure Article 198(1) dealing with a suspects right to leave once

In the *Right to Counsel (No coerced confession—X & 5 Others)* case,[332] the Supreme Court made clear that suspects have an *obligation* to submit to questioning even when they have requested to see counsel and have stated their refusal to answer questions. Suspects have a *duty to attend interrogation*—merely being present and subjected to questioning was not inconsistent with the privilege against self-incrimination.[333]

Once the suspect's obligation to submit to questioning is added to the suspect's inability to have counsel present when he is questioned and the prosecutor's ability to question the suspect for at least 23 days, it is easily seen why most suspects in Japan eventually confess. Torture is not used[334] but long hours under physically and psychologically exhausting conditions are used. Prosecutors can go at the interrogation for many hours of virtually uninterrupted questioning and a confession obtained under such questioning is admissible in evidence.[335] The Japanese Supreme Court's decision in *Right to Counsel (No coerced confession)* places responsibility for determining when a confession is coerced in the Legislative rather than the Judicial Branch.

[4] Immunity from Prosecution

One investigative tool that Japanese prosecutors do not possess but which is a staple of American investigative technique is the ability to grant a suspect immunity in exchange for testimony against others. The Supreme Court has held that a grant of immunity is not permitted under Japanese law and further held that witness statements obtained under such a grant were inadmissible in a criminal proceeding. The case involved the infamous Lockheed political bribery scandal and the ruling threw out deposition testimony taken in the U.S. and given under a grant of immunity implicating the indicted former prime minister.[336]

[Where properly obtained, witnesses' statements taken abroad are admissible in Japanese criminal trials.][337] The court recognized that in some circumstances the grant of immunity had practical criminal justice value but concluded that adoption was a legislative not judicial function. As the Code of Criminal Procedure had no provisions

questioning has commenced see Daniel H. Foote, *Confessions and the Right to Silence in Japan*, 21 Georgia Journal of International and Comparative Law 415, 435–436 (1991).

332. *Right to Counsel (No coerced confession) case, X and Five Others v. Japan*, Judgment of Case No. 1993 (0) No. 1189. (G.B., Mar. 24, 1999), http://www.courts.go.jp/english/judgments/text/1999.03.24-1993-O-No.1189.html.
333. While inconsistent with the U.S. view, this approach is not inconsistent with the view recently stated by the Supreme Court of Canada. See, *R. v. Sinclair*, 2010 SCC, http://www.canlii.org/en/ca/scc/doc/2010/2010scc35/2010scc35.pdf.
334. There have been some cases where 'overzealous' prosecutors have been punished for striking a suspect but as a general rule there appears to be little evidence of actual physical force used during interrogation sessions.
335. Daniel H. Foote, *Confessions and the Right to Silence in Japan*, 21 Georgia Journal of International and Comparative Law 415, 460–461 (1991).
336. *Lockheed Criminal Immunity case*, Case No. (A) 1351 of 1987, http://www.courts.go.jp/english/judgments/text/1995.02.22-1987-A-No.1351.html (G.B., Feb. 22, 1995).
337. *Admissibility of Witness Statements Taken Abroad case*, Case No. 1999 (A) No. 400 (Sup. Ct. P.B. 31 October 2000) 54 Keishu 735.

for an immunity system, testimony obtained under a grant of immunity was inadmissible as evidence.

The Judicial Reform Council recognized that immunity may be an effective mechanism against organized crime but also noted that such system might not be compatible with the values of the Japanese population and could be inconsistent with norms concerning fairness of the criminal process. Further consideration of an immunity system was recommended.[338] No action has been taken to date.

[5] Bail

There is no Constitutional provision concerning bail. The Code of Criminal Procedure allows bail in certain situations at the discretion of the judge. Some crimes and defendants are not bailable. For example, serious crimes, habitual defendants, those previously sentenced to imprisonment for over 10 years and those without a fixed address are not bailable. Judges may deny bail if there is danger that a defendant will destroy evidence or could cause harm to others once released.[339] The Supreme Court has stated the purposes of such detention as prevention of the concealment and/or destruction of evidence; of course such detention also assures that the defendant will not escape.[340] The concealment and destruction of evidence criteria is particularly flexible and in many cases where the prosecutor does not wish to see an indicted defendant released on bail this provision is used as an excuse to oppose and deny bail. Bail may even be denied a suspect who has been acquitted at the initial trial and the prosecutor has appealed. In such a case, the High Court's determination is de novo and need give no deference to the acquittal.[341] This power has been utilized particularly against non-citizens. There is an open question of whether the court system will apply a different standard for bail to a defendant who has been cleared by a Saiban'in Panel. If the function of the *saiban'in* system is to give the public a meaningful role in deciding criminal cases, it would appear that bail determinations should take into account the views of the lay judges. The Supreme Court has held that the High Court should give significant weight to the mixed panel's findings of innocence when hearing the appeal[342] and it would appear the same should apply to bail. The most significant bail problems are (1) bail is not available until the suspect has become an accused. To grant

338. Recommendations of the Justice System Reform Council—For a Justice System to Support Japan in the 21st Century 12 June 2001 www.kantei.go.jp/foreign/judiciary/2001/0612report.html last accessed Sept. 17, 2012.

339. Article 89, Code of Criminal Procedure.

340. *Censoring of Prisoner's Newspapers Acceptable*, Case No. 1977 (O) No. 927 (22 June 1983) 37 Minshu 793. The Court found the censoring of newspapers to be within the rational judgment of the prison authorities.

341. *Denial of Bail on Prosecutor's Appeal 2011 case,* Case No. 2011 (Shi) No. 376, Keishu Vol. 65, No. 7 (P.B., Oct. 5, 2011), http://www.courts.go.jp/english/judgments/text/2011.10.05-2011.-Shi-.No..376.html; *Denial of Bail on Prosecutor's Appeal* case, Case No. 2000 (shi) No. 94, http://www.courts.go.jp/english/judgments/text/2000.06.27-2000.-Shi-.No..94.html (P.B. 27 June 2000).

342. *Deference to be given to Mixed Panel's findings case,* Case No. 2011 (A) No. 757, Keishu Vol. 66, No. 2 (P.B., Feb. 13, 2012), http://www.courts.go.jp/english/judgments/text/2012.02.13-2011.-A-.No..757.html; Mainichi Daily News, Feb. 14, 2012, Top court urges high court to

bail during this stage would deter investigation and interrogation.[343] (2) Because of the nature of Japanese trials, a defendant denied bail may be held in custody for several years while the trial is in progress. Considering the leniency granted to confessed convicted defendants, an innocent defendant might wish to either shorten the time of trial (and thus the period of incarceration) or obtain bail by confessing and getting the case over with.

[6] Speedy Trial

Article 37(1) of the Constitution provides accused persons the right to a "speedy and public trial" (the exact words used in the United States Constitution). In the United States the "speedy trial clock" begins to run as soon as the defendant is indicted. Prior to indictment the applicable time limit is set by the statute of limitations, if any. There are, of course, exceptions to speedy trial, such as flight by the defendant or agreement for extension of time by the defendant or defendant's counsel.[344] In the United States the speedy trial obligation is generally applied as written[345] and there is a Speedy Trial Act[346] that carries forward the Constitutional grant by requiring as a general matter that a defendant be tried within 70 days of public indictment or information charging a crime or appearance before a judge or magistrate, whichever is later.[347]

In Japan where trials are not continuous affairs but rather where there can be long periods of delay between trial sessions, speedy trial is, by necessity, interpreted differently—although for crimes subject to the mixed panel trial (saiban'in) the rationale for different treatment is missing. In *Park* et al. *v. Japan*,[348] trial was begun under defendant's indictment but then put on hold for a period of 15 years. Defendant moved to have the indictment dismissed arguing that his right to a speedy trial had been denied. The District Court dismissed the indictment, finding that the delay in trial exceeded the statute of limitations for the crime. The High Court reversed but the Supreme Court affirmed the dismissal. As a rule, courts in Japan do not dismiss cases for failure to provide a speedy trial notwithstanding that some cases may take well over a decade to try.

---

respect citizens' viewpoints, scraps acquittal overturn, http://mdn.mainichi.jp/perspectives/news/20120214p2a00m0na020000c.html.

343. See, Tsuyoshi Kinoshita, *Legal System and Legal Culture in Japanese Law*, 44 Comp. L. Rev. 25, 107 (2010) noting that the purpose of the 20+ day detention period was originally to enable the authorities to question the subject and hence bail would defeat the purpose.
344. *Doggett v. United States*, 505 U.S. 647 (1992); *Vermont v. Brillon*, 556 U.S. 81 (2009).
345. *Barker v. Wingo*, 407 U.S. 514 (1972); *Zedner v. United States*, 547 U.S. 489, 126 S. Ct. 1976 (2006).
346. 18 U.S.C. sections 3161 et seq.
347. The statute has tolling provisions that can extend the time, such as pretrial motions that must be decided within a certain period, etc. *United States v. Tinklenberg*, 563 U.S. ___ (2011); *Henderson v. United States*, 476 U.S. 321 (1986).
348. *Speedy Trial case, Park* et al. *v. Japan*, Case No. 1970 (A) No. 1700 26 Keishu 631, http://www.courts.go.jp/english/judgments/text/1972.12.20-1970.-A-.No..1700.html (G.B., Dec. 20, 1972).

[7] Double Jeopardy Prohibited

Article 39 of the Japanese Constitution provides that a person acquitted of a crime cannot be later held criminally responsible for the same act. The Article specifically grants a right against double jeopardy.

In the United States, a prosecutor may not appeal from a jury determination that the defendant is not guilty. When the jury has found the defendant guilty and on appeal the conviction is reversed or where the jury cannot agree on a verdict the state may prosecute again as the appeal is considered a waiver and no double jeopardy problem arises.[349] If a defendant refuses to comply with his obligations under a plea agreement (such as the obligation to testify against another person) the prosecution may vitiate the agreement and try the defendant notwithstanding sentencing under the plea agreement has already taken place.[350]

In Japan the meaning of double jeopardy is different from that of the United States in a critical way—a prosecutor unhappy with a decision or sentence of the lower court may appeal to a higher court as Japan follows the European rather than the Anglo-American double jeopardy concept.[351] This reading of the Constitution is consistent with the intent of the American drafters.[352]

A person found guilty of a crime by a foreign court may be punished in Japan for the same crime, although the penalty should be modified or even forgiven to take into account the foreign judgment and sentence.[353]

Appeal by the prosecutor should provide due process to the defendant, but what you see may not be what you get. In 2012 the Supreme Court acknowledged that the Code of Criminal Procedure requires that the charges against the defendant state the basis for the charge. In an arson case the basis was stated as releasing gas from the stove and then pressed down the ignition. There was no evidence of the defendant causing the fire in the manner charged. Defendant was convicted of starting the fire by "a certain means" although the charge basis had not been amended. The Supreme Court affirmed the conviction finding that it would not have mattered to the defense. As the dissenting judge noted it might well have changed the basis for the defense, took

349. *United States v. Perez*, 9 Wheat. 579 (1824); *Green v. United States*, 355 U.S. 184 (1957); *Renico v. Lett*, 559 U.S. ___ (2010) See also, *Arizona v. Washington*, 434 U.S. 497 (1978); *Richardson v. United States*, 468 U.S. 317 (1984). If the defense is responsible for a mistrial then retrial is probably not double jeopardy, *United States v. Dinitz*, 424 U.S. 600 (1976). If the mistrial is caused by the prosecution's actions the defendant is more likely to succeed on a double jeopardy motion—especially if the defense can show that the prosecutor intended to create a mistrial—but the cases are confusing. Compare e.g., *Oregon v. Kennedy*, 456 U.S. 667 (1982) with *Downum v. United States*, 372 U.S. 734 (1963). The American federal trial requirement of a unanimous verdict for either conviction or acquittal while not unique is the exception to the general rule followed by countries that have adopted some form of lay participation in reaching a criminal law judgment. Ethan J. Leib, *A Comparison of Criminal Jury Decision Rules in Democratic Countries*, 5 Ohio St. J. Crim. L 630 (2008).

350. *Ricketts v. Adamson*, 483 U.S. 1 (1987).

351. *Double Jeopardy case*, 4 Keishu 1805 (Sup. Ct. G.B., 27 September 1950) for an English language translation see John M. Maki, *Court and Constitution In Japan* 219 (University of Washington Press 1964).

352. Alfred C. Oppler, *Legal Reform in Occupied Japan* 144 (Princeton University Press 1976).

353. Penal Code Article 5.

the defense by surprise and significantly mattered. What you see a requirement for charging facts and Code provision for a mechanism of making needed amendments—is not what you get. Amendment need not be made as long as the court is convinced the defendant is guilty.[354]

[E] Reform Proposals and Action Taken on Proposals

The Judicial Reform Council has made a number of recommendations concerning the criminal justice system many of which, but especially the use of lay persons in deciding cases, have been adopted. Noticeably absent was any recommendation for adopting a full interrogation recording system. Other matters not resolved in the Council Report were issues relating to the confinement of suspects in police jails (the substitute prison system), whether bail should be permitted pre-indictment, the rules under which counsel can meet with suspects, and whether the rules for post-indictment bail should be changed.

The substitute prison system (known as *Daiyo Kangoku)* has been criticized by the international community and the JFBA for failure to provide an effective protection for suspects. In an effort to deflect criticism the Japanese government enacted legislation in 2005 under which the word *Kangoku* was no longer used to describe Japanese prisons. Instead a new term was used so that prisons have now become "penal institutions." As a consequence the institution known as the *Daiyo Kangoku* or substitute prison has been abolished. In its place there is a new institution namely the substitute penal institution and no substantive change has been effected.[355] The actual situation, namely a suspect held in police holding cells for purposes of 23 days of interrogation has not changed. What you see may not be what you get.

The most significant change brought about by the Council's report is the Saiban'in system under which certain serious crimes are tried to panel of six lay persons and three judges (when only penalty is involved to a smaller Panel) that has had surprising and unanticipated positive effects (although the effect on defendants tried before the system has not changed from the Judge only system, i.e., 99+% conviction rate). These include the greater production of exculpatory evidence by the prosecutor leading to reversals of previous convictions, a tightening of the prosecutor's burden of proof in circumstantial evidence cases tried to a saiban'in panel and raising questions about the current interrogation without recording system. Lay judges have recommended changes in criminal procedure concerning exculpatory evidence and interrogation recording and have recommended adding other crimes to Saiban'in procedures. Even greater production of evidence in all criminal cases (not simply

354. *Amendment of Charging Document as Provided by the Code of Criminal Procedure not Required Case*, Case Number 2011 (A) No. 775, Keishu Vol. 66, No. 2, (Sup. Ct. 2nd Petty Bench, Feb. 29, 2012). http://www.courts.go.jp/english/judgments/text/2012.02.29-2011.-A-.No..775.html.

355. http://64.233.169.104/search?q=cache:e4or9q3yW2gJ:www.ohchr.org/english/bodies/cat/docs/ngos/JFBA containing the report of the Japan Federation of Bar Associations commenting on the government's fifth period report paragraphs 107 and 108.

Saiban'in cases) is to be anticipated and under easier procedural requirements while full recording of interrogations is likely to be in Japan's future.

One aspect of Judicial Reform that the American legal system would be wise to examine in light of the Japanese experience is effect of confession and repentance on rehabilitation. The Japanese experience indicates that repentance associated with keeping the offender out of prison has a positive effect on both the offender and the society. It is a matter worthy of study and experimentation in the United States.

CHAPTER 17

Administrative Law

§17.01 UNITED STATES

The United States Constitution makes no mention of administrative agencies. All Executive power is given to the president. However, it was clear, even as early as the late eighteenth century, that the president could not manage the Executive Branch on his own. President Washington appointed cabinet members to assist him and the Departments of Government, the first administrative agencies, were created. These agencies were a part of the Executive Branch and they were supervised and run by Executive Branch officials who were responsible to the president.

As the government's responsibilities grew, a new form of administrative agency was created. This form of agency was headed not by a cabinet officer but by a collegial body representing the two major political parties. The first such agency was the Interstate Commerce Commission created to deal with issues arising out of expansion of the railroad monopolies across the country. Government regulation was considered necessary to control the power of the monopoly. As railroad competitors, airlines and trucks operating over the interstate highway system advanced the ICC was abolished.

Other "independent agencies" followed on the heels of the ICC. Referred to sometimes as "alphabet agencies" because they tend to be referred to by their initials, such agencies included the CAB, SEC, FCC, CPSC, etc. Typically agencies were given either of two authorities: (a) to deal with a specific industry e.g., FCC to deal with communications, or (b) to deal with a specific problem that cuts across industry lines (e.g., CPSC—dealing with consumer product safety issues whether involving the toy industry or electronics, etc.). More recent agencies appear to fall into the second category. An agency might be created within a cabinet department and under the supervision of a cabinet secretary (i.e., OSHA is under the Department of Labor). There have even been agencies created that are neither collegial in character, nor under the control of a cabinet secretary (i.e., the EPA).

Administrative agencies are created by legislation. The law that creates an administrative agency will specifically delegate the areas of responsibility and authority that the agency is given. Agencies have no authority other than that given to them in the authorizing statute or later statutes that grant additional authority. Only the Executive (president) can appoint agency members—although such appointments may require the advice and consent of the Senate.[1] The Congress (including the Senate) has no power to remove an agency member or head except through the impeachment power.[2] Nor is the president's power to remove an official appointed with advice and consent subject to advice and consent on removal.[3] Members of collegial "independent agencies" may be removable only for cause if the Congress so states in the authorizing legislation.[4] In such case, there may be restrictions on the president's power to remove.[5]

Because "independent agencies" are nowhere mentioned in the Constitution, questions have arisen as to the Constitutionality of the agency system. The Constitutional doctrine that has arisen to validate the system is the "delegation" doctrine.[6] The Congress and the president, through legislation, can delegate to the agency certain authority provided the delegation is cabined by sufficiently specific standards that the Congressional will is clear and the basic policy choices have been made in the legislation. The agency lacks authority to act outside the delegated authority given to it. Modern cases have broadly interpreted the standards requirement and some judges have raised questions about whether Congress may be delegating too broad an authority to some agencies.[7]

An agency may be granted, within its delegated authority, the power to make rules and regulations, which once promulgated have the effect of law. Similarly an agency may be delegated the power to decide specific cases that may arise under its authority. The rule-making authority resembles "legislative power" and the decision making power resembles "judicial" power. To avoid Constitutional issues these powers are referred to as "quasi-legislative" and "quasi-judicial." Quasi-judicial decisions cannot be final and binding. Because of the Constitutional requirement that all judicial power is in the court system quasi-judicial agency decisions are subject to judicial review.

The statute that authorizes the agency may establish the procedures under which the agency must operate. Where the authorizing statute fails to establish procedures or establishes only partial procedures, The Administrative Procedures Act is a "fall back"

1. *Buckley v. Valeo*, 424 U.S. 1 (1976).
2. *Bowsher v. Synar*, 478 U.S. 714 (1986).
3. *Myers v. United States*, 272 U.S. 52 (1926).
4. While Congress may not appoint Executive Department or Agency officers, the Congress and President through legislation may give the Judicial Branch the power to appoint an Independent Counsel, *Morrison v. Olsen*, 487 U.S. 654 (1988).
5. See *Humphrey's Executor v. United States*, 299 U.S. 602 (1935); *Wiener v. United States*, 357 U.S. 349 (1958).
6. See e.g., *Yakus v. United States*, 321 U.S. 414 (1944); *Chevron, USA v. Natural Resources Council, Inc.*, 467 U.S. 837 (1984).
7. See, e.g., *Industrial Union Dep't. v. American Petroleum Institute*, 448 U.S. 607, 686 (Rehnquist J., dissenting).

statute and fills in the procedural blanks. Traditionally agency procedures fell into two broad categories depending on the type of power the agency was proposing to utilize. For "adjudications" (typically a determination affecting a specific individual or entity) made on the basis of a record, the agency must follow "formal adjudication" procedures.[8] The end result of adjudication is the promulgation of an order affecting the parties to the adjudication. These procedures resemble the procedures used in a court case, including the adversary system, an independent judicial type officer to take testimony and make an initial decision (an Administrative Law Judge, (ALJ)) and ex parte rules to prohibit one side from discussing the case with the decision-maker. An ALJ recommendation is subject to review by the collegial agency heads that compose the juristic body, the agency. A dissatisfied party can appeal to the Court of Appeals. The standard for review is a "substantial evidence" test.[9]

For rule making (a rule is a general statement of policy that affects the public or segments of the public in general and is then applied to individuals, entities, or circumstances) the typical procedure is "notice and comment" also known as "informal rulemaking."[10] [For certain limited categories of cases an agency may be required to follow "formal rule-making procedures" that are similar to formal adjudication procedures.] Notice and comment requires the agency to publish proposed rules (or regulations) and give the public an opportunity to comment. After taking into account the public's comments, the agency can then publish a final rule. The agency must explain its decision making process in making the final rule and publish its reasons for rejecting certain arguments against the rule, etc. Virtually all rule-making determinations are subject to judicial review in a Court of Appeals. The standard for review is whether the agency determination was "arbitrary, capricious or unreasonable." When acting within its delegated authority the agency has broad discretion to make policy decisions but the court may take a "hard look" at the facts and the decision to determine whether the decision is arbitrary.[11] Failure to follow appropriate procedures, failure to act within delegated authority, failure to explain a determination, failure to make a rational decision that is supported by logical analysis of the facts are all reasons why rule-making determinations may be found to be arbitrary, although review is deferential to the agency.[12] The same standard of review applies whether agency action is the initial rule making or a change in an existing rule.[13]

When Congress has specifically or by implication delegated to the agency the determination of an issue and the agency does so, its discretionary choice is entitled to great deference and the court is not permitted to substitute its own view for that of the

8. The APA does not cover informal adjudications, such as a park policeman's determination to give a motorist a warning rather than a traffic citation.
9. For a discussion of the Substantial Evidence Test see *Universal Camera Corp. v. NLRB*, 340 U.S. 474 (1951).
10. Compare *Londoner v. Denver*, 210 U.S. 373 (1908) with *Bi-Metallic Investment Co. v. State Board of Equalization*, 239 U.S. 441 (1915) for the distinction between rule making and adjudication.
11. *Motor Vehicle Manufacturers Association v. State Farm Mutual*, 403 U.S. 29 (1983).
12. *National Association of Home Builders v. Defenders of Wildlife*, No. 06–340 (25 June 2007), 551 U.S. 644 (2007).
13. *FCC v. Fox Television*, 556 U.S. ___ (2009).

agency. As long as the agency's interpretation is reasonable the court must abide by that interpretation.[14] It is not uncommon for statutes to leave regulatory gaps and it is then the function of the agency to fill those gaps through regulations that are entitled to be treated with the force and effect of law.[15] Where an agency properly regulates, violation of the regulation is the equivalent of violating the substantive statute under which the regulation is issued.[16]

When an agency issues a "policy statement" as distinguished from following notice and comment and issuing a rule, such "informal rule" is entitled to very little deference. On the other hand, when the court is confronted with a dispute as to the meaning of an agency's regulation, the agency's interpretation of its own regulation is entitled to deference.[17]

Sometimes Congress will subject the fact-finding determinations of an agency in a rule-making proceeding to a substantial evidence test. In such a case, the agency must grant parties additional procedural rights dealing with a fact-finding hearing. Such procedures are called "hybrid rule-making" because they are a mix of notice and comment procedures and more formal adjudicatory type procedures dealing with the facts that are subject to the substantial evidence standard.[18] More recently Congress has allowed agencies to follow a negotiated regulation procedure (reg-neg) in certain rule-making contexts. Under this procedure the parties and the agency will attempt to negotiate a rule that all feel should be applied to the situation under review. The theoretical basis of reg-neg is to bring the parties that have interests in the rule making into the process before the agency sets forth its proposal and thus sets out a "target" for interest groups to attack in an adversarial context. By bringing the affected industry and consumer and opposing interests into a negotiation with the agency it is hoped that the parties can arrive at a regulatory regime that meets both the requirements of the agency as the proxy for the public interest and that the parties are prepared to follow without judicial challenge and hostility. This kind of collaborative governance is praised by some as less confrontational and more likely to result in effective regulation and conformance with the regulatory regime, while attacked by others as a sell out by the regulators to the regulated industry interests. While around for more than 20 years, the dispute concerning reg-neg continues and there is not much in the way of empirical evidence to prove whether it advances regulatory regimes.[19]

14. *Chevron, USA v. Natural Resources Council, Inc.* 467 U.S. 837 (1984); *National Cable & Telecommunications Association v. Brand X*, 545 U.S. 967 (2005); *National Cable & Telecom v. Gulf Power*, 534 U.S. 327 (2002); *Barnhart v. Walton*, 535 U.S.212 (2002).
15. *Entergy Corp. v. Riverkeeper, Inc.*, 556 U.S. ___ (2009); *Long Island Care at Home LTD. v. Coke*, 551 U.S. 158 (2007).
16. *Global Crossings Telecommunications Inc. v. Metrophones Telecommunications Inc.*, 550 U.S. 45 (2007).
17. *Talk America, Inc. v. Michigan Bell Telephone Co.*, 564 U.S. ___ (2011); *Chase Bank USA, N. A. v. McCoy*, 562 U.S. (2011).
18. When Congress has not mandated procedures, the APA procedures are to be used and the courts have no authority to require more than the APA requires. *Vermont Yankee Nuclear Power Corp., v. NRDC*, 435 U.S. 519 (1978).
19. See Remarks by Professor Jody Freeman to *Japanese American Society*, 83 Wash. U. L. Q. 1859 (2005).

Review of adjudications and rule making is in a Court of Appeals because the factual record in each circumstance is made in the agency and there is no need for a District Court proceeding. Administrative cases are handled like any other case there are no special panels to hear such cases and judges are selected by lottery amongst all the active judges of the court. United States courts may even review an agency's failure to regulate when required by law to do so.[20]

Administrative agencies (including cabinet departments) are subject to the Freedom of Information Act (FOIA) pursuant to which the public is entitled to obtain access to records of the agency unless the records fall within certain narrow exceptions set out in the rules. Agencies must act quickly to resolve FOIA requests and failure to make production is subject to judicial review. There is also a Privacy Act[21] that, subject to certain statutory exceptions, protects from disclosure private information in the possession of the government that is identifiable with individuals. The law permits persons to request copies of their own private records and to request amendments to correct such records. Adversely affected parties may sue the government agency. More general privacy laws apply to the private sector, including the Fair Credit Reporting Act that requires companies to inform consumers when an adverse action is taken based on information in the person's credit report. The purpose of the law is to allow for consumers to demand corrections of inaccurate information in the reports.[22] Under certain conditions persons adversely affected by the failure of companies to comply with the law may sue.[23]

The distinguishing characteristics of administrative agency law in the United States are:

- The agency has only such authority as is delegated to it by legislation;
- Rulemaking and adjudication are governed by procedures that provide for party access and that result in the making of 'agency law';
- There is no secret agency law and all such law must be available to the public;
- Virtually all agency determinations are subject to judicial review (in certain limited circumstances, such as when there is no law to apply, or in limited situations where Congress specifically provides that administrative action is not subject to review, there may be no avenue to seek judicial review).

§17.02 JAPAN

The Meiji Constitution placed power in the hands of the Emperor. It also provided for a Cabinet. The administrative organs of government operated under the Cabinet and the Cabinet and Diet could create other agencies. The new government structure required a trained civil service. One of the first orders of business was to create a prestigious bureaucracy, which quickly became a powerful part of the government.[24]

20. *Massachusetts v. EPA*,549 U.S. 497 (2007).
21. 5 U.S.C. 552 (a).
22. 15 U.S.C. 1681m(a).
23. See *Safeco Insurance Co. v. Burr*, 551 U.S. 47 (2007).
24. John M. Maki, *The Japanese Constitutional style in* Dan Fenno Henderson, *The Constitution of Japan, The First Twenty Years 1947–1967* (University of Washington Press, 1969); 22.

Following the European tradition, Japan had a separate Administrative Court located in the administrative branch of government that was not a judicial body.[25] The regular judiciary was denied the power to interfere with governmental or administrative actions. The Administrative Court was subservient to the executive so that it could not unduly disrupt government plans and operations. The Occupation abolished the Administrative Court and placed administrative litigation in the hands of the regular court system.[26] This was one of the few Constitutional changes recommended by the Matsumoto draft of the amended Meiji Constitution.

The Occupation created a number of regulatory agencies similar in function to American agencies and relied on a purged Japanese bureaucracy to manage the affairs of government. Pre-war and wartime bureaucrats became an important power in the governmental structure and their power continued after Occupation.[27] Many bureaucrats entered government in political positions after retiring from the bureaucracy and Japan has had several postwar prime and other ministers who were previously bureaucrats. Many Japanese bureaucrats "descend from heaven" upon retirement and join private or public companies. Thus the relation between the bureaucracy and industry is close. (The process of "descending" is under attack, but continues in part because bureaucrats, like private sector employees, are subject to relatively young mandatory retirement policies and a career "lifetime employment" system making their ability to find places in the private sector difficult unless they are allowed to "descend.")[28]

Because of the political system's reliance on the bureaucracy in many areas, Japan's bureaucracy holds a higher position of power vis-à-vis the elected officials than is the case in the United States. As a consequence of the Fukushima nuclear disaster the bureaucracy has suffered a loss of public confidence as the public has become aware of the shortcomings of METI and its subsidiary agency NISA to assure nuclear safety.

There has been a drive for regulatory reform in Japan with emphasis on reducing the power of the bureaucracy, increasing the transparency of government actions and subjecting government determinations to judicial review. The Judicial Reform Council recommended changes to make judicial review more easily obtainable and the role of the court more relevant. Some legislative changes were made designed to liberalize the confining rules governing standing that served to prevent most administrative law cases from being considered by the judicial system. A privacy law [Personal Information Protection Act][29] has been passed (but the law has little effect on government

25. This followed the French model for administrative adjudication. While in France this has generally resulted in a body of administrative doctrine that checks abuse of power by the bureaucracy, the same could not be said of pre-war Japan.
26. Alfred C. Oppler, *Legal Reform in Occupied Japan* 134 (Princeton University Press 1976). Oppler overstates the case when he refers to Japan as a police state during the war. It is true that there were severe restrictions on civil liberties but Japan never reached the totalitarian state level of fascist Italy or Germany.
27. John W. Dower, *Embracing Defeat* 212–213 (W.W. Norton & Co. 1999); James L. McClain, *A Modern History of Japan* 535 (W.W. Norton & Co. 2002).
28. Gregory W. Noble, *Koizumi and the Neo-liberal Economic Reform*, Soc. Sci. Japan 6–9 (March 2006).
29. Law No. 57 of 2003.

records), a national FOIA [Law Concerning Access to Information Held by Administrative Organs][30] was adopted after a wave of local Freedom of Information Ordinances were put in place at the prefecture and local levels, and an Administrative Procedure Law has been adopted.

Most senior bureaucracy officials and most judges are graduates of the prestigious Tokyo University and many are from that University's faculty of law.

§17.03 WHAT YOU SEE MAY NOT BE WHAT YOU GET

[A] Kokoku Suits to Review Administrative Action

The Administrative Case Litigation Law [ACLL], on its face, provides a comprehensive mechanism for reviewing actions of administrative agencies. A significant number of administrative cases are dismissed at an early stage for lack of standing or mootness grounds, and few plaintiffs are successful at the District Court level. Because the High Court rules in favor of agencies more frequently than in favor of plaintiffs fewer cases survive appeal.[31]

It is questionable whether the changes in administrative law and procedures that the Occupation made were as sweeping as the Occupation thought. Others have referred to the slogan, "although the Constitution has changed, administrative law continues" as showing that the pre-war, German legal theory approach to Administrative Law remains a constant in modern Japan.[32] This remains the case notwithstanding the reforms recommended by the Judicial Reform Council and the legislation adopted since the Council's report—although as disclosed later herein the rules regarding standing and what decisions are subject to review are loosening.

Administrative cases are now brought in the one court system but separate panels of judges handle administrative cases under the overarching authority of the Supreme Court. Administrative cases are not treated, either procedurally or substantively like ordinary civil suits. Thus, the shorter statute of limitations in administrative law cases, (six months) the circumstance decision, the high hurdles that must be navigated to obtain "suspension" (similar to prohibitory injunction) rather than reliance on the same terms as an ordinary civil suit, the prime minister's ability to set aside a temporary suspension, etc. are all designed to prevent the judiciary from interfering with the administrative process.[33] Among the major problems a plaintiff confronts

---

30. Law No. 42 of 1999.
31. Hiroyuki Hata & Go Nakagawa & Takehisa Nakagawa, *Japan Constitutional Law* 164–165 (Kluwer Law International 2001).
32. See Hiroya Endo, *Administrative Law Theory During the Thirty Years After the War: A Reappraisal* (Lawrence Repeta trans.), 14 L. Japan 82,102 (1981). [Endo suggests that the response to the slogan is that matters are seen through German law theories even when Anglo-American legal concepts are studied.]
33. *Osaka Airport Noise* case, *Minister of Transportation v. Ueda*, 35 Minshu 1369, Case No. 1976 (O) No.395, http://www.courts.go.jp/english/judgments/text/1981.12.16-1976-O-No.395.html (G.B. Dec. 16, 1981).

when bringing a kokoku suit is that most administrative action is not subject to judicial review.

Two problems with jurisdiction are presented under the ACLL—(i) the question of standing and (ii) courts when they take jurisdiction are influenced by pre-war distinctions between administrative dispositions and other administrative actions.

The primary lawsuit permitted by the ACLL for review of administrative action is the "kokoku" suit. Kokoku suits may be brought to overturn administrative action or to declare an administrative disposition invalid or illegal.[34] Such a suit must be filed under the ACLL and cannot be filed under the ordinary civil procedure rules. A kokoku suit directly challenges the exercise of government power and seeks to have a change made in how the government power is or is not exercised.

[1] Standing

To bring a case under the ACLL a plaintiff must have standing to sue. As in the United States standing has a Constitutional component because Japan's judiciary demands a case or controversy to proceed.[35]

Standing in the United States is more liberal than in Japan.[36] In the United States a plaintiff must have more than a generalized interest as a taxpayer or an interest common to all members of the public. But, when a plaintiff can show a particularized injury in fact along with causation and that the injury can be redressed by judicial decision standing is established.[37] When seeking injunctive relief, a plaintiff must demonstrate a threat of "injury in fact" that is both concrete and particularized as well as actual and imminent as distinguished from conjectural or hypothetical. The plaintiff must show that the threatened action of the defendant if enjoined will in all likelihood prevent or at least redress the injury. These requirements assure that "there is a real need to exercise the power of judicial review in order to protect the interests of the complaining party …."[38]

A plaintiff in an ACLL suit must have a "legal interest" as distinguished from a "reflex interest" that is damaged. Injury in fact is not sufficient. The requirement for a

34. Hiroyuki Hata & Go Nakagawa & Takehisa Nakagawa, *Japan Constitutional Law* 161 (Kluwer Law International 2001). There are other categories of cases where administrative action may be involved, such as a suit between parties where an administrative determination may be at issue. But for challenges of governmental action the kokoku suit is the principal mechanism for challenge.
35. *National Police Reserve case*, 6 Minshu 783, Case No. 1952 (Ma) No.23 (G.B. Oct. 8, 1952).
36. In *Massachusetts v. EPA*, 549 U.S. 497 (2007) Massachusetts had standing to challenge the failure of EPA to regulate greenhouse gases that cause global warming. Failure to regulate created a risk of harm to Massachusetts both in its position of property owner and its sovereign position as a State whose interests the EPA was required to take into account in light of the fact that the statute under which EPA operates took from Massachusetts certain authorities in the air pollution area. Although the Court did not require the EPA to take global warming into effect when regulating, it did require EPA, if it did not regulate concerning global warming to explain why.
37. *Lance v. Coffman*, 549 U.S. 437 (2007).
38. *Summers v. Earth Island Institute*, 555 U.S. ___ (2009); see also *Monsanto Co. v. Geertson Seed Farms*, 561 U.S. ___ (2010).

legal interest comes from the ACLL itself. Where an agency acts on a matter that is not specifically related to the plaintiff but affects the public in general, the fact that the plaintiff may have suffered an injury as a consequence does not give the plaintiff a legal interest. The injury in such a situation is as a consequence of a "reflex action." The agency's action must adversely deal with a legal interest possessed by plaintiff. Like the doctrine of *shobunsai* discussed *infra*, the *legal interest v. reflex interest* serves to push back the time when a party can sue to challenge administrative action and thus serves to impede the ability of parties to obtain a judicial reversal of administrative action. In the *Sakamoto* case,[39] the plaintiffs challenged a land use plan that could adversely affect the plaintiff. However, until the plan was put into effect, the plaintiff merely had a reflex interest and not a legal interest injured. Plaintiff lacked standing until action under the plan was taken. The timing of judicial review was a matter of legislative discretion so failure to provide review at an early stage was not a violation of the Constitution. Only when the administrative action had a direct effect on a legal interest of the plaintiff was a suit challenging the action permitted.

The *Bathhouse* case,[40] serves to highlight the difference between a legal and a reflex interest. The licensing requirements for bathhouses required that bathhouses not be closer than 250 meters from each other. The stated purpose of the distance requirement was to protect health of bathhouse users since too many bathhouses in a small area were thought to create potential health risks. A competing bathhouse owner challenged the grant of a license to a competitor. Because of the general public health purpose of the law, lower courts found the competitor's interest to be merely a reflex interest. The Supreme Court found otherwise. Because the licensing scheme was designed, in part, to protect competing bathhouse owners the legal interest of such competitors was injured and they had standing to sue. The legal interest of the bathhouse owner was adversely affected by the license to a competitor.

Similarly, in the *Hiroshima Pharmacy* case,[41] the party challenging the Hiroshima restriction on location of pharmacies had a legal interest affected because the license application filed by the plaintiff had been denied the agency acted on his personal legal interest. Competing pharmacies similarly would have legal interests. But a local resident, who objected to a new pharmacy or bathhouse because of concerns that the new business would create traffic congestion, would not have a legal interest. A consumer who wanted more pharmacies because additional competitors would drive down price similarly would have no legal interest at stake. A community resident who would be forced to drive miles out of his way if a railroad was constructed cutting off local streets has, in the absence of a statute or ordinance, no legal interest injured by

39. *Bathhouse* case II, *Sakamoto v. Governor of Tokyo Prefecture*, 20 Minshu 271 (G.B.. Feb. 23, 1966). For a partial English translation see Dan Fenno Henderson, 'The Constitution of Japan Its First 20 Years,' Ichiro Ogawa, *Judicial Review of Administrative Actions in Japan* 197.
40. *Bathhouse Case*, *Sakamoto v. Japan*, 16 Minshu 57 (Sup. Ct. 19 January 1962). For a partial English translation see Hideo Tanaka (assisted by Malcolm D.H. Smith), *The Japanese Legal System* 689 (University of Tokyo Press 1976).
41. *Hiroshima Pharmacy* case, *Suniyoshi, v. Governor*, 29 Minshu 572, Case No. 1968 (Gyo-Tsu) No. 120http://www.courts.go.jp/english/judgments/text/1975.04.30-1968-Gyo-Tsu-No.120.html (. G.B. Apr. 30, 1975).

the decision to construct or the construction itself notwithstanding the injury in fact inflicted by the decision.

Even an individual who can show actual personal injury cannot bring a kokoku suit under the ACLL unless the individual can show a nexus between the statutory authority of the agency and the *legal interest of the individual plaintiff.*[42] It is a very stringent test for standing. On the other hand, in Japan taxpayer suits are permitted when challenging public expenditures by local government. Thus, an Osaka taxpayer challenged an Osaka supplemental budget because it provided funds to carry out the Police Law, which he alleged had been passed unlawfully because the Diet had had no authority to extend its session to enable it to pass the law. The Supreme Court refused to consider whether the Diet could extend its session (this was a political question) but the Court reviewed the substantive provisions of the law to see if the law was unconstitutional.[43]

While lower courts in the 1970s began to loosen this standing requirement,[44] the Supreme Court in 1978 reaffirmed the stringent nature of the standing rule by holding that an interest protected by statute that was shared by all citizens—such as an interest in protecting the general welfare—was a reflex interest and thus could not provide standing to a consumer group that sought to challenge administrative action under the Fair Labeling Law.[45] In a case involving a challenge to Administrative Guidance[46] that permitted a shopping center to be built in competition with local merchants, those merchants were held not to have standing to sue under the Large-Scale Retail Store Law, even though that law was designed to protect local merchants. The reasoning was that the "guidance" did not have binding effect on the shopping center and thus could not have affected a legal interest of the merchants.[47] The standing doctrine has been a major impediment to kokoku suits.

In 2004 the Diet enacted several modifications as amendments to the ACLL. The most significant loosened the standing requirement. The background of the amendment may serve to help in understanding its reach. Although a party must, as discussed above, show an injury to a legal interest in order to have standing, the Japanese courts

42. Frank K. Upham, *The Legal Framework of Japan's Declining Industries Policy: The Problem of Transparency in Administrative Process*, 27 Harvard Intl. L. J. 425, 430–431 (1986).
43. *Extension of Diet Session* case, *Shimizu v. Governor of Osaka*, 16 Minshu 445 (G.B. Mar. 7, 1962). In addition, under the Local Autonomy Act, voters may request audits of allegedly improper expenditures by local government. If dissatisfied by the audit results, the voter may file a 'resident's suit' challenging the expenditure. For a discussion of resident's suit, see Hiroyuki Hata & Go Nakagawa & Takehisa Nakagawa, *Japan Constitutional Law* 91, 163 (Kluwer Law International 2001).
44. See cases cited and discussed in Hideo Tanaka (assisted by Malcolm D.H. Smith), *The Japanese Legal System* 691–692 (University of Tokyo Press 1976).
45. The *Juice* case, 880 Hanrei Jiho 3 (Mar. 14, 1978). For a discussion of the Juice case see Frank K. Upham, *After Minamata: Current Prospects and Problems in Japanese Environmental Litigation*, 8 Ecology L. Q. 213, 243 (1979).
46. The concept of Administrative Guidance is discussed *infra* in this section 17.03[B].
47. Frank K. Upham, *Privatizing Regulation: The Implementation of the Large-Scale Retail Stores Law, in Political Dynamics in Contemporary Japan* (Gary D. Allinson & Yasunori Sone ed., Cornell University Press 1993) reprinted in part in Yukio Yanagida, Daniel H. Foote, Edward Stokes Johnson, Jr., J. Mark Ramseyer & Hugh T. Scogin, Jr., *Law And Investment In Japan* 129–133 (Harvard University Press 1994).

recognized that in some unusual cases there were parties without a legal interest who had such a strong interest in the matter that they should be protected. If a nuclear power plant was being built in a community, members of the community had no legal interest that was being affected unless the plant would pollute their property or the government was taking private property they owned or effluent from the plant would injure the complaining resident's health. There were, of course, rules for obtaining building permits that were designed to assure that the plant was properly constructed and the power plant operator needed to comply with such permitting process. However, the building standards provisions did not give local residents a legal interest that would be adversely affected if the operator failed to build in accord with the permitting process. Yet it is clear that the danger to local residents was real and present and that the permitting requirements were designed, in part, to protect the life and safety of the local residents. In such an unusual and potentially catastrophic accident situation the legal interest rule was expanded to recognize an interest of the local residents.[48] And, the fact that the decision of the administrative body did not directly affect them that is they were not the subject of any *shobun*—could also be put aside in determining standing. The interest was said to arise from the purpose of the permitting rules/ordinances/laws combined with the potential catastrophic accident that would directly impact the local community and the decision on permitting could be considered to directly affect the residents because of their exposure to the danger. The rule was limited to potentially catastrophic accident situations. Taken together with this exceptional situation rule, was a 2001 decision of the Supreme Court that recognized standing on the part of a specific group when it was the intent of the legislation involved to protect that group rather than the public in general.[49]

The 2004 legislation modifies the standing rule by joining these two strands and making them a general rule for standing. Standing is permitted when there exists any law (including local ordinance) that is designed to protect the right of the party suing and that law is relevant to the administrative determination being reviewed. The party suing need not be a party to the administrative determination. Standing comes not from the permit process but from some other law, perhaps an environmental law or local ordinance, or even from the licensing law that has as its purpose protecting a person or entity not a party to the permitting process. The court is to look beyond the words of the licensing statute to its purpose and the purpose of other laws that may be related. Where the degree of potential injury is great the court should be more liberal than when the potential injury is small.

The *Odakyu Railroad* case is a case in point. The city of Tokyo approved the construction of an above ground railroad line that would cut across a section of Tokyo.

48. Supreme Court decision in *Monju I Nuclear Power Plant* case, Case No. 1989 (Gyo-Tsu) No.130,(P.B. Sept. 22, 1992), http://www.courts.go.jp/english/judgments/text/1992.9.22-1989-Gyo-Tsu-.No.130.html; Case No. 1989(Gyo-Tsu) No.131 http://www.courts.go.jp/english/judgments/text/1992.9.22-1989-Gyo-Tsu-.No.131.html (P.B. Sept. 22, 1992) finding standing for residents inside a 60 kilometer ring around the plant.

49. *Standing of Group Protected by Law Permitted*, Case No. 180 Gyo-tsu 1996, 55 Minshu 283, http://www.courts.go.jp/english/judgments/text/2001.03.13-1996.-Gyo-Tsu-.No.180.html (P.B. Mar. 13, 2001).

Group 1-Property owners along the line, whose property would be directly affected by the line sued to challenge the administrative determination to build the line above ground. Group 2-landowners near the line whose property would not be directly affected and whose health would not be directly affected but who were covered by a Tokyo City Ordinance dealing with planning sued challenging the line. Group 3—landowners near the line but not covered by the Tokyo Ordinance also sued. On appeal the determination of no standing was reversed in part. The Supreme Court held that Group 1, residents along the line had a legal interest and thus had standing to challenge the line's approved route. Group 2 residents who were not along the line also had standing because of various Tokyo City Ordinances that showed the planning process was designed to take into account the interests of neighboring residents. Thus while these residents were not parties to the planning and permitting process and had no specific property injured by the project, because they were the beneficiaries of ordinances that were related to the line they had standing to challenge the line. Although the language of the Court appears limited (and one Justice challenged such limiting language) the decision itself grants standing where none was allowed previously and may open up the standing doctrine as hoped for by the Law Reform Council.[50] Like the amendment to the ACLL[51] the Court looked beyond the licensing statute to other statutes or in this case City Ordinances—to find standing. On the other hand, Group 3 residents who were outside the zone affected by the city ordinance lacked standing notwithstanding the line would significantly affect their daily lives by blocking traffic routes previously used by them.

In a later case[52] the Grand Bench recognized that a project plan for a land readjustment project, while it does not itself take property or require that owners agree to a swap of property, makes it possible to predict how the project will affect individual land owners whose property is within the zone in which swaps will be required. Once a determination is made to adopt a land readjustment project plan there are immediate effects on land within the zone of the plan such that certain activities on such land cannot go forward. As a consequence, such owners are deemed to have a legal right affected by the plan and thus have standing and the plan itself can be considered an administrative disposition subject to review. To the argument that until the swap is actually required there has been no injury to the asserted legal right and no disposition the Supreme Court recognized the effect that the circumstance decision doctrine can have in making it impossible to sue after the event. Thus the Court held that standing existed when the Plan was adopted rather than when it was put into effect. This

50. *Odakyo Railroad* case, Case No. 114 (Gyo-Hi) of 2004, 59 Minshu No. 10 http://www.courts.go.jp/english/judgments/text/2006.11.02-2004.-Gyo-Hi-.No..114.html (P.B., Dec. 7, 2005). The opinion of concurring Justice Fujita would have gone further than the majority and extended standing based on a much broader basis.

51. Administrative Case Litigation Law Article 9 subpart 2.

52. *Standing Permitted to Contest Land Readjustment Plan Case*, Case No. 397 (Gyo-Hi) of 2005, Minshu Vol. 62, No. 8, (Grand Bench, Sept. 10, 2008). http://www.courts.go.jp/english/judgments/text/2008.09.10-2005.-Gyo-Hi-.No..397.html.

constitutes a significant opening of standing to a time when challenge to the administrative act may actually have an effect of preventing the act from moving forward. In this regard the intent of the Law Reform Council is furthered by the Court's decision.[53]

[2] Disposition or Shobun

If there is no "disposition" then there is no administrative action to be challenged. The doctrine of administrative disposition (*shobun*) has its roots in Japanese pre-war administrative court determinations.[54] Under this doctrine, which is statutorily provided for in the ACLL and the more recent Administrative Procedure Law (APL) a case must involve an exercise of public power and must dispose of a matter in a manner that creates, vitiates or enforces rights of a member of the public.[55] Because of this focus on individual right, the doctrine of *shobunsai* is closely related to standing.[56] The Administrative Guidance case discussed above shows a clear interrelation between *shobun* and standing because the guidance was not legally binding on the person to whom it was given it was not an administrative disposition and since it was not binding it could not have affected the legal rights of third persons and thus they had no standing. Even the party to whom the guidance was given would lack standing and there would be no disposition. Where an adverse disposition is consented to by the party affected, it is no longer considered an adverse disposition.[57]

The doctrine serves to make "internal" government directives free from legal challenge. An internal order or directive simply affects the agency (or agencies) involved and by itself does not create any rights in anyone outside the agency. It creates no rights and takes no rights from persons outside the government establishment.[58]

53. In its 2012 decision approving the saiban'in system (*Lay Judge System Constitutional Case, Case No. 2010 (A) No. 1299, Keishu Vol. 66, No. 1* (P.B., Jan. 13, 2012) Japan, http://www.courts.go.jp/english/judgments/text/2012.01.13-2010.-A-.No..1299.html) (see also, *Lay Judge System Constitutional Case*, Case No. 2010 (A) No. 1196, Keishu Vol. 65, No. 8 (Nov. 16, 2011), http://www.courts.go.jp/english/judgments/text/2011.11.16-2010.-A-.No..1196.html) the court entertained the convicted defendant's claim that the system was unconstitutional because it imposed involuntary servitude on the lay judges. While the Court could have simply noted that the appellant lacked standing to make the claim as she was not a lay judge and thus had no right being adversely affected by involuntary servitude, the Court nonetheless entertained the claim and rejected it.
54. Itsuo Sonobe, *Comparative Administrative Law: Trends and Features in Administrative Law Studies (Japan)*, 19 L. Japan 40, (1986) (Kevin Hansen trans., from 1 Gendai gyoseiho taikei, I. Ogawa, H. Shiono, I. Sonobe, eds. 121–146 (1983) Itsuo Sonobe, *Comparative Administrative Law: Trends and Features in Administrative Law Studies (Japan)*, 19 L. Japan 40, 45 (1986) (Kevin Hansen trans., from 1 Gendai gyoseiho taikei, I. Ogawa, H. Shiono, I. Sonobe eds., 121–146 (1983).
55. APL Article 2 (2)..
56. For a general discussion of how the doctrine of *shobunsai* has rendered kokoku suits unavailable in most situations see Robert W. Dziubla, *The Impotent Sword of Japanese Justice: The Doctrine of Shobunsei as a Barrier to Administrative Litigation*, 18 Cornell Intl. L. J. 37 (1985).
57. APL Article 2 (4).
58. When the Tokyo Board of Education issued a circular to school principals telling them what to do regarding disciplining teachers who refused to stand and sing or play the National Anthem on the piano, suit under the ACLL to challenge the circular was not permitted as this was no

Until action that takes rights, the internal communication is without "legal rights" affect and is not a disposition. This doctrine differs substantially from the American approach to administrative law, where a rule or regulation may be challenged as arbitrary, capricious and unreasonable when promulgated because it will have the force and effect of law when applied in individual cases. It is similar to American law in situations where the rule has no binding effect but is simply an informal internal communication that has no force and effect as law.

The doctrine serves to push back the time when an individual or group may challenge an administrative determination to the time when the agency actually acts on its determination or applies it to an individual. While conceptually this may be viewed as simply a time problem, in many cases it serves to shield administrative action from any meaningful review. This follows from the effect that time delay has under Japanese law.

First, once "action" is taken and a disposition has been made it is very difficult to get "injunctive relief" to stop action from moving forward. There is no general equity power in the courts in Japan and thus injunction must come from legislative sources. In the administrative area a court can issue the equivalent of a preliminary injunction—a temporary suspension of a disposition. The initiation of a kokoku suit does not automatically suspend the disposition; the plaintiff must apply for a temporary suspension that should not be granted if to do so would have an adverse effect on the public welfare. Although the Occupation sought, as a general rule, to have administrative cases handled the same as ordinary civil cases, the Occupation objected to a temporary injunction issued to prevent removal of an official purged by the Occupation until after a due process procedure. This led the Occupation to support enactment of a special law for administrative cases (which later became the 1962 "ACLL") which contained limits on injunctions in administrative cases. The rules for obtaining a temporary suspension in an administrative case are much more stringent than for a normal civil suit. A party seeking a temporary suspension must show urgent necessity to avoid irreparable injury as well as a basis on the merits for success.[59] Suspension will not be granted if to do so would threaten a serious adverse effect on the public. While sounding like the American rule that preliminary injunction will not be granted except where plaintiff can show reasonable likelihood of success on the merits and irreparable injury and that a balancing of the equities (taking into account the public interest) favors plaintiff, the Japanese rule is much more difficult for a plaintiff to meet.

shobun or disposition. Even the Official Orders issued pursuant to the Circular by school principals requiring teachers to stand and sing the Anthem were not dispositions as no action against teachers was taken until after the teachers violated the orders and thus the rights and obligations of teachers are not affected by the Orders. It is only when the disciplinary action is taken that there is a disposition that is subject to review. *Board of Education Circular to Principals not a Disposition*, 2011 (Gyo-Tsu) No. 177 and No. 178, and 2011 (Gyo-Hi) No. 182, Minshu Vol. 66, No. 2 (P.B., Feb. 9, 2012)., http://www.courts.go.jp/english/judgments/text/2012.02.09-2011.-Gyo-Tsu-.No..177.and.No..178%2C.and.2011.-Gyo-Hi-.No..182.html.

59. Article 25 of the ACLL. For an English language translation see Robert W. Dziubla, *The Impotent Sword of Japanese Justice: The Doctrine of Shobunsai as a Barrier to Administrative Litigation*, 18 Cornell Intl. L. J. 37 (1985).

In the *Board of Education Circular to Principals not a Disposition* case the teachers sought an injunction to prevent the taking of certain disciplinary actions based on the Official Orders issued by school principals based on the Board's Circular (the issuance of the circular was held not to involve a *shobun*). The Supreme Court held that under the liberalization of the injunction rules brought about by the 2004 amendment to the ACLL the party seeking an injunction must first show that there is a likelihood that a disposition adverse to that party will be issued. Those teachers subject to discipline other than dismissal were able to do this because such discipline had been meted out in the past (there has never been a case of dismissal for violation per the court decision). Next the teachers must show that serious damage is likely to be caused by the disposition. The Court held that to meet this requirement the teachers must show that the damage likely to occur through the disposition sought to be enjoined cannot be remedied by some other means (such as a suit to revoke the disposition together with a stay of execution of the disposition). The damage must be such that it cannot be remedied unless injunction prior to issuance is obtained. This is similar to but more difficult to show than the United States standard of showing "no adequate remedy at law" before an equitable remedy of injunction is permitted. The teachers met this test because past practice showed that serial disciplinary action had occurred in the past and was likely to occur in the future affecting large numbers of teachers. Actions after the event were thus not a viable remedy. Finally, the teachers needed to show a reasonable likelihood of success. This they were unable to do because of the series of Supreme Court decisions holding that it was Constitutional to require the teachers to stand and sing the Anthem at ceremonial school events. (See discussion in Chapter 7 Freedom of Expression §17.03[B].

Second, once an administrative action has been taken it may be too late to obtain effective relief. The "circumstance decision," in which the court decides the case against the government but, because the circumstances make reversal of the administrative action contrary to the public interest, is an example of the problem. Where reversal of the administrative action is harmful to the public interest, the court can hold the action unlawful and then withhold the remedy to prevent such harm leaving the "winning" plaintiff a monetary remedy the administrative action has taken place and remains in place. In effect, the failure to obtain a temporary suspension and the need to have a disposition can easily lead to the administrative action becoming a *fait accompli*.[60]

Because of the difficulty in getting injunctive relief under the ACLL some plaintiffs have tried to obtain injunctions against administrative action under the normal civil suit provisions of the Civil Procedure Code. The Supreme Court held that

60. United States law also raises issues of when an administrative action may be challenged. In *Sackett v. EPA*, 566 U.S. ___ (2012) the government argued that an EPA Administrative Compliance Order under the Clean Water Act was not subject to review by suit from the property owner but was only reviewable when the government sought to enforce the order by judicial action. The Court unanimously held that the Order had all the earmarks of final agency action as the homeowner was subject to fines immediately assuming the EPA eventually sought judicial enforcement. In essence the Court found that the order was what in Japanese would be referred to as a *shobun*.

such suits were not permitted when the effect of the suit was to review the action of the administrative body. In the *Osaka Airport* case the Ministry of Transportation both operated the airport as proprietor and regulated the airport as the airports regulator in Japan. The Airport's residential neighbors sued to enjoin certain operations, governed by regulations issued by the ministry, arguing that the operations caused the residents environmental damage. Plaintiffs framed their complaint as a case against the ministry as the operator of the airport and argued that it was a normal civil lawsuit to prevent the operator of a facility from causing damaging pollution that affected the lives and health of neighbors (who thus had standing as a legal interest was being adversely affected). The ministry argued that the suit challenged the rules under which the airport operated and the ministry set those rules in its regulatory capacity. The Court sided with the ministry and held that suit under the ACLL was the exclusive remedy and thus any injunction would have to comply with the ACLL's stringent standards.[61]

The 2004 amendment also addressed in small measure the question of delay in obtaining an administrative determination that might then be subjected to judicial review.[62] Under this provision a party seeking an administrative determination that has been pending without decision for an unreasonably long period of time (an undefined term) may seek an order requiring the agency to act. To obtain relief the applicant must show that the administrative arm abused its discretion by not taking action or that failure to act is itself the violation of some law.

Where an administrative body has denied an application, the aggrieved party may seek an order requiring the agency to determine the matter in the applicant's favor. The standard of review is abuse of discretion. But, the plaintiff must join its request for action granting the application with a request for a declaration that the administrative determination is erroneous—the only form of relief allowed prior to the 2004 amendment. This alternative relief gives the court authority to deny the plaintiff's request for an order directing the agency to grant the application and leave the applicant with a declaratory judgment. But declaratory relief does not necessarily mean that the agency will be required to grant the application—indeed, this was the problem that the 2004 amendment was supposed to cure and as originally drafted would have cured. The alternative relief requirement was a compromise made to allow (but not require) the court to order the agency to grant the application. What you see is not what you get.

The issue of delay and timing of litigation to seek a remedy is critical. Thus, while in the United States a suit seeking reapportionment may be filed as soon as a redistricting plan is filed, in Japan the suit must await a disposition the election itself. The election would affect rights—the plan would not. The *Nibutani dam* case discussed in Chapter 8 is another illustration of how the need for a disposition can result in failure to obtain relief to prevent administrative action. In that case there was no disposition until the plaintiffs' land was expropriated. At that time suit was brought

61. *Osaka Airport Noise* case, *Minister of Transportation v. Ueda*, 35 Minshu 1369, Case No. 1976 (O) No.395, http://www.courts.go.jp/english/judgments/text/1981.12.16-1976-O-No.395.html (G.B. Dec. 16, 1981).
62. Article 6.2.

but no temporary suspension of plans to build the dam was obtained. By the time the court ruled that the government expropriation was improper the dam had been built and it would be against public interest to remove the dam.

An administrative body seeking to shield itself from potential judicial oversight may frame what would be rules with binding effect in the United States as internal communications. When prosecutors used "general designations" served on counsel to prevent counsel from visiting its client at a police jail (Chapter 16) there was a disposition reviewable in-court as it affected the counsel's legal right to communicate with the client and affected the client's legal interest to meet with counsel. By simply changing the disposition notice to an internal memo to the jail authorities advising them not to allow the meeting until after the counsel had communicated with the prosecutor, the same objective was achieved but there was no "disposition" and thus no action that was judicially reviewable. To assure that prosecutorial determinations such as designating the time when counsel may meet with a client is not subjected to the new procedures required by the APL, the law specifically excepts from its coverage both dispositions as well as Administrative Guidance by public prosecutors and police personnel acting under criminal law and criminal procedural law statutes.[63] Where a prosecutor determines not to prosecute but the PRC twice determines that prosecution should be undertaken, the determination of the PRC is not subject to review under the ACLL but must be challenged in the criminal proceeding[64] (where it is unlikely to be set aside if the court finds the defendant committed the crime).

Even "external guidelines" i.e., government guidelines that set forth how an administrative body will handle permit applications, are not subject to challenge until the actual denial of a permit. The rationale is that until a permit is denied the guidelines have no legally binding effect—no legal interest of any party has been injured by the guidelines.[65]

More recently the Supreme Court of Japan has opened the window of what constitutes a disposition. When a Prefecture Governor who had authority to determine which hospitals would be eligible for payments under the national health system "suggested" that a certain hospital should not be built, the Court found such action to be a "determination" a "*shobun*" and hence subject to review. The hospital did not have to invest in the construction and then apply for recognition and when it was denied then bring suit. Rather, the so-called recommendation was of sufficiently binding character because of the authority of the governor that it constituted administrative action.[66]

63. APL Article 3 (1) (5) discussed *infra*.
64. *Prosecution Review Commission Challenge Case*, Case No. 2010 (Gyo-To) No. 63, 2010 (Gyo-Fu) No. 4, 64Minshu No. 8, http://www.courts.go.jp/english/judgments/text/2010.11.25-2010.-Gyo-To-.No..63%2C.2010.-Gyo-Fu-.No..4.html (P.B. Nov. 25, 2010).
65. The *Osaka Small Business Restraint* case, *Marushin Industries, Inc. v. Japan*, 26 Keishu 9 (Sup. Ct. G.B. Nov. 22, 1972) reported in Lawrence W. Beer & Hiroshi Itoh, *The Constitutional Case Law Of Japan, 1970 Through 1990* 183 (University of Washington Press 1996).
66. *Governor's 'Guidance' is actually a Shobun Case*, Case No. 2002 (Gyo-Hi) No. 207, 59 Minshu No. 6, http://www.courts.go.jp/english/judgments/text/2005.07.15-2002.-Gyo-Hi-.No..207.html (P.B., July 15, 2000).

So too, the Supreme Court recognized that the adoption of an ordinance by a local governing body was in the nature of legislative action and hence was, as a general matter, not a disposition. However, when the subject matter of the Ordinance was the closing of existing day care centers the Court found that the adverse effect of the Ordinance was basically focused on the children who attended the center and as such the ordinance was sufficiently similar to a disposition so that it could be considered a disposition and thus reviewed under the ACLL.[67]

The Grand Bench recently reversed a previous authority in holding that a resident could sue a local government body based on the body's acceptance of a plan for a land readjustment project. Previous authority had held that as the resident was not actually injured by the Plan's acceptance—injury would come when the resident's property was taken pursuant to the land readjustment project. The Supreme Court specifically recognized the effect that its prior decision had in inhibiting relief. The Court noted that for residents to have to wait would mean that when they sued the project would already have been started and even if the resident was successful the court would likely issue a "circumstance decision" thus effectively denying residents real judicial review. To protect the right of meaningful review, the Court held the acceptance of the Plan by the local government was a *shobun*—a disposition and hence was immediately subject to judicial review. Moreover (as discussed *supra*) this *shobun* affected legal rights even though no rights in the land had been taken yet. This is a significant departure from previous law. Whether it heralds making other actions that previously were not subject to immediate review reviewable at a time when judicial action can be effective remains to be seen.

As a separate opinion points out, the effect of the court's decision is to require that suit to challenge the Plan be filed within six months of the adoption of the Plan (the ACLL has a six month statute of limitations). Those who wait to file suit until after their property is actually subjected to readjustment may have lost their right to sue. In this sense, the separate opinion treats the Readjustment Plan much like an American court would treat rule making, i.e., suit must be brought when the rule is made not when it is applied, and the Plan once adopted and having passed judicial review will be binding in future actions challenging the Plan and/or its effect.

Justice Fujita filed a separate concurring opinion noting that a preliminary process prior to adoption of the Plan might be a good legislative solution for how to deal with a land readjustment plan. After the preliminary step there could be a disposition and an opportunity to file suit and get a court determination prior to action being taken that compels a circumstance decision even if the landowner wins. This suggests a process not dissimilar from Notice and Comment rulemaking in the United States with the Plan taking the place of an American Rule. As there is no such preliminary step

67. *Ordinance Closing Day Care Center is a Shobun Case*, Case Number 2009 (Gyo-Hi) No. 75, Minshu Vol. 63, No. 9, http://www.courts.go.jp/english/judgments/text/2009.11.26-2009.-Gyo-Hi-.No..75.html (P.B., Nov. 26, 2009).

provided for legislatively, Justice Fujita concurs that the Court's action making judicial review meaningful.[68]

The Supreme Court, in 2011, set aside an administrative disposition that had withdrawn the license of an architect. The Court held that the APL requires as a general matter that when a disposition is entered the reason for the disposition must be provided to the party who is a party to the disposition.[69] The agency relied on various potions of publicly available Tables as containing the basis for suspension of an architect's license. However the Tables were so complicated that unless the details of the reason for application of a specific Table item to the architect was made known it was impossible to know the basis for the administrative action. Of great importance was the Court's acknowledgment that the purpose of making reasons known is to assure that arbitrary action is not taken by the administrative agency. The Court recognized that the subject of the disposition has a right to know the basis for the administrative action so that it can appeal from the disposition.[70]

It is estimated that a combination of standing and lack of disposition had resulted in approximately 25% of all administrative cases being dismissed.[71] Whether the court's approach in the *Odakyu Railroad, Governor's Disposition, Land Readjustment Plan* and *Reasons for Disposition* cases will reduce this percentage is uncertain.

[3] Judicial Restraint: Substitutes for Administrative Review

The doctrine of "free discretion," a rule of judicial self-restraint under which courts defer to administrative action in the policy and technical arenas and the use of the doctrine of "mootness" to terminate litigation against the government, limit review of administrative action. Japanese substantive administrative law carries forward pre-war notions of distinctions between questions of law (subject to judicial scrutiny) and questions of discretion (not subject to scrutiny). Many issues that in the United States would be treated as subject to review are treated in Japan as belonging to the discretion of the agency and thus not subject to review.[72] The bureaucrats who will administer the statute also draft most statutes that grant agencies authority to act. By imprecise drafting the statutes leave significant room for consensual arrangements between the administrators and the administrated. Whether for these or other reasons, legislation

68. *Standing Permitted to Contest Land Readjustment Plan Case,* Case No. 397 of 2006, http://www.courts.go.jp/english/judgments/text/2008.09.10-2005.-Gyo-Hi-.No..397.html (G.B., Sept. 10, 2008).
69. Article 12 of the Administrative Procedure Act calls upon administrative agencies to adopt standards for dispositions and to make such standards public. Article 14 calls on administrative bodies to set out the reasons for an adverse disposition in most cases.
70. *Reasons for disposition must be made known case,* Case No. 2009 (Gyo-Hi) No. 91, Minshu Vol. 65, No. 4 http://www.courts.go.jp/english/judgments/text/2011.06.07-2009.-Gyo-Hi-.No..91.html (P.B. June 7, 2011).
71. Hiroyuki Hata & Go Nakagawa & Takehisa Nakagawa, *Japan Constitutional Law* 164 (Kluwer Law International 2001).
72. Itsuo Sonobe, *Comparative Administrative Law: Trends and Features in Administrative Law Studies (Japan)*, 19 L. Japan 40, 47 (1986) (translated by Kevin Hansen, from 1 Gendai gyoseiho taikei, I. Ogawa, H. Shiono, I. Sonobe, eds 121–146 (1983).

tends to be very broad, leaving administrators great discretion. How the courts will treat "free discretion" in cases brought under the new section 6.2 that allows suit to compel action after the agency has delayed an unreasonable period of time is unknown. But it is not unreasonable to believe that at least some courts will defer to agency considerations that more time is needed to make an appropriate decision.

Japanese courts also have a broader view of the doctrine of mootness than do American courts. Thus, if a party dies during the course of litigation against the State the action can be dismissed for mootness. So too, if the administrative action being challenged has already had the effect that the suit seeks to avoid, such as the date to hold a march passes before the court has heard the suit challenging denial of the permit for the march, the case is moot. The American doctrine under which a suit that challenges an action that is likely to be repeated remains viable even if the specific event is now moot is not followed in Japan. Litigants cannot challenge legislation "on its face" but rather must wait until action is taken under the legislation and then challenge the law in an "as applied" lawsuit. The result is that many government actions cannot be judicially challenged. However, in the *Overseas Voting* case, the Supreme Court opened up the ability to challenge actions that would have a future effect. There the Court held that challenges based on failure to provide plaintiffs with voting rights in past elections were moot and properly dismissed, so too a suit seeking declaration that the law was unconstitutional as applied to the just concluded election was not proper, but a suit seeking a declaration that the law was unconstitutional as it would be applied in the next general election was proper because otherwise the right to vote could be effectively blocked.[73] Whether this ruling will apply in other situations is uncertain.

The inability to bring *kokoku* litigation has not dissuaded Japanese lawyers from seeking alternative means of challenging administrative action. One mechanism frequently used is the civil suit for damages based on negligence or other improper conduct. Such money damages suits were the backbone of attempts to obtain modifications of the "designation" practices of prosecutors. While such suits do not overturn the administrative decision they do draw attention to the problem and can, over time, bring about change in policy.[74]

The 2010 Great East Japan Earthquake and Tsunami and the Fukushima nuclear disaster brought into sharp focus the inability of litigants to stop government sponsored and authorized projects. Thus, although many lawsuits have been brought in Japan in an effort to stop the construction of nuclear plants based on positioning near fault lines raising safety concerns, none has been successful in stopping construction. In great part this failure to obtain meaningful Judicial Review is based on the court's reliance on expert opinions issued by the supposedly expert government agencies involved. While

73. *Overseas Voting* case, Case No. 82 and 83 (Gyo-Tsu) and 76 and 77 (Gyo-Hi) of 2001, http://www.courts.go.jp/english/judgments/text/2005.09.14-2001.-Gyo-Tsu-.No..82%2C.2001.-Gyo-Hi-.No..76%2C.2001.-Gyo-Tsu-.No..83%2C.2001.-Gyo-Hi-.No..77.html (G.B., Sept. 14, 2005).

74. See *Prosecutor Designation case, (Meeting should have been allowed)* Case No. 1995 (O) No. 105, 54 Minshu 1653 http://www.courts.go.jp/english/judgments/text/2000.06.13-1995.-O-.No..105.html (P.B. June 13, 2000).

in the United States such expert opinions of the agency would be subjected to cross-examination and conflicting expert opinions and application of a substantial evidence or arbitrary test, in Japan the judicial system has been loath to reject the government's expert advice—which is sometimes written by the regulated entity. It remains to be seen whether the tragedy of the Fukushima nuclear plant will lead to more searching judicial review.[75]

[4] Judicial Reform

The Judicial Reform Council noted some of the problems a plaintiff faces when seeking to bring a *kokoku* suit. Among these were the special consideration courts give to determinations of administrative officials and the deference shown to administrative decisions, the failure of the law to keep pace with the changing nature of administrative disputes, and structural problems in the court system for dealing with administrative challenges. The Council called for strengthening the judiciary's power to review administrative actions.[76] The 2004 amendment to the ACLL was a legislative response to the Council's recommendations. To the extent that the law has loosened the standing requirement and to the extent that the law has spurred courts to find *shobuns* where in the past they would not, it has advanced the Council's agenda, but still leaves administrative agencies wide latitude and courts with discretion to avoid conflict with the bureaucracy. The legislation's principle shortcomings are the retention of the concept of legal injury as a standing requirement, its failure to define circumstances that are considered as abuse of discretion and to fail to deal with Administrative Guidance—the primary engine of administration/regulation in Japan.

[B] Administrative Guidance

In many regards Japan is a much more highly regulated society than is the United States. Ministries such as METI claim a broad authority over industrial policy. The regulation of Japanese industry and what American's viewed as unfair restrictions against American entry into some industries—was a subject of the trade talks between Japan and the United States in the 1990s. Deregulation became a subject of political discussion and a policy objective of various LDP governments. But deregulation has proceeded slowly. Many regulatory hurdles are not formalized by legislation or formal policy directives but rather are creations of informal Administrative Guidance.[77]

75. For a discussion of recent cases where plaintiffs were unsuccessful in stopping nuclear plant construction and the deference the court gives to the agency expert opinion see, Kyodo News, *Suits to Halt Atomic Plants Have All Failed*, Japan Times (Apr. 26, 2011), http://search.japantimes.co.jp/cgi-bin/nn20110426a2.html.
76. Recommendations of the Justice System Reform Council—For a Justice System to Support Japan in the 21st Century, 12 June 2001, The Justice System Reform Council at www.kantei.go.jp/foreign/judiciary/2001/0612report.html 34.
77. Akira Negishi, *The Reception in Japan of the American Law and Its Transformation in the Fifty Years Since the End of World War II*, Econ. L., 26 L. Japan 34, 39 (2000).

Unlike many American administrative bodies that possess cease and desist authority, most administrative bodies in Japan lack the compulsory processes that compel compliance with agency determinations.[78] A regulation adopted by an administrative agency in the United States, acting within its authority has the force and effect of law and is as binding on the public and industry groups to which it is directed as a statute. Japanese agencies as a rule do not have enforcement tools available to them. They are left with "Administrative Guidance" as their means of regulating.[79]

Administrative Guidance is typically not an act but a process wherein an administrative body attempts, through negotiation, cajoling, and consultation, to effect change in conduct by a company, industry or individual in order to carry out a policy objective of the agency.[80] The subject matter on which the agency may apply its guidance may, or may not, technically fall within the scope of the specific statutory authority given to the administrative body. The subject matter may be outside a specific programmatic delegation but the party (parties) who are the subject of the guidance may be within the agency's general scope of responsibility. The agency may lack specific enforcement authority to compel action on the part of the subject of the guidance and, as a general rule such enforcement authority is lacking. For this reason Administrative Guidance is "voluntary" on the part of the subject of the guidance. Administrative Guidance is the preferred means used by Japanese bureaucrats to achieve their policy goals. It has been estimated that as much as 80% of administrative activity in Japan is through the use of Administrative Guidance.[81]

Administrative Guidance existed long before there was any statute that defined the term giving rise to debate as to its meaning. Reminiscent of the debate over the Japanese characters used to translate Western words dealing with legal rights, the Japanese phrase "*Gyosei Shido*" was parsed to come up with an acceptable definition.[82]

---

78. See John O. Haley, *Authority without Power: Law and the Japanese Paradox* (Oxford University Press 1991) Bureaucrats and Business: Administrative Power Constrained, 139 et seq.
79. Guidance is not unknown to American Administrative Agencies. In decrying the lack of Congressional action to define the term "the waters of the United States" in the Clean Water Act Justice Alito noted: "But Congress did not define what it meant by "the waters of the United States"; the phrase was not a term of art with a known meaning; and the words themselves are hopelessly indeterminate. Unsurprisingly, the EPA and the Army Corps of Engineers interpreted the phrase as an essentially limitless grant of authority. We rejected that boundless view ... EPA has not seen fit to promulgate a rule providing a clear and sufficiently limited definition of the phrase. Instead, the agency has relied on informal guidance. But far from providing clarity and predictability, the agency's latest informal guidance advises property owners that many jurisdictional determinations concerning wetlands can only be made on a case-by-case basis by EPA field staff. ... Allowing aggrieved property owners to sue under the Administrative Procedure Act is better than nothing, but only clarification of the reach of the Clean Water Act can rectify the underlying problem." *Sackett v. EPA.*, 566 U.S. ___ (2012) (Alito J., concurring).
80. Professor Nakagawa defines Administrative Guidance as either written or oral action by an agency to persuade private parties to cooperate on a voluntary basis with a policy the agency views as desirable. Takehisa Nakagawa, *Administrative Guidance: A Tentative Model of How Japanese Lawyers Understand it*, 32 Kobe U. L. Rev. 1 (1998).
81. Tsuyoshi Kinoshita, *Legal System and Legal culture in Japanese Law*, 44 Comp. L. Rev. 25, 151 (2010); Michael K. Young, *Judicial Review of Administrative Guidance: Governmentally Encouraged Consensual Dispute Resolution in Japan* 84 Columbia L. Rev. 923, 935 n. 50 (1984).
82. See Wolfgang Pape, *Gyosei Shido and the Antimonopoly Law*, 15 L. Japan 12, 13 (1982); Russell Allen Yeomans, *Administrative Guidance: A Peregrine View*, 19 L. Japan 125, 130–137 (1986).

The APL is the first statutory definition[83] and it makes clear that the defining aspects of Administrative Guidance are: (a) the guidance cannot be a disposition (*shobun*)—it cannot determine and adversely affect legal rights; (b) it must fall within the scope of the agency's duties or functions (but not necessarily within specific program delegation); (c) it must be non-compulsory and must seek voluntary compliance; (d) it must have as its objective obtaining a result to further an agency's goal.[84] Guidance may be given by an administrative "organ" which is defined as a state organization provided for or created by a body provided for in the National Government Organization Law or a body under the jurisdiction of or created by a body under the jurisdiction of the Cabinet. Individual bureaucrats who are granted authority to act in a matter are also considered as an administrative organ covered by the law.[85] While local government bodies and agencies created by local government are included in the general definition of bodies subject to the law, an encompassing exception is made so that disposition and Administrative Guidance given by such local government bodies is exempt from the Act.[86]

The substantive section of the Act that deals with Administrative Guidance, Article 32, emphasizes that guidance cannot exceed the duties and functions of the administrative body (but again not limiting guidance to the specific programmatic duties delegated to the agency), and requires that the desired effect can only be achieved by voluntary action. The law is emphatic that failure to agree with guidance cannot be punished and that a party who refuses cannot be disadvantaged in any way. What you see may not be what you get. While Administrative Guidance is voluntary action, at the same time it may be "imposed" by a government official.[87]

Thus, Administrative Guidance involves action by an administrative body that has as its objective action or inaction by the subject of the guidance. The guidance must

83. For a discussion of the reasons for passage of an Administrative Procedure Law, the provisions of the new law and the author's view of the effect of the law see Lorenz Kodderitzsch, *Japan's New Administrative Procedure Law: Reasons for its Enactment and Likely Implications*, 24 L. Japan 105 (1991). At the time of the article there was no English translation of the APL. Since then the Management and Coordination Agency has put out an English language translation of the law.
84. APL Article 2 (6).
85. APL Article 2 (5).
86. APL Article 3 (2). In addition to the exemption for local public entities, the Act contains sixteen exemptions including such things as dispositions in statutes or court decisions, dispositions and guidance by prosecutors, tax determinations, educational oriented guidance and dispositions, dispositions and guidance having to do with administration of the prison system, public personnel matters, etc. APL Article 3 (1).
87. APL Article 32. In several places the Management and Coordination Agency English language translation of the APL uses the term 'imposes' or a variant thereof. In Lorenz Kodderitzsch, *Japan's New Administrative Procedure Law: Reasons for its Enactment and Likely Implications*, 24 L. Japan 105 (1991) written before there was an English language translation of the law, the term 'imposed' was also used when discussing the statutory provisions of Article 32 but only to assert that an agency cannot 'impose' disadvantage to a party that refuses to comply. The matter is probably just a translation problem, but it may also reflect the view of administrative officials (at least at this one translating agency) that when they conduct business through Administrative Guidance, although persons and entities subject to the guidance are free to refuse to comply there is some subtle force at work that will compel compliance.

be within the scope of the duties or functions of the administrative body and the ultimate decision regarding the guidance must be "voluntary."

Two terms must be defined before Administrative Guidance can be understood. They are "duties or functions" and "voluntary." Before there was an APL there was Administrative Guidance. The law seems to deal with a *fait accompli* and seeks to try to put some procedural boundaries on it. So what was (is) it and how does it operate?

The concept of government officials giving guidance as to what they believe should be done is not uniquely Japanese (although many Japanese commentators believe that Administrative Guidance as used in Japan is unique—and they may be correct). On the international level it has become commonplace for leaders to tell others over whom they are believed to have some influence how to act. On the domestic front the president may engage in "jaw boning" to get an industry to roll back a price increase or the Securities and Exchange Commission might suggest to the stock exchange that it tighten its rules on accounting practices. Guidance is commonplace. On the other hand, while international leaders may wish others follow their advice there is no "legal base" for the guidance. On the domestic level, industry may follow the government's advice in the hope of avoiding legislation that might be "worse." In either case there is no "compulsion" to do as guided.

The APL would seem to be the same—it specifically enshrines voluntariness as the hallmark of guidance. It specifically prohibits sanction if the guidance is not followed. So what is the big deal? If a party who receives Administrative Guidance is unhappy, the party can refuse to comply and the agency either seeks to compel action through a means that provides the party an opportunity to challenge the agency; or the agency goes away. It has been argued that Administrative Guidance is no big deal and the agency giving guidance either does nothing with a refusal or sues to compel compliance with the guidance. If nothing is done the subject of the guidance wins and if suit is brought it gets judicial review. So what is the fuss?[88] But, what if the recipient of the guidance does not want to acquiesce but is compelled (or at least feels compelled) by social or at least perceived social or other constraints to acquiesce?[89] Is that voluntary action? In a sense yes, but in another sense, no. Is there some reason for law and lawyers to be concerned? The answer is probably yes. Does voluntary really mean voluntary—considering the high value placed on harmony in Japan and the great respect given to bureaucrats and bearing in mind the social pressures to follow guidance. If guidance is a process, the administrator is not asking for a yes or no—it is

88. J. Mark Ramseyer & Minoru Nakazato, *Japanese Law an Economic Approach* (University of Chicago Press 1999) 205.

89. In *Citizens United v. Federal Election Commission*, 558 U.S. ___ (2010) the Supreme court of the United States said the following concerning "guidance" (in the form of advisory opinion) given by the FEC "when the FEC issues advisory opinions that prohibit speech, '[m]any persons, rather than undertake the considerable burden(and sometimes risk) of vindicating their rights through case-by-case litigation, will choose simply to abstain from protected speech—harming not only themselves but society as a whole, which is deprived of an uninhibited marketplace of ideas.' *Virginia v. Hicks*, 539 U.S. 113, 119 (2003) (citation omitted). Consequently, 'the censor's determination may in practice be final.'" While the above quote related to free speech and there is a chilling effect component to free speech cases, it illustrates the point that guidance can in fact be final action.

asking for a discussion, negotiation and consultation. In such case saying no may not be a viable alternative. Indeed, there may be a legal requirement to at least talk about the issue.[90]

In practice, Japanese law leaves much to the bureaucracy and guidance is the chief means by which the bureaucracy acts.[91] As discussed in Chapter 16 herein it is the bureaucracy that is the enforcer of substantive law in Japan. As the discussion of sex discrimination in the workplace revealed, mediation before a government agency and the fear of being named a discriminator who fails to follow the agency's advice are the sanctions behind the EOL. Japanese law leaves many matters to the bureaucracy to handle and the bureaucracy, like bureaucracies everywhere is ever mindful of its "turf" and the expansion of that turf if possible. Accordingly, the bureaucracy may "insinuate" itself into matters or may be called upon for its advice as to how to deal with a problem. Its "guidance" while not binding is certainly entitled to consideration by the recipient thereof and guidance is given great weight.

Because many Japanese statutes are written in hortatory or policy directional terms, leaving discretion in the bureaucratic organization, the actual requirement of what an entity should do may be less than clear. Before acting the entity will want to know that the responsible agency is in agreement with its plans. Or the opponents of a plan may want to get the responsible government entity to express its disapproval so that negotiations for modifications can take place in a more "receptive" climate. Or the government may have plans of its own and may wish to suggest to an industry that it focus on production of a particular type of product or that a particular company should devote less R&D money to a product because someone else is already working in that area and R&D in a different arena would be more "in the public interest." To protect against big swings in the world price of a commodity, the government may wish to create a "buying" cartel of interested companies or even a selling cartel of certain products to assure supply and reasonable pricing. Guidance from administrative bodies is plentiful in Japan. Issues that in the United States would be handled by a rule adopted after procedural due process through notice and comment and maybe some hybrid of witness testimony, may be handled over a series of lunches in central Tokyo. And, many matters may be handled over lunch in Tokyo that a government bureaucrat would never consider raising in the United States either because of views that such matters are not for the government in a capitalistic society or a society based on individual rights or simply because to have been discovered doing so would not look good on page 1 of the New York Times. But what does not look good in the Times may be completely acceptable indeed laudable in the local *shimbun*. The point is that guidance is ubiquitous in Japan and permeates many decisions made by business and

---

90. See Takehisa Nakagawa, *Administrative Guidance: A Tentative Model of How Japanese Lawyers Understand it*, 32 Kobe U. L. Rev. 1, 12 (1998) referring to the 1985 Supreme Court decision in the *Nakatami* case and interpreting it as implying that in certain circumstances there may be a social obligation to at least cooperate if not fully comply with Guidance. The *Nakatami* case (*Administrative Guidance Nakatani* case, 39 Minshu 989 (Sup. Ct. 16 July 85)) is discussed *infra*.

91. For the view that Guidance is constitutional and further that it is de facto binding see, Shigenori Matsui, *The Constitution of Japan* 70–71 (Hart Publishing 2011).

others in the society. In a study made in 1981 the Administrative Management Agency found that informality via Administrative Guidance is preferred over formal procedures in every aspect of contact between those in and those outside government.[92]

The definition of Administrative Guidance set out in the APL recognizes but does not resolve a problem that existed prior to the law's enactment. Namely, must there be a statutory basis for an agency to give guidance? Clearly there need be no statute that says "agency you have the power to give guidance." The power to give guidance is assumed. The issue is whether there must be a statutory base to give guidance in the area where it is offered. To an American lawyer the answer would lie in the delegation doctrine. An examination of the Japanese Constitution might logically lead to the same result. Article 41 makes the Diet the sole law-making organ of the State, while Article 73(6) gives the Cabinet the power to enact Cabinet orders to execute the Constitution and the laws. This contemplates delegation and limits the delegation by prohibiting penal provisions in such orders unless authorized by law. Moreover local governments are given specific authority to make "regulations" as long as they comply with the law. It would seem unreasonable to allow local government a regulation authority and deny the same to the national government.

The Japanese government has acted on its Constitutional right and has created agencies, departments, and "alphabet agencies." But unlike American legislation, Japanese legislation is much less specific as to the powers and duties of the agencies created. Broad discretion has been delegated to the agencies and sometimes that delegation is not found in the substantive statute. Whereas in the United States courts and lawyers would look to the statute to determine the "duties" of the agency under the delegation doctrine, in Japan the agency may have greater authority than simply the "duties" set out in law. For one thing, the agency may have "functions" (as that term is used in the APL) that are broader than its specified duties. For example, the Ministry of Finance may have duties in regulating financial matters, but it has the general function of dealing with banks. As a consequence some matters that affect banks but do not come within the Ministry's statutory duties may be functions that the ministry is concerned with. In such case, although not within the duties that the agency has been directed by legislation to carry out, the guidance may fall within the broader functions of the agency. In other words, an agency's program responsibilities as defined by statute may be narrower than its functions or duties. Although statutorily authorized programs may come to an agency via specific legislation, the agency's authorizing statute may generally designate its "business" or "functions." As a consequence the function or business of an agency can greatly exceed its specific

92. See Frank K. Upham, *The Legal Framework of Japan's Declining Industries Policy: The Problem of Transparency in Administrative Process*, 27 Harvard Intl. L. J. 425 (1986); for a discussion of Administrative Guidance in connection with investment advisors see J. Robert Brown Jr., *Bureaucratic Practices in Japan and the United States and the Regulation of Advertisements by Investment Advisors*, 12 UCLA Pacific Basin L. J. 237 (1994); for Foreign Exchange transactions see Allen D. Smith, *The Japanese Foreign Exchange and Foreign Trade Control Law and Administrative Guidance: The Labyrinth and the Castle*, 16 L. & Policy Intl. Bus. 417 (1984).

programmatic statutory grants of power.[93] Agencies may interpret their establishment laws quite broadly. METI, for example has enabling authority to effectuate a uniform administration of and promotion of commerce.[94] Differing agencies may claim responsibility for promoting commerce as well. Agencies with authority over a particular industry will likely have a function that includes promoting that industry and thus promoting commerce. The same activity may be part of the business of many agencies including METI. METI has no specific statutory authority to deal with issues of corporate governance, but as we saw in Chapter 13 METI has been the guiding influence behind and the issuer of guidelines concerning hostile takeover defenses. Even when there is a statute that "specifically" delegates authority, the delegation is typically so broad that there are little if any guidelines to cabin the authority given.[95] Where administrative bodies have conflicting or overlapping "business" or "functions," they will try to work with each other to avoid conflicts. The recipient of guidance may use such overlap to try to change the playing field to get a more accommodating solution from a more accommodating administrative body giving more accommodating guidance.

In pre APL discussions of Administrative Guidance there was debate about whether guidance was limited to those areas where the agency had a statutory basis for its action or whether it included both areas where an agency did and did not have statutory authority.[96] It now appears that the relevant question is not whether there is a statutory base for the agency's action but how much water an agency's broadly worded authorizing statute can carry. The answer would appear to be a great deal. Certainly the authorizing statute can carry more than the admittedly broad interpretation American courts have given to the delegation doctrine in the United States. As a consequence it is not uncommon to see an agency give guidance in areas that are outside the strict legal definitions of its authorization.

In analyzing the scope of the agency's "authority" to give guidance, it seems clear that where the agency initiates contact, the first decision-maker is the agency itself. Once the agency has made its own determination that it will give guidance or has taken an action making it clear that it wants some action to be taken or stopped, the recipient is in the Administrative Guidance process. It either complies or it refuses or more frequently the parties start a consultative negotiation process. There is no forum to go to, to argue nice legal points such as lack of jurisdiction. Any attempt to go to a court would be met with the defense that no disposition has been made; there is no legally binding action that affects the legal rights of any party. So while the subject is intriguing, it hardly serves as a legal restraint on agency Administrative Guidance. Of course, where an industry or company seeks guidance, it can hardly complain about lack of statutory jurisdiction on the part of the party it went to.

93. Takehisa Nakagawa, *Administrative Informality in Japan: Governmental Activities Outside Statutory Authorization*, 52 Administrative L. Rev. 175, 186 n. 30 (2000).
94. Michael K. Young, *Judicial Review of Administrative Guidance: Governmentally Encouraged Consensual Dispute Resolution in Japan*, 84 Columbia L. Rev. 923, 927 n. 12 (1984).
95. Yoshihara Matsuura, *Law and Bureaucracy in Modern Japan*, 41 Stanford L. Rev. 1627 (1989).
96. See Yoriaki Narita, *Administrative Guidance*, 2 L. Japan 45 (1968) quoted in Russell Allen Yeomans, *Administrative Guidance: A Peregrine View*, 19 L. Japan 125, 133–134 (1986).

The second issue concerns voluntariness. The APL has a bit of "protest too much" character to it when the issue of voluntary action is considered. The Administrative Guidance to the greatest degree must be realized by voluntary cooperation. Persons who refuse to cooperate cannot be placed at a "disadvantage." But even before the APL it was generally agreed that Administrative Guidance could only be utilized in a situation where the guided party cooperated and acquiesced. Whether there was a statutory base or not, guidance required voluntary or consensual action.[97] Pape defined Administrative Guidance as involving non-binding directives.[98] Upham stresses the voluntary nature of guidance.[99] Young similarly stressed the voluntary aspect of guidance.[100] Why the statutory emphasis on voluntary action?

The answer may lie in whether what you see is what you get. After all, the whole purpose of guidance is to achieve a result that the administrative agency seeks. The agency or its agent has an end in mind. This is not simply an academic exercise. The mere fact that a government agent is requesting action carries with it certain baggage. This is all the more so in Japan, which is a vertically structured society that values relationships. One is careful in Japan not to ask for too many favors as granting of favors by others leads to a feeling of necessity to reciprocate. A favor involves two parties who are under obligations—if you ask me for a favor I have an obligation to deal with the request fairly and hopefully in a way that can accommodate you. The harmony between us mandates such consideration. Of course, you have an obligation also as you know the stress you are placing on me by asking. This balancing of stresses can serve to moderate the need to act positively if possible. I must consider your position before I ask you. This later point is, however, modified if I am the bureaucrat because presumably I have not my interest but the interest of the body politic—the people of Japan in mind. This makes it easier for me to guide and more difficult for you to reject. One does not have to go as far as one commentator who suggests that voluntary action in Administrative Guidance is a fiction[101] (and indeed Administrative Guidance does not always achieve the objectives sought by administrators) to acknowledge that there exists subtle but great unspoken pressure to meet a government request.

The fact is that in all societies a request emanating from government carries with it its own "command" character. All the statutory language conceivable will not change the fact that the first reaction when a government official asks is desire not to alienate the official.[102] This is why we answer questions when a police officer asks and why we

97. See *ibid.*

98. Wolfgang Pape, *Gyosei Shido and the Antimonopoly Law*, 15 L. Japan 12, 14 (1982).

99. Frank K. Upham, *The Legal Framework of Japan's Declining Industries Policy: The Problem of Transparency in Administrative Process*, 27 Harvard International L. J. 425 (1986).

100. Michael K. Young, *Judicial Review of Administrative Guidance: Governmentally Encouraged Consensual Dispute Resolution in Japan* 84 Columbia L. Rev. 923 (1984).

101. Russell Allen Yeomans, *Administrative Guidance: A Peregrine View*, 19 L. Japan 125, 134 (1986).

102. The APL appears to assume that parties will comply with guidance even though voluntariness is stressed. Thus, guidance may be given that seeks action on the spot (APL Article 35(3)), an entity receiving guidance may ask for it to be placed in writing but cannot insist on a writing if it is administratively inconvenient (APL Article 35 (2)).

give over our driver's license when the officer requests instead of asserting our Constitutional right to know "why" before we act. The request comes from authority and when that authority is as highly respected and carries the public interest, as does the Japanese bureaucrat, it takes a strong will to say no. Moreover institutional memory is long and a denial of "understanding" today may not lead to disadvantage tomorrow but who knows what will happen 10 years from now when the official who gave guidance is the head of the department your company must deal with on a regular basis? The official may not create compulsion, the circumstance does and the APL cannot change that fact no matter how much emphasis it places on voluntary action.[103]

In addition, there are leaks from the Japanese government just as there are leaks from the United States government. Reporters are always seeking to break a story. In a country where reputation is important does one wish to put its company in a position where it may have to explain why it did not follow governmental guidance? And what if failure to follow guidance actually had a negative effect on the Japanese economy, or a segment thereof, or could be blamed for that effect five years from now? Is it easier to have understanding and recreate the harmony that existed before the guidance was given then worry about a sword of Damocles hanging over the company? Of course leaks can operate in both directions and the power to go to the press with stories of administrative "strong arming" helps keep the bureaucracy in check.

The statute itself raises questions that an astute businessperson may want to consider before rejecting guidance. The subject of rejected guidance cannot be treated "disadvantageously" because of the rejection. But can the subject of guidance who accepts be treated advantageously? For example could a company that decides to divert its R&D activity as the administrator guides receive low interest loan money to support its R&D efforts? Companies that fail to comply might be left with higher interest costs. If a company agrees to divert steel output from the United States market, might it receive a subsidy to assist it in defraying shipping costs to other markets? Five years from now may the complying company ask for and receive a benefit that it might not otherwise have received except that administrators remember its understanding attitude?

If the subject of guidance is one that affects many companies can one company afford to stay out of the negotiations? If the objective of guidance is to come to a consensual regulatory scheme, can a company refuse to voice its opinions as to what the consensus should be? Perhaps if the issue is substantive enough the company may refuse to go along with the ultimate regulatory actions, but certainly it will engage in the negotiation. From the administrator's perspective that is a good first step since one purpose of the guidance process is to get a change of conduct that will in fact garner support among those regulated so that they will in fact carry it out. Further, once the process of negotiation is underway there is not simply governmental pressure to agree there can be peer pressure as well. Ultimate compliance may be a "voluntary" matter

103. For a discussion of factors that can affect a decision to accept guidance see Steven M. Spaeth, *Industrial Policy, Continuing Surveillance, and Raised Eyebrows: A Comparison of Informality in Administrative Procedure in Japan and the United States*, 20 Ohio N. U. L. Rev. 931, 934–937 (1994).

as the agency may lack authority to get a court order to compel compliance, but negotiation and engagement in the process may not be "voluntary."

There in fact may be situations where a company given guidance does not have the option of saying no—perhaps it does not have to say yes, a maybe (*tabun*) will do. That is to say, the guidance given is not the last word—it may be the first step in a negotiation process. There may be situations where negotiation is required even if consent is not. If guidance is viewed as part of a process of regulation through cooperative negotiation and consultation—and this is a very good way to look at some Administrative Guidance—than it would appear that negotiation is called for. Especially in a society where conciliation and compromise to achieve consensus and harmony are viewed as positive characteristics, guidance as a means of negotiation is favored by both administrators and administered.

In the *Nakatani* case[104] the court recognized that a building permit must be issued within 21 days after request if conditions for the permit were met but nonetheless held that the city authorities had not acted unlawfully by withholding such permit for several months to allow negotiations (suggested by the city authorities) between the builder and neighbors over the issue of sunlight. Only after negotiations had irrevocably broken down and the builder made it clear that he would not negotiate further was there an obligation to issue the permit. Not only must the builder be clear in his rejection of further negotiation but such rejection must be sincerely made. A rejection of negotiation at too early a stage may be viewed as merely tactical or psychological and thus not sincere.

The city had a right to give Administrative Guidance that the developer should negotiate with abutters and a right to hold up the permit process for a reasonable period to level the playing field between the abutters and the construction company. Granting the permit within 21 days would shift the leverage in the negotiation entirely on the builder's side and successful negotiation could not be had. The builder *was required to negotiate* in good faith and only when it was clear that no negotiated agreement could be reached could he say "NO—give me my permit." At that point the city was required to grant the permit. Where did the requirement to negotiate come from? Certainly not from the Building Standards Law, which was concerned solely with technical matters and required the city to act within 21 days? The requirement to negotiate had to come from the Administrative Guidance given by the city. Accordingly, Administrative Guidance may have to be followed in certain cases, even if the ultimate determination is voluntary. The issue of what negotiated settlement, if any, would be the product of the negotiation was voluntary—the issue of negotiation itself was not.

Since there was no statute giving the city authority to deal with zoning issues or to deal with light, air and sunlight access questions where did the city get the authority to give guidance? The answer lies in the general purposes clause of the Local Autonomy Law under which all cities are to preserve health and welfare of residents. This tied to

104. *Administrative Guidance Nakatani* case, *Nakatani v. Tokyo-to*, 39 Minshu 989 (Sup. Ct. 16 July 1985). For a discussion of the Nakatani case see Takehisa Nakagawa, *Administrative Informality in Japan: Governmental Activities Outside Statutory Authorization*, 52 Administrative L. Rev. 175 (2000).

the Building Standards Law's purpose of protecting life and health and furthering public welfare created the necessary legal authority for the city to give guidance. But this "legal basis" for guidance would have done the city no good if the court had not concluded that the matter of guidance was one that had popular support. In other words, the general view of society (as determined by the court) was that sunlight was a matter that should be considered by the parties—society understood there was a problem and the city acted properly in trying to get the parties to resolve that problem through negotiation.

What is critical is not the statutory authority of the city but rather whether the city's actions conform to the generally accepted view of society.[105] The determination of what is generally accepted is apparently a legal decision that can be based on extra-legal sources. Societal acceptance need not be found in a rule, regulation or statute; it need not be the product of notice and comment or any other procedural device. It is the product of the judge's knowledge. Nor for that matter does it appear that testimony on the question is either proper or allowed. No social science expert witness appears to have appeared to testify to scientifically valid surveys of the view of the public.[106]

It may be that *Nakatani* does not state a general rule of administrative law giving agencies authority to require some action even if the end result is left to voluntary resolution. It may be that *Nakatani* is limited to situations where the guidance given is intended to resolve disputes between competing interests and the role of government is to temporarily level the playing field so that a negotiated settlement may be possible. Given Japanese law's preference for mediation and conciliation over litigation, for negotiation over rupture, it may well be that *Nakatani* should be limited to guidance that requires negotiation to resolve a dispute between private parties. Still, it demonstrates that some guidance may have to be followed, at least guidance that says negotiate before action is taken that makes negotiation impossible.

Nakatani does not change the general landscape of review of administrative action. It was not a *kokoku* suit under the ACLL to restrain or reverse administrative action. Rather, it was a civil action seeking damages on the theory that the city officials acted improperly and outside their authority. *Nakatani* appears to endorse in the administrative context the same kind of "substantive justice" idea that underlies criminal litigation in Japan. The court in reviewing the action of the city focused in on the "right and wrong" of the matter rather than the technical rules that an American court would apply. There was no attempt to determine whether "procedural due process" had been given the builder, or whether the technical 21-day limit of the Building Standards Law was a restriction on the city's action. Rather, the key aspect of

105. Michael K. Young, *Judicial Review of Administrative Guidance: Governmentally Encouraged Consensual Dispute Resolution in Japan*, 84 Columbia L. Rev. 923, 966 (1984) discussing the *Yoshina v. Nakano Ward* decision, 886 Hanrei Jiho 15 (Tokyo District Court, 1973).

106. American judges may be called upon to make similar community standards type determinations in an obscenity case. But in an American trial, evidence on the issue would be presented and subjected to cross-examination before a determination was reached. An American trial would treat the consensus of society as a fact issue to be determined through hearing fact witnesses.

the case was community values as represented by the view of society. The city, by holding up the permit process, provided the correct atmosphere for negotiation. Accordingly, its action was acceptable to the court. [One is left to wonder what the effect of the 21-day limit specifically written into the Building Standards law is. Perhaps the answer is that what you see is not what you get and that 21 days only means 21 days when a problem does not arise that society thinks needs more time to resolve, even if that problem has nothing to do with the permit application or the Building Standards Law.]

It is unclear whether the rule of the *Nakatani* case is changed or confirmed by the APL. Article 33 provides that in dealing with applications those giving guidance must act in a manner consistent with the applicant's expressed intent not to comply with the guidance. In such a case the guiding administrator cannot continue to give guidance. By implication this could be read to mean that absent the statutory bar, agencies giving guidance could, under circumstances not stated, disregard the applicant's "NO." This is consistent with *Nakatani* where the view of society compels negotiation. Since Article 33 is not applicable to actions of city authority such as that involved in *Nakatani*[107] it is unlikely to negatively affect the rule in the case and may by implication support the rule. Indeed, it is unlikely that the question will be litigated.

Nakatani involved a situation where the administrative arm was not a party to the dispute and was not giving "substantive guidance." Where the administrative arm is a party to the dispute and gives substantive guidance, the rule appears to be the same—except that the court may take a closer ("harder"?) look at whether the administrative arm was forcing the subject of guidance to comply, in other words was the guidance really a shobun as held in the *Governor's "Guidance" is actually a Shobun Case* mentioned earlier.[108] It would thus appear that the *Nakatani* rule might have broader application than simply cases where the government is attempting to get parties to negotiate a reasonable settlement. The rule would appear to apply where the administrative body has its own policy objectives in mind. An agency may give guidance in situations where it has no specific authority so long as the public supports the action. And, once guidance is given, as long as the agency does not cross the

107. APL Article 3 (2).
108. In the *Administrative Guidance Masashino case*, 36 Minshu 727 (Sup. Ct. Apr. 23, 1993) it was held that the City crossed the line when it made a "suggested" payment by builders a compulsory payment. This was not Guidance but a *shobun* in an area where the city had no authority and hence a tort for which money damages were available. For a discussion of the case see Takehisa Nakagawa,*Administrative Informality in Japan: Governmental Activities Outside Statutory Authorization*, 52 Administrative L. Rev. 175 (2000) and Yoshiro Miwa & J. Mark Ramseyer, *Deregulation and Market Response in Contemporary Japan: Administrative Guidance, Keiretsu, and Main Banks*, NELLCO Legal Scholarship Repository, ch. 6, at 10–12, (Mar. 29, 2004), http://lsr.nellco.org/cgi/viewcontent.cgi?article=1250&context=harvard_olin &sei-redir=1&referer=http%3A%2F%2Fwww.google.com%2Furl%3Fsa%3Dt%26rct%3Dj% 26q%3Dadministrative%2520guidance%2520japan%2520written%26source%3Dweb%26cd %3D19%26ved%3D0CFgQFjAIOAo%26url%3Dhttp%253A%252F%252Flsr.nellco.org%252 Fcgi%252Fviewcontent.cgi%253Farticle%253D1250%2526context%253Dharvard_olin%26ei %3DTxBNT-CUIcjniAK_9MjEDw%26usg%3DAFQjCNFYdTXeHgnbnN-S_eMy6d7QEQgL8g# search=%22administrative%20guidance%20japan%20written%22.

"voluntary/compulsory" line, no improper action has been taken. No reason exists to believe that this rule is any different for national government agencies.

Perhaps equally important is the effect that guidance, such as METI's anti-takeover guidance, has on courts. Japan has no *Chevron* doctrine as such, but the reality is that the judges look to the bureaucracy just as they look to the Diet to resolve matters by applying the consensus of society. It is likely that courts will look with favor on poison pills that track METI's guidance simply because they track METI's guidance. Poison pills that are inconsistent with METI's guidance will have a significantly more difficult time in passing judicial muster unless the court sees them as consistent with community values, such as the corporate community value (as was the situation in the *Steel Partners/Bull Dog* litigation discussed in Chapter 13). While in the middle will be poison pills that neither follow nor are contradicted by METI's guidance.

The Fukushima nuclear disaster has thrown a sharp light on the way the administrative agencies in Japan carry out (or fail to carry out) their regulatory responsibilities. Nuclear policy including the expansion of nuclear energy as a greater portion of Japan's energy mix was a function of METI. But METI was also the regulator of nuclear plants. In its regulatory role NISA (the regulatory portion of METI) relied in great measure on TEPCO (the power company) and the reports it received from TEPCO rather than conducting its own independent on site reviews. This continued even after it was disclosed that TEPCO had failed to properly make certain reports. After the Kobe earthquake of the 1990s NISA and METI made stress test evaluations of nuclear plants. Yet these tests did not take into account the question of whether the plants could survive a tsunami, even though a tsunami in size and strength not dissimilar to the Great East Japan Earthquake and Tsunami that disabled the Fukushima plant had been recorded some centuries earlier in the Fukushima area—in fact it now appears that a government committee report urging greater tsunami concern may have been watered down at the request of power companies so as not to disturb or confuse the public.[109] A review of safety standards for nuclear plants prepared in the 1990s failed to require safety steps if there were a failure of power at a nuclear plant causing a "blackout" for more than 30 minutes. Such standards were adopted in other countries but not Japan. It is reported that the government regulators permitted the power industry to write the portion of the report dealing with why such standards were not necessary.[110] After the Fukushima tragedy NISA was spun out of METI because of concerns about conflict of interest. But other regulatory issues were not addressed. NISA has responsibility for many areas involving energy companies and is not exclusively a nuclear power safety agency. Indeed at the time of the Fukushima tragedy the head of NISA was not someone trained in the nuclear field or indeed in any scientific discipline. NISA does not have a great store of nuclear experts on staff and must rely on the power companies themselves. The Japanese philosophy of training staff in-house so that they can handle all aspects of a company or agency responsibility favors generalists over specialists and

109. Kyodo, *Japan quake report worried utilities, Tsunami alert softened days before 3/11*, Japan Times, (Feb. 27, 2012), http://www.japantimes.co.jp/text/nn20120227a2.html.
110. *Nuclear power plant collusion*, Japan Times Editorial (June 23, 2012), http://www.japantimes.co.jp/text/ed20120623a1.html.

downplays narrow technical expertise; the lifetime employment system in both companies and government agencies means that employees must leave their positions when reaching an age at which they still want (need?) to be actively employed. Because the lifetime employment system supports a restricted market many bureaucrats retire to the senior ranks of the companies they regulated when in government service. This practice of "descending from heaven" makes guidance regulation easier to do but also means that agencies can be compromised in their regulatory function[111] either by relying on personnel to whom current regulators may owe loyalty obligations or by placing reliance on such personnel in the belief they will support the agency's goals over the company's goals—an assumption that may not be accurate—or for other reasons. These former agency officials may influence agency policy in ways that advantage their current employer but may prove not to be in the public interest.

In the summer of 2012 legislation was enacted that created a new independent five person commission to deal with nuclear safety issues. The commission is to adopt new safety regulations for nuclear plants within 10 months of establishment and while under the Cabinet office, the Commission is granted significant independence even from the Cabinet. Members of the Commission will be appointed by the government but must be approved by the Diet and it is expected that nuclear experts will be appointed. The legislation separates NISA from METI and places NISA under the Nuclear Energy Safety Commission, where it will have a relationship with, but not be subservient to, the Environment Ministry.[112]

Nor does the APL change the rule that Administrative Guidance is not subject to review under the ACLL because it is only advice and not a determination. Indeed, the APL confirms that judicial review under the ACLL is not available. Where an entity seeks guidance from government and acts on that guidance, a third party may not attribute the private party's action to the government entity. Thus, where the national broadcasting station NHK sought guidance as to whether they should air derogatory remarks in a political broadcast and thereafter deleted such remarks from the broadcast

111. Kyodo, *Watchdog let utilities justify omitting nuclear plant power supply safety steps*, Japan Times, (June 6, 2012), http://www.japantimes.co.jp/text/nn20120606a3.html, reporting that the nuclear watchdog agency allowed the electric utilities to write portions of the guidelines omitting consideration of a sustained power loss; Walter Hatch, *Regionalizing the State: Japanese Administrative and Financial Guidance for Asia*, 5 Soc. Sci. Japan J. 197 (2002).

112. Jji Press, *Diet Passes Bill on New Nuclear Agency*, Daily Yomiuri (June 22, 2012), http://www.yomiuri.co.jp/dy/national/T120621004052.htm. The new law also gives the new commission authority to deal with nuclear matters as a part of Japan's "security" causing some to question whether this language may someday be interpreted to mean that material created through use of nuclear plants could be used for weaponization, a position strongly denied by both the government and the opposition LDP which had sought to security language. See, Mizuho Aoki, Japan Times (June 22, 2012), *'Security' Wording in Nuke Power Law Change Raises Arms Questions*, http://www.japantimes.co.jp/text/nn20120622a3.htm; Revised nuclear law stipulates aim to ensure Japanese national security, The Mainichi (June 22, 2012), http://mainichi.jp/english/english/newsselect/news/20120622p2a00m0na015000c.html; *'National security' amendment to nuclear law raises fears of military use*, Asahi Shimbun, http://ajw.asahi.com/article/0311disaster/fukushima/AJ201206210061.

there was no inappropriate "censorship" since it was private action and not action by an administrative organ.[113]

Because compliance with guidance is by definition voluntary, companies must be aware of the pitfalls of compliance. For example, in the oil cartel litigation the Japanese FTC pressed its anti-monopoly case against the cartel members even though the cartel argued that it was simply following the guidance of MITI. The companies themselves had come to MITI with the prices they had fixed and had gotten guidance that the prices were acceptable. The court found that MITI was not sufficiently involved to insulate the companies and their executives from price fixing.[114] MITI's more direct involvement in setting production limits could be raised as a defense.[115] In the shareholder litigation brought against the directors of Daiwa Bank, the bank argued that the heart of their alleged wrongful conduct—the failure to timely inform American officials of the problem—was based on guidance received from the Finance Ministry. The Bank executives had met with the Finance Ministry and, there was some evidence that the ministry may have indicated that this was not a good time to make disclosure to the Americans.[116] Even if the ministry had made such a "suggestion" it would not avail the executives. The District Court was of the view that corporate management had to make its own decision and could not rely on the guidance allegedly received from the ministry.[117]

The few Administrative Guidance cases that have been decided by the courts throw an interesting light on judicial review of guidance. Critical is to distinguish guidance from *shobun*. Thus, in the textbook censoring controversy the Supreme Court held that it is proper for the Ministry of Education to *suggest* changes in textbooks and the Court refused to consider whether such *suggestions* were valid in the sense of following historic fact. It was only when the ministry crossed the line and ordered a change that the Court could consider whether the change required was consistent with historic fact.[118]

113. *NHK Censorship* case, Case No. 1986 (0) No. 800, http://www.courts.go.jp/english/judgments/text/1990.4.17-1986.-0-.No..800.html (P.B. Apr. 17, 1990).
114. *Oil Cartel case, Japan v. Idemitsu Kosan*, 985 Hanrei Jiho 3 (Tokyo High Court Sept. 26, 2980) (partial translation in Yukio Yanagida, Daniel H. Foote, Edward Stokes Johnson, Jr., J. Mark Ramseyer & Hugh T. Scogin, Jr., *Law and Investment in Japan* 141–147 (Harvard University Press 1994).
115. See Michael K. Young, *Judicial Review of Administrative Guidance: Governmentally Encouraged Consensual Dispute Resolution in Japan*, 84 Columbia L. Rev. 923, 940 n. 74 for a discussion of the oil cartel litigation (1984).
116. A discussion of the meeting between Daiwa executives and the Ministry of Finance and its relationship to Administrative Guidance can be found at Mitsuru Misawa, *Daiwa Bank Scandal in New York: Its Causes, Significance, and Lessons in the International Society*, 29 Vanderbilt J. Transntl. L. 1023, 1048–1053 (1996).
117. The *Japan Times* Sept. 21, 2000 *Execs to Repay USD 775 million. Shareholders win in rogue-trader case*. The parties settled while an appeal was pending.
118. Compare, *Textbook Screening* case, Case No. 1428 (O) of 1986, 47 Minshu No. 5 at 3483, http://www.courts.go.jp/english/judgments/text/1993.03.16-1986-O.-No.1428.html (P.B. Mar. 16, 1993) with *Textbook Suggestions are Guidance but Mandatory Order Reversed*, Case No 1119 (O) of 1994, 51 Minshu No. 7 2921, http://www.courts.go.jp/english/judgments/text/1997.8.29-1994-O-No.1119-170618.html (P.B. Aug. 29, 1997).

[C] Administrative Procedure

The APL divides administrative matters into two categories—(a) dispositions and (b) Administrative Guidance. As to guidance, there is very little in the way of procedure except for cautionary statements that guidance must involve voluntary actions.[119] In addition the APL provides that, barring extraordinary administrative inconvenience when the party being guided asks for written guidance, the guidance should be put in writing containing both the contents of the guidance and its purpose.[120] Written guidance is not required where the guidance seeks to have an action carried out immediately.[121] Administrative Guidance applied to several parties to carry out a common objective should be made available to the general public.[122] The making of such rules publicly available is a big step forward in abolishing "secret agency law." A form of written guidance would be the guidance provided by METI concerning hostile takeover defense measures discussed in Chapter 13. The publication of guidance may lead to giving agencies a "rule-making authority" similar to rule making in the United States, but without the procedural protections of notice and opportunity to be heard and judicial review of the rules.[123] At all events, it is likely that the Act has had little effect on Administrative Guidance.[124]

For covered dispositions,[125] which are typically in the nature of what would be considered "adjudication" in the United States; the APL provides substantial procedural rights. Included in those rights are the requirements that the administrative entity establish standards for review of applications, provide reasons for an adverse determination, and in some cases of adverse disposition provide "formal hearings." In such a formal hearing the party adversely affected may provide oral and/or written arguments and documents. Questions may even be put to officials of the agency involved (if the presiding official permits). In rendering its final disposition the agency must carefully consider the record compiled by the hearing official and must take into account the opinion of the hearing officer.

The APL has no provision allowing for judicial review of the disposition determination. However, it would appear that a disposition under the APL would meet the definition of a disposition under the ACLL and would be reviewable under that

119. APL Article 34.
120. APL Article 35.
121. APL Article 35 (3).
122. APL Article 36.
123. A form of "notice and opportunity to be heard" is contained in a Cabinet Order regarding guidance to a large group but there are many exceptions to the requirement (e.g. ex parte oral comments are not subject to the rule) and no effective enforcement mechanism. The reality is that Japanese regulators tend to rely on oral guidance except when it suits their purpose to use more formal written guidance.
124. For a discussion see, Cynthia Day Wallace, *The Multinational Enterprise and Legal Control* 346–348 (Kluwer Law International 2002).
125. Not all dispositions are covered by the law. Article 3, Scope of Application contains an impressive list of sixteen categories of administrative action that are not covered, including dispositions by the political branches of government and the judiciary, dispositions by audit committees, prosecutorial, police, and tax dispositions, certain educational matters, prison administration, public employment, emigration and immigration matters, etc.

law—although there is no guaranty that failure to provide the procedural rights set out in the APL is a ground for reversal of the administrative determination. Moreover, the ACLL was originally conceived of as a transitional measure to be replaced by a comprehensive procedure law. With passage of an APL with no judicial review features and in areas where there was no amendments to the ACLL in 2004, these transitional matters appear to be permanent.

[D] Damage Suits against the Government

The Japanese Constitution provides that persons who have been injured as a consequence of illegal action by government officials shall have the right to sue the State or public entity responsible for such injury.[126] Persons who are tried for a crime but found not guilty are also entitled to compensation.[127] The Law Concerning State Liability for Compensation carries out these rights.[128] Because of the difficulty in suing to prohibit the government from following through on administrative determinations, those who complain of governmental action are forced in many instances to seek damages for alleged illegal governmental action under the usual tort law concepts and the Law Concerning State Liability for Compensation. While success in such a suit may not prevent the government action objected to, the plaintiff can highlight the alleged illegality through suing and may obtain a judicial decision that will influence future government action. Because government officials in Japan are delegated extensive discretionary authorities the question of when a decision, action or inaction becomes "illegal" so as to trigger liability under the Law is critical to plaintiff's success. Many cases have turned on the inaction of government officials and while such cases have provided the plaintiffs with some monetary relief the more important relief would appear to be the recognition that the government did wrong and must make amends.

Among the principal cases dealing with government liability for inaction is the *Minamata disease* case discussed in the Chapter 14. Here we note that suit was brought not simply against the owner of the plant that discharged the chemical that caused the disease but also that the plaintiffs sued the government (MITI, now renamed METI) for failure to properly regulate the discharge of the pollutant that was the cause of the disease. In 2004 the Supreme Court upheld the Osaka High Court's judgment finding the government liable for failure to properly regulate.[129] MITI was granted authority to regulate the discharge of pollutants under various laws such as the Law Concerning Conservation of Water Quality in Public Waters (before amendment by Law No. 108 of 1970) and the Law Concerning Conservation of Water Quality in Public Waters and Plant Effluent Control Law. The High Court had found as a matter of fact that as of the end of November 1959 there were sufficient facts available to the governing authorities

126. Article 19.
127. Article 40.
128. Law No. 125, Oct. 27, 1947.
129. *Minamata Disease Government Liability Case*, Case No. 2001(O)Nos. 1194 and 1196, and 2001(Ju)Nos. 1172 and 1174, 58 Minshu No. 7, (Sup. Ct. P.B. Oct. 15, 2004), http://www.courts.go.jp/english/judgments/text/2004.10.15-2001-O-Nos..1194.and.1196%2C.and.2001-Ju-Nos..1172.and.1174.html.

that they should have exercised their authority to stop the company from continuing to discharge the chemical responsible for the disease. The Supreme Court reaffirmed an earlier decision setting the parameters for governmental liability for failure to act the failure to act must be beyond permissible limits, extremely unreasonable in light of the purpose of the laws to be administered and the circumstances of the case and must lead to the damages sued for. If these conditions are met then there exists governmental liability. Because of the facts known or that should have been known by the government, failure of the government to exercise its authority to stop the further dumping of the chemical made the government liable for damages caused after November 1959.

Government liability for failure to exercise discretion may even apply to failure of the Diet to act in unusual circumstances. In The *Overseas Voting* Case[130] the Supreme Court in addition to requiring that Overseas Japanese be allowed to vote in single seat district contests for the Diet also found that the failure of the Diet to act to provide such right in the unusual circumstances of the case was sufficiently egregious that the State was responsible in damages. The factors that led the Court to this conclusion were: the seriousness of the right to vote as a Constitutional right, the failure of the legislature to act for more than 10 years without any justifiable reason, and the obvious need to act to comply with the Constitution. Although the Court was clear that damages should only be awarded as a consequence of Diet inaction in exceptional situations, its ruling makes clear that the Constitutional right of the citizen to sue the State for illegal acts of State representatives that cause injury even extends to the elected Diet's failure to act.

Government liability has been assessed in numerous other situations where the government has failed in its role as regulator, particularly in regulating medical matters. Government liability may be established where private entities follow Administrative Guidance and such action results in damage.[131]

Perhaps mindful of the likelihood that the nuclear disaster at the TEPCO plant in Fukushima would spawn litigation not just against the company but also against the government since METI was responsible for regulating TEPCO's plant operations, the government has established an administrative compensation system for sufferers of the Fukushima nuclear disaster.

Although the Constitution guarantees a right to sue, the damages awarded in such suits are both against the government not the bureaucrats and the amount of damages is not commensurate with the injury suffered, so too damages allowed when a criminal defendant has been found not guilty are inadequate. The real goal of many of these suits is not money but influencing a change in government policy or attitudes.

130. *Overseas Election* case, Case No. 82 and 83 (Gyo-Tsu) and 76 and 77 (Gyo-Hi) of 2001, http://www.courts.go.jp/english/judgments/text/2005.09.14-2001.-Gyo-Tsu-.No..82%2C.2001.-Gyo-Hi-.No..76%2C.2001.-Gyo-Tsu-.No..83%2C.2001.-Gyo-Hi-.No..77.html (Grand Bench Sept. 14, 2005).

131. See, e.g., Seeichi Yishikawa, translation of Judge Kobe's *Proposed Settlement Terms in the S.M.O.N. Case*, 11 L. Japan 765–90 rejecting the government's argument that the government played no role in the distribution of the drug responsible for plaintiffs' injury when the government had given the company Administrative Guidance finding that Guidance has the effect of regulating.

[E] Other Administrative Matters

Clearly with an eye toward United States practice, Japan has enacted a national FOIA[132] to complement information ordinances adopted in numerous municipalities and other local governments. Similarly a privacy law (the Personal Information Protection Act) has been enacted.[133] The Privacy Law deals mainly with personal data held by private entities, unlike the United States Privacy Law that basically deals with data held by the government. These private entities (businesses basically) are required to define and then make public their policy as to how they use private information concerning persons (called purpose of use in the law).[134] Uses beyond the so-called purpose of use are prohibited, unless the person whose information is implicated agrees to such use. The law requires business entities to safeguard personal data in its possession and although personal data may be shared with others, sharing requires consent of the person whose data is involved who must be given the opportunity to refuse to permit sharing.[135] The law contains exceptions to both the sharing and restricted to "purpose of use" provisions of the law—basically to permit use that is allowed or required by other laws, where use is required to protect life, safety or health of a person or persons or to protect property and there is not time to obtain consent, public health purposes or where use is made in cooperation with public authorities.[136] Entities handling personal data must take steps so that the data is accurate and must provide the subject of the data an opportunity to object and have corrections made.[137]

The draft law specifically excluded from its coverage information held by government entities; national and local.[138] However, as enacted the law requires that local public entities "endeavor" to take steps to protect personal information and ensure its proper handling.[139] An interesting aspect of the law is that it permits national authorities to admonish entities that fail to comply and after such admonishment allows the national entity to "order" implementation measures to carry out the admonishment and in emergency situations permits entry of an Order prior to any admonishment.[140] The draft of the law raised concerns that it would restrict access to newsworthy data.[141] As enacted, the administrative enforcement measures of the law[142] are limited so that the administrative authority does not abridge freedom of speech, religion, political activity or academic freedom[143] and news organizations and

132. Law Concerning Access to Information Held by Administrative Organs.
133. Law No. 57 of 2003.
134. Article 15.
135. Article 25.
136. Article 16 (3) subparts 1-4; Article 23 (1) subparts 1-4.
137. Article 19, 26, 31.
138. Proposed Law Article 11.
139. Act Article 11.
140. Article 34.
141. Restrictions Worry Media, Bill on Data Protection Approved by Cabinet, *Japan Times* 28 March 2001.
142. Article 34.
143. Article 35.

journalists are specifically exempted from the provisions of the law giving administrative entities cease and desist authority or the authority to make orders affecting their disclosure of information.[144] Although the law contains penal sanctions for certain violations, there are no provisions allowing for civil suit to enforce the law or to challenge a government order issued under the law. Provision is made for mediation of grievances between business and those whose personal data is held by both local entities and the national government.[145]

Some in the bureaucracy were apparently not convinced that privacy and freedom of information represent rights that should be applied against the government. In the spring of 2002 it was revealed that the Self-Defense Force regularly kept dossiers on people who requested information under the FOIA,[146] an action that could well chill the ardor of those who might wish to exercise their rights under the law. Similarly, the review of documents in the Foreign Ministry failed to locate the secret agreements entered into between the United States and Japan at the time of the Okinawa reversion. It is likely that such documents were destroyed in the lead up to the adoption of the FOIA.[147] In the aftermath of the Great East Japan Earthquake and Tsunami it was disclosed that notes of meetings were not kept and thus could not be made available under the FOIA law only to have some notes made public at a later date.

Although the new Personal Information Protection Act creates the impression that personal information is protected in Japan, what you see may not be what you get. The Act does provide protection when privacy data is held by private entities,[148] but the biggest threat to personal information in Japan is not a threat from private business (although even after passage the government has had to admonish financial and other institutions for failures to protect personal private information) but a threat that stems from the government's national database—Juki Net—and the law does not cover it. The Supreme Court of Japan has upheld Juki Net.[149] In July 2012 medium and long-term foreign residents of Japan were incorporated into the Juki Net system.[150]

Japan's version of the FOIA follows the United States pattern of listing exemptions from required disclosure. The act contains six general categories for exempted material among which is documents relating to internal deliberations of the government in situations where disclosure might adversely affect the open and honest exchange of views or opinions.[151] Thus internal government decision making materials

144. Article 50 (1).
145. Article 9, 13.
146. *Japan Times*, May 30, 2002 Data Routinely Collected on Info Seekers: MSDF.
147. See, e.g., Kyodo News, *Secret pact documents likely discarded: report*, Japan Times (June 6, 2010), http://search.japantimes.co.jp/cgi-bin/nn20100606a8.html.
148. For a discussion of the history and provisions in the Act see, Carol Lawson, *Japan's New Privacy Act in Context*, 29 UNSW L. Rev. 88 (2006).
149. *Juki Net Case*, Case No. 2007 (O) No. 403, 2007 (Ju) No. 454, Minshu Vol. 62, No. 3 (P.B., Mar. 6, 2008), http://www.courts.go.jp/english/judgments/text/2008.03.06-2007.-O-.No..403%2C.2007.-Ju-.No..454.html.
150. Ashley Thompson and Angela Jeffs, Bye-bye to the *gaijin* card, welcome to the Juki Net in '12, Japan Times, July 21, 2012, http://www.japantimes.co.jp/text/fl20110712at.html.
151. Law Concerning Access to Information Held by Administrative Organs, Law No. 42 of 1999 ('FOIA').See, Carl F. Goodman, *The Evolving Law of Document Production in Japanese Civil Procedure: Context, Culture, and Community*, 33 Brooklyn J. Intl. L. 125, 202 (2007).

are not subject to disclosure under the Japanese Act. (See Chapter 14) Unlike United States law, there is no stringent timetable for making production. The Act does however significantly advance Freedom of Information and disclosure of government materials in Japan.

The National Environmental Impact Assessments Law (1997) unifies procedures under which environmental assessments will be performed when licenses are sought for certain large-scale projects such as roads, power plants, etc., that could potentially have a serious impact on the environment. The Law applies to both private and public large-scale projects and gives the Administrator of the Environmental Agency the authority to express opinions as to all such projects. Citizens are also given a greater right to participate in the licensing process to express views on the environmental impact.[152] This law may have an effect on standing rules as discussed earlier.

Japan may appear to outsiders to be a society where bureaucrats have unfettered power, such is not the case. Japan is undoubtedly a more bureaucratic society than the United States and its economy certainly has more governmental involvement than in the United States. To the outsider bureaucratic power appears ubiquitous. While bureaucrat authority may be ubiquitous, power may not be.[153] When you see authority you may not be seeing ability to enforce that authority. Bureaucrats may guide—indeed they may even guide in areas where there is no programmatic grant of authority but there is little power to enforce guidance. As for judicial review, while the ACLL appears to provide for review of administrative determinations, there is little that can actually be reviewed in a direct assault on administrative action. Even where suit is permitted it is likely that by the time the suit is completed many cases will have become moot or a circumstance decision may be called for. Still, where there has been a disposition it is possible to get review by a court and where the agency is not exercising an unreviewable discretion the court may overturn the agency determination.[154] Such things have happened—but they are not the rule no matter how much judicial review the ACLL may seem to provide. Whether the Supreme Court's opening of review by loosening standing will change matters remains to be seen.

152. Developments in 1997, 18 Waseda Bull. Comp. L. 45–47.
153. John Owen Haley, *Authority without Power*ch. 7 (Oxford University Press 1991).
154. In the *Jehovah's Witness* case, Case No. 1995 (Gyo-Tsu) No. 74 (Sup. Ct. P.B. 8 March 1996) 50 Minshu 469, http://www.courts.go.jp/english/judgments/text/1996.3.8-1995.-Gyo-Tsu-.No..74.html.

CHAPTER 18

Unifying Factors

A landlord in Tokyo enters into a lease of a residential apartment with a tenant who is a senior at the University and plans on staying only one year until graduation. The lease contains a one year term and requires the student to give up the apartment at the end of the year. When the end of the lease term arrives the student determines not to leave. The landlord points to the contract term. But the courts will not enforce the contract even though in Japan the concept of freedom of contract and freedom of will in making contracts is well accepted. What you see is not what you get.

A manufacturer and its exclusive distributor are having a dispute. The distributor has violated a term of the distributorship agreement and the contract provides that for such a violation the manufacturer may terminate. The manufacturer terminates but the distributor sues. The court recognizes that the contract allows termination for the violation. Nonetheless, the court finds that the distributor has devoted time and energy and resources to the business and concludes the violation is not so serious. Termination is not permitted.

A broadcast company wants to discharge a newscaster who on a number of occasions has slept through the time when he was supposed to be on air. The contract allows for discharge for failure to meet the contract terms. Clearly the terms have been violated. But the newscaster has not been malicious in his failure and the failure was caused in part by other reporters failing to wake him at the time requested. Discharge would be too great a penalty and besides he had apologized for missing the programs. Discharge was not permitted.[1]

A real estate broker has brokered a deal that will grant him a large commission. After orally agreeing to the deal the seller sells the property to a third party. The broker sues asserting that, as a written agreement is not required under the Civil Code, which recognizes oral agreements, it has a contractual right to a commission. The court holds

1. *Reporter who Overslept* case, *Shioda v. Kochi Broadcasting* 268 Rodo Hanrei (Sup. Ct. Jan. 31, 1977) discussed in Frank K. Upham, Visions of Justice in Postwar Japan: A Preliminary Inquiry, *Law in East and West* 145 (Waseda University Press 1988).

that there is no contract because there is no writing—although it is clear that the Civil Code does not require writing. [However the court finds another reason to grant the broker the part of the commission the seller was responsible for.][2]

What you see is not what you get. But this is not limited to contract, which might be explained by the abuse of rights doctrine or good faith requirements of the Civil Code.The Civil Code provides that a marriage that has not been registered in the Family Register is void and further than an uncle and niece cannot marry. Nonetheless when an uncle and his niece lived together as husband and wife and failed to register the marriage the Supreme Court noting that such "de facto marriages" supported certain social values in small farming communities (such as keeping the farm land in the family) and that the local community and its community leaders as well as the family of the "husband" and "wife" supported the "marriage" held that they were in de facto marriage relationship and thus the "spouse" was entitled to certain welfare and insurance benefits under a law that allowed such benefits to a de facto spouse. On the other hand the Civil Code contains a presumption that the husband of the woman who gives birth is the father of her child. But when the husband sought to have the child registered as his, the Registrar refused because the husband had been a woman and thus could not produce sperm.

The Building Safety Law requires that a building permit issue in 21 days if the safety aspects of the construction conform to the law. The building conforms but the permit is delayed beyond the 21 days to permit a leveling of the playing field between the builder and neighbors so they can attempt to negotiate a reasonable compromise. The city's action in delaying the permit is appropriate and not a violation of the law.

The Constitution provides for freedom of expression and forbids censorship of any type. But political candidates are severely restricted as to when they can speak, about what they can say, how much they can spend on campaigns, what media they can use, even the size of pictures of themselves that can be posted. All this is found Constitutional on the grounds that the rules level the playing field. But the playing field for independent candidates who run against political party candidates is not level and independents are put at a significant disadvantage in campaigning. So too, while censorship is forbidden textbooks must pass muster before the Ministry of Education and historic facts that are found inconvenient and are objected to by the government either do not find their way into certified texts or must be written in a way that waters down the event. The books may of course be published but cannot be used as texts but who would publish a textbook that cannot be used as such? The action of the Ministry is acceptable as it is not a formal rejection it is simply guidance and guidance cannot be challenged.

The new Companies Law allows for triangular mergers and thus opens the possibility to hostile takeovers. Courts have held that an abusive acquirer (an undefined term) can be prevented from such acquisition and shareholders may put in place

2. *Brokerage Commission (Real Estate)* case, *Suehiro Shoji v. Seisho Gakuen*, 790 Hanrei Jiho 63 (Tokyo High Court, 30 June 1975) discussed in Veronica L. Taylor, 'Continuing Transactions and persistent Myths: Contracts in Contemporary Japan,' 19 *Melbourne University* L. Rev. 352, 368–369 (1993).

a takeover defense in the midst of a takeover battle and tender offer. The reality is that there is yet to be a successful hostile takeover in Japan.

The Constitution specifically provides for equality of the sexes and the EOL requires non-discrimination. But two track-hiring systems keep many women out of senior executive positions, even after the amendment to the Act recognizing certain limited forms of "indirect discrimination." Bureaucrats lack power to force companies to follow Administrative Guidance, but as a rule guidance is followed and all would admit that the bureaucracy is quite powerful. The Constitution provides for equality and non-discrimination based on social status and background. But Burakumin and Ainu are not included in the Equal Opportunity Law. Supreme Court Justices are to be placed before voters after serving 10 years but as most Justices are appointed after reaching 60 and mandatory retirement is 70, few if any are presented to voters as the Constitution contemplates. It is a violation of the Constitution not to follow a modified one-person, one-vote election system. Diet elections almost never conform to the rule and the Supreme Court while finding the elections unconstitutional does not require a new election or overturn an old election. What you see is not what you get.

The Occupation modified the Rules of Civil Procedure to create a more Americanized adversary system. But Japanese judges control trials and can even set the order of questioning of witnesses. The Civil Procedure Code is amended to provide greater production of documents but the exemption from production of the most important self-use documents, namely those incorporating the opinions of employees engaged in the decision making process, swallows the new rule for "smoking gun" documents. The Code of Criminal Procedure was amended to abolish "trial by dossier" but prosecutors regularly submit their dossier, including defendant's confession and the police report with witness statements attached, at the start of the criminal trial and the burden then moves to the defense to undo the damage. The Code also prohibits hearsay under most circumstances but prosecutors regularly submit their own version of what suspects have said under interrogation without having to be cross examined as to the accuracy of such statements—accuracy is not always the case as the Ozawa prosecution has illustrated. The law requires speedy trial but the saran gas case continued to be tried 10 years after the events. The Administrative Court was abolished by the Occupation and administrative cases are to be tried in normal civil court. But the court system has created specialist District Court panels to try administrative cases rather than having them tried by judges who hear ordinary civil cases. The Occupation's theory was to make government action subject to judicial review but the doctrine of *shobunsai* and the circumstance decision lead to either the dismissal of or the failure to provide adequate relief in most administrative cases. What you see is not what you get.

The Japanese equivalent of the FOIA requires the production of certain government documents. But it was only revealed in 2010 that certain secret agreements that had been declassified by the United States and thus were publicly available (and no longer secret) were acknowledged to have been effective. And when the government was requested to produce such documents it asserted their non-existence and likely destroyed the documents before the FOIA went into effect so they could not be produced. Although required the government reported that no minutes were taken of high level meetings dealing with the Fukushima nuclear tragedy only to have some minutes of some meetings produced months later by Ministries that attended the meetings.

Criminal statutes must specifically define crimes and analogy is not permitted to expand the statutes' reach. But through "interpretation" some statutes have been greatly enlarged so that they may reach to 180 degrees away from the original intent. Suspects have a right not to answer questions but because they cannot stop the questioning and no counsel is present during questioning and because they can be held for questioning for 23 days or maybe longer almost all defendants eventually confess, thereby testifying against themselves. The Constitution requires a right to counsel in criminal cases but the right only attaches after indictment—when the defendant has typically already confessed and provided the necessary evidence for the prosecution to prove its case. The Penal Code contains stiff penalties for some crimes and mandatory minimums for others but hardly anyone, except repeat offenders, those who commit serious crimes and an entrepreneur who bucked the establishment, goes to jail. What you see is not what you get.

Under generally accepted principles treaties are the law of the land and override statutes—but by interpretation virtually no treaty ever overrides a statute. Treaties that might override statutes are found to not be effective but programmatic. Civil lawsuits are permitted for many types of disputes but damage awards are low and suits are expensive with the result that many cases that might be won if brought are simply never brought. And even if successful another procedure must be undertaken to obtain execution on the judgment and execution is difficult to obtain. So judges suggest and parties are well advised to accept compromise, which includes actual payment. Article 566(3) of the Civil Code constitutes a statute of limitations. But suit need not be brought within the time set out. All that is required is that the buyer clearly indicates its intention to make the seller accountable within the limitation period.[3] Under pressure from medical groups Japan passed a law permitting organ transplants—but because brain death was not recognized as "death" doctors who removed an organ from a brain dead person in order to transplant were accused of murder.[4] Organ transplants became impossible. So the law was changed to permit people to make their own decision as to whether they wished to donate organs when brain dead. But the law also requires family consent before an organ can be removed. As a result, the card solves one end of the problem but not the problem and transplant surgery is not covered by Japan's otherwise broad public medical insurance program.[5] The practical result is that while brain death has been recognized as such—for some purposes—since 1997, the law permitting transplants is not as effective as it should be.[6]

3. *Statute of Limitations* case, Case No. 1988 (0) No. 1543 (Sup. Ct. P.B. Oct. 20, 1992), http://www.courts.go.jp/english/judgments/text/1992.10.20-1988.-O-.No.1543.html.
4. Kazumasa Hoshino, *Legal Status of Brain Death in Japan: Why Many Japanese Do Not Accept 'Brain Death' As A Definition of Death*, 7 Bioethics Number 2/3 at 234, 236 (1993); Margaret Lock, *Deadly Disputes: Hybrid Selves and the Calculation of Death in Japan and North America (The History of Science Society)*, 13 Osiris 410 (1999).
5. *Japan Times*, Feb. 10, 2002 Transplant Expert Rues Cadaveric Donor, Social Charity Dearth.
6. Hiroshi Sakagami & Akemi Ari, *Donors' rights must be guarded / Greater legal protection required to ensure organs given up willingly*, Yomiuri Shimbun (Nov. 13, 2007), www.yomiuri.co.jp/dy/national/20071113TDY04303.htm.

A Japanese mother and a Japanese father donate the egg and sperm transplanted into a surrogate who gives birth to a child who is the biological child of the Japanese couple. But the family registrar refuses to register the child as the natural child of the Japanese genetic donors. The surrogate who delivered the child does not want the child. Clearly the best interests of the child are for recognition but the Court upholds the registrar's refusal.

Corporate law reform tracks the American model of reform and utilizes the hostile takeover model as one means of enforcement of director responsibility to shareholders. But, although triangular mergers and hostile takeovers are legally permitted hedge funds from the United States are stymied by poison pills that make successful hostile takeovers virtually impossible.

And yet Japanese citizens do not as a rule complain. And yet, the judiciary is the most respected branch of government. And yet, judicial decisions on issues of social policy or treaty interpretation affect changes at the political and legislative level. Japan's criminal justice system seems to work unusually well in protecting citizens and assisting criminals to rehabilitate. Japanese industry does not overly complain about Administrative Guidance and the public, at least until the Fukushima meltdown, had no great objection to the way the bureaucracy works. The Judicial Branch is overworked, is respected, is doing the public's business, disputes get resolved either at law or through ADR, Japan is a very free society with a strong democracy. What is happening and why does the judicial system work well in the face of what to many Americans may appear to be a system where law does not mean what it says and thus the Rule of Law is, at best, dormant?

Law may mean what it says in Japan, at least to the Japanese as understood by the Japanese. It is just that the principles used in the United States to understand the meaning of law is different from the operative principles at work in Japan. This does not mean that either set of principles is "correct" or that one operates better than the other does. In fact each seems to operate reasonably well in its own sphere. To the Japanese what you see may be what you get when you look at what you see through the lens of harmony, balancing of social values and norms, requirements of good faith, communitarian ideas and group dynamics. To Americans, who view law through the lens of individual rights and strict interpretation of words, the situation may appear different. But then, to Japanese what Americans get through their interpretation of law is not what it appears that it should be. And, for students and observers of comparative systems there may be much each can learn from the other—would not the United States benefit from a crime rate similar to that of Japan, from a repeat offender rate similar to that of Japan, to a prison population whose numbers are similar to that of Japan, to more apologies and less litigation?

Once again history is a good guide to understanding present day Japan. In Tokugawa Japan application of the law (such as it was) respected the letter of the law while the law's substance might be modified to reach a result that was in harmony with the prevailing views of society.[7]

7. Yoshiro Hiramatsu, *Tokugawa Law* (Dan Fenno Henderson trans.), 14 L. Japan 1, 43 (1981).

§18.01 HARMONY AND A BALANCING OF SOCIETAL INTERESTS VERSUS INDIVIDUAL RIGHTS

It is the function of the Japanese civil and criminal litigation systems to restore harmony. In the case of civil lawsuits, the effort is to restore harmony between litigants who have come to disagreement over an issue. If the litigants do not know each other, as in an auto case, the function of the system is to restore a sense of harmony in the society they both exist in. By restoring harmony in individual cases, a greater societal harmony can be achieved. Not only is this a function of the civil litigation system it is consistent with the "attitude" of Japanese society.[8]

This may sound strange to Americans but the goal of the common law appeal judge is similarly societal through individual cases. In each case the judge decides the "right and wrong" of the situation and through that decision sets out guidance for future application. By knowing what the law is, parties may negotiate with the rules in mind and come to agreements that take the rules into account. By knowing what the judges have decided, individuals have a better understanding of what is permitted and what is prohibited. It is for this reason that precedents are published and discussed, taught in law schools and parsed by lawyers on competing sides of cases and reported on in the New York Times. It is the collective experience of litigants, as determined by judges, that creates the common law. Societal purposes are served through individual cases.

Similarly judges use individual cases to establish, restore and systematize harmony in Japan. When possible, the legal system and courts attempt to bring about harmony between the litigants through mediation and compromise. When it is not possible, the system structures damage awards in ways that make the amount that can be expected in a future situation reasonably clear. With this clarity disputants need not go to the litigation system to resolve disputes but can go to some less "hostile" form of dispute resolution for closure.

It is axiomatic that litigation is confrontational. The adversary system is based on the assumption that the parties are adversaries—they are in conflict. Cross-examination assumes the witness is not telling the truth or at least not the whole truth on direct examination. The lawyer and witness are in an adversarial relationship, although good cross-examiners typically do not want that to appear to be the case. In such a setting, harmony is difficult to find and opportunities to bring the parties to a harmonious closure are difficult.

Where the judge is the trier of fact and can question witnesses freely, the adversary parties need not be so adversarial. Cross-examination losses much of its

8. Takeo Tanase, *Community and the Law: a Critical Reassessment of American Liberalism and Japanese Modernity* 147–148 (Luke Nottage & Leon Wolff trans. & eds., Edward Elgar Publishing Ltd. 2010). While Tanase does not refer to harmony and balance he argues that there is a Japanese attitude that leads to less litigation and has supported a legal system that does not encourage litigation. Tanase suggests that such "attitude" reflects a legal consciousness that may be unique to Japan. Such a consciousness that is not rooted in excessive regard for "rights" would, I suggest, be closely linked to harmony and consensus—strong Japanese values.

"hostile" nature when there is no jury to play to. Repeated appearances before the judge over an extended period of time may be frustrating to lawyers and clients but it tends to unite them and the judge in the quest for a shorter, easier and less hostile solution. Moreover it gives the parties and their lawyer a better opportunity to communicate so that the lawyer can better understand not just the legal nature of the party's complaint but the personal affront that might lie at the base of the litigation. This then better arms the lawyer to play a significant role in resolving the matter through a compromise. A series of meetings allows the judge to get to the root of the issue, which may not be legal at all but could well be interpersonal. A "legal" analysis may provide a correct "legal" resolution but understanding the emotional component of a dispute allows for a resolution that each side can walk away from as a winner. The frustrations of the Japanese trial system assist in the search for a less hostile more harmonious solution than an American style trial. Recent "reforms" that have as their goal a streamlined judicial process that brings cases to resolution quickly may serve a valuable bureaucratic or governmental purpose and may be useful in complex litigations between major companies but the speed of the process may disserve the interests of the litigants, without their recognizing this effect.

It is of course best to restore harmony as quickly as possible. The legal system has mechanisms available to do that. Apology, which is interpreted as "admission against interest" in the United States, is a useful lubricant to harmony. In Japan one can apologize and not have it used against the party at trial in the event apology and other actions are not sufficient to restore harmony. It may seem that what you see—the admission of wrong—is not what you get—it is not an admission of wrong at the trial—but that is not the case. Apology is not admission as much as it is sincere sorrow at the event and a showing of contrition. It does not have to have "legal" consequences to retain its apologetic character. This seeing of apology as two different things may be difficult for Americans but it does not mean that others cannot have a different (deeper, better?) understanding of the human relationship that is involved in simply saying "I am sorry."

The Japanese legal system also demands that parties work out their problems in a cooperative fashion before the breach of harmony implicit in a lawsuit occurs. Thus, the requirement that changed circumstances require new negotiations to account for those circumstances is an implicit part of each contract. That is why contracts contain good faith meet and negotiate provisions, backed up by the "sanction of law" through the interpretation of the Civil Code's abuse of rights and good faith provisions.

The administrative law system seeks to achieve harmony by placing a high premium on negotiated agreements. The goal of an administrative official giving Administrative Guidance is to achieve a certain end, but the goal of the guidance process is to get the agreement of the party being given guidance to that end. Guidance to many over a single goal seeks to get common action toward that goal. Even guidance to one has commonality as its end—the common objective of the administrator and the administrated. A "directive" from an administrative official is subject to discussion, negotiation and compromise for the sake of a harmonious relationship going forward.

Similarly, guidance from cities to construction companies that calls on them to negotiate with neighbors may not have a "statutory base" but they certainly help get the parties together to talk and try to reach a harmonious resolution of the problem.

Whether Japan is or is not as "harmonious" a society as is reflected in statements about harmony, and whether harmony in relationships is a "myth," is not of importance in understanding the role of harmony as a unifying factor in understanding Japanese law. Myth becomes reality when it is utilized to bind concepts together. Indeed, it may be argued that one of the functions of myth is to help a society explain itself to itself. As long as law professors, lawyers and judges continue to rely on the notion of harmony as an important element in the application of law, it will be an important element. The use of harmony is ubiquitous in legal discussion of Japan.

Regardless of the specific terms of the anti-trust laws, it is harmony and cooperation not anticompetitive legislation that is at the foundation of Japan's economic system and the relationships between companies and the government.[9] The Supreme Court in *The Osaka Small Business Restraint* case[10] referred to the statute involved as a measure designed to achieve "harmonious" development of the economy by taking into account the special problems of small- and medium-size business.

The circumstance decision may appear to be useless to Americans who simply see the plaintiff as having lost the case. But the reality is that the decision has great meaning. The respect for the judiciary means that changes will likely take place to achieve some if not all of the plaintiff's objectives, while the defendant is not faced with a loss of face. The need for consensus in board decisions at most Japanese companies is a reflection of the need to achieve harmony. The process may be infuriating to the American businessperson who wants a decision NOW, but once consensus is achieved, the carrying out of the policy is eased. Semi-annual bonuses may be an act of grace by management as a matter of law, but negotiating the amount of the bonus and coming to agreement on the bonus creates a more harmonious relationship with the employee force and is better for the company, the workers and the society.

Moreover consensus is required for judicial decisions at the District Court, High Court and even in the new saiban'in panels for criminal cases. Only at the Supreme Court can dissenting opinions be presented and even here the decision is usually announced as unanimous with separate dissenting opinions by Justices ____ and ____. The Cabinet also works on a consensus basis with Cabinet decisions being signed by all members of the Cabinet. Where a member refuses to sign the Prime Minister must use his authority to remove the Cabinet member to get the needed unanimity.[11]

---

9. Akira Negishi, *The Reception in Japan of the American Law and Its Transformation in the Fifty Years Since the End of World War II*, Econ. L., 26 L. Japan 34, 37 (2000).
10. *Osaka Small Business Restraint* case, *Marushin Industries, Inc. v. Japan*, 26 Keishu 586 (Sup. Ct. G.B. Nov. 22, 1972) reported in Lawrence W. Beer & Hiroshi Itoh, *The Constitutional Case Law of Japan, 1970 through 1990* 183, 187 (University of Washington Press 1996).
11. It is reported that when Prime Minister Koizumi determined to dissolve the House of Representatives because the Upper House had rejected a Bill that Koizumi wanted passed a Cabinet Member refused to go along with the dissolution. As a consequence Koizumi sacked the Minister to achieve the needed unanimity. See, Shigenori Matsui, *The Constitution of Japan* 100–103 (Hart Publishing 2011).

Similarly the Japanese criminal law system has harmony as its goal. A criminal is outside the harmony that should exist in society. It is the function of the criminal justice system to restore the offender to society. Where the victim of the crime can be brought into the process of restoration of harmony the criminal justice system will do so. Thus, apology and restitution are important aspect of Japanese criminal procedure. Unlike the United States, which places persons at the heart of the criminal justice system and insists on punishment for the harm caused, the Japanese system places the society and the defendant's place in society at the heart of the system and does not demand punishment but demands a restoration of harmony. Long sentences take defendants out of the community and into an anti-social world that harms the effort at rehabilitation. So judges use discretion to suspend sentences or reduce them to the point of suspension or at least as short as possible. Prosecutors know that confession is the first step on the road to rehabilitation, and thus the restoration of harmony with the rest of society, so it is important to obtain confession.

Harmony also affects the separation of powers and relations between the branches of government. This is especially true of Judicial/Diet relations. Japan, with a modern civil law tradition has found it necessary to incorporate in that tradition the American common law notion of "Judicial Review." The court exercising that right might well decide than the American concept of how to exercise judicial review is not consistent with the Civil Law respect for elected assemblies. The end result may be different from what Americans would expect from a court but it is not necessarily a case of not getting what the Japanese see in their Constitution. Added to that is the need to maintain harmony between the branches. A court more circumspect than an American court in determining when to say the legislature has exceeded the bounds of its legislative power will undoubtedly not upset harmony in governmental circles as much as a United States style judicial "activism." Such a court may resort to sending "warning shots" across the bow of the Diet before exercising the strong judicial power the framers of the Japanese Constitution intended the court to have. This does not mean that the rights in the Constitution are being laid aside; it simply may be another (different) means for achieving the Constitutional result.

Harmonious relations require that the parties take into account the context in which they find themselves. The context in turn may help to define the "right" asserted. And, in some contexts the "right" may be very different from what it otherwise would appear to be. For example, the right to freely contract is an important right. Exercising this right, parties may agree to what terms should be in the contract and one such term may permit cancellation of the contract if certain events happen. But when such an event happens the context in which the parties find themselves may have changed. This contextual change may bring about a change in the interpretation of the right. The exclusive distributor may have spent large sums to support the product after the contract was entered into. Cancellation in the context of the circumstance may be excessively harsh. Some other action may better serve to restore harmonious relations between the parties than termination, which breaks the relationship and puts the parties irrevocably out of harmony with each other. In such a case it is true that the parties have the freedom to contract but it is also true that the right to terminate may no longer mean a right to terminate at will. It may now be interpreted to take into account the circumstances and in so doing may mean that termination is not permitted.

Likewise context must take account of custom. Custom is in fact an integral part of Japanese law. When contracting in Japan (or in other business relations as well) one must know the customs that could attach to the contract and conform to them. Custom extends well beyond commercial law. In the *Tsu City Groundbreaking Purification* case[12], the court relied on custom and public consciousness in finding the ceremony not to violate the separation of Church and State.

Once it is understood that to create, restore or maintain harmony, all rights are contextual, the concept of rights in Japanese law becomes more understandable. American insistence on rights as written regardless of the context in which the rights are sought to be exercised creates confusion and a lack of understanding on the part of many Japanese just as the Japanese insistence that rights must be understood in context creates lack of understanding on the part of many Americans.

Any parent of more than one child knows that technical definition of rights does not always win out. That peace in the family, the ability for us all to live together in harmony may require that one child give up its "rights" to another at times to restore harmony. If need be the parent may have to intervene with a "creative interpretation" (based on the context in which the family finds itself) to restore harmony. Negotiation between the family members may be the best way to resolve problems no matter who is technically right. Of course the child with the abstract right may have more chips to bring to the negotiation table, and that is probably as it should be, but insistence on absolute right may be more harmful than compromise. The same is true among adults. Married couples that wish to stay married do not insist on their individual "abstract rights" in relationship with each other. When something is important for one the other may give up a right and there is the daily need to negotiate around some situations. The same is true in larger settings like the office,[13] the tennis club, etc. Why should it not be true in societal relations in general? Does it mean that the party with rights has no rights? Not at all. Does it mean that the vehicles for creating those rights have no meaning? Not at all. Does it mean that what you see is not what you get? Not if you interpret the right as flexible, contextual and changing with the situation and those affected by the right in a quest for harmonious relations.

§18.02 THE COMMON SENSE OF SOCIETY VERSUS STRICT INTERPRETATION: THE CONSENSUS OF THE COMMUNITY

Closely associated with harmony is the social value of considering the common sense of the community, or the norms of the society, or the consensus judgment of the community on an issue. After all, applying that common sense or consensus judgment

12. *Tsu City Ground Purification* case, *Kakunaga v. Sekiguchi*, Case No. 1971 (Gyo-Tsu) No. 69, 31 Minshu 533 (G.B. Jul. 13, 1977); http://www.courts.go.jp/english/judgments/text/1977.7.13-1971.-Gyo-Tsu-.No..69.html.
13. Takao Tanase, *Global Markets and the Evolution of Law in China and Japan,*' 27 Michigan J. Intl. L. 873 (2006).

to legal situations has the effect of harmonizing society with the law and parties to a dispute with society in general. If the meaning of law is contextual, then one important context is the view of society as to the issue presented. Thus, the courts' reference to norms of society[14] or the common sense judgment of society can be seen as a reference to the culture of the society as norms reflect a society's culture. In recent years the study of Japanese law has seen the pendulum swing away from a reliance on custom to a more structural or institutional analysis—but the pendulum may be returning to a kind of equilibrium.[15] Culture plays a role—even in the case of rationale for why there is less litigation in Japan than in the United States. Some types of litigation may be avoided for cultural reasons (as well as institutional reasons). Minamata disease sufferers may have initially avoided litigation because they did not want to parade the symptoms of their disease in public through the medium of a public trial.[16] As the society moderates its cultural values so too the prosecutors, potential litigants and judges will moderate their conduct—so we see longer sentences in rape cases in the twenty-first century than was true at the close of the 20th.

Japanese judges typically look to the law-making organ of the state to define a change in culture through legislation and see it as their role to support cultural values that have not been the subject of legislative change. Thus, the science behind tobacco damages suits will be treated almost with distain until the Diet or Cabinet deals with the issue (as it is now doing), just as the science behind brain death or surrogate birth is given a back seat to cultural values that spring from the family system of pre-Meiji Japan. Cultural values appear to underlie the Supreme Court's jurisprudence that prohibits the disclosure of internal company decision making documents for a viable operating entity but permits such disclosure once the entity has gone out of business or which prohibits production of documents used in the decision making process but permits production of documents disclosing the decision and actions to be taken based on the decision. By enforcing the norms of society or at least the Judiciary's perceived norms of society, the Japanese judicial system makes those norms rules of law—much as British common law judges made law in the heyday of British common law. This explains how and why Japanese judges made and continue to refine the legal rules dealing with continuing relationships and *"stronger" v. "weaker"* relationships such as distributorship law, landlord-tenant law and employer-employee law.

14. See, Carol Gluck, *Top Ten Things to know about Japan in the Early Twenty-First Century*, 13 Educ. About Asia 4 (2008). Gluck notes that one of the critically important thing to know is the primacy of society, including the preservation of social order, in Japan.
15. See e.g., Nicholas C. Howson & Mark D. West, *Law, Norms, and Legal Change: Global and Local in China and Japan*, 27 Michigan J. Intl. L. 687 (2006); John O. Haley, *Law and Culture in China and Japan: A Framework for Analysis*, 27 Michigan J. Intl. L. 895 (2006); Eric A. Feldman, *The Culture of Legal Change: A Case Study of Tobacco Control in Twenty-First Century Japan*, 27 Michigan J. Intl. L. 1 (2006); Leon Wolff, *Book Review of Burns, Sexual Violence and the Law in Japan*, 32 J. Japanese Stud. 447–451 (2006); Tsuyoshi Kinoshita, *Legal System and Legal Culture in Japanese Law*, 44 Comp. L. Rev. 25 (The Institute of Comparative Law in Japan 2010).
16. John O. Haley, *Comment, Law and Culture in China and Japan: A Framework for Analysis*,' 27 Michigan J. Intl. L. 895, 897 (2006).

This concept of common sense of the society is relevant to any contextual relationship between parties who have a relationship. Perhaps it applies to prevent the government from exercising its eminent domain powers over elderly farmers to build runways for congested airports. There appears to be no reason why it could not apply to other situations where the public would expect a party to act in a certain way or not act in a particular way. When the common sense judgment of society is that the reliance on a "right," even a right set forth in a statute, is generally appropriate but not appropriate in the circumstances, the "right" may have to be "reinterpreted" or even set aside. Accordingly, although a news reporter has a right to gather news, even secret documents, and report his findings to the public, and although the law permits him to continuously attempt to persuade a government employee to make such secrets available to him in violation of the law, and although newsgathering by its nature may involve incitement and inducement and such gathering supports the need of the public in a democracy to get information, when the news reporter exceeds socially acceptable ideas as to how to induce and incite when a reporter used sexual seduction of the public employee as part of a plan to obtain secret documents and terminated the affair after getting the documents, he may be guilty of a crime.[17] It was only after the DPJ came to power in 2010 that evidence emerged showing that the reporter's disclosure was in fact true and that official government documents had been destroyed to conceal the payments. Nonetheless truth was not the issue but method of discovery was the issue and the method exceeded the mores of society. So notwithstanding the truth of the reporting no new trial was permitted.[18]

The common sense of society has also been used by the Supreme Court to both support the administrative authority of school officials to dismiss students and to overrule administrative action in discharging students. A private woman's college was within its rights in discharging students who protested school policies in a paper because the school acted within its discretionary powers in finding such paper inconsistent with the college's educational goals. On the other hand, the president of Kyoto Prefecture Medical College expelled a student. The student challenged the expulsion and while the Supreme Court recognized that, as a rule, disciplinary action was within the university's discretion, it reversed the president's determination because the punishment was unsound as a matter of social norms as reflected in the common sense of society.[19]

This can be viewed as another form of contextualism, as the common sense consensus of society is part of the context. The common sense of society is what

17. *Nishiyama Official Secrets* case, *Nishiyama v. Japan*, 32 Keishu 457 (P.B. May 31, 1978). For an English language translation see Lawrence W. Beer and Hiroshi Itoh, *The Constitutional Case Law of Japan, 1970–1990* (University of Washington Press 1996) 543. See also, Shigenori Matsui, *Freedom of Expression in Japan*, 38 Osaka U. L. Rev. 13, 38 (1991).
18. See *Reporter Fails to Clear Name over '72 Scoop*, Japan Times (May 28, 2007).
19. Ichiro Ogawa, *Judicial Review of Administrative Actions in Japan* 196, discussing *Fukuda v. President Kyoto Prefecture Medical College*, 8 Minshu 1501 (Sup. Ct. July 30, 1954) (*Kyoto Prefecture Medical College Student Expulsion* case, 8 Minshu 1501 (Sup. Ct. July 30, 1954 in Dan Fenno Henderson, *The Constitution of Japan its First Twenty Years, 1947–1967*(University of Washington Press 1969).

establishes the norms of society and examination of norms includes an understanding of the customs of a society as well as its written laws.[20]

So too the failure of the society to have as yet coalesced around a consensus to change a cultural value is included in context—for the Japanese Supreme Court to compel society to move in one direction or another when consensus has not yet been achieved is unlikely. For the Court to strongly suggest to the government that it act to create a consensus and embody that consensus in a law is much more likely. But when the Court's perception is that there is a societal consensus or that a rule of law is consistent with the judiciary's perception of a cultural value it will act.

Thus the right of employers to fire at will employees may have to succumb to the common sense judgment of society that it is inappropriate in the circumstance. The right of a manufacturer to discharge the offending exclusive distributor may succumb to the consensus of society that in the circumstance the penalty does not fit the wrong. The right of a tortfeasor to rely on previous decisions that set forth a high standard of proof on the part of the plaintiff may have to give way to the consensus of society that the wrong committed is so great the plaintiffs should have relief from such rules (as in the *Minamata* disease and other big four pollution cases). The rule can, of course, work in both directions. The Constitutional right of women to equal treatment may give way to the consensus of society that existed at the time the allegedly wrongful act took place and thus the employer may not be responsible for damages. The consensus of society as to the rights of aliens may override what appear to be clear Constitutional rights granted to such aliens who are permanent residents of Japan.

American law, which has much less regard for context in these terms, may find granting such power to a judge inconsistent with the "right" that persons have a right to rely on. Moreover, it may appear to be far too great a power to give judicial officers, as their view of societies' judgments is not necessarily correct. On the other hand, giving judges the power to overturn statutes passed by elected representatives of the people is a broad and strong power. Just as use of a "common sense judgment of society" or "consensus of the public" or "norms of society" standard strikes American lawyers as rule of man and not Rule of Law, a lack of understanding and appreciating contextualism may be viewed from a Japanese prospective as a failure of law to reflect societal values.[21]

Of course, in a Constitutional democracy the first place to look for norms of society would appear to be in legislative enactments of the popularly elected Legislative Branch. As the representatives of the people at large, it would be expected that these representatives incorporate the norms of society in the laws they write. Because the winds of emotion can affect public perceptions and appear to change norms over the short term, written Constitutions are viewed as preventing a temporary majority from

20. See Shigemitsu Dando, *The Criminal Law of Japan: The General Part* 85 (B. J. George trans., Rothman & Co. 1997).
21. There are times when the Supreme Court of the United States may use a consensus of society approach to a problem. But they are rare. *Atkins v. Virginia*, 536 U.S. 304 (2002).

infringing fundamental rights under the guise of norms or common sense judgment of society.[22] To this end Constitutions may require super majorities for amendment.

When Constitutional issues are not involved it would appear reasonable to look to the legislation as being the best guide for the common sense judgment of society. The Judicial Branch in Japan, while paying great respect to the Legislative Branch in refusing to find laws unconstitutional or resolve on its own social issues best left for legislation is sometimes prepared to lead when convinced that societal views have changed and the legislature has not acted.[23] There is in fact no inconsistency in this position. Deference is paid to the Legislative Branch when broad policy issues are involved. However, once those broad issues are resolved, the judiciary is free to apply the common sense of society as to how to interpret and apply those norms. In a sense, the professional judicial bureaucracy plays the same role in dealing with judicial issues as the professional administrative bureaucracy plays in dealing with administrative issues. This may explain, at least in part, why the judiciary is so circumspect when questions are raised as to the administrative bureaucracy's judgment and prodding of private parties.

This judicial "prodding of the legislature" to deal with broad policy issues or to modify positions as the norms of and consensus of society have changed has exerted pressure on the Legislative Branch to catch up with the judicially understood common sense judgment of the society as a whole. Although it can be explained as a form of contextualism, the policy holds potential dangers, as there may be inconsistent application of the rule. Moreover, the court acts without a complete record on the issue of the common sense judgment of society. Judges can and frequently do make errors in gauging the temper of the times—and the temper of the times may not reflect society's view over the longer term. Nonetheless, Japanese courts appear to have adopted a "long-term" view of what societal norms are composed of and are cautious in their approach to what has been accepted as a consensus of the community most affected by its decision.[24] This long-term approach and the slowness with which matters are decided in the Japanese judiciary gives the judiciary and the Diet an opportunity to test the public's view of lower court determinations.

When there has been coalescence by society around an idea as acceptable, it becomes part of the common sense experience of the society to accept that idea. The Japanese society as a whole (there are of course always some who disagree), whether out of concern for tensions faced in Japan's geographic neighborhood from an assertive neighbor (North Korea) and/or a developing and much bigger neighbor (China) or for reasons of performing the role required of a major economic power, has accepted the

22. Cf. *McCulloch v. Maryland*, 17 U.S. ___ (4 Wheat.) 316, 407 (1819) ('We must never forget that it is a *constitution* we are expounding.' Marshall, C.J.).
23. For a general discussion of judicial philosophy in Japan see Hiroshi Itoh, *How Judges Think in Japan*, 18 Am. J. Comp. L. 775 (1970). Itoh traces Japanese judicial philosophy from the Minshoho school, which he states viewed the role of judges as fact finding, law interpretation and then application of law to the facts to reach a conclusion, to a more value oriented process ('experimentalist') where value orientation is a major determining factor in choosing what rule of law to apply.
24. Takao Tanase, *Global Markets and the Evolution of Law in China and Japan*, 27 Michigan J. Intl. L. 873, 884 (2006).

idea that Japan needs a sophisticated military force for purposes of self-defense. This view is consistent with the government's policy of maintaining such a force. Thus, it is the consensus of society (the common sense judgment of the society) that the SDF is a legitimate and legal organization and that its existence and contracts are not violations of the pacifist Constitution, public policy, or otherwise inconsistent with Article 90 of the Civil Code. However, there is yet to be a consensus about the proper role of the SDF—especially about its deployment abroad. Here there appears to be agreement that the SDF can be used when its mission is solely humanitarian or to maintain a peace already agreed to by parties and the SDF is dispatched under the umbrella of the United Nations. But when the SDF is not used under the auspices of the UN and there is armed conflict, the consensus breaks down. In such situation it is likely that the judicial system will refrain from taking any action that is inconsistent with the policy established by the Diet, the Supreme Organ of the State, and the elected representative of the society.

And the idea of common sense of the society and need for a consensus affects not only the Judicial Branch but also the law-making Legislative Branch. Bills may take years moving through the policy group, committee, and Diet process before being enacted so that views of all sides may be heard and compromised so that a consensus position may be formed as the basis for legislation. To do this compromises are made that may require the Judicial Branch to define the terms of the compromise (as is the case with the document production provisions of the Civil Procedure Code and recently enacted legislation dealing with employment). But when a consensus cannot be found by the Legislature and the issue finds its way into the judicial arena the court tends to send the issue back to the legislature and to rely on: (a) the older more comfortable rule that harkens back to Japan's history, (b) the position of the government in the case, or (c) private ordering. This is the situation with modern medical techniques that raise ethical questions and questions going to the heart of Japan's notions of family, family law and the natural order. Thus, when the court denies the biological parents of a child delivered by a surrogate mother the right to register the child in the Family Register it does not do so out of a failure to recognize the genetics of the child but rather does so in the shadow of a disagreement in the Japanese society as to how to deal with surrogacy. That is, there is no consensus of society and hence no common sense judgment of society that something as "unnatural" as surrogacy is acceptable and if so in what situations.

In looking for the consensus of society and the society's common sense judgments the Supreme Court and the Legislature will be guided to some extent by Japan's feudal as well as Meiji era past. Marriage between an uncle and niece to preserve agriculture was permitted and practiced in Tokugawa Japan and this forms a predicate for recognizing a de facto relationship when statutes grant benefits to de facto spouses in agricultural communities today where it may serve the same purpose.

[A] Liberal Individualism versus Communitarianism[25]

The philosophical debate between liberal individualism, represented by the works of Kant and Rawls[26] and the counterattack to such approach by those who have been characterized as communitarian such as MacIntyre[27], Taylor[28] and Sandel[29] may be a useful mirror in which to look at Japanese law.[30] While liberal individualism focuses on the interests of the self—on the individual who is bound because she agrees to be bound (a contractual theory such as the social contract) and who owes certain universal obligations such as by way of natural law —as well as self-sufficiency, communitarians find that there is a moral value to community in and of itself. That members of society owe certain obligations to other members of the community to which they belong whether they have agreed to be bound by such obligations or not. These are not universal obligations that arise out of natural law but are obligations limited to the community of which the individual is a part. When confronted with a moral choice in which either of two alternatives is possible but not both and equal good in an abstract sense will follow from either choice it is appropriate to choose that which protects a member of your community rather than the stranger. Individual good may need to be sacrificed in favor of the community good. Thus community values and community norms are important and so too is community good as distinguished from the individual good.

Professor Tanase, a foremost thinker and philosopher of Japanese law, also sees community as central to a modern legal system and in this regard sees United States rights based law at odds with community but finds community in much of Japanese law. He points out that it is important that those who are governed by a legal interpretation consider that interpretation as correct or put another way that the community affected by the law approves of the law as interpreted by the courts and as applied in real life situations.[31] Thus the voice of the community is relevant in

---

25. For a Brief introduction to communitarianism see, D. Bell, *Communitarianism, Stanford Encyclopedia of Philosophy*, http://plato.stanford.edu/entries/communitarianism/, last accessed Sept. 17, 2012; See also, *Communitarianism in Law and Society*, Paul van Seters ed., Rowman and Littlefield 2006); For communitarianism and Japan see generally, Takeo Tanase, *Community and the Law: a Critical Reassessment of American Liberalism and Japanese Modernity*, translated and edited by Luke Nottage and Leon Wolff (Edward Elgar Publishing Ltd., 2010); John O. Haley, *A Spiral of Success, In Context, http://www.context.org/ICLIB/IC38/Haley.htm.*; John O. Haley, *Law and Culture in China and Japan: A Framework for Analysis*, 27 Michigan J. Intl. L. 895 (2006).
26. E.g., John Rawls, *A Theory of Justice* (Harvard University Press 1971); John Rawls, *The Law of Peoples* (Harvard University Press 1999).
27. Alasdair MacIntyre, *After Virtue* (2d ed., University of Notre Dame Press 1984); Alasdair MacIntyre, *Whose Justice? Which Rationality* (University of Notre Dame Press 1988).
28. Charles Taylor, *Philosophy and the Human Sciences, Philosophical Papers* 2 (Cambridge University Press 1985).
29. Michael Sandel, *Liberalism and the Limits of Justice* (2d ed., Cambridge University Press 1998); Michael Sandel, *Justice: What's the Right Thing to Do?*, (Farrar, Strau, and Giroux 2009).
30. See, Sharyn L. Roach Anleu, *Law and Social Change* 121–123 (2d ed., SAGE Publications 2010).
31. Takeo Tanase, *Community and the Law: A Critical Reassessment of American Liberalism and Japanese Modernity*, 108 (Luke Nottage & Leon Wolff trans.& eds.,Edward Elgar Publishing Ltd. 2010) hereinafter cited as Tanase, *Community and the Law*).

determining what a law means and whether a law comports with the Constitution. However, this view of communitarianism runs the risk of replacing communitarian ideals with majoritarian dogma—a vice that can adversely affect a minority or a disenfranchised group not recognized as part of the "community," a vice that most modern liberal Constitutions seeks to avoid through providing rights for the minority that cannot be abrogated by the majority. Tanase's view of communitarianism would bring together both ideas of public and private law and action to do away with discrimination.[32]

In a society less concerned by "rights" than is the United States and more concerned with society's view of what is seen as just or the good, the rights of the minority may nonetheless sometimes be sacrificed for the majority's notion of the good, although certain essential rights should remain above the fray. Thus it is postulated that in the United States "best interests of the child" a standard that reflects the good is watered down by the rights that *each parent asserts* in a visitation or custody dispute, as distinguished from the interests of the child. In Japan a ban on visitation may be justified by the idea that such ban is in the interests of the child without being distracted by the parents' differing claims. Although Tanase believes that Japanese law should give greater weight to visitation by non-custodial parents he would find support for such visitation outside the "parental right" dialogue.[33]

Tanase sees the hand of the community as significant in interpersonal relations that are implicated in situations that are handled in the United States through resort to law. The community may be as small as the players in litigation. Thus lawyers should devote more time trying to understand the emotion of their client and how that emotion is related to the litigation not only the emotions of their client but the emotions of the other side as well so that a compromise resolution that deals with emotions that may lie at the heart of the "legal" dispute may be taken into account. A "just" result involves more than simply monetary compensation and indeed the monetary aspect may detract from the good because what may really be at stake is not money but other interpersonal or emotional or non-monetary considerations. To achieve the appropriate relief resort to law or at least adherence to having law rule the outcome may be counterproductive.[34] To Tanase Japan's legal system reflects, at least in part, a search for community that can be found through societal values.[35] For example, the idea of what is in the best interest of the child—i.e., a ban on visitation in Japan is determined at least in part by the social norm that rejects shared custody or visitation.[36] But, while it may be correct

32. Tanase, *id.* at 10.
33. Tanase, *id.* at 91. See also, Takao Tanase, *Divorce and the Best Interest of the Child: Disputes Over Visitation and the Japanese Family Courts*, (Matthew J. McCauley trans.) 20 Pacific Rim Law & Policy J. 563 (2011) where Tanase appears to give more weight than in the past to the right of the child as distinguished from the right of the parents or the rights of the society.
34. Tanase, *Community and the Law*, at 44–49 and 60–62.
35. Tanase, *id.* at 57.
36. Tanase, *id.* at pages 64 and 65. That custody to the mother, the prevailing view of the Japanese judiciary is consistent with norms of the society see, Allison Alexy, *The Door my Wife Closed* (Chapter 12) *Home and Family in Japan* (Richard Ronald, and Allison Alexy eds., Routledge 2011).

that rights doctrine may interfere with the good, a basic idea of Tanase's communitarianism, it is questionable whether the good can be determined from a norm of the society, especially if the norm is contrary to facts or morality. In visitation for example the determination of the good should flow, at least in part, from modern science or other objective studies—such as sociological and psychological studies and reports that reflect what is truly in the best interests of the child—rather than a court's *ex cathedra* announcement of the prevailing social norm—even if that announcement correctly captures the public's current view.

In many regards Tanase's view of communitarianism is different from that of some Western exponents of the philosophy—something Tanase accepts.[37] Indeed, it lies at the heart of many of his essays that are brought together in the text cited in the footnotes. Nonetheless, the difference in approach should not obscure the fact that Tanase (and judicial precedent and reasoning in Japan) as well as the Western adherents of communitarianism share the basic idea that community matters and that it matters in legal affairs just as it does in everyday life and that it is important to take community into account when striving for the good in judicial determinations.

By emphasizing common good of the community, communitarians diminish the role of individual good and individual rights in favor of community good and community rights. This does not mean that communitarians reject the notion that some rights are so fundamental that they cannot be rejected by a majority vote of the relevant community (thus communitarians can recognize universal obligations and values such as those arising from natural law) nor that community values at a specific point in time should dominate over other interests. Nor are all communitarians committed to the idea that values of a community determine how to define justice in any particular case. Some argue that it is the moral significance of the end to be achieved that defines a right.[38] Others argue that there is room for a coming together of communitarian ideas and liberal individualism in a way that leads to a liberal communitarianism or a communitarian liberalism in which changed circumstances as well as communal needs are relevant.[39] Nonetheless communitarians tend to believe that traditions and culture of the particular society or community to which one belongs are relevant to moral, social, political and even legal judgments.

Communitarians are not convinced that liberal individualism is a universal ideal and are prepared to focus more on values of individual communities and the norms of such communities as determined by community members themselves as well as the effect of actions on persons as members of a community as an aid in determining the moral significance of the end sought to be achieved. This, of course raises the question of what is the relevant community and various forms of communities have been suggested as communities to be valued—not the least of which are communities described by geography both large (the world community, the nation state, etc.) and

37. See, e.g., Tanase *id*,, at 135 fn. 4.
38. See, e.g., Michael Sandel, *Liberalism and the Limits of Justice* at x (2d ed., Cambridge University Press 1998).
39. See, e.g., *The Jurisprudence of Communitarian Liberalism*, Philip Selznic in *Communitarianism in Law and Society* 19, 29 (Paul van Seters ed., Rowman and Littlefield 2006).

small (a local farming community, the company to which one is committed, etc.); and communities tied together by a common history or language. Communitarianism does not reject the idea of democracy and/or equality as each member of the community needs to be considered when a community norm is evaluated and looked to. Similar ideas can be found in the history of Japan (such as the significance, role of and governing principles of the village in Tokugawa Japan,[40] the family law institution of the *Ie* which itself forms a relevant community whose members are tied together, or the pre-war Emperor system and State Shinto in which all members of the society were deemed members of a community that shared Emperor and religious values as a family)[41] and in aspects of Japanese society that tend to emphasize group togetherness (such as the modern company/employee relationship).[42]

This may explain, at least in part, the phenomenon in Japan of the government delegating to private organizations responsibilities that in the United States are considered the responsibility of the State. Thus the unwillingness (to date) of the Japan Society of Obstetrics and Gynecology to find in vitro fertilization or surrogate birth ethical plays a significant role in the Supreme Court's rejection of surrogacy and posthumous in vitro conception and the government's rejection of surrogacy and in vitro fertilization (except in the case of those suffering from Gender Identity Disorder—where the Society recognizes in vitro as acceptable and so too does the government—but not so acceptable that the child should be registered as the natural child of the father whose sperm was not used as he had no sperm to contribute).

It is not the point here to debate the intricacies of the differing philosophies or to argue for or against either approach or aspects of either approach. Rather it is the point to note that Japan, has been and is much more a communitarian society than is the United States, notwithstanding that its Constitution clearly embodies the ideals of liberal individualism[43] although it may be argued that Article 13 of the Constitution while recognizing individualism subjects such individualism to a communitarian limitation.[44] The Supreme Court of Japan has approached many legal issues with a more communitarian approach than the Supreme Court of the United States, in the sense that the Supreme Court of Japan looks at community values and persons as parts

40. Carol Gluck, *Japan's Modern Myths: Ideology in the Late Meiji Period* 211 (Princeton University Press 1985).
41. See, e.g., Toshio Ochi, *Communitarian Liberalism in America and Conservative Political Thought and Discourse in Japan*, Paper presented at the annual meeting of the American Political Science Association, Marriott Wardman Park, Omni Shoreham, Washington Hilton, Washington, DC, Sept. 1, 2005, http://www.allacademic.com/meta/p_mla_apa_research_citation/0/4/2/6/8/p42685_index.html.
42. See, John O. Haley, *Why Study Japanese Law?*, 58 Am. J. Comp. L. 1 5–6 (2010).
43. For a general discussion of Communitarianism and Japanese law see, Toon Peters, *Law and Society in Japan*, in *Communitarianism in Law and Society* 49 et seq. (Paul van Seters ed., Rowman and Littlefield 2006); See also, Tatsuo Inoue, *Predicament of Communality*, in *Communitarian Politics in Asia* 46–56 (Routledge 2004) noting that a communitarian mode of conflict resolution as well as labor relations, etc., dominates Japanese society.
44. For a view that American's are not as individualistic as they think and that Japanese are indeed imbued with the idea of individualism—comparing Article 13's "public welfare" with American "communitarians" "general welfare"—see, Lawrence W. Beer & John Maki, *From Imperial Myth to Democracy* 125 (University of Colorado 2002).

of a community as well as the effect of its decision on the "relevant" community in considering the justice of a matter. However, the use of community mores and community sense of what is right while making use of community is not necessarily communitarian. The substitution of majoritarianism (as reflected for example in an act of the Diet that presumably represents the consensus of the Japanese public) for individualism is not consistent with much of communitarian thought and fails to address the critical question of the "justice" interest in the Court's decision. Moreover, an act of the Diet may not reflect the actual will of the majority in Japan's population. This is especially so considering the nature of Japanese politics, the role of money in Japanese politics and the power of special interest groups in Japan's political parties and factions of parties as well as the role of the bureaucracy in the law-making process.

Communitarian values have also found their way into the 2006 amendment of the Fundamental Law on Education. Amendment of the Occupation influenced law dealing with education had been a prime objective of some of the conservative forces in Japan's ruling LDP for many years. The 2006 amendments specifically make contributing to the society's development based on communal spirit an objective of education and specifically make patriotism (a love of one's country as the relevant community) an objective of education. In the Japanese context this is designed to make a turn away from individuality and towards communitarianism part of the Japanese education system.

Communitarian concepts confuse Japan's acknowledgment of its wartime conduct. While in an individualistic society the objection to acknowledgment of a prior generation's actions (and the need to apologize for such actions) may be grounded in the idea that the current generation was not responsible for the prior generation's wrongful conduct and thus has nothing to apologize for, such rationale is not as readily available to a communitarian society, especially one rooted in generational continuity ideas. It appears easier for individual rights and autonomy societies to apologize for past wrongs than for Japan. Thus the United States has apologized for its horrific treatment of Japanese-American citizens during the war, has built monuments to recognize the courage of those who suffered as a consequence thereof, has reopened past records to find and properly honor Japanese-American soldiers whose bravery during the war warranted the Medal of Honor, and has paid compensation for its prior improper actions. So too some States have adopted resolutions apologizing for slavery—although the question of payment of compensation to African-Americans runs into opposition based on individualism (this generation did not own slaves—an argument met with the claim that this generation derives benefits from the labor of slaves because that labor laid the foundation for current benefits—in the United States the debate is further complicated by the fact that not only did the current generation not own slaves but most current citizens are the offspring of immigrants who arrived in the U.S. after both slavery and Jim Crow laws were made illegal). As the textbook debate in Japan shows it appears more difficult for the current generation to acknowledge wrongdoing by a prior generation in Japan. The answer may be as simple as the fact many of Japan's political elite are the offspring of the political elite whose actions would have to be acknowledged in an apology. But it is also possible that the communitarian nature of Japanese society makes apology for a prior generation more difficult. It is the community of Japan that would be seen as responsible for prior actions and the community of Japan that is apologizing. Perhaps the notion of communitarianism is why the lack of an apology does not have the same impact on the United States (an individualistic society) as it does for some of Japan's Far East neighbors who suffered during the war (such as China, Indonesia, the Philippines) and who share a communitarian approach to many issues.

Common sense of the society as used by the Supreme Court of Japan does not necessarily mean the entirety of the Japanese society. What is relevant is membership in and/or the consensus of the important or relevant Japanese community. Thus for some issues—surrogate pregnancy for example the entire nation is likely to be considered the important community rather than the community of women who cannot carry a child through pregnancy to birth. It may mean the portion of society that has the most interest in the issue. Thus, when an uncle and niece live in a de facto marriage relationship the court will try to determine what is acceptable to the community with most at stake by looking not at the Civil Code or the rules that apply in the big cities but rather by looking at the local society where the parties live, work and raise their family. It is in the mirror of that society that the acceptability of the relationship, at least for purposes of welfare benefits will be judged. Many Japanese workers identify more strongly with their company then they do with their family. In turn Japanese companies embody the community of the company and its workers. In such situation it is not acceptable to throw workers out of work simply because the company is suffering an economic set back and it is not acceptable to require the company to produce internal decision making documents as that may adversely affect the communal relationship between employees and employer.[45] On the other hand, the relative strength of identity with company (very strong) versus with nuclear family (relatively weak) creates societal problems and may well be related to the declining birth rate in Japan that in turn adversely affects the entire community of the Japanese. Here the Diet has acted to try to create a more balanced family/company relationship in order to increase the greater good of the larger Japanese community. And the Court has followed suit by recognizing the responsibility of the employer when a worker has literally worked himself to death and by refusing to offset against compensation in such a case certain matters that would be offset in typical tort cases.

Take for example the Japanese approach to the rights of a spouse whose husband was killed while a member of the SDF vis-à-vis the rights of the community as represented in part by the husband's family and the community where he was raised. In the *Gokoku Enshrinement case* the Supreme Court of Japan focused on the rights of the community and found a primacy in the community's right to have the deceased soldier venerated at the shrine. The common sense of the local community was that the family of a deceased SDF member (and local community where he grew up) should have the right to honor his death in a Shinto fashion, even if his wife is Christian. The

45. For a discussion of the company as community between employer and employee see Goodman, *The Evolving Law of Document Production in Japanese Civil Procedure: Context, Culture, and Community*, 33 Brooklyn J. Intl. L. 125 (2007); Daniel A. Bell, *Beyond Liberal Democracy* 279 (Princeton University Press 2006).

consensus judgment of the community would appear to be to allow the wife to honor her husband in the way she sees fit while at the same time allowing his parents and local community the right to honor him the way they see fit. That the Self-Defense establishment may have assisted the family and community in carrying out their desires to have a shrine deify him will not rise to a level of sufficient government involvement to implicate separation of Church and State issues while the action of the shrine will not be inconsistent with Article 90's good faith and morals requirement. This is not to say that the wife's rights were totally disregarded—rather the Court in dealing with the competing rights of the individual (spouse) and the community found the community's right to be paramount and found that the right of the spouse could be accommodated by allowing her to worship her deceased husband as she pleased without forcing the community to either follow her belief or be left without a way to celebrate the deceased as a departed community member. In more philosophical terms the community good was enhanced and while the individual good was diminished it was not totally rejected or discarded. Looked at in more legal terms the individual "rights" of the spouse were found not to be superior to the "community rights" of the parents and others in the local community where the deceased was raised and brought up. At the same time, the Court did not take sides in the dispute about the relative worth of the self-defense force while recognizing that the community does not find the SDF to be immoral.

So too in the corporate takeover poison pill context of the *Bull-Dog case*, values of the community of shareholders and other stakeholders take precedence over the interests of individual shareholders—even if the community of shareholders has to be constructed. When a tender to take over a company is made the shareholders individually have the right to accept or reject the tender. Each makes its own decision individually. But when the takeover target intervenes in the process by injecting a takeover defense that needs approval of the general meeting of shareholders, the anonymity of the individual shareholder decision may be lost at the general meeting where each votes. In each case—tender of the shares or vote in favor of the takeover defense—it is the body of shareholders that makes the ultimate decision but in tendering its own shares the shareholders act individually and in voting at the shareholders' meeting they reject the tender offer as a community. The need to take the decision as a community rather than as individuals is so strong that the Supreme Court is prepared to allow that decision to be made by a community although it may in fact not be the relevant community at the time of the vote. That is to say, shareholders attending and allowed to vote at the general meeting may in fact have sold their shares between the date of the closing of the company's books and the date of the meeting. This fact, which clearly must have been known to the Supreme Court in the *Bull-Dog/ Steel Partners* case, was neither mentioned in the Court's decision nor was it allowed to stand in the way of the over 80% vote in favor of the defense and thus against Steel Partners' plan.

Steel Partners/ Bull Dog represents communitarianism in another aspect. Although the Supreme Court focused on the majoritarian aspects of the shareholder's vote, the case may reflect a broader community than simply shareholders. The Bull Dog shareholders overwhelmingly accepted the takeover defense, which in essence was the payment of green mail in exchange for shares. Viewed on a purely economic basis the tender offer price provided a significant premium over the market price and the cost was so great to Bull Dog that it has not yet recovered to its pre-takeover defense value. Why then did shareholders so overwhelmingly adopt a rejection of the take over? The answer might be found in the effect the takeover would have on the relevant Bull Dog community. While shareholders selling out might benefit, the effect on the Bull Dog employees of an ownership that might not respect and carry forward the Japanese core employee "lifetime" employment system and/or the relationships with other companies who also form a part of the Bull Dog community might suffer. Shareholders might well have seen themselves as part of a broader community of Bull Dog stakeholders that needed to be protected even if shareholders had to suffer some economic loss.

Similarly, when the mixed lay/professional judge panel system for determining certain criminal cases was challenged on Constitutional grounds the basic thrust of the arguments against the system's validity were directed to the burden the system placed on the lay judges rather than on the question of whether the use of lay personnel infringed the accused's right to a fair and impartial trial. And, in upholding the system the Tokyo High Court, while it found that the rights of the accused were not violated appears to have been more concerned about the utility of the system in fostering the public good by improving the confidence society has in the judicial system and improving trust in the judicial system while at the same time minimizing the burden on lay jurors.[46]

The individual rights of children with health issues who need organ transplants were subordinated to the perceived community objection to harvesting the organs of deceased children. As a consequence harvesting organs from children was prohibited. Even the new law allowing the harvesting of such organs from children is worded in such a way as to recognize the rights of family—just as the organ donation system recognizes the rights of the family of the deceased—even when the (adult) deceased during life made it clear that the deceased wished organs to be harvested and transplanted.

The smaller community of the family appears to be the dominant community when Japanese law considers the rights of patients to full information from their physician. The doctrine of informed consent—based on the patient's individual right to choose the medical course to be followed for the patient's treatment is gaining support in Japanese legal circles but in a modified form that recognizes community. Thus while doctors are now required to give information on which informed consent can be based,

46. *High court rules lay judge system constitutional, upholds murder conviction*, Mainicnhi News (Apr. 22, 2010), http://mdn.mainichi.jp/mdnnews/news/20100422p2a00m0na010000c.html; Kyodo News, *High court rules lay judge trial constitutional*, Japan Times (Apr. 23, 2010), http://search.japantimes.co.jp/cgi-bin/nn20100423a6.html. The Supreme Court has held the Lay Judge system is Constitutional in two cases, Lay Judge System Constitutional Case, Case No. 2010 (A) No. 1196, Keishu Vol. 65, No. 8 (11/ 16/11), http://www.courts.go.jp/english/judgments/text/2011.11.16-2010.-A-.No..1196.html and *Lay Judge System Constitutional Case*, Case No. 2010 (A) No. 1299, Keishu Vol. 66, No. 1 (P.B., Jan. 13, 2012) http://www.courts.go.jp/english/judgments/text/2012.01.13-2010.-A-.No..1299.html.

such information need not be given to the individual patient. Rather, by informing the patient's family and leaving it to the family to determine how to or even whether to inform the patient, the medical practitioner's duty has been met. In a sense the individual patient is not in control of her treatment but the community of the patient's family is placed in charge of such decision. So too, the individual is not in full control of the decision as to whether to donate organs—the family is brought into the picture and has a say on the donation decision.To recognize the importance of community values, norms and the community good does not diminish the fact that sometimes community values do not represent moral imperatives and that community values may conflict. Where they conflict the Japanese legal system appears to recognize that some community values may create obligations that in turn create severe hardship that must be acted against to protect a larger community good. There are cases where it is necessary to diminish the importance of one community tie in favor of other community ties, such as diminishing the company community in favor of the family community.[47] Where community values may not lead to a "just" decision the Supreme Court may be willing to give too great a value on the community and not enough value on the individual. Thus, the best interests of the child in the Surrogate birth case are not realistically considered and the best interests of the child in the posthumous in vitro fertilization case are treated cavalierly at best.

Community in Japan is also used as a means of protecting individuals, especially when they are being thrust out of a relevant community—especially when there is no alternative community reliably available. Thus, core employees cannot be thrust out of the company/employee community simply because of economic benefit to the employing company. Rather there must be a necessity that requires this action and even then it can only be taken after all alternatives have been tried and have failed. Survival of the company must be truly at stake.

Consensus and community are such fundamental ideas that the new *saiban'in* system for criminal cases has no provision dealing with the possible situation where a majority of the nine-judge mixed panel votes in one way but the decision cannot be carried out because no professional judge on the panel will vote consistent with the majority of the lay panel members. In other words there can be no "hung jury" or

47. See, Daniel A. Bell, *Beyond Liberal Democracy*, 279 (Princeton University Press 2006). One aspect of communitarianism challenges the idea that liberal individualism is a universal value. Some have used the idea of "Asian values" that are less liberal and less individual and less accommodating to human rights and have tried to tie communitarianism to approval of such values. However communitarianism is not a basis for or support for antidemocratic values or degrading basic human rights—the community is likely better served by having the community, on a basis of equality, elect its representatives. As properly understood communitarianism need not be either "liberal" or "conservative." This is demonstrated by the powerful overtones of community in Justice Steven's dissent in *Citizens United v. Federal Election Commission*: "In a democratic society, the longstanding consensus on the need to limit corporate campaign spending should outweigh the wooden application of judge-made rules. ... At bottom, the Court's opinion is thus a rejection of the common sense of the American people, who have recognized a need to prevent corporations from undermining self-government since the founding, and who have fought against the distinctive corrupting potential of corporate electioneering since the days of Theodore Roosevelt. It is a strange time to repudiate that common sense."

"hung panel." In fact, decisions of the mixed panel will be announced, as all District Court and High Court decisions are, as decisions of the panel with no dissents. To remedy the situation the Judicial Secretariat stepped in to decide that in such "hung jury" situations the professional judges should vote with the lay participants.

Contextualism, community and consensus are not unknown in the United States, although they may go under different names and are hardly as widely respected as in Japan. When used they must be used with great care, especially when applied to Constitutional rights in a Constitutional democracy. The Constitution is designed to grant individual rights that cannot be taken away and there is always a temptation for a government to bend to popular will. That will is affected by the immediacy of emotional circumstances and thus can result in dangers to liberties. At the same time it may result in an expansion of rights such as when the Supreme Court of the United States finds that a right exists although not specifically mentioned in the Constitution. Yet it is precisely such decisions of highest courts in the United States that tend to create political divides and fractures in the society—abortion, homosexuality, same sex marriage immediately come to mind. At times of war, the context may lead to terrible mistakes such as was the case in the infamous *Japanese Internment* cases of the Second World War.

§18.03 GROUP VERSUS PERSONAL INTERESTS

The significance of group affiliation cannot be overestimated in Japan, while the significance of individuality cannot be overestimated in the United States.[48] Numerous provisions of the Japanese Constitution contain public welfare exceptions to rights granted to individuals in the Constitution. And, while the Constitution seeks to enshrine the American idea of individuality as a Constitutional imperative through requiring respect for individuality ("all of the people shall be respected as individuals") and by granting rights to "every person" in various places, the fact remains that group identity is a vital part of Japanese life, and hence of Japanese law.

When the rights of the individual conflict with the rights of the group, the individual's rights must take a backseat to preservation of the greater good of the group. The Christian wife of a deceased SDF officer must recognize the right of his family and the local community where he was raised to have him enshrined as a Shinto Deity and worshipped at the local Gokoku shrine, even though it conflicts with her personal religious beliefs. When the group is identified as the entire Japanese population—as it is in the context of the criminal law—then the individual right of the accused must be interpreted so as not to unduly restrict the group's protection. In the balancing of interests in criminal cases, the right of the accused is secondary while the

48. In an article published since the first edition of this book it is argued that the "groupism" of Japan is an outgrowth of its agrarian past and a fundamental part of the Japanese character that affects Japanese legal culture. The author suggests that while Japan may have borrowed a written Western Law this has resulted in tension between legal structure and legal culture in Japan. This leads the author to the conclusion that Japan should be placed in the East Asian circle of legal culture and that Japanese law is in fact not "Western Law." See, Tsuyoshi Kinoshita, *Legal Systems and Legal Culture in Japanese Law*, 44 Comparative L. Rev. 25 (2010).

right of the public to be free of crime is primary. The Constitutional guarantees given to suspects and the indicted accused is sharply different in the Japanese and American society, regardless of the fact that they have the same basic language and were both written by Americans. Indeed, the concept of crime itself may be broadly interpreted to protect the public from fear—even when the fear is engendered by activities that implicate the Constitutionally protected right to freedom of expression and association. The most recent illustration of this is the Supreme Court of Japan's three to two decision upholding Hiroshima's ordinance on Eliminating Motorcycle Gangs. The ordinance contains criminal penalties for the acts of congregating and/or assembling in public places without governmental approval when the assembly would instill fear in the public and cause the public to feel insecure. Of the three Justices in the majority, one noted his concern for the public's feelings if the accused were found to be not guilty while another Justice in the majority voted to uphold the ordinance, although he found its broad sweep exceeded that allowed by the Constitution. This Justice concluded that all that was required to cure this Constitutional issue was to ask the City Government to voluntarily revise the Ordinance.[49]

In Japanese law the right of the individual may sometimes not be seen as a separate right from the right of the group. Individual rights are dependent on the rights of the group and when the rights of the group are threatened, so too are the rights of the individual.[50] Accordingly, individual rights must be interpreted in such a way as to recognize the more important and more fundamental rights of the group. This has the effect of moderating individual rights when they conflict with the rights of the greater society, such as is the case in criminal law enforcement.

The right of the group is in part a function of the need to find consensus in the group. In other words the group itself represents different individuals and in finding a group dynamic the notion of harmony leads individuals to a consensus approach. The need to find this consensus—or at least to attempt to find the consensus—will lead the law to favor consensus oriented approaches to matters that in the United States would involve individual rights. Such an approach can explain the use of Administrative Guidance by cities and localities to "compel" negotiations between construction companies and residents over fears that new construction will adversely affect established residents. Although the cities and localities lack power to compel a resolution—and indeed may have no zoning authority or power to stop construction—the courts will recognize a power to enable the group dynamic to attempt to find a solution and will require the builder to set aside his "right" to a building permit until it has negotiated in good faith with residents to try and come to consensus.

A majority of a corporate board may have the right to take action because they "have the votes" but the group dynamic will result in seemingly endless meetings and

49. *Hiroshima Motorcycle Ordinance Case,* Case No. 1819(A) of 2005, 61 Keishu No. 6, (P.B., Sept. 18, 2007), http://www.courts.go.jp/english/judgments/text/2007.09.18-2005.-A-.No..1819.html).

50. See e.g., Takeshi Ishida, *Fundamental Human Rights and the Development of Legal Thought in Japan,* 8 L. Japan 39, 65 (1975) (Hiroshi Wagatsuma & Beverly Braverman trans.). See also, Lawrence Beer, *Group Rights and Individual Rights in Japan,* 21 Asian survey No. 4 437 (1981).

delays so that objecting members can be brought into a consensus decision. At the national level, the party or coalition in power may have the votes to pass its legislative proposal but attempts to pass the proposal over objection by the minority in the Diet without first giving that minority ample opportunity to voice its disagreement and to postpone decisions for greater discussion will be seen as "ramming" the matter through and will be considered as undemocratic.

The government may have the power to take property to build Narita airport and may later take property outside the airport to build an additional runway, but it will delay action over objection of neighboring farmers hoping to achieve some kind of consensus. Of course, once the "string" of negotiation has run out and action is taken in the "public interest" the rights of the objectors must give way to the rights of the group—namely the society as a whole. Thus, once the airport is built it is proper for the government to restrict private property use outside the airport facility for fear that property can be used for protest activities against the airport. Such restrictions clearly invade property rights and rights of free expression but they are deemed warranted by the need to protect the interests of the greater society, which requires the airport facility.[51]

In addition, group membership implies obligations between group members. Whether considered as *giri* obligations[52] or simply as group affiliation obligations, group membership requires conduct conducive to harmony and consensus. As workers are part of a group that includes their corporation, workers have a duty to work hard for their company's benefit that transcends their rights under the labor laws. Company management in turn has obligations to the company workers that transcend their duty to shareholders to maximize profits. Keiretsu companies are independent companies, part of a larger group of companies and as such owe obligations to other members of the keiretsu that may transcend their obligation to stockholders to maximize profits. Keiretsu members may have no legal duty to buy each other's products—indeed such a legal duty might violate the anti-trust laws—but surely decision makers at each level will feel some obligation to the organization to purchase from a member company if the opportunity presents itself—and surely to avoid purchasing from a competing keiretsu entity. Among members of the group informal contracts will suffice even if such contracts do not meet the technical requirements of the Civil and Commercial Codes. Companies are part of the greater Japanese society and have an obligation to at least consider the Administrative Guidance received, although there may be no legal right for the administrator to deal with the subject and no legal obligation to follow the administrator's suggestions.

51. See e.g., The *Narita Airport* case, as discussed in Colin P.A. Jones, *Narita Airport and the Japanese Constitution: A Case Study*, 24 L. Japan 39 (1991). See decision of the Supreme Court of Japan in *Sanrizuka-Shibayama Anti-Airport League case*, Case No. 1986 (Gyo-Tsu) No. 11 (G.B., Jul. 1, 1992), http://www.courts.go.jp/english/judgments/text/1992.07.01-1986-Gyo-Tsu-No.11-163553.html) (freedom of association is subject to a public welfare exception—and the airport is necessary for the welfare of the public).
52. See, Yosiyuki Noda *Introduction to Japanese Law* 174–183 (Anthony H. Angelo trans. & ed., University of Tokyo Press 1976).

§18.04 SUBSTANTIVE JUSTICE

American law is greatly concerned with procedural due process. Procedural due process dominates American criminal law as well as administrative law. Resident aliens may not enjoy all of the substantive Constitutional law protections of American nationals when it comes to matters of nationality, immigration and deportation, but they are entitled to procedural due process under the Constitution. This focus on procedure means that the Constitutional guarantees that affect procedure—whether it be procedure in the courts, procedure in the administrative process, procedure in the criminal law investigation, etc.—will tend to be given broad meaning to assure a fair process, if not a "just" result.

Japan, on the other hand, has a more substantive approach to the law. Procedure is secondary. As a consequence legal provisions that focus on procedure tend to get short shrift from both the authorities and the courts. More important is to get the "correct" answer, even if procedural short cuts may be required to get there. Thus, a criminal defendant in Japan will not get all of the procedural protections that the Constitution appears to grant and courts will not read the Constitution to grant wide procedural protections if such protections get in the way of a correct decision. In other words, if the defendant is guilty the defendant should be found guilty. To exclude evidence that proves guilt is akin to throwing out the baby with the bath water—unless there has been such a breach by the police that the greater community good is served by prohibiting such shocking to the conscience conduct to lead to admissible evidence (and in such case there is typically other evidence of either the same or a different crime to assure that a conviction of the guilty will follow). The end result of letting the guilty go free is to deny the public its right to substantive justice. The inevitable confession will be examined not to determine whether it was given in antiseptic circumstances but rather to determine whether it is reliable—in other words did the confessing defendant actually commit the crime. Too many times this means that substantive justice is denied the innocent are not set free—those who did not commit the crime give false confessions. The criminal is still among the population to commit more crime.

In the administrative law arena courts tend not to examine procedure and even the new Administrative Procedure Law says precious little about the procedures for Administrative Guidance, the primary method of administering. Again the focus is on substantive justice. The issue is not whether the municipality or other local government held open hearings and obtained views of a wide spectrum of the public before determining how much money they would suggest builders contribute to offset the costs to the community of the new housing they are building. The issue is whether it is right, proper, just, appropriate for the city to make such suggestion. The procedure by which an agency determines what guidance to give is not relevant to legal questions raised by the guidance; the relevant issue is whether the subject of the guidance is within the general frame of reference for government involvement. Is the government involving itself in a matter in which the government should be involving itself—is it correct for the government to be involved. If it is then it is just for the recipient of guidance to give good faith consideration to that guidance before it acts. The fact that the agency has not been specifically delegated program authority to deal with the issue is secondary to the question of whether the issue falls within the broad subject that the agency deals with.

And, procedure at the private level is also limited when the correct result has been achieved. Thus, restrictions on poison pill protections against hostile takeovers are likely to be disregarded when an overwhelming majority of shareholders agree to pass a poison pill resolution aimed at a specific hostile bidder.

The Fukushima nuclear tragedy has brought procedure into focus in the sense that the public demands to be heard about the subject of nuclear power and does not want public hearings to be matter of form over substance or dominated by power companies who send representatives as members of the public to support the company's position.

CHAPTER 19

Conclusion

Like so many things Japanese, Japan's feudal past, or myth about Japan's feudal past, exerts a strong pressure on Japanese law. The importance of the past cannot be ignored when analyzing any legal system. But in Japan the past is particularly influential as custom is an established part of the law and custom includes the past or at least myths about the past. In many ways Japan is a new country on the territory of a very old country. Modern Japan is said to have begun with the Meiji Restoration, but the first three quarters of a century following the Restoration may be viewed as a failed governmental experiment. The political/military structure based on a German model selected by the Meiji oligarchs was wiped at out Hiroshima and Nagasaki and the American Occupation that followed. Modern Japan is the postwar Japan and that is only some 70 years old. Just as Meiji Japan adopted Civil Law Codes out of necessity rather than indigenous experience and just as Tokugawa Japan reinterpreted myths and Confucianism to support the Shogun based political system and Meiji Japan retold old myths to support the new Emperor-based system, so modern Japan is reformulating those myths to support a more democratic modern State. In doing so Japan is utilizing its legal system to support its modern view of itself. This is nothing new. The United States (and in all likelihood all modern developed countries) uses the legal system to reinforce its views of itself and support its chosen legal, economic, political and social system. In Japan the choosing of these systems is in an earlier stage of development. Japan is still in the process of determining which of its new American imports and which of its older European imports it wishes to retain, which it wishes to discard and which must be reinterpreted to fit the evolving modern Japan. As it moves forward, its legal system adapts itself to this evolution and supports what the Judiciary views as the political and social evolution of the society. Thus, the power of evolving legal doctrine to influence the political branches of government to adopt laws that reflect modern and changing social views is particularly strong in Japan while at the same time the Judicial Branch is, to American eyes, overly deferential to the political branches when it comes to exercising the power of judicial review. So too the borrowed or "imposed" (if not by force than by circumstance) written law must be interpreted, massaged and if necessary jettisoned in favor of a more indigenous solution to problems.

As it attempts to define itself in the modern age, Japan has undertaken a series of reform programs. In economic reform to find a "correct" balance between a mercantile system that favors domestic industry and underlies the postwar recovery and globalization which is demanded by its trading partners without whom Japan's export based economy cannot thrive; in the administrative and political arenas—seeking the "correct" balance between a highly influential bureaucracy that has lost much of its glow as a consequence of two decades of economic stagnation and the more recent Fukushima nuclear meltdown and a political leadership that has failed to exercise leadership but is entrenched. A change in Party government from the LDP, which ruled as the governing party for almost the entirety of the Post-Occupation period until 2009 has done little to change the public's frustration with indecisive and lack luster political leadership. (Whether the new electoral system which puts greater emphasis on Party and Party doctrine will lead to stronger and more charismatic Party leaders with Party platforms remains to be seen, and if so whether such change is good is uncertain.) Similarly with the rise of an opposition political party with the capacity to rule and with the public's choice of divided government Japan is looking for the correct balance between the Upper and Lower House as well as between rival political parties with public support. As a supporter of the Kyoto Protocols and an environmentally sensitive society Japan is seeking for the appropriate balance between its need for clean energy and the lessons of the Fukushima nuclear tragedy. Accordingly Japan finds itself in continual efforts at political reform and administrative reform. The economic, bureaucratic, political and judicial reforms of the past decade are part of the tug and haul process by which modern Japan is defining itself. When those reforms appear to have moved too fast or appear to have copied too closely a culture that is not comfortable to Japan's society the Judicial Branch may act to give the society another chance to rethink were it is going.

Japan has adopted as a goal the establishment of the Rule of Law as the guiding principle for its legal reform efforts. The Judicial Reform Council has set as its goal the transformation of the "spirit of the law and the Rule of Law into the flesh and blood of this country." It appears that the Rule of Law referred to by the Council is the kind of Rule of Law society found in Western Europe and the United States. If it truly adopts this Rule of Law philosophy it will need to do more than simply better train a more numerous legal profession. It will need to do more than increase the number of judges and speed up the judicial process. With an indecisive Diet and a Supreme Court loath to enter the vacuum and enforce individual rights that the public in general may have reservations about (such as in dealing with the issue of Surrogate Birth or In Vitro fertilization) or even that the public may favor, hopes for relief through the Rule of Law remain stymied. Rather than relying on the philosophy of the legal system that guided its Postwar Constitution, namely respect for the views of the majority but also respect for fundamental rights that are not subject to the whims of the majority, Japan's Supreme Court has adopted a more "majoritarian" approach leaving it to the majoritarian elected government and the powerful bureaucracy to decide how to deal with modern issues and fundamental rights issues, even when the government is unable or unwilling to resolve and in some cases to recognize the existence of those issues.

A Rule of Law system requires a fundamental shift in legal philosophy and judicial thinking. The Rule of Law has as its foundation the concept of rights that are, if not fixed at least not so malleable that enforcement through litigation is seen as an unsatisfactory option leading to use of "extra-legal" models for resolving issues. To achieve a Rule of Law society such as is envisioned by the Judicial Reform Council changes in the way Japan's bureaucracy works and a searching judicial review of both the substantive decisions of that bureaucracy (both civil and prosecutorial) as well as the creation of and judicial review of procedural norms followed by the bureaucracy will be needed. To achieve the Rule of Law society envisioned by the Council, legislation must set forth judicially enforceable rights that parties may rely on rather than merely a set of hortatory objectives for action. And judges must look to the Constitution and legislation as setting forth the consensus of society rather than the amorphous societal norms divined by the judicial system. The Council's view appears to contemplate a more transparent system where everyone—whether Japanese or not—can look at the law as written in the Constitution, Codes and Statutes and know that when they seek enforcement what they see is actually what they will get without having to divine rules based on a mythical past or a judge's view of what the particular social norm is when the case is decided. Until parties have judicially enforceable rights that are consistently interpreted and enforced, a Rule of Law society such as is contemplated by the Judicial Reform Council is difficult to envision. While numerous pieces of legislation have followed in the wake of the Reform Council's recommendations such legislation is yet to adopt the "radical" changes needed to carry out the Council's goal. In short, much more remains to be done if Japan is to achieve the goals of the Council.

Understanding the basis for judicial decisions that do not appear consistent with the written law may help to understand a society and its legal system but it does not resolve the issue of whether the legal system needs change. To a lesser or greater extent we are all captives of our own system and our own myths and the value judgments that underlie our system. This captivity makes it difficult for a society to understand its own system in the abstract—it is too distracted by the "givens" that underlie its thought process about the system. One of the challenges of a comparative study of legal systems is to try to think "outside the box" of one's own preconceived notions and philosophies. By looking at how others deal with the same or similar issues and understanding why they deal with them differently we may be able to gain insight into what and why we are doing what we are doing. This insight may help us in modifying and restructuring not just our system but also our thought process about our system.

Japan has adopted the goal of making its legal system more of a Rule of Law system and incorporating the notion of the Rule of Law into differing aspects of its society. It remains to be seen whether the suggestions made for how to do this are "outside the box" or simply modifications that strengthens and improve the workings of the prevailing system. To date not much "outside the box" solutions have been forthcoming from the Diet although much has been done to strengthen the existing system. In other words, is what you see what you get when you see the suggestion of the Law Reform Council that the Rule of Law should be strengthened in Japan?

There is no doubt but that the Judicial Reform Council has made a valuable contribution to the furthering the kind of Rule of Law Society in Japan envisioned by the Council. To achieve such a society issues touched on but not resolved in the Council's Report will need to be addressed—bureaucrats will have to give up some of their authority, judges will have to become more aggressive in upholding legal norms and rights of individuals, including but not limited to those accused of crimes, on a consistent basis and will need to find the consensus of society in the Constitution and legislation, and legislators will have to deal with issues that are compelling but where a clearly defined public opinion is not available and in some cases reject a public opinion that fails to take into account Japan's needs as a nation and its international obligations undertaken in treaties that will be viewed with a Rule of Law mentality by treaty partners. Steps in this direction have been taken, such as the Supreme Court's determinations loosening standing requirements in Administrative Law cases as well as its recent decision recognizing the importance of providing public and understandable reasons for dispositions such as the taking away of an architect's license, and requiring evidence that meets the prosecutor's burden of proof in circumstantial evidence cases. The recognition that reasoned decision making is required both to allow the subject of a disposition to defend itself and so that an Agency's actions are deliberate and reasonable rather than arbitrary and capricious is a significant step forward. So too, the mixed lay/professional criminal panel process has had benefits beyond the cases for which it was designed and has helped in loosening the tight grip on evidence that prosecutors have had in Japan. Scandals involving the prosecution service have been responsible for an experiment in recording the entirety of interrogation of witnesses and the Supreme Court has rendered important decisions requiring High Courts to give deference to the findings of mixed lay/professional panels and by defining the proof required in circumstantial evidence cases may have taken a big step towards reinvigorating the presumption of innocence.

The Diet must legislate rights that are judicially enforceable and provide for greater and more meaningful judicial review of administrative actions and expand recent efforts to create a meaningful civil judicial forum with meaningful remedies for those who have suffered wrongs and against those violating the law and thereby causing damage to others. That does not mean that Japan must jettison the values that presently underlie its judicial system and which serve its society well. To achieve the transformation that is the philosophical base of the Council's recommendations, the values that underlie legal determinations in Japan today—societal norms, common sense of society, harmony, consensus, group identification, communitarian values and an effort to obtain a "correct" decision—must be harmonized with the rights, understandability, consistency, reliability and enforceability demanded by the Rule of Law.

Table of Japanese Cases

Editors Note: Unlike United States reporters, Japanese cases are not reported using the names of the parties. To aid the reader, this Table of Cases uses descriptive titles for the cases cited (and in some situations the names of the parties.) Where cases have been translated and reported in English language collections of cases, such as in Lawrence W. Beer And Hiroshi Itoh, *The Constitutional Case Law of Japan, 1970 through 1990* (University of Washington Press, 1996), or are discussed in English language Law Review articles or books, an attempt has been made to use the same descriptive title of the case as may be found in such compilations or readings so that the reader may be better able to understand that the same case is being discussed. In other situations a descriptive name has been given in the hope that this will assist the reader in locating cases in the text by the subject matter covered in the case. In the text, attempt is made to cite cases to the Japanese reporter and attempt is made to also cite to English language translations or discussion of the case in books, articles and the web site for the Japanese Supreme Court. In this Table attempt is made to cite the Japanese reporter system. Where the case is cited to the case number and date, an English language translation probably can be found on the Internet through the web site for the Japanese Supreme Court. For other English language translations (if any) the reader should refer to the text.

Case Name or Descriptive Title

Table of United States Cases

Index

J

K

L

P